ETHNIC
GENEALOGY

ETHNIC GENEALOGY

A Research Guide

Edited by
Jessie Carney Smith
Foreword by
Alex Haley

Greenwood Press
Westport, Connecticut·London, England

Library of Congress Cataloging in Publication Data
Main entry under title:

Ethnic genealogy.

  Bibliography: p.
  Includes index.
  1. United States—Genealogy—Handbooks, manuals, etc.
  2. United States—Genealogy—Library resources.
  3. Afro-Americans—Genealogy—Handbooks, manuals, etc.
  4. Asian Americans—Genealogy—Handbooks, manuals, etc.
  5. Hispanic Americans—Genealogy—Handbooks, manuals, etc.
  6. Indians of North America—Genealogy—Handbooks,
  manuals, etc. I. Smith, Jessie Carney.
  CS49.E83 1983   929′.1′072073   82-12145
  ISBN 0-313-22593-1

Library of Congress Catalog Card Number: 82-12145
ISBN: 0-313-22593-1

First published in 1983

Greenwood Press
A division of Congressional Information Service, Inc.
88 Post Road West
Westport, Connecticut 06881

Printed in the United States of America

10 9 8 7 6 5 4 3 2 1

To
my black, American Indian, and Anglo-Saxon ancestors

"You-all means a race or
  section,
Family, party, tribe or clan;
You-all means the whole
  connection
Of the individual man."

Anonymous.
Quoted in *Richmond Times-Dispatch*

Contents

Figures and Tables   ix

Foreword   xiii

Preface   xvii

Introduction   xxi

**I General Information on Sources, Procedures, and Genealogical   1
    Research**

1 Librarians and Genealogical Research   3
   RUSSELL E. BIDLACK

2 Basic Sources for Genealogical Research   21
   JEAN ELDER CAZORT

3 Library Records and Research   59
   CASPER L. JORDAN

4 Researching Family History   91
   BOBBY L. LOVETT

II Utilizing Major Repositories for Genealogical Research   121

5 The National Archives and Records Service   123
   JAMES D. WALKER

6   The Genealogical Society of Utah Library   175
    ROGER SCANLAND

III **Sources Available to Specific Ethnic Groups**   207

7   American Indian Records and Research   209
    JIMMY B. PARKER

8   Asian-American Records and Research   239
    GREG GUBLER

9   Black American Records and Research   309
    CHARLES L. BLOCKSON

10 Hispanic-American Records and Research   365
    LYMAN DE PLATT

    Index   403

    About the Contributors   437

Figures and Tables

FIGURES

1.1	Memorandum, Enoch Pratt Free Library	7
2.1	Four Generation Pedigree Chart	22
2.2	Family Group Sheet	26
2.3	Individual History Sheet	28
2.4	Research Record	29
2.5	Correspondence Record	30
2.6	Birth Registration in Tennessee, 1935	33
2.7	Certificate of Live Birth	34
2.8	Record of Early Marriages	35
2.9	Certificate of Death	36
2.10	Evidence of Family Relationship in a Deed	39
2.11	Michael Garber's Will	41
4.1	Bank Depositor's Card	102
4.2	Family History Deposit Agreement Form	113
5.1	Passenger Arrival Record Form	137
7.1	Deed for Sale of Indian Lands	213
7.2	Annuity Payroll	215
7.3	Annuity Payroll	216
7.4	Annuity Payroll	217
7.5	Annual School Census Report	218
7.6	Indian Census Roll	219
7.7	Indian Allotment Register	220
7.8	Register of Indian Families	222
7.9	Marriage Card	223
7.10	Record of Deaths	224
7.11	Certificate of Death	225

7.12   Birth Report   226
7.13   Letter Verifying Birth Dates of Children   227
7.14   Sanitary Record of Sick, Injured, Births,   228
          Deaths, etc.
7.15   Data for Heirship Finding   230
7.16   Will   231
8.1   Application for Verification of Information   253
          from Immigration and Naturalization Service Records
8.2   Document Granting Permission to Travel Abroad   260
8.3   Chinese Pedigree Chart   265
8.4   Brief Approximation of 1886-Type *Koseki*   268
8.5   Page from a *Kakochō*   271
8.6   *Ihai* (Mortuary Tablet)   272
8.7   Korean Genealogical Table   276
8.8   Chinese Pedigree Chart (Blank)   280
8.9   Chinese Pedigree Chart (Partially Completed)   281
8.10   Chinese Family Group Sheet   282
8.11   Catalog Card Entry for Chinese Records   284
8.12   Japanese Pedigree Chart (Blank)   286
8.13   Japanese Pedigree Chart (Partially Completed)   287
8.14   Japanese Family Group Sheet   288
8.15   Catalog Card for a Japanese Genealogy   289
9.1   Illustration of Use of Classical Names for Slaves   312
9.2   Sample Page from a Bastardy Casebook Showing   314
          Mulatto Mother and Free Negro Father
9.3   Bible Record Showing Names of Slaves   318
9.4   Church Record, Works Projects Administration,   320
          1939–41, Showing Black Members of White Congregation
9.5   U.S. Census Report, Slave Schedule, 1850   322
9.6   Slave Labor Contract for Private Employer   324
9.7   Slave Labor Contract for Work in State Office   324
9.8   Bondage Record for Black Bound in Servitude   325
9.9   Receipt for Sale of Estate Property Showing   326
          Value of Slave Boy and Girl
9.10   Bill of Sale of Slaves   327
9.11   Will Showing Disposition of Slave Girl   328
9.12   Inventory and Appraisal of Estate Property,   330
          Including Nineteen Named Slaves
9.13   Insurance Policy for Slaves   332
9.14   Manumission, or ''Free,'' Papers for Former Slaves 334
9.15   Letter Regarding Runaway Slave on Indian Reservation 345

TABLES

6.1   Geographic Distribution of LDS Library Microfilms   178
8.1   Personal Papers and Documents (Japanese)   259

Foreword

Tracing ancestors as far back as possible has brought to many people great satisfaction and pleasure. Even documenting one's family thoroughly for but a few generations can prove just as exciting and fulfilling as a more sketchy documentation across two or three centuries. Each individual ancestral relative previously unknown and genealogically discovered is its own special thrill! No less thrilling is the discovery of records rich with information, which would have remained untouched, which would never have come to light, unless you had gotten caught up in the multiple, magnetic lures of genealogy.

Young and old alike find that knowing one's roots, and thus coming better to know who one is, provides a personally rewarding experience. But even more is involved than uncovering a family history, for each discovered United States family history becomes a newly revealed small piece of American history. Stated simply: a nation's history is only the collective histories of all of its people. It is only through an unfolding of the peoples' histories that a nation's culture can be studied in its fullest meaning.

Serious search for one's roots requires strong dedication; genuine longing to unfold the past; some would say a nigh-fanatical pursuit of each lead. The result is a sense of fulfillment as ancestors become real, coupled with a sense of disappointment because yet so much remains unknown. Moreover, one's pleasant, comfortable, and regular routines must be altered, if not sacrificed, in order to submerge one's self in libraries, archives, and other repositories of information. Finally, there must be a deep commitment and sense of purpose, which must not diminish until the final lead has obviously been exhausted. Even then, the serious genealogical researcher must retain an optimism—a real hope that one day may present some brand-new lead to be explored to the fullest, of course. Indeed, optimists rather than defeatists have produced the results for which serious genealogical research is best known.

Every genealogical researcher shares one frustration that I know I will always live with: Was there something else I should have uncovered? My long curiosity about my family's roots and the twelve years of obsessively pursuing and writing about them surely have not ended my curiosity. Again, put simply: I have learned to live with my genealogical addiction. Among the reasons that I so sincerely admire and endorse *Ethnic Genealogy: A Research Guide* are that it encourages others to develop this most positive addiction; and this volume also guides and instructs one in some of the ways to truly enjoy coping with it.

My book *Roots* likely would never have been realized without conscious assistance from some living family elders and, I truly believe, an unconscious inspiration from ancestors in their graves. Oral history, the telling and retelling of family stories, was practiced throughout my family's generations; the elders fed the interest of their children and their grandchildren in continuing the tradition—this is how the stories finally reached me.

I feel that our tradition passed along the family historian role to me, who happened to be a writer. Somehow as a writer I felt that a book fusing the history and the genealogy of the Kunta Kinte family in Africa and then in America might have some impact. But I repeat: It never could have happened unless our family's earlier generations had preserved our history orally. So that's another reason why I praise *Ethnic Genealogy*: It promotes oral history and family history as solid, valid genealogical research methods. The authors rightly stress the importance of talking with older family members and recording all possible information now, while they remain with us. Moreover, *Ethnic Genealogy* illustrates how oral and written family records can attest to ancestral family unity.

Many people assisted my *Roots* research, none more than the genealogists and librarians, who often seemed as obsessed with my roots as I was, as they helped me to pursue clues and to document my forebears. They simply helped me to illuminate my family's past.

This volume pays tribute to these professionals, acknowledging that, without them, successful genealogical search ranges from difficult to impossible in some cases. Nonetheless, *Ethnic Genealogy* is an assistance tool not only for genealogists, but also for librarians and researchers desiring to hone their skills in this particular specialty. Genealogists, librarians, and researchers sometimes have experienced appreciable differences in their individual approaches to research challenges and even in their appreciation and respect for each other's professions, but *Ethnic Genealogy* clarifies these groups' common interests and shows particularly how, united, they present an incomparable resource for the amateur and professional genealogical researcher.

Ethnic Genealogy is not only timely, it is necessary. Had this work appeared long before now, many a genealogical researcher could have experienced far less frustration. Now, this volume can immensely aid countless researchers who are just beginning their search, or others who have become muddled and confused in the pursuit.

The authors describe the special research approaches that should be observed in these specific ethnic quests, along with some of the classic pitfalls that ethnic specialty researchers may expect to encounter, and demonstrate that American Indian, Asian American, black or Hispanic genealogical research can be successfully pursued. Basic research steps are discussed for each ethnic heritage.

Several of the authors remind us how the work of family historians has led to many family reunions—an event which I strongly endorse.

This single reference volume lists and describes libraries, archives, and other repository sources of data in selected sites across the United States. The authors note that some records are accessible regardless of one's location. At least two of the authors discuss records beyond American shores, especially important for Asian American and Hispanic research.

Finally, *Ethnic Genealogy* surely will spur many new genealogical searchers along their way, thus making a significant and healthy impact on many families. Together with being vital to any well-rounded genealogical collection, this work is an important text for courses in family history, genealogy, and ethnic culture. It is, in fact, a volume that will balance anyone's personal library.

Alex Haley
Los Angeles

Preface

Researchers who pursue genealogical projects, whether in search of ancestors or for other informational or exploratory reasons, soon learn that the literature of genealogy varies widely in scope, in depth, in recency of publication, and in usefulness. Those who traditionally have searched for information on mainstream Americans and certain ethnic groups have had at their disposal numerous documents, which has led to the publication of family histories or to the building of rather complete family trees. Those who pursue genealogical research on other ethnic groups, however, often have done so with much greater difficulty, as the obstacles to reasonably complete research seemed insurmountable. This has been especially true for those in pursuit of black genealogy, as researchers and some of the published literature have proven only in recent years that such pursuit can be followed and can lead to bona fide research and well-documented projects.

The recognition of black genealogy as a virgin field is indeed a discovery which is not exclusive to the study of that group. For ethnic groups such as American Indians, Hispanics, and others who may or may not appear in full discussion in this work, too little attention has been given to their heritage and the search for their ancestors in published literature, in conferences, and in training sessions. On the other hand, Asian Americans, whose roots have been preserved for centuries in clan genealogies and other works, also have received far too little attention in the field of genealogy in this country. While it is true that for many groups records vital to a complete genealogical study have been lost or destroyed over the years, the problem has been compounded, especially for some ethnic groups. During the period of slavery in America, for example, genealogical documentation for blacks was virtually unknown, as slaves may have been unable to provide written clues to their origins, as the slave/master mixtures generally were unrecorded in official records (although this work demonstrates that some were recorded), and as slave names were often lost over the years. Extant documents on the American slave can be used to complete some family lines and can lead the researcher to very early periods of black life in America, in Africa, and elsewhere.

Genealogical searches for ethnic groups are further complicated by the admixture of the groups, particularly in certain geographical areas of this country and in foreign countries as well. For example, the frequent mixture of blacks, whites, and Indians in North Carolina, Virginia, and Maryland; of Chicanos and Indians in Mexico; of Africans, Indians, and Spanish in Puerto Rico; and of blacks or whites and Japanese in Japan during World War II makes it difficult to trace family histories which can provide a new and enlightening addition to American culture.

The popularity of and necessity for genealogical searches in America have been well documented. Problems peculiar to ethnic groups in the quest for genealogical information are compounded and point to the need for special attention to a series of problems. For librarians, the importance of genealogical activities looms large. Because libraries aim to preserve and to interpret information regardless of its form, oral history and family history projects should become permanent additions to archives. Various documents already in archival collections are potentially useful sources for genealogical searches. The oral and family history projects, as well as the archival materials in libraries, must be indexed to facilitate use by searchers. In addition, those who are involved in such projects often uncover valuable and obscure materials which might have been lost to searchers. Such materials include letters, business ledgers, photographs, early city directories, and similar items valuable for genealogical and other study. When possible, these materials should also become a permanent part of archival or reference collections.

Genealogical researchers often require the professional assistance of genealogists and of librarians. While librarians are not necessarily genealogists by training, to enhance their service capability to patrons and to help address the immediate and pressing needs of the researcher, they need to develop particular expertise. In doing so, librarians may well develop an interest in searching their own family lines. On the other hand, new and seasoned researchers often are able to avoid the pitfalls of endless searches and dead-end leads by acquiring a firm grasp of the rich resources contained in various types of libraries and repositories, by learning that a rare item may emerge in an obscure library, and by taking advantage of the exposure that librarians, archivists, and other personnel in various information centers have to a multitude of records.

A variety of activities and episodes led to the compilation of this work. For example, over the years I have been curious about who people really are, about how one's ancestry can produce brown skin, straight hair, and blue eyes; or straight black hair, reddish skin, and high cheek bones, while the descendants are variously referred to as "colored," "Negro," or "black." My curiosity led me to question why family offspring came in so many colors and how historical truths allowed generations to pass and offspring to retain their African or white, Anglo-Saxon appearance, which became more marked as time passed. Several years in advance of the publication of *Roots*, Alex Haley lectured extensively on what the nation could expect both in the written work and in the television adaptation of it. Both his lectures and the resulting book meant that a new day was dawning—for Haley as a writer and television producer; for young and older Americans of all races, creeds and colors; and for me, because I was spurred to find ways to address some of the curiosities which lingered.

Thus, with some persistent anxieties and with the confidence that everyone's roots could and should be searched, as demonstrated by Haley, I applied for and received funds from the U.S. Office of Education to direct an Institute on Ethnic Genealogy for Librarians. Held at Fisk University in the summer of 1979, the training program aimed to develop in librarians particular expertise, to enhance their service capability to patrons, and to help address an area of popular interest. The institute brought to the campus twenty librarians and library researchers whose genuine interest in genealogy was unquestionable and well demonstrated. It brought also a group of librarians, historians, archivists, and amateur and professional genealogists, who shared their wisdom, expertise and visual resources with the institute participants.

The program enabled the participants to visit some of the nation's leading repositories of genealogical resources, such as the Library of Congress, the National Archives, and the Genealogical Library of the Church of Jesus Christ of Latter-day Saints, or LDS. Exposure to these vast resources; to librarians, archivists, and subject specialists who knew their areas well; to other researchers who were searching the vast records; and to practical experience in searching census records, family histories, marriage records, and other documents helped the participants to enhance their own research skills and sealed their interest in genealogy. Many returned to their places of employment and sponsored conferences, training sessions, lectures, and tours of historical sites for their colleagues or area residents. Several immediately embarked on preparation and publication of family histories, and one has completed a biography of one of her ancestors, Hazel Harrison, the noted black pianist of the 1920s.

Simultaneous with the library training institute, I took initial steps to identify a group of writers who would be invited to prepare papers on various aspects of ethnic genealogy. Some of the writers lectured in the library training institute. The resulting work embraces most of the topics the institute addressed. The authors are scholars who have published previously, who have had some experience in genealogical research, and who are genealogists, historians, or librarians.

Thus, the reader or researcher who utilizes *Ethnic Genealogy: A Research Guide* should be cognizant of the audience the work addresses as well as the purposes for which the work has been prepared. The work is designed as a handy reference volume for librarians, researchers, archivists, genealogists (both amateur and professional), historians, oral historians, and interested readers, whose knowledge of ethnic history and genealogy may vary. While professional genealogists, seasoned historians, experienced librarians, and other readers may have considerable knowledge in some of the areas addressed in this reference work, the writers assume that their awareness of the different areas covered varies in scope and in depth. Those who are less experienced will find the work much more helpful than others may. Regardless of the researcher's level of expertise in ethnic genealogy, however, the work presents an introduction to the problems which may be encountered when searching for ancestors who are American Indian, Asian American, black American, or Hispanic. It enumerates steps to be taken when exploring genealogical research on these groups and describes the types and identifies the location of resources which should be used to support the research. Obscure items as well as more popular ones are identified. Numerous references are made to works which give more comprehensive coverage of an area than this volume aims to present, thus reducing the need for listing items or for discussions which are covered elsewhere. The work concentrates on those ethnic groups mentioned above and is restricted further to the particular Asian-American or Hispanic groups included. Some helpful discussions on other ethnic and religious groups emerge in one or two sections. The authors and I acknowledge the desirability of a much more comprehensive work which would also embrace other ethnic groups but chose to focus on four as examples which present particular problems in genealogical research.

I acknowledge the assistance and support of a number of individuals whose contributions made this work possible. Special thanks are extended to the authors of the various chapters, whose extremely heavy responsibilities as historians, librarians, subject area specialists in ethnic genealogy, lecturers, and authors doubtless provided little time for extra activity, but who recognized the importance of this work and therefore did their part in creating it. I am grateful also to the following persons: Beth M. Howse of Fisk University Library's Special Collections for gathering certain historical documents; John L. Heflin of Brentwood, Tennessee, dealer in rare manuscripts, books and memorabilia, for making his documents available for reproduction in this work; Marilyn Bell, Tennessee State Library and Archives, for her assistance in locating materials needed to document parts of this volume; Joanne A. Mattern, Bureau of Archives and Records, Hall of Records of Delaware, for supplying illustrations; Ann Reinert, Nebraska State Historical Society, for supplying information on the Reference and Adult Services Division, History Section, American Library Association; Jean Elder Cazort for her editorial assistance; Vickie Heritzer and Helena Carney Lambeth for proofreading the manuscript; Sheila Baxter, Linda Burton, and Gwendolyn Houston of Fisk University Library and Vallie P. Pursley of the Tennessee State University Library for typing the manuscript; and Cynthia Harris, James T. Sabin, and others of Greenwood Press for their patience when deadline after deadline for submitting the manuscript was missed and for their continuing words of encouragement as the work developed.

Jessie Carney Smith
Fisk University

Introduction

As one learns the techniques of genealogical research, it becomes obvious very early that certain procedures must be followed when tracing any ethnic background. Most of the authors of the ten chapters of this guide to research emphasize the logical procedure which the researcher must observe; that is, to begin the search with one's self and to move backward in time. In other words, one works from the known to the unknown. The reader or researcher who utilizes this work will note additional similarities in the history, culture, or record-keeping practices of those who prepared the documents which we use now to trace ethnic ancestry. For example, the writers call attention to some similarities in census-taking practices. Census records, one of the researcher's most important resource documents, should be acknowledged for the long periods of time they span and in some years for the detailed information they yield. On the other hand, such records must be examined with caution, as census enumerators have often recorded the names of blacks, Indians, Orientals, and other immigrants whose speech patterns were different from their own in a manner that resembled what they heard, or exactly as they heard them. Thus, names frequently have been misspelled and inaccurately recorded. Some immigrants aided in this misrepresentation. As Greg Gubler points out in chapter 8, some Asian Americans merely adopted Western-type names to simplify pronunciation, to eliminate problems in various records, and to gain social acceptance.

The reader will note further that slavery was an institution known in many civilizations and cultures. While for the American black, slavery was the vehicle which brought most of one's black ancestors to this country, American Indians sometimes knew the system from experience in their native land. Asian and Mexican immigrants were also subjected to it prior to their arrival in America.

Another common element among the authors' discussions is the matter of records for the study of ethnic genealogy. Where the Asian American, the American Indian, the black American, and the Hispanic are concerned, the authors carefully dispel the notion that the tracing of one's ancestry is impossible and that no suitable records are extant. The problems of certain records notwithstanding, each author demonstrates that the researchers can be successful in genealogical pursuit, and they document their claims by identifying a variety of sources and by locating them for the researcher.

This research guide is arranged under three broad sections, under which chapters relating to the headings are grouped. The sections are Part I, General Information on Sources, Procedures, and Genealogical Research; Part II, Utilizing Major Repositories for Genealogical Research, and Part III, Sources Available to Specific Ethnic Groups.

As a logical point of departure for this research guide, Russell E. Bidlack explores the topic "Librarians and Genealogical Research." He notes the radical change in philosophy and attitudes of librarians as they move to accept genealogy as a field of research and proceeds to explain this remarkable change. While those who know Bidlack well have heard his familiar classification of himself as an amateur genealogist, they know also that for numerous years he has devoted considerable time to genealogical research and publication and to editing a newsletter on genealogy. To him genealogy has been a hobby, yet Bidlack distinguishes between genealogy and other hobbies. Rather than collect objects, like those who gather art items, stamps, and other pieces, the genealogist collects information from written and oral records. Rather than collect ancestors, the genealogist gathers data about them.

The roots of America lie in part in the immigrants, who escaped societies where tradition and caste offered little opportunity for self-improvement. The early immigrants wanted to forget their unhappy past, while those of later generations now want to preserve it. Accordingly, Bidlack quotes a saying among genealogists: "The grandson often wants to remember what the grandfather wants to forget." Among the activities which mitigated against the study of genealogy were, according to Bidlack, slavery, which deprived black Americans of a knowledge of their heritage; the success of the American Revolution, which hampers genealogists, despite the efforts of the Daughters of the American Revolution (DAR) and Sons of the American Revolution (SAR) to preserve the past, because it sometimes meant that titles and coats of arms from the old country received no status in American law; and the tendency of Americans to migrate and in doing so to leave behind family Bibles and other items of importance to genealogical research.

Bidlack's account of the history of genealogy shows that most Americans of the past two centuries professed a disregard for the subject; however, as the surviving pioneers of the nineteenth century became fewer in number, local historical societies were often established to preserve the past. There were approximately 400 published family histories in 1876; today the nation has among its resources more than 25,000 such records. Only in recent times have libraries moved to develop collections in genealogy, to help individuals study their past and to publish their accounts. This may be due in part to limited library budgets and to the expense of certain items needed.

Among those libraries which for a number of years have catered to the genealogist are the Newberry Library of Chicago, the Detroit Public Library, the New York Public Library, the Library of Congress, the Public Library of Fort Wayne and Allen County in Indiana, and the Genealogical Department Library, Church of Jesus Christ of Latter-day Saints, in Salt Lake City.

Whether or not genealogy is for all people has been debated by many groups. Bidlack demonstrates that it is, and that activities supporting this claim include Alex Haley's *Roots;* the U.S. bicentennial celebration; the appearance of Milton Rubincam, past-president of the National Genealogical Society, on the "Today" show; a cover story in *Newsweek;* the seventy-fifth birthday of the National Genealogical Society, at which celebration the society's then vice-president, James D. Walker, who is black, presided over one of its ceremonies; the acceptance of Karen Farmer as the DAR's first acknowledged black member, and the trend away from suppressing Indian ancestry to open acknowledgment of and pride in it.

While some of the activities mentioned above have served as catalysts in bringing genealogy and libraries together, they have by no means been the only forces behind the change. Bidlack cites the increasing interest of libraries in having genealogical collections as early as the 1960s. As certification of genealogists by the American Society for Genealogists, and the National Genealogical Society's *Code of Ethics,* have helped to separate genealogists from charlatans, the reputation of genealogical research has been enhanced significantly and has helped to bring together the genealogist and the librarian.

To build collections in public libraries, Bidlack suggests a minimum number of how-to-do-it books, guides to periodicals, and manuals and guides relating to groups of different ethnic or geographical origin. After acquiring such resources and working with genealogists and researchers, Bidlack concludes that public and academic librarians "will do well to recognize that genealogy is here to stay."

Jean Elder Cazort helps the researcher begin in the pursuit of genealogical research through her discussion of "Basic Sources for Genealogical Research." She calls upon the researcher to have a knowledge of the special sources and problems of the ethnic group which is being examined, but she acknowledges that some sources and techniques are basic to genealogy in general. It is these techniques and tools which are introduced at the beginning of this research guide through the Cazort chapter.

The beginner will ask, "How?" Cazort advises the reader that genealogical research generates considerable paperwork and good organization. Using the ancestor chart (sometimes called the pedigree chart), the researcher should provide for recording data on several generations. Beginning with the searcher's self, the search then records parents, grandparents, and so on, and this data is documented through use of a variety of written records. The search actually begins at home in the examination of family sources (old letters, diaries, family Bibles, school records, and other items) to document what is known and to record what is needed but unknown.

Correspondence with other relatives to fill in blanks, visits to courthouses, libraries, government record offices, and elsewhere will be needed to obtain additional data and as a part of the verification process. Family group sheets will require the searcher to identify multiple marriages, married siblings, birth and death dates, maiden names of wives, listing of adoptees, and other data. Individual worksheets also require mention of military service, religious affiliation, education, and other information, which will provide rather complete information for a family's history.

Cazort cautions against use of dates from early records and warns the searcher that some dating practices can be confusing and misleading. For example, 4–7–76 can be July 4 or April 7, and the genealogist's system (4 July 1776) should be used to avoid that pitfall.

Among the variety of records and sources which the genealogist needs are local histories, maps and atlases, directories, genealogical guides, vital records (birth, marriage, divorce, and death records), county records (land and property records), probate records (wills, administrations, and other documents relating to settling an estate), other county records (civil and criminal court records, voter registration, tax rolls), federal records (war and pension records, bounty land records), church records, cemetery records, and miscellaneous records (newspapers, school reports, private organizations, records on adoptees, and records on the blind and physically handicapped).

The selected bibliography which Cazort includes contains an annotated list of the basic genealogical texts and primary reference works which will need to be consulted. Realizing the importance of periodicals to genealogical research, the section includes a selected list of such works and refers the reader to more complete lists which appear in a variety of references. Major genealogical repositories which contain records on a variety of ethnic groups are given. Their addresses, the scope of their holdings, and other brief information are included. Following, Cazort gives a selected list of general, state, regional, and special-interest genealogical societies, their addresses, and a brief description of their focuses and resources.

Frequently the beginning genealogist is unfamiliar with the supplies which are needed for the investigation. Cazort's brief list of genealogical bookstores and dealers will be useful. She advises the reader, however, to visit local bookstores in search of supplies, as more and more of these businesses are adding pedigree charts and other documents to their stock.

Concluding the chapter is a brief list of training programs in genealogy as examples of courses which both beginning and experienced researchers may wish to pursue.

In preparing a work which is designed for the genealogist, the family historian, the researcher, and the librarian, it follows that some discussion must be given to the topic "Library Records and Research." Casper L. Jordan addresses this topic by exploring current trends in collection development and services. He notes that barriers to information access have often prevented librarians from meeting the informational needs of users researching genealogical and family history and stresses the need to find ways to remove such barriers. This might be done through the development and enforcement of policy statements which describe the collecting practices and define services to users. Such statements should be distributed widely, especially to other libraries and repositories and to professional organizations.

Jordan cites the need for researchers to explore the basic resources in libraries, but also to consider the special bibliographies, published family histories, and other materials. This means that the mechanism for identifying such works may well come through reference services which libraries provide to the genealogist or family historian. Thus the need for a genealogical reference interview looms large, and should come early in the patron's visit to the library. Jordan stresses the importance of conferring with users on the various research approaches as search strategies. Service programs to users may well introduce them to other repositories that collect resources more appropriate to the researcher's needs or that extend those materials already consulted in a particular library.

The stormy, treacherous road of genealogical librarianship is reviewed. Jordan sees merit in the joint ventures which genealogists and librarians have undertaken to meet genealogical reference needs. Further, he notes a dearth of literature on the library's role in service to genealogists and reviews a recent work which takes a giant step in filling this void. The American Library Association (ALA) in recent years also has addressed genealogists' needs. Jordan identifies several ALA publications in genealogy. In addition, he reviews a recent preconference which the History Section of its Reference and Adult Services Division (RASD) held before ALA's annual conference in 1981. The preconference was designed to assist reference librarians in analyzing the genealogist's needs and in creating programs to meet these needs. The comprehensive syllabus which was distributed to participants is especially suited to the issues at hand. Thus, plans are underway to publish the document so that it will be available to libraries and researchers.

Further, the RASD History Section drafted a revision of its statement to editors of family newsletters and called for editors to give special attention to contents, correct form, an appropriate numbering system for each issue, and other specific items.

"Types of Libraries and Their Resources" is a major heading in Jordan's chapter. Here he discusses academic, public, and state libraries and historical societies as repositories of genealogical materials and gives examples of the materials libraries are likely to collect. Although academic libraries generally are designed to support the institutions' curricular and research interests, many collect genealogical materials, and indeed, their own archives are genealogical sources. Such primary materials as academic archives will provide researchers with information on relatives who worked or studied at these institutions. Sometimes papers of families with no connections with the institution are also housed in an academic library.

Jordan states that public libraries, an arm of local government, are designed to serve the interests of the entire community. Thus, the collecting of genealogical materials may be standard practice. Their collections are important for the attention which they give to local history; however, some may have a much broader focus and assemble rather extensive collections in genealogy.

An arm of state government, state libraries and archives are concerned with service to state officials and legislators. They are also open and free to the public. Their collections may center around governors, governmental officials and other political figures, notable figures who live or have lived in the state, and other areas of interest at the state level. It is not unusual to find resources from local historical societies deposited in state libraries.

Libraries in genealogical societies may focus on local history, family history, and genealogy. The societies promote their own work, yet such activities may well fall within the interests of other genealogists. Jordan notes the popularity of historical societies and points out that 5,865 were identified in 1982. Some are much more specialized than others, as, for example, those that relate to religious and ethnic groups.

Included is a discussion of library aids to genealogical research in which Jordan identifies the type of work (handbook, family history, periodical index) and goes on to give examples. The chapter ends with a list of selected libraries and historical societies with genealogical collections. This section is introduced by a discussion of several tools which will lead the reader to more extensive lists, but it also identifies, alphabetically by state, examples of libraries in academic, public, and state settings and in historical societies, which expands the list of a few such libraries in Cazort's chapter. At the end of the chapter Jordan reminds the reader that library staff members must collect genealogical materials in a responsible manner and then assume responsibility for promoting their use, so that patrons will have access to many more resources needed for studying the family.

Bobby L. Lovett provides an in-depth approach in chapter 4, "Researching Family History." He uses researching ethnic history as an example of his approach. The discussion begins by addressing the origins of family history, as Lovett notes that family histories have for a long time appealed to historians, lay citizens, and social scientists. Some families who came to this country brought their coats of arms with them to certify their pedigrees, while many others were of lower classes or descended from indentured servants. Still others came as African slaves. Lovett cites the Revolutionary War and Civil War as two great stimuli for the pursuit of family history, as families began to develop a sense of firm roots in this country. Tracing one's ancestry to the period of either war became a popular activity. Newer conflicts, such as the Spanish-American War and the two world wars, seem to have generated less enthusiasm for the search for ancestors.

Ethnic families of the 1960s began to think more of their unique position in American society, and this awakened them to the fact that they knew little of their family or racial origins. By the late 1970s, interest in ethnic family history had mushroomed. Thus the need to teach family history became pronounced, and later books were written and workshops held which included the study of ethnic family history and approaches to ethnic genealogy.

Lovett distinguishes family history from genealogy and pedigree. Accordingly, he defines pedigree as the lineage, the family tree, the line of descent, and notes that genealogy traces lineal descent. Figuratively, the family history puts flesh on the bare bones of the genealogical chart and enables one to breathe life into deceased ancestors. Genealogy is the chart with chronological and annotated explanations, while family history is the narrative—the saga of a family going through various periods of history.

To complete a genealogy, Lovett advises the searcher to follow six basic steps: (1) construct a pedigree chart, which begins with one's self; (2) collect the research tools needed; (3) acquire the necessary supplies; (4) begin the search at home and use family records; (5) utilize libraries; and (6) investigate records in local, state, and national archives. Creating a family history from a genealogy can be time consuming. However, Lovett notes that the genealogy—a listing of facts and dates about each ancestor—will read like a chronicle or even an obituary. The family history will be much longer because of the detailed information about people's lives and life styles which it will contain. The family historian must develop the same techniques any other biographer uses. As illustrated, Lovett notes the techniques Alex Haley followed in tracing his roots, as he used sources creatively and tried to relive some of Kunta Kinte's experiences as a means of visualizing the background of his ancestor's home. Haley, like other family historians, became a detective, and he interviewed relatives; pinpointed periods in time to begin the search; explored the passage of ships between Gambia and Annapolis; cross-checked data; searched newspapers, deeds, plantation records, and other documents; and was able to weave a story around his findings.

Lovett explores various methods which the family historian should follow in the search. The researcher will need to identify and use the appropriate sources, which will include oral interviews with relatives and family friends, memoirs, books, newspapers, and bank records. These sources will vary according to the researcher's ethnic background. For example, a black may need to search plantation records and missionary society reports, while an American Indian will need to search tribal records. The importance of the oral interview is emphasized. Lovett identifies some of the oral history collections which include ethnic groups, and he points out their potential importance to the family history researcher.

Cemetery records, computer banks, and photoanalysis (of old photographs, paintings, and drawings) are discussed as important sources of information for the family historian. Even though the researcher may utilize the various sources given, Lovett warns that there may be some roadblocks to successful research. Problems may result from the absence of records on ethnic groups. Ethnic history becomes difficult as one examines the migration patterns of families; thus Lovett advises researchers to understand the black and Japanese migration patterns during earlier and later periods in history. Further, the researcher will need to question the reliability of sources used and check and authenticate dates and other information by finding supporting sources. One must question unsupported dates, inflated figures, and doubtful details, as unreliable evidence can lead in the wrong direction, making the family history which results from the search inaccurate.

At this juncture the researcher is ready to write the family history. Lovett recommends several tools which one should use to begin the writing process. Next the relevant data are selected and the irrelevant discarded. The writer should explain why certain events occurred, present information in a strict chronology, gain a sense of the complete history surrounding the family, and, when possible, illustrate the work. Once the history has been written in final form, Lovett suggests depositing a copy of the work in a library. The chapter concludes with a selected and annotated bibliography, which is useful for researching and writing ethnic family history.

Among the various genealogical repositories in the nation are two which have much more extensive collections and are by far the most resourceful for comprehensive study of genealogy, including ethnic genealogy. These are the National Archives in Washington, D.C., and the Genealogical Society of Utah Library in Salt Lake City. These two leading centers are discussed in separate chapters under the general title of Part II, ''Utilizing Major Repositories for Genealogical Research.'' James D. Walker opens the discussion with his review of ''The National Archives and Records Service.'' He identifies the archives as that part of the General Services Administration that has responsibility for retaining the permanently valuable records of the federal government. Divided into three parts, the National Archives and Records Service embraces the National Archives Building in Washington, D.C., seventeen Federal Records Centers, and eight presidential libraries. Walker notes that these are vital sources of information on individuals and families of ethnic origin and can contribute to successful pursuit of family history or genealogy. He stresses the importance of understanding the archives and the record group format, which includes or separates the records of various federal agencies, offices, bureaus, services, and so forth.

Various guides to the National Archives are discussed early in Walker's chapter. While some are outdated and may have limited value to the librarian and researcher, others are effective indexes to the vast resources located in the archives. Thus the published guides, inventories, information leaflets, and other publications serve as an introduction to the holdings of the National Archives and can be used successfully in research there.

To aid the librarian and researcher in utilizing the archives, Walker stresses the importance of knowing at least the names, dates, places, and events which cause information about a person to be included in a federal record. Once this is known, a variety of sources may be used to gather information. Such sources include the Federal Census Schedules, which Walker lists and describes. Data included in the schedules are given from the first census in 1790 to the most recent census available for public use—the 1910 census. Further, Walker describes the various supplemental schedules, such as manufacturing schedules, mortality schedules, agriculture schedules, and others which relate to a segment of the population (Civil War enumerations, enumerations of American Indians, records of the Bureau of Refugees, Freedmen, and Abandoned Lands, and so forth).

In addition to the census schedules, there are in the archives extensive records which relate to aliens and immigrants. These include federal immigration records, passenger lists, crew lists, ship manifests, naturalization records, passport records, and seamen's passports.

For an account of the extensive military records located in the National Archives, Walker's chapter is especially useful. He describes the various federal military services records and their importance as sources of information about aliens, unnaturalized residents, and U.S. citizens who served in the various wars. Whether these people were called to serve in the armed forces or participated with a group known as volunteers, the records are extremely beneficial. Walker notes that members of volunteer units served in every major conflict. The records of battles he describes are those of the Revolutionary War, the 1784–1811 war, the War of 1812, the Indian wars, the Mexican War, the Civil War (Union), the Spanish-American War, and the Philippine Insurrection.

Papers relating to specific military units are described in detail. These units and records relating to them include the U.S. Army (enlistment registers, medical records, and other documents), U.S. Navy and U.S. Marine Corps (officers' records, prisoner-of-war records, enlistment registers, and others), and U.S. Coast Guard and U.S. Merchant Marine (records include information about duties and services rendered).

Military records also include documents relating to pension application files, bounty land warrant application files, domiciliary care and hospitalization, and other veterans' benefits. Civilian personnel records are significant sources of data on ethnic groups, and Walker discusses the various records which relate to citizens who were employed by the federal government.

The final portion of Walker's discussion relates to the particular series of federal records that are valuable to ethnic family history. For the Afro-American, Walker notes that all the records discussed throughout the chapter are important.

He notes, however, that the most desired information on Afro-Americans is excluded from federal records. Papers which are in federal records include those of the Freedmen's Bureau, the Freedmen's Savings and Trust Company, Afro-American military unit records, intercoastal slave manifests, census records (for slaves and free blacks), Civil War records (including especially those of the U.S. Colored Troops), various court records, District of Columbia slave records, and Confederate States government records.

The most important records which aid in the study of American Indian family history are among those of the Bureau of Indian Affairs. Walker notes, however, that many separate series of military records, veterans' benefits records, censuses, and other record groups contain valuable information on American Indians. Since 1870 American Indians have been included in the federal decennial population schedules, and since then there have been various censuses of Indian tribes. Some quasi-censuses also exist in the form of enrollments, lists of tribal members who signed treaties, departure and arrival rolls of Indians removed from the East Coast to reservations in the West, various treaty records, and others.

Records of American trust territories included in the archives relate to Hawaii, the Philippine Islands and other former possessions, and Puerto Rico. Most of these records remain in the territory or are among the territorial records of the departments of Interior and State. Those of Puerto Rico have been transferred to the island, while those of the Philippines were returned to that country after its independence. Other ethnic groups represented in the archives are the Chinese, Japanese, Latin Americans, Danes, and others.

Walker ends the chapter with an extensive bibliography of items published by the National Archives. Included are guides, indexes, reference information papers, preliminary inventories, special lists, Archives Conference Papers, and other sources which are vital to the utilization of the National Archives for genealogical research.

"The Genealogical Society of Utah Library," by Roger Scanland, describes, in his words, "the world's largest genealogical library" and the contents of "the world's largest collection of ethnic genealogical data." Without actual count, Scanland estimates that there are over 200,000 reels of microfilm in the library's ethnic holdings. In addition, the collection contains thousands of family group sheets and hundreds of taped or transcribed oral pedigrees.

Of the groups addressed in this reference work, American Indians, black Americans, and Hispanic Americans are particularly well represented. Because of the library's global acquisition program, some smaller groups are also represented in the collection. Included also are records from Samoa, Tonga, Indonesia, and Korea. Located in the Church Office Building, the headquarters of the Church of Jesus Christ of Latter-day Saints (LDS, the Mormons), the library, which is referred to as the LDS Library, is open to the public regardless of race or creed.

Interestingly, the library is currently divided into ten collections, most of which have full-time specialists and staffs. In addition to the General Reference Collection and the United States Collection, related to this reference work and housed in the library are the Africa-Asia Collection, the Oriental Collection, and the Latin America Collection. The United States reference staff includes specialists in American Indian and Afro-American research, while the Latin America–Iberian Peninsula staff assists the researcher in Hispanic-American studies. Reference service at the main desk is currently available in a variety of languages, including English, Spanish, French, Chinese, and Japanese.

In keeping with the trend toward computerization, in 1979 the library's card catalog was discontinued except for entries in non-Roman-alphabet languages, and some 10 million cards were placed in an automated catalog. Full conversion into all-Roman-alphabet entries is in process. The library's International Genealogical Index, a computerized worldwide listing of millions of births, christenings, and marriages, is increased annually by several million new entries. There are also over 8 million family group records in the Family Group Record Archives. Many minorities are represented in the files. The main library's collection also houses over 117,000 volumes and bound periodicals, and microfilms. It also retains genealogical books and manuscripts which individuals lend to the library for research purposes.

The library for the past ten years has maintained an oral genealogy program. Most projects completed through 1979 are on tape and in transcribed copy. The book collection, the oral genealogy collection, and the Family Group Record Archives cover fairly recent histories of families.

The researcher will find the library system and its branches particularly interesting and useful for research regardless of his or her own location. While the main library is located in Salt Lake City, branch libraries are in Mormon meetinghouses throughout the United States and in some foreign countries. Branch libraries maintain small collections of basic genealogical books and microforms and copies of the library's catalogs and the International Genealogical Index. Copies of microfilms which are housed in the main library may be borrowed through the branch system for use in the branch libraries. Some of the larger branches provide photocopies, both for books which are out of copyright and for microforms. Staff members in the branch libraries provide assistance to the beginning genealogist and to some extent to the experienced researcher.

American Indian records in the library include microfilmed resources from the National Archives, materials microfilmed in Oklahoma and elsewhere, and several hundred works on American Indians. Most are histories of tribes, but some biographies are included. Resources on black Americans include birth registers, marriage books, death registers, wills and deeds (from every southern state), census and tax rolls, court records, church records, and other records. Military records housed in the National Archives have been microfilmed and are available in the LDS Library. Scanland points out the importance of the library's vast holdings in black genealogy and that these resources have gone largely unrecognized.

The nation's largest collection of Hispanic-American genealogical resources is also in the Genealogical Department, LDS Library. According to Scanland, extensive microfilming is still underway to preserve the Spanish influence in Texas and California; however, on hand already are copies of Spanish censuses of eastern Florida, Alabama, and Mississippi; records of the Spanish governmental organization in Louisiana; parish records from Arkansas; and marriage records, church records, church lists, census records, and other items from Texas. Similar records for New Mexico, Arizona, Colorado, and California are included.

For the Oriental American, the extensiveness of records depends on how mobile people were after arriving in the United States. If Oriental Americans tended to remain in the same place, their genealogies are easier to trace in the library through church records, organization records, and other sources. Until a few years ago microfilmed records in the United States concentrated almost wholly on eastern states, but now they are moving to western states. For those who have traced their Oriental ancestry to the water's edge and require pursuit of records in the mother countries, the library has an extensive collection of Oriental genealogies and related resources.

Other records are included on the Caribbean, Spain, Portugal, Mexico, Central America, South America, certain African countries, other countries in Central Africa, Southeast Asia, the Orient (China, Japan, Korea, the Philippines), and elsewhere.

Scanland's discussion concludes with an annotated list of works that describe the library's ethnic collection and notes that many others have been prepared but are unpublished.

Opening the discussion of special-subject genealogy in Part III is Jimmy B. Parker, in his chapter entitled "American Indian Records and Research." Parker notes early that one can no more be an American Indian expert than one can be an expert in genealogical and historical research on all of Europe. One need not become an expert on the history of all American Indian tribes but must know the commonalities that exist among the records and research relating to the various tribes.

He points out that many people believe that no records on the American Indian are extant, but he emphasizes that they do indeed exist and in many cases are much more complete and accurate than those which relate to non-Indian ancestors. It is usually possible to trace an American Indian line as far back as the early 1800s or late 1700s.

In preparing for American Indian research, one must know how to find the tribal group, study the tribe's history and locality, study the types and locations of records, and remember that the attitudes of both Indians and non-Indians will affect the records that exist. To identify the various tribes, Parker cites several notable reference works on American Indians and goes on to explain that the term "tribe" often has no uniform application in the eastern United States, that one term may embrace several groups.

Parker stresses the historical background of Indian tribes and notes that one must know the background of the tribe with which the ancestor was affiliated. Thus one must know naming customs, kinship systems, migration patterns, and other features of the tribe. As tribes migrated, their records and the responsibility for maintaining them fell into the hands of different agencies.

Intermingling or conversion is important in American Indian history. Parker notes the basic intention of whites to intermingle all Indians with white society, to convert them to Christianity, and to remove them entirely from their own society. Church records may prove important references for the genealogists, yet caution must be exercised in identifying persons whose Indian names were replaced by Christian names. Further, as Indians were removed from their lands and established in other geographical areas, their existence may well have been recorded on census rolls and muster lists. Once placed on reservations, their whereabouts were monitored on a set of records known as annuity rolls. As the Bureau of Indian Affairs became concerned about Indian education, the school census records of those who were educated were kept. Beginning in 1865 and continuing to 1940, the federal government maintained censuses for most reservations.

The allotment period, 1887–1930, a time in which the federal government gave a parcel of land to each individual Indian, also produced a valuable set of records which identified the tribe, the death of an Indian with an allotment, all heirs, and their relationship to the deceased. Registers of families were maintained by the Indian agents and usually included both the Indian and English names, ages or birthdates, and information regarding brothers, sisters, parents, uncles, aunts, and other relatives.

Parker cites the importance of records that fall outside the various policy periods he describes. These are called vital records, and some were kept by non-Indians and some by tribal governments. The information they contain varies according to the particular reservation, thus increasing the importance of understanding the historical background of a particular tribe. Parker notes other types of records, such as the Sanitary Record of Sick, Injured, Births, Deaths; the claims records (legal cases against the United States); wills; and other documents.

To determine where American Indian records are located, Parker cites family records; Bureau of Indian Affairs records; tribal offices; the National Archives and its branches; churches; private collections, including historical societies, universities, genealogical libraries, and other repositories; the Doris Duke Oral History Project, which involves seven universities; and the LDS Library. The discussion concludes with an annotated list of works on the American Indian.

One of the most extensive discussions on Asian-American genealogy to be found in any source is Greg Gubler's "Asian-American Records and Research." Noting that Pacific migration is a relatively recent phenomenon, that the immigrants received hostile treatment, and that assimilation has been difficult to achieve, Gubler concludes that racial bars and prejudices have caused Asian Americans to keep close ethnic ties and to strive for a sense of community as a security measure in mainstream America. It is the relatively recent arrival of the Asian immigrant that makes it difficult to divorce these new residents from the Asian past. Vestiges of the past are needed to provide clues for family research; yet for many Asian Americans, research to determine their origin is not an easy task. Complex languages and the lack of direction and information about records and procedures hamper the research process.

As the genealogical research begins, the researcher must remember that, as with other groups, the number of ancestors doubles with each generation. Thus the research project is soon likely to grow into a sizeable undertaking. Asian research may require a great deal of imagination and detective work. Photographs, for example, may contain clues about dress styles, traits, and other elements of people's life styles. Home sources for the Asian American may include those common to other groups, such as photographs, clippings, certificates, passports, and diaries, but for the Japanese American may mean traditional family crests (*kamon* or *iemon*), family genealogies (*kafu* or *keizu*), and paper or wooden mortuary tablets (*ihai*); Chinese Americans may have clan or family genealogies (*chia-p'u* or *tsu-p'u*), family registers, or other pertinent materials; Korean Americans may have family genealogies (*chopko* or *ga-jung*); while some Vietnamese refugees may have little or no records, having escaped with nothing more than the clothes on their backs.

Gubler's account of the research problems and approaches, or the barriers and solutions to Asian-American genealogical research, stresses the language barrier and the difficulty which Asian Americans encounter in developing enough expertise to do advanced research in the languages of their ancestors. As most Asian immigrants struggled with English, they made errors in completing simple immigration papers. Immigration officials were unable to understand the Asians' poor English and often made errors in paperwork, in spellings, and in the entire record systems they maintained. The absence of library materials for Asian immigrants is cited as a critical problem, and when materials have been gathered, they tend to relate more to the larger groups. The stronger collections are few in number and their contents generally unknown. In many cases, Gubler notes, there is simply nothing to collect, as no records exist.

The reader will find Gubler's brief overview of the history of the various Asian-American groups informative, as he moves from a brief history of the Chinese to histories of the Japanese, Koreans, Indochinese (refugees from Vietnam, Cambodia, and Laos), and Asian groups from the Indian subcontinent (India, Pakistan, and Bangladesh), from Indonesia, and from Thailand.

Records on Asian Americans which are found in the continental United States and Hawaii include vital records (births, deaths, marriages, divorces) in the Hawaii State Archives and in the LDS Library; immigration records in the Japanese Consulate-General's offices in Honolulu; census records in the Hawaii State Archives, the Genealogical Department, LDS Library, and the National

Archives and its branches; other immigration records (arrival and registration records, ship manifests, passenger manifests) located in the Hawaii State Archives and at the LDS Library; other records kept by the Chinese Bureau in Hawaii; "segregated Chinese files" at the National Archives; Japanese immigration records kept at the University of California–Los Angeles (UCLA); and so on.

Also useful for Asian-American genealogical research are ethnic newspapers, cemetery and funerary records, local records (criminal and civil judgments, land records, wills, adoptions, agreements, miners' taxes), city directories, other personal records (work permits, applications, certificates of identification, voter registrations), and a variety of other sources. Gubler lists in tabular form a group of personal papers and documents, their purpose, notations of their contents, and their origin.

Crossing the waters, Gubler discusses the history of Asians in their native lands and the types of records which are useful for genealogical purposes. These include Chinese clan genealogies, ancestral tablets, tombstone inscriptions, and other documents; Japanese family or household registers (earlier noted), Buddhist death registers, mortuary tablets, tombstone inscriptions, genealogies, and other early sources; modern Korean records such as the family or household register, genealogies, local histories; Catholic Church registers in the Philippines and Philippines immigration and naturalization records; and records of other Asian groups, such as the Vietnamese, Thais, and East Indians. The Genealogical Department, LDS Library, maintains extensive microfilmed records from the native lands of many of these groups.

Useful to the researcher and the librarian is Gubler's typical Chinese- and Japanese-American search, which guides one in genealogical pursuit; his extensive and well-annotated selected list of books, monographs, and articles on the various Asian-American groups; his list and description of major repositories on these groups; his list of major societies and ethnic organizations, together with statements about their work; and his list of bookstores and suppliers, with a discussion of their resources.

Still a developing field, black genealogy is discussed in Charles L. Blockson's chapter on "Black American Records and Research." Appropriately, Blockson begins the chapter by citing James D. Walker's earlier published definition of black genealogy as "the history of the person or family, slave or free, whose ancestry includes at least one person of African blood." While the literature of genealogy generally notes the importance of the book *Roots* and the television presentation "Miss Jane Pittman" to the field of genealogy, Blockson especially notes the value of these two sagas to the field of black genealogy. Further, he points out the nation's slow acceptance of black genealogy as a viable field and goes on to demonstrate that black genealogy is, in fact, a recognized field of study.

Black genealogy has its peculiarities. As Blockson describes, black Americans have encountered a variety of problems in tracing their roots. These include their multiethnic backgrounds; the various difficulties in tracing ancestors through the period of slavery; the separations of families; the changes in names which occurred during slavery, as well as the use of classical names, the use of a single name, and the use of the names of various slave masters; lost or mixed ancestry, with admixtures including whites, Spaniards, and American Indians; and the practice of crossing over into mainstream America, or "passing," which some blacks have been able to do. Sample documents from plantation and other records are used in the chapter to illustrate these problems.

The black oral tradition is emphasized in the pursuit of black genealogy, especially because of the absence of systematic records on blacks during their early years in this country, because slaves were forbidden to read and write, and because oral transmission of information was the only means by which certain information could be preserved. The slave narrative, which was written down for former slaves by whites, by some of the few blacks who could write and who managed to record their history, and later by others who interviewed former slaves, can be important sources of information about early black life in America.

Blacks who pursue their family lines must remember that not all blacks were slaves. Accordingly, they will need to search for genealogical information on free blacks, as can be found in publications such as *List of Free Black Heads of Families in the First Census of the United States, 1790* and *Free Negro Heads of Families in the United States in 1830*. Blockson notes also that some free blacks were slave owners themselves. Thus the researcher will have to examine a variety of records on such ancestors and, in doing so, will be able to capture a picture of the position free blacks held in American history.

Considerable discussion is given to a variety of black genealogical records. Among these are family Bibles (those kept by black families as well as those which were owned by white families and which listed slaves), church records (those of black churches as well as those of white churches, some of which maintained black memberships), cemetery records (for blacks and for whites, especially those cemetery records which listed slaves buried there), census records (especially slave schedules and notations of free black heads of households), and plantation records. The records plantation owners kept vary widely in scope and content and include records of bondage, ownership, breeding, and branding; labor contracts; bills of sale of slaves; wills; estate inventories; insurance records; medical records; employment records; emancipation records, or "free papers"; and sharecropping records. Plantation records have been preserved in many libraries and archives, yet many have been scattered, and they often appear at flea markets and elsewhere, thus fragmenting an important source of information on black history.

Blockson also identifies documents from other activities involving blacks, such as war or military records (including those of the pension bureau and elsewhere); Underground Railroad records; early city directories; photographs;

papers of the Freedmen's Bureau; bank records (especially those of the early black banks); Negro court and criminal records; prison, workhouse, and inebriate asylum records; and county orphan records. The relationship between blacks and Indians is also discussed, and the researcher is referred to American Indian documents as a source of information on Indian ancestors. As seen earlier in the discussion on American Indian records and research, one must know the tribal affiliation of one's American Indian ancestor or the search will be fruitless.

Appropriately, Blockson discusses blacks and the Canadian connection, noting that as early as 1720 blacks resided in Canada. Some went there from the United States through the efforts of the Underground Railroad; others who were free also settled there. Records on black Canadians can be traced in a number of primary and secondary sources, some of which are discussed in the chapter.

As example of the pursuit of records of an early black immigrant, Blockson presents a case study of two members of the Jamestown Group which shows that the male immigrant, who later married and had a son and possibly other children, was an early landowner and that his family owned land as late as 1660. The case study cites the need to search wills, deeds, and other records from Virginia's early history and proves also that black genealogy can take one far back into this nation's history.

Of particular importance to the study of black genealogy, Blockson lists several black or ethnic programs which have helped to foster the study of black genealogy; several black genealogical societies (and gives a notation of their work and their publications); and black organizations. He provides a selected and annotated bibliography, which guides the librarian and the researcher to some of the numerous works on black history, black family history, and black genealogy and includes sections on black periodicals and retrospective and current black newspapers, which are useful for their account of black history.

The concluding section in this research guide is Lyman De Platt's "Hispanic-American Records and Research." Platt defines such records as those which deal with Americans of Spanish and Mexican origin, with emphasis on those found in the United States and Mexico and with some mention of the vast repositories in Spain. Like the earlier authors who discussed the genealogy of particular ethnic groups, Platt makes it clear that genealogical and historical research on Hispanic Americans can be successfully pursued throughout the United States and other countries. As with any group, not every ancestor can be traced across the border or through the extant records; yet Platt asserts that tracing the pedigrees of Hispanic Americans is just as easy as tracing those of Anglo-Europeans, blacks, or Orientals, if not more so.

As he gives accounts of Hispanic-American history, Platt mixes his discussions with case studies and with detailed expanations of the records which reveal specific information. In doing so, he notes where the appropriate records are located; for example, the Archivo General de la Nación (AGN) in Mexico City contains records of twenty-one orphan children in Mexico, or New Spain as it was called. Further, Platt cites attempts to persuade large groups (families) to immigrate en masse into California, New Mexico, Arizona, and Texas.

Records of Spaniards who chose to settle in the United States west of Mexico are called emigration records and were kept at Cadiz and Seville in Spain. Today they are housed at the Archivo General de Indias in Seville. Numerous individual records are maintained in the Immigration and Naturalization Service (INS) office in El Paso, Texas, for those Spaniards or Mexicans who entered the United States between 1902 and 1953. Legislation that deals with the transfer or resettlement of Mexicans living in California, Arizona, New Mexico, and Texas; and the northern Mexican states of Baja California, Sonora, Coahuila, Durango, Nuevo Leon, and Tamaulipas are in the Archivo Historico de Sonora. Records of Spaniards who entered the United States through New Orleans (1820–1903) have been recorded in official lists that are available in the New Orleans Public Library, while microfilm copies are in the LDS Library. Early lists (1830–1923) also have been published.

Of particular value to the researcher is the AGN, which houses a variety of documents dealing with immigrants entering the United States through New Mexico and Arizona. Its archives contain the majority of those documents relating to the northern part of Mexico during the colonial period. The extensive records of the AGN also contain passports and passport information, lists of garrisons, detachments, crews, and other information and documents. Further, Platt notes that the Spanish took many censuses during the colonial period, thousands of which are extant in Spain, Mexico, and the United States. Spanish censuses tend to be informative much earlier than those of the English-speaking world. They include family names, ages, relationships, and civil status, and they date from the beginning of European civilization in the northern area. Microfilm copies of these censuses are available in the LDS Library.

Notable among the genealogical sources that include data on families are the military records. Such records are located in numerous major archives as well as in minor ones and also in the LDS Library. In addition to records located in state, regional, or national archives, Platt notes the location of Hispanic-American records at the libraries of the University of Texas and the University of California–Berkeley and at the State Records Center and Archives in Santa Fe, the Huntington Library, the Texas History Research Library, St. Mary's University library in San Antonio, and other libraries in Mexico. Reference is made to several sources which locate Hispanic-American materials in libraries in the United States.

Noting the problems Hispanic-American genealogy is likely to produce, Platt states that it is difficult to extend a pedigree when the origin of the family is unknown. Mexican and Spanish lines in the United States often go back two or three generations and then leave the country. Records in the United States give little or no information on the whereabouts of their ancestry. To some extent the 1900 census and the International Genealogical Index at the LDS Genealogical Library help shed some light on the problem. In addition, many children of

Hispanic-American parents were born of unions that were not legally recorded, thus frequently making the father permanently lost or, if known, omitted from earlier records. Subsequent records, such as marriages or deaths, may provide this information.

The searcher must review vital records, censuses, land records, cemetery records, local histories, and other documents that would be used in genealogical searches. Further, the researcher must know that in parts of Mexico separate parish registers were maintained for Spaniards, Indians, and Negroes and their admixtures. Separation was necessary for tax purposes as well as for proper dispensations of contracts to parties who wished to marry, as it was unlawful for many years for Spaniards to marry Negroes or anyone of Negro ancestry.

Platt concludes his discussion with an extensive annotated bibliography, which is important for successful pursuit of Hispanic-American genealogy.

I

GENERAL INFORMATION ON SOURCES, PROCEDURES, AND GENEALOGICAL RESEARCH

1

Librarians and Genealogical Research

RUSSELL E. BIDLACK

In no area of library service has there been a more dramatic change in philosophy and attitude on the part of librarians than that relating to genealogy. The "hands-off" policy that was so typical among libraries just a decade or two ago has been largely transformed into one of "open arms." This remarkable change of attitude toward the study of family history deserves some explanation.

As one who has been fascinated by genealogical research for forty years, I am convinced that it is part of human nature to have some curiosity regarding one's ancestry. While for many this curiosity extends no further than remembering a grandparent's account of family legends and passing them on to one's children, for others it means research extending over a lifetime.

GENEALOGICAL INFORMATION

Unlike most other hobbies, genealogy involves searching for information rather than for collectable objects. Philatelists and numismatists, like collectors of antiques, autographs, or Indian relics, seek the objects themselves. While they may use the written record to improve their technique or to classify and describe their findings, the information contained in those records serves only to assist them in reaching their real goal, that of locating and acquiring the objects. For the genealogist the information contained in the written record constitutes the end result, to be recorded and interpreted and then to be shared with others. We do not collect our ancestors, only data about them. What better patron than the genealogist might a librarian seek to serve? Perhaps a better question would be: Why was the genealogist so unwelcome in so many libraries for so long?

There is an old Chinese proverb that reads: "To forget one's ancestors is to be a brook without a source, a tree without a root." While most of us have a natural curiosity regarding our roots and the sources of our heritage, until rather recently there were forces in America that dampened that curiosity.

THE ROOTS OF AMERICA

The United States was settled largely by people who were running away, escaping from societies where tradition and caste offered little opportunity for improvement of their lot. Our ancestors who came to America of their own free will, came in search of a life better than that which their forebears had experienced, and they frequently brought with them bitterness toward aristocracies that had been beyond their own reach, aristocracies that relied upon ancestry and inheritance for preserving their favored place. Few individuals with titles, pedigrees, and property left England, Europe, and Asia to settle in America. Those who ventured forth tended to have little to lose, and if they survived in the New World it was because they "made it" on their own, not because of a heritage passed on to them from the past. In many instances the immigrant to America did not want to remember an unhappy past in the "old country." Life would begin anew in a new land. The immigrant would be the beginning, not a continuation, of an ancestral line of descendants.

For the European and Oriental immigrants of the nineteenth century, the "melting pot" ideal of America also discouraged the preservation of family traditions and history. I can recall second-generation German families in the Iowa of my youth whose embarrassment caused by their parents' heavy accents took the form of total disinterest in their parents' origins. But all of that has changed. There is a saying among genealogists: The grandson often wants to remember what the grandfather wants to forget.

That portion of our population brought unwillingly to America, uprooted from its African heritage and enslaved, was of course systematically deprived of a knowledge of its heritage. The slave who remembers and takes pride in ancestral achievements is a constant threat to the master, as Kunta Kinte was so ably shown to be in *Roots*.

The success of the American Revolution represented a further blow to the study of genealogy. While today the Daughters of the American Revolution (DAR) and Sons of the American Revolution (SAR) take pride in tracing their descent from soldiers who fought the British, few of those soldiers would have professed an interest in tracing their own ancestry. To our ancestors who fought the redcoats, England represented all the evils of a closed society based upon birthright, and it is not surprising that the victorious Americans saw to it that the legal foundations of their new country contained none of the vestiges of inherited privilege—titles and coats of arms were given no status in American law, and the abandonment of the custom of primogeniture made the eldest son the equal of the youngest.

Another American characteristic that has tended to mitigate against an interest in genealogy has been our tendency to move from one part of the country to another. Family ties were constantly broken by the westward movement, and family traditions were often short-lived. In many instances, even the family Bible was left behind or was lost during the journey.

"I am a self-made man," was the motto of the typical American pioneer and remains today as the badge of honor for many a politician and industrial entrepreneur. The self-made person presumably has little regard for ancestry. "I am more interested in what the grandson will become than in what his grandfather was." Abraham Lincoln is said to have used this observation on more than one occasion for political advantage, but despite his public utterances, several of Honest Abe's private letters reveal a genuine interest in, and close knowledge of, the Lincoln family history. In the Lincoln tomb today, each state in which the Lincoln family resided during its movement westward is represented by that state's flag.

HISTORICAL DEVELOPMENT OF GENEALOGY

While the majority of eighteenth- and nineteenth-century Americans professed a disregard for genealogy, a minority gradually became interested. There was actually a family history published in 1731 by James Blake, Jr., as an appendix to his *Memoirs of Roger Clap,* and a broadside is known to have been published in German in Lancaster County, Pennsylvania, in 1763 devoted to the genealogical records of the Bollinger family.

In 1845 the New England Historic Genealogical Society was founded in Boston, and by the time of the nation's centennial in 1876, it was estimated that some 400 family histories had been published in the United States. In 1903 the National Genealogical Society was founded by twenty-four individuals in Washington, D.C., and nine years later it began publishing a quarterly journal. When that society celebrated its fiftieth birthday in 1953, it could boast of a membership of 600; in 1978, when it celebrated its diamond jubilee, its membership numbered over 4,000.

By the turn of the century a number of hereditary and patriotic societies had been established. These groups limit membership to individuals who can prove that an ancestor participated in a certain event or was living in a particular place prior to a given date. It was our centennial in 1876 that stimulated the formation of the DAR and SAR, followed by the General Society of Colonial Wars, the Colonial Dames of America, the Mayflower Society, and a score of others. More recently the Daughters of the Barons of Runnemede, the Magna Charta Dames, and the Order of the Crown of Charlemagne in the United States of America have made their appearance. There is even the Society of Descendants of the Illegitimate Sons and Daughters of the Kings of Britain, members of which are often called the Royal Bastards. While few hereditary and patriotic societies were established to promote the study of genealogy, in order for one to become a member such investigation has been required, and this experience has often proved to be the stimulant for more extensive genealogical research.

Wars have a tendency to promote genealogical investigation—a soldier finding himself in a place where his ancestors once lived, whether a Union soldier in

Virginia in 1863 or an American GI in Germany in 1945, may become curious to know more about those ancestors.

During the later decades of the nineteenth century, as every community's surviving pioneers were becoming fewer, local historical societies were often established to preserve the memories of the past. Local history and genealogy are closely bound together, and a heightened interest in one always stimulates activity in the other. Improved communication in the early twentieth century also helped to bring branches of families in touch with one another again. Ease of travel by automobile, coupled with the growing tendency for more and more families to take annual vacations, have enabled distant cousins to become acquainted personally and to share the knowledge of their families' past.

LIBRARIES AND GENEALOGY

Whereas in 1876 the number of published family histories amounted to about 400, by 1915 the number had grown to over 3,000. Today that figure stands at over 25,000. As increasing numbers of Americans became interested in tracing their roots, it would seem to follow that libraries, especially public libraries, should have developed genealogical collections and welcomed researchers. With but relatively few exceptions, however, this seems to have happened only recently. The policy regarding genealogy at the Enoch Pratt Free Library of Baltimore, as expressed in its 1950 "General Reference Department Staff Manual," was typical: "No genealogical searching is done by the library, either for residents or non-residents. Inquirers are given the printed memorandum (Form 78) explaining our policy on the subject and are supplied with a list of local genealogists. The staff should make it clear to patrons that the list is not to constitute a recommendation of their services."

The "printed memorandum" mentioned in this statement is reproduced in figure 1.1.

How does one account for this lack of enthusiasm for genealogy and genealogists as library patrons as expressed in the Enoch Pratt policy, a disinterest that has been so typical of public libraries? I have attempted to answer this question in another publication, an article entitled, "Genealogy As It Relates to Library Service," appearing in the American Library Association's yearbook of 1978:

She, less often he, tended to be elderly or at least middle-aged and usually possessed an imperfect knowledge of and respect for essentials of proper library usage such as the card catalog and the *Readers' Guide*. Genealogists were not considered serious readers in that they never read a book thoroughly—in fact, they often demanded as many as a dozen volumes at a time only to examine the indexes (and complain mightily if an index were wanting). If the stacks were closed, they demanded access because they were never quite sure what it was they wanted, nor did they trust the page to find it. If there were several genealogists in the reading room at one time, they tended to be noisy—they talked out loud as they shared with each other their discoveries and their frustrations. The fact that

Figure 1.1
Memorandum, Enoch Pratt Free Library

ENOCH PRATT FREE LIBRARY
Baltimore's Public Library
CATHEDRAL AND MULBERRY STREETS, BALTIMORE 1, MD.

Genealogical Research

A Survey of Libraries in the United States, conducted by the American Library Association and published in 1926, shows that as a general custom the public libraries of the country find it inadvisable to devote any considerable amount of time to genealogical work or to specialize in genealogical departments or collections.

In accordance with this custom, The Enoch Pratt Free Library does not buy books that are narrowly and technically genealogical. For such books the reader must turn to the collections in the libraries of the Peabody Institute and the Maryland Historical Society. If genealogical books are purchased by the Pratt Library, it is because they contain a liberal amount of biographical (as contrasted with strictly genealogical) information about important individuals or families of Maryland.

Furthermore, as the Pratt Library does not maintain a genealogical department and on its present budget cannot afford to have a trained genealogist on its staff, the Library feels regretfully forced to explain that it is not at present equipped to do research work of a genealogical nature.

78 8-47-200

Courtesy Enoch Pratt Free Library of Baltimore.

they often appeared to be hard of hearing added to the aggravation. Furthermore, they never wanted to leave when it was time to close the reading room—there was always one more note to take or another index to check.

The prim little old lady, or the elderly gentleman with a cane, was always, of course, a Wasp. While there were a few genealogists who did their research as thoroughly as the serious historian, many seemed to search for ancestors merely to use them as badges to join exclusive societies, such as the DAR, the Society of Mayflower Descendants, the National Society of Colonial Dames of America, or the Society of the Cincinnati. Genealogy was often dismissed by librarians as "the sport of Brahmins."[1]

In further defense of the public library's lack of enthusiasm for genealogy, it must also be noted that printed materials in this area have always been expensive and have often been difficult to acquire. Published family histories constitute a small portion of the research materials required by the genealogist, which include state, county, and town histories; indexes and abstracts of probate records, deeds, and court proceedings; cemetery transcriptions; military rosters and pension applications; church records—in fact, any record pertaining to people who lived in the past, especially obscure people whose presence on this earth left but a small mark, can serve as a vital source for genealogical research. (Most of us descend from a remarkably large number of obscure people.) An awareness of the vast store of materials necessary for extensive genealogical research has frightened many a librarian with a limited book budget.

For many years, however, a few libraries have catered specifically to the genealogist. The Newberry Library of Chicago; the Detroit Public Library, with its famous Burton Historical Collection; and the New York Public Library are notable examples. The Library of Congress, with its vast collection of books in every field, has long been a haven for the genealogist. A more recent example of a library providing unusual service to the genealogist is that of the Public Library of Fort Wayne and Allen County in Indiana. Assistant librarian Rick Ashton has reported: "We acquire all the genealogical books and periodicals we can afford and provide full reference service for these materials in a separate reading room. Our collection now approaches 200,000 volumes and exceeds 20,000 rolls of microfilm."[2] Ashton further wrote that many of the happy users of the Fort Wayne library "believe that only Washington, D.C., with the combined resources of the Library of Congress and the National Archives, and Salt Lake City, with the vast collection put together by the Mormons, offer greater opportunities for the genealogist." In 1971 the library board at Fort Wayne named the collection after the library's director, Fred Reynolds, in recognition of his work in building and maintaining it.

Following World War II, interest in genealogy in the United States increased dramatically. An element in this phenomenon was surely the work of the Church of Jesus Christ of Latter-day Saints. The Mormons have long emphasized the importance of the family structure, both in this life and in the hereafter, as one of their religious convictions. The expenditures of the church in collecting vital records from around the world, largely on microfilm (now numbering over one million rolls), have dramatically increased the availability of research materials for the genealogist, whether Mormon or gentile. The 1969 World Conference on Records sponsored by the LDS Church in Salt Lake City played an important role in promoting scholarship in genealogical research. The second such world conference in August 1980, with the theme "Preserving Our Heritage," made a similar contribution.

IN PURSUIT OF GENEALOGY

While genealogists today are separated from our colonial ancestors by three centuries, the opportunity to do research regarding those colonial ancestors is vastly superior to that of our great-grandparents. The technology that has given us microfilm, the copying machine, and the computer, along with easy travel and quick communication, has made genealogical source materials accessible at a price and on a scale never dreamed of by the nineteenth-century family historian.

Two recent events have given the pursuit of genealogy in the United States an unparalleled boost: the celebration of the nation's bicentennial in 1976 and the publication and dramatization of Alex Haley's *Roots* shortly thereafter. While *Roots* was a major force in attracting black people and other minorities to genealogical study, it seems to have had a similar effect upon nonminorities as well. To many members of nonminorities its message seems to have been: If Alex Haley could succeed in discovering his roots against the odds that he faced, surely I can trace mine. Both events, the bicentennial and the appearance of *Roots,* had the effect of legitimizing genealogy in the eyes of many librarians as an area worthy of serious study. The appearance of Milton Rubincam, past-president of the National Genealogical Society, on the "Today" show and a cover story in *Newsweek* (4 July 1977) entitled "Everybody's Search for Roots" provided further proof that the study of one's ancestry has wide popular appeal. The fact that *Newsweek*'s cover illustrating its story was a photograph of a nineteenth century Italian immigrant family rather than that of an old Virginia household or a New England Puritan surrounded by his progeny was further proof of the democratization of genealogy. Appropriately, the theme of the three-day conference held by the National Genealogical Society to celebrate its seventy-fifth birthday in 1978 was "Genealogy for All People."

Two short decades ago the National Genealogical Society was nearly torn asunder over the issue of whether, indeed, genealogy is for all people, as it debated the possibility of black membership. To many members the idea that black people could be interested in their ancestry was beyond comprehension, as was also the possibility of their being able to trace their forebears. How satisfying it was to note that the society's vice-president, James D. Walker, served as master of ceremonies at its diamond jubilee banquet in 1978. Walker, who recently retired from the directorship of the National Institute of Genealogical

Research at the National Archives, is black. Further proof that genealogy is for all of us is found in the "warm welcome" extended by the DAR in 1977 to Karen Farmer, a descendant of William Hood of the Continental Army. She became the first acknowledged black member of the society that once forbade the appearance of Marian Anderson in Constitution Hall.

Whereas the presence of American Indian blood in a family was a matter seldom openly discussed or even acknowledged by our grandparents, it has become a matter of family pride today. While its suppression in the past makes such research more difficult, records have survived, and many a family's heritage is now enriched by the presence in the ancestral line of some of America's first inhabitants.

To account for the marked change in the attitude of librarians toward the genealogy patron, we must not give complete credit to the bicentennial and *Roots*. As Mary K. Meyer, genealogical reference librarian for the Museum and Library of Maryland History, has pointed out, these events were "the catalyst which brought the steady increase in popularity of the subject to full flower."[3] In the 1960s it became increasingly apparent in libraries having genealogical collections that their patrons were growing younger at the same time that their number was increasing. As a World War II soldier stationed in Chicago and a frequent evening visitor to the Newberry Library in 1944, I recall feeling uncomfortably youthful in the reading room devoted to local and family history. A quarter-century later, when I had occasion in 1969 to return to the Newberry and happily found Ellen Chase still supervising the genealogical collection, I was amazed that she remembered me. The uniform had helped, of course, but Chase said she remembered me primarily because "you were so young." She pointed out, however, that a quarter-century later I would not have had that distinction—in the reading room of 1969 youth was well represented, while today the young genealogists may actually outnumber those of my own generation.

Donald Lines Jacobus, America's most respected genealogist of the twentieth century and the first professional genealogist to be included in *Who's Who in America*, claimed that the beginning of modern genealogical research dates from about 1930. The "new school of genealogists," of which Jacobus was the leading member,

showed by example how problems should be solved, what sources should be used, and how records should be interpreted; they attacked many of the absurdities and atrocities committed in the name of genealogy by the armchair dilettantes who conjured lines of descent from their own fervid imaginations working upon the poorest printed sources.[4]

The "absurdities and atrocities" to which Milton Rubincam referred in the above quotation included such works as that of Albert Welles, who in 1879 traced the Washington ancestry of the Father of our Country back to the Norse god Odin. A Cadwalader family of Philadelphia claimed descent not only from Adam but from the god Jupiter. Had the *Mayflower* really carried all the passengers that have been claimed as ancestors, it would of course have sunk within sight of England, and had as many colonial Americans possessed royal blood as has been claimed, surely we would not have fought the Revolution. Furthermore, if the claims of genealogists of the early 1900s could be believed, the officers considerably outnumbered the privates in our war for independence.

These genealogical "absurdities and atrocities" have constituted splendid ammunition for the critics of genealogical study and have been responsible in part for the low esteem in which genealogists have been held by librarians.

THE NEW SCHOOL OF GENEALOGY

If Jacobus was correct in stating that a "new school" of genealogy came on the scene about 1930, we can say that some fifty years later the goals of that "new school" have been largely achieved. The place of genealogy in libraries across the country today provides ample evidence of the change. Earlier the policy regarding genealogy of the Enoch Pratt Free Library of 1950 was quoted; in 1966 the Peabody Institute Library was merged with Pratt, and with that collection came 20,000 volumes of genealogical materials. Quite naturally, the attitude toward genealogy at Pratt quickly changed. John S. Burgan, chief of the central library of Pratt, has described that library's present policy:

As a subject with popular, no longer esoteric, appeal and one on which we already have a fairly rich collection of material, we think genealogy an appropriate part of public library service."

Burgan goes on to describe that service:

Increased interest in genealogy was apparent even before the publication and subsequent televising of Haley's *Roots*. My feeling is that this interest will continue to grow as more and more American family lines lengthen and their founders' circumstances become shadowy with the passage of time. Whether or not this feeling is well founded, it is certain that the library users now searching for their ancestors are more representative of the general population than formerly. No longer is the group largely restricted to professional genealogists and persons seeking admission to the DAR or Daughters of the Confederacy. Members of virtually every ethnic group prominent in the Baltimore population—Black, British, Chinese, German, Greek, Italian, Jewish, Polish—are found in our current crop of searchers. In age they now range from adolescents to the very old; in fact, staff have observed that fairly often teenager and grandparent work as a team in seeking out the family line.[5]

In the statement just quoted, Burgan refers to the professional genealogist. This is the individual whose income derives from searching for other people's ancestors. Services may extend from searching a specified record for a specific name or date for a client in a distant city to preparing a complete family history ready for publication for a wealthy patron. Typically charges are by the hour, from $5 up. Libraries having large genealogical collections may find that professional genealogists spend their entire working days in their stacks and reading room. While these people tend to be highly knowledgeable in their use of the library's resources and demand little of the library staff other than ready access, it is sometimes disconcerting to realize that professional genealogists are making their living in the free public library. The fact that, in the past, professional genealogists often outnumbered the amateurs has contributed to the sometimes hostile attitude of librarians toward genealogy. The charlatans in the group, of which there have been a fair number, who have even invented ancestors for gullible clients, elevating privates to generals and transfusing royal blood where desired, have especially damaged the reputation of genealogical research. The joint creation in 1965 of the nonprofit Board for Certification of Genealogists by the American Society for Genealogists and the National Genealogical Society, with its code of ethics published in 1971,[6] has done much to weed out the charlatans.

With the cleansing of genealogy's reputation that has occurred in recent years, how should the library proceed that now desires to provide service in this area where little was provided in the past? Such service requires major budgetary commitment, of course, and plans should be carefully laid.

PUBLIC LIBRARY RESOURCES

Every public library should provide a number of how-to books on genealogy. With the popularization of the topic, there are now scores of such works from which to choose, from the old and scholarly Donald Lines Jacobus, *Genealogy as Pastime and Profession*[7] and *Searching for Your Ancestors* co-authored by one-time library director Gilbert H. Doane,[8] to the pamphlet that one can pick up for fifty cents at the check-out counter of the supermarket. A brief introduction to genealogical research and accompanying selected bibliography by Kip Sperry appear as chapter 1 in his *Survey of American Genealogical Periodicals and Periodical Indexes*.[9] Of equal value is his excellent bibliography entitled "Sources for American Genealogists and Family Historians."[10] The new convert to genealogy should begin by reading one or more of these basic works, and the reference librarian should be able to offer guidance in their selection. Besides the general manuals, there are dozens of more specific guides, depending upon one's ethnic or geographical origins. Examples include James D. Walker's *Black Genealogy: How to Begin; Finding Our Fathers: A Guidebook to Jewish Genealogy*, by Dan Rottenberg; and Lyman De Platt's *Genealogical-Historical Guide to Latin America*.[11] Two recent paperbacks, *Finding Your Roots: Every American Can Trace His Ancestors—At Home and Abroad*, by Jeane Eddy Westin, and *The Family Historian's Handbook* by Yaffa Draznin (1978), offer clues for tracing ancestry for a number of ethnic groups.[12] Major genealogical periodicals now regularly carry articles on ethnic genealogy, examples being "How to Use the Card Catalog of the LDS Genealogical Library for Polish Research," by Zdenka Kucera, and the article by Jimmy B. Parker in the *National Genealogical Society Quarterly* of March 1975 entitled "American Indian Genealogical Research."[13]

For the small library, genealogical service may not extend much beyond the how-to shelf, but even that small library should assume responsibility for acquiring local materials, including the maintenance of a file of the local newspaper, along with a record of persons in the community whose interest in local history extends to helping others. The genealogist is constantly confronted with the need to know whether someone of the name being researched may still live in the community of the ancestor in question or whether anyone has transcribed the tombstone inscriptions in a given cemetery. Nearly every community has its unofficial local historian who can answer such questions. The public library should be able to provide that individual's name and address in response to a letter of inquiry. Where some agency other than the public library has assumed responsibility for collecting and preserving local history and genealogy, such as a historical society or nearby academic library, duplication of such service is obviously unnecessary.

As a library extends its genealogical collection beyond materials pertaining to its own community, that expansion should probably continue to be closely related to geography. The Burton Historical Collection of the Detroit Public Library specializes, for example, in the history and genealogy of the Old Northwest, which of course includes Michigan and several neighboring states. Beyond the Old Northwest, the collection has long given first priority to materials relating to New York and New England, the sections of the country from which Michigan's early settlers came in especially large numbers. Responding to changing clientele, increased emphasis has been given in recent years to the southern states.

Public libraries have long emphasized the value of community analysis in responding to the informational needs of their users, including potential users. A part of the library's community analysis should relate to family origins in order to anticipate its genealogical interests.

Genealogists are contributing their full share to the information explosion (or paper explosion if you will), about which librarians have expressed such great concern in recent years. Vast stores of vital records long available only in courthouses and church basements or in the National Archives in Washington are being indexed, abstracted, and copied in unprecedented numbers by individuals and groups. Inexpensive methods of printing, from the mimeograph to the multilith, have made their reproduction remarkably easy. Furthermore, genealogical works and local histories long out of print are being reproduced through the offset process at reasonable cost. At least 500 serial publications relating to genealogy are currently being published, from the single-family magazine, such as the *Sparks Quarterly*, which I have edited for a quarter-century, to the scholarly journal called the *National Genealogical Society Quarterly*. As noted earlier, microfilm has been a particular boon to the genealogist. For example, the federal census, taken every decade from 1790, is available from the National Archives on microfilm through 1910, as are all pension applications of the soldiers of the American Revolution. While the genealogist would hope that the entire census file might be available in the local library, it is not unreasonable to expect that the library will have at least the reels for the county in which it is located, if not for those for the entire state. Remember that it was in a census record that Alex Haley first found his Aunt Liz (Elizabeth, age six), a discovery that spurred him on to further research.

GENEALOGICAL SOCIETIES

Genealogists are highly gregarious, in large part because they can so often be helpful to each other in sharing data. Dozens of serial publications exist that serve to put genealogists in touch with one another, through queries and directories of ancestral lines. The *Genealogical Helper* is perhaps the best-known example and is a publication that should be available in libraries. Their gregarious nature also encourages genealogists to form groups, not only to share experiences and information, but to launch cooperative projects to preserve, index, and copy local records. The membership of the Ohio Genealogical Society now numbers over 3,000. One of the most productive groups is the Detroit Society for Genealogical Research, formed in 1947. From the start, this society has had a close working relationship with the Detroit Public Library, a relationship that has benefited the library much beyond an improved service to genealogists. Kenneth King, director of the Mount Clemens (Michigan) Public Library, where a similar genealogical society exists, has noted: "These people tend to represent some of the community's most influential families, and it follows that their prolibrary stance can be very helpful."[14] A public library needs all the friends that it can attract within its community. What better group to attract than those persons interested in genealogy?

A recent bequest of a member of the Detroit Society for Genealogical Research has permitted the Detroit Public Library to expand its file of the federal census to include all states through 1880. Patricia Chadwell, head of the Southwest and Genealogy Department of the Fort Worth Public Library, has reported: "We receive extensive support from a very active local genealogical society which provides us with 140 periodical titles, a number of review copies, and funds to purchase supplies and equipment which cannot be obtained through city funding."[15] Private gifts to libraries now frequently pertain to history and genealogy.

Because of the widespread interest in genealogy, speakers on the subject are in constant demand. A librarian with a personal interest in genealogy experiences no difficulty in being invited to appear before community groups. What better way to win friends for the public library?

GENEALOGY, GENEALOGISTS, AND LIBRARIANS

Not only are libraries serving genealogists through increased acquisitions and reference assistance, but many are conducting workshops for the beginning genealogist. Lucia Patrick, a consultant for the Readers Service Division, Public Library Services, Georgia Department of Education, reports that "several public libraries have held or sponsored workshops on how to get started in tracing your family's roots, and a number of high schools and colleges are giving assignments or courses in genealogy."[16] Daniel A. Yanchisin, head of the History and Travel Department of the Memphis/Shelby County Public Library and Information Center, reports that his library sponsors an annual genealogical workshop.[17] As many as 600 people have attended the five sessions.

Many libraries have prepared leaflets and brochures for their patrons describing their genealogical collections, along with hints on how to start the search. The forty-seven-page booklet entitled "Genealogy Beginner's Manual" prepared by the Public Library of Fort Wayne and Allen County is a fine example.[18]

As is true of the service extended to any library user, it is not, nor can it become, the policy of a public library to do actual genealogical research for the amateur family historian, no matter how inexperienced the historian may be. But the librarian should be able to offer guidance. Peggy Tuck Sinko, supervisor of the Local and Family History Division of the Newberry Library, a library long famous for its genealogical collection, has given sound advice regarding today's library service to genealogists:

A major problem facing all libraries with genealogical collections is the lack of preparation of many novice genealogists. With the exception of five or six professional genealogists who use the Newberry regularly, the rest of our readers are amateurs, and I imagine this is true in most institutions. Many are very competent and highly sophisticated researchers, but there is still a problem in dealing with unprepared readers. Unfortunately these readers often have very unrealistic expectations of what they will find, and go away disappointed and frustrated when they discover how much work is involved in a genealogical search. Besides unprepared readers, I believe the other major problem facing genealogical libraries is the question of bibliographic control. This is a very serious problem and one for which I wish I had some good answers. The boom in genealogical publishing has been phenomenal, but much of the material is locally or privately printed, often in limited editions. This makes it difficult and time consuming for the librarian who wants to build a local history and genealogy collection to identify and locate important items.[19]

One of the papers presented at the National Genealogical Society Jubilee Conference in 1978 was entitled "A Professional Code for Genealogical Libraries and Librarians," by Gary Boyd Roberts. Roberts suggests that the genealogy librarian should feel obligated to serve the patron in four ways. Such a librarian should

(1) point out any obvious and major errors in the patron's work (tactfully, of course, and with guidance to corrective references); (2) direct the patron to any sources, especially periodicals and multi-ancestor compendia, that will add to the patron's essentially correct but extendable research; (3) bring together any two patrons he knows of who are working on the same or related problems and are eager to consult with other researchers . . . and (4) give as much help as possible within his time limitations to correspondents who seem to be elderly, confined, without extensive funds, and yet genealogically eager.[20]

On the latter point many librarians would have to disagree, especially as the number of persons interested in genealogy has increased. John L. Ferguson, the state librarian of Arkansas, while noting that "persons seeking genealogical information constitute three-fourths of our patronage," adds: "We do not undertake research for inquirers. Instead we refer them to the Arkansas Genealogical Society, whose membership has soared to more than a thousand."[21] The Detroit Public Library likewise turns over to the Detroit Society for Genealogical Research letters received seeking genealogical assistance, a further illustration of the benefits of having the library work closely with a local genealogical society. On the other hand, Cynthia Arnold, head of reference services for the Maine State Library, reports: "We have tried to limit our research to one-half hour, after which we suggest the patron contact one of many local genealogists who provide research service for a fee."[22]

As suggested here, many public libraries provide a list of local genealogists willing to work for hire in response to letters requesting assistance. Of course, any time a library provides information of this nature, care must be taken not to evaluate the work of these individuals—the library cannot be in the business of recommending the best professional genealogist, any more than it can recommend the best lawyer in town.

I can recall almost with embarrassment the extensive help provided me in the 1950s by Ellen Hill, a librarian in the Genealogical Society of Utah who spent hours responding to my letters of inquiry. The fact that I identified myself as "an ex-GI going to school under the GI Bill and with limited resources" doubtless made her sympathetic toward my research. Today librarians in that library, with its million reels of microfilm, even though they number in the scores, find it impossible to provide the personal assistance that Hill gave me in the 1950s. Thomas E. Daniels, manager of public relations for the Genealogy Department of the LDS Church, has described that library's present clientele:

Ten years ago our main library was serving approximately 700 patrons per day. This number steadily inclined each year until in 1972, when we moved into our new facilities, we were serving 1,200 to 1,400 per day on the average. During 1976 and into early 1977 the daily patronage reached about 2,000. Then along came a man named Alex Haley, and things haven't been the same since, nor will they ever be. After the telecast of *Roots* and Haley's appearance on the Johnny Carson "Tonight" show, the news media beat a path to our door. The extensive coverage heightened the interest of the public who also began to come in great numbers in search of their roots. Those who didn't come in wrote letters asking for help at the rate of 4,000 per month. Patronage increased to 3,000 per day, then to over 4,000 a day during the tourist season in August. It has since leveled back to about 3,000 per day.[23]

Mention perhaps should be made at this point of the nearly 300 LDS branch libraries scattered around the country, where the genealogist can arrange to use in the branch library any of the microfilm on file in Salt Lake City.

Librarians who serve genealogists and are responsible for genealogical collections are themselves subject to the bite of the genealogical bug. I well remember my own introduction to genealogy in 1939, when my favorite college professor, whose enthusiasm for history had obviously been greatly enhanced by the study of his own family history, responded to my after-class query, "Dr. Watson, how does one go about tracing his family history?" Dr. Watson paused and observed, "I hesitate to tell you, because if I do and the genealogy bug bites, you will be lost forever." He did tell me, however, and the next Saturday I hitchhiked to Des Moines to pay my first of many visits to the Iowa Historical Society Library—the bug did bite, and, indeed, I have been lost ever since. I often think how much longer my bibliography of scholarly writings on librarianship would have been had I devoted the time that I have spent on genealogy to, say, the theory of classification or the history of printing. My only consolation is that I have had a lot more fun this way.

Many genealogy librarians are interested in the subject before accepting their professional assignment, but if not, they are quite likely to develop a curiosity about their own ancestry as they assist others in their search. I recall asking Ellen Chase of the Newberry Library, whom I mentioned earlier, whether she was interested in her own family history. "Oh, yes," she replied, "I help other people with their research all day and then I go home at night and work on my own." While it is inappropriate for a librarian to pursue his or her own genealogical interests while on the job, one can scarcely avoid the discovery of items of personal interest while assisting others. A practical problem sometimes faced by the genealogically smitten librarian is, how to spend a day off in the library researching one's own family tree without being distracted constantly by the patrons one has helped while on duty? Another practical matter, on which there should probably be a library policy, relates to whether a librarian should undertake private commissions; that is, should the genealogy librarian, while not on duty, be permitted to serve clients for a fee? This is an unresolved issue in a number of libraries.

It is currently estimated that only stamp and coin collectors outnumber genealogists in the pursuit of their hobby. As in any hobby, of course, some people quickly lost interest, as happened some years ago to Dagwood Bumstead of comic page fame. As Blondie explained, "The poor dear . . . shook his family tree and a bunch of nuts fell out." Dagwood's was not a unique experience, although most beginning genealogists find that, once they start, regardless of the discovery of horse thieves and closet skeletons, the thrill of the search never ends. After all, the number of one's ancestors doubles with each generation. After one becomes truly immersed in the subject, one discovers that assisting a colleague to solve a genealogical problem provides pleasure and satisfaction equal to solving a problem of one's own. And then one can be diverted from climbing the family tree to reversing the direction by tracing other descendants of a favorite ancestor.

Public librarians, even academic librarians, will do well to recognize that genealogy is here to stay, that it is no passing fancy, and that constantly improved library service in this area will be demanded with a louder and louder voice. Furthermore, librarians are discovering that working with genealogists brings many satisfactions. The observation of Wrenette Whartenby, genealogy librarian for the Shreve Memorial Library of Shreveport, Louisiana, is typical:

Most of our patrons are people for whom genealogy becomes a long-term, even a lifetime, project. They are interested in researching their family history simply for the sake of the knowledge itself. For the most part these people are intelligent, patient and a pleasure to work with. Of my four years of professional experience in libraries, the time I have spent in the genealogy department has been the most pleasant and the most rewarding.[24]

"Pleasant" and "rewarding"—these are the words that best describe the work of most genealogy librarians today.

NOTES

1. Russell E. Bidlack, "Genealogy as It Relates to Library Service," in *The ALA Yearbook, 1978* (Chicago: American Library Association, 1978), pp. xxiv–xxv.

2. Rick J. Ashton, letter to author, 10 October 1978.

3. Mary K. Meyer, letter to author, 27 October 1977.

4. Quoted by Milton Rubincam in his "Genealogy for All People," *National Genealogical Society Quarterly* 66 (December 1978), p. 246.

5. John S. Burgan, letter to author, 7 November 1977.

6. "The Genealogist's Code," adopted in 1971 by the Board of Certification, reprinted in the *National Genealogical Society Quarterly* 61 (March 1972), p. 64.

7. Donald Lines Jacobus, *Genealogy as Pastime and Profession*, 2d ed. (Baltimore: Genealogical Publishing Co., 1978).

8. Gilbert H. Doane and James B. Bell, *Searching for Your Ancestors: The How and Why of Genealogy*, 5th ed. (Minneapolis: University of Minnesota Press, 1980).

9. Kip Sperry, *A Survey of American Genealogical Periodicals and Periodical Indexes* (Detroit: Gale Research Co., 1978).

10. Kip Sperry, "Sources for American Genealogists and Family Historians," *Genealogical Helper* 33 (May–June 1979), pp. 15–17.

11. James D. Walker, *Black Genealogy: How to Begin* (Athens: University of Georgia Center for Continuing Education, 1977); Dan Rottenberg, *Finding Our Fathers: A Guidebook to Jewish Genealogy* (New York: Random House, 1977); Lyman De Platt, *Genealogical-Historical Guide to Latin America* (Detroit: Gale Research Co., 1978).

12. Jeane Eddy Westin, *Finding Your Roots: Every American Can Trace His Ancestry—At Home and Abroad* (Los Angeles: J. P. Tarcher, 1977); Yaffa Draznin, *The Family Historian's Handbook* (New York: Jove Publications, 1977).

13. Zdenka Kucera, "How to Use the Card Catalog of the LDS Genealogical Library for Polish Research," *Genealogical Helper* 33 (March–April 1979), pp. 9–10; Jimmy B. Parker, "American Indian Genealogical Research," *National Genealogical Society Quarterly* 63 (March 1975), pp. 15–21.

14. Kenneth King, letter to author, 15 January 1980.

15. Patricia Chadwell, letter to author, 16 November 1977.

16. Lucia Patrick, letter to author, 28 October 1977.

17. Daniel A. Yanchisin, letter to author, 28 October 1977.

18. Public Library of Fort Wayne and Allen County, "Genealogy Beginner's Manual" (Fort Wayne, Ind.: The Library, 1975).

19. Peggy Tuck Sinko, letter to author, 1 November 1977.

20. Gary Boyd Roberts, "A Professional Code for Genealogical Libraries and Librarians," *National Genealogical Society Quarterly* 67 (March 1979), pp. 11–13.

21. John L. Ferguson, letter to author, 15 November 1977.

22. Cynthia Arnold, letter to author, 15 November 1977.

23. Thomas E. Daniels, letter to author, 18 October 1977.

24. Wrenette Whartenby, letter to author, 16 November 1977.

2

Basic Sources for Genealogical Research

JEAN ELDER CAZORT

While research into ethnic genealogy will most certainly have to depend upon a knowledge of the special sources and problems of each ethnic group, it must necessarily begin with a knowledge of sources and techniques which are basic to genealogy in general. In most instances it will be these general sources and techniques which will form the basis for beginning the research into ethnic genealogy and which will support the search for one's ancestry for one or more generations back, at which point a more specialized knowledge will become necessary. It would seem appropriate, then, at the beginning of a book on ethnic genealogy, to introduce the general techniques and tools of genealogy. This chapter will discuss the basic equipment needed for getting started; it will also discuss what the researcher should know before getting started and the sources of genealogical information.

GETTING STARTED

Getting started is the biggest step. The question one immediately asks is "How?" First of all, it is important to recognize at the outset that genealogical research is going to generate a lot of records and paperwork and that the necessity for good organization from the beginning is paramount. When it is further realized that this work may extend over eight or ten generations, fanning out as it proceeds, it will be evident that not only must the work be organized in some manner, but it should also be arranged for easy access. For an overview of what is known and what is not known about a family, and as a clue to where one's own search might begin, the first step is to fill out a pedigree chart.

Pedigree Chart

Sometimes called an ancestor chart, the pedigree chart (figure 2.1) is a good beginning. It is a simple and graphic representation of the linkage between

Figure 2.1
Four Generation Pedigree Chart

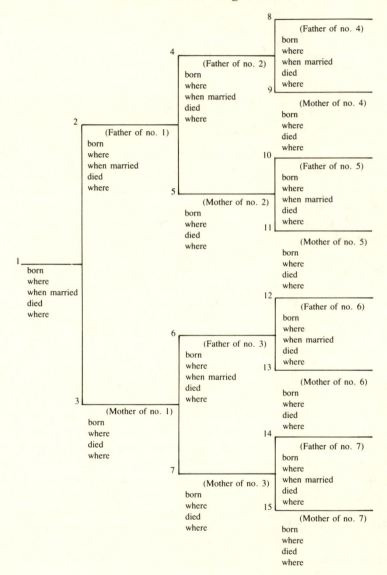

generations and will show at a glance the state of ready information about a family. As the blanks on the chart are filled, there will be visual evidence of progress and a graphic representation of family relationships. Pedigree charts come in a variety of printed formats, up to ten generations, and they may be purchased from a genealogical supply house or drawn up at home. The four- or five-generation chart will be adequate in the beginning. Note that there are spaces for genealogical data for each ancestor: name, date, and place of birth and death, and date of marriage. The search should always begin with one's self, writing the name on the pedigree chart on line 1, then adding the names of the searcher's parents and grandparents in the proper spaces. Then the dates and places of birth, marriage, and death for each person are recorded, working from facts that are already known. When all that is known from personal knowledge is recorded, the unfilled spaces will indicate the information that has to be looked for, and this is where the search actually begins.

Genealogy begins at home. It is important that the search begin with family sources, as nearly every family has some evidence of the activities of its ancestors. Begin by examining old letters, diaries and journals, scrapbooks, family Bibles, school records, military discharges, or anything else that is likely to be of value. Old letters can be valuable sources of information, especially in the South, where many other genealogical records were destroyed by the Civil War. The researcher should be sure to correspond with older relatives or interview them when possible, not only for their help in locating some of these records but also to have the benefit of their knowledge of family matters. After all possible information has been located in family sources, the verification process begins, and the search expands into courthouses, government record offices, libraries and archives, and historical societies and to other sources which will be discussed in this chapter.

Note that for each name on the pedigree chart there is a number. This is the thread that runs throughout the records and ties them all together. The number that a person has on the pedigree chart will always be the same for that person and will serve as identification on a family group record, on the individual biography sheet, on the backs of photographs, and on other records and research materials. This coding system is especially helpful, too, in keeping family members with the same name from becoming confused. In filling out the pedigree chart, the genealogist is always number 1, the father number 2, and the mother number 3. Paternal grandparents are 4 (grandfather) and 5 (grandmother); the maternal grandparents, 6 (grandfather) and 7 (grandmother). And so the numbering proceeds for each generation, always beginning with the male member. As the pedigree chart is filled in, be careful to use full names whenever possible, recording married women by their maiden names and putting any nicknames in parentheses. Always remember the basic rule for genealogical research: Work from the known to the unknown.

The vital information on the pedigree chart—places and dates of birth and death and date of marriage—will have to be verified and documented, as absolute accuracy is essential for the success of the whole project. Any errors made at this point will lead to difficulty later on. Occasionally, however, birth and death certificates contain errors. In such cases, corrections can eventually be made by means of other documents or sources that give dependable evidence on the same points. Sources of verification are usually provided for on family group sheets and individual work sheets. If the space allotted is insufficient, the information may be continued on the back of the sheet. Until the information has been verified, it should be written in pencil. As data are sought out from family sources to complete the pedigree chart, hopefully a great deal more than vital statistics will emerge. This additional information may be recorded on family group sheets and individual work sheets.

Family Group Sheet

The family group sheet (figure 2.2) brings each family unit together on one page, and it requires almost all of the information needed to develop a family history: names, dates, and places of birth, death, and marriage for parents and also children. As the family sheets are completed, the pedigree chart can be filled in. A good supply of family sheets will be needed, as genealogical search includes all of the family, not just the two parents and four grandparents. Each marriage in the family, past and present, will require a family group record: parents, married siblings, maternal and paternal grandparents, and so on. These should begin with the researcher's own family, and the blanks should be filled in for husband, wife, and children. If some dates are uncertain, they should be verified through sources such as birth, death, and marriage certificates, family Bibles, and census records, and the sources should be recorded. Children, living or dead, should be recorded in order of birth. After the researcher's immediate family has been completed, he or she should proceed in the same way to develop group sheets for all other family units, on both the maternal and the paternal lines.

Other Marriages

In recording multiple marriages, remember that each marriage must have a family group sheet. The husband or wife in question will have a family group record for each spouse, on which will be recorded any children of the marriage. Thus, on the group sheet showing his family with his first wife, the second and third wives would appear on the line calling for the husband's other wives as #2, with the maiden name, and #3, with the maiden name.

Adoptees

If a child is adopted, that fact should appear in parentheses beside the adoptee's name on a family group sheet. Blood parents, if they are known, may be recorded on the back. If the parents are unknown, that fact, too, should be recorded.

Dating

Genealogical practice records dates with the day first and then the month, spelled out or abbreviated (except May, June, and July), and then the year: 4 July 1776. As the practice of indicating the day as well as the month with numerals varies from place to place, 4-7-76 can mean July 4 or it can mean April 7. Using the genealogist's system will avoid that pitfall. The year should not be shortened to its last two digits, because genealogists cover centuries, and '76 could mean 1776, 1876, or 1976.

Family group records are filed by code number for the head of the household, traditionally the husband. The number sequence will be 1 (the genealogist), 2, 4, 6, 8, 10, and so forth. Individual work sheets are filed in numerical sequence: 1, 2, 3, 4, and so forth.

Other Records

Additional research aids may include individual work sheets, research records, and correspondence records. The individual work sheets (figure 2.3) should contain as much pertinent information as possible about the person, such as date and place of birth, parents, military service, marriage, spouse's name, residences, and additional biographical information such as religious affiliation, education, and membership in organizations. There is room on the sheet for documentation, which will come from the appropriate records. Proceed as far as possible for each member of the family. List all of the children of a marriage on the father's work sheet, with a "see" reference on the mother's work sheet in the space for children. Thus, by the time the individual and family group sheets have been compiled for three generations, the pedigree chart can be completed up to the same point.

A research register (figure 2.4) is essential. All vital, census, military, and church records, deeds, wills, and so on which have been consulted will have to be noted in the research record, as memory cannot possibly retain it all. Always record the exact source of every bit of information. For printed sources this information will consist of the author's full name and the title, publisher, date, volume, and page. Archival sources should be identified by name of repository, record series, and file number. This procedure will enable the researcher to recheck, if necessary, when dates or names or places are at variance.

Correspondence

Letter writing is essential. Early in genealogical research one realizes the necessity for correspondence—for copies of birth certificates and wills, for assistance in locating information and in requesting information of persons. It would be a good idea to have some kind of organization and record keeping, however simple, for the correspondence. Figure 2.5 is one method which can be used effectively and which seems to do the job.

Figure 2.2
Family Group Sheet

Husband	occupation	code no.	
Born	place, date		sources of information
Married	place, date		
Died	place, date		
Buried	place, date		
Husband's father	husband's mother		
Husband's other wives			
Wife	occupation	code no.	
Born	place, date		
Died	place, date		
Buried	place, date		
Wife's father	wife's mother		
Wife's other husbands			

Children (in order of birth)	Sex	Day Month Year	Town County State or Country	Marriage	Died Day Month Year

	Date:	Date:	Date:	Date:	Date:	Date:	Date:	Date:	Date:	Date:
	To:	To:	To:	To:	To:	To:	To:	To:	To:	To:
	1.	2.	3.	4.	5.	6.	7.	8.	9.	10.

27

Figure 2.3
Individual History Sheet

Name in full _____ code no. _____
Birthdate and place _____
Mother's name _____ code no. _____
Father's name _____ code no. _____
Occupation(s) _____ date, place _____
                           _____ date, place _____
                           _____ date, place _____
Military service _____
Married _____ code no. _____ date, place _____
                _____ code no. _____ date, place _____
Died _____ date, place _____

Education

Name of school	dates attended	diploma or degree

Residences

Street address	town	county	state	dates

Additional information (memberships, travel, honors):
_____
_____
_____
_____

Sources of information (Bibles; birth, death, and marriage certificates):
_____
_____
_____

Date:

Information requests by mail should be specific and brief, and care should be taken to provide the proper information for retrieval of the record. That usually will include the full name of the person about whom the information is being sought, taking care in the case of married women to give the proper name, and the date and place of the event. The fee should be enclosed. Many books on genealogy contain the names and addresses of county, state, and local offices having jurisdiction over different records, along with the fees they charge. Noel

Stevenson's *Search and Research*[1] and the Cache Genealogical Library's *Handbook of Genealogical Correspondence*[2] are particularly helpful, containing state-by-state listings of records and services available from libraries, public archives, and historical societies.

The best way to keep all of these record sheets together is in a three-ring binder, which allows for easy filing as well as for portability. Dividers should separate the types of records. Finally, it may become necessary to establish a miscellaneous file to accommodate the sundry photographs, legal documents, and old letters that will turn up in the searching process. This file may be a box, a file drawer, or a large folder, and the items should be arranged according to the code numbers of the ancestors to whom they pertain.

Regarding old photographs: pleasant though it is to look at old pictures of

Figure 2.4
Research Record

Ancestor _____ code no. _____
Place _____
Researcher _____

Place of Research	Date	Research Completed	Call No./ File No.

Figure 2.5
Correspondence Record

Ancestor _____ Code no. _____

Date Sent	Addressee/Address	Purpose	Date of Reply	Results

unknown persons, they do provide a lesson for the present-day genealogist, and that is to identify all of one's own photographs now with names and dates. In a few years today's certainty that the persons and dates will never be forgotten will have blurred, and the problem will have been perpetuated.

HISTORY FOR GENEALOGISTS

With notebooks and work sheets in hand and a knowledge of the areas of family history that remain to be filled in, the searcher is almost ready to turn to outside sources, but should make an intermediate stop at the public library to become acquainted with some sources that will save much time and misdirected searching. Among the basic tools essential to almost every genealogical search are local histories, maps and atlases, directories, and genealogical guides. Our country has undergone many changes—colonization and revolution, westward expansion, and urbanization—and these changes have been reflected in changing boundaries, changes in names of some towns and cities, and the disappearance of others. Changes continue today as congressional districts are redrawn to reflect shifts in population. Before the history of a family can be pursued, there must be some knowledge of the history of the states and counties in which the ancestors lived. Generally, the records pertaining to a family will be located in the court-house of the home county. But before embarking on an examination of local records, the geography must be right. Even though the family continued to occupy the same house, it is possible that a hundred years ago that location was part of another county.

It will be important to consult atlases and gazetteers of the period of the search, and it will also be important to read a history of the county, to become acquainted not only with what happened, but also with migration patterns, with the establishment and growth of industries and churches, and with the activities of the leading citizens, all of which could be helpful in piecing together a family picture.

City maps of the period will be especially helpful if one's ancestors lived in a large city, as the time will come when they will be searched for in federal census schedules, where urban addresses are arranged by wards. If the number of the ward of an ancestor's residence is known, it can mean the difference between locating that ancestor in a federal census with relative ease or spending hours in the search.

City directories began appearing in America in the eighteenth century, listing the names, addresses, and occupations of the working people in a city. It is possible to learn a great deal about an ancestor by examining successive city directories to determine when the person may have moved away or died. City directory listing is an additional aid to locating an ancestor in the federal census. After locating the ancestor's address in the directory, it will be possible to determine the ward from an old city map and then to proceed directly to the corresponding listing in the federal census.

Other kinds of directories can be helpful, as they are compilations of data about specific groups of persons or organizations. Bibliographies aid the researcher in bringing together titles of potential usefulness, and indexes provide access to information that otherwise would be as accessible as a needle in a haystack. An effort should always be made to ascertain what help exists in the form of these reference works. The list of references at the end of this section will provide the titles of a few of them, and more extensive listings may be found in most genealogical primers. The reader is also referred to Bobby L. Lovett's discussion on family histories, which appears as chapter 4.

Double Dating

After working back to records which date before 1752, the searcher is likely to encounter the practice of "double dating." In many early colonial American records there are entries like "19 March 1732/33" or "10 January 1740/41." Double dating was an effort to reconcile the differences between the Julian and Gregorian calendars. The calendar devised by Julius Caesar attempted to bring together lunar and solar time, but his calculations were off by 11 minutes and 14 seconds, and over the years lunar and solar time began to drift apart again. By 1582, when Pope Gregory reformed the calendar, the deviation had become ten days. Pope Gregory eliminated the ten-day discrepancy by having the day after October 4 become October 15. The time discrepancy of 11 minutes and 14 seconds, which amounted to about three days every 400 years, was adjusted by eliminating the years 1700, 1800, 1900, and so on, as leap years. Thus lunar and solar time were brought together. However, England and its colonies continued to use the Julian calendar until 1752, by which time there was an eleven-day discrepancy between the two systems. When Parliament decided to adopt the Gregorian calendar, it was directed that eleven days be dropped from the calendar and that New Year's Day, then celebrated by the civil authorites on March 25, be changed to January 1, the popular date for the beginning of the new year. In order to maintain some kind of clarity in all this confusion, people frequently used double dates, such as 1735/36, to clarify dates falling within the first three months of years prior to 1752, thus indicating that while it was officially 1735, many people considered it to be 1736.[3]

Spelling Variations

Every surname may be spelled several ways, and the researcher should always be alert to spelling variations when searching records. Consider how, even in these days of standardization, one's own mail may arrive under a variety of spellings. It is even more likely that a name will be spelled in a number of different ways in earlier record keeping. The census taker or minister or county clerk would spell a name as it sounded to him or her, and the same name might be spelled one way on a deed, another way in a will, and still another on a marriage license. The name Cazort, for instance, regularly appears as Cozart, Cuzzort, Kazort, Karzort, Carzort, and Karsort.

VITAL RECORDS

Those records which will be of the most value in locating or verifying names and dates on the family pedigree chart are vital records. These are birth (figures 2.6 and 2.7), marriage (figure 2.8), and death records. They deal with the vital statistics of people and are one of the first sources a genealogist pursues. These records will substantiate facts already uncovered and sometimes advance the search into another generation. Vital records may contain some, but not all, of the following facts about a person: name, sex, age, birthplace, father's name, mother's maiden name, father's birthplace, mother's birthplace, age of father, age of mother, date and place of parents' marriage, and place of parents' residence. For example, a death certificate (figure 2.9) will contain much of this information, as well as the name of the funeral director and the place of interment, which will lead to cemetery records. One should always be on the alert, however, to the possibility that some of the certificates will have incomplete

Figure 2.6
Birth Registration in Tennessee, 1935

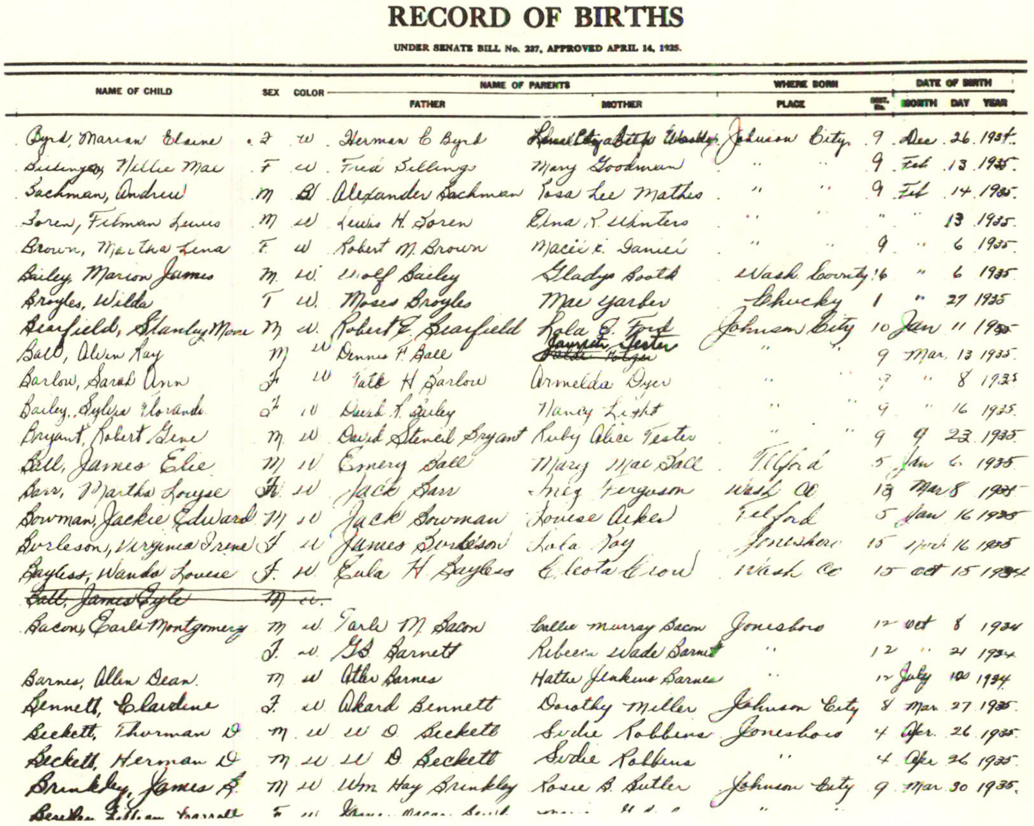

RECORD OF BIRTHS

UNDER SENATE BILL No. 237, APPROVED APRIL 14, 1925.

NAME OF CHILD	SEX	COLOR	NAME OF PARENTS: FATHER	NAME OF PARENTS: MOTHER	WHERE BORN: PLACE	DIST. No.	DATE OF BIRTH: MONTH	DAY	YEAR
Byrd, Marian Elaine	F	W	Herman C Byrd	~~Hazel Eliza~~ Betty Woolsey	Johnson City	9	Dec	26	1934
Billings, Nellie Mae	F	W	Fred Billings	Mary Goodman	" "	9	Feb	13	1935
Bachman, Andrew	M	Bl	Alexander Bachman	Rosa Lee Mathes	" "	9	Feb	14	1935
Boren, Filmore Lewis	M	W	Lewis H. Boren	Elna R. Winters	" "	"	"	13	1935
Brown, Martha Lena	F	W	Robert M. Brown	Macie E. Daniel	" "	9	"	6	1935
Bailey, Marion James	M	W	Wolf Bailey	Gladys Booth	Wash. County	16	"	6	1935
Broyles, Wilda	F	W	Moses Broyles	Mae Yarber	Chucky	1	"	27	1935
Bearfield, Stanley Moore	M	W	Robert E. Bearfield	Lola E. Ford	Johnson City	10	Jan	11	1935
Ball, Alvin Ray	M	W	Dennis F. Ball	~~Jeanette Tester~~ [illegible]	"	9	Mar.	13	1935
Barlow, Sarah Ann	F	W	Tate H Barlow	Armelda Dyer	" "	9	"	8	1935
Bailey, Sylvia Florinda	F	W	Daniel F. Bailey	Nancy Light	" "	9	"	16	1935
Bryant, Robert Gene	M	W	David Stencil Bryant	Ruby Alice Tester	" "	9	9	23	1935
Ball, James Elie	M	W	Emery Ball	Mary Mae Ball	Telford	5	Jan	6	1935
Barr, Martha Louise	F	W	Jack Barr	Inez Ferguson	Wash. Co.	13	Mar	8	1935
Bowman, Jackie Edward	M	W	Jack Bowman	Louise Aiken	Telford	5	Jan	16	1935
Burleson, Virginia Irene	F	W	James Burleson	Lola Fry	Jonesboro	15	April	16	1935
Bayless, Wanda Louise	F	W	Eula H. Bayless	Cleota Crow	Wash. Co	15	Oct	15	1934
~~Ball, James Lyle~~	~~M~~	~~W~~							
Bacon, Earle Montgomery	M	W	Earle M. Bacon	Callie Murray Bacon	Jonesboro	12	Oct	8	1934
	F	W	G.B. Barnett	Rebecca Wade Barnett	"	12	"	21	1934
Barnes, Allen Dean	M	W	Otter Barnes	Hattie Jenkins Barnes	"	12	July	10	1934
Bennett, Claudine	F	W	Okard Bennett	Dorothy Miller	Johnson City	8	Mar.	27	1935
Beckett, Thurman D	M	W	W D Beckett	Sudie Robbins	Jonesboro	4	Apr.	26	1935
Beckett, Herman D	M	W	W D Beckett	Sudie Robbins	"	4	Apr	26	1935
Brinkley, James A	M	W	Wm Hay Brinkley	Rosie B. Butler	Johnson City	9	Mar.	30	1935
[illegible]	F	W	[illegible]	[illegible]	"				

Courtesy Tennessee State Library and Archives.

Figure 2.7
Certificate of Live Birth

VITAL RECORDS

THIS BECOMES A LEGAL RECORD WHEN PROPERLY EXECUTED AND FILED.

TYPE OR PRINT IN PERMANENT BLACK INK.

PREPARE SEPARATE FORM FOR EACH CHILD IF MULTIPLE BIRTH.

ATTENDANT MUST SIGN IN PERMANENT BLACK INK.

ALL ITEMS 1-26 MUST BE COMPLETED.

THE CERTIFICATE MUST BE FILED WITH THE LOCAL REGISTRAR WITHIN 10 DAYS AFTER BIRTH

CHILD

CHILD — NAME — FIRST — MIDDLE — LAST — 1.
DATE OF BIRTH (MONTH, DAY, YEAR) — 2a.
HOUR — 2b. — M.

SEX — 3.
THIS BIRTH — SINGLE, TWIN, TRIPLET, ETC. (SPECIFY) — 4a.
IF NOT SINGLE BIRTH — BORN FIRST, SECOND, ETC. (SPECIFY) — 4b.

COUNTY OF BIRTH — 5a.
CITY, TOWN, OR LOCATION OF BIRTH — 5b.
INSIDE CITY LIMITS (SPECIFY YES OR NO) — 5c.
HOSPITAL — NAME (IF NOT IN HOSPITAL, SPECIFY PRIVATE RESIDENCE, DOCTOR'S OFFICE, ETC.) — 5d.

MOTHER

MOTHER — MAIDEN NAME — FIRST — MIDDLE — LAST — 6a.
AGE (AT TIME OF THIS BIRTH) — 6b.
STATE OF BIRTH (IF NOT IN U.S.A. NAME COUNTRY) — 6c.

RESIDENCE — STATE — 7a.
COUNTY — 7b.
CITY, TOWN, OR LOCATION — 7c.
INSIDE CITY LIMITS (SPECIFY YES OR NO) — 7e.
CENSUS TRACT NO. — 7f.

FATHER

FATHER — NAME — FIRST — MIDDLE — LAST — 8a.
AGE (AT TIME OF THIS BIRTH) — 8b.
STATE OF BIRTH (IF NOT IN U.S.A. NAME COUNTRY) — 8c.

CERTIFIER

9. MOTHER'S SIGNATURE

I CERTIFY THAT I HAVE INSPECTED THIS CERTIFICATE FOR ACCURACY

I CERTIFY THAT THE ABOVE NAMED CHILD WAS BORN ALIVE AT THE PLACE AND TIME AND ON THE DATE STATED ABOVE

10a. SIGNATURE
ATTENDANT — M.D. OTHER (SPECIFY) — 10b.
DATE SIGNED (MONTH, DAY, YEAR) — 10c.

NAME (TYPE OR PRINT) — 10d.
MAILING ADDRESS (STREET OR R.F.D. NO., CITY OR TOWN, STATE, ZIP) — 10e.

REGISTRAR — SIGNATURE — 11a.
DATE RECEIVED BY LOCAL REGISTRAR (MONTH, DAY, YEAR) — 11b.

MOTHER'S MAILING ADDRESS (STREET OR R.F.D. NO., CITY OR TOWN, STATE, ZIP) — 12.

CONFIDENTIAL INFORMATION FOR MEDICAL AND HEALTH USE ONLY

FATHER

FATHER — RACE WHITE, BLACK, AMERICAN INDIAN, ETC. (SPECIFY) — 13a.
HISPANIC/SPANISH ORIGIN OR DESCENT — YES ☐ NO ☐ — 13b.
EDUCATION HIGHEST GRADE COMPLETED — ELEMENTARY OR SECONDARY (0-12) COLLEGE (1-4 OR 5+) — 14.

MOTHER

MOTHER — RACE WHITE, BLACK, AMERICAN INDIAN, ETC. (SPECIFY) — 15a.
HISPANIC/SPANISH ORIGIN OR DESCENT — YES ☐ NO ☐ — 15b.
EDUCATION HIGHEST GRADE COMPLETED — ELEMENTARY OR SECONDARY (0-12) COLLEGE (1-4 OR 5+) — 16.

DATE LAST NORMAL MENSES BEGAN — (MO.) (DAY) (YR.) — 18.
MONTH OF PREGNANCY PRENATAL CARE BEGAN (1ST, 2D, ETC. SPECIFY) — 19a.
PRENATAL VISITS TOTAL NUMBER (IF NONE SO STATE) — 19b.

PREGNANCY HISTORY

LIVE BIRTHS (DO NOT INCLUDE THIS CHILD) — 17a.
NOW LIVING NUMBER ☐ NONE ☐ — 17b.
NOW DEAD NUMBER ☐ NONE ☐ — 17c.
DATE OF LAST LIVE BIRTH (MONTH, YEAR) — 17f.

OTHER TERMINATIONS (SPONTANEOUS AND INDUCED) — 17d.
LESS THAN 20 WKS. NUMBER ☐ NONE ☐ — 20 WKS. OR MORE NUMBER ☐ NONE ☐ — 17e.
DATE OF LAST OTHER TERMINATION (MONTH, YEAR)

LEGITIMATE (SPECIFY YES OR NO) — 23.

COMPLICATIONS OF PREGNANCY — 20. (DESCRIBE OR WRITE "NONE")

CONCURRENT ILLNESSES OR CONDITIONS AFFECTING THE PREGNANCY — 21. (DESCRIBE OR WRITE "NONE")

COMPLICATIONS OF LABOR AND/OR DELIVERY — 22. (DESCRIBE OR WRITE "NONE")

APGAR SCORE — AT 1 MINUTE — 24a. — AT 5 MINUTE — 24b.
BIRTH WEIGHT — 25.

CONGENITAL MALFORMATIONS OF CHILD — 26. (DESCRIBE OR WRITE "NONE")

PH-1651
VR Rev. 7/79

Courtesy Department of Public Health, State of Tennessee.

Figure 2.8
Record of Early Marriages

RECORD OF MARRIAGES,

No.	Date of Marriage. Month. Day. Year.	Where Married.	Names of Parties. Give full name of each, and if Widow, also give maiden name.	Color.	Age.	Birth Place of each Party.
9	1 1881	Washington Co Tenn	John L Hice To 8/31/81 Lidia C Crouch	W W	27 17	Washington Co Tenn Washington Co Tenn
			James R Metcalf To 4/3/81 Catherine M Hensley			
9	1 1881	Washington Co Tennessee	S C White To 9/1/81 Mollie E Young	W W		Washington Co Tenn Washington Co Tenn
			Joseph H Monaker To 9/6/81 Castella Carnock			
9	8 1881	Washington Co Tenn	John Sovergrove To Mary A Christie	W W	40 31	Washington Co Tenn Washington Co Tenn
9	13 1881	Washington Co Tenn	John Taylor To Col 9/13/81 Eva Moore	Col Col	30 16	Virginia Tennessee
9	13 1881	Washington Co Tenn	Jasper Call To Col. 9/13/81 Malinda Wallace	Col 58 Col 66		Sullivan Co Tenn Washington Co Tenn
9	22 1881	Washington Co Tenn	Thomas M Brabson To 9/9/81 Margaret A Miller	W W	43 21	Washington Co Tenn Washington Co Tenn
9	29 1881	Washington Co Tenn	Jacob Krous To 9/29/81 Martha J. Pritchett	W W	28 28	Washington Co Tenn Washington Co Tenn
9	28 81	Washn Co Tenn	D L Miller To 9/28/81 Mollie Harris	W W	28 22	Washn Co Tenn Washn Co Tenn

Courtesy Tennessee State Library and Archives.

Figure 2.9
Certificate of Death

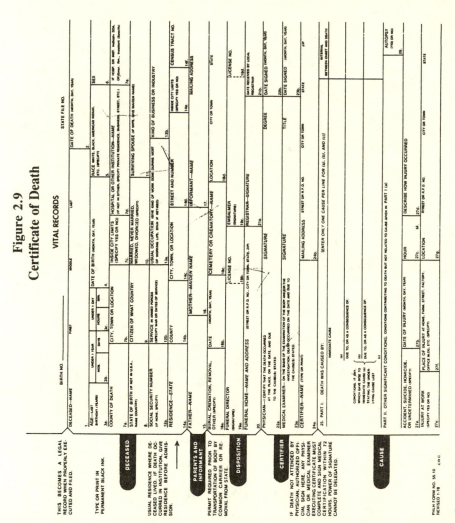

Courtesy Department of Public Health, State of Tennessee.

information due to lack of information on the part of the informant or that some of the information itself may be incorrect.

Many states began vital statistics registration during the latter part of the nineteenth century and others much later, so the value of vital records is usually limited to recent research. As vital records were never kept on a national basis, each state developed its own registration system, beginning with Massachusetts in 1841; the last state to institute such a system was Georgia, in 1919. Every birth, death, and marriage within a state since that state began vital registration should be on file in that state's bureau of vital statistics. Most useful in the location of vital records are three pamphlets published by the National Center for Health Statistics and available from the superintendent of documents: "Where to Write for Birth and Death Records: United States and Outlying Areas"; "Where to Write for Marriage Records: United States and Outlying Areas"; and "Where to Write for Divorce Records: United States and Outlying Areas." These booklets, which are frequently revised, contain information on registration areas and on the cost of certified copies of certificates, addresses of record custodians, and information regarding the time period and completeness of the records. A fourth pamphlet, "Where to Write for Birth and Death Records of U.S. Citizens Who Were Born or Died Outside of the United States and Birth Certificates for Alien Children Adopted by U.S. Citizens," may be useful in different circumstances. (These four booklets also appear in the bibliography at the end of this chapter.)

Locating vital records prior to statewide registration is more difficult. Probably most helpful are the Works Projects Administration (WPA) guides to vital statistics records, which provide information regarding the location of existing vital statistics for the counties, cities, and towns of the forty states which participated. These inventories are usually found in the genealogical collections of larger libraries, especially in the states concerned.

After determining who has jurisdiction over the records for a particular time period, the searcher may direct a request to the proper office, along with the proper fee. For the most part, states file their records in chronological order, and in general, if the name of the person and the date and place of the event are known, there should be no problem in getting the necessary certificates. Correct names are, of course, important, particularly for women, as a remarriage may have been overlooked or forgotten. And efforts to secure a death certificate for a married woman under her maiden name will be fruitless. Once an official death record has been obtained, for example, one can then attempt to locate the obituary in the local newspaper for additional information, such as names of survivors. In writing to a vital statistics office for a certificate, it would be a good idea to state one's relation to the person and reason for the request, as some vital statistics offices will supply records only to relatives. Some states issue copies of marriage certificates only to the parties involved. Birth certificates in some states may be under similar restrictions, requiring the written consent of the concerned party or else that a certain number of years will have elapsed, before the certificate is issued.

Divorce records are also considered as vital records providing useful genealogical information: dates and places of birth for both parties, the date and place of the marriage, and the names and ages of the children. In addition, there will be information regarding the grounds for the divorce, custody of the children, and distribution of property. Divorce records are recorded in the county in which the divorce was granted, but the office varies from state to state, the most frequent locations being the offices of county clerks, superior court clerks, and district court clerks; the Public Health Service pamphlets previously mentioned will be especially useful in determining the proper office. In many states, divorce records are centrally filed.

COUNTY RECORDS

Land and Property Records

Known as "the genealogist's bread and butter," land records constitute a very important approach to family history. They include records such as deeds, mortgages, leases, liens, contracts, and other documents that affect title to the land. They are usually located in the office of the county recorder or register of deeds. In some states early land records have been put on microfilm and copies placed in the state archives. Although land records exclude primary genealogical facts such as exact birth and death dates, they include information as to times, places, and relationships.

Deeds and other land records prior to 1800 tend to give more historical and genealogical information than recent ones. One of their most useful services is the statement of relationships (figure 2.10). For example, as land is usually held jointly by a husband and wife, the deeds will include both names and often the wife's maiden name. Also included will be the names of the buyers (grantees) or sellers (grantors) and sometimes the names of relatives and their kinship and the names of friends and associates. Frequently a statement such as the one describing land as "lately in the possession of James Hughes senior, father of James Hughes junior" may be all that is needed to extend a genealogical search back one generation.

When land is divided among heirs, the names of the children, and frequently their addresses, are included in the deed. In the case of someone's dying without a will when there is real estate involved, it becomes necessary to "quiet the title," that is, to contact all living children to secure their releases before the property can be sold. These releases will sometimes include not only the signatures of the heirs, but their addresses and the names of their spouses as well.

Other general information which may turn up in property records can be references to previous places of residence, places of residence of relatives and associates, dates and places of death, occupation, church affiliation, social status—all clues to additional information.

Mortgages frequently accompany land purchases and can contain information

Figure 2.10
Evidence of Family Relationship in a Deed

State of Tennessee) November 28" 1908 11, O'clock A. M. then
Washington County) was the foregoing Deed received for
registration with certificate thereon entered in note book
no 2 page 343 recorded in vol 100 pages 13 +14.

W. F. Vines
Register.

Deed) For and in consideration of one dollar
Sarah J. Rogers) cash in hand paid and the love
    To   and good will that I have for my son
J. H. Rogers   J. H. Rogers, I, Sarah J. Rogers have
this day sold given transfered and conveyed unto my
son the said J. H. Rogers, all the right, title, claim and
interest (except such rights and interest herein after
named) that I have in and to a certain tract or parcel
of land situated and lying in the 14 Civil district of
Washington County and State of Tennessee adjoining
the lands of hisenbery I. J. Campbell Mc adam
Conley, Ross Campbell and mrs. E. L. Basket and
bounded as follows Beginning at a planted Rock
corner to Basket and in hisenbery's line thence
with his line and I. J. Campbell's line North 18 west
38 1/2 poles to a large black oak tree Campbell's corner
thence South 85 west 14 poles and 9 links to a double
white oak Thence North 38 west 10 4 1/5 poles to a stake
in Conleys line. Thence South 40 west 52 poles to a
Stake corner to Campbell and Rogers thence South
35 east 75 poles to a double Black oak. Thence North
x5 E. 27 1/2 poles to a planted rock w. a. Keys corner
thence with his line South 1 1/2 west 27 1/5 poles to a
planted rock corner this day made Thence with a line
this day established North 83 1/2 east 54 poles to the place
of the Beginning Containing forty and three furths (40 3/4)
acres be the same more or less. To have and
to hold unto him the said J. H. Rogers his heirs
and assigns forever in fee simple I agree and bind myself
to warrant and forever defend the title to said tract of land
unto him the said J. H. Rogers against the lawful claims
of all persons whomsoever (This tract of land is a part of the
land convey to said Sarah J. Rogers by her father Henry
Buchanan by will now it is understood and agreed by
both parties herein named that the said Sarah J.
Rogers is to have one third of all the grain and hay
that is produced on said land during the natural
life of said Sarah J. Rogers. The grain and hay to be
delivered in good condition at barn of the said Sarah
J. Rogers, I, the said Sarah J. Rogers give unto the said

(continued)

Figure 2.10—*Continued*

J. H. Rogers a right of way to pass to and from a spring that is on a tract of land that I am this day conveying to my daughter C. L. Basket I also give unto the said J. H. Rogers a right of way to the spring branch for the purpose of watering stock, said Right of way to be wide enough for a good wagon Road to be located as Follows: Beg. at a planted Rock corner to Basket and in Lisenbery's line Thence with his lines South 1 east 6½ poles to a stake Thence South 34 east 18½ poles to a stake then South 25 W 11½ poles to a stake Thence South 10 west 19 poles to a stake Thence South 87 west 14 poles to a planted stone on the South west side of the spring branch. said Right of way to be Ten(10) feet wide This the third day of April in the year A.D. 1908.

                                                  Sarah J. Rogers.

State of Tennessee) Personally appeared before me Wm
Washington County) S. Bacon a notary public in and
for said county and State, the within named bargainor
Sarah J. Rogers with whom I am personally acquainted
and who acknowledges that she executed the within
instrument for the purposes herein contained. Witness
my hand and notarial seal at office this 3rd. day of
April 1908.

                                        Wm S. Bacon.
                                        notary public.

Courtesy Tennessee State Library and Archives.

which will aid the search. Sometimes they yield information on family relationships or land transfers which are omitted from deed records. Bills of sale involving transfer of slaves were frequently recorded in deed books.

Probate Records

Probate records consist largely of wills, administrations, and other documents relating to the settlement of estates and deceased persons. They are especially useful in providing information for the period prior to the registration of vital records. The most important of the probate records is the will (figure 2.11), as it contains almost indisputable evidence of relationships. However, some wills are more informative than others. Some meticulously list all living (and some deceased) relatives, while others consist of little more than the statement, "I leave my entire estate to my loving wife and children." Usually there is a statement of relationship between the person making the will (testator) and the person receiv-

Figure 2.11
Michael Garber's Will

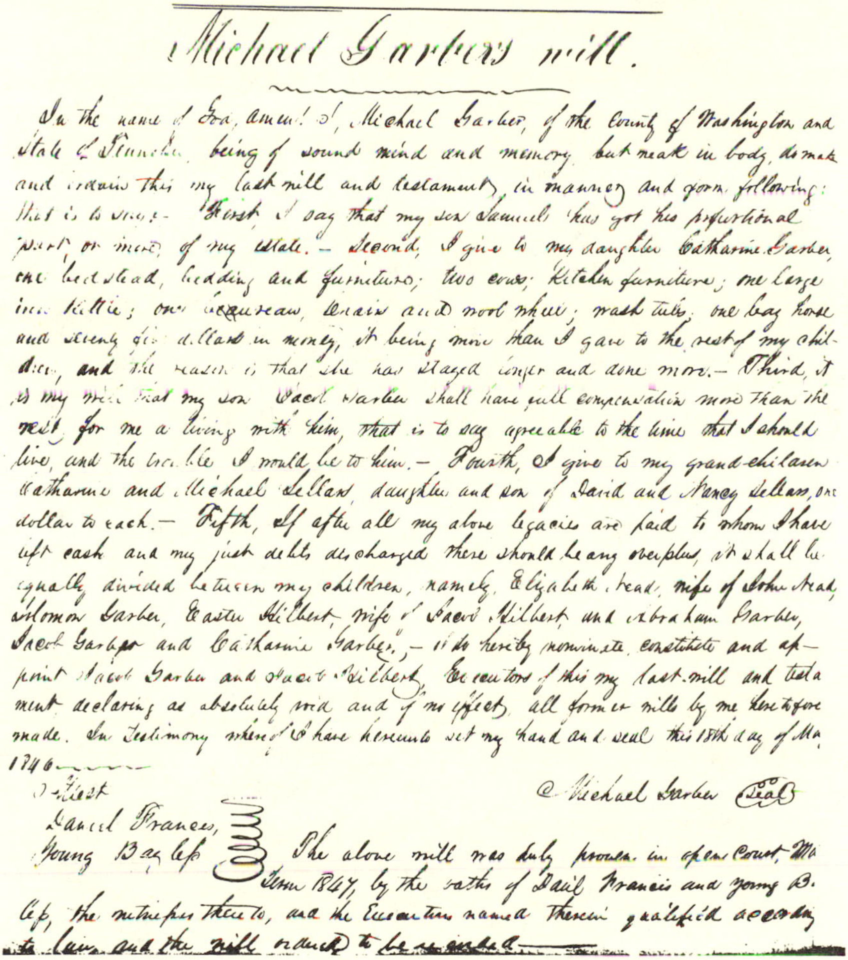

Michael Garber's will.

In the name of God, amen! I, Michael Garber, of the County of Washington and State of Tennessee being of sound mind and memory but weak in body, do make and ordain this my last will and testament, in manner and form following: that is to say: – First, I say that my son Samuel has got his proportional part, or more, of my estate. – Second, I give to my daughter Catharine Garber, one bedstead, bedding and furniture; two cows; Kitchen furniture; one large iron kettle; one bureau, chair and wool wheel; wash tubs, one bay horse and seventy five dollars in money, it being more than I gave to the rest of my children, and the reason is that she has stayed longer and done more. – Third, it is my will that my son Jacob Garber shall have full compensation more than the rest for me a living with him, that is to say agreeable to the time that I should live, and the trouble I would be to him. – Fourth, I give to my grand-children Catharine and Michael Sellars, daughter and son of David and Nancy Sellars, one dollar to each. – Fifth, If after all my above legacies are paid to whom I have left cash and my just debts discharged there should be any overplus, it shall be equally divided between my children, namely, Elizabeth Read, wife of John Read, Solomon Garber, Easter Hilbert, wife of Jacob Hilbert, and Abraham Garber, Jacob Garber and Catharine Garber, – I do hereby nominate, constitute and appoint Jacob Garber and Jacob Hilbert Executors of this my last will and testament declaring as absolutely void and of no effect, all former wills by me heretofore made. In Testimony whereof I have hereunto set my hand and seal this 18th day of Ma[illegible] 1846

Attest

Michael Garber (Seal)

Daniel Frances,
Young Bayless

The above will was duly proven in open Court, Ma[illegible] Term 1847, by the oaths of David Francis and Young B. Bayless, the witnesses thereto, and the Executors named therein qualified according to law and the will ordered to be recorded.

Courtesy Tennessee State Library and Archives.

ing the property. Each child may be named, along with the property to be received. Sometimes grandchildren, nieces and nephews, brothers, sisters, and parents are named. A fairly straightforward example of the statement of immediate family relationships appears in a codicil to Robert Cowan's will in 1841, when having directed that certain property be sold, he instructs that

> the proceeds when collected shall be equally divided among my children; that is, they shall receive share and share alike the share coming to my Daughter Polly Newberry shall

be given to her children, as their family would receive more benefit from the same, and the share coming to my Son James C who has departed this life shall be given to his two children, Elizabeth P and Robert C Cowan, Second. With a view to secure to my sons Ross B and Samuel P and my daughter Sirena the full title and interest to the land and negros devised to them, . . . I have thought proper to make to them an absolute deed of gift.[4]

To die without leaving a will is to die intestate. In that case an administrator is appointed by the court to oversee the disposition of property and is required by law to account for it. Thereby another source of information is generated, as there may be letters of administration, records of litigation, inventories, notices to creditors, and so forth.

Wills are usually on file at the courthouse of the county in which they were probated, where copies are kept in large bound volumes called libers. Other probate records are likewise located in the county courthouse having jurisdiction over the proceedings. Photographic copies of wills are available by mail. It is necessary to know the proper jurisdiction and the approximate date of death. They are usually indexed by testator.

The language of older wills may be misleading, as many terms now in common use have changed meaning over the years. For example, the term "brother," in addition to its twentieth century meaning, may also refer to brother-in-law, stepbrother, husband of a sister-in-law, brother in the church, or good friend.

Other County Records

Although vital, land, and probate records are the most useful to the genealogist, another possible source of information, civil and criminal court records, should not be overlooked. Civil court records, which pertain to action between private parties, consist of files, dockets, registers of action, reporters' transcripts, and exhibits, and they are most often in the custody of the county clerk. Since the parties to civil action are either plaintiffs or defendants, there is an index by plaintiff and an index by defendant.

Criminal records speak for themselves. Usually of little value, they would be a last resort. But judging from the number of persons who boast of their colorful ancestors who were outside the law, they should be considered as a possibility.

Voter registration records give the name and address of the voter, the state or county of birth, and any naturalization information.

Tax rolls are another source of name and address information, but unless an ancestor owned property, it is unlikely that the name will appear. Earlier tax records sometimes leave something to be desired in their completeness, so they are not a source for every problem, but they should be kept in mind. Used in conjunction with other records, such as marriage records and deeds, they may be just what is needed to piece a puzzle together.

STATE LIBRARIES

Concentrating on a state's history and preserving all manner of primary and secondary materials relative to it, state libraries and archives may be of great help in locating an ancestor. They are usually divided into areas according to the function each performs, the library containing published material and the archives, state and county records, frequently with a manuscript section containing the private papers of citizens of the state. The state library and archives is a storehouse for family histories, both published and manuscript; state histories; state censuses; county records; genealogical and family association periodicals; state land, vital, and census records; tax lists; legislative records; military service records; muster rolls; and pension applications for the state's soldiers. The list goes on and varies somewhat from state to state, but the extent and variety of the resources of state libraries and archives make them invaluable.

FEDERAL RECORDS

Census Records

Census taking goes back as far as Babylónia and ancient China, usually for the purposes of taxation or raising an army. It was a function of government in the days of the Romans, beginning about 550 B.C., and was extended under Caesar Augustus to include the entire Roman Empire. It was in response to the decree that "all the world should be taxed" that Mary and Joseph traveled to Bethlehem to be counted among the descendants of David. Modern censuses have been taken from about 1580 in Mexico, 1635 in Finland, and 1703 in Iceland. Some of these records are yet extant.[5] The data and their accuracy vary from country to country. In the United States a federal population census has been taken every ten years since 1790, and they reflect the change and growth of the country: the westward movement, the status of free and slave labor, immigration, urbanization, and changing population trends. Genealogists as well as social scientists and historians find a mother lode in census records.

Eventually everyone doing family research has to use federal census records. They are invaluable for the information they contain about persons and families during the nineteenth and early twentieth centuries. The originals are in the National Archives located in Washington, D.C., but microfilm copies have been made of the originals to protect them from handling. Census records are public property and may be examined by anyone who wishes to see them. However, to protect their confidentiality, they are made public only after seventy-five years have passed. The latest census records available to the public are those for 1910. Microfilm copies of census records are also deposited at the eleven regional branches of the National Archives and are available for research at each branch.

Many state libraries and historical societies have complete or partial census records. Census data that is collected but not publicly available may be obtained from the Bureau of Census in Pittsburg, Kansas. Specific information and proven relationships are required (on Form BC-600) before a search can be undertaken. For a full discussion on the contents of the various census records, the reader is referred to chapter 5 of this book.

Mortality Schedules

Beginning with the 1850 census, enumerators collected information on persons who had died in the twelve-month period prior to the census. Known as the mortality schedules, these data were taken for the censuses of 1850 through 1890. They recorded the name, age, sex, color, birthplace, occupation, marital status, month, and cause of death. The primary purpose was to gather information in the fight against disease: death rate, prevalence of disease, longevity, and so forth. The value of mortality schedules in family history research is the fact that they predate many state vital records and can provide vital information that may appear nowhere else. They may pinpoint a death date, which may lead to other records. These special schedules should be searched if an ancestor's name fails to appear in the regular decennial censuses for 1850–1880, since the ancestor may have died during one of the time periods covered by the mortality schedules. The user should be alert to the fact that information in these schedules is only for the year prior to June 1 of the census year. That adds up to one year out of ten, and four years altogether for the entire 1850–1880 period (the 1890 schedules having been destroyed by fire), covering only about 13 percent of the deaths over the thirty-year period.

After 1900 most states had established central registration of deaths and the mortality schedules were discontinued. Records for each state were returned to the states to be placed in the state's archives. Chapter 5 also makes reference to the mortality schedules.

Military Service Records

Military records are a valuable source for the location of male ancestors, especially if they were of military age during a major war. The National Archives contains the military service records of men who saw service, chiefly in the federal government's interest, from 1775 to 1917. Records of later service are in the custody of the National Personnel Records Center in St. Louis. There are also some surviving colonial and militia records, primarily rosters containing names and military units. Early service records, however, are fragmentary. Many were lost in a War Department fire in 1800 or when the British army burned and ransacked U.S. government buildings in 1814. More extant records date from 1800. The wealth of information contained in these records may be located through indexes, and if there is any possibility that an ancestor served, the records should be searched.

The service records for volunteer soldiers cover the period from 1775 to 1902 and are compilations of information from a variety of military records, such as muster rolls, hospital records, prison records, and so forth, gathered together for easier searching. Yet despite efforts to assure their comprehensiveness, many compiled records are incomplete. Information from these records will vary but will most often show name, age, rank, military unit, term of service, and place of enlistment.

The information in Regular Army records covers the period from 1789 to 1917 for officers and from 1789 to 1912 for enlisted men and has not been organized into compiled service records. It is to be found in scattered and diverse sources, usually enlistments, muster rolls, and medical and other records, and will show for each man his name, age, place of birth, occupation at enlistment, military unit, physical description, and date of discharge or date of death.

There are likewise records of the men who have served in the U.S. Navy, Marine Corps, Air Force, and Coast Guard, the earlier records being located at the National Archives and the later ones at the National Personnel Records Center. All Air Force records are at the center.

Service records, usually compiled, also exist for men who served in the Confederate Army. Their genealogical value is confined to proof of military service, age, and place of enlistment. Additional service records of Confederate soldiers may be found in the archives of each southern state.

Before undertaking research into military records, the researcher should consult a copy of the very useful publication by Meredith Colket and Frank E. Bridgers, *Guide to Genealogical Records in the National Archives.*[6] It will steer one easily through the maze of record groups, series, indexes, and so forth, so necessary for successful and expeditious searching. For a general introduction to military records in the National Archives, its pamphlet, "Military Service Records in the National Archives of the United States,"[7] will be useful. Chapter 5 is also helpful.

CHURCH RECORDS

Church records of genealogical value are those dealing with the vital milestones of birth, marriage, and death: christenings or baptisms, marriages, and burials. They constitute an important source of this information, as they often predate vital statistics registration or may cover years for which official records have been destroyed.

The genealogical information provided by church records varies according to denomination, but most records provide a baptismal date, possibly the date and place of birth, and the names of the parents. Marriage records usually include the names of the parents and the witnesses, and burial records include the date of burial and frequently the date of death. It should be kept in mind as one uses church records that a baptismal date is not a birth date nor a burial date a death date, although they are good indicators of the actual dates. Marriage banns were frequently recorded in church records, but they are expressions of intent to marry and do not constitute proof of marriage.

A great deal of trial and error goes into the location of church records, due to the number of denominations, the transient nature of many denominations, and the lack of uniformity in storing records. U.S. church records are most commonly found in the local churches, and contact should be made with the pastor. Sometimes older records have been transferred to a central location, very often a church archives or historical society. If the church of an ancestor no longer exists, the local historical society may know of the location of its records. If that fails, the state organization of the church should be contacted.

Frequently entered into church records were arrivals from and departures to other congregations, thus allowing the researcher to trace a family from one location to another. As one of the frustrations of genealogy is to have a family disappear without leaving a trace, this recording of arrivals and departures is especially important. Other types of church records may include membership lists, minutes, and disciplinary actions.

Church denominations tend to handle records variously. The records of Quakers, for example, yield extensive genealogical information relating to births, marriages, transfers to other congregations, and disciplinary actions. Baptist records are congregationally owned and lately have been microfilmed and deposited in Baptist historical libraries or in regional centers. They usually lack vital data, but that may be recorded in the minister's journal. Methodist records are being gathered into regional centers. They, too, exclude vital records, but these may have been entered voluntarily into the record by the minister. As the LDS Genealogical Society has been microfilming all church records, many denominational records are included in its holdings at Salt Lake City.

During the 1930s the WPA inventoried church records. Much of the information is now out of date, but they are still a valuable source of information and are to be found in large libraries and historical societies of the state concerned. Kirkham's *A Survey of American Church Records: Major Denominations Before 1860* is useful for locating early records. Many denominations publish their own directories, which give the addresses of their churches throughout the United States.

CEMETERY RECORDS

Cemeteries can be valuable sources of genealogical information, and sometimes they are the only clue to an ancestor. As already noted, early vital statistics records are incomplete, and other records that could have yielded the information may have been lost or destroyed. Unfortunately, many cemeteries have been casualties of shopping centers and interstate highways, and locating the place of burial of an ancestor may present some problem. For more recent deaths, the information may come from death certificates, obituaries, or a funeral director's records. For earlier ancestors, the historical society in the area may be helpful.

Information on tombstones can vary widely. Older ones tend to give more information. They may include place and date of birth, marriage date, names of children, spouse(s), religious affiliation, and military service. If the family lived in the area for a long time, there might be a family plot, with all members of the family buried there. Be aware, as with other records, of the possibility of error, such as the reversal of numbers in a date. Errors in stone carving, once made, are not easily corrected.

It is well to check with the cemetery superintendent, or sexton, to see if the records contain additional information. They frequently have information as to who purchased the lot, who pays for its upkeep, burials, and locations of graves.

If a cemetery no longer exists, it is possible that transcripts were made of the inscriptions. The Daughters of the American Revolution (DAR) has collected volumes of gravestone inscriptions from cemeteries across the country. The WPA undertook a similar project, as have many other organizations, and the results have been deposited in state libraries, academic libraries, and historical societies.

MISCELLANEOUS RECORDS

Newspapers

Local newspapers can provide a wealth of genealogical information: obituaries; engagement, wedding, and birth announcements; legal notices, divorces; and so forth. Unfortunately, most newspapers are unindexed, and if one is to avoid a lengthy day-by-day search for information in a newspaper, it is necessary to have a reasonably close date for a birth, marriage, or death. Fortunately, however, with the upsurge of interest in genealogy, there has been considerable progress recently in the microfilming and indexing of old newspapers.

Another feature of genealogical interest sometimes found in newspapers is the genealogy column, usually consisting of queries and answers. It is possible, through a query or advertisement placed in a local newspaper or genealogical publication, to achieve very satisfactory progress toward the solution of a research problem. Among older newspapers, the *Boston Evening Transcript's* genealogy column, begun in 1876, was extremely successful, eventually becoming an entire department in 1895 and continuing until the *Transcript* ceased publication in 1941. It has been microfilmed and indexed. The American Antiquarian Society of Worcester, Massachusetts, has indexed many early newspapers, including the *Columbian Centinel* of Boston (1784–1840), which printed notices of marriages and deaths from all over the country, with an index of some 80,000 names. Its indexes are to be found in the Library of Congress, the New York Public Library, and the New England Historic Genealogical Society.[8] To find the name of the local newspaper which may be of value in a genealogical search, there are several directories, covering the years 1690 to the present, which will aid in the search and which are found in the reference departments of most libraries.

School Records

Schools and colleges can yield information from their enrollment records, yearbooks, alumni publications, and other sources. This information will serve primarily to verify dates of attendance and give some biographical details. Very often schools have published alumni directories, which may provide some necessary verification. Local histories and local historical societies can be of help in finding out what schools were in the area at the time an ancestor was of school age. If the school is no longer in existence, the local board of education or historical society may have custody of the records.

Private Organizations

Records of private organizations such as fraternities, clubs, professional societies, and so forth are also sources of genealogical data. Particularly if the organization is a national one, such as the Elks, Masons, or American Legion, there is a greater likelihood of records which will provide information, such as name, address, date and place of joining, family and educational data, and religious affiliation.

Fortunately there exist numerous directories of schools and organizations, which can be invaluable as locators and time savers. Again, a trip to the library is in order, this time to take advantage of information already compiled. Libraries themselves are compiled into directories, which give data such as location, holdings, and special strengths. Before doing any kind of field work, the libraries in a locality should be pinpointed for possible support in the project.

ADOPTEES

The subject of open or closed adoption records is under vigorous discussion now. While its resolution does not appear to be imminent, the subject and its urgency have at least been placed in the public eye. The founding of the Adoptees' Liberation Movement Association (ALMA) has as its aim the opening of adoption records for any person over eighteen years of age who wishes to see them. ALMA maintains a date-of-birth registry and acts as a clearinghouse for research tips. The law as written, however, seeks to retain the confidentiality that was assured at the time a child was given up for adoption. Adoptees maintain that they are interested in their heritage, medical and cultural, and not in reunions.

An adoptee who would like the facts of his or her parentage should contact ALMA, P.O. Box 154, Washington Bridge Station, New York, NY 10033, to find the nearest chapter.

BLIND AND PHYSICALLY HANDICAPPED

A library was formed in 1976 with the aim of providing assistance to the blind and physically handicapped who desire to pursue genealogical research. The Genealogical Library for the Blind and Physically Handicapped in Atlanta began by producing genealogical instructional material for the blind and deaf and went on to create a genealogical lending library for the handicapped. Books and magazines are cataloged by title, and cards are created for any item within them of genealogical interest that may pertain to a location or surname. This locality and surname information is computerized to provide printouts of all titles in the library pertaining to a certain name or area. Additional information may be secured from the Genealogical Library for the Blind and Physically Handicapped, 15 Dunwoody Park Road, Suite 130, Atlanta, GA 30338.

CHECKLIST OF SOURCES OF GENEALOGICAL INFORMATION

Family sources	Bibles
	letters
	diaries
	photographs
	scrapbooks
	interviews
	documents such as marriage licenses, birth certificates, divorce papers, death certificates, military discharges, deeds, mortgages, wills, and tax receipts
Local sources	city directories
	telephone directories
	newspaper files, including genealogical columns
	cemetery records and tombstone inscriptions
	school records
	hospital records
	church records
	tax lists
	voter lists
	local histories
	lodge records
County sources	vital records
	land records

	probate records
	court records, civil and criminal
	other recorders' records
	voter registration
State sources	vital records
	state censuses
	state library and archives
	state historical societies
	land office records
	legislative records
National sources	censuses
	mortality schedules
	military records
	pension records
	passenger lists
	immigration records
	land records
	Greek-letter organizations

NOTES

1. Noel C. Stevenson, *Search and Research* (Salt Lake City, Utah: Deseret Book Co., 1979).
2. Cache Genealogical Library, *Handbook of Genealogical Correspondence*, rev. ed. (Logan, Utah: Everton Publishers, 1974).
3. Gilbert H. Doane and James B. Bell, *Searching for Your Ancestors* (New York: Bantam Books, by arrangement with University of Minnesota Press, 1974), pp. 138–39.
4. *Records of Franklin County Will Book,* vols. 1–2, 1808–1876 (Nashville, Tennessee: Historical Records Survey, 1936), p. 167.
5. Timothy Field Beard, *How to Find Your Family Roots* (New York: McGraw-Hill Book Co., 1977), p. 84.
6. Meredith B. Colket, Jr., and Frank E. Bridgers, *Guide to Genealogical Records in the National Archives* (Washington, D.C.: National Archives and Records Service, 1964). The National Archives has published an expanded and updated edition of this work under the title *Guide to Research in the National Archives.*
7. U.S., National Archives, "Military Service Records in the National Archives of the United States," pamphlet (Washington, D.C.: National Archives and Records Service. reprint ed., 1976).
8. American Genealogical Research Institute, *How to Trace Your Family Tree* (New York: Doubleday and Co., 1973), p. 151.

BIBLIOGRAPHY

Basic Genealogical Texts

Beard, Timothy Field, and Demong, Denise. *How to Find Your Family Roots.* New York: McGraw-Hill Book Co., 1977.
General introduction, with chapters on Jewish, black, and American Indian ancestry. The lists of sources of information, by state and by country, are especially helpful.

Doane, Gilbert H., and Bell, James B. *Searching for Your Ancestors.* 5th ed. Minneapolis, Minn.: University of Minnesota Press, 1980.

Informal, conversational approach to genealogical research sources and techniques.

Everton, George B., ed. *The How Book for Genealogists.* 7th ed. Logan, Utah: Everton Publishers, 1971.

Handy, concise primer. Contains genealogical dictionary.

Greenwood, Val D. *The Researcher's Guide to American Genealogy.* Baltimore: Genealogical Publishing Co., 1978.

Comprehensive and scholarly. Covers all aspects of genealogical research.

Helmbold, F. Wilbur. *Tracing Your Ancestry: Step-by-Step Guide to Researching Your Family History.* Birmingham, Ala.: Oxmoor House, 1976.

General introduction; easy to follow. Useful bibliography.

————. *Tracing Your Ancestry Logbook.* Birmingham, Ala.: Oxmoor House, 1976.

A companion (or workbook) to the first Helmbold work, and very useful as a ready reference of appropriate forms.

Hinshaw, William Wade. *Encyclopedia of American Quaker Genealogy.* 7 vols. in 8. Ann Arbor, Mich.: Edwards Brothers, distributed by Friends Supply House, Richmond, Ind., 1936. Available on microfilm from Frederic Luther Co., Indianapolis, Indiana.

Rubincam, Milton, and Stephenson, Jean, eds. *Genealogical Research: Methods and Sources.* Washington, D.C.: American Society of Genealogists, 1960.

Discusses general considerations and research materials; special emphasis on regional and state resources.

Stryker-Rodda, Kenn. *Genealogy; A Boy Scouts of America Handbook.* North Brunswick, N.J.: Boy Scouts of America, 1973.

A basic primer for the beginning genealogical researcher.

Westin, Jeane Eddy. *Finding Your Roots: How Every American Can Trace His Ancestors—At Home and Abroad.* Los Angeles: J. P. Tarcher, 1977.

General introduction; contains a great deal of information. Easy to follow.

Williams, Ethel W. *Know Your Ancestors: A Guide to Genealogical Research.* Rutland, Vt.: Charles E. Tuttle Co., 1976.

Fundamental instruction for tracing ancestry and compiling family records. Special chapters on New York State, New Jersey, Pennsylvania, and Ohio.

Wright, Norman Edgar. *Building an American Pedigree: A Study in Genealogy.* Provo, Utah: Brigham Young University Press, 1974.

A practical book for the person who wants to bypass theory and background. Extensive illustrations.

Reference Works

Adams, James Truslow, ed. *Atlas of American History.* New York: Charles Scribner's Sons, 1943.

Akey, Nancy, and Akey, Denis. *Encyclopedia of Associations.* 16th ed. 3 vols. Detroit: Gale Research Co., 1981.

American Library Directory. New York: R. R. Bowker Co., published biennially.

American Newspapers, 1821–1936: A Union List of Files Available in the United States and Canada. Edited by Winifred Gregory. New York: H. W. Wilson Co., 1937.

Cache Genealogical Library. *Handbook for Genealogical Correspondence.* Rev. ed. Logan, Utah: Everton Publishers, 1974.

Colket, Meredith B., and Bridgers, Frank E. *Guide to Genealogical Records in the National Archives.* Washington, D.C.: National Archives and Records Service, 1964. (An expanded edition is now available.)

Columbia Lippincott Gazetteer of the World. Edited by Leon E. Seltzer. New York: Columbia University Press, 1952.

Directory of Historical Societies and Agencies in the United States and Canada. Nashville, Tenn.: American Association for State and Local History, published biennially.

Hamer, Philip M., ed. *A Guide to Archives and Manuscripts in the United States.* New Haven, Conn.: Yale University Press, 1961.

Herbert, Miranda C., and McNeil, Barbara, eds. *Biography and Genealogy Master Index.* 2d ed. 8 vols. Detroit: Gale Research Co., 1980–81.

————. Supplement to the Second Edition. 3 vols. Rev. 2nd ed. Detroit: Gale Research Co., 1982.

Joramo, Marjorie K. *A Directory of Ethnic Publishers and Resource Organizations.* 2d ed. Chicago: Office for Library Service to the Disadvantaged, American Library Association, 1979.

Kaminkow, Marion H., ed. *Genealogies in the Library of Congress: A Bibliography.* 2 vols. Baltimore: Magna Carta Book Co., 1972. Supplement 1972–1976 (1977).

————. *United States Local Histories in the Library of Congress.* 5 vols. Baltimore: Magna Carta Book Co., 1975.

Kirkham, E. Kay. *The Counties of the United States and Their Genealogical Value.* 2d ed. Salt Lake City, Utah: Deseret Book Co., 1965.

————. *A Handy Guide to Record Searching in the Larger Cities of the United States.* Logan, Utah: Everton Publishers, 1974.

————. *How to Read the Handwriting and Records of Early America.* Rev. ed. Salt Lake City, Utah: Deseret Book Co., 1965.

————. *The Land Records of America and Their Genealogical Value.* Salt Lake City, Utah: Deseret Book Co., 1964.

————. *Some of the Military Records of America Before 1900: Their Use and Value in Genealogical and Historical Research.* Salt Lake City, Utah: Deseret Book Co., 1964.

————. *A Survey of American Church Records.* 2 vols. Salt Lake City, Utah: Deseret Book Co., 1959–60.

Konrad, J., ed. *A Directory of Genealogical Periodicals.* Munroe Falls, Ohio: Summitt Publications, 1975.

Meyer, Mary Keysor, ed. *Directory of Genealogical Societies in the United States and Canada.* Rev. ed. Baltimore: Maryland Historical Society, 1980.

Milner, Anita Clark. *Newspaper Genealogical Column Directory.* Bowie, Md.: Heritage Books, 1979.

Munsell's, Joel, sons. *The American Genealogist, Being a Catalogue of Family Histories.* 5th ed. Albany, N.Y.: 1900; Baltimore, Genealogical Publishing Co., 1967. Supplement: 1900–1908 (1967).

N. W. Ayer and Son's Directory, Newspapers and Periodicals. Philadelphia: N. W. Ayer and Son, published annually.

Newberry Library (Chicago). *The Genealogical Index.* 4 vols. Boston: G. K. Hall and Co., 1960.

New York Public Library, Local History and Genealogy Division. *Dictionary Catalog of the Local History and Genealogy Division.* 20 vols. Boston: G. K. Hall and Co., 1974.

Spear, Dorothea N. *Bibliography of American Directories Through 1860.* Worcester, Mass.: American Antiquarian Society, 1961.

Sperry, Kip. *A Survey of American Genealogical Periodicals and Periodical Indexes.* Detroit: Gale Research Co., 1978.

Stevenson, Noel C. *Search and Research.* Salt Lake City, Utah: Deseret Book Co., 1979.

U.S., National Center for Health Statistics. "Where to Write for Birth and Death Records of U.S. Citizens Who Were Born or Died Outside of the United States and Birth Certificates for Alien Children Adopted by U.S. Citizens." Washington, D.C.: Government Printing Office, 1979.

————. "Where to Write for Birth and Death Records, United States and Outlying Areas." Washington, D.C.: Government Printing Office, 1979.

————. "Where to Write for Divorce Records, United States and Outlying Areas." Washington, D.C.: Government Printing Office, 1979.

————. "Where to Write for Marriage Records, United States and Outlying Areas." Washington, D.C.: Government Printing Office, 1979.

Young, Margaret L., ed. *Directory of Special Libraries and Information Centers in the United States and Canada.* 2 vols. Detroit: Gale Research Co., 1981.

Periodicals

Genealogical periodicals are as varied in content and style as the nation itself. They may be the publications of genealogical societies or privately printed; scholarly or folksy; national, regional, or statewide in scope. They may be newsletters concerned with a single family surname. The following list of periodicals presents examples in each category, with the year in which they first appeared. Most are indexed in the *Genealogical Periodical Annual Index.* For a full listing of genealogical periodicals, consult J. Konrad, ed., *A Directory of Genealogical Periodicals,* or Kip Sperry, *A Survey of American Genealogical Periodicals and Periodical Indexes* (in preceding section of bibliography).

The American Genealogist (1922)
1232 39th Street
Des Moines, IA 50311
Genealogy and related subjects; emphasis on articles reporting individual family research.

Ansearchin News (1954)
Tennessee Genealogical Society
Box 1214
Memphis, TN 38112
Genealogical records and Tennessee source data.

Cousin Huntin' (1961)
Central New York Genealogical Society
Box 104 Colvin Station
Syracuse, NY 13205
Current research problems of members; queries.

The Genealogical Helper (1947)
Everton Publishers
P.O. Box 368
Logan, UT 84321
Exchange medium for genealogists; queries, lists of family associations, directories of genealogists and societies.

The Hoosier Genealogist (1961)
Indiana Historical Society
315 West Ohio Street, Room 350
Indianapolis, IN 46202
Marriage, will, probate, land, tax, and census records of Indiana counties; family records, Bible records, some cemetery records.

Journal of North Carolina Genealogy (1966)
P.O. Box 1770
Raleigh, NC 27602
Source material of North Carolina 1663–1900.

The Murphree Quarterly (1963)
Murphree Genealogical Association
1370 Bryan Avenue
Salt Lake City, UT 84105
Genealogical research on the Murphree family; data on all known Murphree family groups.

National Genealogical Society Quarterly (1912)
National Genealogical Society
1921 Sunderland Place, N.W.
Washington, DC 20036
Articles of general genealogical interest and previously unpublished source materials.

New England Historical and Genealogical Register (1847)
New England Historic Genealogical Society
101 Newbury Street
Boston, MA 02116
  Scholarly articles on genealogy and history of New England, primarily pre-1800.

New York Genealogical and Biographical Record (1870)
New York Genealogical and Biographical Society
122 East 58th Street
New York, NY 10022
  Family histories and transcripts of various types of New York records, including those of the Dutch
  in New York.

Orange County California Genealogical Society Quarterly (1964)
Orange County California Genealogical Society
P.O. Box 1587
Orange, CA 92668
  Emphasis on California and the Far West, including vital statistics, cemetery records, old letters,
  Bible records.

St. Louis Genealogical Society Quarterly (1966)
St. Louis Genealogical Society
1617 South Brentwood Boulevard, Room 261
St. Louis, MO 63114
  Genealogical indexes, lists, cemeteries, Bible records, censuses, family histories.

Virginia Genealogist (1957)
Box 4883
Washington, DC 20008
  Abstracts of source materials and articles on early generations of families of Virginia and West
  Virginia.

MAJOR GENEALOGICAL REPOSITORIES

American Antiquarian Society
185 Salisbury Street
Worcester, MA 01609
  National in scope. Open without charge to serious adult researchers. Noncirculating.

Detroit Public Library
Burton Historical Collection
5201 Woodward Avenue
Detroit, MI 48202
  National in scope; strong emphasis on Michigan and Detroit area genealogy. Noncirculating.

Genealogical Department Library, (LDS) Utah
50 East North Temple
Salt Lake City, UT 84150
  World's largest collection of primary genealogical records; international in scope. Numerous
  branches. Open to public without charge.

Library of Congress
Genealogy and Local History Collection
Washington, DC 20540
  International in scope. World's largest collection of published family histories. Open to adults.

National Archives (GSA)
Pennsylvania Avenue at 8th Street, N.W.
Washington, DC 20408
   Federal census schedules, military records, passenger lists, and other federal records of genealogical value. Open to the public.

National Genealogical Society
1921 Sunderland Place, N.W.
Washington, DC 20036
   Emphasis on U.S. sources. Members in good standing may borrow for a nominal fee. Open to public; nonmembers pay daily fee.

National Society, Daughters of the American Revolution Library
1776 D Street, N.W.
Washington, DC 20006
   The collection extends to colonial America. Open to the public except during the month of April; nonmembers pay a fee.

New England Historical Genealogical Society
101 Newbury Street
Boston, MA 02116
   One of the largest, containing 300,000 volumes. Emphasis on New England families and history. Open to public; nonmembers pay daily fee.

New York Public Library
Local History and Genealogy Division
5th Avenue and 42nd Street
New York, NY 10018
   Emphasis on local history for United States and Great Britain; genealogies worldwide. Local histories outside United States and Great Britain in other collections in library.

Newberry Library
Local and Family History Collection
60 West Walton Street
Chicago, IL 60610
   Especially strong in local history, genealogy, and biography of the Midwest. Open to public.

Public Library of Fort Wayne and Allen County
900 Webster Street
Fort Wayne, IN 46802
   National in scope, with local emphasis on Fort Wayne, Allen County, and Indiana materials. Complete set of U.S. federal census records and many census indexes. Open to public.

   For additional information consult the following directories, which are listed in the bibliography to this chapter:
   American Library Directory
   Directory of Historical Societies and Agencies in the United States and Canada
   Mary Keysor Meyer, ed., *Directory of Genealogical Societies in the United States and Canada*
   Margaret L. Young, ed., *Directory of Special Libraries and Information Centers in the United States and Canada*

GENEALOGICAL SOCIETIES

   The following list of genealogical societies will give some indication of their variety: general, state, regional, and special interest. For a complete listing, consult a directory of genealogical societies such as Mary K. Meyer, ed., *Directory of Genealogical Societies in the United States.*

Ark-La-Tex Genealogical Association
P.O. Box 4462
Shreveport, LA 71104

> Founded 1955; 500 members. Primary interest in southern research, especially Arkansas, Louisiana, Texas; collects, preserves, and makes available genealogical materials, documents, and records. Publishes *The Genie,* quarterly.

Genealogy Club of America
19 West South Temple
Union Pacific Annex, Suite 600
Salt Lake City, UT 84101

> Founded 1969; 2,500 members; 6 staff. Membership consists of genealogists, libraries, groups, and individuals interested in tracing family ancestry; gives assistance with personal research problems; maintains 2,000-volume library. Publishes *Genealogy Digest,* bimonthly.

National Genealogical Society
1921 Sunderland Place, N.W.
Washington, DC 20036

> Founded 1903; 4,500 members. Purpose is to create interest in genealogical research; maintains library of approximately 80,000 volumes of genealogy, local history, and source material. Publishes *National Genealogical Society Quarterly,* newsletter, books.

Polish Genealogical Society
984 Milwaukee Avenue
Chicago, IL 60622

> Founded 1978; 200 members. Promotes Polish genealogical study and establishes communication among those doing research; conducts annual workshop. Publishes semiannual newsletter.

Southern Arizona Genealogical Society
P.O. Box 6027
Tucson, AZ 85716

> Maintains cemetery, mortuary, Bible, and some family records. Publishes *Copper State Bulletin,* quarterly.

Unitarian and Universalist Genealogical Society
10605 Lakespring Way
Cockeysville, MD 21030

> Founded 1971; 231 members. Purpose is to collect, organize, and make available genealogical records on Unitarians and Universalists. Maintains 1,100-volume library.

Vesterheim Genealogical Center
4909 Sherwood Road
Madison, WI 53711

> Founded 1975; 450 members. Promotes study of Norwegian heritage and ethnic background; serves as clearinghouse for inquiries. Publishes *Norwegian Tracks* (newsletter), quarterly.

GENEALOGICAL SUPPLIES

Very often local bookstores may stock genealogical supplies. Listed below are a few which offer a variety of charts, kits, binders, and so forth, as well as genealogical books.

Bookcraft
1186 South Main Street
Salt Lake City, UT 84101

Charles E. Tuttle Company, Inc.
Rutland, VT 05701

Deseret Book Company
Personal Shopping Service
P.O. Box 30178
Salt Lake City, UT 84125

Everton Publishers
P.O. Box 368
Logan, UT 84321

Goodspeed's Book Shop, Inc.
18 Beacon Street
Boston, MA 02180

OPPORTUNITIES FOR STUDY

Genealogical study may take several forms. It may be carried on at home by correspondence or it may be a short course, such as those offered by a variety of organizations. Increasingly it is being offered on college campuses. Below are listed examples of the various formats in which it is possible to begin or extend one's study of genealogy.

Brigham Young University
Provo, UT 84601
  Offers an annual family history and genealogical research seminar with instruction at the basic, intermediate, and advanced levels; covers the United States, Britain, Germanic Europe, Scandanavia. University credit available.

National Genealogical Society
Education Division
1921 Sunderland Place, N.W.
Washington, DC 20036
  Offers a home study course which serves as an introduction to basic genealogical sources and techniques. The society's Conferences in the States, begun in 1981, have been held each spring and in a different city each year. Now called the National Genealogical Society National Conference, the 1984 program will be held in San Francisco. Contact the society for additional information.

Samford University
Institute of Genealogy and Historical Research
800 Lakeshore Drive
Birmingham, AL 35229
  Sponsors an annual institute with the Board of Certification of Genealogists. Academically and professionally oriented. Admission to courses requires faculty approval.

Smithsonian Institution
Washington, DC 20005
  Offers a brief course in genealogical research in which participants learn how to conduct research in the major genealogical repositories in the Washington area, such as the National Archives, the Library of Congress, and the DAR library.

3

Library Records and Research

CASPER L. JORDAN

To undertake genealogical research in a logical and appropriate manner, the researcher must exhaust many sources of information, correspond with relatives and family friends, and examine various types of records and papers. Once the search begins, notebooks soon bulge with notes and charts. At this point the family historian is ready to consult reference works and other printed sources available in libraries or to engage in research requiring the use of other types of library materials.

This chapter focuses on library records and research by exploring some of the current trends in collecting genealogical materials in libraries, services which libraries provide to genealogical researchers, efforts of the American Library Association (ALA) to promote the development of genealogical collections, publications, and research, and the role that academic, public and state libraries, and libraries in genealogical societies play in promoting genealogical research. Further, the chapter refers the reader to selected repositories which contain significant collections in genealogy and publications which libraries may acquire.

Those who undertake genealogical research should visit the library early in the search process and become familiar with its resources. If the researcher lives in a large urban area, well-developed genealogical collections may be available in the local public library. If there is no special genealogical collection in the local public library, the librarian in any area library must be prepared to refer the researcher to another repository where genealogical needs may be met. This may include libraries in nearby historical societies, genealogical societies, state organizations, and academic institutions.

The library is an invaluable resource for genealogical research as long as the user remembers its place in the total genealogical process. Courthouses, archives, and records centers are the primary sources for certain kinds of evidence; however, libraries may contain other original research resources which are unavailable elsewhere. The library is also the resource center which aids in the interpretation of data, and it contains many types of indexes, printed records, genealogies, and histories. The researcher should select the library that has the potential for being most beneficial in resolving immediate problems and then move on to other repositories which will enable him or her to complete more of the family's history. Because it is virtually impossible to do all of one's research in a particular repository, it is necessary to investigate thoroughly the resources of various libraries and information centers, such as those described in chapter 2 and subsequently in this chapter.

Genealogists generally agree that the search for one's past begins at home and with one's self. On the other hand, genealogical literature tends to present conflicting views on the extent to which one must use libraries for research. One view is that most of the research is conducted outside libraries. Another view is that, once basic facts are compiled from home and family sources and external sources are investigated, a considerable amount of the genealogical researcher's time is spent in library research, and one is wise to become familiar with collections which will be useful and with the procedures and policies for using them. Regardless of the view taken, the importance of libraries in genealogical research is well documented.

As noted in chapter 1, the merging of minds between genealogists and librarians in locating and interpreting genealogical materials has far-reaching benefits. Differences which in the past have separated the interests of these two groups are giving way to mutual interests and respect for research or data collecting for whatever the purpose. Considering the focus of this reference work, it follows that this relationship should be given further exploration, and the librarian's role in supporting and promoting genealogical research should be studied. To strengthen further its commitment to service, the library profession should reexamine its service role to genealogists and researchers and eliminate any barriers to successful research which may linger.

CURRENT TRENDS IN COLLECTION DEVELOPMENT AND SERVICES

In many libraries and repositories, barriers to information access have prevented the filling of the informational needs of users researching genealogy and family history. These deterrents may be the product of inadequate reference staffs or inexperienced library users, or they may be the product of deficiencies in the library's genealogical holdings. Browsing in collections is frequently prohibited, and the user is limited to access through library catalogs and other indexes. If such indexes are outdated and refer to older works on family history, their value may be minimal. These problems are compounded when an out-of-town user is pressed for time, thus emphasizing the need for researchers to allow adequate time for their research. Interlibrary loan procedures also present barriers to resources and information because of restrictions placed on the circulation of rare and out-of-print materials; in fact, it is common policy in many libraries to make genealogical materials noncirculating.

The similarities between genealogical and historical research can scarcely be overlooked: the two disciplines employ the same material. Thus genealogical collections often address some of the needs of the historian as well as the genealogist and support the research strategies and techniques of the two types of users. Sometimes, however, those who are employed in genealogical research may expect the impossible—that a single library will solve all of their informational needs. On the other hand, few historical researchers expect that any one library, and at the same time the nearest and most convenient, will satisfy their informational needs to any great extent. The same constraints which confront the historical researcher also face the genealogist; yet the genealogist will find that the resulting problems are compounded. The historian can tailor his or her research to the resources at hand; this option eludes the genealogist who is preparing a modest family history, because families migrate and records are scattered in diverse places, both foreign and domestic. Family research can be stymied, because many records and documents have never been published or otherwise identified. Charles L. Blockson illuminates this point in his discussion of black American records in chapter 9.

Developing Policy Statements

Does the library have a role to play in providing information for family historians, local history authors, and genealogists? It is readily apparent that this is a legitimate concern of public libraries, some of which may have a problem in providing a mission statement that embraces these researchers' needs. On the other hand, the problem may be that the policy makers have not clearly analyzed the library's relationship to the subject or have not arrived at the conclusion that a realistic policy on the topic is needed. The academic libraries' mission is less public oriented, since it focuses on the educational and research needs of the institution or its clientele, but an academic library may collect local history in its aim toward diversity or toward some community service.

Genealogy is an area of public activity in which a clearly defined, written, realistic policy statement is critically needed. Such a statement might include a number of items, but especially two which Robert E. Wagenknecht suggests for consideration—the acquisition policy (including gifts) and the degree to which reference help will be available.[1] Such policy statements should be reviewed periodically and revised as needed. They should be distributed to patrons who come to use the library and also to historical societies, genealogical societies, family history associations, other libraries and repositories, and organizations such as the ALA and the American Historical Association (AHA).

A library's acquisition policy statement and dissemination of the statement go hand in hand. Fortunately patrons are aware of this policy statement in some libraries, or at least inquire into the nature of the library's holdings as they pursue genealogical research. In its newsletter the Tennessee State Library and Archives notes various collections that have been received, as well as requests for use of the collection through visits or correspondence. For example, the newsletter of 1 April 1978 notes that

more than 3,000 letters have been received in the Library and Archives recently, and a great many of these contain genealogical questions about Tennessee families or families which have their roots in Tennessee. The letters from Tennessee taxpayers are given top priority and are answered as promptly as possible. Letters from researchers in other states are answered in the order in which they are received after the Tennessee Correspondence is completed. In spite of the staff's best efforts a backlog exists in both the Library and Archives, for the number [of] employees has not increased to keep pace with the increased desire for knowledge about family roots. Patrons will be notified by postcard if an answer is not mailed within a month.

The staff is happy to see that the public is aware and appreciative of the holdings of the Library and Archives, but recognizes a need to ask continued patience from patrons awaiting an answer. Patrons are also encouraged to come to the Library and Archives in person whenever possible to do their own research.[2]

Collection Development

Generally, public libraries should collect at least those titles which are of an introductory nature. Practicality would dictate that most libraries, regardless of their clientele or type (that is, whether public, state, or academic), would find collecting primary and secondary source materials, except of a local nature, an expensive project. Networks, county library systems, and consortia should dictate that at least one library in a service area attempt to collect source material for that particular area. Happy is the area which is fortunate to have one or more genealogical-historical libraries which seek out and acquire source material on a multicounty or statewide basis, and academic or special libraries, the primary resources of which round out the weak spots in genealogical-historical repositories.

Numerous bibliographies, lists of published family histories, and other documents have been published and will aid the genealogical collection development librarian in building the library's resources in that area. Many such titles are given subsequently in this chapter, and other titles are included in other chapters in this reference work. Still others are referred to in various parts of this book, whether or not they are annotated or described fully. In addition to these lists, the librarian would profit from an extensive search through library literature, including *Books in Print*,[3] to expand the list of resources and to pull together titles which may or may not be listed in basic or even comprehensive bibliographies in genealogy. Particular attention should be given to those which address ethnic genealogy.

A search could be made to identify and obtain copies of ethnic family histories, which may or may not be published. Their usefulness to the researcher in ethnic genealogy is obvious, as the scattered and obscure sources which many researchers must use may have been identified already by those who have com-

pleted ethnic family histories. Fortunately, some libraries and genealogical societies have included in their collection development practices the acquisition of
family histories.

Reference Service in Genealogy

An important area which needs examination is the library's policy governing
the degree to which reference assistance will be made available to genealogical
users. The primary service of the reference librarian should be identical to that
provided to a nongenealogical user: to make suggestions and to make available
and interpret material in the library's holdings which furthers the user's research.
As noted earlier, when local resources have been exhausted, the librarian may
suggest interlibrary loans or refer the user to other libraries having additional
genealogical resources.

THE GENEALOGICAL REFERENCE INTERVIEW

As the reference librarian provides assistance to the genealogical researcher,
the genealogical reference interview becomes extremely important. A skillful
interviewer—the reference librarian—learns how to ferret out unasked questions.
Along with a wise patron, a skilled librarian can offer assistance in early pedigree
analysis. Teaching family history research from the reference counter becomes a
reality. Conferring on research approaches widens the research horizons for
many. What the patron knows already and what is needed from the reference
librarian are what finally determine a proper mix of reference services.

By the time the reference librarian is approached, it is assumed that the
researcher has followed the procedures Cazort presents in chapter 2 and is now
ready for serious, detailed, and thorough work outside the home. Thus the
researcher will maximize use of the reference librarian and of the library, and the
librarian's time more appropriately may be spent in professional activity. The
beginner's checklist, which has been prepared by this time (and which includes
the various approaches and sources that will be utilized) will make the researcher's work much more effective.

Genealogists are sometimes unaware of local sources that are gold mines of
information in their search. Librarians are able to assist them in finding these
sources, such as vital statistics from city and state records. National, state, and
local sources can be suggested, and frequently microfilms of the records can be
borrowed for use at a local library. A librarian can also offer assistance by
referring the user to regional or even foreign centers and to record repositories
which are more suitable for the user's research needs. Finally, the genealogical
reference interview may provide an opportunity to introduce the patron to oral
evidence and its importance in the search process. Reference tools on oral interview techniques are readily available to the librarian and patron, and successful
interview techniques are easily learned. Chapter 4 provides additional details for
the family historian who is about to embark on this important phase of the
research process.

Sometimes the special or unique document the researcher needs will be found in the most unlikely library, where the collection is poorly publicized but known to the knowledgeable and resourceful librarian. In other instances the document is located in the appropriate library, yet the user may not consider the library a likely genealogical resource. Consider, for example, the descendants of Fisk University's original Jubilee Singers who came from various parts of the South and became internationally known, and whose letters, diaries, and other documents are housed in Fisk's Special Collections. The logical repository for materials on the Jubilee Singers is the Fisk collections, and those who are searching for information on one of them would write to or visit Fisk. Papers in the collection would shed important light on various activities of the group or of an individual singer while at Fisk or during the singers' extensive tours. It is these papers which enabled one researcher to complete a rather detailed account of one of her ancestors who was a member of the group. Others whose ancestors were connected with the singers have also written to obtain genealogical information on them from the collection.

Similarly, the name "Fisk" would invite searchers who are pursuing family lines or information on family members' activities to write to the institution for information on certain ancestors. The Fisk library received an inquiry for information relating to William Shreve Bailey, and for a biography of him written by Reverend Photius Fisk. The searcher described the monument which was erected at Bailey's grave in Nashville:

This monument was Erected to the Memory of William S. Bailey, By His Life-Long Anti-Slavery Friend, Rev. Photius Fisk of Boston, at Mt. Olivet Cemetery, Nashville, Tennessee. William Shreve Bailey, born Feb 10th, 1806. Died Feb 20th, 1886 Aged 80 years and 10 days. One of the Bravest Pioneers of Abolitionism for Chattel Slavery And Of Freethought for Mental Slavery. Though often Outraged and Martyred for his Principles He was Never Conquered, Suppressed, Nor Discouraged. It was through the efforts of such Heroes that the world has been made fit for the abode of humanity. He rests in the Peace and Honor so nobly won. This monument is erected to his Memory by his Hellenic friend Photius Fisk.[4]

Unless the researcher knew that the Fisk biography of Bailey existed, Fisk University may be an unlikely source of information on him. As another illustration indicates, the Fisk collection is not among those which have extensive slave papers, and one would scarcely write to Fisk for a copy of the free papers of Martha Jackson, though these papers are indeed housed at Fisk.

Should a patron prove totally helpless, a library can fulfill its goal of service to users by providing names of professional and amateur local genealogists who might offer assistance or by directing the patron to the nearest genealogical society. The library, as part of an outreach program, might sponsor a beginner's workshop in conjunction with experienced genealogists and societies. This method would establish a rapport with groups and individuals in the community and gain new friends and possible support for the library. Examples of some of the workshops libraries have offered are given in other chapters of this work. (See chapters 2, 4, and 9.)

Genealogical librarianship has had a treacherous road to travel over the years. Little or no direction has been given to library reference, due in part to the chaotic pattern of publishing in genealogy, family history, and local history. "How we do it good" articles have tended to dominate the corpus of professional literature. Further in the matter of library service to genealogists, Ashton opines that the "history of library activities in genealogy . . . is a story of irregular growth."[5] Moreover, my own search through library literature for accounts of library activities in the world of genealogy has provided few leads. So pressing is the need for published accounts of such activities, for reference works which assist both the genealogist and the librarian in their joint ventures, and for policy and procedure handbooks which delineate genealogical reference needs that it will take some time to deal with these matters properly.

J. Carlyle Parker's recent publication, *Library Service to Genealogists,* takes a giant step in filling this void.[6] While his work is basically a bibliography, Parker begins with a discussion of library administration (including supplies for genealogists, staffing, circulation, budgeting, facilities, services, and volunteers), devotes an entire chapter to collection development, reviews the library's role in genealogy and local history, discusses the reference interview, and opens each succeeding chapter with an introductory statement which will guide the librarian in handling the records and resources discussed. The concluding chapter, "Typical Genealogical Research Problems and Reference Questions," provides some solutions to inquiries librarians may receive.

THE AMERICAN LIBRARY ASSOCIATION AND GENEALOGY

Fortunately, the ALA and its Reference and Adult Service Division (RASD) have addressed some of the library profession's needs in the field of genealogy. As evidence of its interest in genealogical research tools, the ALA for a number of years has published and distributed important titles which are useful to genealogical collections and to the researcher.

Clifford Neal Smith's *Federal Land Series* is an excellent example of an ALA publishing venture. It records federal land grants to early U.S. settlers between 1788 and 1835 and includes maps to illustrate various lands. Genealogists, biographers, historians, archivists, land-title searchers, and librarians will find the set an important tool for tracing the westward movement of families during this early period.[7]

P. William Filby's, *American and British Genealogy and Heraldry,* is another example of the ALA's publications in genealogy. Included in this work are over

5,200 of the best-known titles in genealogy and heraldry. Notable works for regional and ethnic groups in the United States (including the American Indian population) and Latin America, Canada, and Great Britain are given. The work has been noted as a major bibliography.[8]

The Genealogist's Guide, compiled by Geoffrey Barrow, lists articles from the periodical publications of all British and Irish genealogical, archaeological, historical, and local history societies that have appeared over the past twenty-five years. The articles are cited under family name and under individual family history.[9]

In addition to its publishing activities, ALA has encouraged and promoted training in genealogical activities for librarians, as seen in the preconference sponsored by the RASD History Section. Held at the University of San Francisco from 24 June to 26 June 1981, immediately before ALA's annual conference, the preconference was specifically designed to assist reference librarians in analyzing the genealogist's needs, in recognizing the references which are already in the collection and which may be useful to the researcher, and in providing the appropriate referral service to other repositories which house unique or special records. Of particular importance also was the guidance the preconference offered to help small libraries develop core collections of genealogical reference materials. Conference participants received a comprehensive syllabus of 200 pages which served as a guide to the topics covered. The syllabus is being revised and includes some of the conference papers, as well as other supporting documents which relate to the topics discussed. Preliminary plans are being made to publish the syllabus so that it may be readily available to librarians and researchers.[10]

Topics addressed during the sessions included "The Need for Improved Genealogy and Local History Reference Services," "Off to a Good Beginning—The Library's Role in Facilitating Genealogical Research," "Collection Development: Building and Maintaining the Core Collection on Genealogy and Local History," "Reference Interview," "Reviewing the Issues in Genealogy and Local History Reference Services: From the Point of View of the Public Library Administrators," and "Reviewing the Issues in Genealogy and Local History Reference Services: From the Point of View of Librarians Representing Our National Collections."

Of equal importance to the librarian and the genealogist is the use which is made of the genealogical information gathered. The Genealogy Committee and the RASD History Section have for several years been concerned with the manner in which certain genealogical materials are preserved and published. Accordingly, the committee and the History Section have drafted a revision of the 1973 statement. Addressed to editors of local history publications, genealogical magazines, and family newsletters, the statement gives ten recommendations which should assist libraries which collect genealogical material and which are responsible for its public use and preservation. Noting the apparent unawareness of family newsletter editors of the wide readership of their publications, the suggestions call for newsletters with titles which are clearly descriptive of the contents, numbering systems dated concurrently for each calendar year, inclusion of the editor's name and address in each issue, a uniform format with clearly specified margin sizes, high-quality and acid-free paper, restrictions on use of staples, correct form for reviewing or citing new works, awareness of the importance of subject and name indexes, and the necessity for seeking lowest possible postal rates for mailing the newsletters.[11]

Thus the work of the ALA and the History Section of RASD is vital to the proper growth of genealogical activities in libraries, both through publications which each has issued and through the preconferences on genealogy which are planned as a continuing activity.

TYPES OF LIBRARIES AND THEIR RESOURCES

A search through selected published sources provides a limited amount of information, which will enable the reader to understand clearly the differences among types of libraries and their collecting practices and services in genealogy. For the most part the discussions give an overview of procedures which should be followed in conducting library research, such as conducting preliminary work in a library to become familiar with its practices, services, and resources; using the card catalog; understanding the arrangement of card catalogs in various libraries; and using library classification systems (the Library of Congress, Dewey Decimal, and Cutter systems). Most of the literature stresses the need to ask for professional assistance in locating materials needed. Here again the discussion of the reference interview given earlier will guide the researcher toward maximizing use of libraries.

Published sources also guide researchers to the basic materials needed for beginning the search (such as those noted in chapter 2) and may include general indexes, genealogical indexes, general reference books and sources, guides to specific records (such as military records, Civil War records, records of local courthouses, and census records), family histories, periodicals, and other works. Notable among these works are two major reference works cited earlier: Newberry Library, Chicago, *The Genealogical Index*, and Marion H. Kaminkow, ed., *Genealogies in the Library of Congress: A Bibliography*.[12] Some of the guides, such as Timothy Field Beard, *How to Find Your Family Roots*, George B. Everton, ed., *The Handy Book for Genealogists*, and Noel C. Stevenson, *Search and Research*, discussed later in this chapter in the section on selected libraries and historical societies with genealogical collections, go a step beyond and list genealogical and historical societies and libraries in the various states which contain resources needed for genealogical research. While the lists are selective, they provide an important index to genealogical resources.

Thus these basic sources provide the researcher with an introduction to library research for family history and genealogy and an index to some of the libraries which are noted for their collections in genealogy. The next step is to analyze types of libraries and the resources they are likely to contain. The discussion which follows focuses on academic, public, and state libraries and archives and historical societies, yet mentions only briefly three major repositories—the National Archives, the Library of Congress, and the Church of Jesus Christ of Latter-day Saints (LDS) Library—which are described in other sections of this work.

Academic Libraries

Academic libraries historically have been regarded as a vital part of advanced learning. Traditionally they have provided access to records and resources which their higher-education clientele needs for support of academic programs. Academic libraries vary in role and scope. For example, undergraduate libraries have more limited resources, while research libraries are much more exhaustive in their collecting practices. Whatever their purpose, both types must serve important roles in the achievement of the educational and research goals of students and faculty. Both may serve research purposes, thus meeting the needs of researchers who are external to the institution. Because educational institutions vary in the scope and diversity of their academic offerings, each must develop for its library a mission statement and objectives which are appropriate for the institution. The mission and objectives may well focus on areas which require the library to collect the important works needed for genealogical research, especially for the local researcher, or to develop exhaustive collections in this area. Some academic libraries in recent years have begun to collect materials to meet the needs of local family historians and genealogists. Examples of academic libraries which are known for their extensive collections are the Brigham Young University Library, University of Utah Library, John Hay Library (Brown University), University of Pennsylvania Library, University of Cincinnati Library, City University of New York libraries, Columbia University libraries, Fordham University Library, New York University Library, Yeshiva University Library, Baker Memorial Library (Dartmouth College), and College of William and Mary Library.

Although academic libraries are primarily concerned with collecting resources which support their curricular and research offerings, increasingly they are also preserving primary research materials which relate to institutional activities. As discussed earlier, some of these libraries collect not only the usual basic reference sources which aid genealogists, such as atlases, dictionaries, and catalogs of other collections, but also beginners' manuals, lists of genealogical sources in the area, obituaries, news clippings, and enough resources for the beginner to get started in the research process. Often these libraries will publish bookmarks and booklists which identify their basic genealogical sources. For example, the Eastern Kentucky University Library issues a brief guide to its genealogical materials. The researcher should be familiar with the types of primary resources academic libraries are likely to collect. This is important because at some point early in the pursuit of a family history the genealogical search will require library use, while in many instances extensive searches of academic records will be necessary.

Regardless of the size of the institution, academic libraries collect their own archives, thus providing researchers with information on relatives who may be former administrators, faculty members, or students. Such resources generally are available in special collections and may be restricted to use within the facility. Copies of some records and resources may be obtained from the institution or its library. Here are examples of records which academic libraries are likely to house:

COLLEGE AND UNIVERSITY ARCHIVES

Audio and video recordings of institutional activities (especially in recent years; however, some older audio recordings may be collected)

Business office records

Clippings of press releases relating to administrators, faculty, or institutional activities

College catalogs

Institutional telephone directories

Minutes of committee meetings

Minutes of faculty meetings

Minutes and reports of boards of trustees' meetings

Papers of former presidents, deans, and other administrators

Personnel records

Photographs of administrators and faculty members, campus scenes, and campus groups

Records of the admissions office

Records of the dean of students

Records of the registrar's office

Reports and records of various academic offices

Various official institutional publications, including faculty research journals, books and monographs, reports, newsletters, and other publications

STUDENT RECORDS

Autograph books (especially in earlier years)

Ephemera (posters, flyers, signs, and other items)

Examples of students' writings (essay contests, short story contests)

Health records

Memorabilia

Photographs (individual and group)

Programs of student activities (art exhibits, concerts, plays)

Records of social organizations (fraternities, sororities, social clubs)

Records of student academic organizations (honor societies and other groups)

Records of student committees

Records of office reports, such as those from admissions, registrar, and other offices showing dates of enrollment, conditions of admission, grades, delinquencies

Scrapbooks showing campus life, student activities, and other activities

Student projects (research projects in the various disciplines)

Student publications (newsletters, school newspapers, yearbooks, literary magazines)

Theses and dissertations

ALUMNI RECORDS

Alumni directories

Alumni drives, fund raisers, and contributions

Ephemera

Memorabilia

Minutes of meetings

Newsletters, journals, and other publications

Obituaries

Photographs

Recordings

Reports from various alumni chapters

Scrapbooks

OTHER INSTITUTIONAL RECORDS AND WORKS

Books and writings by and about administrators, faculty members, and former students

Ephemera

Family histories of former administrators, faculty members, and students

Memorabilia

Miscellaneous works

Oral histories of current and former administrators, faculty members, and students

Paintings, sculpture, and other works of art

Personal papers of former administrators, faculty members, or students, including manuscripts, photographs, publications, scrapbooks, correspondence, memorabilia, and ephemera

Public Libraries

The public library is an arm of local government. Like academic libraries, public libraries are concerned with the proper acquisition, maintenance, or provision of resources (books and other materials), but they are designed to serve the needs and interests of the entire community. Social and educational advancement are major thrusts of public library service. This is all-important because it is a primary justification for public support: enrichment of the person, and thereby enrichment of the community and society. The library is maintained with the hope that the quality of life of the community is enhanced. Thus, to promote their use, such libraries are provided free of charge to users.

Generally, public libraries are much more community oriented than academic libraries, in that information which is important to the larger community is sought and preserved. Regardless of size, public libraries may collect resources which enhance and promote genealogical research. The collections in some of these libraries are exhaustive, while those in others are important for local use, and one of the latter may well provide the only source of information needed to complete a genealogical search. A few examples of public libraries which contain important genealogical collections are those in Atlanta; Detroit; Los Angeles; San Francisco; Denver; Greenwich, Connecticut; Fort Wayne, Indiana; New York (including the Schomburg Center for Research in Black Culture); and Dallas. A more extensive list is given in this chapter in the section below on selected libraries and historical societies with genealogical collections.

Examples of genealogical records which public libraries are likely to house include the following:

Business records (local)

Catalogs of other genealogical collections

Census records (local)

Church histories

Church records

City maps (early)

Community newsletters

Community surveys and studies, including works on ethnic groups

Directories (local)

Family histories (local)

Family papers (private papers of local residents which may or may not supplement those in the local academic library)

Guides to municipal records

Handbills

Histories (city and county)

Information on early settlers

Information on early schools

Letters, diaries, and mimeographed and typewritten materials

Newspapers (local)

Oral histories (local)

Photographs

Professional genealogists (lists of)

Programs, playbills, and information on other cultural activities

Records of early social and political organizations

Scrapbooks, clippings, and ephemera

Works by and about local authors

Works of local historical societies

WPA inventories, guides, and other publications

State Libraries and Archives

To some extent, state libraries and archives parallel the function of public libraries. They also differ somewhat in focus and yet expand the efforts of the local public library. Essentially, a state library is an arm of state government. It is concerned with service to the state government, to state officials, and to legislators. It may administer a statewide system of regional libraries which takes its resources to various areas across the state, enabling the regional libraries to serve as local public libraries. State libraries maintain open and free access to the public and serve legislative, social, and educational purposes.

Archival units in state libraries collect and preserve papers of governors, governmental officials, and other political figures, and they may also include in their collections papers of other notable figures and families who live or have lived in the state. There is no clear distinction between state libraries and public libraries in the types of nongovernmental papers they gather. Additionally, whether or not local historical societies deposit their papers and literary effects in either type of library is a matter the society and the library must determine. Some societies prefer to maintain separate and distinct libraries for their archives. Whatever the decision, the pattern varies in states across the nation.

The state library is supported by tax dollars, which are channeled through the state's government, and it provides service to the public. Some state libraries may require use cards and identification, but without an aim toward restricting service. Often identification is requested to record the types of users and the resources needed. Analysis of the registration book which the archives and reference divisions maintain, for example, shows that currently a significant number of users are pursuing genealogical research.

Examples of some of the notable state libraries which house sizeable collections in genealogy include the Alabama State Department of Archives and History; California State Library; Delaware State Archives; Iowa State Department of History and Archives; Mississippi State Department of Archives and History; New York State Library; North Carolina Department of Cultural Resources, Division of Archives and History; and Tennessee State Library and Archives. Some, though not all, of these libraries also house resources from state historical societies.

While chapter 2 gives a brief description of the genealogical holdings in state libraries, the genealogical researcher will benefit from the more extensive list that follows:

Archives, library, and society publications

Checklist of imprints from various localities within the state

Church and parish records

Census records (state and federal)

Courthouse records (local and state)

Courthouse records (from surrounding states)

Directories (municipal and state)

Ephemera

Family histories and genealogies

Family papers

Genealogical society records (local)

Guides to manuscripts in other libraries and archives

Guides to manuscripts in the state library and archives

Guides to public vital statistics

Hispanic records (depending on the particular region in which the repository is located)

Indian claims, land records, and other information on Indian residents of the state

Information on early settlers

Information on the history and social and economic conditions of the state

Inventories of church archives

Inventories of county archives (for each county in the state)

Land and property records (may duplicate those found in family papers)

Maps (early city, county, and state)

Marriage records

Memorabilia

Municipal histories

Newspapers (state, including ethnic)

Oral histories

Pension records

Plantation records (for the slave states)

Photographs

Records of organizations

Records of governors and other state officials

Scrapbooks

Slave documents

State histories

State imprints (and checklists of such imprints)

Tax records

Township records

Transcriptions of public archives

War records (state regiments and militia)

WPA records (cemeteries, church memberships, and church histories)

Historical Societies

Genealogists and family historians owe a debt of gratitude to city, county, state, regional, and special historical societies. These organizations have pioneered in collecting, preserving, and promoting the particular aspects of history which they were founded to serve. In many cases this may mean that local history, family history, and genealogy are a part of their focus. Their resources include items published by the society and may also include copies of extensive primary and secondary materials collected and published elsewhere. As noted especially in chapters 1 and 6 of this book, the Genealogical Society of Utah Library, known as the LDS Library, is a prime example of a historical society with extensive activities in preserving and in promoting ethnic genealogical research materials.

As discussed in chapter 2, a number of directories and guides which locate and describe historical societies have been published. In the 1982 list of historical societies, 5,865 historical organizations were identified, which attests to popular interest in promoting areas of history. The founding of specialized historical and genealogical societies in recent years may have eluded the published guides, and these societies often are identified through close contact with academic, public, and state libraries in the geographic areas in which the societies are located. Such societies also may publish important guides and indexes to their resources and descriptions of their services. The importance, therefore, of current directories of historical societies and their publications cannot be overemphasized.

Examples of city historical societies include the Birmingham Historical Society (Alabama), Santa Barbara Historical Society (California), Atlanta Historical Society (Georgia), Detroit Historical Society (Michigan), Lowell Historical Society (Massachusetts), and Historical Commission of Charleston (South Carolina). Among the various county historical societies are the Historical Society of Frederick County (Maryland), Madison County Historical Society (Nebraska), Historical Society of Hudson County (New Jersey), Westchester County Historical Society (New York), and Historical Society of York County (Pennsylvania). State historical societies include the Historical Society of Delaware, Indiana Historical Society, Maryland Historical Society, Michigan Historical Commission, Missouri Historical Society, New York Historical Society, and Oklahoma Historical Society. There are also regional historical associations, such as the Southern Historical Association (University of Kentucky, Lexington).

Some of the important genealogical collections which have been assembled are located in private and special genealogical or historical society libraries, such as the Filson Club (Louisville, Kentucky), the American Antiquarian Society (Worcester, Massachusetts), Western Reserve Historical Society Library (Cleveland, Ohio), Friends Historical Association (Swarthmore College, Pennsylvania), Disciples of Christ Historical Society (Nashville, Tennessee), Genealogical Society of Utah Library (the LDS Genealogical Library, Salt Lake City), the Daughters of the American Revolution Library (Washington, D.C.) and the National Genealogical Society Library (also in Washington).

Even more specialized are the various black family history associations and black historical societies which Charles L. Blockson describes in chapter 9. Such organizations are particularly important for teaching the techniques of successful pursuit of black family history and for the interests of researchers in the geographical areas these societies serve. Thus far their work has emphasized techniques and sources rather than building library collections. Other ethnic historical associations include the Chinese Historical Society of America and the American Indian Historical Society. Names of additional city, county, and other historical societies are given subsequently in this chapter in the section on selected libraries and historical societies with genealogical collections.

Historical society libraries are likely to include the following resources in their collections:

Catalogs of other libraries

Cemetery records (including WPA records)

Census reports (local, state, and federal)

Directories

Ethnic histories

Genealogical indexes (computerized and printed)

Genealogies and family histories (published and unpublished)

Geographical materials (maps, atlases, and gazetteers)

Information on pioneers of a locality

Local histories

Military records (state and federal)

Newspapers (on film)

Official records of the organization

Oral histories

Periodicals (genealogical)

Reference books (basic works, works on heraldry, books on genealogy, and dictionaries of place names)

LIBRARY AIDS TO GENEALOGICAL RESEARCH

Aids to genealogical research in libraries appear in several forms. These include written aids which lead users to local research activities, guides and indexes to major collections, genealogical indexes, and other items described throughout this book. While many items which are useful for genealogical research are basic in libraries, those repositories which aim toward building more comprehensive collections in genealogy also seek specialized works in genealogy. Whatever the focus, there are available numerous types of resources which the researcher will find in libraries. Examples of these follow.

Handbooks on Genealogy

Handbooks on genealogy are fairly numerous and give an introduction to this area of study and to genealogical holdings in various repositories. Examples are Janice T. Dixon and Dora D. Flack, *Preserving Your Past: A Painless Guide to Writing Your Autobiography and Family History* (Garden City, NY: Doubleday and Co., 1977); Gilbert H. Doane and James B. Bell, *Searching for Your Ancestors: The How and the Why of Genealogy* (Minneapolis: University of Minnesota Press, 1980); and James D. Walker, *Black Genealogy: How to Begin* (Athens: University of Georgia Center for Continuing Education, 1977).

Gazetteers and Dictionaries of Places

The gazetteer, or dictionary of places, is an interesting and valuable reference tool in a genealogical collection. This is a work in which the most recently revised edition and the older issues are of almost equal value, although for different reasons. If the question calls for current information about a place, only the most recent works should be consulted; conversely, the older gazetteer is often very useful for historical information about place names that have since changed or for bits of local history that are elusive. Examples are the *Columbia-Lippincott Gazetteer of the World* (New York: Columbia University Press, 1952), published in various editions since 1855; Times of London, *Index-Gazetteer of the World* (Boston: Houghton Mifflin Co., 1966); U.S. Board of Geographical Names, *Gazetteer* (Washington, D.C.: Government Printing Office, 1955–73); and Joseph W. Kane, *American Countries* (Metuchen, N.J.: Scarecrow Press, 1972).

Atlases

Atlases are necessary reference books in any genealogical collection, and as with gazetteers, older maps are very important. National Geographic Society, *Atlas of the World* (Washington, D.C.: Government Printing Office, 1970), and U.S. Geological Survey, *The National Atlas of the U.S.A.* (Washington, D.C.: Government Printing Office, 1970) are two recognized works.

Research Exchange Files

Research exchange files are of paramount importance to a genealogist. Libraries maintain such files to show research undertaken at the library, research in progress, and research completed. These files help other researchers tremendously.

Catalogs of Genealogical Collections

Catalogs of genealogical holdings elsewhere are welcome reference works. These cooperative efforts direct the user to other repositories which can be of assistance. Works such as St. Louis Public Library, *Genealogical and Local Histories in the St. Louis Public Library* (St. Louis: the Library, 1965), and Marion H. Kaminkow, ed., *Genealogies in the Library of Congress*, 2 vols. and supplement (previously described) are examples of the genre. The Newberry Library's monumental catalog has already been mentioned.

Inventories, Registers, and Indexes

Inventories, registers, and indexes help the user by analyzing collections, compilations, newspapers, records, and other sources or documents. As stated earlier, many of these works are privately printed and may be difficult to find, but the effort is worthwhile; others are published by state libraries and archives, public libraries, governmental agencies, and other institutions.

Family Histories

Family histories contain a wealth of material at best; at worst they can be duds. Let the buyer beware. Many families are happy to present copies of their histories to libraries. Care should also be taken to collect those from families of local interest and, in the focus of this book, to collect ethnic family histories. W. P. Phillimore, *How to Write the History of a Family: A Guide for the Genealogist* (1876; reprint ed., Detroit: Gale Research Co., 1972), is an excellent work for researchers who are about to embark on such a project.

Local Histories

Local histories, like family histories, can be of great use to patrons seeking knowledge about the "old home place."

Resources for Advanced Research

WORKS PROJECTS ADMINISTRATION GUIDES

Items that are needed for more advanced research include Works Projects Administration (WPA) guides. One of the most worthwhile projects sponsored by the New Deal administration of Franklin D. Roosevelt was the WPA program. Some of the useful WPA projects were state guides to local cemeteries and other records, and other compilations, such as the Soundex system, which aids accessibility to census records, and the collection of recorded interviews with former slaves.

ENCYCLOPEDIAS OF ASSOCIATIONS

Information is frequently sought in libraries regarding the organization, officers, publications, addresses, and history of various associations and societies, and for such inquiries the directories to these groups are invaluable. *The En-*

cyclopedia of Associations (Detroit: Gale Research Co., 1956–) is the most comprehensive tool of this type for the United States, giving details about associations in many fields. Gale has also published a *Directory of European Associations* (1971–).

DIRECTORIES OF FOREIGN ARCHIVES

Many searches lead to archival collections on foreign shores, and directories of these organizations can orient possible visitors. Leendert Brummel, *Guide to Union Catalogues and International Loan Centers* (The Hague: International Federation of Library Associations, 1961), lists some 200 citations.

FOREIGN GENEALOGICAL HANDBOOKS

Foreign genealogical handbooks expand the coverage offered by domestic efforts. David E. Gardner and Frank Smith, *Genealogical Research in England and Wales* (Salt Lake City, Utah: Bookcraft Publishers, 1964–65), note the principal genealogical sources for the two countries.

LANGUAGE DICTIONARIES (ENGLISH AND FOREIGN)

Dictionaries are the main sources for information about words and are often encyclopedic, giving information about items as well as about words—combining the features of two types of reference books. "Webster's" dictionaries are myriad. Paramount among dictionaries useful for historical research is the *Oxford English Dictionary*, familiarly known as the OED.

FOREIGN GENEALOGICAL REGISTERS

Foreign genealogical registers vary in scope from the venerable *Burke's Genealogical and Heraldic History of the Landed Gentry* (London: Burke, 1837–   ; reprint ed., 1972), and the *Almanach de Gotha,* 181 vols. (Gotha, Germany: Justus Perthes, etc., 1794–1944), to *Debrett's Peerage of England, Scotland and Ireland,* John Debrett, comp. (London: John Debrett, beginning in 1802).

REGISTERS OF PATRIOTIC SOCIETIES

The American patriotic societies have published registers of their members, and these sources offer a great deal of assistance to those connected with these groups. The *Roster of Revolutionary Soldiers and Patriots in Alabama* (Montgomery, Ala.: Parchment Press, 1979) and *Membership Rolls and Register of Ancestors of the Georgia State Society of the DAR* (Atlanta: Georgia State Society, 1976) are just two examples of the many publications in this category.

PUBLISHED CENSUS REPORTS

Census reports at the U.S. National Archives and Records Service are a natural beginning for a genealogical project. The microfilm series of the decennial reports are gold mines of information. U.S. Census Bureau, *Heads of Families at the First Census, 1790* (Washington, D.C.: Government Printing Office, 1907–9) is of a great value for reference work, while Carter G. Woodson attends to another phase in his *Free Negro Heads of Families in the United States in 1830* (Washington, D.C.: Association for the Study of Negro Life and History, 1925) and *Free Negro Owners of Slaves in the United States in 1830, Together with Absentee Ownership of Slaves in the United States in 1830* (1924; reprint ed., New York: Negro Universities Press, 1968).

PUBLISHED VITAL RECORDS

Published vital records contain basic data on natality, marriage, divorce, and mortality and can save a great deal of research and travel time. Many state archives are attempting to consolidate these records on microfilm and deposit them in the state capitols.

PERIODICAL INDEXES

Indexes to periodicals provide a key to the plethora of genealogical serials available for research. The "mainstream" indexing services give short shrift to the subject. *Readers' Guide to Periodical Literature* provides access to information in general articles appearing in the periodicals indexed; however, my search of *Library Literature* provided very few items. Donald Lines Jacobus, *Index to Genealogical Periodicals*, 3 vols. (New Haven: Jacobus, 1932–53; reprint ed., Baltimore: Genealogical Publishing Co., 1963–65), covers the years 1932–53, and *The Genealogical Periodical Annual Index*, edited by Ellen Stanley Rogers and George Ely Russell (Bladensburg and Bowie, Md.: Genealogical Recorders), begins with 1962. Kip Sperry, *Index to Genealogical Periodical Literature, 1960–1977* (Detroit: Gale Research Co., 1979) is a fairly current source for checking purposes.

DIRECTORIES

Directories of all sorts are of great use to the researcher: city directories, educational directories, and biographical directories are only a few examples which libraries should offer users.

FOREIGN HISTORIES

Histories of foreign areas where local ethnic groups originated, foreign genealogical periodicals, family histories, local histories, atlases, maps, and gazetteers enlarge the resources of those wishing to extend their research beyond America's shores.

PALEOGRAPHY MANUALS

Paleography manuals assist in the study and interpretation of ancient written documents and offer valuable help to serious scholars. Leighton D. Reynolds and

Nigel G. Wilson, *Scribes and Scholars: A Guide to the Transmission of Greek and Latin Literature* (Oxford: Oxford University Press, 1968) is a very readable guide for beginners in the field.

IMMIGRATION RECORDS AND PASSENGER LISTS

Immigration records and passenger lists give invaluable aid to patrons looking for ancestors who immigrated to America. P. William Filby, *Passenger and Immigration Lists Index,* 3 vols. (Detroit: Gale Research Co., 1981), is a guide to the published arrival records of 300,000 passengers who came to the United States and Canada in the seventeenth, eighteenth, and nineteenth centuries.

LAND, COURT, AND TAX RECORDS

Land, court, and tax records are another source of genealogical information which may have to be searched to complete a family history.

CHURCH AND OTHER RECORDS

Church records, cemetery records, hospital records, and mortuary records can provide birth, marriage, christening, health, and death data.

SCHOOL RECORDS

Records of schools at all levels can give a different and personal slant on a person's development.

MILITARY RECORDS

Most military records are available through the National Archives and are treasure troves of information on those who fought in the various American conflicts. These records include those of men in grey who fought for the Confederacy in the Civil War; various southern archives also have material on these soldiers. Draft records are an added boon to the researcher; World War I draft cards are at the Record Center in Atlanta. Additional discussion of military records is given in Walker's account of resources in the National Archives, which appears later in this work.

SELECTED LIBRARIES AND HISTORICAL SOCIETIES WITH GENEALOGICAL COLLECTIONS

Lists of academic, special, public, private, state, and historical society libraries which contain important genealogical collections are readily available to the researcher. For a more complete list of the repositories, the reader should consult the following works:

Beard, Timothy Field. *How to Find Your Family Roots.* New York: McGraw-Hill Book Co., 1977.
    Lists types of records (family, local sources, and others) and indicates libraries in which these records are located. Includes also record sources on various ethnic groups (emerging groups, black, and Jewish), pp. 267–309, and an extensive section on "Genealogical Sources in Every State," pp.

371–555. Concludes with a list of reference tools and libraries which enable the researcher to trace ancestry abroad (to Africa, Central America, Asia, Europe, and elsewhere), pp. 559–1000.

Everton, George B., ed. *The Handy Book for Genealogists.* 7th ed., Logan, Utah: Everton Publishers, 1971.

A state-by-state account of the printed sources, archives, libraries, and societies which house useful genealogical information. County maps of each state are included.

Greenwood, Val D. *The Researcher's Guide to American Genealogy.* Baltimore: Genealogical Publishing Co., 1978.

Gives a brief list of libraries in the United States which house large, important collections of printed genealogical materials and archives, pp. 52–54. These include public, state, and society libraries. The Library of Congress and the Newberry Library are given in the list.

Stevenson, Noel C. *Search and Research.* Salt Lake City, Utah: Deseret Book Co., 1979.

An alphabetical listing by state which gives libraries, historical societies, and archives in each state; in certain U.S. territories and possessions, such as Cuba and the Philippines; and in several foreign countries. Briefly notes records on American Indians and on Puerto Rico. Refers to more complete lists which identify records in each state and also describes research resources and records such as reference works, military rosters (rolls and records), official records, and federal and state census records.

As ready reference, the researcher should consider the following state-by-state list of selected libraries which support genealogical research. Excluded from the list are the National Archives and Records Service, its regional centers, and the LDS branch libraries, which may be available in one's local area, because these repositories are discussed elsewhere in this book.

Alabama

Alabama State Department of Archives and
History
624 Washington Avenue
Montgomery, AL 36104
205/832–6510

Birmingham Public Library
2020 Park Avenue
Birmingham, AL 35203
205/254–2551

Arizona

Arizona Branch Genealogical Library
464 East First Avenue
Mesa, AZ 85201
602/964–1200

Arizona State Department of Libraries and
Archives
1700 West Washington Street
Phoenix, AZ 85007
602/255–4035

The Cox Library
302 West Elm Street
Tucson, AZ 85705
602/792–1393

Arkansas

Arkansas State History Commission
One Capitol Mall
Little Rock, AR 72201
501/371–1524

California

California Historical Society
2090 Jackson Street
San Francisco, CA 94109
415/567–1848

California State Library
914 Capitol Mall
Sacramento, CA 95809
916/445–2585

California State Library–Sutro Library
2495 Golden Gate Avenue
San Francisco, CA 94118
415/557–0374

Los Angeles Public Library
630 West Fifth Street
Los Angeles, CA 90017
213/626–7555

Pasadena Public Library
285 East Walnut Street
Pasadena, CA 91101
213/577–4066

Pomona Public Library
625 South Garey Avenue
Pomona, CA 91766
714/620–2033

San Diego Public Library
820 E Street
San Diego, CA 92101
714/236–5800

San Francisco Public Library
Civic Center
San Francisco, CA 94102
415/558–4235

Santa Barbara Mission Archive/Library
Old Mission
Santa Barbara, CA 93105
805/682–4713

Colorado

Denver Public Library
1357 Broadway
Denver, CO 80203
303/573–5152

Pikes Peak Regional District Library
20 North Cascade Street
Colorado Springs, CO 80903
303/473–2080

Connecticut

Connecticut State Library
231 Capitol Avenue
Hartford, CT 06115
203/566–4301

Fairfield Historical Society
636 Old Post Road
Fairfield, CT 06430
203/259–1598

Godfrey Memorial Library
134 Newfield Street
Middletown, CT 06457
203/346–4375

Greenwich Public Library
101 West Putnam Avenue
Greenwich, CT 06830
203/622–7900

New London County Historical Society
Blinman Street
New London, CT 06320
203/443–1209

Otis Library
261 Main Street
Norwich, CT 06360
203/889–2365

West Hartford Public Library
20 South Main Street
West Hartford, CT 06107
203/236–6286

Delaware

Delaware State Archives
Dover, DE 19963
302/736–5318

Historical Society of Delaware
505 Market Street
Wilmington, DE 19801
302/655–7161

District of Columbia

District of Columbia Public Library
901 G Street, N.W.
Washington, DC 20001
202/727–1101

Library of Congress
Genealogy and Local History Collection
Washington, DC 20540
202/287–5000

National Genealogical Society Library
1921 Sunderland Place, N.W.
Washington, DC 20036
202/785–2123

National Society of Daughters of the American
   Revolution Library
1776 D Street, N.W.
Washington, DC 20006
202/628–1776

Sons of the American Revolution Library
2412 Massachusetts Avenue, N.W.
Washington, D.C. 20008
202/462–1776

Florida

Florida State Library
Tallahassee, FL 32304
904/487-2651

Jacksonville Free Public Library
122 North Ocean Street
Jacksonville, FL 32202
904/633-6870

Miami-Dade Public Library
One Biscayne Boulevard
Miami, FL 33132
305/579 5001

Georgia

Atlanta Public Library
One Margaret Mitchell Square, N.W.
Atlanta, GA 30303
404/688-4636

Georgia Historical Society
501 Whitaker Street
Savannah, GA 31401
912/944-2128

Hawaii

Church College of Hawaii
Laie, HI 96762
808/293-9211

Idaho

Idaho State Historical Society
325 West State Street
Boise, ID 83702
208/334-3356

Illinois

Illinois State Library
Centennial Building
Springfield, IL 62706
217/782-2994

Newberry Library
Local and Family History Collection
60 West Walton Street
Chicago, IL 60610
312/943-9090

Indiana

Indiana State Library
140 North Senate Avenue
Indianapolis, IN 46204
317/232-3675

Indianapolis Public Library
40 East St. Clair Street
Indianapolis, IN 46204
317/635-5662

La Porte Public Library
904 Indiana Avenue
La Porte, IN 46350
219/362-6156

Public Library of Fort Wayne and Allen
    County
960 Webster Street
Fort Wayne, IN 46802
219/424-7241

Iowa

Iowa State Department of History and
    Archives
East 12th Street and Grand Avenue
Des Moines, IA 50319
515/281-5472

State Historical Society of Iowa
402 Iowa Street
Iowa City, IA 52240
319/338-5471

Kansas

Kansas State Historical Society
120 West 10th Street
Topeka, KS 66612
913/296-3251

Wichita Public Library
223 South Main Street
Wichita, KS 67202
316/262-0611

Kentucky

Eastern Kentucky University Library
Richmond, KY 40475
606/622-3606

Louisiana

New Orleans Public Library
219 Loyola Avenue
New Orleans, LA 70140
504/586-4905

Maine

Bangor Public Library
145 Harlow Street
Bangor, ME 04401
207/947–8336

Brick Store Museum
117 Main Street
Kennebunk, ME 04043
207/985–4802

Maine State Library
LMA Building
Augusta, ME 04333
207/289–3561

Maryland

Genealogical Periodicals Library
3800 Enterprise Road
Mitchellville, MD 20716
301/464–8225

Maryland Historical Society
201 West Monument Street
Baltimore, MD 21201
301/685–3750

Maryland State Library
College Avenue and St. John's Street
Annapolis, MD 21404
301/269–3916

Milbourne and Tull Genealogical Library
3608 Clifmar Road
Baltimore, MD 21207
301/655–7449

Unitarian and Universalist Genealogical
   Society
10605 Lakespring Way
Cockeysville, MD 21030
301/628–2490

Massachusetts

American Antiquarian Society Library
185 Salisbury Street
Worcester, MA 01609
617/755–5221

Berkshire Athenaeum
One Wendell Avenue
Pittsfield, MA 01202
413/442–1559

Beverly Historical Society
117 Cabot Street

Beverly, MA 01915
617/922–1186

Boston Public Library
666 Boylston Street
Boston, MA 02117
617/536–5400

Canton Historical Society
1400 Washington Street
Canton, MA 02021
617/828–4962

Cape Ann Historical Association
27 Pleasant Street
Gloucester, MA 01930
617/283–0455

Dedham Historical Society
612 High Street
Dedham, MA 02026
617/326–1385

Essex Institute
132–34 Essex Street
Salem, MA 01970
617/744–1240

Forbes Library
20 West Street
Northampton, MA 01060
413/584–8399

Haverhill Public Library
99 Main Street
Haverhill, MA 01830
617/373–1586

Historical Society of Old Newbury
98 High Street
Newbury, MA 01950
603/462–2681

Lucius M. Boltwood Genealogical and
   Historical Collection
Jones Library
Amherst, MA 01002
413/253–3101

Lynn Public Library
5 North Common Street
Lynn, MA 01902
617/595–0567

Massachusetts State Library
341 State House
Boston, MA 02133
617/727–2590

New Bedford Free Public Library
613 Pleasant Street
New Bedford, MA 02740
617/999–6291

New England Historical Genealogical Society
101 Newbury Street
Boston, MA 02116
617/536–5740

Michigan

Detroit Public Library
Burton Historical Collection
5201 Woodward Avenue
Detroit, MI 48202
313/321–1000

Flint Public Library
1026 East Kearsley Street
Flint, MI 48502
313/232–7111

Grand Rapids Public Library
60 Library Plaza, N.E.
Grand Rapids, MI 49503
616/456–4400

Minnesota

Minnesota Historical Society
690 Cedar Street
St. Paul, MN 55101
612/296–2150

Olmsted County Historical Society
3103 Salem Road, S.W.
Rochester, MN 55901
507/282–9447

Missouri

Missouri Historical Society
Jefferson Memorial Building
St. Louis, MO 63112
314/361–1424

St. Louis Public Library
1301 Olive Street
St. Louis, MO 63103
314/241–2288

Mississippi

Mississippi State Department of Archives and
  History
100 South State Street

Jackson, MS 39205
601/354–6218

Rogers (Lauren) Library and Museum of Art
Fifth Avenue and Seventh Street
Laurel, MS 39440
601/428–4875

New Hampshire

New Hampshire State Library
20 Park Street
Concord, NH 03301
603/271–2392

Portsmouth Athenaeum
9 Market Square
Portsmouth, NH 03801
603/964–8284

New Jersey

Cape May County Historical Society and
  Museum
Court House
Cape May, NJ 08204
609/465–7111

Genealogical Society of New Jersey
Rutgers University Library
New Brunswick, NJ 08903
201/932–7505

Glassboro State College
Savit 2, Learning Resource Center
Glassboro, NJ 08028
609/445–6101

Hunterdon County Historical Society
114 Main Street
Flemington, NJ 08822
201/282–1091

Monmouth County Historical Association
70 Court Street
Freehold, NJ 07728
201/402–1466

New Jersey Historical Society
230 Broadway
Newark, NJ 07104
201/483–3939

New Jersey State Department of Education,
  Division of the State Library
185 West State Street
Trenton, NJ 08625
609/292–6200

Plainfield Free Public Library
Eighth Street and Park Avenue
Plainfield, NJ 07060
201/757–1111

New York

Buffalo and Erie County Public Library
Lafayette Square
Buffalo, NY 14203
716/856–7525

Chemung County Historical Society
304 William Street
Elmira, NY 14901
607/737–2900

Genesee County Department of History
19 Ross Street
Batavia, NY 14020
716/343–9550

Holland Society of New York
122 East 58 Street
New York, NY 10022
212/758–1675

Long Island Historical Society
128 Pierrepont Street
Brooklyn, NY 11201
212/624–0890

New York Genealogical and Biographical
  Society
122 East 58 Street
New York, NY 10022
212/755–8532

New York Historical Society
170 Central Park West
New York, NY 10024
212/873–3400

New York Public Library
Local History and Genealogy Division
Fifth Avenue and 42 Street
New York, NY 10018
212/790–6262

New York State Library
Cultural Education Center
Albany, NY 12230
518/474–5930

Queensborough Public Library
89-11 Merrick Boulevard
Jamaica, NY 11432
212/990–0700

Rochester Public Library
115 South Avenue
Rochester, NY 14604
716/428–7300

Smithtown Public Library
One North Country Road
Smithtown, NY 11787
516/265–2072

Syracuse Public Library
335 Montgomery Street
Syracuse, NY 13202
315/473–2702

North Carolina

North Carolina State Library
109 East Jones Street
Raleigh, NC 27611
919/733–2570

Ohio

Allen County Historical Society
620 West Market Street
Lima, OH 45801
419/222–9426

Bluffton College–Mennonite Historical Library
Musselman Library
Bluffton, OH 45817
419/358–8015

Cleveland Public Library
325 Superior Avenue
Cleveland, OH 44114
216/623–2800

Free Public Library
1320 First Avenue
Middletown, OH 45042
513/424–1251

Ohio State Library
65 South Front Street
Columbus, OH 43215
614/466–2693

Pickaway County District Library
165 East Main Street
Circleville, OH 43113
614/477–1644

Public Library of Cincinnati and Hamilton
  County
800 Vine Street
Cincinnati, OH 45202
513/369–6000

Rutherford B. Hayes Library
1337 Hayes Avenue
Fremont, OH 43420
419/332–2081

Toledo-Lucas County Public Library
325 Michigan Street
Toledo, OH 43624
419/255–7055

Western Reserve Historical Society
10825 East Boulevard
Cleveland, OH 44106
216/721–5722

Oklahoma

Tulsa City-County Library
400 Civic Center
Tulsa, OK 74103
918/581–5221

Pennsylvania

Bucks County Historical Society
Pine and Ashland Streets
Doylestown, PA 18901
215/345–0210

Cameron County Historical Society
R.R. 2
Emporium, PA 15834
814/483–3636

Cambria County Historical Society
201 West Sample Street
Ebensburg, PA 15931
814/472–6674

Carnegie Library of Pittsburgh
4400 Forbes Avenue
Pittsburgh, PA 15213
412/627–3100

Genealogical Society of Pennsylvania
1300 Locust Street
Philadelphia, PA 19107
215/545–0391

Historical Society of Pennsylvania
1300 Locust Street
Philadelphia, PA 19107
215/732–6200

Historical Society of York County
250 East Market Street
York, PA 17403
717/848–1587

Pennsylvania State Library
Walnut Street and Commonwealth Avenue
Harrisburg, PA 17120
717/787–2646

Rhode Island

Bristol Historical and Preservation Society
48 Court Street
Bristol, RI 02809
401/253–6948

Rhode Island Historical Society
121 Hope Street
Providence, RI 02906
401/331–0448

South Carolina

Calhoun County Museum
208 North Harry C. Kayson Drive
St. Matthews, SC 29135
803/874–3389

Huguenot Society of South Carolina
25 Chalmers Street
Charleston, SC 29401
803/723–3235

Tennessee

Chattanooga Public Library
1001 Broad Street
Chattanooga, TN 37402
615/757–5320

Cossitt-Goodwyn Library
33 South Front Street
Memphis, TN 38103
901/528–2994

Lawson McGhee Memorial Library
500 West Church Avenue
Knoxville, TN 37902
615/523–0781

Tennessee State Library and Archives
403 Seventh Avenue, North
Nashville, TN 37219
615/741–2561

Texas

Dallas Public Library
1954 Commerce Street
Dallas, TX 75201
214/748–9071

Fort Worth Public Library
300 Taylor Street
Fort Worth, TX 76102
817/870–7700

Houston Public Library
500 McKinney Avenue
Houston, TX 77002
713/224–5441

McMurry College Library
14th Street at Sayles Street
Abileen, TX 49697
915/692–4130

San Antonio Public Library
203 South St. Mary's Street
San Antonio, TX 78205
512/299–7790

Texas State Library
1200 Brazos Street
Austin, TX 78711
512/475–2166

Utah

Genealogical Department Library
Church of Jesus Christ of Latter-day
  Saints (LDS)
50 East North Temple Street
Salt Lake City, UT 84150
801/531–2323

Virginia

Virginia State Library
12th and Capitol Streets
Richmond, VA 23219
804/770–2300

Vermont

Bennington Museum–Genealogical Library
Bennington, VT 05201
802/442–2180

Washington

Seattle Public Library
1000 Fourth Avenue
Seattle, WA 98104
206/625–2665

Spokane Public Library
906 Main Street
Spokane, WA 99201
509/838–3361

West Virginia

West Virginia University, West Virginia
  Collection
University Library
Morgantown, WV 26506
304/293–4040

Wisconsin

Beloit Historical Society
2149 St. Lawrence Avenue
Beloit, WI 53511
608/365–3811

Milwaukee Public Library
814 West Wisconsin Avenue
Milwaukee, WI 53233
414/278–3000

State Historical Society of Wisconsin
816 State Street
Madison, WI 53706
608/262–3421

Waukesha County Historical Museum
101 West Main Street
Waukesha, WI 53186
414/544–8430

Wyoming

Wyoming State Library
Supreme Court and Library Building
Cheyenne, WY 82002
307/777–7281

SUMMARY

The challenges and opportunities presented by the genealogical movement are many. Acquiring a valid mix of useful information requires that the genealogical researcher become familiar with the range of materials on family history and then attempt to assimilate those which are relevant and receive the stimulation to write as many thorough and accurate family histories as possible. It is for the family historian to make the final assessment of the merit of any document for the research at hand. Library staff members must collect genealogical materials in a responsible manner and then assume responsibility for promoting their use. Whether or not a library collects such resources in depth, its staff must make at least basic resources (dictionaries, atlases, guides, directories, and other reference tools) available to the family historian. Once this has been done, users will have access to many more resources and a higher level of reference service as they try to arrive at some findings about that important but mercurial social institution, the family.

NOTES

1. Robert E. Wagenknecht, "Genealogy Reconsidered," *Illinois Libraries* 58 (June 1976), pp. 456–58.

2. *TSL&A Newsletter* (Nashville: Tennessee State Library and Archives, 1 April 1978), p. 4.

3. *Books in Print* (New York: R. R. Bowker Co., 1982).

4. Letter to the library, Fisk University, from Louise P. Pence, dated 30 November 1977.

5. Rick J. Ashton, "Curators, Hobbyists, and Historians: Ninety Years of Genealogy at the Newberry Library," *Library Quarterly* 47 (April 1977), pp. 149–62.

6. J. Carlyle Parker, *Library Service to Genealogists* (Detroit: Gale Research Co., 1981). Another recent handbook of value to librarians is Richard Harvey, *Genealogy for Librarians* (London: C. Bingley, 1983).

7. Clifford Neal Smith, Federal Land Series, 3 vols. (Chicago: American Library Association, 1972–80).

8. P. William Filby, *American and British Genealogy and Heraldry*, 2d ed. (Chicago: American Library Association, 1976).

9. Geoffrey Barrow, comp., *The Genealogist's Guide* (London: Fudge and Co., dist. by the American Library Association, 1977).

10. The RASD History Section held a second preconference on July 9, 1982 before its Annual Meeting in Philadelphia. For additional information on the preconference, "Four Centuries of Genealogy," write to the Reference and Adult Services Division, History Section, American Library Association, 50 East Huron Street, Chicago, IL 60611.

11. For a copy of the statement entitled "To: Editors of Local History Publications, Genealogical Magazines, and Family Newsletters," write to the Reference and Adult Services Division, History Section, ALA. The statement cites two additional sources which should be consulted for more information. These are Russell E. Bidlack, "Publishing the Family Genealogical Magazine," *Stirpes* 7, nos. 1–3 (1967), available from the Texas State Genealogical Society, 2528 University Drive South, Fort Worth, TX 76109, and George Ely Russell, ed., *Genealogical Periodical Advisory Bulletin*, nos. 1–3 (January 1968—February 1969), available from the editor at 2906 Stonybrook Drive, Bowie, MD 20715.

12. Newberry Library, *The Genealogical Index*, 4 vols. (Boston: G. K. Hall and Co., 1960); Marion H. Kaminkow, ed., *Genealogies in the Library of Congress: A Bibliography*, 2 vols. (Baltimore: Magna Carta Book Co., 1972; supplement 1972–76 issued 1977).

4

Researching Family History

BOBBY L. LOVETT

The purpose of this chapter is to provide an in-depth approach to researching family history, using ethnic history as an example. Further, this chapter gives a background for the historical development of genealogy, family history, and teaching of family history, as well as the background for researching ethnic history. The discussion differentiates between a genealogy and a family history and illustrates and discusses the approaches, methods, and techniques used to research and write a history.

In many ways the techniques for historical research are the same as the basic steps for genealogical research. For this reason, therefore, the basic steps of genealogical research are mentioned briefly in this section. They are illustrated much more vividly in chapter 2 and in other sections of this work.

ORIGINS OF FAMILY HISTORY

Historians, lay citizens, and social scientists have long been interested in the history of the American family. Some families brought their coats of arms across the Atlantic Ocean to certify their pedigrees. On the other hand, more than half of the early settlers of the thirteen colonies were of the lower classes or descended from indentured servants. Some 25 percent of them came as African slaves. Since so many of the original settlers had been involuntarily cut off from their roots, successful families became interested in their origins.

In the nineteenth century the American Revolution (1770–83) became a focus of increased interest in the roots of families and individuals. Because this had been the nation's most glorious and most romantic war, citizens were quite anxious to be associated with its noble results. Families took steps to document or at least to claim that one of their ancestors had fought in it. To stimulate the development of American genealogy, in 1829 John Farmer wrote *A Genealogi-*

cal Register of the First Settlers of New England.[1] In 1845 the New England Historic and Genealogy Society was founded, and it began publishing the *New England Historic and Genealogical Register* in Boston in January 1847. The Sons of the American Revolution (SAR) and Daughters of the American Revolution (DAR), founded in 1889 and 1890, respectively, based their entrance requirements upon the ability of the potential member to trace his or her ancestry to one who had fought in the war.

As non-English immigrants increasingly began to enter the United States during the second quarter of the eighteenth century, the prejudices generated by nativist movements and the desire of the "original settlers" to be distinct and exclusive aided further the growth in genealogy. But as Americans were busy moving westward and class distinctions were minimal on the frontiers, the pursuit of genealogy in America was still not an organized and consistent activity among the nation's best families.

In 1861, however, a great historical event occurred that gave impetus to the pursuit of genealogy and family history, and that event was the start of the Civil War (1861–65). Nearly 1,000,000 Northern citizens participated, and some 500,000 Southerners. Nearly 200,000 black Americans fought on the Union side, while thousands of Indians served in the Confederate Army. Additionally, millions of civilians who were black, white, or members of other ethnic groups serviced the fighting men. Indeed, here was a war during which upper- and lower-class families, native settlers, and newly arrived immigrant groups could claim to have participated in one of the nation's most dramatic events. Accordingly, participation in the Civil War, as well as in the Revolutionary War, gave the families involved a sense of firm roots in this country.

Tracing one's ancestry back to the Civil War, therefore, generated more interest in genealogy and family history. It was unthinkable for any respectable southern family not to have had some relative who had served in the Confederate Army, and Northerners eagerly sought photographs of a relative holding the tattered flag named "Old Glory." Post–Civil War organizations such as the Sons and Daughters of the Confederacy and similar Union groups dignified themselves by requiring their members each to locate an ancestor who had fought in the great war. The enormous volume of records that this war had generated caused Congress to appropriate monies for the organization, preservation, and publication of the military and other records that individual citizens were increasingly inquiring about soon after the war ended. So too did state governments begin to preserve and make available Confederate and Union public records on the men who had fought in the state regiments.

As new conflicts, such as the Spanish-American War (1898–99), World War I (1917–19), and World War II (1941–45), overshadowed the memories of the Civil War, some of this interest in family history waned. Yet these modern wars generated less enthusiasm in the search for ancestors than the Civil War had done. Not until the Civil War centennial celebration of the 1960s and the bicentennial celebration of the Declaration of Independence in 1976 did thousands more become interested in the pursuit of family history research.

By the early 1970s the study of family history and genealogy of the white American family was well developed but did not parallel that seen among German and other European families. Nonetheless, all kinds of aids, pedigree charts, publications, printed records, and computerized surname reference files rapidly became available. These activities and records were augmented by the collecting and printing of other records, such as marriage records, records kept in Bibles, tombstone inscriptions, church records, deeds, wills, cemetery records, and local histories, under the direction of the Federal Writers' Project and the Works Projects Administration (WPA) during the New Deal of the 1930s. Because much material on former slaves and freedmen was included, these WPA sources are valuable to the genealogy of blacks.[2]

ORIGINS OF ETHNIC FAMILY HISTORY

Notwithstanding increased white interest in genealogy, during the 1960s blacks and other ethnics, especially Indians and Mexican Americans, did not have enough leisure time, wealth, or exposure to their historical backgrounds to become interested in tracing their family origins. Paradoxically, the Civil Rights Movement of the 1960s had made blacks and other minorities conscious of their unique positions in American society and also awakened them to the fact that they knew very little of their racial, group, and family origins. Soon after emancipation of the slaves and until the Supreme Court case *Brown* v. *Board of Education* (1954), blacks had been so segregated and made to feel so inferior that few of them believed they had any roots or significant origins which warranted examination.

Although most people have viewed America as populated by a continuous stream of immigrants who came mainly from Europe, America also has a history of people added through slavery, annexation, purchase, and territorial conquest. America's history includes a migration of people from non-European countries, including Asia. Since 1965, when the country ended its national origin quotas, some 500,000 people annually have come into the land as legal immigrants. America, therefore, is a complex nation of various ethnic groups.[3] This fact was vividly magnified by the fervent 1960s, when minority groups became more involved politically. Soon American Indians, Mexican Americans, and other non-European ethnic groups realized their uniqueness and differences in origin. Belatedly these groups became conscious of a need to find their roots and revive their histories.

The attention given to the more popularly known minorities during the 1960s also stimulated a white ethnic consciousness. A flood of publications on ethnic history further catalyzed white ethnic fever. Dissertations, books, and college courses were the logical results of this heightened ethnic cultural awareness among groups such as the Basques, Greeks, Armenians, Serbs, Croats, Sovenes, Lithuanians, Portuguese, and Swiss. These had been America's invisible ethnic minorities, who soon wanted to publicize openly their historical backgrounds and trace their family histories. Certainly in the pursuit of ethnic European family history one will find interesting topics and themes to include in the narrative, such as the ethnic family's encounter with immigration policies and restrictions, settlement in the cities, old ethnic attitudes, early political behavior, and religious practices; the material progress of each generation after migration; and the family's occupations, education, and connections to the old country and its traditions.

Finally the arrival of *Roots: The Saga of an American Family*, by Alex Haley, signaled the beginning of an avalanche of interest in genealogy, family history, and ethnic history. Thus genealogy had its needed renaissance. The serialization of *Roots* on television before millions of viewers further moved ethnics to begin to try and find proud African or Indian warriors, defiant slaves, courageous soldiers, or industrious European men and women in their family trees. Soon the pursuit of genealogy and family history became firmly established as a worthwhile objective for many American families, including minorities, blacks, and other ethnics. Accordingly, black American writers took the lead in advancing the cause of black and ethnic family history research. Such writers and their works include James D. Walker, *Black Genealogy: How to Begin*, a well organized and useful manual,[4] and Charles L. Blockson, with Ron Fry, *Black Genealogy*, the first in a proposed series of volumes intended to support the study of various ethnic groups' genealogies, including those of Mexican Americans and American Indians.[5]

TEACHING FAMILY HISTORY

Notwithstanding the intellectual impact of *Roots*, other efforts in the direction of the study of family history had already been initiated in the academic arena. As early as 1973, students at Louisiana State University and Tennessee State University, among others, had been writing histories of their families as part of their history class assignments. By the late 1970s the use of family history assignments was common as a college and high school teaching tool. Many libraries soon developed new techniques and stocked sources for the study of family history. By 1977 a Gallup Poll indicated that from 29 to 40 percent of Americans were interested in tracing their families' histories. Teachers made more creative use of the students' time in the classroom by applying various approaches to family history, including brief family history questionnaires on the elementary and secondary school levels; allowing students to trace their family origins on maps; preparing histories of local and ethnic communities; and developing bibliographies.[6]

Soon the scholarly community became interested in the research and organization of genealogical sources, ethnic history, and family history. In April 1974, for example, Kirk Jeffrey of Carleton College led a workshop on undergraduate family history projects during the annual meeting of the Organization of American Historians. Several textbooks and research handbooks appeared, such as

David E. Kyvig and Myron A. Marty, *Your Family History: A Handbook for Research and Writing.*[7] The major purpose of the manual was to help writers of family histories find potential sources of information and answer typical genealogical questions. This book instructs the student researcher on gathering information, utilizing research techniques, writing family histories, solving potential problems, and documenting the final manuscript. Jim Watts, a professor at City College of New York, and Allen F. Davis of Temple University collaborated to publish *Generations: Your Family in Modern American History,*[8] which was based upon their years of college teaching and on the contributions of their students who had made studies on the histories of their families. Watts and Davis assembled the book to engage the readers in asking questions about themselves, their own families, and the historical events surrounding their families. The book also engages a unique strategy to teach the family history researcher to look at the world or the environment that surrounds the family or the individual. In doing so, the researcher has to use primary literature and primary sources to reconstruct contemporary times as accurately as possible. A few other books on the basics of researching family history appeared, including F. Wilbur Helmbold, *Tracing Your Ancestry: Step by Step Guide to Researching Your Family History,*[9] and Janice T. Dixon and Dora D. Flack, *Preserving Your Past: A Painless Guide to Writing Your Autobiography and Family History.*[10]

In recent years various scholarly workshops for the promotion of ethnic genealogy and family history research on blacks and minorities have been sponsored. As example may be cited Fisk University's Institute on Ethnic Genealogy for Librarians, held in June 1979 and designed to prepare librarians to assist genealogists and family history researchers. In 1980–81 the North Carolina Committee on the Humanities supported the Afro-American Family History Project: Grassroots Genealogy Workshop. Further, Afro-American family history associations were established in a few cities, including Atlanta and New York. Still, other special skills workshops and courses in various aspects of genealogy and family history have been offered at various sites throughout the nation and have enhanced the research skills of amateur, developing, and experienced genealogical researchers. (For additional details on workshops in basic and ethnic genealogy, see chapters 2 and 9.) By 1980 the study of black and ethnic family heritage was significantly increased, creating demands for more guides, handbooks, and reference and other works to support these developing or continuing interests.[11]

DEFINITION OF FAMILY HISTORY

Several different kinds of history exist, including biographical, economic, ethnic, psychological, and social history. One of the earliest forms of historical inquiry and writing, biographical history examines the records and achievements of an individual. Family history, which is similar, examines the records and achievements of a group of people who are related. Further, family history attempts to establish a continuity of descent as well as patterns of relationship among several individuals. Because of these objectives, family history research requires the combined skills of the genealogist and the historian.

Just as the genealogist must be a good historian, the family historian also must be a devout genealogist. Since the main objective of historical research is to ascertain the truth, the research must be systematic—a deliberate process of collecting, sifting, organizing, and presenting the facts. Equally important, the family historian must be inquisitive, persistent, skeptical about the origins of sources, and determined to unearth as many sources as possible.

History in its roots means inquiry, and the study of ethnic family history follows the patterns established in historical research. Even so, the divergent patterns inherent in the study of ethnic history, and especially Afro-American history, require some variation in source material and in the methods the researcher employs when using those materials. As an illustration, the black family's historical patterns are made complex by 246 years of bondage and the lack of good records on blacks of that period. Similarly, the patterns of family history of many nonblack ethnic groups were broken by long periods of indentured servitude in the period between 1607 and the 1820s. Nevertheless, ethnic family history research still requires basic approaches, methods, steps, and techniques that are identical with those of general historical research.

A logical question is, How are family history, genealogy, and pedigree defined? The pedigree is the lineage, the family tree, the line of descent. Genealogy traces the lineal descent, often in chart form; it is a chronological record that traces the descent of a person or family from particular ancestors. Genealogy, therefore, emphasizes the relevance of history, which lends its techniques and knowledge of sources to the study of genealogy. The family history puts the flesh on the bare bones of the genealogical chart. In other words, the family history breathes life into the dead ancestors and tells the complete story of the family and its origins, problems, progress, and achievements. Genealogy is the chart with chronological and annotated explanations, while family history is the narrative, the saga, of a family going through various periods of history.[12]

RESEARCH STEPS

To complete a genealogy, the researcher should begin with a pedigree chart, as described and illustrated in chapter 2. Next, the searcher is advised to follow these basic research steps:

1. Construct a pedigree chart which begins with yourself, your parents and your grandparents.
2. Collect the research tools needed: family chart, correspondence log, research log, research continuation log, census manuscript sheets, and other forms.
3. Acquire the necessary supplies and materials to organize the data collected. These

include pencils, bibliography and note cards, notebooks, typing paper, and a file box.

4. Begin the search at home by using vital family records, by contacting distant relatives by telephone or letter, and by conducting oral interviews with family members.

5. Proceed to libraries and search reference sources, manuscripts, and archives.

6. Investigate the records in local, state, and national archives.

One may execute the above steps more effectively by consulting the appropriate chapters in this book. Chapter 2, especially, will aid the genealogical researcher in the use of the proper forms and sources. Additionally, consult the bibliography at the end of this chapter for books on genealogical and historical research methodology.

CREATING A FAMILY HISTORY FROM A GENEALOGY

Genealogy and family history can require a tremendous amount of research. However, one's genealogy usually reads like a chronicle—a chronological listing of facts and dates about each of the ancestors. On the other hand, the family history is much more lengthy, because it fills in information about the people's lives, including their personalities, life styles, character, and activities. Thus the bare genealogy will often read like an obituary, while the family history brings it to life through narrative of the family's past, not necessarily in chronological order, but with emphasis upon dates and direct descendants. In fact, the family history may be topical rather than chronological; one might focus on children, on women in the family, or on periods of history or specific aspects of history, such as economics, politics, or social development. In other words, unlike the genealogy, the writer does more than simply list the information gleaned from his or her sources. Instead that data is used to create a story of great interest and great value to the readers.

In this manner the family history writer should take note of the writing of biographical history—read or scan a few biographies in order to get the essence of what experienced writers have to say about individuals. Biography is the reconstruction of a human life. It attempts to describe and evaluate an individual's career, image, personality, and character. The biographer also must attempt to evaluate that individual's impact upon the world in which he or she lived and interpret the impact of that world upon the individual. Thus the writer must assume the role of a god, by breathing life into the dead ancestor. Surely the biographer must be part novelist as well as a historian in order to portray the individual in a lively, dynamic manner.[13]

The techniques the biographer employs are also similar to those of a portrait painter. To illustrate, Alex Haley, the author of *Roots,* used the combined techniques of a biographer, historian, novelist, and portrait painter to transform a simple genealogy into a story about Kunta Kinte and his ancestors. By using his sources creatively, Haley painted a portrait of Kinte and his African village. Haley even lay in the hull of a ship, *The African Star,* to attempt to sense how young Kinte reacted to his bondage. He visited Gambia, Kinte's homeland, as a means of visualizing the background of his ancestor's home.[14]

Similarly, in researching facts about individuals, one should attempt to find detailed information about the person's childhood, education, marriage, off-spring, family life, occupations, politics, religion, and other aspects of life. Utilize memoirs, personal papers, oral interviews, and the usual history sources mentioned in chapter 2.

To gather data for a meaningful history, the researcher must ask meaningful questions. Historical research is analytical; it is not simple and mechanical, as genealogical research can often be, but is a creative process in which the searcher must think and reflect upon the sources that should or should not be used. One must ask the right questions and decide which sources are likely to yield the most information for that specific set of questions.[15] Thinking out the process one is to follow in daily research will save time and yield more fruitful results. For example, to discover whether or not a certain ancestor was free or slave in 1850, it is better to consult census manuscripts instead of a city directory. Again, to learn the origin of the slave ancestor's surname, the researcher should avoid searching for birth certificates but try to find out who the parents and owners were by searching planters' diaries, census manuscripts, deeds, and bills of sale. The family history researcher must constantly think about how to proceed and how to unearth answers. Undoubtedly, the creative thought process is critical to saving time and pursuing the next logical source for answers, for quite often some answers create other questions.

To some extent, then, historical methodology uses scientific methods, includ-ing the gathering of facts, organizing of facts, making of generalizations, form-ing of hypotheses, and drawing of conclusions based on those facts. But what are facts? Facts are pieces of information, the raw materials of historical inquiry. The family history, therefore, is an interpretive study of the facts about a group of ancestors, a series of related biographies in which interrelationships are estab-lished in a meaningful pattern. Without interpretation and the establishment of trends, relationships, and patterns, however, the family history would be a mere chronicle, or a dull diary, of events, dates, and names.

THE FAMILY HISTORY RESEARCH PROCESS

Like the genealogist, the family historian must be a detective—one who gathers the sources, organizes the clues, and interprets the facts to reach a conclusion. The best illustration of this process of researching a family geneal-ogy and turning that genealogy into a family history is Haley's search for his African roots.

Haley's search began with the simple oral history of his ancestors, as he heard it on his grandmother's front porch in Henning, Tennessee. After becoming interested in the authenticity of the stories, Haley followed these steps of historical inquiry, which eventually brought Kunta Kinte and other ancestors to life.

1. Relatives were interviewed to add more details to Grandmother Haley's stories. These oral interviews were carefully noted and studied for clues to further research. Two valuable pieces of information were ascertained, through a keen eye and a good ear: (a) the name of the oldest ancestor identified was Kunta Kinte and (b) he came from West Africa to Annapolis, Maryland, as a slave.

2. A time period in which to begin the search was pinpointed. This was determined by Haley after carefully noting that the African probably came from near the Gambia River of West Africa. By consulting a griot—an oral historian in West Africa— Haley learned that Kinte disappeared "about the time the King's soldiers came." A search of British military records was the next logical source. These records revealed that a consignment of English troops was sent to the Gambia area in 1767.

3. Next the task was to determine which ships in 1767 sailed between Gambia and Annapolis. By researching British slave ship records, Haley learned that a *Lord Ligonier* had sailed on 5 July 1767 from the Gambia River to Annapolis.

4. The data had to be cross-checked and confirmed. Haley consulted a book, *Shipping in the Port of Annapolis,* which was in the Library of Congress. As a result he confirmed that the *Lord Ligonier* had cleared the Annapolis customs house on 29 September 1767.

5. A contemporary newspaper was searched to fill in details about the ship's arrival and cargo. A microfilm copy of the *Maryland Gazette* (October 1, 1767) advertised that the *Lord Ligonier* had arrived from Gambia, Africa, with a cargo of slaves for sale and was available to transport local tobacco to England.

6. More documents were researched, to provide even more details about the ship's cargo. This sixth step was necessary because Haley needed to know as much as possible about the slaves aboard to get clues to whether this was indeed the ship that brought his ancestor to America. Although the ship's records revealed no names for African slaves, Haley was able to determine the number of slaves aboard the vessel upon its arrival in Maryland and the number it took from Africa.

7. Although it appears that the historical researcher would be at a dead end here, such is not the case. The seventh step was logical—refer back to the oral history notes for further clues. Haley took note of the fact that his relatives had told him that this "Kunta Kinte" was first sold to a "massa John Waller" of Virginia and renamed "Toby." At this point the historian has to make a connection between the time the ship arrived and the subsequent sale of the slaves in the area.

8. Haley researched Virginia deeds for the year 1767 and thereafter. A connection was made! A Virginia deed dated 5 September 1768 documented the facts that John Waller and his wife had transferred to William Waller 240 acres of land and a Negro slave named Toby.

9. From this point Haley, the historian, traced Kinte's descendants, using plantation records and government documents to ascertain the complete genealogy of births,

marriages, children, ages, and deaths. Oral history and family papers helped to fill in details about important events in the life of the family and in the lives of individuals. Finally, Haley sat down to write these facts into a history by fleshing the story around the bones of the genealogy.[16]

Thus, when creating a family history from a genealogy, one can see how Alex Haley systematically searched, sifted, checked, cross-checked, and investigated numerous leads and sources. By skillfully using bits and pieces of information from oral history interviews, a historian can ask additional questions from other source materials. Similarly, the family historian takes this approach after determining a genealogical pattern for the family; that is, the historian finds out more and more about the individuals in the genealogy and asks the right questions. The study and research of history is a series of questions: Who, what, when, why, and how? By asking such questions and using the right documents to seek correct answers, Haley was able to include seven generations in his genealogy and dozens of persons in his family history. Furthermore, he used textural details, periods of history in which the family lived, personal data, and general topographical, social, and cultural information to write a lively, interesting saga of the descendants of Kunta Kinte. In a like manner the genealogist can turn his or her work into a family history.

METHODOLOGY IN HISTORICAL RESEARCH

To proceed further the family history researcher must become familiar with a few of the various methods of historical research, including those already mentioned, such as oral interviewing and traditional search of documents. The craft or methodology of history involves skill developed through a hands-on approach. The general craft of historical research can be learned by reading several books on the subject, including Louis Gottschalk, *Understanding History: A Primer of Historical Research*,[17] but personal techniques must be developed by actually experiencing the process.

Sources of Data

Using the right sources saves time and helps to obtain the most accurate answers to specific questions. For example, to obtain a true picture of the town in which the ancestor lived, one should not rely solely upon oral accounts from relatives but should consult memoirs, books, and newspapers. There is a tendency in writing family history and biography for the writer to see the subject's times through the subject's eyes. Such an error can make that individual too much the center of action and lead to too many apologies or too much condemnation.[18] Thus the researcher should seek sources independent of the ancestor's views and take into account social, cultural, and the psychological forces that affected the subject's point of view. Always attempt to corroborate oral history sources with written accounts.

To illustrate further, in compiling a family history for American ethnics, one might have to use some obscure and unusual sources. In other words, certain documents that yield information for specific questions on white Americans may exclude similar data for black Americans or American Indians. For example, census documents prior to 1860 reveal white family names but only first names for slaves. Private white family papers are better sources for identifying black family names prior to 1860 than are census manuscripts alone. To go further, black Americans, as one ethnic example, may find more data for countries such as the United States, Great Britain, Denmark, France, the Netherlands, and Portugal in customs records than in census documents. Moreover, the black American may have to use white family records for the antebellum period, along with overseers' diaires, mistresses' journals, Indian tribal records, newspaper advertisements for runaway slaves, Freedmen's Bureau marriage records (1865–68), northern missionary society reports, and even records of the Freedmen's Savings and Trust Company (1865–74).

In particular, the Freedmen's Bank records vividly illustrate the point of using unusual sources for ethnic family history. Although business records of various kinds, such as cancelled checks, are useful in researching any family's history, the Freedmen's Bank records contain an extraordinary amount of biographical data on the depositors. Established by Congress in March 1865 to serve former slaves, the bank's tellers were careful to record as much information as possible about the individual depositors in order to identify them or their heirs. Remember that some 95 percent of the former slaves could neither read nor write; therefore they could not always be identified by signature. For this reason a depositor's card reads like a biographical sketch.[19] (See figure 4.1.)

Oral History

As noted earlier, another important method for the family history researcher is oral history interviewing. The researcher should be reminded, however, that oral history can be helpful in painting a general picture as well as in providing otherwise unobtainable facts. It is not to be relied upon as a single and unsubstantiated source for family history or historical research in general. To strengthen the interviewee's story, it is suggested, therefore, that the family history researcher use some printed or manuscript sources.

A good example of oral history for an ethnic group is the slave narratives collection, or interviews with more than 2,000 former slaves who were alive between 1919 and 1941. Transcripts of these narratives are stored at the Library of Congress; some are at Fisk University Library and at Hampton Institute's library, Hampton, Virginia. Over thirty volumes have been published in *A Composite Autobiography of Slavery: The Slave Narratives*, edited by George P. Rawick.[20] Again, a note of caution: oral history is not an end in itself, but only

Figure 4.1
Bank Depositor's Card

```
FREEDMAN'S SAVINGS AND TRUST COMPANY              MEMPHIS, TENNESSEE

Number  0001                          Date:  February 2, 1866

Name of Depositor:  Henry Prince      Born:  January 3, 1841?

Where:  Richmond, Virginia            Raised:  Fayette County, Tenn.

Master's Name:  John Randolph         Complexion:  light brown

Age:  25 or thereabouts

Residence:  109 rear Beale Street, Memphis

Employer:  self (works sometimes for Mr. James Overton

Married:  Susie

Children:  Samuel, Mary, Sukie, Caesar

Parents:  don't remember mother; but her name was Mary Mason; father a

            man named Henry Mason.

Brothers and Sisters:  know father's children--Sam and Bell Mason

Remarks:  do not permit anyone to withdraw funds but me and Susie.

                                      Signature:  Henry Prince

                                      (His mark  X  )
```

NOTE: The amount and kinds of information on the cards at the Freedmen's Bank varied among the thirty-three branches in the United States and according to the style and exactness of the branch cashier or teller. Because the microfilmed copies of the original depositors' cards are often handwritten and difficult to read, the illustration is a reconstructed example of a typical card.

SOURCE: Freedmen's Savings and Trust Company (Washington, D.C.), *Registers of Signatures of Depositors in Branches of the Freedmen's Savings and Trust Company, 1865–74, Tennessee Accounts*, record group no. 101, National Archives and Records Service, Washington, D.C. (available on microfilm)

one of the means to the end of the research. Information gleaned from this source should be corroborated.

There exist throughout the nation numerous oral history projects and collections which will aid the researcher in understanding oral interview techniques and which will provide vital information for the study of family history or genealogy. Among these are the Black Women Oral History Project, Schlesinger Library, Radcliffe College, which consists of interviews with older women who have made a notable contribution to the shaping of the nation. Twenty colleges and universities across the country are receiving copies of the transcribed tapes, which makes the collection accessible to many more scholars and serious researchers. These collections may or may not be of value to the genealogical researcher or to specific relatives; however, the general accounts of local events and history given by the interviewees can sometimes prove vital in piecing together background material for a family history. For example, the interviewer often asks the interviewee, "How was it back then in that town?" And the person often responds with an overview of social, cultural, economic, and even racial conditions for that period of history.

Somewhat older than the Radcliffe collection is the Fisk University Library's Black Oral History Project. Established in 1969, the project focuses on men and women whose work has been germane to the black experience. While only a portion of the tapes has been transcribed, the researcher will find the collection useful in genealogical research for the information which the tapes include on the intimate lives of the interviewees. For persons searching for their family backgrounds in Tennessee and in other states where the subjects lived, these tapes could provide some clues.

More recently (1980), the Instructional Services Center of the University of South Carolina at Columbia has made available on audio and videotape "The Oral Recollections of Black South Carolinians," edited by Grace J. McFadden. Some of these interviews discuss black historical developments in South Carolina as far back as the 1860s and through the Civil Rights Movement of the 1960s.

In chapter 7 Jimmie B. Parker discusses the Doris Duke Oral History Project, in which seven universities are involved and which preserves Indian history through oral interviews with tribal groups.

Some private collections also exist. Among them is the collection of Virginia Sanchez-Korrol, Department of Black and Puerto Rican Studies, Brooklyn College. As a part of her doctoral research, Sanchez-Korrol conducted oral interviews with a number of Puerto Ricans.

Perhaps the most extensive oral history collection has been acquired by Columbia University. Numerous library facilities also have copies of the collection, thus making the resources available for genealogical and family historical research.[21]

The use of these stored and transcribed oral history collections is one way to pursue the oral interview method of history. But it is more likely that the beginning family historian will have to create his or her own oral history sources by taping interviews with relatives and other persons. For this reason, the next two paragraphs will describe how one should proceed in using this method.

First, to obtain as much information as possible from interviews, one must be diplomatic and alert. The potential relative or interviewee should be contacted in advance. The interview session should be planned; for instance, written questions should be prepared and the recording equipment should be checked. Consult a handbook on conducting oral history interviews (see the bibliography for this chapter) and prepare to use the proper techniques for the session.

Second, follow the suggestions given below for focusing on the most important questions to ask when preparing for a family history interview. Be reminded also that the objective of the questions is to provide details to fill in the genealogy and to turn it into a family history.

1. Narrow the theme of your family history to focus on specifics: women, children, distinguished ancestors, historical themes such as war years or depressions, slavery, and other topics.

2. Inquire about the family members' occupations, their religions, the daily routines of earlier years, family feuds, the first machines and appliances, community life, courtship and marriage, and general but favorite reminiscences of the interviewee.

3. Relate the questions and the family's history to specific historical events that may have affected the family, including migration, political participation, labor unions, and other activities.

4. Acquire a copy of Willa K. Baum, *Transcribing and Editing Oral History*, American Association of State and Local History, 1400 Eighth Avenue, South, Nashville, TN 37203.

Oral interviews with relatives and acquaintances of relatives add flavor to the finished product. Yet the interviewer must be careful to separate fact from fiction and must exercise careful judgment in deciding what to use and what not to use in the final family history narrative. A good selection of live dialogue sprinkled throughout the narrative will prevent the essay from being a dull exposition of facts, dates, and charts. Good answers to the right oral history questions will help the writer to place the family members within their proper context of history by showing how they affected history and how history affected their lives. (See also chapter 9, which includes techniques for conducting black oral history interviews.)

Utilizing Cemetery Records

Cemetery transcribing is a historical method that is often used in genealogical research. Many states have no birth or death records for the periods prior to 1900. Other vital statistics are sometimes incomplete, and Bible records and newspapers for the years prior to 1900 are often lost. Even some county and state census manuscripts are unavailable, due to human mistakes and to natural disasters such as courthouse fires. Further, unlike Catholic, Episcopal, and some Presbyterian churches, most Baptist churches and many other Protestant churches, especially in the South, saw no need to preserve birth and death dates for their members. In addition to newspapers and obituaries, a good source of birth and death dates for relatives is the cemetery tombstone.

Cemeteries can be located through county and state records, maps, and surveyor's records. In some states, especially southern states, the WPA compiled lists of private cemeteries, slave cemeteries, inscriptions of tombstones, and registers of the dead. Ethnic cemeteries usually can be located in the vicinities of old ethnic neighborhoods. Jewish deaths, for example, can be easily located because the death dates of ancestors are annually commemorated. On the other hand, numerous rural black cemeteries are lost because of the crudeness of the plots, the lack of durable headstones, and the absence of permanent employees to maintain the burial places. It is relatively easy to locate deceased black soldiers, however. As explained in chapter 2 and in other sections of this book, several printed registers are available on the nation's war dead. For instance, Civil War dead are listed in the multivolume document called *The Roll of Honor*, which lists all Union Army soldiers interred in several national cemeteries. These Union rolls include the names, graveyard sections, and tombstone numbers for the U.S. Colored Troops as well as for the white troops.[22]

Many ethnic cemeteries, however, have been affected adversely by urbanization. The expansion of commercial districts has caused many small cemeteries to be removed, often destroying the markers and reinterring the dead elsewhere in unmarked graves. For this reason oral interviewing might be necessary to gain information about the whereabouts of the removed graves. Better still, consult city maps if available. One might also use a reference work which lists the state mortician association members or the national directory of funeral home directors. Church and newspaper accounts of the funeral also may be used.

If the researcher is successful in locating the tombstones of relatives, the following historical research procedures should be used:

1. Acquire a copy of *Cemetery Transcribing: Preparations and Procedures,* by John J. Newman, technical leaflet no. 9, American Association of State and Local History, 1400 Eighth Avenue, South, Nashville, TN 37203.

2. Use a steel rod to probe the soil for sunken tombstones in old graveyards.

3. Use a garden spade to unearth headstones that are found below the soil.

4. Use a wire brush, white chalk, and a small knife to clean, magnify, and read the weather-beaten inscriptions.

5. Copy all information, including poems and Bible verses, exactly as it is spelled, because these data are a legitimate historical source and could provide clues to further research sources.

Computer Banks

A fourth historical methodology is the use of information stored in computer banks. Computerized methods of storing and analyzing records and machine-readable data is one of the latest of historical research methodologies. For example, the Soundex system of tracing surnames is discussed in chapter 5. To illustrate further, some slave ship records have been machine coded by the University of Wisconsin and can yield ports of departure, ports of arrival, numbers of slaves bought and sold, and other pieces of information. Further, as explained in other chapters of this work, some large genealogical depositories contain computerized data entry systems. Although most of this kind of data is statistical and in bits and pieces useful mostly for genealogical research, some of the information can be used creatively by the writer to fill in parts of the family history.

Photoanalysis

Photoanalysis is a fifth historical research method that is quite useful for researching and writing the family history. Old photographs, paintings, drawings, and sketches can yield the precise information one is searching for. However, the researcher must be alert to interpret such visual evidence. Consult Robert Akeret, *Photoanalysis: How to Interpret the Hidden Psychological Meaning of Personal and Public Photographs,*[23] or similar works. Be reminded also that the newspapers carried sketches of local scenes, local personalities, buildings, and pictures of events and people. For example, a college student who was researching a family history had no picture of her grandfather until she remembered that in 1916 the man had been involved in a tragic municipal accident. The local newspaper had published a photograph of the victim, one of her grandfather, and a complete account of the incident. The historian uses a photograph to note background features: type and condition of houses, terrain, dress, personal features, and even the socioeconomic status of the individuals.

Finally, it is up to the researcher to choose the best methods in conducting the family history project. However, familiarity with various historical research methods and techniques will make the job easier and the results more accurate. Consult some of the books in this chapter's bibliography on historical methods and on the study and craft of history in general.

TYPICAL RESEARCH PROBLEMS

In all historical research, including that of ethnic family history, one certainly will encounter numerous roadblocks and problems. These problems result from the absence of private and public records on blacks, Indians, and Mexican-American and other non-European ethnic groups as well as from the peculiar historical experience of American ethnic history. For instance, the absence of records could present problems as one seeks to ascertain the following: physical descriptions, racial origins, places of residence, levels of education, and linking of surnames. Moreover, language can prove to be a barrier for persons researching ethnic history, where old country records are not only in the old language but also in an old dialect of that language. Lengthy translations may have to be done by hired experts, but small translation jobs can be handled by the family history researcher by using various language dictionaries, such as *The New Cassell's French Dictionary.*[24] Because African history once was completely oral, black family history researchers must rely on the records of the slave trading and colonial nations. These records may have been written in Swedish, French, Russian, German, Portuguese, or another foreign language. Various printed dictionaries and language translation tools, including verb wheels and pocket dictionaries, are available for the modern researcher's use.

ETHNIC HISTORY

A needless problem that often presents obstacles to the historical researcher is lack of general background knowledge about the topic under investigation. The researcher must also be aware of the ethnic historical background, general historical background, and migration patterns of the family under study. It is recommended, therefore, that the family history researcher prepare for work by reading a general history on the ethnic group under study and a history of the country and locality in which the ancestors lived. For instance, if one is preparing to conduct research on the history of a Japanese family in Arizona, it is wise to read a general history of Japan, a book on Arizona history, a book on Japanese-American history, and a general American history book. If one is researching a black American family history, it is wise to read a general American history book, a book on the areas where the family resided, and a general history of black Americans such as John Hope Franklin, *From Slavery to Freedom: A History of Negro Americans.*[25]

Such reading should prepare the researcher to be alert to general facts that have a bearing on the study in progress. Examples of general facts which concern the accurate evaluation of ethnic history and the role of ethnic families in that history follow.

1. Germans migrated into the early thirteen colonies but also populated the Midwest and southern states such as Texas and Tennessee. Although many Germans were antislavery advocates, some were pro-Confederate. For example, a Nashville, Tennessee, German Regiment fought in the Confederate Army of Tennessee.

2. Many Scandinavians migrated into Iowa; some, such as the Swedes, settled in the original thirteen colonies.

3. Some 95 percent of black Americans lived in the southern states prior to 1865; yet blacks migrated to the Far West during the black exodus of the late 1870s. Rural southern blacks began to move into southern towns during the Civil War years and continued that migration into the second half of the twentieth century; subsequent generations of these southern city blacks led the black migration to northern industrial cities beginning near the turn of the present century.

4. Japanese-American families were highly concentrated on the West Coast prior to 1940.

It is evident that unless the researcher is aware of the history of the ethnic group, its migration patterns, and its geographical and demographical backgrounds, some difficulties may be encountered in the research and writing of the family history. (See specific discussions in other chapters concerning various ethnic groups and research on their families.)

Recent interest in the histories of ethnic groups has caused an increase in publications on such groups, both European and non-European. The ethnic family history researcher can benefit greatly by consulting some of these works. Before embarking upon study, the researcher should read selected works on specific ethnic groups and their history, which are given in chapters 7–10. Additionally, various publishing companies have catalogs on ethnic studies which list books and government publications on ethnic and immigrant histories.

ETHNIC RECORDS

The research problems for European ethnic groups will be considerably less than those for non-European ethnic groups. Most European countries have much better records and archives than African and Asian nations. Moreover, many Western European nations are steeped in the tradition of studying genealogy and preserving records pertaining to family history. In the United States, unlike records on African slaves and Asiatic immigrant laborers, records for European immigrants were systematically retained. There are guides to the published arrival records of hundreds of thousands of seventeenth- and eighteenth-century immigrants,[26] published guides to genealogical research on Czech and Slovak Americans,[27] and even personal name indexes to certain city directories of the nineteenth century.[28] To be sure, the use of such published sources will minimize the problems inherent in ethnic family history research as far as European ethnic groups are concerned.

Such printed indexes and easy reference tools are not yet available for non-European Americans, such as Asiatics, blacks, and Indians; yet a few microfilmed sources are beginning to appear to help alleviate this problem. For example, *The Major Council Meetings of American Indian Tribes* (in two parts) is available on microfilm from University Publications of America (44 North Market Street, Frederick, MD 21701) and contains topics of importance to American Indian history, including tribal disputes, crimes, religion, education, and the election of tribal delegates—the kind of material needed to turn a genealogy into a family history. Additionally, the same company offers *The British Colonial Office Manuscript Records of Early Indian Affairs,* which contains government hearings, surveys of Indian conditions on the reservations, and various reports of Indian commissioners. Some of these documents contain photographs of Indians as well as data on members of the Arapaho, Blackfoot, California, Cherokee, Cheyenne, Chickasaw, Chippewa, Choctaw, Creek, Crow, Delaware, Iowa, Kaw, Klamath, Menominee, New York, Omaha, Oneida, Osage, Otoe, Ottawa, Pawnee, Ponca, Potawatamie, Sac, Seminole, Shawnee, Shoshone, Sioux, and Winnebago tribes. (See also chapter 7.)

Military records can solve some of the problems of dead ends in family history research. Write to the General Services Administration, Washington, D.C. 20408, for the National Archives and Records Service's General Information Leaflet no. 7, *Military Service Records in the National Archives of the United States*. Military records list name, age, place of birth, date and place of enlistment, occupation, regiment and company, physical description, discharge date, medical information, and some pension information on other family members. Sometimes a photocopy of a military record fills in that bit of information needed to complete a section of the genealogy or the family history. (See also the discussion on sources in chapters 2 and 5.)

RELIABILITY OF SOURCES

Finally, the reliability of the sources used is a key to completing an accurate and professional family history. The genealogist and the family historian should be cautious when judging the reliability of sources encountered during the course of research. Reliability is the trustworthiness, the authenticity, or the accuracy of the historical document or data. Therefore it is important to evaluate critically the evidence collected. This also relates to the previous discussion on using the right sources to answer specific questions. The quality and reliability of the sources used determines the quality and reliability of the final family history. One should attempt to use mostly primary sources.

Regardless of the source used, always check and authenticate dates and other information by finding another supporting source. If a diary says that 17 December 1864 was a Monday and a very warm day, check a newspaper or an almanac to verify that information. Obviously all witnesses are not equally competent. For example, the size of the army with which Xerxes invaded Greece in 480 B.C. was said by Herodotus to have numbered 1,700,000, but it is unlikely that such a large army was raised at that period of history when local populations were very small and the world's population was counted in the millions. The historian and the genealogist must, therefore, be skeptical of dates, inflated figures, and doubtful details. Unreliable evidence can lead the researcher in the wrong direction and force the writer to commit errors that distort the final product.

WRITING THE FAMILY HISTORY

Once the researcher has collected all available information, data, and records, it is time to begin the essay, the family history. Again, remember that one can write the family history in chronological form, according to the organization of the genealogical data, or in topical form, according to areas of interest or special aspects of history.

Prior to beginning this process, consult some of the handbooks and guides used by professional historians and students of history, which are also useful to the family historian. These include Jacques Barzun and Henry F. Graff, *The Modern Research;* F. N. McCoy, *Researching and Writing History: A Practical Handbook for Students;* Peter M. Roget, *The Original Roget's Thesaurus of English Words and Phrases;* and William S. Strunk, Jr., and E. B. White, *The Elements of Style.*[29] Additionally, to produce the best possible family history narrative, the writer should follow the instructions in historical research handbooks and writing manuals, including the *MLA Style Sheet*[30] and the bibliography at the end of this chapter for other useful guides and reference tools.

Again, all historical writing consists of selecting the relevant and discarding the irrelevant. The information should be organized in a meaningful as well as a chronological or topical pattern. Connections, patterns, and developments should be clearly established within the narrative. Again, the family history is the attempt to put flesh on the bare bones of the genealogy, to turn sterile dates, names, and otherwise impersonal data into a complete and interesting story.

The narrative can be written in a style that denotes painstaking, precise, impersonal reporting, filled with details in a strict chronology. On the other hand, the family history can get beneath and behind the facts to uncover the realities and issues of the time. For instance, if a relative was a fireman during the 1890s, more should be researched on that role, its effects upon the relative, and the manner in which the relative affected the role. Indeed, a fireman's job was a prestigious and political one in many nineteenth-century American communities. The writer should try to understand the historic events and their significance as they related to the family and convey that understanding through the narrative and to the reader of the family history.

One of the most difficult problems for the historian as a writer is explaining why a certain event occurred. While the genealogy might simply list the death date for a person, the family history would attempt to conclude why and what about that event. The family history, therefore, is not as objective or as impersonal as a genealogy; yet the writer of the family history must be careful to avoid substituting personal opinion for historical interpretation. The writer also must try to avoid becoming too sympathetic toward any one relative and avoid taking sides. Any bias will be obvious throughout the narrative and will impair the value of the family history.

The writer should strive to gain a sense of the whole history that surrounded the individuals of that family. One must learn to imagine past realities to present the family members in an accurate manner, as well as to interpret their achievements, roles, and shortcomings in that society. This includes telling or being willing to tell the complete truth and avoiding intentional omissions merely to please or displease surviving relatives or others. Such insight into the whole past will also enable the writer to avoid judging the morals, achievements, and shortcomings of ancestors according to current or personal standards. For example, although today's citizen would call a duelist who shot and killed his opponent in the streets a murderer, early nineteenth-century neighbors might not necessarily have called the duelist a murderer if the opponent was fairly shot. Without doubt such knowledge of the historical realities of that period in which the ancestor lived will equip the family history writer to present the facts in an objective rather than a subjective manner. Indeed, objectivity and subjectivity are major problems in the writing of a family history.

The format of the family history is usually in the manner of a good history essay, book, or paper: (1) title page, (2) dedication page, (3) table of contents, (4) genealogy chart(s), (5) introduction, (6) text, (7) appendices, (8) footnotes, if any, and (9) bibliography.

There are, however, various ways in which to organize the final manuscript. The family historian should review genealogies and family histories in libraries or private collections. Some family histories, for instance, break the monotony of narration through periodic insertions of charts, illustrations, maps, direct quotes, and photographs. Certainly, the writer may be as creative as desired.

One of the most important parts of the narrative will be the introduction. Here is where the writer establishes the background and attracts the reader's interest. This is the section in which the writer uses the maps, background information, and general and local history information. For example, Haley's *Roots* skillfully established a geographical and cultural background for Kunta Kinte's homeland prior to presenting any genealogical data on his birth.

Early in the spring of 1750, in the village of Juffre, four days upriver from the coast of the Gambia, West Africa, a manchild was born to Omoro and Binta Kinte. . . . The thin blue smoke went curling up, pungent and pleasant, over the small dusty village of round mud huts as the nasal wailing of Kajili Demba, the village alimamo, began, calling men to the first of the five daily prayers that had been offered up to Allah for as long as anyone living could remember.[31]

Note the technique of using general information to add to and fill out the few bits of specific information on Kunta's birth. The specific information Haley had was simply the time of year, date, place, and names of the child's parents, Omoro and Binta Kinte. It is obvious that the author obtained the bulk of the information in the paragraph from oral and written history of the area where the child was born. In this manner, one line of genealogical data became the center of an entire page and more of the story about Kunta Kinte's childhood.

Another example of setting the background in a family or biographical history appears in the introduction to *Pen and Sword: The Life and Journals of Randal W. McGavock*, about a Scottish-Irishman of the nineteenth century.

The northeast coast of County Antrim rises quickly from the Irish sea. Almost at once the hills begin. If the traveller follows the coast road ambling north from Belfast, he sees misty mountains rising in the west, and the road seems commanded from these high craggy places.[32]

The editors of the book continue by describing the environment and circumstances of McGavock's earliest known ancestors, who migrated to America during the late eighteenth century and ultimately to Tennessee, where Randal was born and buried. Again, it is clear that the information contained in the above introductory paragraph was taken from maps and geographical accounts of that part of Northern Ireland.

As one can see, a family history should not be written in a sterile, lifeless environment; the narrative should be brought to life. Truly, the family history recreates as many of the facets of the ancestors' lives and surroundings as possible.

This whole picture helps the reader to understand more fully the role of the ancestors in history.

It is important, too, that the writer provide an adequate physical and character description of the principal individuals in the family history. This is quite essential in the absence of pictures or photographs. Another example from the McGavock biography follows.

Hugh, the eldest son of James and Mary Cloyd McGavock, was born in Rockbridge County in 1761. . . . As a growing lad he learned to dig out stumps for new ground and to plow a straight furrow. . . . Like his father, Hugh was tall and fleet. . . . Hugh was a God-fearing righteous man.[33]

Again the simple and brief genealogical data about place of birth, parents, and date of birth were expanded with interesting information on the person's character and personal attributes. The objective is to transform the genealogical data into as complete a description of the ancestor as possible. Some imagination can be used; however, one should avoid inventing data where no sources exist.

It is important to determine and to illustrate in the narrative important historical events involving members of the family. In *Roots* Haley discusses his family through the Revolutionary War and the Civil War. These parts of the narrative will be developed according to the kinds of questions posed and answers gained during the research process. Naturally, one should be interested in major historical events such as wars, economic periods and conditions, and political changes as they affected the family members. To a great extent, the structure of the final essay will be dictated according to the questions posed by the researcher.

In summary, the following steps should be followed in writing the history itself:

1. Consult a manual of style and a book on writing history.

2. Organize the note cards in chronological or logical order.

3. Form a working outline that furnishes a unified theme and creates logical interrelationships of the subordinate parts. Include a definitive introduction, a detailed narrative based upon chronological or topical methods, and a concise, clear conclusion that summarizes developments and changes in the family's history.

4. Follow a style which conforms to ordinary rules of grammar and rhetoric. Consult a manual on expository writing.

5. Write clearly.

6. As noted earlier, accuracy is quite important in historical writing. Keep the sequence of events logical and consistent. Check, double-check, and cross-reference pertinent facts. Use footnotes where necessary.

7. Avoid opinions and be as objective as possible. Objectivity is a most valued quality for any historical account. Be impartial in tone, but attempt to interpret events where needed.

8. Avoid filling in space with meaningless rhetoric and irrelevant information. The

Figure 4.2
Family History Deposit Agreement Form

NAME OF FAMILY HISTORY COLLECTION OR LIBRARY

_____

FAMILY HISTORY DEPOSIT AGREEMENT

I agree to donate this family history, entitled _____

_____ ,

19__ and all rights thereof to _____ ,

Through its acceptance of this family history, the receiving institution
agrees to take all necessary precautions to safeguard this document and
agrees to allow only qualified persons and researchers to use this family
history for research purposes. The user agrees not to identify living
persons herein, nor will he or she use the information contained in this
family history to degrade, slander, or defame the living relatives of the
persons mentioned herein.

Signed _____

Dated _____

length of the manuscript is not equated with its quality. Length will be determined
by the amount of data, the number of generations covered, and the time periods
under study.

9. Use standard (8½ × 11-inch) typewriter paper of good quality and double space the
   manuscript. Use a solid black ribbon and follow the guidelines established by
   recognized manuals of style.

In conclusion, proofread, correct, and make several copies of this valuable
document. The copies may be bound in hardcover by a local company. Additionally, the family may wish to donate a copy to the local library or to the state
archives. If so, it is desirable to include a written Family History Deposit Agreement form. (See figure 4.2.) Finally, consult the librarian about obtaining
copyrights to the completed family history.

NOTES

1. John Farmer, _A Genealogical Register of the First Settlers of New England_ (Lancaster, Mass.:
Carter, Andrews and Co., 1829).
2. See U.S., Works Projects Administration, _Bibliography of Research Projects, Reports,
Checklist of Historical Records Survey Publications_ (Washington, D.C.: National Archives and
Records Service, 1943).

3. *Ethnic Groups in the United States*, Report of the 61st American Assembly on Ethnic Groups in the United States, New York, N.Y., 12–15 November 1981, p. 5.

4. James D. Walker, *Black Genealogy: How to Begin* (Athens: University of Georgia, Center for Continuing Education, 1977).

5. Charles L. Blockson with Ron Fry, *Black Genealogy* (Englewood Cliffs, N.J.: Prentice-Hall, 1977).

6. David H. Culbert, "Family History Projects: The Scholarly Value of the Informal Sample," *American Archivist* 39 (October 1975): 533–41.

7. David E. Kyvig and Myron A. Marty, *Your Family History: A Handbook for Research and Writing* (Arlington Heights, Ill.: AHM Publishing Co., 1978).

8. Jim Watts and Allen F. Davis, *Generations: Your Family in Modern American History*, 2d ed. (New York: Alfred A. Knopf, 1978).

9. F. Wilbur Helmbold, *Tracing Your Ancestry: Step-by-Step Guide to Researching Your Family History* (Birmingham, Ala.: Oxmoor House, 1976).

10. Janice T. Dixon and Dora Flack, *Preserving Your Past: A Painless Guide to Writing Your Autobiography and Family History* (Garden City, N.Y.: Doubleday and Co., 1977).

11. See Fisk University, Institute on Ethnic Genealogy for Librarians, June 3–22, 1979, "Guide for Participants," (Nashville, Tenn.: Fisk University Library, 1979); The North Carolina Afro-American Family History Project was directed by Tommie Young, North Carolina Agricultural and Technical State University, Greensboro.

12. Ethel W. Williams, *Know Your Ancestors: A Guide to Genealogical Research* (Rutland, Vt.: Charles E. Tuttle Co., 1960), pp. 1–14; *Webster's Third New International Dictionary* (Springfield, Mass.: G. and C. Merriam Co., 1972).

13. See A. S. Eisenstadt, ed., *The Craft of American History*, 2 vols. (New York: Harper and Row, 1966), which discusses various approaches to the study of history, including biography.

14. Alex Haley, *Roots: The Saga of an American Family* (New York: Doubleday and Co., 1976), pp. 574–84.

15. The researcher should consult Donald V. Gawronski, *History: Meaning and Method* (Glenview, Ill.: Scott, Foresman and Co., 1969), pp. 1–30, for a discussion on various historical research methodologies.

16. Haley, *Roots*, 682–88; Vaughan Brown, *Shipping in the Port of Annapolis, 1748–1775* (Annapolis, Md.: U.S. Naval Institute, 1965).

17. Louis Gottschalk, *Understanding History: A Primer of Historical Research* (New York: Alfred A. Knopf, 1967).

18. Ibid, pp. 136–70.

19. U.S., Records of the Comptroller of the Currency, *Registers of Signatures of Depositors in Branches of the Freedmen's Savings and Trust Company, Tennessee Accounts (Memphis), 1865–1874*, record group no. 101 (Washington, D.C.: National Archives and Records Service), microfilm.

20. *A Composite Autobiography of Slavery: The Slave Narratives*, edited by George P. Rawick, 19 vols., 11 supplements (Westport, Conn.: Greenwood Press, 1975–79).

21. The collection has been identified and described in Columbia University, Oral History Research Office, *Oral History Collection of Columbia University* (New York: Columbia University, 1960; supplement, 1962).

22. U.S., *Roll of Honor: Names of Soldiers Who Died in Defense of the American Union Interred in the National Cemeteries at Memphis, Tennessee and Chalmette, Louisiana*, vol. 21 (Washington, D.C.: Government Printing Office, 1869). A volume exists for each of the national cemeteries where Civil War soldiers are interred.

23. Robert Akeret, *Photoanalysis: How to Interpret the Hidden Psychological Meaning of Personal and Public Photographs* (New York: Pocket Books, 1973).

24. *The New Cassell's French Dictionary: French-English, English-French* (New York: Funk and Wagnalls, 1971).

25. John Hope Franklin, *From Slavery to Freedom: A History of Negro Americans*, 5th ed. (New York: Alfred A. Knopf, 1980).

26. See P. William Filby, *Passenger and Immigration Lists Index*, 5th ed., 3 vols. (Detroit: Gale Research Co., 1980). This work contains guides to the published records of nearly 500,000 passengers who came into the United States during the seventeenth and eighteenth centuries.

27. Oga K. Miller, *Genealogical Research for Czech and Slovak Americans* (Detroit: Gale Research Co., 1978).

28. Moderate size cities have published directories since the early nineteenth century. A microfilm project is under way to copy all directories before 1840. Public libraries and city archives usually have files of local directories.

29. Jacques Barzun and Henry F. Graff, *The Modern Researcher* (New York: Harcourt, Brace and World, 1970); F. N. McCoy, *Researching and Writing History: A Practical Handbook for Students* (Berkeley: University of California Press, 1974); Peter M. Roget, *The Original Roget's Thesaurus of English Words and Phrases* (New York: St. Martin's Press, 1964); William S. Strunk, Jr., and E. B. White, *The Elements of Style* (New York: Macmillan Co., 1972).

30. *The MLA Style Sheet*, 2d ed. (New York: Modern Language Association, 1970).

31. Haley, *Roots*, p. 1.

32. Herschel Gower and Jack Allen, eds., *Pen and Sword: The Life and Journals of Randal W. McGavock* (Nashville: Tennessee Historical Commission, 1959), p. 5.

33. Ibid, pp. 16–17.

BIBLIOGRAPHY

Akeret, Robert. *Photoanalysis: How to Interpret the Hidden Psychological Meaning of Personal and Public Photographs*. New York: Pocket Books, 1973.
  Describes how to use photographs as historical source materials.
The American Slave: A Composite Autobiography. Edited by George P. Rawick. 19 vols. Westport, Conn.: Greenwood Press, 1972. *Index to the American Slave*. Edited by Donald M. Jacobs. Westport, Conn.: Greenwood Press, 1982.
  A collection of transcriptions of slave narratives prepared by the Federal Writer's Project in the 1930s and deposited in the Library of Congress. The separated index is arranged by slave name identification, a name index by state and by subject.
Appel, John J. *Immigrant Historical Societies in the United States, 1880–1950*. Ph.D. diss., University of Pennsylvania, 1960; New York: Arno Press, 1981.
  An example of the numerous printed studies available on American ethnic history. This dissertation studies selected historical societies founded by Scotch-Irish, Irish, Jews, Germans, and Scandinavians in America.
Barth, Gunther. *Bitter Strength: A History of the Chinese in the United States, 1850–1870*. Cambridge, Mass.: Harvard University Press, 1964.
  A study of Chinese immigrants, beginning with their early entry to help build Western American railroads, until 1870, just prior to passage of federal laws to exclude Chinese from immigrating into the United States.
Baum, Willa K. *Transcribing and Editing Oral History*. Nashville, Tenn.: American Association for State and Local History, 1977.
  A small and inexpensive leaflet of less than ten pages that provides a convenient overview of how to use oral interviews.
Brandon, William. *The American Heritage Book of Indians*. New York: Dell Publishing Co., 1978.
  A survey of American Indian history.
Brown, Barbara W., and Rose, James M. *Black Roots in Eastern Connecticut, 1650–1900*. Detroit: Gale Research Co., 1980.

An example of the many new printed sources beginning to appear for historical and family history research on the Afro-Americans. Contains every piece of information that could be found on blacks in this particular location.

Cantor, Norman F. *How to Study History*. Arlington Heights, Ill.: AHM Publishing Co., 1981.
A guide to the study of history.

Castelli, Joseph Roy. *Basques in the Western United States: A Functional Approach to Determination of Cultural Presence in the Geographical Landscape*. Ph.D. diss., University of Colorado, 1970; New York: Arno Press, 1981.
An example of studies available on the Basque ethnic group in Wyoming.

Colket, Meredith B., Jr. "Creating a Worthwhile Family Genealogy." Special Publication no. 42. Washington, D.C.: National Genealogical Society, n.d.
A useful guide for persons wishing to publish genealogies. Includes selection of titles, illustrations, format, content, evidence of identity, documentation, and some methods of production and indexing.

Culbert, David H. "Family History Projects: The Scholarly Value of the Informal Sample." *American Archivist* 38 (October 1975): 533–41.
This article discusses the increased interest in oral history, family history, and genealogy as methods of teaching history in schools and colleges.

Current, Richard N.; Williams, T. Harry; and Freidel, Frank. *American History: A Survey*. 4th ed. 2 vols. New York: Alfred A. Knopf, 1979.
A survey history book that is the type to be read prior to completing a family history project.

Davis, Cullom; Back, Kathryn; and MacLean, Kay. *Oral History: From Tape to Type*. Chicago: American Library Association, 1977.
Examines the state of this new method of studying history.

Dixon, Janice T., and Flack, Dora D. *Preserving Your Past: A Painless Guide to Writing Your Family History*. Garden City, N.Y.: Doubleday and Co., 1977.
A manual that outlines and discusses clearly and concisely the procedures and sources for writing personal and family history.

Dossick, Jesse. *Doctoral Research on Puerto Rico and Puerto Ricans*. New York: New York University, School of Education, 1967.
A useful reference source to help locate theses and dissertations on Puerto Rican history.

DuBester, Henry J. *State Censuses: An Annotated Bibliography of Censuses of Population After the Year 1790 of States and Territories of the United States*. Washington, D.C.: Library of Congress, 1948; New York: Burt Franklin, 1969.
An example of one of the many reference tools the family historical researcher uses in libraries.

Edner, Michael H. "Students as Oral Historians." *History Teacher* 9 (February 1976): 196–201.
Useful for students and beginners who desire to conduct oral interviews during the course of researching a family history.

Eisenstadt, A. S., ed. *The Craft of American History*. 2 vols. New York: Harper and Row, 1966.
Discusses various approaches to the study of history.

Faust, Albert B., and Vrumbaugh, G. M. *Lists of Swiss Emigrants in the Eighteenth Century to American Colonies*. 2 vols. Baltimore: Genealogical Publishing Co., 1968.
An example of a valuable guide available for use by researchers in ethnic family history.

Filby, P. William. *Passenger and Immigration Lists Index*. 5th ed. 3 vols. Detroit: Gale Research Co., 1980.
An example of reference material available for researching the family histories of European ethnics. These volumes are guides to the published materials and arrival records of nearly 500,000 passengers who came to the United States and Canada in the seventeenth, eighteenth, and nineteenth centuries.

Franklin, John Hope. *From Slavery to Freedom: A History of Negro Americans*. 5th ed. New York: Alfred A. Knopf, 1980.
The best survey of Afro-American history and useful to those who wish to trace the black

American experience, from Africa to the present. This book is the kind that should be used as preparatory reading before writing an ethnic family history paper.

Fry, Gladys-Marie. *Night Riders in Black Folk History*. Knoxville: University of Tennessee Press, 1975.

A unique usage of oral history to reconstruct blacks' experiences with local terrorists. Often, questions about race relations and racial violence come up in the process of researching a black American family history.

Fulcher, Richard C. *Basic Workbook for United States Genealogical Research*. Brentwood, Tenn.: Richard C. Fulcher, 1979.

A small and locally produced book written for lay historians and amateur genealogists.

Gawronski, Donald V. *History: Meaning and Method*. Glenview, Ill.: Scott, Foresman and Co., 1969.

Discusses in detail historical research methodology and the rules of the craft of history.

Gordon, Michael, ed. *The American Family in Social-Historical Perspective*. 2d ed. New York: St. Martin's Press, 1974.

This collection of articles by scholars explores the various aspects of the history of the American family.

Gottschalk, Louis. *Understanding History: A Primer of Historical Method*. New York: Alfred A. Knopf, 1967.

An older but useful book that provides an in-depth lesson on historical methodology. It also explains the principles of the craft of history. These rules and principles are the same ones the family historian should follow during research and writing.

Gower, Herschel, and Allen, Jack, eds. *Pen and Sword: The Life and Journals of Randal W. McGavock*. Nashville: Tennessee Historical Commission, 1959.

McGavock's biographical history and journal is preceded by an excellently written history of the McGavock family. A book such as this one should be reviewed by the family history researcher to get a sense of the kind of information needed and the style to be followed in the narrative.

Hartley, William G. *Preparing a Personal History*. Salt Lake City, Utah: Primer Publications, 1976.

A brief guide that also includes numerous suggestions for interview topics. The work points out that it is essential for the family history researcher to ask the proper questions when interviewing family members.

Helbold, F. Wilbur. *Tracing Your Ancestry: A Step-by-Step Guide to Researching Your Family History*. Birmingham, Ala.: Oxmoor House, 1976.

A useful guide and manual for beginning family history research.

Holway, John. *Voices from the Great Black Baseball Leagues*. New York: Dodd, Mead and Co., 1976.

A collection of interviews with Afro-American men who participated in the old Negro baseball leagues during the days of segregation (prior to 1964). This volume is one in the growing number of collections on ethnic oral history. Such a volume could be used to provide background material for a family history.

Hoopes, James. *Oral History: An Introduction for Students*. Chapel Hill: University of North Carolina Press, 1979.

A very useful manual on how to use oral history sources and techniques.

Hurt, Peyton. *Bibliography and Footnotes: A Style Manual for Students and Writers*. 3d ed. Berkeley: University of California Press, 1968.

Useful for writing family histories as well as general history papers.

Ichibashi, Yamato. *Japanese in the United States*. American Immigration Collection, vol. 28. Palo Alto, Calif.: Stanford University Press, 1932; reprint ed. New York: Arno Press, 1969.

A history of Japanese Americans and another example of the type of history book which one would use as preparatory reading before researching ethnic family history.

Johnson, Leanor B. "Search for Values in Black Family Research." *Western Journal of Black Studies* (June 1977): 98–104.

Discusses the procedures, time, and money needed to study the complexities of the black family in America. Such an article should be read by the black family historian who needs to become familiar with the research problems inherent in Afro-American history.

Kyvig, David E. "Family History: New Opportunities for Archivists." *American Archivist* 30 (October 1975): 509–19.

Reviews the trends in collecting and writing family history sources and narratives as well as new directions in using various methods for the teaching of family history.

————, and Marty, Myron A. *Your Family History: A Handbook for Research Writing.* Arlington Heights, Ill.: AHM Publishing Co., 1978.

A short book of less than 70 pages that serves as a guide; includes examples from family histories written by the authors' college students.

Lasker, Bruno. *Filipino Immigration to the Continental United States and Hawaii.* Chicago: Institute of Pacific Relations, University of Chicago Press, 1931; reprint ed., New York: New York Times/Arno Press, 1969.

A history of Filipino peoples in America. A minority history that is useful for reading prior to conducting research on this specific American ethnic group.

Lewis, Marcus W. *The Development of Early Emigrant Trails in the United States East of the Mississippi.* Washington, D.C.: National Genealogical Society, 1962.

This type of book is useful for solving research problems in tracing ancestors from the Eastern to the Western United States. Such precise background information saves time by helping the searcher keep the investigation on the right track.

Lichtman, Allan J. *Your Family History: How to Use Oral History Family Archives, and Public Documents to Discover Your Heritage.* New York: Vintage Books, 1978.

One of the best guides to family history. Includes chapters on the methodology described in this chapter: oral history, printed records, photograph usage, and other methods of research.

————, and French, Valerie. *Historians and the Living Past: The Theory and Practice of Historical Study.* Arlington Heights, Ill.: AHM Publishing Co., 1978.

Discusses skills for analyzing historical events and communicating the results effectively; includes sections on family and local history, historical research, and history writing.

Matthews, William, and Pearch, Roy. *American Diaries: An Annotated Bibliography of American Diaries Written Prior to the Year 1861.* Berkeley: University of California Press, 1945.

Diaries are important historical sources for piecing together the daily events in the lives of ancestors and their neighbors, friends, and families.

McCoy, F. N. *Researching and Writing History: A Practical Handbook for Students.* Berkeley: University of California Press, 1974.

A handbook for researching and writing history papers.

Meckler, Alan, and McMullin, Ruth. *Oral History Collections.* New York: R. R. Bowker Co., 1975.

Locates oral history collections housed in various parts of the United States.

Meier, Matt S., and Feliciano, Rivera. *The Chicanos: A History of Mexican Americans.* New York: Hill and Wang, 1972.

A survey of Mexican-American history; good background reading for conducting such an ethnic family history. (For further sources, see chapter 10 of this book.)

Meltzer, Milton. *Taking Root: Jewish Immigrants in America.* New York: Farrar, Straus and Giroux, 1980.

An overview of Jewish immigrant life in America during the late nineteenth and early twentieth centuries and another example of background reading in preparation for pursuing an ethnic family history project. (See chapter 2 of this book for additional references to ethnic histories.)

————. *World of Our Fathers: The Jews of Eastern Europe.* New York: Farrar, Straus and Giroux, 1980.

A panoramic view of Jewish life in Eastern Europe through the mass migration to the United States in the early 1900s.

Miller, Oga K. *Genealogical Research for Czech and Slovak Americans*. Detroit: Gale Research Co., 1978.

A comprehensive research guide.

Morrissey, Charles T. "Oral History as a Classroom Tool." *Social Education* 32 (October 1968): 546–49.

Discusses how to use oral history to teach children to appreciate local and family history.

Murphy, E. Jefferson. *History of African Civilization*. New York: Dell Publishing Co., 1974.

One of the many survey books on the African background. Again, such a book should be used to familiarize the black family history researcher with African history, culture, and places. (For further sources, see chapter 9 of this book.)

Murray, Pauli. *Proud Shoes: The Story of an American Family*. New York: Harper & Row Publishers, 1956.

A history of a family of racially mixed ancestors which includes an interesting account of various family members and which places the story in perspective by presenting vivid accounts of local, regional and national history of the era. For example, discussions of the Civil War are included. Contains photographs and other documents which have meaning to the author's family.

Newman, John J. *Cemetery Transcribing: Preparations and Procedures*. Technical leaflet no. 9. Nashville, Tenn.: American Association for State and Local History, 1971.

A technical leaflet that describes what a historical researcher does to utilize data from cemetery tombstones.

Newman, Richard. *Black Index: Afro-Americana in Selected Periodicals, 1907–1949*. New York: Garland Publishing, 1981.

A multiple-subject index that provides access to over 1,000 articles on Afro-Americana located in over 350 American, Canadian, and British periodicals published in the early 1900s. Such articles and periodicals often included information on state and local history, black life and culture, and personal histories that could provide valuable background material for certain family history researchers. (Such reference sources are given also in chapter 2 of this book.)

Phillimore, W.P.W. *How to Write the History of a Family: A Guide for the Genealogist*. 1876; reprint ed., Detroit: Gale Research Co., 1972.

Contains naming practices; laws and customs; and all types of records, manuscripts, and registers. Gives procedures that guarantee accuracy in tracing family history. Illustrations and bibliographies included.

Platt, Lyman De. *Genealogical Historical Guide to Latin America*. Detroit: Gale Research Co., 1978.

A detailed guide to the use and availability of genealogical records in twenty Latin American countries. (See chapters 2, 6, and 10 of this book for further sources on this specific ethnic group.)

Poulton, Helen J. *The Historian's Handbook: A Descriptive Guide to Reference Works*. Norman: University of Oklahoma Press, 1972.

A research manual.

Rose, James M., and Eicholz, Alice. *Black Genesis*. Detroit: Gale Research Co., 1978.

Contains a survey of the types of records known to be available for black genealogical research.

Schelbert, Leo. *Swiss Migration to America: The Swiss Mennonites*. Ph.D. diss., Columbia University, 1966; New York: Arno Press, 1981.

An attempt to write a comprehensive history of Swiss migration to preindustrial America and an example of the numerous printed sources appearing on European ethnic groups.

Schiavo, Giovanni Ermenegildo. *The Italians in America Before the Civil War*. New York: Arno Press, 1934.

One of the many studies on the Italian Americans published by Arno Press. The author has completed several books on this subject and intends to write a total of fifteen such monographs on the Italians.

Shopes, Linda. *Using Oral History for a Family History Project.* Nashville, Tenn.: American Association for State and Local History, 1980.

A small, useful, and inexpensive leaflet that describes in less than nine pages how to assimilate oral interviews into the family history paper.

Shumway, Gary L. *Oral History in the United States: A Directory.* New York: Oral History Association, 1971.

A guide to collections.

Slave Testimony: Two Centuries of Letters, Speeches, Interviews, and Autobiographies. Edited by John W. Blassingame. Baton Rouge: Louisiana State University Press, 1977.

Selected essays and descriptions of available oral history on the black experience in America.

Steckmesser, Kent L. *The Westward Movement: A Short History.* New York: McGraw-Hill Book Co., 1969.

A textbook, but also valuable as background reading for persons interested in researching family history in the Western states. A book on Western American history is especially important for gaining a needed perception of how various ethnic groups, including Asiatics, blacks, Mexican Americans, and Indians, migrated into the Western states and contributed to the transmission of civilization and culture.

Steele, D. J. *Sources for Scottish Genealogy and Family History.* London: Phillimore and Co., 1970.

A reference tool.

Turabian, Kate L. *A Manual for Writers of Term Papers, Theses, and Dissertations.* Chicago: University of Chicago Press, 1967.

A manual on style, footnotes, bibliography, and other mechanics of writing a history paper.

U.S., Work Projects Administration. *Bibliography of Research Projects, Reports, and Checklist of Historical Records Survey Publications.* Washington, D.C.: National Archives and Records Service, 1943.

A valuable guide to the numerous historical reports and studies completed by members of the Federal Writers' Project during the New Deal period. Some of these reports and publications are stored in state libraries and local archives or in the National Archives and include church, cemetery, marriage, and plantation records as well as interviews with former slaves. These old WPA records often included local histories and surveys or compilations or county records that are not otherwise available to the family history researcher. Sometimes the information contained therein provides the family history filling for the genealogical crust. (See chapter 2 of this book for similar records.)

Walker, James D. *Black Genealogy: How to Begin.* Athens: University of Georgia, Center for Continuing Education, 1977.

A small but useful manual; includes instructions, examples of charts, important addresses, and a brief bibliography.

Washburn, Wilcomb E. "Ethnohistory: History in the Round." *Ethnohistory* 8 (Winter 1961): 31–48.

A discussion of various approaches to the study of ethnic history.

Weinstein, Robert A., and Booth, Larry. *Collection, Use and Care of Historical Photographs.* Nashville, Tenn.: American Association for State and Local History, 1979.

A technical leaflet.

Young, Tommie M. "Ten Steps in Rooting Out the Past of the Black Family." *North Carolina Society Papers* (August 1980): 150–59.

Discusses the differences in the procedures the black family researcher must use from those used by genealogists and majority American family history researchers. Provides examples from the research of the author's own black family history.

II

UTILIZING MAJOR REPOSITORIES FOR GENEALOGICAL RESEARCH

5

The National Archives and Records Service

JAMES D. WALKER

Since 1976, thanks to Alex Haley, along with the White House, U.S. Capitol building, the Washington and Lincoln monuments, the National Archives has become a household word. It is that part of the General Services Administration formally titled the National Archives and Records Service, which has the responsibility for retaining the permanently valuable records of the federal government. The three parts of the National Archives and Records Service which serve as depositories for the records are the National Archives Building in Washington, D.C., the seventeen Federal Records Centers, and the eight Presidential Libraries. To date, billions of cubic feet of records are contained in the depositories, some with enduring legal and historical value, others pertinent to the presidential administrations to which they relate, and the remainder records of undetermined permanent or temporary value which must be retained for a period of years to satisfy audits or other needs. Today the records of the first two centuries of the nation's existence serve as a principal resource for the study of our political and historical past and for an understanding of the programs of the national government, including those involved with the study of family history and genealogy.

Only some of the older records have survived, primarily due to the lateness of the establishment of a permanent archives and also due to the general lack of regard for such records over the century and a half when the records remained in the hands of the agencies responsible for them. Yet the surviving records, which sometimes predate the existence of the federal government, (1) are an important resource for information about individuals and families of ethnic origin (and thus can contribute immeasurably to the study of family history or genealogy), (2) are of value for many legal purposes, and (3) generally prove worth investigating for whatever study is undertaken relating to Americans and to the United States. Foremost in the successful use of the records, however, is an understanding of the methods and systems employed in keeping and controlling the records and an understanding of the kinds of records excluded from the National Archives.

Records which have been formally accepted into the National Archives repositories are mentioned in the *Guide to the National Archives of the United States*.[1] This publication describes in brief terms the various federal agency and other records which were on deposit as of 1972. A long-awaited update of that volume will reflect both a significant increase and some reductions, the latter because the records were either destroyed or given away to other depositories. The guide serves only as a general catalogue to the records. A more complete aid to the identification, description, arrangement, volume, chronological coverage, and so forth, of records is called an inventory. These inventories are also available. As a further aid, the National Archives has sometimes prepared reference information papers, subject guides, special publications, pamphlets, and staff information papers, many of which can be found in state, university, college, reference, historical, and genealogical libraries here and abroad. Additional aids to use of the records have been prepared by scholars, and others are available to consult in many libraries.

THE RECORD GROUP FORMAT

The National Archives of the United States is described by the agency in the record group format, a system which permits the inclusion or separation of the records of one agency or one of its offices, bureaus, services, and so forth, into a separate records entity. A record group has a formal title, chronological coverage, and a number, and it may contain records of a continuing agency, one of the predecessors to an existing agency, or a now-defunct agency. Under the record group format the records are retained in or restored to their original filing scheme and maintained in this manner forever. Unlike a library, the National Archives is not described in a catalogue, nor is it described in calendars as they are by manuscript depositories. A National Archives final or preliminary inventory usually includes a history, the description and function of the whole agency or one of its parts (the office or the bureau), the records of which comprise the record group. As it can logically be assumed, in some instances several parts of the same agency or two or more agencies may have been involved in a given program, and as a result sometimes two or more series of records or documents exist pertinent to a given government program and therefore to the individuals or families involved.

In spite of the confusing description of the record group system, most federal archives available for public use can be consulted with a minimum of effort and with good results. The importance of this understanding to the researcher must be highlighted, for in some instances, without the knowledge of the whole picture, researchers may assume that because the information desired was not found in the sources checked, no other source exists for the information in the depository. Alluded to but not yet explained here is the word "series." A series is a unique group of records in the record group. An example would be Federal Population Census Schedules, which is a series of the Records of the Bureau of the Census, Record Group 29. The Bureau of the Census is currently an agency of the U.S. Department of Commerce; thus one can see that the records of an agency may also be a separate record group. For a more detailed description of the record group system and its use by the National Archives, the researcher should consult the numerous publications by and about the National Archives. (For examples, see the bibliography to this chapter.)

GUIDE TO THE NATIONAL ARCHIVES

In specific research areas the National Archives Conference Papers and its guides are effective tools for the genealogist. These documents are few and occasionally too outdated to serve useful research purposes. Such is true for the *Guide to Genealogical Records in the National Archives*, published in 1964. This incomplete, often confusing guide is in no measure a tribute to its compilers, but rather the product of editors who failed to understand the records and the National Archives record group system. The recent revised version is more complete, inclusive of most of the series of records of genealogical value, and published in a useful format.[2]

Other guides include the *Guide to Records in the National Archives Relating to the American Indian*, the *Guide to Federal Archives Records Relating to the Civil War*, the *Guide to the Archives of the Government of the Confederate States of America;* and the numerous guides to the records of the German and Italian governments, which describe records captured during World War II, which for the most part have been returned to the successor governments of those countries. Two additional guides are in preparation, but their actual publication and publication dates are uncertain. These are guides to records relating to Afro-Americans and to Cherokee Indians.[3]

In addition to the published guides, inventories, and other publications mentioned, the National Archives has prepared for the general public a series of general information leaflets. The leaflets list the locations of the National Archives facilities and their telephone numbers, hours of operation, regulations, and restrictions and give other useful information about them. These are listed in a special section of the bibliography.

The various publications available serve as an introduction to the National Archives holdings and can be used successfully in preparing to do research at the archives. Two other avenues are also available for information preliminary to genealogical research. The federal information operators located in federal buildings throughout the United States and the archivists located in the eleven regional branches of the National Archives can generally field questions and obtain answers to simple questions for the researcher. Neither the operators nor the archivists can undertake research for the patron. Research must be done in person or by correspondence, and either of the two sources can provide the correct mailing address for the depository or branch of the National Archives Building which has custody of the records pertinent to one's study. In many instances a simple, uncomplicated request can be handled by the staff, but detailed research will not be performed. Many records series are possible resources for an answer to a given research problem. Some series, however, are unindexed, have no name and subject arrangement, and generally lack the systematic arrangement needed to allow the staff to determine the potential for locating an answer without the expenditure of many hours of research time. In such cases an explanation of the research problem will be given, and then the requestor must examine the records series in person or employ a private researcher to do it.

National Archives and Records Service, Locations and Areas Served

Headquarters
Central Reference Division
7th and Pennsylvania Avenue, N.W.
Washington, DC 20408
202/523-3218
8:45 A.M.–9:45 P.M., Monday–Friday;
9:00 A.M.–5:00 P.M., Saturday

Branches and Areas Served: For each of the following, address inquiries to:
Chief, Archives Branch
Federal Archives and Records Center

Boston
380 Trapelo Road
Waltham, MA 02154
817/223-2657
8:00 A.M.–4:30 P.M., Monday–Friday
Serves Connecticut, Maine, Massachusetts, New Hampshire, Rhode Island, and Vermont.

New York
Building 22-MOT Bayonne
Bayonne, NJ 07002
201/858-7245
8:00 A.M.–5:00 P.M., Monday–Friday
Serves New Jersey, New York, Puerto Rico, and the Virgin Islands.

Philadelphia
5000 Wissahickon Avenue

Philadelphia, PA 19144
214/438-5200, ext. 591
8:00 A.M.–4:30 P.M., Monday–Friday
Serves Delaware and Pennsylvania; for microfilm loans, also serves the District of Columbia, Maryland, Virginia, and West Virginia.

Atlanta
1557 St. Joseph Avenue
East Point, GA 30344
404/526-7477
8:00 A.M.–4:30 P.M., Monday–Friday
Serves Alabama, Georgia, Florida, Kentucky, Mississippi, North Carolina, South Carolina, and Tennessee.

Chicago
7358 South Pulaski Road
Chicago, IL 60629
312/353-8541
8:00 A.M.–4:30 P.M., Monday–Friday
Serves Illinois, Indiana, Michigan, Minnesota, Ohio, and Wisconsin.

Kansas City
2306 East Bannister Road
Kansas City, MO 64131
816/926-7271
8:00 A.M.–4:30 P.M., Monday–Friday
Serves Iowa, Kansas, Missouri, and Nebraska.

Fort Worth
4900 Hemphill Street (building address)
P.O. Box 6216 (mailing address)
Fort Worth, TX 76115
817/334-5515
8:00 A.M.–4:30 P.M., Monday–Friday
Serves Arkansas, Louisiana, New Mexico, Oklahoma, and Texas.

Denver
Building 48, Denver Federal Center
Denver, CO 80225
303/234-5271
7:30 A.M.–4:00 P.M., Monday–Friday
Serves Colorado, Montana, North Dakota, South Dakota, Utah, and Wyoming.

San Francisco
  1000 Commodore Drive
  San Bruno, CA 94066
  415/876-9001
  7:45 A.M.–4:15 P.M., Monday–Friday
  Serves California (except southern California), Hawaii, Nevada (except Clark
  County), and the Pacific Ocean area.

Los Angeles
  24000 Avila Road
  Laguna Niguel, CA 92677
  714/831-4220
  8:00 A.M.–4:30 P.M., Monday–Friday
  Serves Arizona, the southern California counties of Imperial, Inyo, Kern, Los
  Angeles, Orange, Riverside, San Bernardino, San Diego, San Luis Obispo,
  Santa Barbara, and Ventura; and Clark County, Nevada.

Seattle
  6125 Sand Point Way NE
  Seattle, WA 98115
  206/442-4502
  8:00 A.M.–4:30 P.M., Monday–Friday
  Serves Alaska, Idaho, Oregon, and Washington.

Utilizing the Archives

In spite of the foregoing, the National Archives remains without peer as a research source for general and specific information about the ethnic groups in the United States. For successful use of the archives, one should at least know the names, dates, places, and the events which should have caused information about the person to be included in a federal record. In most cases the answer is very simple. Any person in the United States at the time the census was enumerated became a part of a federal population census by name or as a statistic. A man between the ages of eighteen and fifty-five may have been enumerated on a draft list in the Civil War, World War I, World War II, or later. A person who immigrated to the United States after 1798, as a single person or as a member of a family, will have been listed in the immigration records. A person may have become part of a record simply by signing a petition, filing a claim, being included in a survey of peoples (special groups and others), or being a resident of a city, town, county, state, or territory. A person may be in the records because of having written to the federal government to seek employment, to express an opinion, to register a complaint, or for another reason. As will be shown in a number of instances in the records to be described here, sometimes such sources reflect a nearly complete personal or family history. By far the most valuable records are those for individuals and groups in which the federal government had a special interest, such as American Indians, freedmen, the political prisoners of war, and aliens in general. While on the other hand no deliberate effort was made by the federal government to create detailed family records, sometimes such records resulted from efforts to qualify persons for one or another federal benefit or under the requirements of certain laws and regulations.

FEDERAL CENSUS SCHEDULES

In general, the records which record ethnicity over several centuries are the Federal Decennial Population Census Schedules. From 1790 and every ten years thereafter, and in 1885, the federal government undertook the enumeration of the nation's population. As a result a group of records known as population census schedules reflects efforts made to enumerate the population in general and in some instances to gather specific information for one or more given needs of the government. There also exist many censuses taken of specific parts of the population; special census schedules are included among the records of the Bureau of the Census, Record Group 29 (1790–1950).

1790–1840

From 1790 to 1840 the enumerators of the decennial population count were instructed to enumerate the names of heads of households and to represent all other household residents as statistics (males, females, free persons, slaves, and Indians not taxed). Only white and black males and females and heads of households are therefore listed by name in the Federal Decennial Population Census Schedules for 1790 through 1840. Some substitutes for the missing 1790 schedules have been compiled and printed. For the lost Virginia schedules, the Census Bureau used Virginia's tax lists for 1782, 1783, and 1785. Lion DeValenger, Jr., used several sources for the 1790 Reconstructed Census of Delaware. Substitutes for some of the other schedules are also available.

The 1810–40 schedules also included occupations (by class), alien status (1820 and 1830), health statistics, welfare status, literacy, and whether those counted were military pensioners (1840). Only in 1820 and 1840 did the statistics gathered result in the preparation of a separate supplemental schedule or report. In 1820 persons engaged in manufacturing answered specific detailed questions about their businesses, their employees, and the value of the business and nature of the products generated. These data were contained in a questionnaire now called the 1820 Census of Manufacturers. While the schedules lacked the names of the employees, they can be used as a means of identifying manufacturers who employed (probably owned) one or more African slaves. These data also may aid in the identification of individuals established in trades they had learned in their countries of origin.

Sixteen of the present states were enumerated in the first census, 1790. They were Vermont, New Hampshire, Maine, Massachusetts, Rhode Island, Connecticut, New York, New Jersey, Pennsylvania, Delaware, Maryland, Virginia, Kentucky, North Carolina, South Carolina, and Georgia. The Southwest Territory and Northwest Territory also were enumerated. Seven of the schedules were lost or destroyed before the surviving schedules were published in the 1900s. Those missing were for New Jersey, Delaware, Virginia, Georgia (including Alabama and Mississippi), Kentucky, Southwest Territory and Northwest Territory (Ohio, Indiana, Illinois, Michigan, Wisconsin, and part of Minnesota). The surviving schedules were indexed and printed. The printed census schedules are on microfilm and in reprints.

1850–60

The census schedules for the second half of the nineteenth century reflect a growth in the detailed information gathered with each successive census enumeration, and this growth of information continued into the present century. As of the 1850 census, the name of each free person in a household was enumerated. Also given were age, sex, race, occupation, health (if impaired), value of real estate, birthplace, and literacy, and a notation was made if the person had been married during the year preceding the taking of the census, attended school during that year, or was either a pauper or a convict. Omitted from inclusion on the 1850 schedule and again on the 1860 schedule (which duplicated the 1850 schedule) were statistics on enslaved persons and Indians on reservations. Several supplementary schedules which list some slaves and American Indians were prepared and will be described below.

1870

In 1870 for the first time all Afro-Americans were enumerated as a part of the general population. The specified details required in 1850 and 1860 were again enumerated in 1870, together with month of birth or marriage if the event occurred during the year preceding the census. Reported also were statistics on male citizens over twenty-one and those who were denied the right to vote. Several supplemental schedules, which will be described below, were also prepared.

1880

In 1880 each person was enumerated by name, age, sex, and race and was further identified by relationship to the head of the household (spouse, son, daughter, mother, father, brother, sister, and so forth). Occupation, street address, birthplace, birthplace of parents, month of birth or marriage if in the year preceding the census, number of months unemployed, temporary illnesses or disabilities, impaired health status, literacy, and school attendance were also added. Because of the inclusion of statistics reflecting relationship to the head of the household, it became possible for the first time to determine the relationships of the household members to each other. Supplemental schedules, described below, were also prepared.

1885

In 1885 the federal government offered to share the expense of taking a middecennial census with the various states and territories. Only Colorado, Dakota (now North and South Dakota), Florida, Nebraska, and New Mexico agreed to do so. Thus for these six states there exists an additional schedule. The categories of information gathered duplicated those in the 1880 census schedules.

1890

Of the 1890 Federal Population Census Schedules, 99 percent were destroyed by fire in 1921 in Washington, D.C. The 1 percent remaining relates to parts of some few towns, counties, and cities. A listing of the surviving fragments is given in the 1790–1890 Census Microfilm Catalogue. An index to the names that could be read on the fragments has also been prepared. The categories of information gathered were duplicated in the 1900 schedules described below. Nearly all of the supplemental schedules prepared were also destroyed. (See listing of supplemental schedules to follow.)

1900

The most useful of the schedules up to that time are those that were prepared for 1900. They include name, age, sex, marital status, number of years married, race, for women the number of children born and number then living; birthplace of individuals and their parents; year of immigration if foreign born; relationship to head of household; naturalization status; months not employed; literacy; school attendance; ability to read, write, and speak English; whether residence was a house or a farm; and if the residence was owned or mortgaged. All supplemental schedules were destroyed.

1910

On January 1, 1982, the 1910 censuses became public property. Their value as a family history tool replaces that of the 1900 schedules because they include much more detailed information: full address; name; age; sex; relationship to head of household; years of current marriage; for women, the number of children born and then living; birthplace; mother tongue of person and parents; if foreign born, year of immigration and whether naturalized; whether able to speak English, or if not, what language spoken; occupation; industry; class of worker, if an employee the number of weeks of employment; school attendance; whether residing in a house or on a farm and if it was rented, mortgaged, or owned; whether a survivor of Union or Confederate military service; and if deaf, dumb, or blind.

Indexes

Ease in using the federal census schedules is dependent upon the availability of an index. The available 1790 schedules were printed and indexed by the federal government. Due to the fact that many names were misread, the index is impaired. In other instances several indexes were prepared by private individuals and groups for all or some of the 1800 through 1860 and some 1870 schedules. Their value is directly in proportion to the care with which they were prepared, and only a few, such as the 1850 Michigan, 1860 Ohio, and 1830 Indiana state indexes, are nearly free of large errors. Many individual county schedules, such as the 1800 Frederick, Maryland (as cited by Volkel[4]), and the 1850 Frederick, Maryland, indexes were also carefully prepared.

The federal government also indexed the 1880, 1900, and later census schedules, but the value of each is in one way or another limited. The 1880, 1900, and 1910 indexes were prepared according to the Soundex system. In 1880, 25 percent of the population was indexed. Only those households were indexed in which one or more persons dwelled who were from one day to ten years of age on the day of the commencement of the census (7 June 1880). In 1900, 65 percent of the population was indexed. An index card was prepared in 1900 for each "different" family within the residence. Thus if a father and his family and one or more sons and their families resided in the same household, an index card was prepared only for the father. On that index card also appear the names of all other residents of the household. If a stranger or a relative with a different surname resided in the same household, a separate index card was prepared for that individual and his or her family. In 1910 an index was prepared similar to that for 1900 but only for the states and territories which then had no law making registration of vital statistics mandatory and in a few other instances; thus it was prepared for only thirty-two of the existing states and territories.

The National Archives and other libraries and repositories which house census records also have available to the researcher a guide to the Soundex filing system. As explained in the guide, the Soundex is a system whereby names are arranged alphabetically by the first letter of the surname and then by a code for the sound of the surname. All names sounding alike, regardless of spelling differences or errors, are interfiled on file cards. The code for the family surname consists of the first letter of the name, followed by three numbers representing consonant sounds, as follows:

1	b, p, f, v							4	l	
2	c, s, k, g, j, q, x, z							5	m, n	
3	d, t							6	r	

There is no code for a, e, i, o, u, y, w, or h. Every Soundex name code must be a 3-digit number. If there are not three codable letters in the name, zeros are added; if there are more than three codable letters, only the first three are considered. The following names are examples of the Soundex coding:

Name	Letters coded	Code No.
Eberhard	b, r, r	E 166
Handselmann	n, s, l	H 524
Lind, Van	n, d	L 530
McDonnell	c, d, n	M 235
McGee	c	M 200
O'Brien	b, r, n	0 165
Oppenheimer	p, n, m	0 155
Riedemanas	d, m, n	R 355
Zita	t	Z 300

There are variations in the coding of the names of American Indians and Orientals. Phonetically spelled Oriental and Indian names were sometimes coded in the normal manner. For example, the American Indian name Shinka-Wa-Sa may have been coded as "Shinka" or "Sa." Researchers should be alert to the various possibilities of coding such names, as well as to the general possibility of errors and omissions. In all cases, whether or not a pertinent entry is found, the original schedule should be examined.

Supplemental Schedules

In addition to the 1820 manufacturing schedules, supplemental schedules survive that were prepared in 1850, 1860, 1870, 1880, and half of the veterans schedules for 1890. While not a supplemental schedule, the information gathered in 1840 relating to Revolutionary War pensioners was published as *A Census of Revolutionary War Pensioners*, and an index to that census was prepared by the Church of Jesus Christ of Latter-day Saints.[5]

Supplemental 1850–80 schedules were prepared for (1) persons who died within the year preceding the taking of the census (mortality schedules), (2) persons engaged in agriculture (agriculture schedules), (3) persons in business and manufacturing (business and manufacturing and industry schedules), and (4) persons who were suffering health impairments (social statistics schedules). In 1850 and 1860 additional schedules were prepared for slave owners (slave schedules), listing the owner's name, but only the age and sex of each slave. In 1958 the National Archives gave to state archives, university libraries, libraries of the Daughters of the American Revolution (DAR), and other repositories the majority of the nonpopulation schedules, as the mortality, agriculture, industry, business and manufacturing schedules are called. The slave schedules were excluded. Since that time, however, the National Archives has acquired microfilm copies of some of the original schedules, and in a few instances the original schedules have been returned. Microfilm copies of many of the individual state and territory schedules are available at the National Archives, at the depositories having custody of the original volumes, and elsewhere.

Other Census Enumerations

On various occasions the federal government has required an enumeration of a segment of the population. The total number of such enumerations is unknown, as many have been taken by individual federal agencies at the orders of agency administrators. Notable are the Civil War enumerations and the various enumerations of American Indians. The American Indian enumerations will be discussed with other records relating to them.

During the Civil War the U.S. Army took censuses of the population in the South, in areas it had just occupied. Many of the enumerations have survived and are a part of the records of the U.S. Army Continental Commands, Record Group 393. Such censuses are not found for every area occupied but exist for some of the areas in the Gulf region. Additional censuses are among the records of the Bureau of Refugees, Freedmen, and Abandoned Lands, Record Group 105. For the most part the schedules list the names, ages, occupations, and residences of those enumerated, with an initial "c" or the word "colored" used to denote Afro-Americans. Also included in Record Group 393 are the censuses of legal voters for the state constitutional conventions, with similar racial descriptors for Afro-Americans. The inventories to the two record groups serve to identify the specific census records series.

Additional censuses are often described in the published "Territorial Papers" series, but they may not be included in the records in the National Archives. Rather, many are found in records of the states as they exist now, or elsewhere. Unlike the population schedules, the territorial censuses provide little detail on ethnic origins, if any, and little more than the names of those enumerated. Yet such schedules could be invaluable to the study of a community in a territory settled primarily by one ethnic group.

Census Schedules as a Value to Ethnic Individual and Family Research

Due in great measure to the failure to record vital statistics, to identify consistently the place of birth of a person's parents in a vital record, at least since 1880 the federal census schedule has been the best source of information on the ethnic origins of people and their parents. Given the limitations normally associated with census records—incompleteness, inaccuracies, misinformation, misspellings of names, and deliberate omissions of specific individuals and families—the census can still be a resource of information which otherwise would be hard to acquire without personal knowledge of the family. If the information recorded on a given schedule is evaluated carefully, the researcher will find that it can serve to provide clues to other record sources which may be more fruitful.

Also, as borne out in numerous schedules, especially those which reflect new ethnic communities, the ethnic origin, specific principality, and name of country of origin will be shown. For European countries, the name of the old country is used instead of the accepted modern name. One noted difference on the general population schedules is failure to identify the ethnic or tribal origin of the Africans and American Indians enumerated. Separate American Indian census enumerations reflect tribal affiliation, however, and in some instances, tribal records or other federal records will give more details about descent than is shown on the census schedules.

FEDERAL IMMIGRATION RECORDS

Since 1798 federal laws have required the enumeration of aliens who immigrate to the United States; however, many valuable records have been lost due to neglect, indifference, and destruction. From 1798 to 1819 few records concerning immigrants were either kept or submitted to the Congress that was to receive them. In 1819 and in succeeding years, new laws were enacted to strengthen the regulations requiring registration of aliens and to provide a means of locating aliens once they had entered the country. The 1819 law required that the customs officials at the ports of entry give quarterly reports with detailed information about both immigrants and Americans entering the United States. The quarterly reports were abstracted and submitted to the U.S. Department of State, which was to give the Congress a statistical breakdown of immigrants periodically.

Under the earlier laws, the name of the entrant and his or her age, sex, occupation, country of origin or nationality, and place of intended habitation were recorded. Under laws and regulations enacted in the latter quarter of the century, the recording became more detailed. Added was the specific destination within the United States, the name of the relative or employer receiving or sponsoring the immigrant, his or her final destination in the United States, and the name and address of the nearest relative overseas. In the twentieth century such refinements include the religious affiliation claimed; language spoken; ability to read, write, and speak English; and country of birth. All records mention the last country from which the ship departed en route to the United States.

Passenger Lists, Crew Lists, and Ship Manifests

Information about persons arriving at U.S. ports by ship was recorded on passenger lists, crew lists, and ship manifests. Until the end of the nineteenth century, passenger lists and cargo manifests lacked general uniformity. Some lists were very detailed and included more information than required (such was the case of many German lists), while others, specifically those for passengers arriving on freighters, lacked all but the immigrant's name, age, and sex; the name of the vessel; and the date and place of arrival.

Pre-1906 passenger lists can be a good source of information about the ethnic origins of immigrants, but post-1906 lists are more reliable in this respect. Much of the confusion is due to the failure of the U.S. Congress and the agencies regulating immigration to detail the manner in which accurate information about an immigrant should be obtained. Since 1926 the basic information reported in immigrant records was taken directly from immigrants' visas and passports. Since 1906 a central record has been kept on all admitted legal aliens; thus postimmigration information is also available.

The chief series of early immigration records are called passenger arrival records. (See form for ordering passenger arrivals reproduced in figure 5.1.) This series consists of three kinds of basic records: (1) original lists received at the port of entry from masters of vessels, 1789–present; (2) abstracts of such lists prepared by the customs officials, 1820–66; and (3) transcripts of the abstracts prepared by the State Department for the U.S. Congress, 1820–66. A fourth record, the crew lists, identifies the ships' complements, some members of which may also have been immigrants. Crew lists do not detail the information gathered from immigrant passengers but include each crew member's name, age, sex, occupation, country of origin, country to which allegiance was owed, date and place of entry, name of the ship, and remarks.

Passenger lists for most ports are generally dated 1820 or later. Only records for ports located on the East Coast and in the Gulf region have survived. The California lists prior to the 1940s, the Great Lakes port records, and those of some time periods for the major East Coast ports have been lost. The chief series are those for Boston, New York, Philadelphia, Baltimore, and New Orleans. Records for eighty-eight minor ports are included in a series known as "Miscellaneous East Coast and Gulf Ports Records." Records also exist for many ports established in the late nineteenth and early twentieth centuries, when many new southern ports were opened and when additional immigration points were established as air passenger travel began.

Unlike census records, passenger arrival records usually give the name by which the country was known, or the portion thereof of the immigrant's origin or residence, at the time the list was prepared. If the language spoken was entered on the record, it may reflect religious belief or a language peculiar to the immigrant's ethnic origin or to that of his or her ancestors. The general language of the country of residence prior to immigration was omitted.

INDEXES

Passenger list indexes reflect the names of the passengers as shown on the arrival records. Such names may or may not be the true names of the immigrants, for many reasons. If an immigrant failed to understand the request to give his or her name, or gave a name which was not readily understood, was too lengthy, was spelled basically with consonants rather than interspersed with vowels, that name may have been entered by the port authority in a distorted manner. The renaming of immigrants at the port of entry is legendary.

Indexes exist for most ports, from 1820 to the ports' termination. Exceptions include the port of New York, where records are unindexed for the period 1847–69; the port of Boston, 1820–47; and the port of New Orleans, 1820–53. Some of the passengers arriving at these ports during the unindexed period are included in the index to the "Miscellaneous East Coast and Gulf Ports Records,

Figure 5.1
Passenger Arrival Record Form

ORDER AND BILLING FOR COPIES OF PASSENGER ARRIVAL RECORDS	Please follow instructions below. Submit a separate set of order forms for each passenger arrival. Do not remove any of the sheets of this 3 part set. You will be billed $3.00 for each list reproduced. Do not mail payment with your order. This form will be returned to you and serves as your bill when we fill your order.	Date received

Mail the complete set of this order to ▶	Passenger Arrival Records (NNCC), Washington, DC 20408

IDENTIFICATION OF ENTRY

DATE OF ARRIVAL		NAME OF IMMIGRANT OR NAMES OF MEMBERS OF IMMIGRANT FAMILY	AGE	SEX
PORT OF ENTRY				
WHERE NATURALIZED (if known)				
SHIP NAME (or carrier line)				
PASSENGER'S COUNTRY OF ORIGIN				

NOTE

The National Archives has customs passenger lists dating back to 1820 with a few as early as 1787. Lists prior to 1820 that are not at the National Archives may be on file at the port of entry or the State archives in the State where the port is located. The **Morton Allan Directory of European Passenger Steamship Arrivals** may be useful in determining the name and arrival date of ships arriving at New York, 1890—1930, and Philadelphia, Baltimore, and Boston, 1904—1926.

Please fill in as much of the information called for above as possible. We will advise you if the information is inadequate to enable us to locate the entry you are seeking.

We do not maintain a list of persons who do research for a fee; however, many researchers advertise their services in genealogical periodicals, usually available in libraries.

YOUR NAME & ADDRESS	DO NOT WRITE BELOW - SPACE IS FOR REPLY TO YOU

Type or print legibly PRESS HARD — Name — Number & Street — City & State — (Zip code) — NUMBER OF BLANK ORDER FORMS YOU WOULD LIKE SENT TO YOU ▶

	ARRIVAL DATE	PORT	SHIP

☐ THIS IS YOUR BILL RECORD ENCLOSED ▶

MICROFILM PUBLICATION — make check or money order payable to NATF (NNCC)

ROLL — PAGE — AMOUNT DUE ▶ $

☐ WE WERE UNABLE TO COMPLETE YOUR ORDER RECORD SEARCHED FOR BUT NOT FOUND ▶

RECORDS SEARCHED

MICROFILM PUBLICATION — SEARCHER

☐ SEE REVERSE ROLL — PAGE — DATE SEARCHED

☐ A SEARCH WAS NOT MADE FOR THE REASON INDICATED:

☐ 1. Our index to New York passenger arrivals covers the periods 1820 — 1846 and 1897 — 1943. We regret that we cannot undertake a page-by-page search of the lists for the period between 1847 — 1896, inclusive.

☐ 2. Masters of vessels departing from U.S. ports were not required to list the names of passengers. Therefore, we would not have a list for the passenger you have cited.

☐ 3. Our holdings of passenger lists do not include any for Pacific coast ports. The San Francisco passenger lists were destroyed by fires in 1851 and 1940. (Consult the two works by Louis J. Pasmussen, **San Francisco Ship Passenger Lists**, 4 vols., 1965; and **Railway Passenger Lists of Overland Trains to San Francisco and the West**, 1 vol., 1966.)

☐ 4. Overland arrivals into the U.S. from Canada and Mexico are not documented in passenger list records.

☐ 5. Justice Department restrictions prohibit us from making searches in Immigration and Naturalization records less than 50 years old. We suggest that you direct an inquiry to: District Director, Immigration and Naturalization Service, New York, NY 10007.

NATIONAL ARCHIVES TRUST FUND BOARD   NATF FORM 40 (12-79)

Courtesy National Archives and Records.

1820–77.'' An additional index to the ''City Passenger Lists for the Port of Baltimore, 1820–66,'' aids in the identification of passengers entering through that port. A transcript, which has been indexed, for the port of New Orleans reflects the names of passengers entering through that port on merchant vessels, 1813–67.

Additional sources of information relating to aliens include naturalization records, federal land records, and federal military records, all of which are discussed below.

NATURALIZATION RECORDS

Naturalization of aliens has been permitted by various U.S. laws since 1789. Except for the 1789 law, nearly all subsequent laws until 1867 required that free white males twenty-one years of age and older who desired citizenship could apply for admission to citizenship status once they met the basic residency requirements. Their wives and children were naturalized automatically. The naturalization process included two steps, the filing of a declaration of intent after a year's residence in a state or territory and the petitioning to be naturalized after five years of total residency. Additional laws enacted after the Civil War allowed for the immediate granting of citizenship to persons who had served at least six months of federal military service and received an honorable discharge. Persons of African descent were allowed to become citizens after the Civil War, and women could be naturalized in their own right after 1922 (and in certain other instances prior to that date).

Under pre-1906 laws, any court of record could naturalize a person if permitted by state or territorial law. Further, the laws did not require the two acts to take place in the same court, state, or territory, but because the act of naturalization was a legal one, several records were created. In the declaration process, the application was made in writing, with a copy becoming a part of the court record and a copy given to the applicant. In the petition procedure, again in writing, a request was made by the applicant who applied for citizenship. If successful, the applicant received a certificate of naturalization, with a facsimile copy becoming a part of the court record. As both actions took place in a court of law and an interrogatory was part of the proceedings, the court should have created a record of the entire proceedings. Such proceedings would normally have been made in the court's minutes. Further, the court docket should reflect the date and disposition of the court's action. If a petition to be naturalized was denied, the petition and a record of the court's rejection should have become a part of the court record.

The general information acquired in the processing of a declaration of intent included the applicant's name, age, sex, place of birth, place of residence, and nationality; the name of the country to which the applicant owed allegiance at immigration; the date and place of entry into the United States; the name of the judge presiding over the petition proceedings; the name of the court; and the date of the event. Sometimes the name of the vessel on which the applicant arrived is also mentioned in the record, but the applicant's name may appear only in the court minutes if it appears at all. In the petition proceedings the information acquired during the declaration proceedings is duplicated in the court record. The proceedings also included the results of an interrogatory made of the two witnesses who avowed the morality and loyalty of the applicant and also of any other witnesses. A written petition was received which indicated the applicant's current address, and if naturalization was approved, a duplicate of the certificate issued to the petitioner was made a part of the court record.

Some pre-1906 declarations and petitions contain incorrect information about the date and place of arrival, age of the applicant, or date and place where the declaration of intent was filed. Many court records have been lost, while others are available in a variety of sources. Some states have created central depositories for old state and municipal records; in other instances the records remain with the court. Federal court records also are variously located. Many remain with the courts, while others are available in the various regional branches of the National Archives. The National Archives is gradually microfilming the older court records, with copies being given to the National Archives Microfilm Reading Room.

Only since 1906 has the federal government attempted to centralize records relating to immigrants. About that time more detailed immigration records were also created. Such records remain with the Department of Justice, Immigration and Naturalization Service, and virtually all such records remain closed to public examination under the Freedom of Information Act. Lists of immigrants, passenger lists, duplicate declarations of intent and petitions to be naturalized, passport information, information relating to the naturalization of other family members or to foreign travel, and other information relating to the immigrant may be included in such records. Access to closed immigrant records can be acquired by those legally entitled to receive such information, through the Immigration and Naturalization Office in one's state of residence only.

No attempt has been made to identify the court records included in the holdings of the National Archives, for in spite of the fact that such records may have been formally accessioned and others are on deposit and awaiting accessioning, a court can at will recall all or part of its records, as has been done in the past. A listing of the court records in the custody of the National Archives can be obtained from any regional branch of the archives.

Naturalization records for the pre-1906 period are not always indexed. Most courts maintained an index to naturalizations in books which covered a span of time, depending upon the number of such actions taking place in the court, with several books being used in a given year, decade, or century. Earlier in this century, the WPA indexed the naturalization records of some large cities. New England naturalizations, 1789–1906, were indexed and also photocopied. Copies of the indexes and photocopies are available in the Federal Records Center,

Waltham, Massachusetts, and in the central reference room of the National Archives. An index to the naturalization records of New York City and Brooklyn, 1800–99, is in the Federal Records Center, Bayonne, New Jersey. An index to naturalizations in Philadelphia, 1800–99, is contained in the Philadelphia Federal Records Center. The index to Indianapolis, Indiana, naturalizations recently has been found in the Indiana State Archives, and preparations to publish the index are being made. New Jersey and Mississippi naturalizations were published by the WPA, with copies being placed in the National Archives and in the state archives. Additional indexes are believed to have been prepared; however, their location is currently unknown. As an aid to the identity of court records existing in about 1940, the WPA prepared inventories of federal, state, county, and municipal records. These identify the records and indicate where they were then located. Such information may aid in determining the current locations of such records.

Naturalization records are invaluable in learning the identity of the place from which a person emigrated. Indeed, they may aid in identifying the person's principal permanent residence prior to arriving at the port of departure and thus in the identification of other members of the immigrant's family. This is especially true for early immigrants, for whom the name of the nearest relative overseas was omitted from the arrival record.

PASSPORT RECORDS

While passports are generally considered documents issued to citizens of the country, such has not always been true. Prior to 1906 a passport could be issued by anyone having a seal of office. Immigrants, persons who had only obtained a declaration of intent document, as well as native and naturalized citizens, could also obtain passports. In general, however, prior to the Civil War a passport was not considered necessary, and prior to World War I many Americans and others leaving the country simply failed to apply for a passport through the U.S. Department of State. As the immigration quotas became stricter, war became imminent, and new laws were enacted, more and more persons sought the protection guaranteed to those having U.S. passports.

Thus, prior to 1906, the records of the State Department reflect only a small percentage of the persons who acquired passports to leave the United States, and it is believed that no sizable collection of other passport applications exists. Further, these early passports implied that the person was native born whether or not it was true, identified only the husband or father by name and only alluded to the wife and children, and may or may not have mentioned the applicant's place of residence, occupation, destination, anticipated date and place of departure, country to which traveling, name of nearest relative at place to which traveling, and name of nearest relative or friend in the United States. Physical descriptions, photographs, and other data found in current passports were nonexistent or, if found, unreliable.

Several series of passports, 1789–1925 or later, are included in the holdings of the National Archives. The restriction I have mentioned concerning alien records, a general restriction for fifty years, limits access to some of the passport records.

Seamen's Passports

One of the most important series of federal records are those relating to the issuance of seamen's passports. Seamen's Protection Certificates, 1798–1866 and 1916–47, which is the correct title of such records, relate to the issuance of documents to persons engaged in maritime trade and naval activities for the purpose of protecting them while at sea and in foreign ports. Many of the sailors who received such passports were foreign born. Upon arrival in the United States, they followed the trade learned in their former home and became sailors, after settling in an area where the principal occupation was the sea.

The earliest records of this group were issued to protect the seamen from capture and imprisonment by French and British ships during the quasi-war with France (1798–1801) and in the War of 1812. Later, as hostilities developed between the United States and other countries, passports were needed to protect the American seamen from countries with which the nation was having a dispute.

The earlier seamen's passports contained the sailor's name, age, place of birth, place of residence, and principal maritime occupation. In later years a physical description, photograph, and fingerprints were added. Many of the earlier records are deposited in the National Archives, while the twentieth century records are deposited in the National Archives branch which serves the state in which the U.S. Bureau of Customs office which issued the record was located.

Errors in birthplace of the person receiving the passport in pre-1812 days may invalidate the record, but later records are believed to be valuable and accurate. Earlier passports were issued by government officials and also by notaries and others having a seal of office.

Indexes to the earliest records available have been prepared for only a few principal port cities. One or more finding aids have been prepared for later records, but such indexes vary in completeness and amount of information.

FEDERAL MILITARY SERVICE RECORDS

Since the inception of a federal military force, aliens and unnaturalized residents have served in the volunteers, U.S. Army, U.S. Navy, U.S. Marine Corps, U.S. Coast Guard, and U.S. Air Force. Until 1941 unnaturalized residents were not compelled to render military service during wartime. An unnaturalized alien resident could serve if he so desired or denounce such service. Native-born and naturalized citizens had no such options. As earlier stated, many aliens sought federal military service as a means of acquiring quick citizenship. Aliens also may have been induced to render military service for the guarantees afforded to discharged veterans of federal military service in the form of pensions and bounty land, as well as for its citizenship benefits.

Federal military service commenced with the Revolutionary War, when the Continental Congress compelled the thirteen original states to supply for its use an army, navy, and marine force. In addition, a large number of civilians were used to conduct the war business.

Similarly, in other periods of national emergency and wars, large military forces have been called from the population to aid in quelling the prevailing disturbances. Most such persons called to serve were employed in the army, but a few were assigned to naval and marine duties. Such persons have been called volunteers by the U.S. War and Navy departments. The volunteers may have been volunteers indeed, or they may have been aliens substituting for persons drafted; draftees; members of an established state, county, or local militia; or later the National Guard (as the post–1898 militia is called).

Since 1789 a permanent army, and since 1898 a permanent naval and marine force, have existed, together with a fleet of customs ships called revenue cutters. The Revenue Cutter Service and other civilian services were combined in 1913 to form the U.S. Coast Guard. Whether or not a general war prevailed, volunteers were used to supplement and complement the permanent forces in time of need.

Volunteers

The larger number of persons employed during an emergency were members of volunteer units. They served in every major conflict and in some instances in lieu of the permanent forces in areas in which the permanent forces were unassigned or were weak. Volunteer service records relate primarily to the Revolutionary War, War of 1812, Mexican War, Indian wars (1816–60), Civil War (Union), Spanish-American War, Philippine Insurrection, and other conflicts during the eighteenth and nineteenth centuries. Service rendered during the twentieth century is included with permanent military service records on deposit with the National Personnel Records Center, St. Louis, Missouri. Such records remain restricted under the Freedom of Information Act and some of the records have been destroyed. They will be discussed below, with other records of the permanent military services.

With the granting of more liberal benefits after the Civil War, the establishment of more and more patriotic societies and other actions, such as creation of state veterans' homes, marking of graves, establishment of scholarships, and provision for free burial plots or burial expenses, the War Department was forced to adopt a more efficient method of providing evidence of military service than by consulting the original records each time a need arose. Because the volunteer records were rapidly deteriorating, the department undertook to abstract them. The records consist of jackets into which have been placed abstracts of information about an individual gleaned from official military service documents, such as muster rolls, payrolls, returns, hospital records, courts-martial documents, prisoner-of-war records, and so forth. Included in the records, if available, are original personal documents relating to the serviceman. The resulting records are called "compiled military service records." They have been arranged by period of service, by state, by unit, and thereunder by the serviceman's name. The several series which have resulted are the Revolutionary War, 1784–1811 (post-Revolutionary War), War of 1812, Indian wars (1816–60), Civil War (Union), Spanish-American War (1898–99), and the Philippine Insurrection (1899–1901). In addition, the available Confederate records were also compiled.

Revolutionary War

The Revolutionary War military service records relate to only a few of the men who actually served. While it is known that French, Polish, Canadian, Afro-Americans (slave and free), and American Indians served in that war for the Americans, a fire which destroyed the War Department archives on 8 November 1800 erased much of the evidence of such service. The records currently available were obtained from many sources, but they are incomplete, confusing, and lack evidence of the total service rendered and personal details. It is virtually impossible, therefore, to identify the ethnic units, persons of foreign birth, and those persons who had not been admitted to citizenship in the colonies of their residence prior to the war. Evidence gleaned from other sources may aid in positively identifying a record on file as that of a particular person, but lacking such outside proof, no conclusions can be made about a given record on file.

The records which have been compiled relate only to those persons who rendered actual military service. Support services were performed by civilians as chaplains, medical personnel, quartermasters, paymasters, attorneys, and so forth. A separate record series (manuscript file) identifies many such persons by name only, with a reference to the service performed. Their records are contained in books and on numbered documents which, like the military service records, can be located through a consolidated name index. In addition, military service records also can be located through a series of state indexes.

1784–1811, War of 1812, Indian Wars, and Mexican War

Due in part to the small size of the U.S. Army, Navy, and the Marine Corps, additional troops were needed to quell most disturbances and to defend the nation in the two or more international wars which erupted between 1784 and 1860. The many scattered incidents necessitated the use of the local militia to defend the residents, to assist the regular troops, and to provide a general defense to thwart ideas of insurrection.

Between 1784 and 1811 many minor Indian engagements, some major ones, and at least one civilian uprising occurred. Most of the troops called into service were needed for only a few days or weeks at most. The records of their service, while complete, lack personal details. The War of 1812 was the second major war to occur on American soil.

The many troops called into service initially served but a few days, but such units included foreigners of various nations, newly arrived immigrants, un-naturalized citizens, American Indians, and Afro-Americans (free and slave). Except in the case of some Indian and Afro-American units, the ethnic origin of such persons cannot be gleaned from the information in the records. Personal details are found on but a few documents, primarily those of officers, and in such instances they pertain only to the officer's residence and family.

While the general discharge of the War of 1812 servicemen who had served in the permanent and volunteer units occurred in 1815, a need for militia to supplement the regular forces and handle activities in areas in which such troops were not stationed continued over the ensuing years. As evidenced in the Indian wars records (1816–60) and the Mexican War records, many were called to render such service. In a few instances, the same people served in two or more incidents.

Records relating to service between 1816 and 1860, as those of the preceding period, reflect no general personal information, thus obscuring the identity of many persons and many ethnic-group-oriented units. Again, however, local and state sources may be of assistance in obtaining such information. In this period the forces were involved in many important historical events, which in a few instances employed Indians against Indians and Americans against Americans. Except in the Mexican War, most military actions were directed against the Indians in their removal to the West.

General indexes aid in the identification of the records contained in the separate post-Revolutionary War series (1784–1811), the War of 1812 (1812–15) series, the Indian wars (1816–60) series, and the Mexican War (1846–48) series. In addition, separate state indexes are available for all but the Mexican War series.

Civil War (Union)

Primarily through the use of volunteers from many nations, the Union Army was able to maintain its needed strength. A draft was also used during this unpopular war, to maintain uniform strength in the Union state and territorial militias. Many of the units were identified by their ethnic names or by the names by which they had been known prior to formal induction into the Union Army. Many reverted to those names when the war ended, and such troops were remanded to state militia duty. Because there were many ethnic units, it is believed that persons of the same ethnic groups overseas may have emigrated to serve in them. Noted ethnic groups with units in the army included the Canadians, American Indians, Irish, Norwegians, Polish, Scotch, Swiss, Swedish, Italians, Afro-Americans, Spanish, Turkish, and others of native or foreign birth, local or foreign residence, and in some instances former members of the opposing forces.

Ethnicity was as important a factor in raising a unit as was pride in local residence; however, under the draft laws only native-born and naturalized citizens and Afro-Americans were required to serve. Unnaturalized aliens, immigrants for the war, often served as substitutes for those subject to the draft. Some such persons may have served more than one enlistment in the same or in different units.

The records of military participation in the Union Army reflect an increase over earlier military records in service data and some personal data as well. For most persons, the name, age, place of birth, residence, and occupation are included in the record, on abstracts, or on personal documents such as enlistment papers. Additional family details may be included for persons hospitalized or killed. Though local pride and ethnicity may have furnished the inspiration to join a particular unit, many served in other units by choice, by draft, or because of consolidation of nearly depleted units in battle. It is possible to identify ethnic-group-oriented and name units from a variety of sources, including in some cases the military service records. Due to the lack of a general all-name index, researching such records can be difficult without knowledge of the unit of service or the state or territory of residence at enlistment. Separate state and several miscellaneous indexes serve to locate the many Union Army individual service records.

Spanish-American War and Philippine Insurrection

Volunteers were again required to serve in the two wars which occurred at the turn of the century. The Spanish-American War (1898–99) included units which were identified by their state or territorial names, some of which may have been basically of one ethnic group, such as the "Colored" regiments, and the Puerto Rican regiments. Such service was limited, however, and may not have included actual combat. In the Philippine Insurrection (1899–1901), service was rendered by volunteers in general regiments, though some such units were composed of persons from one residential area or one ethnic group, such as the "colored" units.

In each of the two separate records series, the records reflect the total service rendered by those actually enlisted or commissioned. Support services to many units were rendered by civilians in uniform serving with the troops. Each serviceman's record also included one or more personal documents and the name, age, place of residence, occupation at enlistment, and name and address of a person to be notified in case of an emergency. Separate indexes to each of the series include both a general name index and separate state indexes (Spanish-American War) or unit indexes (Philippine Insurrection). Evidence of civilian support service is sometimes shown in supplemental records and on the official muster rolls of the units. Unlike the records of the regularly enlisted and commissioned personnel, civilian support service records were uncompiled.

U.S. Army

Though established in 1789, in peacetime the U.S. Army was seldom of sufficient strength and in the correct locality when a disturbance occurred. The size of such units was increased in time of war, however, and later reduced when the war was terminated. Unlike some of the volunteer units, until the Civil War the U.S. Army was racially and ethnically mixed. Service in the army was by contract or commission. Enlisted personnel generally were required to serve at least three years or until the end of the war. Officers were allowed to serve only as long as they desired. The records of officers and enlisted personnel were separate; however, some evidence of officers' service is found in the pre-1821 enlistment registers.

Enlisted service is generally reflected in a series of enlistment registers (1798–1814); from 1818 are also generally found enlistment papers; from 1812, medical records; and from 1815, courts-martial records. The two-page enlistment register entry serves as the basic record of enlisted service. It includes the soldier's name, age at enlistment, place of birth, place or residence at enlistment, term of enlistment, physical description, and name and place of enlistment, together with the name of the recruiting officer. The second page of the register identifies the units in which the man served during that enlistment, pertinent misconduct if a court-martial decreed imprisonment, and information about the date, place, and reason for separation. In 1884 the recruit indicated for the medical examination record a full date of birth and pertinent information about deceased parents, brothers, and sisters. In some instances such records name the individual family members. Also provided was the name of the recruit's last employer prior to enlistment. In 1894 the name and relationship of a person to be notified in case of an emergency was added.

Enlistment registers, enlistment papers, and medical records are arranged in separate series, and the series are arranged by chronological periods and thereunder by name or military unit designation. Additional details about a given serviceman are found in the records of his unit. Such records include muster rolls, orders, payrolls, and various unit-maintained correspondence and/or historical records.

Except as noted above for the pre-1822 period, and especially for the pre-1863 period, officers' records are not consolidated; rather, evidence of such service is contained in general routine office records. Published directories, biographies, registers, and other works aid in identifying the basic service information. For the pre-1863 period, unless later consolidated, evidence of actual service must be gleaned from an examination of the basic correspondence records arranged chronologically by year. Beginning in 1863, consolidation of many records relating to officers' service was made if needed. Since 1890 general consolidation of records has been made. Since 1916 individual personnel folders have been maintained.

For the earlier period, unless an officer attended the U.S. Military Academy, the basic information always to be found includes a commission, perhaps an application for a commission, a letter of acceptance of a commission, and an oath of office. Additional records generally found in consolidated officers' files are orders, reports, leave records, and a tender of resignation or notice of death. Personal information of various kinds is often included in correspondence from family members after separation. From the basic record the officer's full name, age, residence, marital status, and education at initial entry can be found on the letter of acceptance of an appointment. Other facts also may be included in the records of officers who served for many years.

The great variety of records, their various methods of indexing, and the numerous supplemental sources which can supply additional details about an officer can require many hours of search and research. Such is reflected in the records of the War Department offices and bureaus, unit records, and records of superior army commands. In a few instances consolidated officers' historical files exist. Also available are records relating to service at the U.S. Military Academy, Civil War generals' reports of their wartime service, medical records, courts-martial records, and prisoner-of-war records. If an officer rendered service in a volunteer unit, such records would also need to be consulted.

While the records mentioned may include birth and residence information, which may indicate foreign ethnic origin or Afro-American descent, it is generally known that during the formative years of the nation and during major war periods many persons who previously had been members of foreign military units received direct commissions into the U.S. Army, primarily for a war, returning to their native lands after the war. Basic birth and residence data alone will generally serve as a clue to ethnicity. In a few instances general recruitment may have resulted in the enlistment of a large number of persons from a single ethnic group into a single regular army unit.

U.S. Navy and U.S. Marine Corps

The naval and marine permanent services were created in 1798, and in keeping with the U.S. Army tradition, separate records of officers and enlisted personnel were maintained. Also as with the U.S. Army, published works similar to those mentioned are the best sources for basic service data about an officer. Official records of the services of both officers and enlisted personnel for the pre-Civil War period are not arranged for easy access. For both, evidence of naval and marine service would be determined best from benefit records, which provide dates, places, and the names of ships and stations to which the men were assigned. Also unlike the U.S. Army, the two services may have maintained separate or mixed records of volunteers when such personnel were included in regular unit complements.

Officers' records are found in a variety of sources, some of which are arranged by the ranks held at various times and others in chronological, subject, and name files, with consolidated files available for only the latter half of the nineteenth century and later. Because rank and/or assignment played an important part in the kinds and numbers of records created, fewer records were created for officers in subordinate positions. In some instances officers' records can be located through consolidated name indexes.

The personal information found in officers' records varies but consists of information gleaned at entrance. Upon acceptance of a commission, an oath of office was taken and a letter of acceptance of the appointment was received. Other records are applications for appointments and termination records. Age, residence at time of acceptance of the appointment, marital status, place of birth, education, and occupation at entrance are normally included in such records. Additional information may be found for graduates of the U.S. Naval Academy and for officers who may also have served in the U.S. Army or in volunteer army units. Ships' records, reports, orders, medical records, prisoner-of-war records, and various office and bureau records may supplement the information found in basic separate officer records series.

Records and information about marine officers are in both naval records and separate corps records. In many instances the corps records include separate officer files. Sometimes access to them is gained through correspondence series, which are arranged alphabetically or chronologically with and without indexes. A few officer histories also are available in corps records.

Naval enlisted records consist of a series of enlistment registers and documents. Many services can be confirmed through correspondence series, and in a few instances separate records were maintained for retired and career personnel. Age restrictions applicable to U.S. Army and U.S. Marine enlistments were inapplicable to naval personnel, some of which may have been as young as eight years of age. As volunteers were included in the regular ranks and ships' complements during war, in a few instances separate volunteer records were created.

For most enlisted personnel, name, age, places of birth and residence, occupation at enlistment, physical description, and marital status are noted in enlistment records. Medical records, courts-martial records, continuous service records, ship and station records, and other documents may provide additional details about a particular enlisted man.

The corps also maintained separate records of its enlisted personnel, though information about such persons is included in naval ship and station records. Many enlisted personnel records of the corps can be located through chronologically arranged name indexes.

Due to the advantages of earlier entitlement to citizenship, and due to training received in a foreign military entity, many newly arrived immigrants and many foreigners rendered service upon arrival, during wartime and otherwise, in a permanent military service unit. Because most records of this type include information about place of birth, ethnic origin can be established. Further, due to the inclusion of race and religion in twentieth-century records, ethnicity can be more easily established. While naval and marine corps units and ships' complements were often racially mixed, it is possible that a large number of people in a given ship's complement or marine unit were from one ethnic group. Racial segregation in naval and marine units began with the Civil War and remained until the end of World War II.

Records reflecting the military services for different chronological periods in the U.S. Army, U.S. Navy, U.S. Marine Corps, and the later U.S. Air Force are in the National Archives Building and the National Personnel Records Center,

St. Louis. Various National Archives publications identify the chronological breaks, while the records are in St. Louis. It should be noted that the basic twentieth-century records relating to service of officers and enlisted men in the U.S. Army and Air Force for the period 1917–56 were destroyed in a fire which in 1972 consumed the sixth floor of the St. Louis facility. Records created by the military units, headquarters commands, support services, and so forth were located on another floor, and records of naval and marine corps personnel escaped that fire. Further, restrictions imposed under the Freedom of Information Act and the Privacy Act limit access to some records.

U.S. Coast Guard and Merchant Marine

Like the U.S. Merchant Marine today, until 1913 the U.S. Coast Guard was basically a civilian service which had commissioned officers at its head. Records relating to persons who served in both services vary greatly according to the period of service, and those for the twentieth century duplicate in content the Seamen's Protection Certificates. They also include information about duties and service rendered.

VETERANS BENEFITS RECORDS

For many reasons, descendants of a serviceman may not have the essential information for locating a military service record; that is, the serviceman's rank, company, regiment, date and place of enlistment, or name of ship. The descendants may know that the individual received a benefit as a result of such service. Through the benefit records, complete service information is sometimes available. Further, the benefit records provide (1) family information unavailable in service records, (2) places of birth and residence, dates and places of death, marriage, and other vital events in the life of the veteran or of other family members, and (3) many other essentials not often found easily in local records of the eighteenth and nineteenth centuries. Many veterans applied for one or more of the benefits to which they were entitled, and even if the benefits were denied, evidence of the claims survives. The number and kinds of benefits offered greatly increased from the initial pension and bounty land grants to include domiciliary care, hospitalization, burial and a grave marker, insurance, education, and home loans. While income determined eligibility for a pension, no such provisions generally affected entitlement to other benefits. Further, the various laws enacted to provide pension benefits were not passed until thirty to ninety years after service, thus limiting the number and kinds of persons entitled to receive the benefit.

Pension Application Files

Since 1776 a limited number of veterans and dependents have been entitled to receive pensions. The limitations have been requisite service, reduced income, legal marriage, continued widowhood, duration of the disability incurred in service, status as widow or orphan (for only a five-year period), and entitlement to only one pension, regardless of the number of times served.

The application initiates consideration for the benefit applied for. Automatic processing of pension or other claims began with World War II. Application evidence is in the form of service documents (discharge certificate, commission, or other evidence), statements of persons who knew or thought the applicant to be a veteran, proof of age of the veteran, spouse, children, or other applicants, proof of birth of children, death certificate, evidence of marriage (certificate, license, banns, or church, minister, or judge's record), and any other documents a person feels will enhance the cause. Information about true family size, marriage of children, residences of various family members, religious affiliation, and sometimes political interests may be evident in the documents found in pension claims.

The pension claims series of records of the Veterans Administration, Record Group 15, currently in the National Archives, is for the period 1775–1934 and sometimes later. The records relate primarily to service rendered between 1775 and 1916. The various series are identified as Revolutionary War (1775–83), Old Wars (1784–1860), War of 1812 (1812–15), Indian wars (1816–93), Mexican War (1846–48), and Civil War and Later. While no dates were given for the Civil War and Later Claims Series, the claims primarily relate to Civil War, Spanish-American War, and Philippine Insurrection service and include a few claims based on World War I service. If a veteran applied for pension based on service in more than one war, the records are generally combined, as are claims by more than one member of the same family. Even if a widow had received a claim based on her first husband's service, remarried, lost the pension, and then reapplied for the pension after the death of her second husband, and even though he, too, may have been a veteran, there should be only one pension claim file.

Indexes serve to locate the various claims files, with a separate index for each series, bearing the same title as that of the pension series. Only the Revolutionary War pension index has been published, but an index to the War of 1812 pension series is in process. Closed pension claims files are generally available based on service performed between 1775 and 1866. But as the last Civil War pension act was not passed until 1958 (for the benefit of five living veterans and many widows of both Union and Confederate service), and because many Spanish-American War and later veterans or their heirs received benefits well into this century, many claims cannot be reviewed or they are accessible to only a few immediate heirs under the Freedom of Information Act. If a claim file has been terminated, even under the Freedom of Information Act, the file may be available to researchers. Claims in the National Archives are generally available, but closed claims files still physically in the custody of the Veterans Administration in most instances may be reviewed in the Veterans Administration Regional Office in one's state of residence. That agency has complete indexes and can easily determine the locations of files in their custody and bring them to a regional office for review. In a few instances privacy laws may prevent access to all of the information in later pension claims or other benefits files.

Bounty Land Warrant Application Files

Veterans of wartime service between 1775 and 3 March 1855, or their heirs, were entitled to receive land from the public domain, if such service was deemed in the federal (previously Continental Congress) interest. Grants of from 40 to 160 or more acres were made to veterans of service after 1783. Revolutionary War veterans received land in accordance with the rank held in service. In every instance, length of service was a factor in the total amount of land given. Both the date on which the awards were made and the date and place in which application was made are significant. Most veterans of wartime service in the period mentioned became entitled to such benefits only with passage of the two key bounty land acts of 1850 and 1855, and many veterans or their heirs applied for such benefits after 1855. Few veterans or heirs actually applied for pensions, but a greater number applied for the free land. Significant also is the fact that many persons sold or traded their right to bounty land even before their applications were filed. Because of the ability to assign bounty land rights for cash or other consideration, a relatively small number of veterans or heirs actually used the warrants received entitling them to land.

The lengthy delay in passage of laws giving benefits (bounty land) to Revolutionary War and War of 1812 veterans and their heirs is of great benefit to family history researchers. In most instances single veterans had married, perhaps moved, and either the veteran and/or his wife had died. Bounty land files will therefore in many instances show a residence different from that of the time of service, evidence of marriage, information about the death of the veteran and/or his spouse, and sometimes the names and addresses of children who applied for the bounty land to which their parents had been entitled.

Bounty land warrant application files are unindexed. Those for veterans or heirs who also received pensions based on Revolutionary War and War of 1812 service have been combined with the pension file. The remaining (450,000) files are arranged in two alphabetical series. Though no index exists, the files are located by the veteran's name, military or naval unit designation, and period of service. The military or naval designation can be obtained from service records. Bounty land warrant application files generally consist of about five pages of documentation. For the reasons stated, they are often the only evidence of postservice information about the veteran and/or his heirs.

Bounty land warrant application files reflect only the effort to obtain bounty land. If a warrant was issued, evidence of the use of the warrant will be found in bounty land warrant records of the General Land Office rather than in the application file. The bounty land warrant files are among the records on file in the General Archives Division of the National Archives and Records Service, which is located in the Washington, D.C., National Records Center. Such records are located through the identification given the file at its creation.

Domiciliary Care and Hospitalization

Residence in a home or treatment in a veterans' hospital were benefits initially given Civil War veterans under an Act of 1863 and later extended to earlier veterans and to most veterans of later service. The National Homes for Disabled Volunteer Soldiers have been renamed in this century Veterans Administration Homes and Hospitals. Located throughout the United States, the homes provide residence and/or treatment to honorably discharged servicemen. Unlike the two previously mentioned benefits, home records series provide little significant postservice information. The case files created while the veterans were residents of the homes have been destroyed, but a record exists which provides some pertinent service and heir information.

The earlier home records located in the National Archives consist of registers of admissions and in rare instances registers of death. The admission register entry for a given veteran generally provides his name, age, military unit designation, date(s) of admission and discharge(s), some information about disabilities (if any), the pension claim number, and the name(s) and address(es) of next of kin. If the veteran was buried in the home cemetery, the plot designation is given. If the veteran's remains were claimed by the family, the name of the consignee and date and place of shipment are entered. Prior knowledge of residence or treatment in a home or hospital generally is the prerequisite to locating a home record, but such information is also found in pension claims files.

The federal government also maintained homes for retired personnel, and many state governments maintained veterans' homes. Therefore a veteran of federal service may have taken residence in either a state or a federal home. State homes and many later federal home records remain with the homes. Freedom of Information and privacy regulations may restrict access to home records. The names and locations of veterans homes are found in many publications.

Other Veterans Benefits

As previously mentioned, many benefits were derived from federal military service, and only the larger, more important series have been singled out for a separate discussion. Records relating to insurance claims; burial in a national, post, or private cemetery; issuance of a headstone or marker; issuance of an artificial appliance; and benefits derived under twentieth-century laws, such as home loans and educational benefits, can also be significant sources of pertinent family information. Such files, however, are limited in providing additional ethnic information, and the time and effort of locating records such as those pertaining to the issuance of a headstone or marker for a veteran's grave may not be worthwhile. The latter records are scattered, variously arranged, and often unindexed. Most other benefit records can be located through indexes in the custody of the regional Veterans Administration office in one's state of residence. Further, as information about Civil War and later military service was often deliberately recorded in the courthouse of residence at the time of discharge, and because many states also gave benefits to their veterans and to veterans of Confederate states' government service, pertinent information may be contained in state and county records.

CIVILIAN PERSONNEL RECORDS

Civilian personnel records are a significant source of pertinent ethnic and sometimes other information. Until the passage of laws restricting employment in the federal government to native-born and naturalized citizens, jobs were made available to anyone who qualified. Also, prior to the passage of the Civil Service laws, employment may have hinged on political affiliation and personal contacts within the government. Fraternalism, political considerations, and nepotism were rampant. This is sometimes evident in the applications, and the files which would significantly reflect appointments for political reasons (postmaster appointments) have been deliberately destroyed, and only a record of each person's appointment remains.

The more significant personnel records relate to workers who served in administrative and clerical positions in headquarters and field offices. Least valuable are the records relating to persons employed on a contractual basis. Records relating to persons employed for the duration of an administration or other temporary appointments, as well as for permanent employees, are now in the National Personnel Records Center, 111 Winnebago Street, St. Louis, MO 63118. Applications by the many unsuccessful and few successful candidates remain in the administrative records of the offices or bureaus to which they applied. Though many persons sought appointments through their elected representatives, relatively few application files or other evidence of such contact remain with the general legislative records. Records of testimony and other information gathered by the U.S. Senate in the act of approving appointments to cabinet and other positions requiring Senate approval remain with the Senate records. Corresponding, supplemental, or duplicate information may also be found in the U.S. Department of State records, since that agency handled such matters for the executive agencies and for the White House. An illustration of the value of such records as a source of ethnic data is given in my paper relating to federal appointment records contained in *Afro-American History: Sources for Research*.[6]

Generally no uniformity is to be found in personnel records from before World War I. During this period written documents were the rule, and thus uniformity, consistency, completeness, and accuracy varied greatly. On the other hand, from World War I onward, forms were used for most purposes from applications to terminations, and information was more uniform. Personnel files of some sort have been in existence since 1880. Records frequently contain a complete biographical description of the applicant, the name and title of the position sought, evidence of political and military service, previous federal employment information, and endorsements by as many political or other influential persons as could be obtained. Full vital statistics, family information, residences, education, promotions, demotions, awards, honors, and other basic vital information can generally be found in twentieth-century employment records. Records reflecting lengthy post-1880 service generally are large files, while records of persons employed in an earlier period may just contain vague references to all or part of their service. Persons employed in regional facilities often were replaced by loyal members of the political party most recently elected, in some instances regaining their old positions when their party returned to office. Every device was used to retain or obtain federal jobs. Thus post-Civil War applications for employment often include detailed accounts of Union Army service and references to membership in Union veterans or political organizations. For this reason, and in instances when a particular candidate may either have been unsuccessful in obtaining the position desired or lost a position in a change of administration, the applicant would file for another position or reapply for the same position when it was vacated. Also, because many rural post offices were located in business establishments, postmaster positions were avidly sought because they would generate a certain amount of continuous business from the community served.

Separate personnel records were maintained by each agency and often by each of its offices and bureaus. Records relating to terminated employees were often gathered into a single series, but the records of one agency were not intermingled with similar records of other agencies unless the agency was redesignated or combined and the employee continued to be employed by the successor agency. Personnel records now in the custody of the National Personnel Records Center are arranged by agency of employment, thereunder by type of position held and/or in a single or several (chronological) series. In some instances cabinet officer records may be with the records of the presidential administration in a government or private depository. Indexes or finding aids of various types are also available in some instances. Freedom of Information regulations apply to records relating to persons whose service terminated in the seventy-five years previous to the time they are sought by the researcher.

Essential to the location of a personnel record is full information about the type of service, agency of employment, dates of entrance and separation, and actual job title. Such information is contained in various published registers of clerical, administrative, postal, and some contractual employees. The general series of registers is called the Register of U.S. Government Employees, 1815–1933, though such registers had many additional titles. Congressional reports, newspapers, and many other publications are also sources of that information. In addition, many agencies maintained lists of employees or periodically compiled them for various purposes.

SPECIAL SERIES OF FEDERAL RECORDS OF ETHNIC
FAMILY HISTORY VALUE

As noted appropriately in the foregoing, many records have value as sources of general ethnic information. In addition, when a government seeks to control a person, group, or whole race, its only means of effective control beyond imprisonment or imposition of martial law is through records. This is significant as it relates to some of the ethnic groups in the United States or its territories. Occasionally, as in instances when the government has sought to aid a given group, special records series have been created or special records made which reflect such actions taken. Such records are created as a byproduct rather than from a deliberate effort; nevertheless, several important records series have resulted, and such records are invaluable to ethnic family history studies. The most voluminous of such series are records relating to Afro-Americans, American Indians, and several immigrant groups. Of immigrant groups of European origin, little may exist except the actual records of arrival. On the other hand, U.S. Department of State records of its diplomatic and consular posts in a foreign country can be invaluable to the study of a person or family who also had U.S. connections through an immigrant or serviceman. Other significant series relate to treaties between the United States and a foreign power, but the value of a treaty series is directly dependent upon the date, nature, and purpose of the treaty, thus somewhat limiting that series.

Afro-Americans

Nearly all of the previously mentioned records series are important to Afro-American families, but in a few instances separate record groups or series are invaluable because of their informational content. The most desired information is not to be found in any significant amount in federal records but in records which identify by name and place of residence Africans who were imported as slaves into the Western Hemisphere. Further, the records of the pre-1870 period seldom contain information about Africans who came to the United States as free immigrants or as bonded servants. Records such as those of the Freedmen's Bureau, the Freedmen's Savings and Trust Company, Afro-American military unit records, and intercoastal slave manifests, as collected series, are invaluable.

The intercoastal slave manifests, as mentioned, are few and invaluable. Ship manifests of slave trade ships document only the number of male and female slaves on board. Occasionally, if a ship was confiscated for breach of U.S. law relating to the importation of slaves or for other purposes, the ship or court records may indicate the origin and destination of the vessel. Only in the records of three ports have separate series of intercoastal slave manifests been found. These records identify the slaves by name, age, sex, previous owner, and new owner or person to whom the slave was consigned. The records are arranged by port, date, and name of vessel. The intercoastal slave manifests are among the records of the U.S. Bureau of Customs in the National Archives.

Perhaps the earliest federal record relating to Afro-Americans is in the papers of the Continental Congress. As shown in the two published indexes to those papers which were recently compiled by the National Archives, many references appear therein to Afro-Americans. The most significant series is the lists of persons evacuated from Staten Island, N.Y., by the British during the Revolutionary War. The informational content and value of such records appear in an article by Debra Newman in the *Journal of the Afro-American Historical and Genealogical Society*.[7] Other references in the indexes to the papers may serve to identify Afro-American servicemen or others who aided the American or British cause.

Mention has been made to federal census records and federal military service records as valuable sources of ethnic information. No need exists, therefore, to point out the significant general sources already mentioned, but special related series should be discussed.

CENSUS RECORDS

In addition to the general population census schedules, several small series of census records exist which are important to Afro-American family history. In the slavery period several special censuses were taken by the territorial governments and perhaps by federal executive or military agencies of the Afro-American population, slave and free. To date, few such tabulations or individual lists have been found, but such may be contained in federal agency records and in territorial records, not all of which are deposited in the National Archives. During the Civil War, in some southern states the Union Army took a census of the population of communities recently acquired through battle. Among the records of the U.S. Army Commands, Record Group 393, and in the records of the Bureau of Refugees, Freedmen and Abandoned Lands (Freedmen's Bureau), Record Group 105, are found several references to censuses. Most of these censuses contain the names, ages, and sexes of the residents and also identify them by race. As will be shown in the inventory entries to the two record groups, many censuses have not been located, thus leaving as a possibility the existence of additional censuses in local or state and perhaps private records.

In addition, in the series of records of Civil War Districts (numbered) of Record Group 393 are entries relating to persons who were voters, eligible or not, in the constitutional conventions of states which seceded from the Union. In some few instances several different lists are found, and additional lists are contained in Record Group 105.

CIVIL WAR RECORDS

The two-volume guides to Civil War records compiled by the National Archives, the *Guide to Federal Archives Relating to the Civil War* and the *Guide to the Archives of the Government of the Confederate States of America*, include in their indexes innumerable references to series significant to Afro-Americans, slave and free. The most important series are those of the records of the Freedmen's Bureau and its predecessor agency; the U.S. Department of the Treasury; Civil War Districts; the U.S. Colored Troops; the Civil War draft; the U.S. courts; the U.S. Veterans Administration; and the Freedmen's Savings and Trust Company.

The Freedmen's Bureau, established in 1863 as the Bureau of Refugees, Freedmen, and Abandoned Lands, inherited from the U.S. Treasury the responsibility for attending to freed slaves and other destitute persons. This general welfare responsibility included provision of food, clothing, shelter, and medical care; reuniting of families; employment; establishment of schools; transportation; negotiation of contracts to handle claims or other legal matters; and marrying or divorcing former slave and free couples. Many records were created as a result of the multifaceted responsibilities of the bureau, but only a portion of them are now on file in the National Archives. Many are located in county, state, university, and private archives and other records depositories.

A four-part (one part published, three parts draft unpublished) inventory serves to identify the various series of headquarters and field records of the Freedmen's Bureau. Some missing or incomplete series are contained in Record Group 393 or are supplemented therein. The three-part draft inventory to the field records (if available) includes an appendix to some important series. Entry numbers are shown in this appendix to prebureau military records, prebureau treasury records, marriage records, Freedmen's Savings Bank records, census records, claims records, contracts, court records, and hospital records. The field records are arranged by state, and the names of the field offices and subdistrict field offices are given. No similar appendix is found in the published inventory of headquarters records. The subjects chosen by the author of the inventory are the larger or more important record series; however, unlike headquarters records or those in Record Group 393, no cross-references appear to records which supplement the series mentioned. Nor are there references to supplemental series of claims, pensions, military service, and other records contained in various groups or located outside the National Archives. As an example, the records relating to marriages solemnized and legalized by the bureau in Kentucky are now divided into three distinct and separate groups. One-third of such records are in the National Archives and include references to marriage, divorce, and the licensing or appointment of ministers to marry those wishing to be wed. One-third are contained in the records of the Kentucky State Archives, Frankfort, and the final one-third remain in variously identified series of records scattered in Kentucky county courthouses.

Marriage records contain the names of persons previously united in marriage during slavery and identify the children born to such unions. They also identify those individuals who wished to be united in marriage for the first time and who were legally eligible to be married (that is, people who were single and of legal age, people who became of legal age, and all people whose divorces were performed by the Freedmen's Bureau agent). The divorce records identify couples united in marriage during slavery or shortly thereafter who wished to be legally divorced. There are included, in a few records series, names and background information on ministers licensed by the bureau agents to perform marriages.

Contracts were negotiated by the agents to assure a fair and equal return for the labor of the freedmen in the form of salary or other compensation, housing, and medical care. Transportation to the new place of employment was furnished if necessary. The contracts are invaluable because they reflect the name of the freedman, his wife and children, place of present residence, place of intended employment, and terms of the contract.

Claims records also are invaluable, for in addition to containing pertinent information about the nature of the claim (reimbursement for military salary or bounty not received, destruction of property, wages due from services performed), sometimes they relate to heirs (pension claims), and they often include references to former and current place of residence. As the agents only initiated the claims for the freedmen, the final disposition of the claim would be reflected in the records of the agency to which the claim was sent.

Court records of the Freedmen's Bureau are similar to such records elsewhere and include both civil and criminal actions. Many relate to atrocities committed by or against slaves, yet some deal with matters of nonpayment under contractual agreements or with the usual two-party suits for a variety of other purposes. Notably, such records include references to land disputes, though separate series of land records are also found in other series. The land records relate to leases or rents and to the sale of lands abandoned or acquired under the amnesty terms imposed on former Confederate officials, military and civilian.

Records relating to the care of individuals for health and other reasons are valuable, for they include the name, age, and sex of the individuals treated. Similarly, names and other information are found in records relating to the furnishing of food and housing. By far the most disappointing of all the records created by the bureau are those relating to the establishment of elementary and grammar schools, and later high schools. The records include information about the school and the teachers and their affiliations, but they exclude the names of the students. Various kinds of statistics on students are given.

Due to the great variation in kinds of information, chronological coverage, subject matter coverage, actual content and volume, and general knowledge of the kinds of information which should be available, the Freedmen's Bureau records are seldom complete for any subdistrict. In a few instances where a complete series is lacking, a few scattered documents are found in the miscellaneous series which follow the general series for a given state.

Finally, it should be remembered that in some instances records were left, turned over to, or have found their way into local records collections. In other instances no records were created.

FREEDMEN'S SAVINGS AND TRUST COMPANY RECORDS

The Freedmen's Savings and Trust Company records, though lacking useful indexes, are by far the most important series of records containing ethnic information available for the Civil War period. Many of the records have been destroyed, such as the individual depositors' passbooks, loan records, applications, and others, but that portion which survives is unique in informational content. The basic record extant is a series of depositors' signature books. The entries contained therein include for each depositor all or most of the following information: name; age; sex; marital status; occupation; residence; names of spouse, children, brothers, sisters, parents, current employer, and former slave owner; physical description; remarks; and signature or mark.

The banks were located in one or two principal cities in each southern state, in Washington, D.C., and in New York. The signature books and a series of index volumes have been microfilmed. Correlation between the numerical account numbers given in the index with those of the signature book entries is impossible.

CIVIL WAR DRAFT RECORDS

In accordance with the laws of Congress, during the Civil War all native-born and naturalized male citizens aged eighteen through fifty-five were subject to the draft. In addition, all male residents in the South were subject to conscription in a Confederate military or civilian capacity, age notwithstanding. Until 1863 the Union forces generally rejected the enlistment of Afro-Americans, but many Afro-Americans served in Union Army units nevertheless. Others served as personal servants to Union and Confederate officers without benefit from the respective governments except for food, clothing, and lodging. Afro-Americans also served the Union forces as cooks, nurses, and launderers; in supply forces, mines, and construction; as general laborers; and as skilled technicians. As of July 1863, formal units of Afro-Americans were accepted into the Union Army, and as towns and states were liberated in the South, the new freedmen were made subject to the draft laws.

The largest and most significant series of federal Civil War draft records are the enrollment records. Draft boards in the various communities were responsible for the enrollment of all native and naturalized male citizens who were between eighteen and fifty-five years of age. After examination, and review of an exemption, if applied for, those found physically able to bear arms were inducted into the Union forces (army, navy, or marines). Those who had served a previous enlistment could become eligible for the draft again under another draft call. For each enrollee there is found his full name, age, place of birth and residence, physical description, and remarks. It is in the remarks column that such words as "exempt" or "drafted," and if drafted, the name of the unit to which assigned, the name of the draft rendezvous, and other information appear.

As the draft laws permitted the hiring of a substitute for a drafted person, sometimes the records would identify a substitute and indicate that the requisite $300 fee had been paid. Many of the substitutes were other family members who were not subject to the draft or aliens who had not declared their intention to become citizens. Thus draft records can be a source of information not found in the actual military service records.

Few records have been found relating to persons who registered for service under the Confederate Conscription Acts. Two volumes of Afro-Americans are included in the Confederate records series, but the bulk of the conscription records are not in federal custody.

DISTRICT OF COLUMBIA SLAVE RECORDS

Under acts of 1862 and 1863, slave owners of the District of Columbia, Maryland, and parts of Virginia could be compensated for the loss of their slaves through manumission, because they ran away, or because they were inducted into federal military service. The records of the District of Columbia are unique in that they are contained in a single records series of the U.S. District Court for the District of Columbia and a single records series of the U.S. General Accounting Office. Between the two series it is possible to determine the exact amount of compensation allowed. The most important series, however, are the actual application records in the district court records. Applicants for reimbursement had to identify each slave by name, sex, occupation, talents, and physical description and evaluate the slave's character and work habits. Some of the records and an index to them have been published in the *Journal of the Afro-American Historical and Genealogical Society*.[8]

Similar records are found for other loyal Union states and some for residents of Confederate states who were loyal to the Union cause, but they are scattered among the War and Treasury Department records groups. Further, in a few instances, information relating to claims has been found in the individual service records of persons who served in the U.S. Colored Troops. The *Guide to Federal Archives Relating to the Civil War* contains many entries relating to records of slave claims.

Also included in the microfilm series slave records of the District of Columbia is a series of court records relating to attempts to recover escaped slaves. Similar fugitive slave case files are located in the federal and state court records of other jurisdictions. Many federal court records of the period are in archives branches of the various Federal Records Centers.

CONFEDERATE STATES GOVERNMENT RECORDS

It is generally concluded that Afro-Americans were prevented from service in either integrated or segregated units of the Confederate forces. Such assumptions are incorrect, as records on file reflect service of both Afro-American individuals and wholly Afro-American units in the Confederate States Army. In addition, innumerable slaves and freedmen were employed at civilian installations and military fortifications as servants, laborers, and skilled technicians. The best evidence of such service is often in the records of states that were part of the Confederacy, as in the published *North Carolina Troops, 1861–1865; A Roster*.[9] Entire or nearly entire Afro-American units of the New Orleans Militia were employed in the defense of that city. Records relating to benefits derived from Confederate service, such as pension files, would be a good source of such information. Some formerly Confederate states and other states gave pensions to Confederate veterans.

Under the conscription laws imposed by the Confederate states, many foreigners, recent immigrants, and immigrants who had not become citizens were forced to serve. The many Confederate records include the places of birth of individual servicemen. Such records, therefore, frequently include the places of birth of recent immigrants and foreign visitors.

A separate series of records entitled "Slave Records" relates to compensation paid owners of slaves employed in various capacities by their owners in behalf of the Confederate government. The records list the owner's full name, the given or full name of the slave, and the dates, places, and types of employment rendered. An index serves only to identify the slave owner and not the slaves themselves. Additional army and navy records reflect employment of slaves on military fortifications. Such records series can be identified in the finding aids for the various record groups containing military and naval records of the Confederate forces.

Many additional Civil War records series exist which are inclusive of records and information relating to the service of Afro-Americans, American Indians, and units composed of persons of Italian, German, Irish, Scotch, Welsh, French, and Scandinavian origin. Units of mixed nationalities were also in service for either side. Many records series of importance are not mentioned in this chapter, such as the voluminous correspondence series of both sides, as reflected in records of the government's individual agencies, bureaus, and offices. Many correspondence series are also located in the records series mentioned, which may be invaluable to the history of given individuals. The identification and location of available aids to the records are important to the determination of the pertinent records series. Therefore, in addition to the use of the published and manuscript finding aids available, advice from knowledgeable archivists is invaluable in the general and specific use of Civil War and related records.

American Indian Records

Except for the actual measurement of major series of American Indian records, the total footage of such records is unknown, and accurate account cannot be given for them. Most of the important records are among those of the Bureau of Indian Affairs, but as indicated, many separate series of military records, veterans benefits records, claims records, censuses, and others are also found in other record groups. The initial responsibility for Indian affairs was inherited from the State and War departments by the Interior Department in 1848. Both the State Department and War Department records groups include many additional records series. Further, due to the number of such tribes and bands and their checkered history with the U.S. government, the identity of many records series is directly dependent on the nature of the tribe's involvement with the federal government.

The principal source of information about many of the more important series of records is the previously cited work, *Guide to Records in the National Archives Relating to American Indians,* compiled by Edwin Hill. A more detailed account of Cherokee Indian records useful for genealogical purposes is in preparation, but the publication data are currently uncertain.

CENSUS RECORDS

Separate censuses of American Indians, or separate schedules of them, have been made for various purposes at various times. Since 1870 American Indians have been included in the federal decennial population schedules as members of the general population (1870) or in a separate population count (1880 and later). Periodically since 1880 the Bureau of Indian Affairs has taken a census of the Indians by tribe, and the schedules dated 1880 to 1940 are currently available for examination. Due to the variety and kinds of data gathered in the individual censuses, a full discussion of their contents census by census will not be given. Their general content includes name, age, sex, residence, occupation, tribal affiliation (sometimes), and similar information for spouses and children.

It should be noted that many quasi-censuses also exist in the form of enrollments; lists of members of tribes signing treaties; lists compiled for various purposes, such as the departure and arrival rolls of Indians removed from the East Coast to reservations in the Far West. Innumerable lists or censuses, rather than a single enumeration, have been the general rule due to the scattering of various bands of members of the same tribes. In a few cases the basic identities of the tribe are by place of residence rather than by name. By far the greater problem is the identity of records of nonrecognized tribes or tribes under state rather than federal control. Further, the records relating to a given tribe may not be found in a depository in the immediate vicinity of the tribe's current or previous location. Finally, many records have seemingly disappeared, such as those relating to the churches which for many years administered schools on Indian reservations.

TREATY RECORDS SERIES AND RELATED RECORDS

Two separate series of ratified and unratified Indian treaties are contained in the records of the U.S. Department of State. As each treaty specifies the terms of the treaty, whether or not they were ratified, each is unique because they contain the names of tribal members who ascribed to the treaty as principals or as adult male members of the tribe. Many related documents are filed with the treaties, and many additional records are in Bureau of Indian Affairs, Department of Interior, War Department, and Treasury Department records. If other federal employees were involved, their records or the records of the agencies they represented are also sources of related records. The two treaty series are indexed, thus establishing the location of the treaties by date and place if not by name. Many publications also assist in this matter.

CLAIMS

Many series of Indian-related claims exist, including claims for damages resulting from Indian depredations. Only claims by and for American Indians will herein be discussed. As a result of treaty negotiations, military service, and special court awards such as the many restitution claims now being allowed for land taken from the Indians, general, collective, and individual claims case files exist. Many claims developed from special congressional acts and resulted in large series being created, such as the Cherokee claims (established after the Dawes Act of 1887, which paved the way for the citizenship of American Indians). The claims are dated at the turn of the twentieth century, and identification of specific claims series is often possible through tribal records on file and through many different federal publications. Claims for reimbursement resulting from military service are in War Department and Veterans Administration records and sometimes in Treasury agencies records or the records of the General Accounting Office.

Since many of the claims were for general settlement and were not paid for many years, it is possible that the records may include information about descendants rather than only the person originally entitled. Thus proof of relationship and other family information would be contained in the records, together with normal documentation showing the right to entitlement to the benefit requested.

Indexes to claims are in various forms in the records of the agencies handling the claims or of the agencies or agents who initiated the claims.

MILITARY SERVICE AND RELATED RECORDS

American Indians have served the United States in all of its major foreign wars. In addition, in instances where Indians were fighting other citizens, the army was aided by Indians, members of loyal bands or tribes. In the Revolutionary War, Maine Indians comprised a whole company; in other instances service was rendered in smaller groups and by individuals. During the War of 1812, whole companies and regiments of Indians served; in the Civil War there were companies and regiments of Indians on both sides. Evidence of Indian military service may also be found in the records for other wars.

Benefits for federal military service were also awarded to American Indian servicemen. Due to the fact that pension claims are contained in the general pension series previously mentioned, to identify and locate a given claims file, it is necessary to know the serviceman's name, military unit, and period of service. A separate series of several thousand bounty land warrant application files, alphabetically arranged, is included in Veterans Administration records. As seen in locating military records, in addition to knowing the Indian's tribal name, frequently it is also necessary to know the Anglicized name. Indian names were spelled phonetically; therefore, even when the correct name is known, locating the person's record is dependent upon translating that name into the phonetical spelling used by the person who prepared the record.

Indian veterans also availed themselves of other veterans' benefits, such as hospitalization, domiciliary care, insurance, loans, and education. Such records are located in the same manner as non-Indian veterans' records.

Many records relating to American Indians are not in the National Archives but are located in the regional archives branch that serves the area in which the reservation is or was located. Records of the Five Civilized Tribes are housed chiefly at the Fort Worth Branch Archives and in the records of the Bureau of Indian Affairs at Telequah, Oklahoma. Additional records are housed in historical societies (one in Oklahoma also serves as a National Archives depository), in college and university archives, and in the archives of most states. Those for Alaskan Indians which were formerly on deposit at the Seattle Archives Branch are now in the State Archives of Alaska.

American Trust Territories and Puerto Rico

Records of the federal agencies relating to trust territories, Hawaii, Puerto Rico, and Philippine Islands, and other former possessions are variously located. Most remain in the territories or are among the territorial records of the departments of Interior and State. In some instances, records which were federal archives or which were due to become federal archives are now in the countries to which they relate. Alaskan and Puerto Rican records have been transferred to the respective state or commonwealth archives. Records relating to the Philippines were returned to that country after its independence.

The Puerto Rican records and those of places such as the Dominican Republic and Alaska may have been dated as early as the seventeenth century. Some records present language difficulties; those of the Dominican Republic are frequently in Danish; those of Alaska, in French; those of Guam, in Spanish, Latin, Togalo, or the Guamanian dialects; and the World War II records, in German, Italian, and other languages. While the series on file in their places of origin or in this country lack many of the valuable records, numerous related series of records are located in federal agencies. In particular where the services functioned as military government authorities, military and naval records often include valuable and vital statistics about individuals, families, and places. Guam and the Marianas had a naval government from their acquisition until 1958; therefore many series of naval records include information about that territory.

Other Ethnic Groups

In some instances specific series of records are particularly valuable to family history studies of given ethnic groups, such as the Chinese, Japanese, Latin Americans, Alaskans, and Danes who inhabited Greenland. The location and identification of specific records series are directly dependent upon knowing the date, place, and reason for the creation of a federal record. Chinese were imported to work on the railroad. They therefore are listed in the censuses of 1850 and later. Notable are the Chinese found in the census of Alaska in 1900. Because a special schedule was used for Alaska, it is possible to learn the individual's name, age, place of birth, residence, occupation, date immigrated, date arrived in Alaska, and whether a naturalized citizen.

Japanese also immigrated to the United States in search of employment. Many had settled in Hawaii or were natives thereof before the general U.S. migration began. As a result of the attack on Pearl Harbor in 1941, sanctions were imposed on persons of Japanese ancestry located in the continental U.S. Western states, but in most instances not on those residing elsewhere in the United States. Internment camps were established in three localities to house such persons, many of whom later were disenfranchised or voluntarily gave up the U.S. citizenship they had inherited as a birthright. Meticulous records were compiled on the internees and on many others of Japanese descent located in the United States and its territories. Most individual case files and other records containing vital statistics remain restricted under the Freedom of Information Act.

Records relating to U.S. relationships with Latin America and other places may include information about families and individuals of those countries. Principally such records relate to general diplomatic functions, but they often include copies of newspapers, some military records, correspondence, and perhaps official records of that country obtained in military or other activities. The *Guide to Materials on Latin America in the National Archives of the United States*, the *Guide to Records in the National Archives Relating to Africa*,[10] and the inventories, microfilm pamphlets, and other publications which describe the various series of diplomatic post records and related series, identify the kinds of information which such records contain for the various countries. (See bibliography.)

SUMMARY

The records in the National Archives pertinent to the study of ethnic family history as discussed here are voluminous, sometimes inaccessible, and otherwise difficult to locate and use, given their limitations or language barriers. In any research, the more information known at the outset of the research project, the better the chances of locating pertinent information about the person or subject being researched. This is certainly true in unearthing information in federal archives. Because such archives are widely scattered and not always indexed, many hours may be needed to exhaust the resource possibilities thoroughly. A comprehensive review of the available printed sources in libraries and collections of government publications, and communication with the archivists in the National Archives and Regional Archives Branches, will enable the researcher to avoid needless trips and fruitless time wasting. Yet the federal archives remain without peer America's largest depository of ethnic family information relating to persons or families residing in this country, or whose homeland was under U.S. protection at one time or another.

NOTES

1. *Guide to the National Archives of the United States* (Washington, D.C.: National Archives and Records Service, 1974).

2. *Guide to Genealogical Records in the National Archives*, compiled by Meredith Bright Colket and Frank T. Bridges (Washington, D.C.: National Archives, 1964). An updated edition of this work was published recently under the title *Guide to Genealogical Research in the National Archives*.

3. *Guide to Records in the National Archives Relating to the American Indian*, compiled by

Edward E. Hill (Washington, D.C.: National Archives, 1982); *Guide to Federal Archives Relating to the Civil War,* compiled by Kenneth W. Munden and Henry P. Beers (Washington, D.C.: National Archives, 1962); *Guide to the Archives of the Government of the Confederate States of America,* compiled by Henry P. Beers (Washington, D.C.: National Archives, 1968). Guides to records of Afro-Americans and Cherokee Indians are forthcoming.

4. Charlotte A. Volkel, Lowell M. Volkel, and Timothy Q. Wilson, comps., *An Index to the 1800 Federal Census of Carolyn, Cecil, Charles, Frederick and Kent Counties, State of Maryland* (Danville, Ill.: 1968).

5. U.S., Census Office, 6th Census, 1840, *A Census of Pensioners for Revolutionary or Military Services, 1840* (Washington, D.C.: Printed by Blair, Rives, 1841; reprint ed., Baltimore: Genealogical Publishing Co., 1967); Genealogical Society of Jesus Christ of Latter-day Saints, *A General Index to a Census of Pensioners for Revolutionary or Military Service, 1840* (Salt Lake City, Utah: 1965).

6. *Afro-American History: Sources for Research,* edited by Robert K. Clarke (Washington, D.C.: Howard University Press, 1981).

7. Debra L. Newman, "An Inspection Roll of Negroes Taken on Board Sundry Vessels at Staten Island Bound for Nova Scotia, 1783," *Journal of the Afro-American Historical and Genealogical Society* 1, no. 2 (1980), pp. 80–84.

8. James D. Walker, "District of Columbia Slave Records," *Journal of the Afro-American Historical and Genealogical Society* 1, no. 2 (1980): 80–84.

9. Louis H. Manarin, *North Carolina Troops, 1861–1865; A Roster,* 8 vols. in progress (Raleigh, N.C.: State Department of Archives, 1966–   ).

10. *Guide to Materials on Latin America in the National Archives of the United States,* compiled by George S. Ulibarri and John P. Harrison (Washington, D.C.: National Archives, 1974); Aloah B. South, *Guide to Records in the National Archives Relating to Africa* (Waltham, Mass.: Crossroads Press, 1977).

BIBLIOGRAPHY

National Archives Publications

GUIDES

Guide to Cartographic Records in the National Archives, 1971.

Guide to Federal Archives Records Relating to the Civil War, compiled by Kenneth W. Munden and Henry P. Beers, 1962.

Guide to Genealogical Records in the National Archives, compiled by Meredith Bright Colket and Frank T. Bridgers, 1964. (An expanded edition is now available.)

Guide to Materials on Latin America in the National Archives of the United States, compiled by George S. Ulibarri and John P. Harrison, 1974.

Guide to Records in the National Archives Relating to the American Indian, compiled by Edward E. Hill, 1982.

Guide to the Archives of the Government of the Confederate States of America, compiled by Henry P. Beers, 1968.

Guide to the National Archives of the United States, 1974.

INDEXES

Index: Journals of the Continental Congress, 1774–1789, compiled by Kenneth E. Harris and Steven D. Tilley, 1976.

Index to the Papers of the Continental Congress, 5 vols., 1976.

OTHERS

List of Record Groups of the National Archives and Records Service, 1981.

The Territorial Papers of the United States, 28 vols., Microcopy 721, 15 rolls.

REFERENCE INFORMATION PAPERS

No. 50. *The Census of Manufacturers, 1810–1890*, 1973.

No. 61. *Vital Statistics in the National Archives Relating to the American Indian*, 1973.

No. 63. *Data Relating to Negro Military Personnel in the Nineteenth Century*, 1973.

No. 64. *Nineteenth-Century Puerto Rican Immigration and Slave Data*, 1973.

No. 67. *Federal Census Schedules, 1850–80: Primary Sources for Historical Research*, 1973.

No. 68. *Cartographic Records in the National Archives of the United States Useful for Urban Studies*, 1973.

No. 69. *The Southeast During the Civil War; Selected War Department Records in the National Archives of the United States*, 1973.

PRELIMINARY INVENTORIES

No. 1. *War Industries Board Records*, 1941 (Record Groups 61 and 113).

No. 2. *Council of National Defense Records, 1916–21*, 1942 (Record Group 62).

No. 3. *Records of the United States Food Administration, 1917–20*, part 1: *The Headquarters Organization*, 1943 (Record Group 4).

No. 4. *War Labor Policies Board Records*, 1943 (Record Group 1).

No. 5. *Records of the National War Labor Board*, 1943 (Record Group 2).

No. 6. *Records of the Bureau of Medicine and Surgery*, 1948 (Record Group 52).

No. 7. *Records of the Federal Trade Commission*, 1948 (Record Group 122).

No. 8. *Records of the Chemical Warfare Service*, 1948 (Record Group 175).

No. 9. *Records of the Office of the Paymaster General*, 1948 (Record Group 99).

No. 10. *Records of the Bureau of Yards and Docks*, 1948 (Record Group 71).

No. 11. *Records of the Civilian Conservation Corps*, 1948, revised 1980 (Record Group 35).

No. 12. *Records of the Senate Committee on Appropriations: Subcommittee on Inquiry in Re Transfer of Employees*, 1942 (Record Group 46).

No. 13. *Records of Naval Establishments Created Overseas During World War II*, 1948 (Record Group 181).

No. 14. *Records of the United States Direct Tax Commission for the District of South Carolina*, 1948 (Record Group 58).

No. 15. *Records of the War Production Board*, 1948 (Record Group 179).

No. 16. *Records of the United States Secret Service*, 1949 (Record Group 87).

No. 17. *Records of the Adjutant General's Office*, 1949 (Record Group 94).

No. 18. *Records of the Forest Service*, revised 1969 (Record Group 95).

No. 19. *Records of the Board of Investigation and Research—Transportation*. 1949 (Record Group 198).

No. 20. *Records of the Maritime Labor Board*, 1949 (Record Group 157).

No. 21. *Records of the United States Council for the Prosecution of Axis Criminality*, 1949 (Record Group 238).

No. 22. *Land-Entry Papers of the General Land Office*, 1949 (Record Group 49).

No. 23. *Records of the United States Senate*, 1950 (Record Group 46).

No. 24. *Records of the United States War Ballot Commission*, 1951 (Record Group 230).

No. 25. *Records of the Office of War Mobilization and Reconversion*, 1951 (Record Group 250).

No. 26. *Records of the Bureau of Aeronautics*, 1951 (Record Group 72).

No. 27. *Records of the Selective Service System, 1940–1947*, 1951 (Record Group 147).

No. 28. *Records of the Retraining and Reemployment Administration*, 1951 (Record Group 244).

No. 29. *Records of the Foreign Economic Administration*, 1951 (Record Group 169).

No. 30. *Records of the War Shipping Administration*, 1951 (Record Group 248).

No. 31. *Records of the Petroleum Administration for War*, 1951 (Record Group 253).

No. 32. *Records of the Accounting Department of the Office of Price Administration*, 1951 (Record Group 188).

No. 33. *Records of the Bureau of Ordinance*, 1951 (Record Group 74).

No. 34. *Records of the Solid Fuels Administration for War*, 1951 (Record Group 245).

No. 35. *Records of the Office of Government Reports,* 1951 (Record Group 44).
No. 37. *Records of the Office for Agricultural War Relations,* 1952 (Record Group 16).
No. 38. *Climatological and Hydrological Records of the Weather Bureau,* 1952 (Record Group 27).
No. 40. *Records of the United States Mint at Philadelphia,* 1952 (Record Group 104).
No. 41. *Records of the Office of Inter-American Affairs,* 1952 (Record Group 229).
No. 42. *Records of the Senate Committee on Education and Labor: Subcommittee on Wartime Health and Education, 1943–46,* 1952 (Record Group 46).
No. 43. *Records of the War Refugee Board,* 1952 (Record Group 220).
No. 44. *Records of the National Recovery Administration,* 1952 (Record Group 9).
No. 45. *Cartographic Records of the Federal Housing Administration,* 1952 (Record Group 31).
No. 46. *Records of the Price Decontrol Board,* 1952 (Record Group 51).
No. 47. *Records of the Court of Claims Section of the Department of Justice,* 1952 (Record Group 205).
No. 48. *Records of the Special Committee of the Senate to Investigate the National Defense Program, 1941–48,* 1952 (Record Group 46).
No. 49. *Records of the President's Air Policy Commission,* 1952 (Record Group 220).
No. 50. *Central Office Records of the National Resources Planning Board,* 1953 (Record Group 187).
No. 51. *Records of the Office of Labor of the War Food Administration,* 1953 (Record Group 224).
No. 52. *"Old Loans" Records of the Bureau of the Public Debt,* 1953 (Record Group 53).
No. 53. *Records of the Bureau of Agricultural Engineering,* 1953 (Record Group 8).
No. 54. *Records of the Office of Censorship,* 1953 (Record Group 216).
No. 55. *Administrative Records of the Bureau of Pensions and the Pension Service,* 1953 (Record Group 15).
No. 56. *Records of the Office of War Information,* 1953 (Record Group 208).
No. 57. *Records of the Federal Writers' Project, Work Projects Administration, 1935–44,* 1953 (Record Group 69).
No. 58. *Records of the United States Court of Claims,* 1953 (Record Group 123).
No. 59. *Records of Certain Committees of the Senate Investigating the Disposal of Surplus Property, 1945–48,* 1953 (Record Group 46).
No. 60. *Records of Selected Foreign Service Posts,* 1953 (Record Group 84).
No. 61. *Records of the Special Committee of the Senate to Investigate Petroleum Resources, 1944–46,* 1953 (Record Group 46).
No. 62. *Records of the Special Committee of the Senate on Atomic Energy, 1945–46,* 1953 (Record Group 46).
No. 63. *Records of the Special Committee of the Senate to Investigate Air-Mail and Ocean-Mail Contracts, 1933–35,* 1953 (Record Group 46).
No. 64. *Records of the Regional Offices of the National Resources Planning Board,* 1954 (Record Group 187).
No. 65. *Records of Certain Committees of the House of Representatives Investigating the Disposal of Surplus Property, 1946–48,* 1954 (Record Group 233).
No. 66. *Records of the Bureau of Plant Industry, Soils, and Agricultural Engineering,* 1954 (Record Group 54).
No. 67. *Records of the Select Committee of the House of Representatives to Investigate Air Accidents, 1941–43,* 1954 (Record Group 233).
No. 68. *Cartographic Records of the American Commission to Negotiate Peace,* 1954 (Record Group 256).
No. 69. *Records of the House Committee on the Civil Service Pertaining to the Investigation of Civilian Employment in the Federal Government, 1942–46,* 1954 (Record Group 233).
No. 70. *Records of the Select Committee of the House of Representatives on Post-War Military Policy, 1944–46,* 1954 (Record Group 233).
No. 71. *Records of the Select Committee of the House of Representatives Investigating National Defense Migration, 1940–43,* 1954 (Record Group 233).
No. 72. *Records of the Wage Adjustment Board,* 1954 (Record Group 236).

No. 73. *Cartographic Records of the United States Marine Corps*, 1954 (Record Group 127).

No. 74. *Records of the Joint Congressional Aviation Policy Board, 1947–48*, 1954 (Record Group 128).

No. 75. *Records of the Senate Committee on Interstate Commerce, Subcommittee to Investigate Interstate Railroads, 1935–43*, 1945 (Record Group 46).

No. 76. *Records of United States Participation in International Conferences, Commissions, and Expositions*, 1955 (Record Group 43).

No. 77. *Records of the War Relocation Authority*, 1955 (Record Group 210).

No. 78. *Records of the National War Labor Board (World War II)*, 1955 (Record Group 202).

No. 79. *Records of the Commission on Fine Arts*, 1976 (Record Group 66).

No. 80. *Records of the Military Affairs Committee of the House of Representatives Relating to an Investigation of the War Department, 1934–36*, 1955 (Record Group 233).

No. 81. *Cartographic Records of the Office of the Secretary of the Interior*, 1955 (Record Group 48).

No. 82. *Records of the Extension Service*, 1955 (Record Group 33).

No. 84. *Records of the Select Committee of the House of Representatives to Investigate Acts of Executive Agencies Beyond the Scope of Their Authority, 1943–46*, 1955 (Record Group 233).

No. 85. *Cartographic Records of the Office of the Chief of Naval Operations*, 1955 (Record Group 38).

No. 86. *Records of the President's Commission on Migratory Labor*, 1955 (Record Group 220).

No. 87. *Records of the Office of the Pardon Attorney*, 1955 (Record Group 204).

No. 88. *Records of the American War Production Mission in China*, 1955 (Record Group 220).

No. 89. *Records of the American Commission to Negotiate Peace*, 1955 (Record Group 256).

No. 90. *Records of the United States Antarctic Service*, 1955 (Record Group 126).

No. 91. *Cartographic Records of the Panama Canal*, 1956 (Record Group 185).

No. 92. *Records of the Office for Emergency Management*, 1956 (Record Group 214).

No. 93. *Records of the Federal Communications Commission*, 1948 (Record Group 173).

No. 94. *Records of the Bureau of Entomology and Plant Quarantine*, 1956 (Record Group 7).

No. 95. *Records of the Price Department of the Office of Price Administration*, 1956 (Record Group 188).

No. 96. *Records of the House of Representatives Select Committee to Investigate Real Estate Bondholders' Reorganizations, 1934–38*, 1956 (Record Group 233).

No. 97. *Records of the United States Shipping Board*, 1956 (Record Group 32).

No. 98. *Records of the Central Bureau of Planning and Statistics*, 1957 (Record Group 1).

No. 100. *Records of the War Trade Board*, 1957 (Record Group 182).

No. 101. *War Department Collection of Confederate Records*, 1957 (Record Group 109).

No. 102. *Records of the Rationing Department of the Office of Price Administration*, 1958 (Record Group 188).

No. 103. *Cartographic Records of the Bureau of the Census*, 1958 (Record Group 29).

No. 104. *Records of the Bureau of Agricultural Economics*, 1958 (Record Group 83).

No. 105. *Records of the Coast and Geodetic Survey*, 1958 (Record Group 23).

No. 106. *Records of the Bureau of Animal Industry*, 1958 (Record Group 17).

No. 107. *Records of the Appropriations Committee of the House of Representatives, Subcommittee on the Works Progress Administration, 1939–41*, 1958 (Record Group 233).

No. 108. *Records of the House of Representatives Select Committee of Inquiry into Operations of the United States Air Services, 1924–25*, 1958 (Record Group 233).

No. 109. *Records of the Bureau of Reclamation*, 1958 (Record Group 115).

No. 110. *Records of the Public Buildings Service*, 1958 (Record Group 121).

No. 111. *Records of the Select Committee of the House of Representatives on Foreign Aid, 1942–48*, 1954 (Record Group 233).

No. 112. *Records of the Commodity Exchange Authority*, 1959 (Record Group 180).

No. 113. *Records of the United States House of Representatives, 1789–1946*, 2 vols., 1959 (Record Group 233).

No. 115. *Records of the Foreign Broadcast Intelligence Service*, 1959 (Record Group 262).

No. 116. *Records of the United States District Court for the Southern District of New York*, 1959 (Record Group 21).

No. 117. *Records of the Commission on the Renovation of the Executive Mansion*, 1959 (Record Group 220).

No. 118. *Records of the Farmers Home Administration*, 1959 (Record Group 96).

No. 119. *Records of the Information Department of the Office of Price Administration*, 1959 (Record Group 188).

No. 120. *Records of the Enforcement Department of the Office of Price Administration*, 1959 (Record Group 188).

No. 121. *Records of the Shipbuilding Stabilization Committee*, 1958 (Record Group 254).

No. 122. *Records of the Collector of Customs, Puget Sound District, in the Federal Records Center, Seattle, Washington*, 1960 (Record Group 36).

No. 123. *Records of the Bureau of Naval Personnel*, 1961 (Record Group 24).

No. 124. *Records of the United States District Court for the Eastern District of Pennsylvania*, 1960 (Record Group 21).

No. 125. *Records of the Public Works Administration*, 1960 (Record Group 135).

No. 126. *Records of the Government of the Virgin Islands of the United States*, 1960 (Record Group 55).

No. 127. *Records of the Headquarters United Nations Command*, 1960 (Record Group 333).

No. 128. *Records of the Committee for Congested Production Areas*, 1960 (Record Group 212).

No. 129. *General Records of the Economic Stabilization Agency*, 1960 (Record Group 296).

No. 132. *Records of the Office of Community War Services*, 1960 (Record Group 215).

No. 133. *Records of the Bureau of Ships*, 1961 (Record Group 19).

No. 134. *Records of the Bureau of Public Roads*, 1962 (Record Group 30).

No. 135. *Records Relating to Civil War Claims, United States and Great Britain*, 1962 (Record Group 76).

No. 136. *Records of United States and Mexican Claims Commissions*, 1962 (Record Group 76).

No. 137. *Records of the President's Organization on Unemployment Relief*, 1962 (Record Group 73).

No. 138. *Records of the Military Government of Veracruz*, 1962 (Record Group 141).

No. 139. *Records of the Supreme Court of the United States*, 1962 (Record Group 267).

No. 140. *Records of the United States Housing Corporation*, 1962 (Record Group 3).

No. 141. *Records of the National Board of Health*, 1962 (Record Group 90).

No. 142. *Records of the Office of the Chief of Finance (Army)*, revised in 1962 (Record Group 203).

No. 143. *Records Relating to United States Claims Against the Central Powers*, 1962 (Record Group 76).

No. 144. *War Department Collection of Revolutionary War Records*, 1970 (Record Group 93).

No. 145. *Records of the Military Government of Cuba*, 1962 (Record Group 140).

No. 146. *Records of the Provisional Government of Cuba*, 1962 (Record Group 199).

No. 147. *Records of the Committee on Fair Employment Practice*, 1962 (Record Group 228).

No. 148. *Records of the Dominican Customs Receivership*, 1962 (Record Group 139).

No. 149. *Records of the Bureau of Agricultural and Industrial Chemistry*, 1962 (Record Group 97).

No. 150. *Sir Henry S. Wellcome Papers in the Federal Records Center, Seattle, Washington*, 1963 (Record Group 200).

No. 151. *Records of the Office of the U.S. High Commissioner to the Philippine Islands*, 1963 (Record Group 126).

No. 152. *Records of the Puerto Rico Reconstruction Administration*, 1963 (Record Group 323).

No. 153. *Textual Records of the Panama Canal*, 1963 (Record Group 185).

No. 154. *Records of the Office of Territories*, 1963 (Record Group 126).

No. 155. *Records of the Office of the Chief Signal Officer*, 1963 (Record Group 111).

No. 156. *Records of the National Bituminous Coal Commission, 1935–36*, 1963 (Record Group 150).

No. 157. *General Records of the Department of State*, 1963 (Record Group 59).

No. 158. *Records of the Commissioner of Railroads,* 1964 (Record Group 193).

No. 159. *United States Government Document Having General Legal Effect,* 1964 (Record Group 11).

No. 160. *Records of the Smaller War Plants Corporation,* 1964 (Record Group 240).

No. 161. *Records of the Bureau of the Census,* 1964 (Record Group 29).

No. 162. *Records of the 1961 Inaugural Committee,* 1964 (Record Group 274).

No. 163. *Records of the Bureau of Indian Affairs,* 2 vols., 1965 (Record Group 75).

No. 164. *General Records of the Housing and Home Finance Agency,* 1965 (Record Group 207).

No. 165. *Cartographic Records of the American Expeditionary Forces, 1917–21,* 1966 (Record Group 120).

No. 166. *Records of the National Park Service,* 1966 (Record Group 79).

No. 167. *Cartographic Records of the Forest Service,* 1967 (Record Group 95).

No. 168. *Records of the Post Office Department,* revised in 1967 (Record Group 28).

No. 169. *Treasury Department Collection of Confederate Records,* 1967 (Record Group 365).

No. 170. *Records Relating to International Boundaries,* 1968 (Record Group 76).

No. 171. *Records of the Solicitor of the Treasury,* 1968 (Record Group 206).

No. 172. *Records of the United States Army Continental Commands, 1821–1920* (Record Group 393), Vol. 1, *Geographical Divisions and Departments and Military (Reconstruction) Districts,* 1973; Vol. 2, *Polyonymous Successions of Commands, 1861–70,* 1973; Vol. 3, *Geographical Districts and Subdistricts,* 1973; Vol. 4, *Military Installations, 1821–81,* 1973.

No. 173. *Records of the Reconstruction Finance Corporation, 1932–64,* 1973 (Record Group 234).

No. 174. *Records of the Bureau of Refugees, Freedmen, and Abandoned Lands, Washington Headquarters,* 1973 (Record Group 105).

No. 175. *Records of the National Capital Planning Commission,* 1973 (Record Group 328).

No. 176. *Records of the 1969 Inaugural Committee,* 1974 (Record Group 274).

No. 177. *Records Relating to International Claims,* 1974 (Record Group 76).

No. 178. *Records of the Office of Education,* 1974 (Record Group 12).

No. 179. *Records of the National Mediation Board,* 1975 (Record Group 13).

No. 180. *Records of the International Military Tribunal for the Far East,* 1975 (Record Group 238).

No. 181. *Records of the Department of Health, Education, and Welfare,* 1975 (Record Group 235).

No. 182. *Records of the 1965 Inaugural Committee,* 1975 (Record Group 274).

No. 183. *Records of the Social Security Administration,* 1976 (Record Group 47).

No. 184. *Records of the Children's Bureau,* 1976 (Record Group 102).

No. 185. *Records of the United States Military Academy,* 1976 (Record Group 404).

No. 186. *Records of the Government of the District of Columbia,* 1976 (Record Group 351).

No. 187. *General Records of the Department of the Treasury,* 1977 (Record Group 56).

No. 188. *Records of the Office of Economic Opportunity,* 1977 (Record Group 381).

No. 189. *Records of the Rural Electrification Administration,* 1977 (Record Group 221).

No. 190. *Records of the National Aeronautics and Space Council,* 1977 (Record Group 220).

No. 191. *Records of the Office of the Secretary of Agriculture,* 1979 (Record Group 16).

No. 192. *Pueblo Records Created by Field Offices of the Bureau of Indian Affairs,* 1980 (Record Group 75).

No. 193. *Records of St. Elizabeth's Hospital* (Washington, D.C.), 1981 (Record Group 351).

No. 194. *General Records of the Department of Justice,* 1981 (Record Group 60).

No. 195. *Cartographic Records of the Soil Conservation Service,* 1981 (Record Group 114).

SPECIAL LISTS

Nos. 2–5. Records of the Bureau of Insular Affairs Relating to:

2. *The Philippine Islands, 1898–1935,* 1942 (Record Group 350).

3. *The United States Military Government of Cuba, 1898–1902, and the United States Provisional Government of Cuba, 1906–9,* 1943 (Record Group 350).

4. *Puerto Rico, 1898–1934*, 1943 (Record Group 350).

5. *The Dominican Customs Receivership, 1905–40*, 1943 (Record Group 350).

No. 6. *List of Documents Concerning the Negotiation of Ratified Indian Treaties, 1801–69*, 1949 (Record Group 75).

No. 8. *Population Schedules, 1800–1870: Volume Index to Counties and Major Cities*, 1951 (Record Group 29).

No. 13. *List of Cartographic Records of the Bureau of Indian Affairs*, 1954 (Record Group 75).

No. 24. *Federal Population and Mortality Census Schedules, 1790–1890, in the National Archives and the States: Outline of a Lecture on Their Availability, Content, and Use*, 1971 (Record Group 29).

No. 26. *Pre-Federal Maps in the National Archives: An Annotated List*, compiled by Patrick D. McLaughlin, 1971 (Record Groups 76, 77, and 360).

No. 29. *List of Selected Maps of States and Territories*, compiled by Janet L. Hargett, 1971 (Record Groups 28, 49, and 77).

No. 31. *List of Pre-1840 Federal District and Circuit Court Records*, compiled by R. Michael McReynolds, 1972 (Record Group 21).

No. 33. *Tabular Analysis of the Records of the U.S. Colored Troops and Their Predecessor Units in the National Archives of the United States*, compiled by Joseph B. Ross, 1973 (Record Groups 94, 105, 110, and 393).

No. 34. *List of Free Black Heads of Families in the First Census of the United States*, compiled by Debra L. Newman, 1973 (Record Group 29).

No. 36. *List of Black Servicemen Compiled from the War Department Collection of Revolutionary War Records*, compiled by Debra L. Newman, 1974 (Record Group 93).

No. 40. *List of Selected Documents Pertaining to Black Workers Among the Records of the Department of Labor and its Component Bureaus, 1902–1969*, compiled by Debra L. Newman, 1977 (Record Group 174).

Documentary Publications

MICROFILM CATALOGUES

The American Indian, 1972.
Black Studies, 1973.
Catalogue of National Archives Microfilm Publications, 1974.
Federal Population Censuses, 1790–1890, 1977.
1900 Federal Population Census, 1978.
Supplementary List of National Archives Microfilm Publications, 1974–80, 1981.

LEAFLETS, GENERAL INFORMATION

No. 1. "The National Archives, Washington, D.C.," 1974.
No. 3. "Select List of Publications of the National Archives and Records Service," revised 1977.
No. 5. "Genealogical Records in the National Archives," revised 1977.
No. 6. "Genealogical Sources Outside the National Archives," revised 1977.
No. 7. "Military Service Records in the National Archives of the United States," 1974.
No. 11. "The Center for Polar Archives," revised 1977.
No. 12. "The Territorial Papers of the United States," 1975.
No. 13. "Reproductions of Historical Documents in the National Archives," revised 1977.
No. 15. "National Audiovisual Center," 1976.
No. 17. "Suggestions for Citing Records in the National Archives of the United States," 1972.
No. 18. "Welcome to the National Archives—Some Facts for Visitors to the Exhibition Area," 1976.
No. 19. "The Washington National Records Center," 1971.
No. 22. "Regional Branches of the National Archives," revised 1977.

No. 24. "National Archives Microfilm Publications," 1972.
No. 25. "Researchers Guide to the National Archives," 1977.
No. 26. "Cartographic Archives Division," 1973.
No. 27. "General Restrictions on Access to Records in the United States," 1976.

National Archives Conference Papers

The National Archives since 1967 has published the papers and proceedings of National Archives conferences. The conferences were held to acquaint scholars with the vast resources in the National Archives and Records Service and its regional branches. The sessions also provided a forum for the discussion of issues and problems of interest to researchers and archivists. All volumes have been edited by the National Archives and Records Service staff. The papers are available from Ohio University Press, Athens, OH 45701, as follows.

No. 1. *United States Polar Exploration,* edited by Herman R. Friis and Shelby G. Bale.
No. 2. *The National Archives and Statistical Research,* edited by Meyer H. Fishbein.
No. 3. *Captured German and Related Records,* edited by Robert Wolfe.
No. 4. *The National Archives and Foreign Relations Research,* edited by Milton O. Gustafson.
No. 5. *The American Territorial System,* edited by John Porter Bloom.
No. 6. *The National Archives and Urban Research,* edited by Jerome Finster.
Papers available from Howard University Press, Washington, D.C. 20001, follow.
No. 7. *Research in the Administration of Public Policy,* edited by Frank B. Evans and Harold T. Pinkett.
No. 8. *Pattern and Process: Research in Historical Geography,* edited by Ralph Ehrenberg.
No. 9. *World War II: An Account of Its Documents,* edited by James E. O'Neill and Robert W. Krauskopf.
No. 10. *Indian-White Relations: A Persistent Paradox,* edited by Jane F. Smith and Robert M. Kvasnicka.

Non-National Archives Publications

Catalogue of U.S. Government Documents. Washington, D.C.: Government Printing Office, 1906.
Genealogical Society of Jesus Christ of Latter-day Saints. *A General Index to a Census of Pensioners for Revolutionary or Military Services, 1840.* Salt Lake City, Utah: 1965.
National Genealogical Society. *Revolutionary War Pensions.* Special Publication No. 40. Washington, D.C.: NGS, 1976.
South, Aloah B. *Guide to Records in the National Archives Relating to Africa.* Waltham, Mass.: Crossroads Press, 1977.
U.S., Census Office., 6th Census, 1840. *A Census of Pensioners for Revolutionary or Military Services, 1840.* Washington, D.C.: Printed by Blair, Rives, 1841; reprint ed., Baltimore: Genealogical Publishing Co., 1967.

6

The Genealogical Society of Utah Library

ROGER SCANLAND

It is now rather widely known that the Genealogical Society of Utah Library, known as the LDS Library and located in Salt Lake City, is the world's largest genealogical library. A lesser-known fact is that it also contains the world's largest collection of ethnic genealogical data. The extent of this material has never been measured, but it is reasonable to conclude that the ethnic holdings include over 200,000 reels of microfilm, several thousand family group records (sheets listing individual couples and their children), and hundreds of orally transmitted pedigrees preserved on tape or in written form.

American Indians, American blacks, and Hispanic Americans are well represented in this collection, although many important records for each of these groups remain to be obtained. Much is being done to fill in the gaps. Of the more than 60,000 reels of microfilm added to the library collection each year, perhaps 10,000 pertain to persons who in the United States would be considered members of minority groups. The vast majority of these records are available at the main library and may be ordered for use at the 300 or more LDS branches located throughout the United States and several other countries. The branch library system will be discussed more extensively later in this section.

Since the record acquisition program of the LDS Library is worldwide in scope, some of America's smallest minorities are surprisingly well represented. To name a few, Samoa, Tonga, Indonesia, and Korea are each represented by hundreds of reels of microfilmed records and, except for Korea, substantial oral genealogy collections.

LOCATION

At present the library's location and mailing address is 50 E. North Temple, Salt Lake City, UT 84150. Currently the library is housed in the four-story west wing of the Church Office Building—the building that houses most of the headquarters of the Church of Jesus Christ of Latter-day Saints (the Mormons). However, in the fall of 1980 plans were announced for a new library building to be located two blocks west of the present facility. This larger library is expected to be completed in two or three years.

PUBLIC ACCESS

The library is open to the public, regardless of race or creed. Special services are being developed for the vision-impaired. Wheelchair access is adequate.

LIBRARY ORGANIZATION

The library is currently divided into the following ten collections, most of which have full-time reference staffs: General Reference and United States, Latin America and Iberian Peninsula, British (including Australia and New Zealand), Scandinavia, Continental Europe, Africa-Asia (including Polynesia), the Orient, the Family Group Record Archives, the LDS Church Record Collection, and Special Collections. The U.S. reference staff includes specialists in American Indian and Afro-American research, and the Latin America–Iberian Peninsula staff provides assistance in Hispanic-American research. In all the collections except Special Collections, library users can obtain printed materials and microforms directly from the bookshelves and microform cabinets without requesting staff assistance.

SERVICES AND FEES

Library orientation classes and guided tours are offered daily in the main library. Classes explaining genealogical research procedures are also offered. Librarians and other staff members are available to assist individuals in locating and using specific materials. Reference service at the main library is currently available in English, Spanish, French, German, Dutch, Danish, Swedish, Polish, Czech, Russian, Chinese, Japanese, and several other languages.

The library offers no paid genealogical research service, nor does it provide extensive document translation services. However, it does provide to patrons a list of qualified professional genealogists. Photocopies of most library materials can be obtained.

CATALOGS

In 1979 the library's card catalog, comprising some ten million cards, was discontinued except for entries in non-Roman-alphabet languages, and an automated catalog was begun. The computerized catalog will eventually include all Roman alphabet entries now in the card catalog; this conversion process is expected to take some ten years. During this time library users will need to consult both the card catalog and the automated catalog, which is being produced on microfiche.

A significant feature of the new catalog, and of the non-Roman portion of the card catalog, is the multilingual approach. Most records are cataloged in the official language of the country in which the record was produced. Even the subject headings are in the native official language, aiding persons with little or no knowledge of English to use the catalogs effectively.

Microfilm copies of the card catalog and microfiche copies of the automated catalog are available at the LDS branch libraries.

INTERNATIONAL GENEALOGICAL INDEX

The International Genealogical Index is a computerized worldwide listing of over 60 million births, christenings, and marriages. Each year the LDS Library adds several million new entries to this file. In the past few years, records from non-English-speaking countries have been added to this file in considerable quantity. The International Genealogical Index is arranged by country, then (for some countries) by state or province, then by person's name, then by the date of the birth/christening or marriage. Microfiche copies of the file, updated periodically, are located in the main library and in the branches.

FAMILY GROUP RECORD ARCHIVES

The Family Group Record Archives, another massive and unique genealogical file, consists of over 8 million family group records filed alphabetically by name of head of household and by birthdate thereunder. These records have been submitted by many individuals and vary considerably in accuracy. Although most pertain to American, British, and Scandinavian families, many minorities are also represented. This file has been microfilmed and may be used through the society's branch library system as well as at the main library.

MICROFILMS

The extent of the library's microfilmed holdings as of 1 January 1980 is given in Table 6.1. Since that date, filming has begun in additional countries.

Table 6.1. Geographic Distribution of LDS Library Microfilms

Area	Country or Region	Microfilm Reels[a]
Western Hemisphere	United States	336,527
	Mexico	111,647
	Central and South America	28,487
	Canada	13,599
	Caribbean	1,380
Europe		
	Scandinavia[b]	149,639
	Great Britain[c]	71,586
	France	66,003
	The Netherlands	64,784
	Germany	58,119
	Belgium	44,317
	Poland	10,431
	Hungary	7,203
	U.S.S.R.[d]	875
	Other European countries	27,170
Mideast		
	Israel	106
Africa		
	Zimbabwe[e]	2,883
	South Africa[f]	513
Asia		
	Japan	7,119
	Philippines	4,490
	China	4,084
	Korea	1,744
	Indonesia	290
Pacific		
	Australia	5,680
	Polynesia (includes New Zealand Maoris)	2,872
	New Zealand (non-Maori)	1,760
Other		538

[a]These figures are for unspliced 100-foot reels of microfilm. The actual number of microfilms after splicing and cataloging is slightly higher.

[b]Denmark, Finland, Iceland, Norway, Sweden.

[c]England, Ireland, Scotland, Wales, Isle of Man.

[d]Most of these microfilms are from western border areas formerly in Poland, Czechoslovakia, Hungary and Rumania.

[e]These films include both blacks and whites. Few contain records prior to 1900. Most Zimbabwe microfilms are presently restricted from public use due to the recent nature of the records.

[f]Microfilming done through 1979 includes records of whites only; filming is continuing.

BOOKS

Supplementing the microfilms is the main library's collection of over 117,000 printed volumes, including bound periodicals (the library subscribes to over 2,000 genealogical, historical, and related periodicals). Most of these printed works pertain to the United States, Great Britain, Scandinavia, and continental Europe, although, as will be explained later, some other countries are also fairly well represented.

The main library also microfilms genealogical books and manuscripts loaned for that purpose by individuals. Over the years a substantial number of items has been added to the collection by this means.

ORAL GENEALOGIES

The LDS Library's oral genealogy program has been underway for about ten years. Most projects completed through 1979 consist of tape recordings accompanied by typed transcripts. Until 1979 the oral genealogy program concentrated on Polynesian areas. During this period several hundred tapes and accompanying transcripts were produced, primarily in New Zealand, the Cook Islands, Tonga, and Samoa. In 1979 the recording medium was changed to a written format somewhat resembling a typical genealogical table or pedigree chart, and the program was expanded to include several Indonesian ethnic groups. Oral genealogy projects are now under consideration for other parts of the world.

The original tape recordings produced through 1979 are not loaned through the branch library system, but microfilms of the typed transcripts are available. Microfilms of the oral genealogy materials produced since 1979 have also been made.

CHRONOLOGICAL COVERAGE

In most cases the records microfilmed in a given country begin with the earliest materials of genealogical value. Generally speaking, the Genealogical Society of Utah's microfilming program aims for a cutoff date as close to 1900 as possible. However, local conditions, particularly the laws that govern public access to records, make it necessary to vary the cutoff date somewhat. For most countries the coverage extends through at least 1875, though records for the third world countries and a few other areas are sometimes filmed through the earlier decades of the twentieth century. The book and oral genealogy collections and the records in the Family Group Record Archives provide more recent coverage of many families.

COLLECTION DEPTH

The basic genealogical materials in a country, particularly records of birth, christening, marriage, death, and burial, are microfilmed as completely as possible up to the predetermined cutoff date. When filming of these basic records is incomplete, this is because some of the original records have not become available for microfilming, have been destroyed, or cannot be located (on the other hand, some original records have been lost to flood, fire, and other perils after filming). In many cases, particularly in the lesser-developed countries, local records have not been gathered into archives and the records must be microfilmed wherever they are housed. Considering the problems this causes in regard to lighting conditions, electricity supply, humidity or dryness, and the condition of the records themselves, the quality and completeness of the microfilming is often remarkably high. At other times, however, these problems are unavoidably reflected in the final product.

Other materials almost as basic to genealogical research—court records, deeds, immigration files, census lists, newspaper and cemetery indexes, and many others—have also been microfilmed in many countries, though in recent years the filming has concentrated on the most essential records. A broader range of records has been filmed in the United States than in most other countries.

THE BRANCH GENEALOGICAL LIBRARY SYSTEM

Most of the LDS branch libraries are located in Mormon meetinghouses throughout the United States and, to a lesser extent, in Canada, Mexico, Great Britain, Australia, New Zealand, and elsewhere. These branch libraries have small collections of basic genealogical reference books and microforms, and copies of the Genealogical Society Library's catalogs and the International Genealogical Index. Copies of most microfilms in the LDS Library catalogs can be borrowed for use on the branch library premises. Books in the main library do not circulate, but many are no longer under copyright protection and will be microfilmed upon request for use at a branch library. Photocopy machines are available in some branches; microfilm photocopiers are available in a few of the largest branch libraries. Staff members in the main library and also the branches can assist the searcher in locating sources of genealogical forms and supplies.

The branch library staff can help a person begin genealogical research and, depending on the local expertise available, may be able to answer more advanced questions or help in the reading of foreign-language documents.

The name, address and telephone number of the nearest branch library is available from the main library upon request.

Preparing to Use the System

Most records in the LDS Library and its branches pertain to the period prior to 1900. To use the genealogical library system most effectively, researchers should, if possible, trace their ancestry back to at least 1900. This preliminary research is normally accomplished by gathering information from older relatives and documenting the information whenever possible by obtaining copies of birth, marriage, and death certificates. The addresses of the state vital statistics offices from which such copies can be obtained, the cost of these copies, and the time period covered by the records are given in two pamphlets available at the nearest branch library and at many other libraries. These pamphlets are "Where to Write for Birth and Death Records, United States and Outlying Areas" and "Where to Write for Marriage Records, United States and Outlying Areas." Copies of the pamphlets may be purchased for a small fee from the Superintendent of Documents, U.S. Government Printing Office, Washington, DC 20402. Also available from the superintendent of documents is a leaflet that will be of particular interest to some ethnic genealogists, "Where to Write for Birth and Death Records of U.S. Citizens Who Were Born or Died Outside of the United States and Birth Certifications for Alien Children Adopted by U.S. Citizens." (See also chapter 2.)

Using the Branch Library System

Persons who live near a branch library and who use it repeatedly over a period of time can sometimes trace their lineage back several more generations with comparatively little difficulty. The types of records used to do this, and the amount of success achieved, will vary depending on the ancestors' ethnic background, social status, places of residence, and the amount of time the researcher is willing to devote to the search.

The prospective branch library user should bear in mind that the hours of operation vary from one branch library to another, because these facilities are staffed and operated by unpaid volunteers. Before making the first visit, the branch should be contacted to determine its hours of operation.

Most branch libraries are small, usually occupying two rooms of a Mormon meetinghouse. As a rule, one room houses the book and microfilm collections. The other, containing study tables and microfilm reading machines, serves as a reading room. Library users begin by deciding which ancestral line to pursue. They can then use the microfilmed and microfiched catalogs of the main library to determine what records are available for the surname and localities involved. The microfilmed card catalog is divided into three segments: surname, locality, and subject. The microfiched (computerized) catalog provides broader coverage, including access by author and title as well as by surname, locality, and subject.

The typical branch library user begins by examining the surname portions of both catalogs. This reveals whether or not the main library has any family histories or similar materials pertaining to the family being researched. If a catalog entry for such an item is found and is available on microfilm (the call number indicates the format), the library user orders the film, using an order form available at the branch library. A modest fee is charged, and the film usually arrives in three to four weeks (as with other interlibrary loan systems, the shipping time varies somewhat). Upon arrival, the microfilm can be used only on the branch library premises.

The locality portion of the catalogs, as the name suggests, is used to determine what records are available for a given locality. The surname and locality portions of the catalog are the ones used most often in genealogical research.

In the locality portion of the catalogs the entries for any given locality are subdivided by record type. The subheadings of greatest value in ethnic research are listed below. Those found most often in the catalog are identified by an asterisk.

Archives and Libraries

Biography

Buddhist Directories

Buddhist Records

Cemeteries*

Census*

Church Directories

Church Records*

Civil Registration*

Court Records*

Directories*

Emigration and Immigration*

Ethnology

Gazetteers

Genealogy*

History*

Inventories, Registers, Catalogs

Islamic Directories

Islamic Records

Jewish Records

Land and Property*

Language and Languages

Maps

Military Records*

Minorities

Native Races

Naturalization and Citizenship*

Newspapers

Notarial Records

Probate Records*

Religion and Religious Life

Shinto Directories

Shinto Records

Slavery and Bondage

Social Life and Customs*

Taxation*

Vital Records*

Using the Main Library

Individual ancestry problems vary widely in difficulty, and the availability of microfilmed records depends upon the time periods and localities being searched. As a result, one person may find a great deal of helpful information on a one-day visit at the main library, while another may spend several days and find much less. In spite of this, there are a few general suggestions that will help a person use the available time to best advantage.

WHEN TO ARRIVE

Most out-of-town visitors use the library during the summer months. However, if time is of the essence, a trip during the fall, winter, or early spring may be advisable. Access to the desired materials, to photocopy machines, and to the library staff is easiest during the nonvacation season.

USING FREE TIME TO ADVANTAGE

The library has found it impractical to house and service over a million reels of microfilm in one building. Thus microfilms from some Central and South American countries, some European countries, and most African and Asian areas have been designated "little-used films" and are kept in storage rather than housed in the main library. These films can be obtained for use within a day or two. To occupy this time to best advantage, library users needing little-used film should have additional research objectives that can be pursued while waiting for such film to arrive at the main library.

HOLDINGS FOR SPECIFIC ETHNIC GROUPS

The remainder of this section is arranged alphabetically by name of ethnic group or country. Under each are listed the major types of genealogical records available through the LDS Library and its branches. The approximate quantity of the records (in microfilm reels or printed volumes) and the time periods they cover are also indicated.

This discussion is based on information available in the fall of 1980. Since then the holdings for some countries will have increased substantially, and microfilming will have commenced in additional countries and concluded in others.

United States

AMERICAN INDIANS (SEE ALSO ESKIMOS)

The U.S. National Archives has microfilmed a tremendous amount of material helpful in American Indian genealogical research. The LDS Library has purchased copies of most of these records and is supplementing this collection with its own microfilming programs in Oklahoma and elsewhere. As a result the library is the most effective single place in the United States in which to conduct American Indian genealogical research.

Anyone planning serious genealogical research in American Indian records should carefully study E. Kay Kirkham's *Our Native Americans and Their Records of Genealogical Value.*[1] As will be seen later, the information collected by Kirkham is essential to effective research in Indian genealogical records.

The core of the LDS Library's Indian holdings is its microfilm copy of National Archives Record Group 75, consisting of Indian census rolls recorded from 1885 through 1940. These 692 reels of microfilm are listed twice in Kirkham's guide. An index on pages 135–48 lists the reels alphabetically by name of tribe or band, with the National Archives reel numbers, while pages 148–96 of the guide list the reels in numerical order, giving the agency names and LDS Library microfilm numbers.

This extensive group of censuses omits the Five Civilized Tribes (Cherokee, Chickasaw, Choctaw, Creek, and Seminole) except for an 1885 census of the Choctaws. The library has other materials pertaining to the Five Civilized Tribes; for example, they are included, along with other tribes, in the 1860 census of "Indian Lands West of Arkansas," an area roughly the same as present-day Oklahoma. The library also has various other enumerations that are separate from the National Archives set of Indian census rolls.

Other Indian materials in the library include records of tribal enrollments, homesteaders, freedmen, and Indian schools, as well as wills, birth and death certificates (for the twentieth century), marriage records, and heirship records. These materials cover various tribes and time periods. Except for the Sioux and the Five Civilized Tribes, these records are listed by state, agency, tribe, or band in pages 91–129 of Kirkham's work. The Sioux materials are listed on pages 88–89, the Five Civilized Tribes on pages 51–83.

American Indian genealogical sources created prior to 1880 are sparse, but the library does have some earlier records. A small number of Aleut Indians are named in several lists, made in the 1870s, of inhabitants of several Alaskan settlements. There is the 1860 census of what is now Oklahoma, mentioned earlier. The library also has several reels of microfilmed land rolls and related records dating from the 1820s and 1830s, pertaining to several of the Five

Civilized Tribes. Also, the regular U.S. census records include those Indians who have left their tribes and reservations to become part of white society.

The library's microfilmed holdings on Indians can be summarized by saying that there are more records for the Five Civilized Tribes, particularly the Cherokees, than for most other tribes, while there is less than average coverage of Southwestern tribes. On the other hand, the library has nearly fifty reels of California mission registers dating roughly from the 1770s through the early decades of the nineteenth century. These registers include baptisms, confirmations, marriages, deaths, burials, and occasionally other records and include Indians as well as the Spanish colonizers.

There are additional records that, while not specifically of Indians, aid in tracing Indian genealogy. In areas where Indians and whites lived in relatively close proximity, records of both groups are often included in the same record books, or at least in similar books kept by the same registrars. Thus among the earliest records of New England one will occasionally locate a volume of Indian deeds, while the county record books of Oklahoma often include the names of Indians as well as whites.

The library's book collection includes several hundred works on American Indians. Most are histories of tribes; a few are biographical. These general works are housed together at the beginning of the main library's United States/Canada book collection. Some additional volumes containing Indian genealogical records from Oklahoma have also been acquired and are housed with other books pertaining to that state. (For additional information on American Indian records, see chapter 7.)

BLACK AMERICANS

Most black American genealogical data is found in the same birth registers, marriage books, death registers, and so forth used to record information on whites. As a result most black materials are not listed separately in the catalog under topical headings, such as "Afro-Americans" or the earlier heading, "Negroes." Instead, the researcher must usually look up the appropriate locality heading.

The records most likely to contain genealogical data on post-Civil War blacks are family records; birth, marriage, and death records; census and tax rolls; court records; newspapers; deeds; and church records (though many Protestant church record books contain relatively little data of genealogical value). The LDS Library has extensive collections of all the above types of records (except, at present, black family records and freedmen's records) for all states east of the Mississippi as well as for Texas, Iowa, Utah, and portions of California. Microfilming is presently underway in several midwestern states. As a result of this wide-ranging record collection program, it is safe to say that black genealogical research, like American Indian research, can be conducted more effectively at the LDS main library than at any other single library or archive.

In most cases American blacks using this library's facilities can trace their ancestry back to 1870 as easily as nonblacks; prior to 1870, research on free black lineages is also similar to nonethnic research, since free blacks and non-blacks are usually listed in the same record books. Thus free black lineages can often be traced back to the Revolutionary War period or possibly earlier.

Research on slave lineages is much more time-consuming and much less likely to produce a documented genealogy spanning hundreds of years. Perseverance, however, will sometimes produce surprising results, and the historical information picked up along the way will make the search worthwhile for many whose research ends before reaching the shores of Africa.

The library has extensive collections of wills and deeds from every southern state (as of 1980 microfilming was still underway in Alabama, Texas, and Oklahoma). Slaves are usually named in the wills of slave owners, as are the persons to whom the slaves were bequeathed. Sometimes a will indicates blood relationship between slaves. Deeds were the other way of transferring ownership of slaves, and sometimes they include physical descriptions of the slaves involved.

The library's family Bible records, cemetery records, newspapers, and church records can occasionally be helpful in southern black research. Some blacks are mentioned in the family Bibles of slave owners, though not often enough to classify this type of record as a significant black source. Cemetery and church records sometimes distinguish between slaves, free blacks, and nonblacks. Newspaper accounts of runaway slaves and slave sales can be helpful, although the chances of finding data relevant to one's own ancestor are minimal. The library has one of the country's best collections of microfilmed newspapers published in Georgia, Tennessee, Kentucky, and West Virginia prior to 1900. Indexes to these papers are lacking, however, and it should be remembered that news pertaining to blacks was generally published only when it would be of interest to whites.

The LDS Library has copies of all known surviving federal census records from 1790 through 1910. While these are helpful in locating free blacks, federal census records prior to 1870 are of little use in southern black genealogy, since slaves were named only under two conditions.

1. The 1860 slave schedules of the federal census, which normally make no identity of slaves by name, include the name, age, and occasionally the state or country of birth of many slaves aged 100 or over, in addition to giving the slave owner's name. About one or two slaves per county are identified in this manner. Some census takers failed to record this information, while some enumerators recorded the names of a few slaves for other reasons, such as to identify those with physical disabilities. The total number of slaves identified by name in the 1860 slave schedules is probably less than 800.

2. The mortality schedules of the 1850 and 1860 censuses included name, age, cause of death, and sometimes other information on all persons reported as having died in the twelve months preceding the taking of the census. While many slave deaths

doubtless went unreported, thousands *were* listed, making this a helpful genealogical source for the two twelve-month periods involved. (Blacks were also included in the mortality schedules of the censuses of 1870 and 1880, as well as the 1885 census of Florida, the Dakotas, New Mexico, Colorado, and Nebraska.) The library has also obtained copies of indexes to the mortality schedules; however, many of these indexes exclude the names of members of racial minorities.

In addition, nineteen slaves are named in the 1850 slave schedules of Utah, four are named in the 1860 population schedules of Kearney County, Nebraska (Fort Kearny Reservation, pp. 11, 17–18), and two are identified (though not by name) in the 1860 population schedules of Ozark Township, Anderson County, Kansas (1860 census of Anderson County, Kansas, p. 47).

The library has purchased, from the National Archives in Washington, D.C., several thousand reels of microfilmed indexes to U.S. military service records and military pension records. These materials relate to conflicts from the Revolutionary War up to, but not including, World War I. Among the indexes is the ninety-eight-reel *Index to Compiled Service Records of Colored Troops* (Civil War soldiers). Blacks are also listed in many of the other military record indexes. The library also has microfilm copies of some of the actual records; information from the remaining records is available through the National Archives. Supplementing this collection is a complete microfilm copy of the 1890 federal census of Union veterans of the Civil War.

To complement this collection of federal-level military records, the Genealogical Society of Utah has microfilmed many military records and additional indexes compiled at the state and local levels. Some of these records date from before the Revolutionary War, and in certain cases they include materials as recent as World War I discharge papers.

The LDS Library's book collections also have some items of value in black research. The standard texts and reference works include James T. De Abajian's *Blacks in Selected Newspapers, Censuses and Other Sources: An Index to Names and Subjects,* James M. Rose and Alice Eichholz's *Black Genesis,* Charles L. Blockson's *Black Genealogy,* and the essential *Directory of Afro-American Resources.*[2] Many historically oriented works are included, consisting primarily of histories of black settlement in various states, though biographical sketches of prominent local blacks are also found in many of the library's county and local histories. The library also has several dozen volumes of published slave narratives. The publishing of Afro-American genealogies is still in its infancy, but the library has obtained copies of those that have come to its attention.

The importance of the LDS Library's vast holdings in black genealogy has gone largely unrecognized. Much of the information fails to call attention to itself, being found within thousands of microfilmed county and municipal record books. When considered collectively, however, the great quantity and variety of this material makes the library in many respects the world's most important black American genealogical repository.

ESKIMOS

The LDS Library's holdings pertaining to Eskimos are thus far limited to census records. The library has a copy of a census of Eskimos at Point Barrow, Alaska, taken in the late nineteenth century, as well as a microfilm copy of the 1910 census of Alaska and its Soundex index.

HAWAIIANS (SEE PACIFIC ISLANDS)

HISPANIC AMERICANS

The LDS Library already has the nation's largest collection of Hispanic-American genealogical source materials, even though microfilming is still under-way in such areas of Spanish influence as Texas and California. Beginning with the southeastern United States and moving westward, the library's Hispanic-American collection can be described as follows:

Florida, Alabama, Mississippi.   The library has copies of several Spanish cen-suses of the eastern Florida seaboard (West Florida was under British control), Alabama, and Mississippi. These records were created from the mideighteenth century through the first decade of the nineteenth century. Most list names of heads of households only, with statistical data on other family members, though a few enumerations were more detailed. The library also has several hundred printed volumes of genealogical materials for each of these states; the earliest of these records go back to the Spanish period.

Louisiana.   The library has over 300 reels of microfilmed Cabildo records. The Cabildo was the Spanish governmental organization for Louisiana. It was orga-nized somewhat like a court system, with civil authorities such as sheriffs at the local level. The record types microfilmed thus far (filming was still in progress as of 1980) include land records, probate records, and some minor civil court records. The library also has copies of several censuses taken while Louisiana was under Spanish control and several hundred volumes of published genealogi-cal and related materials of many kinds pertaining to Louisiana. Among these published records are transcribed births, marriages, deaths, church records, cen-sus indexes, land records, and probate records. The book collection also includes county and local histories and compiled family records. Coverage includes the entire state, with emphasis on the New Orleans area.

Arkansas.   The library has a published copy of the parish records of Arkansas Post, a military garrison in southeastern Arkansas that was chaplained by Span-ish priests during the latter decades of the eighteenth century. Many names in the register are French or Spanish. The library also has a microfilm copy of a portion of the original parish register.

Texas.   Although the society's microfilming in Texas was less than half com-plete at the end of 1980, most of the filming accomplished to that point was in the eastern and southern areas, where the Hispanic population is heaviest. The library's Texas materials also include several dozen reels of purchased microfilms, consisting mostly of marriages and church records of northeastern Texas and some western parts of the state. The library also has microfilm copies of many of the records of the Austin colony, as well as several printed volumes of genealogical and historical records pertaining to the Texas colonies established by Austin and other impresarios. Many of the microfilmed Austin colony materials are found in the records of Austin County, which, with other Texas counties, replaced the colony. The library also has several printed Texas tax lists, taken in the 1830s while the area was still a Mexican province, and the 1840 census of the Republic of Texas. Microfilm copies of the U.S. censuses of 1850–80 and 1910 are also available. The census indexes available include a printed index to the 1850 census and microfilmed Soundex indexes to the 1880 and 1910 censuses. The library also has an extensive collection of books on Texas, consisting of several thousand volumes, including the extensive Worth S. Ray Collection.

New Mexico and Arizona. Hispanic records of New Mexico and Arizona include microfilmed parish records of the Archdiocese of Santa Fe, which included part of west Texas, dating from the 1600s through the midnineteenth century, and the U.S. censuses of 1850–80, 1900, and 1910. The library's book collection for these states includes transcribed vital records, church registers, census indexes, local histories, and other materials. More filming remains to be done, particularly in Arizona, before the holdings for these states can be said to be comprehensive.

Colorado. The San Luis Valley and other areas of Hispanic settlement are the subject of several historical and genealogical volumes in the library's book collection. The library also has microfilm copies of the 1860 censuses of Nebraska, which included the northern half of Colorado, and Kansas, which included the southern half. Microfilm copies of the Colorado censuses of 1870, 1880, 1900, and 1910 and their indexes are also available in the library.

California. In 1980 microfilming had just begun in California. Among the materials now available on microfilm are the records of thirteen Spanish missions, on some forty-seven microfilm reels. These materials cover the mideighteenth century through the earlier decades of the nineteenth century and include baptisms, marriages, death and burial records, confirmations, and other church records. Microfilming of city and county vital records is now underway. The early records filmed thus far, particularly in the Los Angeles area, are in Spanish. The library's California book collection, comprising several hundred volumes, includes the state census of 1852 and an index to the federal census of 1850. Microfilmed census records in the library include the 1850–80, 1900 and 1910. U.S. censuses, as well as the Soundex indexes to the 1880 and 1900–1910 enumerations.

JEWISH RECORDS

The Genealogical Society of Utah has recently begun an American Jewish record microfilming program. Already available is the Judah L. Magnes genealogical collection, filmed at the University of California–Berkeley. Microfilming at Jewish-American archives has not yet progressed to the point where the overall scope of the society's Jewish collection can be accurately stated. However, synagogue records from various parts of the eastern and midwestern United States are already appearing in the library catalog. Among these are eleven reels of synagogue and cemetery records, 1684–1905, and several thousand pages of genealogies of Jews in the United States and elsewhere, filmed at the American Jewish archives in Cincinnati. However, most of the microfilmed records begin much later, typically in the middle decades of the nineteenth century. The library's Jewish-American book holdings include the extensive works compiled and edited by Rabbi Malcolm Stern, America's foremost Jewish genealogist, as well as published histories of Jewish settlement in various parts of the United States. The ultimate strength of the library's Jewish-American collection, however, lies in the fact that it is buttressed by the library's 350,000 reels of local, county, state, and federal records microfilmed throughout the United States. Success in Jewish-American genealogical research, as for most minorities, often lies in combining the use of specifically ethnic materials with the use of other more general source records. These include military service and pension records, census rolls, deeds, tax records, probates, cemetery records, business records, biographical and historical accounts, and other materials.

ORIENTAL AMERICANS

The initial steps in Oriental-American genealogical research are the same as in other American research; however, there are a few differences in how those steps are applied.

For Oriental Americans whose families have been in the United States for a generation or more, the initial steps in genealogical research are the same as in other American research. As a rule the same types of records are examined, except that an occasional person may be fortunate enough to find family shrine records or other ethnic family records of genealogical value. "American" records, however, are often more difficult to use where Oriental Americans are involved. Oriental names are often misspelled, and the other information in the records may be less accurate or less complete than expected. United States census records from 1850 through 1880 are a good example. The census enumerators recorded the names as they heard them, using any spelling that seemed to convey the sounds they were hearing. Since Oriental names usually make no mention of a person's sex in a manner understandable to an American, the census taker was more likely to record an Oriental person's sex incorrectly. Ages likewise are less often correct, particularly when, as sometimes happened, the information was furnished by an intermediary. Finally, when a person was born outside the United States, the country of birth was listed, but not the province, prefecture, or city. Census records are perhaps the worst example of these problems; vital records are usually somewhat better; court and probate records are sometimes even more accurate.

With all this as prologue, how helpful are the LDS Library records to a person conducting Oriental-American research? To some extent this depends on how mobile the ancestors were after arriving in the United States. Regardless of ethnic background, ancestors are easier to trace when they stayed in one location, easier still if they joined record-keeping organizations such as churches or social organizations, and yet easier if they became prosperous. In terms of using LDS Library facilities, it is obviously very helpful if the ancestors lived in places where the society has conducted microfilming programs.

While many Oriental persons who immigrated to the United States in the nineteenth century fall outside these categories, the library's collection is none-theless becoming more and more useful in Oriental-American research. The society's U.S. record filming program, which until a few years ago concentrated almost wholly on the eastern half of the country, is now moving westward. Some filming has already been done in California and other western states; much more is likely to follow. The library's book collections for the western states are also helpful, since they contain printed transcriptions of many local genealogical source records. The main library's staff, of course, is another important asset for the Oriental-American researcher. Depending on the individual situation, the library's holdings may or may not provide what such a person needs, but the staff is definitely a resource not to be overlooked. If the needed records are unavail-able on microfilm, it is entirely possible (again, depending on the situation) that the library staff can indicate how to obtain a copy of the needed information.

For those who have traced their Oriental ancestry to the water's edge and want to pursue research in the records of the mother country, the library has amassed a tremendous collection of Oriental genealogies and related source records. These are not written in English, of course, and as a rule the upper-class families receive the best coverage in these materials. Unfortunately, historical factors such as wars—internal and external—have resulted in the loss of many helpful records. Nonetheless, Oriental genealogical research, if not simple, is at least more practical now than in the past. (The library's Oriental records are described later in this chapter in a section on the Orient.)

Canada

The library has microfilm copies of most Canadian census records through 1871, as well as substantial collections of Canadian church records (mainly Anglican, Baptist, and Catholic) and land records. Blacks, Canadian Indians, and members of other ethnic minorities are included in these records. The library also has a number of printed volumes dealing with the history of Jewish and black settlements in various parts of Canada and a collection of compiled genea-logical records pertaining to the Blood and other Indians of Alberta.

The Caribbean

At the end of 1979 the LDS Library had obtained almost 1,400 reels of microfilmed Caribbean area records. Most of these are from Barbados, Bermuda, and Haiti, with some from Jamaica and a few each from Guadeloupe, Puerto Rico, Martinique, the Dominican Republic, and other islands. The Barbados materials include 110 reels of Anglican and Jewish registers, 1660–1887, with indexes. Blacks are included in the Anglican records. The Bermuda materials likewise consist largely of church records. The library's Haitian records consist of about 100 reels of civil registers of birth, marriage, and death, 1666–1803, as well as notarial records (legal contracts of various kinds) and other materials. The eighteen reels of film now on hand from Jamaica include several reels of Jewish birth, death, and circumcision records, 1796–1950. Among the eleven reels of microfilm recently received from the American Jewish Archives in Cincinnati are cemetery and synagogue records from the Virgin Islands, Curaçao, and Jamaica. The Dominican Republic holdings consist of Catholic parish registers of Santo Domingo, 1590–1903.

Mexico

As of the end of 1980 the LDS Library had some 120,000 reels of cataloged Mexican microfilm, making this the largest of the society's collections for areas outside the United States. The bulk of this material consists of parish registers and civil registers of births, marriages, and deaths, supplemented by notarial records for some larger cities and a few other types of records. The notarial records are the earliest, beginning in the early 1500s in some areas. These were microfilmed through about 1920. The earliest parish registers date from the 1600s; the registers were usually filmed through about 1965–70. Civil registration of births, marriages, and deaths began in the late nineteenth century; and these records were filmed into the early twentieth century. The library also has copies of some civil censuses taken in the late nineteenth and early twentieth centuries, and the church records include some *padrones* (church censuses) taken at irregular intervals, usually as dictated by local needs.

The library's Mexican book collection consists of some 2,000 volumes, helpful primarily for background information. The books include general histories, atlases, gazetteers, collected biographical works often similar to "Who's Who" publications, census statistics, and church directories. The church directories give names of parishes, priests, addresses, and sometimes maps of the parishes.

A recently published guide to the library's Mexican film collection is *Preliminary Survey of the Mexican Collection*, edited by Roger M. Haigh. The guide's introduction explains in general terms the nature, time period, and completeness of the records. The bulk of the work is arranged alphabetically by state, then by *municipio*. For each group of records pertaining to a *municipio*, the following information is given: dates covered, number of microfilm reels, and the types of records included.[3]

Central America

As of mid-1980 the Genealogical Society of Utah had microfilmed nearly 7,500 reels of records in Guatemala, nearly 700 in Costa Rica, 350 in Panama, over 200 in Honduras, and over 150 in El Salvador. Microfilming had not yet been completed in El Salvador, Guatemala, and Honduras. In those same three countries civil registrations of births, marriages, and deaths, as well as parish registers, had been acquired. In Costa Rica and Panama only church records had been filmed. The time period covered by the records, as in Mexico, extends generally from the 1600s into the twentieth century. The library's book collection for Central America is small and contains primarily church directories, gazetteers, general histories, and newsletters of historical organizations and a few genealogical societies.

South America

By mid-1980 the society had microfilmed over 6,600 reels of records in Argentina, over 1,600 in Bolivia, nearly 3,100 in Brazil, over 7,500 in Chile, over 200 in Paraguay, and over 1,100 in Peru. In Chile and Peru both civil registration and church records were filmed; in the other countries only church records were acquired. Microfilming had not been completed in Bolivia, Chile, and Paraguay.

The church records microfilmed in Brazil sometimes include records of slaves, usually in separate registers. The Brazilian records are more complete for freemen, who were listed in the same registers as whites.

The library's book collection for South America, consisting of several hundred volumes, contains the same types of materials as for Central America.

Europe

SPAIN AND PORTUGAL

At this writing, Catholic Church records for the Diocese of Barcelona and the Basque region of Spain were beginning to appear in the library catalog. The records begin as early as 1300 for the diocese-level records (*informaciónes matrimoniales*, or marriage records) and as early as the 1500s for parish records. The records are being filmed through about 1900. Some 600 reels have been received thus far from Portugal, mostly from the island of Madeira. These also are Catholic parish registers and usually date from the 1600s, though a few begin earlier. An interesting feature of the Madeira records is that in at least some parishes the baptismal records list the names of the child's grandparents as well as parents.

The library's book collection for Spain and Portugal is small and consists mostly of general histories, gazetteers, and church directories.

EUROPEAN JEWISH RECORDS

Considering the troubled history of the Jews in Europe, a surprising quantity of European Jewish records have survived long enough for microfilm cameras to reach them, although in many cases the records are only part of what once existed and in some instances all Jewish records for a given locality appear to be lost. The society's German, Polish, and Hungarian record collections each include hundreds of reels of Jewish records, some kept by religious authorities and many by civil officials.

The German-Jewish records are surveyed in two publications. The first, an article that appeared in *Toledot: The Journal of Jewish Genealogy,* lists the records alphabetically by town and includes names of provinces, record types, date spans, and microfilm reel numbers.[4] The second inventory is *Preliminary Survey of the German Collection,* edited by Roger M. Haigh. This survey covers all the area in the former German empire, consisting of present-day East and West Germany and areas now in France, Poland, and the USSR. In Haigh's volume the records are arranged by province and alphabetically by locality thereunder. The record types, places of filming (that is, names of cities or towns), date spans, and total number of microfilm reels are indicated. In this work, specifically Jewish records are usually indicated by the abbreviations *Synagogen-Gem* (synagogue records) or *JüdGem* (Jewish records). Such records are shown for over sixty localities. Inasmuch as the work lacks an index, the researcher should have a specific locality in mind.[5]

The Hungarian Jewish records include the surviving portion of the 1848 census of Jews, covering twenty-three of the empire's sixty counties, and many records kept at the local level. These materials are surveyed in *Toledot.*[6] They will also be covered in a projected volume on Hungary to be issued as part of the Finding Aids series, to which Haigh's work on Germany belongs.

For other European countries such as England, France, and Austria, the society's Jewish holdings are smaller but still helpful.

GREECE

As of 1980 the society's Greek record microfilming program had filmed about 500 reels of materials. Most of these are Greek Orthodox parish registers from about 1650 to about 1950 for the islands of Kephallenia and Corfu.

Africa

MALAWI

The LDS Library has citizenship records of Malawi for the years 1953–63, the period during which the country was part of the Federation of Rhodesia and Nyasaland. However, these microfilms, produced as part of the society's Rhodesia microfilming project, are presently restricted from public use because they are so recent.

SOUTH AFRICA

The records microfilmed in South Africa thus far pertain to whites only. Comprising over 300 reels, with filming continuing, the records received to date can be summarized as follows:

1. Records filmed at the Government Archives, Capetown. Death notices, 1902–12 (death notices are documents used in estate proceedings and include the information usually found in a death certificate, with some additional information such as names of children); census or tax records covering various dates between 1692 and 1845; an index of estates, 1834–1912; an index to death notices, 1758–1833; applications for letters of naturalization, 1865–1911; certificates of registration of marriages, 1857–82, and an index of matrimonial court proceedings, 1818–82.

2. Records filmed at the Natal Archives Depot, Pietermaritzburg. Miscellaneous records, 1845–1918.

3. Records filmed at the Orange Free State Archives, Bloemfontein. Birth, death, and marriage registers and miscellaneous records, 1848–1933.

4. Records filmed at the Transvaal Government Archives, Pretoria. An index to estates of deceased persons (death notices), 1873–1958; death notices, 1835–1939.

SOUTH WEST AFRICA (NAMIBIA)

The library has over 450 reels of microfilm from this area. Most of these cover the period during which South West Africa was under German dominion. The records include both blacks and whites, usually in separate registers. At least the following tribal groups are included: Noma, Herero, Omaruru, and Camaru. The records include Lutheran church registers covering various dates between 1850 and 1959, as well as vital, military, and land records of the following areas: Okahandja, 1894–1915; Rehoboth, 1897–1915; and Keetmanshoop, 1890–1915. The library also has a small group of microfilmed records covering the whole of South West Africa; this includes citizenship, military, and other records obtained from the Zentralbureau at Windhoek. These records cover various dates. The bulk of the South West Africa collection, however, consists of almost 350 reels of miscellaneous records from the state archives at Windhoek, dating from 1891 to 1915. Many of these materials cannot be considered as genealogical sources but often can provide background information about the country. Additional records of white persons living in South West Africa are included in the earlier records of South Africa discussed previously.

ZAMBIA

Some records of persons living in what is now Zambia are included in the earlier records of South Africa, discussed previously, and the records of Zimbabwe, which will be discussed next. No microfilming has been undertaken in Zambia itself as yet.

ZIMBABWE

Over 2,800 reels of materials have been microfilmed in Zimbabwe. These records pertain to both blacks and whites and are usually divided into three groups—those pertaining to blacks, coloureds (persons of mixed blood), and whites. At the present most of the Zimbabwe microfilms are restricted from public use because the records are recent. The records filmed include birth notices, 1890–1976; death notices, 1904–76; marriage registers, 1894–1976; citizenship rolls, 1902–76; voter rolls, 1899–1973 (blacks were excluded until 1938); and Church of England parish registers, 1890–1942 (a few were filmed to 1954).

OTHER AFRICAN COUNTRIES

The library's holdings for other parts of Africa are undeveloped and consist of a small collection of general histories, gazetteers, and miscellaneous printed works.

Middle East

ISRAELI AND PALESTINIAN RECORDS

As of 1980 the library had obtained 135 reels of microfilm from Israel. The bulk of this collection consists of 84 reels of microfilmed Nūfūs records (Ottoman census registers) purchased from the Israel state archives. These registers cover approximately the period from 1887 to 1919 and include the former Palestine area. The records include registers of birth, marriage, and divorce; changes of address; registers of men of military age; registers of foreigners; and Muhktars' registers.

For governmental and record-keeping purposes Palestine was divided into ten districts, which were subdivided by city, then by neighborhood, then by religious affiliation—Moslem, Jewish, and Christian—and by sect or denomination thereunder. The microfilmed records include a catalog in English prepared by the Israel state archives which further explains the organization and content of the records.

The library has also obtained forty-eight reels of German consulate records, 1843–1939 (most date from 1926 to 1939) and two reels of British consulate records, 1838–1914. The consulate records include births, marriages, and deaths of German (or English) Jews residing in Palestine; the German materials include records of German Jews assuming Palestinian citizenship. The library also has one reel of Roman Catholic records of Acre, Israel.

AZIZ S. ATIYA LIBRARY FOR MIDDLE EAST STUDIES

Those interested in Arab historical and genealogical research should be aware that one of the nation's best Arabic book collections is located elsewhere in Salt Lake City. This is the Aziz S. Atiya Library for Middle East Studies, located at the University of Utah. The printed catalog of this collection, issued in several volumes beginning in 1971 by the University of Utah Press, includes many regional and local histories and biographical works, almost all in Arabic.

Western Asia

ARMENIANS

The history of the Armenians is much like that of the Jews; both have been driven from their homelands and decimated in large-scale massacres. Both have been heavily engaged in commercial and business pursuits throughout much of the world. As a result of this heritage, the historical and genealogical records of both have suffered great losses and the remaining records are scattered throughout many countries. This has virtually prohibited any systematic approach to Armenian genealogical research. However, the Genealogical Society of Utah, with the assistance of the Armenian Genealogical Records Search Foundation of Provo, Utah, has thus far microfilmed the following Armenian materials.

1. India. A parish register of the Armenians in Madras, India, spanning most of the nineteenth century.

2. Lebanon. Two volumes of Armenian midwives' records of Beirut, Lebanon, covering primarily the first decades of the twentieth century.

3. Turkey. Censuses of Armenians living in Istanbul. These enumerations were conducted at irregular intervals from 1856 through 1915. Other Turkish Armenian records filmed include those of the Armenian Church and the Armenian Catholic Church (Eastern Rite), for Istanbul and a few other cities. For both of these churches the records generally begin in the 1860s and have been microfilmed to 1980. However, a few of the registers begin considerably earlier. The earliest microfilmed Armenian Church register begins in 1771, while the earliest microfilmed Armenian Catholic Church register dates back to 1821. The library has also microfilmed a register of the Armenian hospital in Istanbul, covering a period from about 1880 to 1980.

TURKEY

In addition to the Turkish Armenian records just discussed, the society recently begun Turkish microfilming program has been filming Roman Catholic parish registers of Istanbul. These records generally begin in the 1600s (the earliest begins about 1662) and were microfilmed through 1980.

Central Asia

INDIA

At present the society has no records from India other than those of the English. However, a sizable Indian population settled in Fiji, and the society has records of this group. See the section below on the Pacific Islands.

SRI LANKA

By mid-1980 some 500 reels of microfilmed records had been received from Sri Lanka. The records for the Dutch period (through 1796) are in Dutch and consist of school records (showing names of parents and often grandparents) and population registers that list names and provide some additional information. The island's British period began in 1796. Records being microfilmed from the time of British dominion include civil registers of birth, marriage, and death, 1867–97, and delayed birth certificates covering births occurring throughout the nineteenth century.

Southeast Asia

INDONESIA

The library's earliest Indonesian materials are from the period of Dutch dominion and consist of parish registers, population registers, and some miscellaneous civil records. These Dutch records appear to be the remainder of what was once a larger body of records. The materials cover the mid-1600s through the 1800s and include several areas of present-day Indonesia.

The Dutch records were purchased from the central archives in Indonesia. The society's own Indonesian microfilming and oral genealogy recording programs have only recently begun, and given the nation's great size and the difficulty of reaching many areas, are likely to continue for some years. The records obtained by the library thus far include

1. Catholic parish registers of the Diocese of Semarang, 1921–60 and later (earlier records apparently have not survived).

2. Yogyakarta Sultanate records, from the early 1900s to 1978. These consist of thirty-three reels of genealogies of persons applying for recognition as descendants of the Sultan's ancestors and therefore eligible to be granted a title of nobility and other honors.

3. Miscellaneous genealogical records.

4. Oral genealogies. By mid-1980 over 113,000 names and other information had been recorded through this program. Three Indonesian oral genealogy projects have been initiated thus far and are centered among the Nias people of the island of Nias, the Batak Toba group of North Sumatra, and the Dayak of Kalimantan Province.

The library's Indonesian book collection consists of about 200 volumes of general histories, sociological and statistical studies, and other background materials.

MALAYSIA

The library's Malaysian materials consist of several dozen reels of microfilmed parish and civil records dating from Malaysia's Dutch period (1600s–1800s) and a continuing oral genealogy project in East Malaysia that by mid-1980 had yielded over 12,500 names. The library has a small Malaysian book collection that provides background information about the country and includes about a dozen genealogies of Chinese families living in Malaysia.

SINGAPORE

The library's records pertaining to the island country of Singapore presently consist of fourteen reels of microfilm and several books. These materials include clan genealogies and other genealogical and historical records.

THAILAND

Although the society has not yet undertaken a microfilming program in Thailand, the library has about ten reels of microfilmed genealogies of Chinese families living in Thailand, two reels of biographies and genealogies of prominent Thais, and a small book collection providing historical and other background information.

The Orient

In 1971 the society began filming over 1,000 reels of Oriental clan genealogies and other materials at the Harvard-Yenching Library. This was followed in 1972 by the filming of over 1,200 reels of Korean clan genealogies at the Central National Library in Seoul, Korea. In Japan extensive filming has been done at the National Diet Library and elsewhere. Much filming has also been done in Taiwan's largest libraries. To augment these collections, clan genealogies in private collections in Japan and Taiwan have also been sought out and microfilmed. As a result, although no filming has been done in mainland China, the LDS Library has amassed the world's largest collection of Oriental genealogies and related materials.

This is not to suggest that genealogical research in Oriental materials has been made easy. Successful Oriental genealogical research is often a drawn-out and complex matter. Having a collection of this magnitude to work with, however, makes the task less formidable.

The following discussion summarizes the LDS Library's Oriental holdings. A more detailed discussion is available in the papers by Basil Yang, Ted Telford, and Kenji Suzuki listed in the bibliography which concludes this section.

CHINA

The library presently has more than 4,000 reels of Chinese materials. Of these the roughly 5,000 clan genealogies are the primary genealogical resource. These works commonly go back to 500 B.C., and almost all—perhaps 95 percent—go back to at least the eleventh century A.D. While upper-class families are dealt with more fully, other families are also included. In Chinese clan genealogies the generations prior to about A.D. 1300 are given in lineal pedigree form. For people living since about A.D. 1300, an effort is made to list all descendants of the ancestor. As with other Oriental countries, however, little information is given on female lines.

Supporting the clan genealogy holdings is a collection of some 5,200 microfilmed local histories. These works customarily include much biographical information and a great deal of information relating to place names and changes in place names. In fact, many of these works can be considered gazetteers with a strong historical focus.

The society has also microfilmed Chinese civil service examination records wherever possible. In these materials the major part of the entry for a given person is the person's genealogy and the identification of the family's place of origin. These records typically cover the Ming Dynasty period (A.D. 1368–1644).

The Chinese holdings also include a small collection of household registration records, a type of record not found in English-speaking countries but similar to the population registers formerly maintained in several European countries and their colonies.

The library's Chinese book collection consists of several thousand volumes, including gazetteers, sociological studies, and other reference works, as well as a number of genealogies and some thirty periodicals and other publications issued by clan associations.

HONG KONG

The library's holdings for this area currently include forty-two reels of wills, over sixty genealogies and clan association publications, and two clan association magazines.

JAPAN

The Japanese materials form the largest of the library's Oriental collections, numbering over 7,000 reels of microfilm. This would be equivalent to some 39,600 volumes of 300 pages each. The bulk of the holdings are clan genealogies and *kafu* (compiled genealogies of imperial, noble, and other upper-class families). The society has also microfilmed local histories and *kakochō* (Buddhist death records) when possible, as well as a number of uniquely Japanese genealogical source records, such as religion registers, individual examination registers, and the Register of Five-Man Units. These latter types of records, which came into being because of a Tokugawa government policy excluding Christian and foreign influences, begin in the mid-1600s and continue until the 1860s and include the upper classes and others as well. Only some of these records have survived to the present, and only a portion have become available for microfilming thus far.

The library also has a collection of Japanese family group records constructed largely from information found in *koseki* (household registration records), which include some 40,000 names.

KOREA

At the 1980 World Conference on Records, sponsored by the Genealogical Society of Utah, the library's Korean collection was described as consisting primarily of clan genealogies—over 16,000 volumes on microfilm (2,050 reels) and nearly 600 more in the library's book collection. This is the largest collection of Korean genealogies anywhere in the world, including Korea. Most of these are written in classical Chinese and are very similar to Chinese clan genealogies. Supplementing this is a collection of nearly 600 microfilmed local histories (29 reels) and nearly 150 local histories in the book collection. The library also has eleven reels of Korean civil service examination rosters dating from 1522 through 1971 and nine reels of household registration records covering the years 1615–1901. The Korean holdings also include over 500 reels of *munjip,* or collected writings of prominent individuals. These writings include such genealogical source material as biographies, epitaphs, obituaries, rosters of various kinds, and genealogical records.

MACAO

Macao, a Portuguese enclave on the mainland China coast, is represented in the library's collection by about 100 reels of microfilmed church records. These generally begin in the late nineteenth century, although a few go back to the 1820s. They were microfilmed to 1975.

ORIENTAL SETTLEMENTS ABROAD

As indicated earlier, the library's microfilmed collections for most southeast Asian countries include clan genealogies and sometimes other materials pertaining to Chinese settlement in these areas. Generally speaking, coverage of such families is minimal thus far.

Oriental peoples who migrated westward are also represented in the library's records. Among the library's Philippine holdings is a collection of *padrones de Chinos* (censuses of Chinese) which begin in the 1500s and extend into the early 1900s. The library's Hawaiian holdings include an extensive collection of emigration records of the Chinese, Japanese, and Filipinos who went there, usually to work on the plantations. The Hawaiian holdings also include birth, marriage, death, and some early census records, as well as indexes to Hawaiian newspapers; all of these records are helpful in identifying members of minority groups. Such persons appear to have been underregistered in the official birth records of Hawaii, and the searcher should consult also the library's microfilm copy of the excellent Hawaiian delayed birth registration records (with index). The birthdates of the people listed in the delayed registrations range from the early 1800s to about 1900. Photographs are included.

THE PHILIPPINES

The library's 4,500 reels of Philippines microfilm consist mainly of parish registers, in Spanish, spanning the late 1700s through about 1970. The more recent records are in English; a few are in Tagalog or other dialects. The library's Philippine book collection consists of about 150 volumes of general histories, atlases, gazetteers, and church directories. Such aids are usually essential in Philippines research due to the great number of boundary and name changes that have occurred in the Philippines in modern times. Also necessary for any in-depth research in Philippine genealogical sources is Lee W. Vance's *Tracing Your Philippine Ancestors.*[7]

A large number of Filipinos migrated to Hawaii to work on the sugar cane plantations. These persons are listed in the library's extensive collection of

Hawaiian sugar cane plantation immigration records. (See the following section on the Pacific Islands.)

Pacific Islands

COOK ISLANDS

The Cook Islands microfilm collection includes civil registers of birth, marriage, and death records dating from 1886 to 1945, with some as early as 1849, and native land court records, 1888–1975. The library also has a collection of about fifty Cook Islands oral genealogy tapes and transcripts.

FIJI

The library's Fijian materials consist primarily of microfilmed civil registers of birth, marriage, and death. Records of (native) Fijians, Indians, and Europeans are kept in separate registers. The records are arranged as follows:

European births, 1875–1969

European marriages, 1871–1969

European deaths, 1880–1969

Fijian births, marriages, and deaths, 1876–1969

Indian births, 1895–1969

Indian marriages, 1920–1968

Indian deaths, 1917–1969

FRENCH POLYNESIA

The records for this area also are composed mainly of microfilmed civil registers of births, marriages, and deaths; however, the holdings also include some native land court records, other court records, and a number of family records and oral genealogy tapes and transcripts. The births, marriages, and deaths begin in the 1870s and end in the early 1900s, except for the death records, which were filmed into the 1970s. The society has also filmed a group of delayed birth records that were filed from 1865 to 1870 and include persons born from the 1830s to 1870.

HAWAII

Almost all of the 1,100 reels of Hawaiian microfilm in the LDS Library pertain to the Kingdom period and cover the 1840s to 1900, with a few records beginning in the 1820s and 1830s. The vital records consist of indexed civil registers of births, marriages, and deaths and a large indexed collection of delayed birth certificates that include births occurring from the early 1800s to 1900, with photographs. Other Kingdom-wide records include the census of 1896 (some records missing), earlier enumerations (still less complete), and an extensive collection of emigration records. Other materials include several Hawaiian and English newspapers and indexes and some church records, including the parish register of Father Damien's leper colony on the island of Molokai. Also microfilmed was the important collection of ancient Hawaiian genealogies in the Bishop Museum in Honolulu.

A most valuable Hawaiian source is the 1910 U.S. census of Hawaii. The library has a microfilm copy of this census and its Soundex index.

THE MAORI

Among the library's 1,700 reels of New Zealand materials are Maori land court records from the 1880s (some as early as the 1860s) to about 1960, as well as several Maori-language newspapers and a number of *whakapapa* (genealogy) books compiled from oral genealogies. The library has also conducted its own oral genealogy program among the Maoris, which has yielded a number of transcripts.

MICRONESIA

At present the library's Micronesian holdings consist primarily of a microfilmed medical survey of the Trust Territory of the Pacific, taken about 1947. This survey includes names, ages, and some medical information about the inhabitants of this area.

SAMOA

Both American and Western Samoa are included in the library's collection of Samoan civil registers of birth, marriage, and death, which begin about 1865 and end in the early 1900s. These registers include some records from the period of German occupation, which ended during World War I.

TONGA

Oral genealogy materials compose the bulk of the library's Tongan materials. As of mid-1980 this program had yielded some 7,500 names. A number of manuscript *whakapapa* (genealogy) books from Tonga have also been microfilmed.

NOTES

1. E. Kay Kirkham, *Our Native Americans and Their Records of Genealogical Value*, vol. 1 (Logan, Utah: Everton Publishers, 1980). Other volumes forthcoming.

2. James T. De Abajian, *Blacks in Selected Newspapers, Censuses and Other Sources: An Index to Names and Subjects* (Boston: G. K. Hall and Co., 1977); James M. Rose and Alice Eichholz, *Black Genesis* (Detroit: Gale Research Co., 1978); Charles L. Blockson, with Ron Fry, *Black Genealogy* (Englewood Cliffs, N.J.: Prentice-Hall, 1977); Walter Schatz, ed., *Directory of Afro-American Resources* (New York: R. R. Bowker Co., 1970).

3. Roger M. Haigh, ed., *Preliminary Survey of the Mexican Collection*, Finding Aids to the Microfilmed Manuscript Collections of the Genealogical Society of Utah, no. 1 (Salt Lake City: University of Utah Press, 1978; supplement, 1979).

4. *Toledot: The Journal of Jewish Genealogy* 2, no. 1 (Summer 1978): 16–25.

5. Roger M. Haigh, ed., *Preliminary Survey of the German Collection,* Finding Aids to the Microfilmed Manuscript Collection of the Genealogical Society of Utah, no. 2 (Salt Lake City: University of Utah Press, 1979). It may aid some researchers to know that the page numbers containing Jewish entries are as follows: 93, 108, 110–14, 116, 120, 131, 137–40, 142, 146, 148, 155, 161, 164–65, 168–70, 173, 175–76, 230, 372, 378, 386–87, 389, 408–9, 411, 478, 497, 501, 504–10, 524–26, 534, and 548.

6. *Toledot: The Journal of Jewish Genealogy* 1, no. 3 (Winter 1977–78): 11, 14–21.

7. Lee W. Vance, *Tracing Your Philippine Ancestors* (Salt Lake City: publisher by the author, 1980).

BIBLIOGRAPHY

Although many genealogical guides and textbooks include descriptions of the LDS Library and its records acquisition programs, few in-depth discussions of the library's ethnic collections have been published. Those works that provide significant coverage are listed below.

Haigh, Roger M., ed. *Preliminary Survey of the German Collection.* Finding Aids to the Micro-filmed Manuscript Collection of the Genealogical Society of Utah, no. 2. Salt Lake City: University of Utah Press, 1979.

Indicates the existence on microfilm of Jewish records from over sixty localities, most in present-day Germany, with a few in areas now in Poland and the Soviet Union. Arranged by province and by locality thereunder, indicating the place (city or town) where the records were filmed, the time span covered, and the number of reels. Microfilm call numbers are excluded.

————. *Preliminary Survey of the Mexican Collection.* Finding Aids to the Microfilmed Manuscript Collection of the Genealogical Society of Utah, no. 1. Salt Lake City: University of Utah Press, 1978; supplement, 1979.

Inventory arranged alphabetically by state and by *municipio* thereunder. The time span covered by the records and the number of reels are included. Microfilm call numbers are excluded.

Kirkham, E. Kay. *Our Native Americans and Their Records of Genealogical Value.* Vol. 1. Logan, Utah: Everton Publishers, 1980. Other vols. forthcoming.

An essential guide for anyone conducting genealogical research in American Indian records. Consists largely of lists and explanations of American Indian genealogical source materials available through the Genealogical Society of Utah library system and the National Archives and its branches. Book and microfilm call numbers are included.

Senekovic, Dagmar. *Handy Guide to Austrian Genealogical Records.* Logan, Utah: Everton Publishers, c1979.

The section on using gazetteers in Austrian genealogical research includes LDS Library call numbers. Pages 14–16 briefly discuss and list the available Austrian Jewish records. Includes location of the original records (name of town and archive). Microfilm call numbers are included.

Suzuki, Kenji. "East Asian Family Sources: The Genealogical Society of Utah Collection: Japan." *World Conference on Records* (2d, 1980) vol. 11, no. 814c. Salt Lake City: Corporation of the President of the Church of Jesus Christ of Latter-day Saints, c1980.

A statistically oriented survey of the society's massive Japanese collection, with descriptions of the various record types and appendices summarizing their quantity and geographic origins within Japan. Microfilm call numbers are excluded.

Telford, Ted A. "East Asian Family Sources: The Genealogical Society of Utah Collection: China." *World Conference on Records* (2d, 1980) vol. 11, no. 814b. Salt Lake City: Corporation of the President of the Church of Jesus Christ of Latter-day Saints, c1980.

A highly informative paper, organized in the same manner as that of Suzuki.

Toledot: The Journal of Jewish Genealogy. Available from Toledot Press, 155 East 93rd St., Suite 3-C, New York, NY 10028.

Established in 1977. The only periodical devoted wholly to Jewish genealogy. Beginning with the Winter 1977–78 issue, a series of articles has discussed and inventoried the Jewish holdings of the Genealogical Society of Utah. Listings are arranged alphabetically by town and include name of province, record type, date span, and beginning and ending microfilm call numbers for each set of records.

Yang, Basil. "East Asian Family Sources: The Genealogical Society of Utah Collection: Korea." *World Conference on Records* (2d, 1980) vol. 11, no. 814a. Salt Lake City: Corporation of the President of the Church of Jesus Christ of Latter-day Saints, c1980. A very helpful guide, organized in the same manner as the Suzuki paper.

III

SOURCES AVAILABLE TO SPECIFIC ETHNIC GROUPS

7

American Indian Records and Research

JIMMY B. PARKER

Those who would do American Indian research are immediately confronted with two facts which, if kept in perspective, will be a help to them as they pursue their research goals. First, it is as impossible to be an American Indian expert as it is to be an expert in genealogical or historical research on all of Europe—Scandinavia, Germany, the Netherlands, France, Italy, Romania, Czechoslovakia, Poland, and all the other countries in that area. One must realize that it is as unnecessary to become an expert on all tribes and that there are some commonalities which exist among the records and research methods relating to the various tribes.

Secondly, many people feel that there are no records on the American Indian. This is simply false. Records are available—in many cases better records than those for non-Indian ancestors—and it usually is quite possible to trace an American Indian line back to the early 1800s or late 1700s.

PREPARATION FOR RESEARCH

To prepare to pursue American Indian research, an individual must know how to find the tribal group, study the historical background on the tribe and the locality, study the types of records available and where they are located, and remember the attitudes on both sides and their effects on records.

Tribal Affiliation

If tribal affiliation is unknown, there are several ways of determining it. First of all, one can use an eight-volume set entitled *Biographical and Historical Index of American Indians and Persons Involved in Indian Affairs*. This set was published by G. K. Hall in 1966 and is arranged in one alphabetical sequence, including the names of tribes that have lived in each state and names of individuals.[1] A second reference is the *Handbook of American Indians North of Mexico,* by Frederick Webb Hodge, which lists the names of North American Indian tribes (with cross-references for variant spellings and other names for the same tribe) and gives a brief history of each.[2] A third reference source is *Indian Tribes of North America,* by John R. Swanton, which contains this explanation of the problem with the term "tribe":

In the eastern United States the term "tribe" is quickly found to have no uniform application. The Creeks were a confederation of a few dominant tribes and a number of subordinate bodies, each formerly independent. The name "Delaware" is commonly said to have covered three tribes or subtribes, but while two of these seem never to have been independent of each other, the third, the Munsee, is often treated as if it were entirely separate. The name "Powhatan" was applied to about thirty tribes or subtribes which had been brought together by conquest only a few years before Virginia was settled, and the term "Chippewa," or "Ojibwa," is used for a multitude of small bands with little claim to any sort of governmental unity. In the case of the Iroquois, on the other hand, the tribe was only a part of the governmental unit, the Iroquois Confederation, or Longhouse.

The Northern Plains tribes present a certain coherence but farther south and west our difficulties multiply. An early explorer in Texas states that in that region, by "nation" was to be understood only a single town or perhaps a few neighboring villages, and in fact the number of tribal names reported from this section seems almost endless. In the governmental sense, each Pueblo community was a tribe, and if we were to attempt the complete list we should have in the first place a large number of existing, or at least recently existing, tribes, little and big, and a still greater number known only through the early writers or by tradition. In California, Kroeber (1925) states that there were no tribes in the strict sense of the term except among the Yokuts of the San Joaquin valley and their immediate neighbors. Elsewhere in California, and in western Oregon and Washington as well, tribe and town might be considered convertible terms. As the number of these was continually shifting, it would be impractical to enter them in that capacity in a work of the present kind.

North of the International Boundary, conditions are, if possible, worse, except in the southern most section of Canada where lived tribes similar to those in the eastern parts of the United States, such as the Huron, Chippewa, Assiniboin, and Blackfoot, though the Chippewa, as already mentioned, require a somewhat elastic extension of our common concept of a tribe. On the north Pacific coast, however, the conditions noted in western Oregon and Washington are continued. We have numerous local groups associated into several major divisions on linguistic grounds alone. Still farther north and east, among the Algonquians, Athapascans, and Eskimo, we are confronted with a bewildering array of bands and local groups, usually confined to one town and taking their name from it or from a certain territory over which its members hunted, and the numbers and names of these are uncertain even at the present time. Nothing remotely resembling scientific accuracy is possible in placing these bands, if we aim at chronological uniformity, and we must either enter great linguistic groups, embracing sometimes almost an entire stock, or make an arbitrary selection of bands with the idea of including those which we esteem the most important.[3]

Another problem in dealing with tribal names is the great variation in their spelling. Hodge's work is extremely valuable in trying to deal with the variant spelling problem.

Historical Background

One of the most critical needs in doing American Indian research is to know the historical background of the tribe with which an ancestor was affiliated. This includes its naming customs and kinship systems, the migration of the tribe, the agencies involved, the churches involved, and all the rest of its history.

Each individual Indian tribe has its own system and custom of naming children. Throughout a lifetime an individual may have undergone a number of name changes. It is important to understand the custom of the tribe of one's ancestor to know when and under what conditions those names may have changed. This will enable one to trace ancestors through a series of records at various periods in life. As the records are searched, it will no doubt become apparent that some of the records keepers were unfamiliar with these naming systems and customs. As a result, they may not have properly cross-referenced records about the same individual in the same set of records.

Types and Location of Records

One must also know where the tribe resided at various time periods to know what agencies were involved. This is, of course, essential if the researcher is to locate the records of the tribe. Many tribes migrated several times during their history, sometimes voluntarily and sometimes involuntarily. The migrations of tribes have caused different agencies to be responsible for their records.

Attitudes on Both Sides and How They Affected Records

The attitudes of the non-Indian toward the Indian had a great deal to do with what records were kept. It is essential, then, for anyone who is serious about American Indian research to have a basic understanding of the policies exercised by non-Indians toward the Indians.

NON-INDIAN POLICIES TOWARD INDIANS

Intermingling or Conversion

The first policy of the non-Indian was that of intermingling, or conversion, as it is sometimes called. The basic idea was to convert all of the Indians to Christianity and have them come right into the non-Indian society.

Christopher Columbus, in a letter to the King and Queen of Spain, wrote: "So attractable, so peaceable are these people that I swear to your Majesties, there is not in the world a better nation. They love their neighbors as themselves and their discourse is very sweet and gentle and accompanied with a smile."[4]

But then he went on and said that these people should "be made to work, sow, and do all that is necessary and to *adopt our ways.*"[5] For four centuries after Christopher Columbus's letter was written, the Europeans and their descendants on this continent did everything in their power to carry out that policy of having the Indians "adopt our ways." This policy of intermingling began with the first contact the white man had with the Indian and continued to about 1830.

Two very important records resulted from the intermingling, or conversion, policy. As one would expect, since one of the basic goals of this policy was to convert the Indian to Christianity, one of the major sources of records is the churches. Unfortunately, sometimes church records were poorly kept. Even when the churches did keep good records, one of the most common things that happened when an Indian was converted to Christianity was that he or she was given a Christian name. Often there is no way to relate the Christian name of a particular Indian to the Indian name or to any other name that the person may have been known by in any other kind of record. Nevertheless, church records are one of the major sources of Indian information for this time period.

Since acquisition of land was always at the root of the Americans' efforts to get the Indians to fight with one another or with the other European groups in America, land records are also one of the major sets of records for this intermingling policy period. The ironic thing about the fact that land cession was an ultimate goal was the initial Indian attitude toward land ownership. Indians had no concept of buying and selling land because they believed that no one had the right to own the land. To them, land was to be used by one and all. They were willing to grant land to the non-Indians because they believed it belonged to everyone anyway—that is, until their generosity was abused. Nevertheless, land records are one of the basic genealogical sources, listing at least heads of families or heads of tribal groups ceding land to the European settlers. (See figure 7.1.)

Removal or Concentration

The second major policy period was the removal or concentration period. This was outlined in President Andrew Jackson's first message to Congress in 1829, when he made this statement: "I suggest the propriety of setting apart an ample district west of the Mississippi . . . to be guaranteed to the Indian tribes as long as they shall occupy it."[6] This policy became law on 28 May 1830 and from 1830 to the middle 1850s was pursued with vigor. Primarily because of the greed of the non-Indians, this policy failed. The Indians were constantly pursued no matter where they were concentrated, and their land or its minerals were expropriated.

For this period, there are two valuable sets of records available at the National Archives in Washington, D.C.—census rolls and muster lists. A very few early censuses were taken prior to the removal of Indians from the eastern part of the United States. Two examples are the 1832 census of the Creek Nation and the 1835 census of the Cherokee Nation, both of which are available in the National Archives and on microfilm. The removal muster rolls, which are lists of indi-

Figure 7.1.
Deed for Sale of Indian Lands

Know all men by these presents y* I Wehanownowit Sagamore of Pusscataquke for a certain sum of money to me in
hand payd and other merchantable commodities which I have
recd as likewise for other good causes and considerations me
y* unto specially moving have graunted bargained alienated
and sould unto John Wheelwright of Piscataqua and Augustine
Storr of Boston all those lands woods meadows marshes
rivers brooks springs with all the appurtenances emolu-
ments pfitts comodytis thereunto belonging lying and situate
within three miles on the Northern side of y* river Meremake
extending thirty miles along by the river from the seaside
and from the said river side to Piscataqua patents thirty miles
up into the country Northwest and so from ffalls of Piscataqua
to Oyster river, thirty miles square every way, to have and to
hould the same to them and y* heirs forever only the ground
which is broken up is excepted and it shall be lawful for y*
said Sagamore to hunt fish and fowle in the said lymits.

In witness wrof I have hereunto sett my hand and seale the
third day of April 1638.

WEHANOWNOWIT, his mrke.
TUMMADOCKYON, his mrke.
the Sagamores son

Signed sealed and delivered and possession given in the
presence of

Sameb † his mrk
Espamabough ‡ his mrke
Edward Colcord
Nicholas Needham
William Ffurbur

SOURCE: *Documents Relating to the Province of New Hampshire,* compiled and edited by George E. Jenks, vol. 1 (Concord: George E. Jenks, State Printer, 1867), p. 135.

viduals removed to the West, are arranged chronologically and are indexed. They list the names of the individuals who emigrated and sometimes the number of persons in each family by age group and sex. For some tribes removed to the West, the original residence of each head of family is recorded.

Reservation

The third basic policy period is the reservation period, which began about 1850 and continued through 1887. The policy of the reservation period was to confine all of the Indians to specific parcels of land called reservations, each individual tribe having an individual reservation. There were many problems with this policy, particularly in the hunting culture of the Plains Indians. They had been accustomed to roaming the plains and seeking the buffalo and other wild game wherever it happened to be living. They were now confined to a specific area and were refused permission to range out into the areas where game was plentiful. Furthermore, the reservations were usually almost worthless lands which the non-Indian did not covet and which the Indians had no use for. Because of this there were many Indian wars and skirmishes, across the plains in particular.

Despite the problems with the policy, this period produced some of the best genealogical and family historical records available on the American Indians.

Probably the largest and most consistently kept set of records belonging to this period is the annuity rolls. As a result of some of the treaties with particular tribes, the U.S. government often guaranteed certain amounts of money or goods in regular payments, sometimes annually, sometimes quarterly, usually to the heads of families. As the payment of these annuities was made, the Indian heads of families had to identify themselves to the government agents, have their names recorded, and sign (usually with a mark), indicating they had received their payment. Often the age and sex of each family member is also given. (See figures 7.2, 7.3, and 7.4.)

The Bureau of Indian Affairs (BIA) also became concerned about educating the Indians, at about the same time as they were being confined to the reservations. The school census records which resulted from this desire to educate the Indian children list their names, their ages, where they were born, and in some cases the names of their parents. (See figure 7.5.) These records started in the 1870s and early 1880s.

Near the close of this period, Congress passed an Act of 4 July 1884 (23 Stat. 98) authorizing the taking of annual Indian censuses. These census records were begun in 1885 and continued on most reservations to 1940. For each Indian the rolls usually show the Indian or English name or sometimes both, sex, relationship to the head of family and sometimes to another Indian named on the rolls, and age. (See figure 7.6.) Some of the earlier rolls are less complete. A name is often assigned to two numbers on a roll, one being the order in which the name appears on the present roll, and the other, the order in which the name appears on the previous roll. Thus one can trace ancestors from one roll backwards in time to the earlier census rolls. The earlier rolls often show the names of persons who were born or died during the year and their dates of birth or death; after 1924 such information was recorded on separate interfiled supplemental rolls.

The size of some reservations and the problems attendant in being isolated in less than favorable conditions did not always allow the agent to do everything that might have been done to keep these census rolls current. For example, the Indian agent on the Navajo Reservation in Arizona took a census in 1885. Thereafter, for thirty years he successfully defended his position that he had no time or staff to record this information on an annual basis. The next census of the Navajo tribe was taken in 1915. Indian agents on other reservations experienced similar problems.

Allotment

The fourth major policy period was the allotment period, which began in 1887 and ended about 1930, although allotments are still honored and administered on those reservations where individual Indians received allotments. (See figure 7.7.) The basic policy of this period was to allot a parcel of land to each individual Indian. This parcel of land was to be held in trust until the Indian had proved capable of handling affairs. Then the individual was issued a government patent giving the owner sole title to it. Unfortunately, the BIA office gave the Indians little training in handling their affairs. The land was allotted to them, and apparently it was then assumed that just because they had a piece of land, they

Figure 7.2
Annuity Payroll

5—322 b.—Form 2.

ANNUITY PAY ROLL.

NO. Last.	NO. Present.	NAMES.		AGE.	SEX.	PER CAPITA.	AMOUNT PAID.	MARKS AND SIGNATURES.	SIGNATURES OF WITNESSES.	DATE OF RECEIPT.	REMARKS.
		Amount Brought Forward					344800				
801	820	George L. Wounded		21	m	3 00	3 00	George L Wounded his x mark	P. S. Everett H. H. Dunbar	APR 21 1897	
805	821	Pretty Laugher		80	f	3 00	3 00	Pretty Laugher her x mark	P. S. Everett H. H. Dunbar	APR 21 1897	
806	822	Mary Tomahawk		71	f	3 00	3 00	Mary Tomahawk her x mark	P. S. Everett H. H. Dunbar	APR 21 1897	
807	823	Wounded Knee		57	m	3 00					
808	824	Face	wife	31	f	3 00					
809	825	Moses Wounded Knee	son	12	m	3 00	9 00	Wounded Knee his x mark	P. S. Everett H. H. Dunbar	APR 21 1897	
810	826	Comes Last		26	m	3 00					
811	827	Day Woman	wife	31	f	3 00					
812	828	Red Spindle	dau	8	f	3 00					
813	829	Savior	son	6	m	3 00					
814	830	Girl	dau		f	3 00	15 00	Comes Last his x mark	P. S. Everett H. H. Dunbar	APR 21 1897	
815	831	Plays With Iron		45	m	3 00					
816	832	Cut Head	wife	44	f	3 00					
817	833	Mamie Coffee	dau	11	f	3 00					
818	834	Highmoon	son	9	m	3 00					
819	835	January	"	7	m	3 00	15 00	Plays with Iron his x mark	P. S. Everett H. H. Dunbar	APR 21 1897	
820	836	Watch		45	f	3 00					
821	837	Pretty Hawk	son	13	m	3 00	6 00	Watch her x mark	P. S. Everett H. H. Dunbar	APR 21 1897	
822	838	Walking Crane		53	m	3 00					
[illegible]	[illegible]	[illegible]	[illegible]	[illegible]	[illegible]	[illegible]					

Courtesy Church of Jesus Christ of Latter-day Saints Library.

Figure 7.3
Annuity Payroll

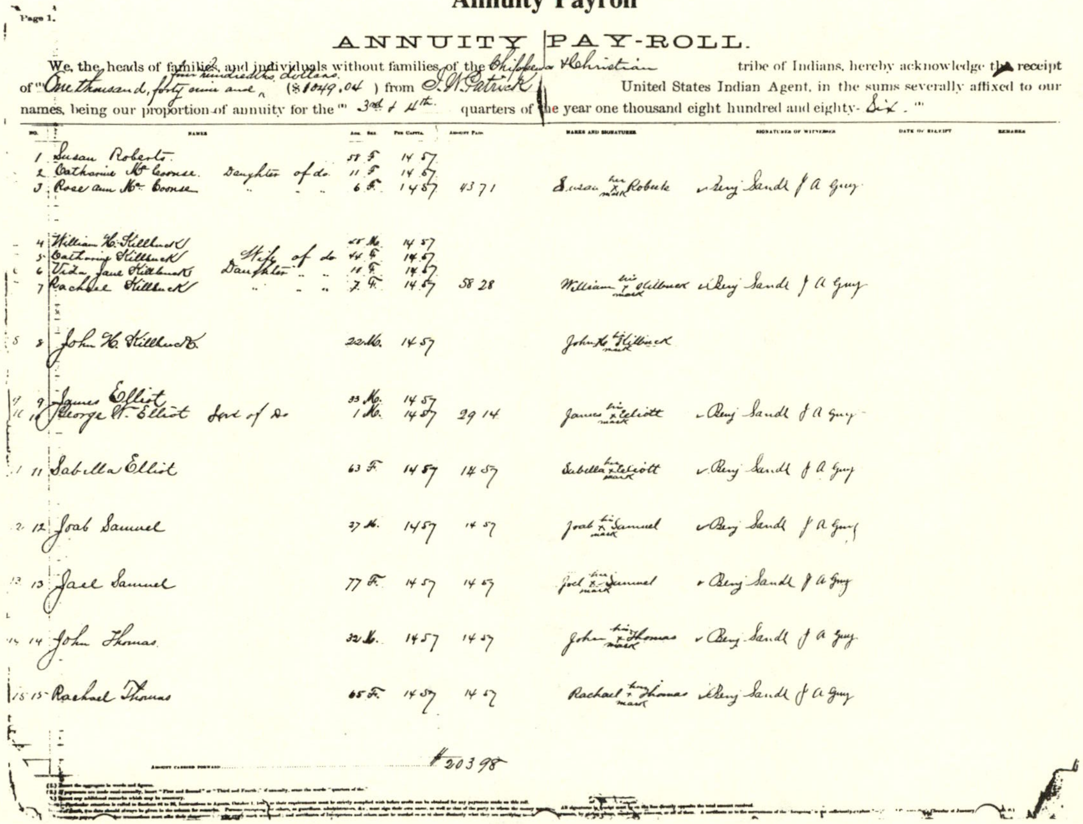

Page 1.

ANNUITY PAY-ROLL.

We, the heads of families, and individuals without families, of the Chippewa & Christian tribe of Indians, hereby acknowledge the receipt of "One thousand, forty nine and four hundredths dollars ($1049.04) from S. W. Patrick United States Indian Agent, in the sums severally affixed to our names, being our proportion of annuity for the " 3rd & 4th quarters of the year one thousand eight hundred and eighty- Six."

No.	Names		Age. Sex.	Per Capita.	Amount Paid.	Marks and Signatures	Signatures of Witnesses	Date of Receipt	Remarks
1	Susan Roberts		58 F.	14 57					
2	Catharine McCoonse	Daughter of do	11 F.	14 57					
3	Rose ann McCoonse	" "	6 F.	14 57	43 71	Susan her x mark Robeke	Benj Sandt J A Guy		
4	William H. Killbuck		45 M.	14 57					
5	Catharine Killbuck	Wife of do	44 F.	14 57					
6	Vida Jane Killbuck	Daughter " "	11 F.	14 57					
7	Rachel Killbuck	" " "	7 F.	14 57	58 28	William his x mark Killbuck	Benj Sandt J A Guy		
8	John H. Killbuck		22 M.	14 57		John H. his mark Killbuck			
9	James Elliot		33 M.	14 57					
10	George W. Elliot	Son of do	1 M.	14 57	29 14	James his x mark Elliott	Benj Sandt J A Guy		
11	Sabella Elliot		63 F.	14 57	14 57	Sabella her x mark Elliott	Benj Sandt J A Guy		
12	Joab Samuel		27 M.	14 57	14 57	Joab his x mark Samuel	Benj Sandt J A Guy		
13	Jael Samuel		77 F.	14 57	14 57	Joel her x mark Samuel	Benj Sandt J A Guy		
14	John Thomas		32 M.	14 57	14 57	John his x mark Thomas	Benj Sandt J A Guy		
15	Rachael Thomas		65 F.	14 57	14 57	Rachael her x mark Thomas	Benj Sandt J A Guy		

Amount carried forward $203 98

Courtesy Church of Jesus Christ of Latter-day Saints Library.

Figure 7.4
Annuity Payroll

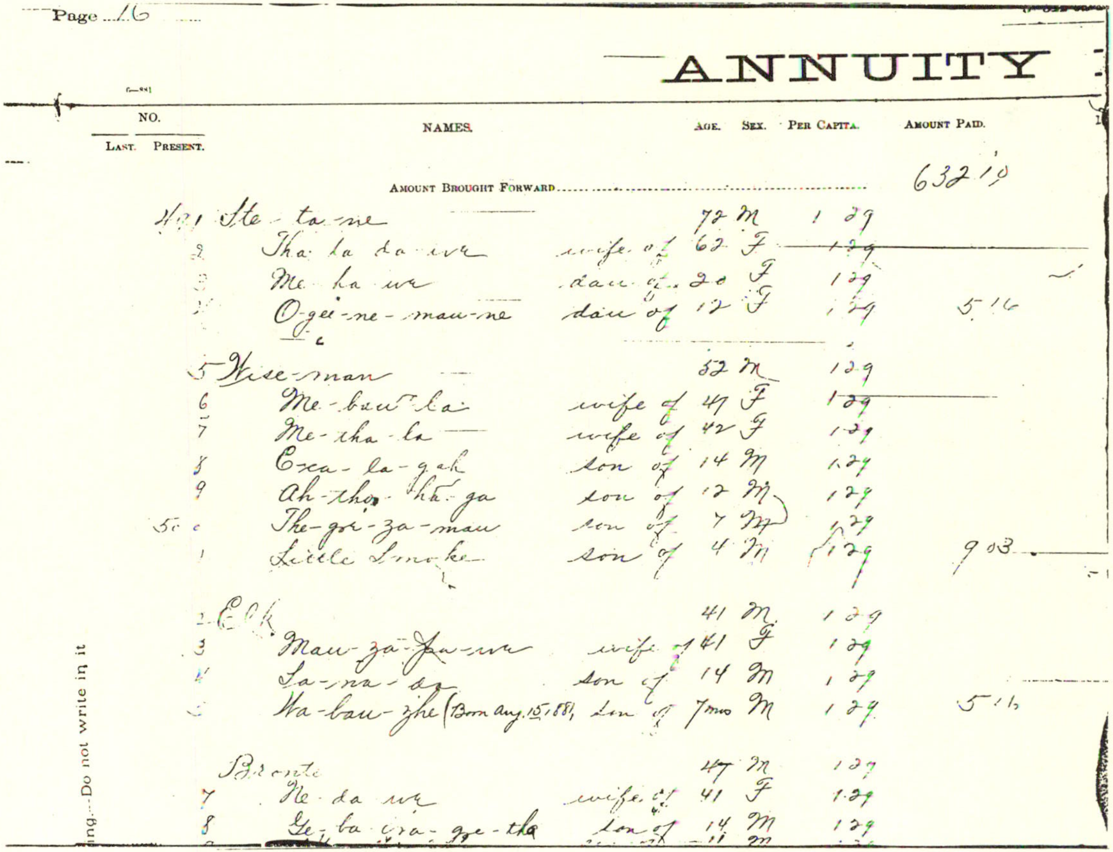

ANNUITY

NO.	NAMES	AGE	SEX	PER CAPITA	AMOUNT PAID
LAST. PRESENT.					
	AMOUNT BROUGHT FORWARD				632 15

...ing—Do not write in it

Figure 7.5
Annual School Census Report

5–255 a

ANNUAL SCHOOL CENSUS REPORT.

-1- Hoopa Valley Indian School

6–3287 H O O P A   V A L L E Y, SUPERINTENDENCY. JESSE B. MORTSOLF, SUPERINTENDENT

No.	Names of all children of school age (5 to 18 years).	Sex.	Age.	Grade.	Tribe and degree of Indian blood.		Citizen or non-citizen.	Restricted or unrestricted.	Distance of child's home from public school.	Name of parent or guardian.	Name or no. of school child is attending.	Length of school term.	Grades taught.	Reasons for nonattendance.	Date of transfer to other school.
	(Boys)														
	(Alphons, Ren No. 521 entered after completion of report.)														
1	Albers, Ernest	M	9	1	Klamath	1/2	Non-Cit.		1 mile	Herman Albers	Hoopa Valley School	10 mo.	7		
2	Bristol, Henry	M	10	2	do	F	do		3 miles	Alex Bristol	do	do	do		
3	do Herman	M	10	3	do	1/2	do		do	do	do	do	do		
4	do Fred	M	7	1	do	1/2	do		do	do	do	do	do		
5	Brown, Amil	M	5	1	Eel River	1/2	do		do	Pearl Seidner Brown	do	do	do		
6	do Harry	M	4	Pr.	do	1/2	do		do	do	do	do	do		
7	Colegrove, Alfred	M	8	1	Hupa	1/2	do		12 miles	Francis Colegrove	do	do	do		
8	do Francis	M	10	1	do	1/2	do		do	do	do	do	do		
9	Carpenter, Walter	M	16	2	do	F	do		do	Tom Marshall	do	do	do		
10	Charles, Edison	M	14	3	Klamath	1/2	do		do	Effie Charles	do	do	do		
11	do Aliangway	M	8	1	do	1/2	do		8 miles	Lillie Charles	do	do	do		
12	Dooley, Cromwell	M	13	5	Coast	1/4	do		1 mile	William Dooley	do	do	do		
13	do Kernan	M	9	2	do	1/4	do		do	do	do	do	do		
14	do Ivan	M	8	1	do	1/4	do		do	do	do	do	do		
15	do George	M	6	1	do	1/4	do		do	do	do	do	do		
16	Davis, Valin	M	9	1	Hupa	F	do		12 miles	John Davis	do	do	do		
17	Effman, Ulysses	M	7	1	Klamath	1/2	do		do	Dan Effman	do	do	do		

Courtesy Church of Jesus Christ of Latter-day Saints Library.

Figure 7.6
Indian Census Roll
5-128

CENSUS of the ......LASSEN COUNTY...... Indians of .....Greenville..... Agency, C al.

on ...June 30........, 19 23, taken by ..Edgar K. Miller, Supt.& S D á
(Name.)

NUMBER		INDIAN NAME.	ENGLISH NAME.	RELATION-SHIP.	DATE OF BIRTH. (Official title.)	SEX.
Last.	Present.					
	1	Alvarez, Lena		W	1874	F
	2	Arnett, Markham		HF	1882	L
	3	" Dorothy		W	1895	F
	4	" Cleveland		S	1913	M
	5	" William		S	1915	M
	6	" Tom		HF	1839	M
	7	" Julia		W	1831	F
	8	Armstrong, Edith		Orph.	1904	F
	9	Augustine, John Sr.		Sing.	1834	M
	10	" John Jr.		"	1889	M
	11	Baker, Billie Sr.		HF	1877	M
	12	" Daisy		W	1879	F

Courtesy Church of Jesus Christ of Latter-day Saints Library.

219

Figure 7.7
Indian Allotment Register

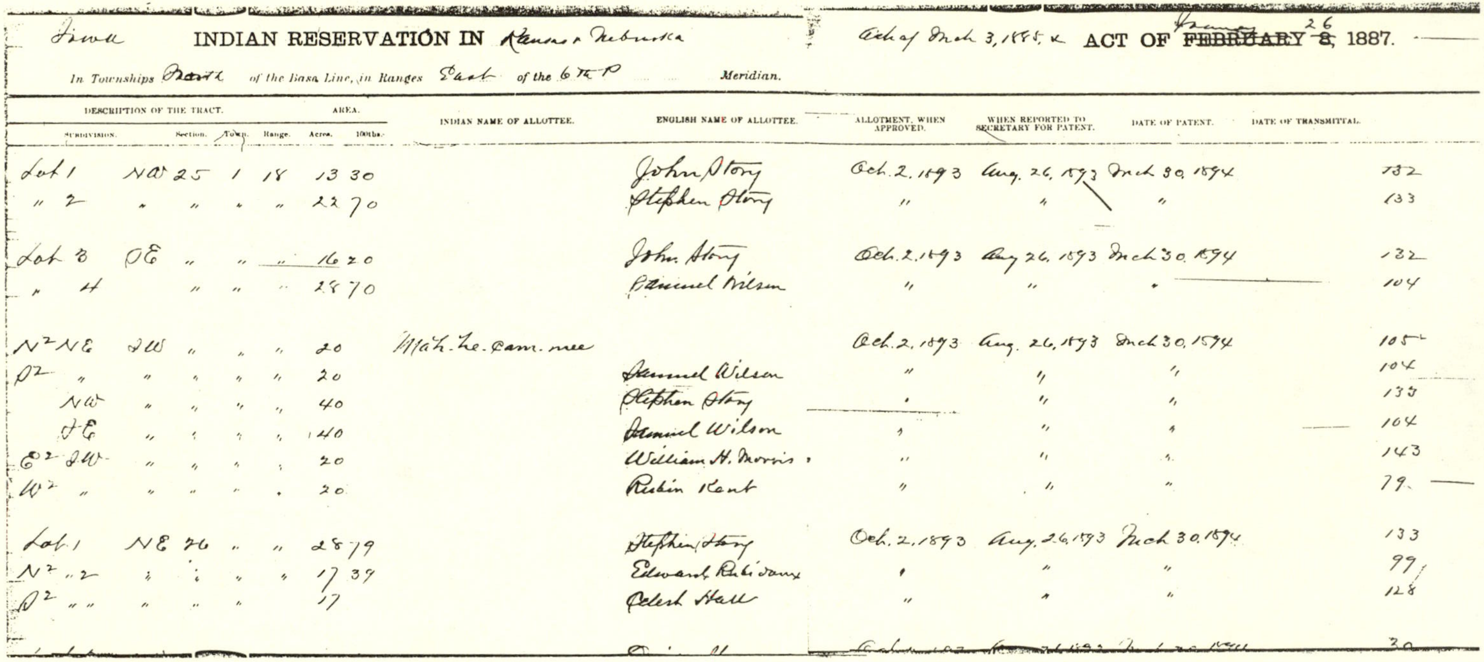
Iowa INDIAN RESERVATION IN Kansas & Nebraska — Act of Mch 3, 1885, & ACT OF ~~FEBRUARY 8~~ 26, 1887.

In Townships North of the Base Line, in Ranges East of the 6th P Meridian.

Description of the Tract: Subdivision	Section	Town.	Range	Area: Acres	100ths	Indian Name of Allottee	English Name of Allottee	Allotment, When Approved	When Reported to Secretary for Patent	Date of Patent	Date of Transmittal	
Lot 1	NW 25	1	18	13	30		John Story	Oct. 2, 1893	Aug. 26, 1893	Mch 30, 1894		132
" 2	"	"	"	22	70		Stephen Story	"	"	"		133
Lot 3	SE "	"	"	16	20		John Story	Oct. 2, 1893	Aug 26, 1893	Mch 30, 1894		132
" 4	"	"	"	28	70		Samuel Wilson	"	"	"		104
N2 NE	SW "	"	"	20		Mah-he-cam-mee		Oct. 2, 1893	Aug. 26, 1893	Mch 30, 1894		105
S2 "	"	"	"	20			Samuel Wilson	"	"	"		104
NW	"	"	"	40			Stephen Story	"	"	"		133
SE	"	"	"	140			Samuel Wilson	"	"	"		104
E2 SW	"	"	"	20			William H. Morris	"	"	"		143
W2 "	"	"	"	20			Rubin Kent	"	"	"		79
Lot 1	NE 26	"	"	28	79		Stephen Story	Oct. 2, 1893	Aug. 26, 1893	Mch 30, 1894		133
N2 " 2	"	"	"	17	39		Edward Robidoux	"	"	"		99
S2 " "	"	"	"	17			Orlesh Hall	"	"	"		128
[illegible]							[illegible]	[illegible]	[illegible]	[illegible]		30

Courtesy Church of Jesus Christ of Latter-day Saints Library.

would automatically become efficient in handling their own affairs. Very few did and very few received patents. But the allotment period produced one of the most significant genealogical records that exists on American Indians.

The records of the allotment period are probably more accurate than the other records mentioned above. Because of the way the General Allotment Act was formulated, an individual Indian who wanted to sell the allotment had to have permission of all Indians who had any interest in that land before the allotment could be sold, even to the tribe. As a result, at the death of an allotted Indian, all heirs and their specific relationships to the deceased had to be identified. Allotments were held in such a way that when an Indian died the deceased's land would not be parceled out among the children. If, for example, a man had four children and forty acres, each of those four children would receive a one-fourth interest in all of the forty acres rather than sole ownership of ten acres each. Relationships were the basis for determination of the fractional interest in the allotment which passed from the deceased allottee to the heirs.

An Indian family sometimes took in other tribal members and raised them as their own children. Because of traditions and kinship systems, they were usually recorded in the censuses as sons or daughters. But in the allotment registers, which were used to determine heirship and therefore the descent of land ownership, the names and relationships were usually recorded more accurately. Although the allotment registers began about 1905, some of the information about the allottees and family members dates as early as the early 1800s.

One of the tools used by the Indian agent to help determine relationships for finding heirship in these allotment cases was called the Register of Families. (See figure 7.8.) Some agents kept no records and had no instructions to do so, but where records were kept and where they still exist, they are a valuable research source. These Registers of Families usually include both the Indian and English names of the individual, the age or birthdate, and the names, ages, relationships, and allotment information regarding parents, brothers, sisters, children, uncles, aunts, and at many times other relatives as well.

In later years the Register of Families sometimes became too bulky and awkward to use, so many agencies began keeping what has been called heirship-finding papers or heirship records, which do essentially the same thing as the Register of Families did earlier.

MISCELLANEOUS RECORDS

There are many other records which do not fit neatly into these policy periods. Vital records, some of which were kept by non-Indians and some by tribal governments, were kept for some Indian tribes. The date they commenced, inclusive dates, information recorded, and so forth, all vary depending upon the reservation in question. (See figures 7.9, 7.10, 7.11, 7.12, and 7.13.) That

Figure 7.8
Register of Indian Families

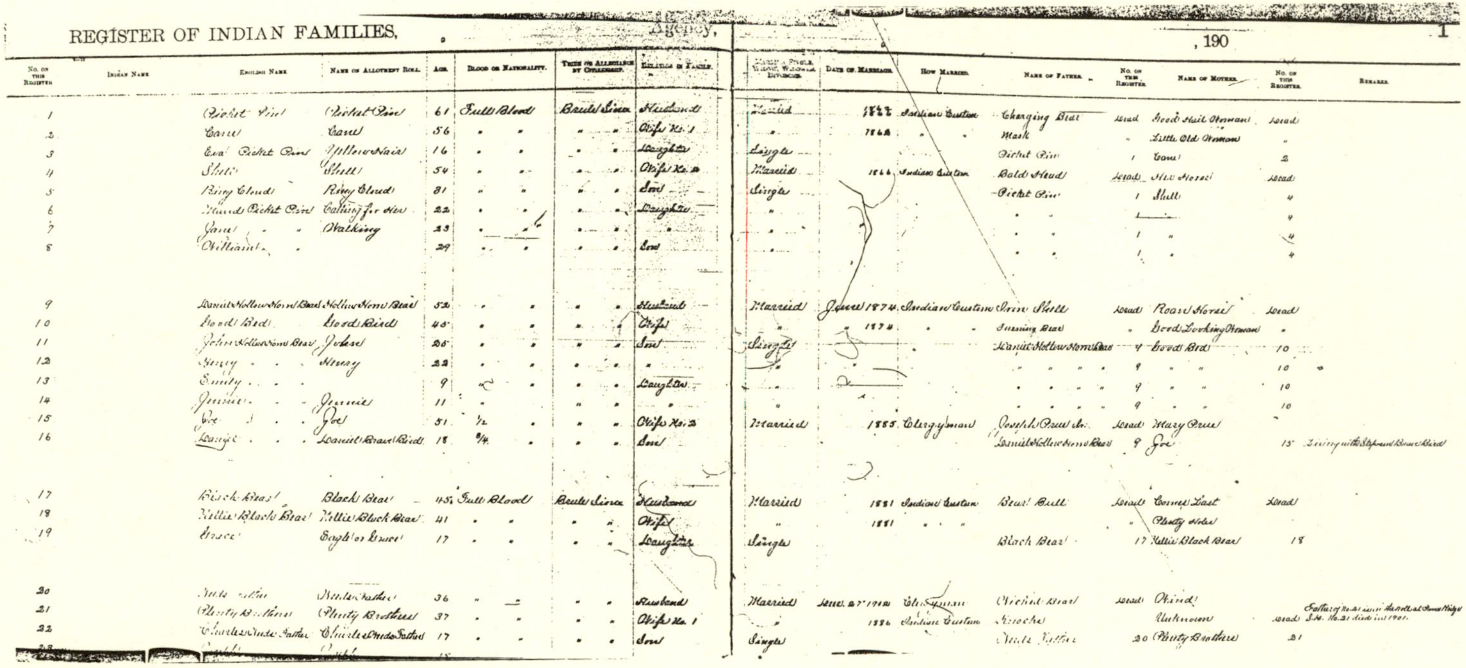

REGISTER OF INDIAN FAMILIES, ________ Agency, ________, 190

No. on this Register	Indian Name	English Name	Name on Allotment Roll	Age	Blood or Nationality	Tribe or Allegiance by Citizenship	Relation in Family	Married, Single, Widow, Widower, Divorced	Date of Marriage	How Married	Name of Father	No. on the Register	Name of Mother	No. on this Register	Remarks
1		Picket Pin	Picket Pin	61	Full Blood	Brule Sioux	Husband	Married	1822?	Indian Custom	Charging Bear	dead	Good Hail Woman	dead	
2		Cane	Cane	56	" "	" "	Wife No. 1	"	1868	" "	Mask	"	Little Old Woman	"	
3		Eva Picket Pin	Yellow Hair	16	" "	" "	Daughter	Single			Picket Pin	1	Cane	2	
4		Shell	Shell	54	" "	" "	Wife No. 2	Married	1866	Indian Custom	Bald Head	dead	Six Horses	dead	
5		Ring Cloud	Ring Cloud	81	" "	" "	Son	Single			Picket Pin	1	Shell	4	
6		Maud Picket Pin	Calling for Her	22	" "	" "	Daughter	"			" "	1	"	4	
7		Jane " "	Walking	23	" "	" "	"	"			" "	1	"	4	
8		William " "		29	" "	" "	Son	"			" "	1	"	4	
9		Daniel Hollow Horn Bear	Hollow Horn Bear	52	" "	" "	Husband	Married	June 1874	Indian Custom	Iron Shell	dead	Road Horse	dead	
10		Good Bird	Good Bird	45	" "	" "	Wife	"	1874	" "	Running Bear	"	Good Looking Woman	"	
11		John Hollow Horn Bear	John	26	" "	" "	Son	Single			Daniel Hollow Horn Bear	9	Good Bird	10	
12		Henry " "	Henry	22	" "	" "	"				" " " "	9	" "	10	
13		Emily " "		9	" "	" "	Daughter				" " " "	9	" "	10	
14		Jennie " "	Jennie	11	"	" "	"	"			" " " "	9	" "	10	
15		Joe " "	Joe	51	1/2	" "	Wife No. 2	Married	1885	Clergyman	Joseph Bruce Sr.	dead	Mary Bruce		
16		Louyie " "	Daniel Brave Bird	18	3/4	" "	Son				Daniel Hollow Horn Bear	9	Joe	15	Living with Stepmother Brave Bird
17		Black Bear	Black Bear	45	Full Blood	Brule Sioux	Husband	Married	1881	Indian Custom	Bear Bull	dead	Comes Last	dead	
18		Nellie Black Bear	Nellie Black Bear	41	" "	" "	Wife	"	1881	" " "			Plenty Holes		
19		Grace	Eagle or Grace	17	" "	" "	Daughter	Single			Black Bear	17	Nellie Black Bear	18	
20		White Father	White Father	36	"	" "	Husband	Married	June 27 1910	Clergyman	Picket Bear	dead	Wind		
21		Plenty Brothers	Plenty Brothers	37	" "	" "	Wife No. 1	"	1886	Indian Custom	Kroche		Unknown	dead	Father of No. 21 ... died in 1901.
22		Charles White Father	Charles White Father	17	" "	" "	Son	Single			White Father	20	Plenty Brothers	21	

Courtesy Church of Jesus Christ of Latter-day Saints Library

Figure 7.9
Marriage Card

8—183 a.

MARRIAGE CARD.

first _____ Marriage. Sex *F* _____ Census or Allotment No. *341*
(1st, 2d, 3d, etc.)

Name *Fader Sadie* _____ Tribe *Sac & Fox full*

Married *April 15 1918* _____ How *Legally*
(By tribal custom, or legally.)

Married to whom *Mark Fader* *White mar* Census or Allotment No. _____

If divorced, When *No* _____ Where _____
(Date.)   (Place.)

If divorced, How _____
(By tribal custom, or legally.)

CHILDREN BORN OF THIS MARRIAGE.

CENSUS OR ALLOTMENT NO.	SEX	NAME	BORN	DIED
		No Children.		

See Marriage Cards Nos. _____ and _____ for half-brothers and half-sisters of these children.
8—184

Courtesy Church of Jesus Christ of Latter-day Saints Library

223

Figure 7.10
Record of Deaths

102

Record of Deaths among Indians of *Fort Berthold.* Agency

Number on Record.	Number on Family Register or Record of Births.	NAME.	AGE.	SEX.	DATE OF DEATH.	MARRIED, SINGLE, WIDOW, WIDOWER, OR DIVORCED.	NAME OF A LIVING RELATIVE.	RELATION.	Kind of Relative or Family Record.
33		Brown Woman	59	F	Mar 29 '02	Widow	Roger Brown	Son	
34		Louis Whiteman	17	M	Apr 13 '02	Single	Old Whiteman	Father	
35		Day Woman	75	F	Apr 7 '02	Widow	Alfred Colson	Brother	
36			42	F	Apr 8 '02	Married	White Arm	Husband	
37		White Bear 1871	31	M	May 7 '02		Jim Brown	Wife	
38		Crackett	6		May 9 '02	Single	No Arm	Father	
39		Jos Hessel	71	M	May 13 '02	Widow	Jumping Hog	Nephew	
40		Oliver Ducton	13	M	May 22 '02	Single	Little Vicene	Father	
41		Eunice Eaton	27	F	June 10 '02	Married	Robert Lincoln	Husband	
42		Wolf Robin	37	M	May 28 '02		Red Striper	Sister	
43		Maggie Annabez	26	F	June 21 '02	Single	White Owl No 2	Bro	
44			6 mo	M	June 7 '02		Break Heart	Father	
45		Yellow Crow			July 27 '02		Owl Comes Out	"	
46		Jos Crait	75	M	July 31 '02	Widower	Miles Anderson	Bro	
47		Owl Woman	64	F	Aug 8 '02	Married	Jimmy Harmon	"	
48		Lurking or Something to Eat	25	M	Sept 20 '02	Single	Old Black Bear	Father	
49		Luci Wolf	10	F	Sept 21 '02		Battles McLains	Mother	

Courtesy Church of Jesus Christ of Latter-day Saints Library.

224

Figure 7.11
Certificate of Death

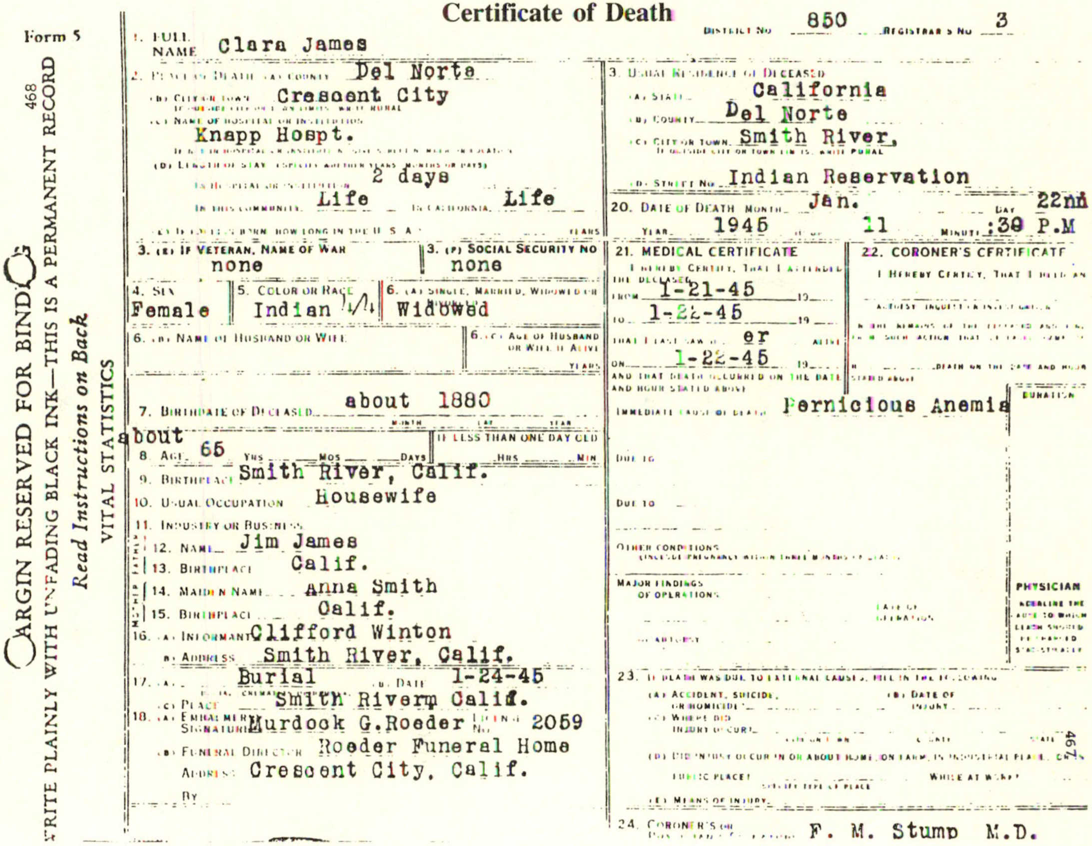

Form 5

District No ___ 850 ___ Register's No ___ 3

1. (a) NAME — Clara James
2. PLACE OF DEATH (a) COUNTY — Del Norte
   (b) CITY OR TOWN — Crescent City
   Name of Hospital or Institution — Knapp Hospt.
   Length of stay — Life — 2 days
   In this community — Life
   How long in the U.S.A. — Life
3. USUAL RESIDENCE OF DECEASED (a) STATE — California
   (b) COUNTY — Del Norte
   (c) CITY OR TOWN — Smith River
   (b) STATE No. — Indian Reservation
20. DATE OF DEATH MONTH — Jan. — Day 11 — YEAR 1945 — Hour 22nd — Minute 30 P.M

4. SEX — Female
5. COLOR OR RACE — Indian
6. (a) SINGLE, MARRIED, WIDOWED — Widowed
3. (f) SOCIAL SECURITY NO — none
3. (d) IF VETERAN, NAME OF WAR — none
6. (b) NAME OF HUSBAND OR WIFE —
6. (c) AGE OF HUSBAND OR WIFE IF ALIVE — YEARS

7. BIRTHDATE OF DECEASED — about 1880
8. AGE — about 65 — LESS THAN ONE DAY
9. BIRTHPLACE — Smith River, Calif.
10. USUAL OCCUPATION — Housewife
11. INDUSTRY OR BUSINESS —
12. NAME — Jim James
13. BIRTHPLACE — Calif.
14. MAIDEN NAME — Anna Smith
15. BIRTHPLACE — Calif.
16. (a) INFORMANT — Clifford Winton
    ADDRESS — Smith River, Calif.
17. (a) BURIAL — Date 1-24-45
    (c) PLACE — Smith River, Calif.
18. (a) SIGNATURE, EMBALMER — Murdock G. Roeder — License 2059
    FUNERAL DIRECTOR — Roeder Funeral Home
    ADDRESS — Crescent City, Calif.

21. MEDICAL CERTIFICATE
    THE DURATION — from 1-21-45 to 1-22-45
    ON 1-22-45 — or — Pernicious Anemia
    IMMEDIATE CAUSE OF DEATH — Pernicious Anemia

22. CORONER'S CERTIFICATE

23. IF DEATH WAS DUE TO EXTERNAL CAUSES
    (a) ACCIDENT, SUICIDE, HOMICIDE

24. CORONER'S (or) — F. M. Stump M.D.

PHYSICIAN

467

Courtesy Church of Jesus Christ of Latter-day Saints Library.

225

Figure 7.12
Birth Report

BIRTH REPORT OF TULE RIVER INDIAN CHILDREN.
1/1/37 to 1938.

NAME		Date of Birth	Tribe	Degree of Blood	Relationship to head of Family
Surname	Given				
20- Dandy,	Antonia (nee Dionicio)	6/13/05	Yawilmani	F	Wife 182
"	Dorothy	5/5/37	Mono & Yawilmani	F	Dau
25- Delgado,	Irene (nee Diaz)	8/15/14	Tejon	1/2	Wife 30
"	Dolores	9/17/36	"	1/4	Dau
39- Eugene,	Mary (nee Dancing)	10/13/14	Wikchamni	F	Wife 61
"	John Paul	3/26/37	Pomo & Wikchamnî	F	Son
78- Franco,	Juan	1903	Yawilmani	1/2	Head 48
44- "	Jennie (Sedillo nee Hunter)	5/28/10	"	F	Wife 149
"	John Robert	9/28/36	"	3/4	Son
"	Pauline	1/18/38	"	3/4	Dau
76- Garfield,	Bennie	5/21/14	Yawilmani	F	Head 51
"	Ida (nee Peyron)		"	1/2	Wife
"	Jennie Lee	6/1/37	"	3/4	Dau

Courtesy Church of Jesus Christ of Latter-day Saints Library.

points up again the importance of understanding the historical background of the particular tribe in which the researcher is interested.

The Wheeler-Howard Act of 18 June 1934 gave the Indians the right to manage their own affairs through tribal councils. Some of the tribes have very active tribal councils and are keeping their own sets of vital records. The dates these records commence and their content vary by tribe, but many are very similar to the vital statistics kept by the states.

Another set of records valuable to genealogists is called the Sanitary Record of Sick, Injured, Births, Deaths, etc. (See figure 7.14.) By 1886 the BIA agents had been requested to record all the Indians who came into the health service for any kind of treatment, physical or mental. The agents were to enter the date the sickness began, the date the sickness ended, the cause of the sickness, how long the Indian was ill, and in the case of death, the date of death. For births, the date of birth and the names of the parents were recorded.

Yet another set of records which have been generated for American Indians are the claims records. Several claims have been filed against the U.S. government by Indians, one of the earliest being the Cherokee claims authorized by an act of 1 July 1902 (32 Stat. 726). The Cherokee Claims Commission Records consist of approximately 48,000 files of individuals who sent in claims. These are at the National Archives in Washington, as is the two-volume index to them. To prove they had a right to receive a portion of the claim they were seeking, each tribal member had to prove descent from an ancestor who appeared on an earlier roll of

Figure 7.13
Letter Verifying Birth Dates of Children

Birth Certificates.

Carnegie,Okla. 3-30-31.

Supt.Kiowa Indian Agency,
Anadarko,Okla.

Dear Sir:

Inclosed herewith Birth Certificate of Perry Jack Hokeah a child born to Barnum Hokeah and Jessie Geimausaddle 5-2-30, as per your recent request. advise that you had a death Certificate,but was unable to find the Birth Certificate. It appears that the Dr.overlooked filing the report, until I took the matter up with Barnum .

There is also inclosed a Birth Certificate of Chester Wallace Horse,son of Harry Horse and Alice Agopetah.
This boy was born in Kiowa Co.west of Carnegie on Nov.1,1930.

Respectfully,
J. F. Haws
Farmer.

RECEIVED
MAR 31 1931
KIOWA AGENCY
ANADARKO, OKL.

Courtesy Church of Jesus Christ of Latter-day Saints Library.

Figure 7.14
Sanitary Record of Sick, Injured, Births, Deaths, etc.

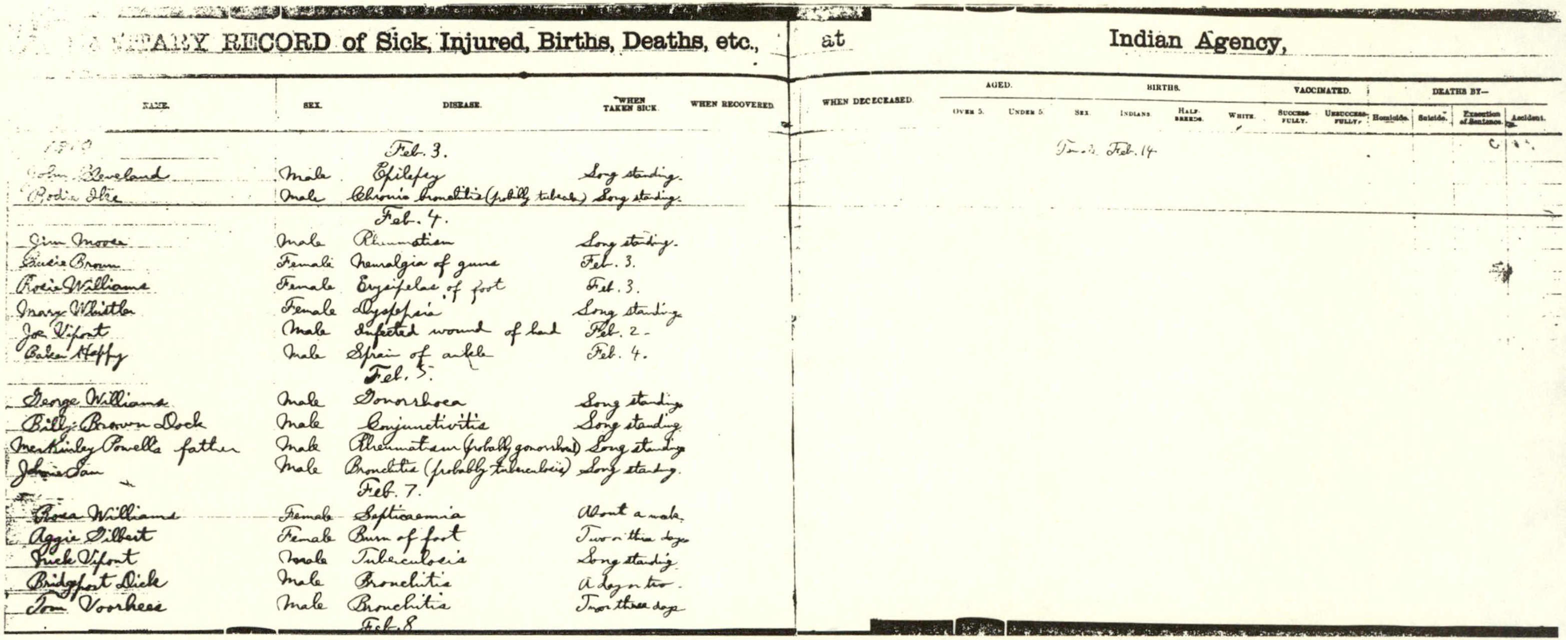

...ITARY RECORD of Sick, Injured, Births, Deaths, etc., at Indian Agency,

NAME.	SEX.	DISEASE.	WHEN TAKEN SICK.	WHEN RECOVERED.	WHEN DECEASED.	AGED. Over 5.	AGED. Under 5.	BIRTHS. Sex.	BIRTHS. Indians.	BIRTHS. Half-breeds.	BIRTHS. White.	VACCINATED. Successfully.	VACCINATED. Unsuccessfully.	DEATHS BY— Homicide.	DEATHS BY— Suicide.	DEATHS BY— Execution of Sentence.	DEATHS BY— Accident.
1910		Feb. 3.						Tom..	Feb. 14								
John Cleveland	Male	Epilepsy	Long standing.														
Bodie Ike	Male	Chronic bronchitis (probably tuberc.)	Long standing.														
		Feb. 4.															
Jim Moore	Male	Rheumatism	Long standing.														
Lucie Brown	Female	Neuralgia of gums	Feb. 3.														
Rosie Williams	Female	Erysipelas of foot	Feb. 3.														
Mary Whittle	Female	Dyspepsia	Long standing														
Joe Vipont	Male	Infected wound of hand	Feb. 2.														
Baker Hoppy	Male	Sprain of ankle	Feb. 4.														
		Feb. 5.															
George Williams	Male	Gonorrhoea	Long standing														
Billy Brown Dock	Male	Conjunctivitis	Long standing														
McKinley Powell's father	Male	Rheumatism (probably gonorrheal)	Long standing														
Johnie Sam	Male	Bronchitis (probably tuberculosis)	Long standing.														
		Feb. 7.															
Rosa Williams	Female	Septicaemia	About a week.														
Aggie Gilbert	Female	Burn of foot	Two or three days														
Dick Vipont	Male	Tuberculosis	Long standing.														
Bridgeport Dick	Male	Bronchitis	A day or two.														
Tom Voorhees	Male	Bronchitis	Two or three days														
		Feb. 8															

Courtesy Church of Jesus Christ of Latter-day Saints Library.

that tribe. These claim files often contain the name of the claimant, the date and place of birth and residence, and names and genealogical information about the claimant's brothers, sisters, parents, grandparents, and children.

There have been many other cases before the U.S. Court of Claims, especially since about 1946. Many of these records for tribes from throughout the United States are in the National Records Center in Suitland, Maryland; some of the records are still in the hands of the attorneys who represented the Indian tribes in the court cases; and many are in the regional archives of the National Archives and Records Service throughout the United States. The general procedure for proving a right of an Indian to receive a portion of a claim is the same as for the Cherokee.

Another set of records is wills. An Indian who desired to make a will after 1910 could do so with the approval of the Commissioner of Indian Affairs. These estate files consist of reports on heirship, wills, and related papers (figures 7.15 and 7.16) and usually include such information as name, tribe, place of residence, date of death, and age at date of death. Other genealogical information is included in the report on heirship, such as name of spouse, date of marriage, names and dates of marriage of parents, and names of brothers, sisters, and children. Most of these records are now part of the National Archives collection and cover Indians from all over the United States.

Other records were kept as well—such documents as journals of the Continental Congress and later the Congressional Reports of Committees, BIA reports, and in later years, reports of the Bureau of American Ethnology. All of these contain at least historical background and, in many cases, names of individual Indians of tribes throughout the country.

INDIAN ATTITUDES TOWARD NON-INDIANS

The attitudes of non-Indians toward Indians affected the records, but the attitudes of Indians toward non-Indians affected the records, too. The Indians' attitudes have changed over the years with their experience with their non-Indian neighbors. Generally, the Indians' attitudes have gone through a sequence such as those described below, some stages of which may have existed concurrently in a given Indian tribe among different members of the tribe.

The usual initial attitude toward the non-Indian was one of helpfulness. This was quite obvious as the original New England settlers came to this continent. For instance, the Indians in that area taught the settlers how to plant corn and other crops that could be grown in that part of the country.

As time went on, however, a gradual degeneration of this attitude of the Indian toward non-Indian became apparent. Helpfulness was succeeded by toleration; toleration by distrust; and distrust by disenchantment, until finally open hostility broke out. By the time open hostility flared up, usually the European settlers (or the American settlers later) were so much better equipped with arms and am-

Figure 7.15
Data for Heirship Finding

5—108 c

DATA FOR HEIRSHIP FINDING.

Tel-my-at,   1856
Allottee..Age...........
                    Not known, died two years before Charley, or Kay-a-kin.
Date of death, her husband...
                    S-369
Allotment No.................... Annuity No............ Vou........... Qr...........
                    SE4 NW4, E2 E2 SW4 NW4, E2 W2 NE4 SW4 NW4, N2 E2 E2
Description of land.........
    SE4 NW4 NW4, S2 N2 E2 W2 SE4 SW4 NW4, and N2 W2 W2 SE4 SW4 NW4,
    Sec. 6, Twp. 29 N., and E2 SW4, Sec. 24, Twp. 31 N., R. 31 E., N.M.,
    Wash., containing 133.125 acres.
Date of patent.... January 10, 1922.
                    March 22, 1906.
Act under which allotted.........

Father's name...Allotment No...........

Mother's name...Allotment No...........
                    Charley, or Kay-a-kin,
Spouse's name...Allotment No. S-381.

Personal property.........

                    PROBABLE HEIRS.   ADDRESSES.

..al quimalx, sister of husband,   Nespelem, Wash.

Paul Timentwa, nephew of husband,   Omak, Wash.

S. B. Susan (Timentwa), nephew of husband,   Mallott (near Omak),
                                                            Wash.

        (Note--The heirs of Charley, or Kay-a-kin, S-381, were   det'd
March 1, 1919, which was prior to issuance of trust patent
to allotment of Tel-my-at, his wife.   The Examiner of
Inheritance, Mr. Stuart H. Elliott, calls attention to the
fact that Charley or Kay-a-kin apparently inherits entire estate
of his predeceased wife, Tel-my-at.)

        Heirs Charley or Kayakin det'd 3-1-19, file 100996-18 JWH.
        I do not find that Tel-my-at had any inherited interests.

Courtesy Church of Jesus Christ of Latter-day Saints Library.

230

Figure 7.16
Will

IN THE NAME OF GOD, AMEN.

I, Maggie Steve, Indian of Hoopa Valley Reservation, County of Humboldt, State of California, of the age of about 50 years, and being of sound and disposing mind and memory, and not acting under duress, menace, fraud, or undue influence of any person whatever, do make , publish and declare this my last will and testiment in the manner following, that is to say:

I give and bequesth to my two children Ada Baldwin, aged 16 years, and Andrew Skaggs, aged 8 years, all of my real property, that is to say, my allotment of land on the Hoopa Valley Indian Reservation, California, to be shared between them equally; provided however, that if my daughter, Ada Baldwin does not return to the Reservation, then my son, Andrew Skaggs, is to have all of said property.

My personal property, consisting of furniture et cetera, in my dwelling is to be given in like manner to my children, subject to the same provision.

My husband, Steve, is to have charge of the property described during the minority of my said children, for their use and benefit.

In witness whereof, I have hereunto set my hand and seal this seventh day of September in the year of our Lord 1900.

Her

(Signed)   Maggie X Steve.   (Seal)

Mark.

The foregoing instrument, consisting of one page besides this was, at the date thereof, by the said Maggie Steve, Indian, signed and sealed and published as, and declared to us to be her last will and testament, in presence of us, who at her request and in her presence, and in the presence of each other have subscribed our names as witnesses thereto.

      (SIGNED) MARY ORR. Residing at Hoopa, California, Teacher in the Hoopa Valley Boarding School.

      (SIGNED) WILLIAM R. FREER. Residing at Hoopa, Calfornia Supt. and Spl. Disb. Agent, in charge of Hoopa Valley Indian Reservati

Courtesy Church of Jesus Christ of Latter-day Saints Library.

munition and other supplies that they were able to defeat the Indians, which left the Indians with a broken spirit. At that point, many of the Indians then accepted the government dole.

Those who lived under government supervision, for whom records were created and kept, are often termed "paper Indians." Paper Indians were those who accepted the reservation or the treaty or the annuities coming from the federal government and therefore had their names recorded on paper. Some who lived among the paper Indians, or at least in the same locality, refused to accept or comply with the government programs. They may have lived on the same reservation, but they refused to have anything to do with the Indian agent. They would not come in to talk to him, and they would not accept the government dole. These were termed "nonpaper Indians," and very few records were created for them.

Naturally, degradation followed the acceptance of the government dole on some reservations. This is one of the non-Indians' most common conceptions of Indians. They think of Indians as degraded and drunk, as having moral problems and drug problems. This degradation has been a long, hard thing to overcome on the part of many of the American Indians.

Recently a very interesting attitude has begun to build among the American Indian tribes throughout this country. At first it was one of rebellion, as in such organizations as the American Indian Movement (AIM), and more recently it has taken the form of a great increase in determination. Many of the younger Indians now are attending college and are determined to go back to help their people on the reservations, rather than seek jobs elsewhere.

WHERE ARE THE RECORDS?

One who begins to search out Indian ancestry must determine where to look for the records discussed above. There are a number of places to look for American Indian records, each significantly important.

The Family

One of the first places to start, in trying to trace an ancestral line, is with the family. To begin any genealogical research task, the researcher should obtain as much information as possible from family members. This is also true with American Indian research. However, problems may be encountered as relatives are asked about someone in their ancestral line.

First, many Indians are reluctant to talk about the dead. There are many reasons and many customs attendant, but many have this aversion. Second, they have a reluctance to discuss what they consider to be moral problems, such as many marriages, a woman having children by several different men during her lifetime, and so forth.

Bureau of Indian Affairs Offices

The BIA is one of the major custodians of American Indian records. There are three levels of BIA offices.

The local office is the agency or subagency. Generally, this is the best source of genealogical or historical information, for researchers who can visit it. Usually an agency (or subagency) has a number of records dating back to its establishment, and the records are often most complete in the agency office itself. There are some problems in using the agency offices. One is the long distance one sometimes has to travel to get to the agency. In many cases the same records may be more logically arranged, indexed, and inventoried, and therefore easier to use, elsewhere. Quite often the attitude of the agent may be less than helpful, unless the request emanates from an Indian enrolled at that agency.

The second level of the BIA is the area office. The area office has only a limited number of records of value to genealogists. It houses land records or lease records or other records relating to the land, which contain very little genealogical information other than that more readily available at the agency.

The third level is, of course, the commissioner's office in Washington, D.C. Over the years the commissioner's office has contained a number of good genealogical records; however, most of them have been transferred to the National Archives and are available for search there.

Tribal Offices

A third records custodian that must be mentioned is the tribal office. Since the Wheeler-Howard Act, or Indian Reorganization Act, in 1934, some tribes have begun keeping their own records; in many cases they have good records which should be searched for genealogy and family history purposes.

National Archives and Records Service

The largest collection of American Indian records in the United States is in the custody of the National Archives and Records Service in Washington, D.C. The National Archives has a large collection of agency records which have been transferred from agencies all over the United States. It also has most of those Bureau of Indian Affairs commissioner's office records that would be of any value to a genealogist or a historian. These include documents such as the correspondence of the commissioner, the correspondence of agents to the commissioner's office, reports from the various agencies with attachments such as the annual census roll and annuity rolls, and wills, which were mentioned earlier.

One of the great pleasures of using the National Archives collections is that it has a fairly complete inventory of its holdings and its collection is reasonably easy to use. Many of its records are also microfilmed and available for purchase.

The regional archives of the National Archives and Records Service are the largest collective holder of Indian records. Their collections consist primarily of the agency records for their respective regions. One notable fact is that the boundaries of these regions have changed over the years, so one needs to determine what the present regional boundaries are and then determine what other states they might have included at an earlier time. Generally the regional archivists are desirous of being helpful to the researcher who comes to their archives. The ten regional archives throughout the country and the states they serve are located and discussed in chapter 5.

Churches

A fifth custodian of records which must be considered is the churches. Many denominations were active in proselyting for Christian converts among the American Indian tribes. Particularly active were the Quakers, the Mormons, and several others. The content of their records varies considerably according to the denomination. A study into the historical background of the particular tribe being researched would be necessary to determine which of those denominations should be consulted.

Private Collections

Private collections, including historical societies, universities, and genealogical libraries, form a sixth category of records custodians. University collections often contain documents pertaining to American Indian affairs. One of the best Indian collections is at the University of Oklahoma in Norman. Other universities should be consulted for collections of Indian documents for their respective areas.

Another fairly recent project is the Doris Duke Oral History Project. Seven universities throughout the country have participated in the project by recording Indian history through oral history interviews of members of tribes in their respective areas. These are the University of Arizona (Tucson), the University of California at Los Angeles (UCLA), the University of Florida (Gainesville), the University of Illinois (Urbana), the University of New Mexico (Albuquerque), the University of South Dakota (Vermillion), and the University of Utah (Salt Lake City). The interviews will help with the historical background of the tribes involved and sometimes include family information as well.

One of the best collections anywhere in the country, as far as size, ease of use, and good indexes are concerned, is in the Oklahoma Historical Society in Oklahoma City. Other historical societies in the areas where tribal groups are located should be checked to see if they have such collections for their respective tribal interests.

The LDS Library in Salt Lake City has in its collections microfilm copies of many of the records from the above types of custodians.

SUMMARY

If the ancestor being researched is associated with a tribal group or a reservation, the research steps to be followed are (1) obtain as much information as possible from living relatives; (2) determine the tribal affiliation of the ancestor; (3) study the historical background of that tribe; (4) determine the agency of the BIA serving the particular tribe; (5) search the records of that agency (or those agencies) at the agency office or at the National Archives or its branches; (6) search records of churches active in proselyting the tribe; and (7) search any private collections relating to the tribe.

If the ancestor is a nonreservation Indian, approach the research in the same way as for any non-Indian ancestor until tribal affiliation is established.

Through it all, remember that American Indian research can be exciting, pleasant, and rewarding.

NOTES

1. U.S. Department of Interior, *Biographical and Historical Index of American Indians and Persons Involved in Indian Affairs* (Boston: G. K. Hall and Co., 1966).

2. Frederick Webb Hodge, *Handbook of American Indians North of Mexico* (1905; reprint ed., New York: Pageant Books, 1959).

3. John R. Swanton, *The Indian Tribes of North America,* Smithsonian Institution, Bureau of American Ethnology, Bulletin No. 145 (Washington, D.C.: Government Printing Office, 1952), pp. 1–2.

4. Quoted in Dee Brown, *Bury My Heart At Wounded Knee: An Indian History of the West* (New York: Bantam Books, 1972), p. 1.

5. Ibid., p. 2.

6. Ibid., p. 5.

BIBLIOGRAPHY

The American Indian: Select Catalog of National Archives Microfilm Publications. Washington, D.C.: National Archives, 1972.

> Presently out of print. A listing of Indian records at the National Archives that have been microfilmed, which includes most of the major classes of records at that depository that would aid the American Indian genealogist.

Carlile, Robert B., III, and Johnson, Jeffery O. "Tribal Sources: Native American Family History." *World Conference on Records* (2d, 1980) vol. 11, no. 313. Salt Lake City: Corporation of the President of the Church of Jesus Christ of Latter-day Saints, c1980.

> Primarily a discussion of the history and sources for Cherokee Indians.

Checklist of United States Public Documents, 1789–1909. 3d ed. 1911; reprint ed., New York: Kraus Reprint Corporation, 1962.

> Includes lists of annual and special reports of the Indian Affairs Office and the Indian Affairs Committee of the U.S. Congress.

Clark, Dick. *Cherokee Ancestor Research.* Modesto, Calif.: Rich-Nor-Lin Publications, 1979.

> Although this work is specific to Cherokee research, some of the information regarding sources is applicable to other tribes as well.

Clark, James R. "The Cultural and Historical Background of the Indian People—A Vital Part of the Genealogical Research Problem." *World Conference on Records and Genealogical Seminar,* area I-40. Salt Lake City: Genealogical Society of the Church of Jesus Christ of Latter-day Saints, c1969.

> Uses Crow and Makah tribes as case studies.

Crampton, C. Gregory. "The Indian Oral History Program Under the Doris Duke Grant." *World Conference on Records and Genealogical Seminar,* area I-39. Salt Lake City: Genealogical Society of the Church of Jesus Christ of Latter-day Saints, c1969.

A description of the oral history effort being carried out among American Indians by several U.S. universities.

Freeman, John R., comp. *A Guide to Manuscripts Relating to the American Indian in the Library of the American Philosophical Society.* Philadelphia: American Philosophical Society, 1966.

A descriptive guide of the manuscripts held by this old and revered society, which began collecting Indian manuscripts as early as 1802, when Thomas Jefferson was its president.

Handbook of North American Indians. Washington, D.C.: Smithsonian Institution, 1978– . vol. 6, June Helm, ed., *Subarctic,* 1981. vol. 8, Robert F. Heizer, ed., *California,* 1978. vol. 9, Alphonso Ortiz, ed., *Southwest,* 1979. vol. 15, Bruce G. Trigger, ed., *Northeast,* 1978.

The handbook is a projected twenty-volume set. Other volumes besides the four listed above may now be available. Titles of the remaining volumes are vol. 1, *Introduction;* vol. 2, *Indians in Contemporary Society;* vol. 3, *Environment, Origins, and Population;* vol. 4, *History of Indian-White Relations;* vol. 5, *Arctic;* vol. 7, *Northwest Coast;* vol. 10, *Southwest;* vol. 11, *Great Basin;* vol. 12, *Plateau;* vol. 13, *Plains;* vol. 14, *Southeast;* vol. 16, *Technology and Visual Arts;* vol. 17, *Languages;* vol. 18, *Biographical Dictionary;* vol. 19, *Biographical Dictionary;* and vol. 20, *Index.*

Hill, Edward E. "American Indian Records in the National Archives." *World Conference on Records and Genealogical Seminar,* area I-38. Salt Lake City: Genealogical Society of the Church of Jesus Christ of Latter-day Saints, c1969.

Description of the records relating to Indians of the BIA, the War Department, the Office of the Secretary of the Interior, and others, all housed at the National Archives in Washington, D.C.

———. *Guide to Records in the National Archives Relating to American Indians.* Washington, D.C.: National Archives, 1982.

A comprehensive descriptive catalog to federal records in the National Archives, and elsewhere, relating to American Indians.

———. *The Office of Indian Affairs, 1824–1880: Historical Sketches.* New York: Clearwater Publishing Co., 1974.

An excellent guide to the history and development of agencies and subagencies of the Office of Indian Affairs. Most genealogical and personal historical records for the American Indians were originated at the agency or subagency level.

———, comp. *Preliminary Inventory of the Records of the Bureau of Indian Affairs.* No. 163. 2 vols. Washington, D.C.: National Archives, 1965.

A comprehensive guide to American Indian records in the National Archives. Includes history and description of records sources and offices generating the records.

Hodge, Frederick Webb, ed. *Handbook of American Indians North of Mexico.* 2 vols. 1905; reprint. ed., New York: Pageant Books, 1959.

Alphabetically arranged listing of tribal groups, clans, villages, settlements, and biographies of tribal leaders. Includes a very comprehensive cross-reference to variant spellings and names of all North American Indian tribes.

Jackson, Curtis E., and Galli, Marcia J. *A History of the Bureau of Indian Affairs and Its Activities Among Indians.* San Francisco: R and E Research Associates, 1977.

The genealogical and historical records of the American Indian are incomprehensible if the researcher does not take into account the history of the various offices of the federal government responsible for Indian affairs. This book goes a long way in providing help in understanding the history of these offices.

Jenness, Diamond. *The Indians of Canada.* 1932; reprint ed., Toronto: University of Toronto Press, 1977.

The most comprehensive work available on Canadian Indians.

Johnson, Steven L. *Guide to American Indian Documents in the Congressional Serial Set: 1817–1899.* New York: Clearwater Publishing Co., 1977.

A fairly comprehensive guide to pre-1900 documents relating to American Indians in the Serial Set.

Kappler, Charles J., ed. *Indian Treaties, 1778–1883*. New York: Interland Publishing Co., 1972.

Treaties usually were the basis upon which the federal government dealt with the Indian tribes and often marked the beginning of the keeping of federal records on tribal members. Includes names of tribal leaders who signed the treaties.

Kelsay, Laura E., comp. *Cartographic Records of the Bureau of Indian Affairs*. Special List 13. Washington, D.C.: National Archives, 1977.

A very helpful guide to maps in the National Archives relating to American Indians.

Kerner, Gaiselle, comp. *Preliminary Inventory of the Records of the United States Court of Claims*. No. 58. Washington, D.C.: National Archives, 1953.

Includes entries relating to American Indian claims cases.

Kirkham, E. Kay. "The Native American: Records That Establish Individual and Family Identity." *World Conference on Records* (2d, 1980) vol. 3, pt. 1, no. 302. Salt Lake City: Corporation of the President of the Church of Jesus Christ of Latter-day Saints, c1980.

A brief discussion of Indian research with an extensive and very helpful glossary of terms relating to American Indian records.

————. *Our Native Americans and Their Records of Genealogical Value*. Vol. 1. Logan, Utah: Everton Publishers, 1980.

A listing of sources for family history of the American Indian.

Klein, Bernard, and Icolari, Daniel, eds. *Reference Encyclopedia of the American Indian*. 2d ed. 2 vols. Rye, N.Y.: Todd Publishers, 1973.

Includes information about reservations and an extensive bibliography.

Maestas, John R. "Growing Up Among the Indians of the American Southwest." *World Conference on Records* (2d, 1980) vol. 3, pt. 1, no. 305. Salt Lake City: Corporation of the President of the Church of Jesus Christ of Latter-day Saints, 1980.

A discussion of the family life and cultural differences of twentieth-century Indians of the Southwest.

"Major Genealogical Record Sources of the Indians of the United States." Rev. ed., 1977. Research Paper, series B, no. 2. Salt Lake City: Genealogical Department, Church of Jesus Christ of Latter-day Saints, 1977.

A brief general listing of the major sources for American Indian genealogy, what they contain and where they can be located.

Miles, Walter. "American Indian Research." *Genealogy* 58 (January 1981): 6–8.

A brief description of American Indian sources for family history research.

Parker, Jimmy B. "American Indian Genealogical Research." *National Genealogical Society Quarterly* 63 (March 1975): 15–21.

Genealogical research methodology and sources.

————. "Sources of American Indian Genealogy." *Genealogical Journal* 6 (September 1977): 120–25.

A description of sources for family history studies of the American Indian.

Prucha, Francis Paul. *A Bibliographical Guide to the History of Indian-White Relations in the United States*. Chicago: University of Chicago Press, 1977.

A monumental work of great help to American Indian researchers. Part 1 lists guides to sources. Part 2 contains a classified and selected bibliography of published works.

Ronda, James P., and Axtell, James, comps. *Indian Missions: A Critical Bibliography*. Bloomington: Indiana University Press, 1978.

Part of a series of bibliographies growing out of the Indian Studies program at Newberry Library.

Schmeckebier, Laurence R. *The Office of Indian Affairs: Its History, Activities, and Organization*. Baltimore: Johns Hopkins Press, 1927; reprint ed., New York: AMS Press, 1972.

Although much of this book is outdated, the very important section dealing with the history of the Office of Indian Affairs is not.

Smith, E. B., comp. *Indian Tribal Claims Decided in the Court of Claims of the United*

States . . . to June 30, 1947. Washington, D.C.: University Publications of America, 1947.
Many Indian tribes have had claims against the federal government settled in this court. It is important to know when those cases were settled, since important genealogical records were often generated in the process of determining how the claims settlements would be made.

Smith, Jane F., ed. *Indian-White Relations; A Persistent Paradox.* Washington, D.C.: Howard University Press, 1976.
Proceedings of the National Archives Conference on Research in the History of Indian-White Relations, held 15–16 June 1972.

Spindel, Donna. *Introductory Guide to Indian-Related Records (to 1876) in the North Carolina State Archives.* Raleigh: North Carolina State Division of Archives and History, 1977.
A description of sources containing North Carolina Indian information, many of which would be very difficult and time-consuming to find without this guide.

Swanton, John R. *The Indian Tribes of North America.* Smithsonian Institution, Bureau of American Ethnology, Bulletin 145. Washington, D.C.: Government Printing Office, 1952.
History, location, and population details for all major tribes. Arranged alphabetically by state and thereunder by tribal name, with cross-reference if a tribe resided in more than one state.

Thernstron, Stephan, and Orlov, Ann, eds. *Harvard Encyclopedia of American Ethnic Groups.* Cambridge, Mass.: Harvard University, Belknap Press, 1980.
Includes sixty-four pages on the American Indian. Every person desiring to do Indian research should read all sixty-four pages, including the portion on federal policy toward Indians.

U.S., Department of Commerce. *Federal and State Indian Reservations and Indian Trust Areas.* Washington, D.C.: Government Printing Office, 1972.
Descriptions of reservations and trust areas. Arranged alphabetically by state, then by name of reservation. Subheadings under reservations include land status, history, culture, government, tribal economy, climate, transportation, community facilities, recreation, and vital statistics.

U.S., Department of Interior. *Biographical and Historical Index of American Indians and Persons Involved in Indian Affairs.* 8 vols. Boston: G. K. Hall and Co., 1966.
A comprehensive index of people mentioned in Indian Office reports and other sources as well. Includes bibliographical entries.

U.S., Department of Interior, Census Office. *Report on Indians Taxed and Indians Not Taxed in the United States (except Alaska) at the Eleventh Census: 1890.* Washington, D.C.: Government Printing Office, 1894.
Excellent history and statistics on the Indians of the United States at that time.

U.S. National Archives. *Preliminary Inventory of the Records Created by the Field Offices of the Bureau of Indian Affairs.* No. 192. Washington, D.C.: National Archives, 1981.

User's Guide to the American Indian Correspondence: The Presbyterian Historical Society's Collection of Missionary's Letters, 1833–1893. Westport, Conn.: Greenwood Press, 1978.
A 100-page guide to the use of a special collection of American Indian manuscripts at the Presbyterian Historical Society in Philadelphia. The entire collection has been microfilmed by Greenwood Press on 35 rolls. The guide includes a reel-by-reel list of contents, author, and subject index and tribal index.

Younkin, C. George. "Historical and Genealogical Records of the Five Civilized Tribes and Other Indian Records." *World Conference on Records and Genealogical Seminar,* area I-42. Salt Lake City: Genealogical Society of the Church of Jesus Christ of Latter-day Saints, 1969.
A comprehensive listing of the records of the Five Civilized Tribes and a brief history of how the records originated.

————. "Researching American Indian Ancestry." In *Recueil de 11ᵉ Congres International des Sciences Genealogique et Heraldique.* Liège, Belgium: Office généalogique et héraldique de Belgique, 1972.
A good description of the use of the regional archives branches of the National Archives.

————. "Searching for American Indian Genealogy." *Stripes* 17 (1977): 167–82.
A general overview of the problems in tracing American Indian genealogy and a general listing of soruces.

8

Asian-American Records and Research

GREG GUBLER

While the Atlantic migration of Americans is chronicled in numerous volumes and is the subject of many genealogical guides, there is little to be found on those coming from the other direction. America was settled from east to west, mainly by whites of European stock. Pacific migration is a relatively recent phenomenon. The participants were fewer, the reception more hostile, and the assimilation process more difficult. As a result of racial bars and prejudices, Asian Americans have kept close ethnic ties and have strived for a sense of community as security in the larger white society. The myths associated with Asia and the Asians have been the source of the majority of the problems Asian Americans have faced in the new country. Only now is genuine acceptance finally becoming a reality. As a result of their experiences, when considered collectively, Asian Americans are, for the most part, a reticent, hard-working group. Understanding and translating the experiences of Asian Americans has never been easy.

Because of the relatively recent arrival of Asian immigrants, it is difficult to divorce them from their Asian past. There are still strong ethnic ties, though in the contemporary world these are beginning to fade. These vestiges of the past can provide clues for family research, but for many Asian Americans, research for their origins is not an easy task. They are hampered by complex languages and a lack of direction and information about records and procedures. Many regard genealogical research much as a high mountain, not knowing the techniques or gadgets available for climbing. But climbing, as with any activity, begins with the first step and proceeds a step at a time. It is the approach and the strategy that lead to successes, however piecemeal they may be. Fortunately, however, these efforts have their own rewards, the discovery of heritage, family, and self.

At the outset it must be emphasized that the term "Asian" includes many diverse and independent peoples, just as the words "European" and "African" do. The traditions cover a wide range, and many traditions exist side by side: Buddhist, Hindu, Confucian, Islamic, or native. The high degree of cultural pluralism in Asia makes it difficult to generalize about Asian records and research.

This chapter focuses on what is available, but the discussion is limited by the lack of source materials and by my own specialized background. I recognize that more precise, practical, and systematic studies, tailored to the needs of the respective Asian-American groups, are sorely needed. I hope this introduction, however limited, will be a step in the right direction.

RESEARCH PROBLEMS AND APPROACHES

Earlier in this work, Jean Elder Cazort introduced the researcher to the basic techniques of genealogical pursuit. Because the majority of Asian immigrants arrived quite recently, many of the American records and techniques she describes may not apply. It may, nonetheless, be wise to review some of the basic steps of research outlined in her chapter before encountering the specific problems and approaches outlined here.

One of the most formidable problems for those contemplating Asian research is the language barrier. Because the great majority of Asian immigrants have arrived within the past century, the language problem is usually encountered fairly soon. There is, furthermore, no relationship between the Asian languages and English, the primary language of Americans. Whereas European immigrants find similar roots and stems in the language structure of English, Asians must start entirely anew, unless they were fortunate enough to learn some English before they arrived.

Succeeding generations of Asian Americans find it almost impossible to develop enough expertise in the language of their ancestors to do more advanced research. Some, indeed, are able to speak the language, but writing it is usually another matter. That is because the largest group of Asian immigrants comes from Japan, China, and Korea, where Chinese characters are an integral part of the language system. These languages require constant use and a great deal of memorizing. For example, basic literacy in Chinese requires the understanding and use of over 5,000 characters, while Japanese need to know at least 2,000, but most of these have multiple readings. The number of characters used in the historical context can exceed this several times, depending on the sources used and the period.

Even though Koreans presently prefer to write in phonetic *han'gul*, the syllabary have their character equivalents, which are still used for names and when more precise meanings are needed. Most older Korean genealogies and documents are written entirely in classical Chinese but are read in Korean. Chinese characters were used in Vietnam, too, before the French instituted Romanization. Romanization was also instituted in other areas under colonial rule, such as

Indonesia, Burma, the Philippines, and parts of India. Separate scripts exist for Thai, Hindi, Tamil, and some other lesser-known languages. Most of these languages can only be mastered and kept up in the home environment or in a similar situation recreated in the new country.

Asian immigrants have usually experienced extreme difficulty in becoming assimilated because of language and cultural differences. Many have continued to use the native language and have preferred to remain close to the ethnic community. Their facility with English has generally been marginal, though a number have had to know enough to survive in the business world. Ethnic publications, including newspapers, directories, and periodic bulletins have kept the immigrants abreast of developments both in the new country and back home. The majority of Asian immigrants before World War II considered themselves temporary sojourners abroad and expected to return after making enough money to establish themselves in the home country, but many were unable to return for one reason or another.

Japanese in the United States considered themselves *dekasegi* (temporarily working away from home), while the Chinese here were referred to as *hua-chiao* (overseas Chinese). The majority of Koreans had no interest in returning because Japan was occupying their homeland. Filipinos, on the other hand, were a colonial people of the United States and as such could immigrate, at least until the Depression produced further legislation against the entry of laborers.

Because the children of the immigrants generally were trained in English-language schools and lacked the enormous commitment required to learn their parents' languages, a large communications gap generally existed between the generations. The next generations were almost totally Americanized. As a result, dealing with local ethnic sources as well as those abroad is usually beyond most Asian Americans. It is imperative, therefore, to identify those few with bilingual capabilities. In addition, scholars need to translate more of the ethnic sources and make them available to later generations. As this point, little has been done in this regard.

A related problem is the Romanization, or Anglicization, of character-based languages. Because several Romanization systems and dialects exist, consistency in spellings and pronunciations is hard to attain. As most Asian immigrants struggled with English, errors were usually made in completing even simple forms. Immigration officials and bureaucrats usually had trouble understanding the immigrants and therefore made errors in their paperwork. Many of the spellings in immigration records bear little resemblance to the actual pronunciation of the characters. The majority of immigrants merely adopted Western-type names to simplify pronunciation and to gain social acceptance. They would still use native names in ethnic circles.

The character name is usually essential if research is to continue, though in some cases correlation can be made with Romanization. This depends on the accuracy of the Romanization and the number of readings in the original language. Because Chinese is tonal and Japanese has multiple readings, research is difficult unless one knows the original characters. While American sources are helpful, it is necessary to correlate them with sources abroad; otherwise research will come to a dead end.

In the conversion of other scripts to the Roman alphabet, intelligence and information are lost. The resulting product is useful only in a phonetic sense and is extremely difficult to convert back. For example, the letters "ma" could be interpreted many ways, including mother, frog, horse, hemp, paralysis, or curse, depending on the specific character used. Moreover, it is difficult to show the various tones represented by these variations of "ma." Although the Pinyin system now used to transliterate Chinese on the mainland is an improvement over the more traditional and confusing Wade-Giles system, the tonal aspects of the language, as well as the large number of fairly precise symbols, make conversion extremely difficult. While those who research European sources at least have a familiar script, most Asian Americans are handicapped by the entirely different language system. Transliteration usually is insufficient; everything has to be translated. This is a very laborious process and it can be quite expensive unless one has relatives or friends who are able and willing to help out.

Another problem of considerable importance is the lack of library materials for Asian immigrants. Since most of those directing library acquisitions efforts are of British or other European origin, those efforts that have been made toward collecting materials of genealogical and family history value (and most have been made by specialty libraries and archives) have generally focused on the so-called larger group. Attention to minority peoples is a relatively recent phenomenon. Librarians are handicapped, too, by their lack of knowledge of the available resources and by shrinking budgets. Thus most libraries have few resources of value for Asian Americans. The few collections that do have certain strengths will be covered separately in this section. Even the stronger collections are few in number and poorly publicized.

Much of the problem concerning the lack of library materials is that in many cases nothing exists to collect. Since Asian research can be quite complex and involved, and traditions and attitudes toward genealogy are considerably different, this is understandable. For example, the Japanese are usually more interested in surname origins and family crests than in delving into their respective lines, while the Chinese are concerned with lineage continuity along the surname line, largely because of their traditions of ancestral veneration and filial piety.

Korean interests are similar to those of the Chinese because of similar Confucian influences. While Westerners are concerned with their various lines of ascent, Chinese and Koreans see a genealogy branching from a founding ancestor or grand patriarch. Their genealogies represent male succession, with women in only a peripheral role. Generation order and linkage ties are common threads, whereas the relationship of the parts is secondary. Because one is only an individual within a large branch, there is no interest beyond the direct patriarchal linkage to the founding ancestor.

Our Western tradition, on the other hand, emphasizes the ego and the need to uncover as many lines as practically possible. To bring the two together, there-fore, Asian-American genealogical research requires a person educated in the Western tradition and aware of Asian traditions. Outside of a few pioneer efforts, there is very little as yet available relating directly to research. There are, of course, items of value of a historical or peripheral nature, but most of them fail to address the research process. Considerable research and effort must be made before the Asian American has anywhere near the information available to the European American.

Even the types of information found in homes may differ in the Asian-Ameri-can context. There are, of course, the usual items found in homes anywhere, such as photographs, clippings, correspondence, certificates, passports, immi-gration papers, family mementos, financial records, journals and diaries, and many other things of a personal or family nature. But what items are unique to Asian Americans? Japanese Americans may have traditional family crests (*ka-mon* or *iemon*), family genealogies (*kafu* or *keizu*), old copies of family registers (*koseki* or *joseki*), paper or wooden mortuary tablets (*ihai*), and any number of ethnic community publications, as well as other items unique to their own tradi-tions. Chinese Americans, on the other hand, may have clan or family gene-alogies (*chia-p'u* or *tsu-p'u*), family registers or individual certificates, publica-tions of Chinese societies and organizations, records relating to immigration, and other pertinent records or materials. Korean Americans may also have access to clan or family genealogies (*chopko* or *ga-jung*), Japanese-era *hojuk* (family registers), immigration records, and so on. Some Vietnamese refugees have escaped with little more than the clothes on their backs, while others were immigrants of means, who have brought many items.

While one may find only a few of these items, there may be clues in them that will help to extend the pedigree and reconstruct family history. The value of an old letter, receipt, or certificate may be minimal, or it may provide clues to the researcher. Those clues which should be sought include the following: places of origin of immigrant families and ancestors, names and addresses of relatives and friends abroad, dates and means of arrival, names of fellow immigrants, names of relatives and friends in this country, dates and places of sojourn or residence, information on citizenship and naturalization, and information on family rela-tionships and traditions, employment, and educational and community matters. It is important to remember that clues can lead to a breakthrough.

Other problems relating to Asian-American genealogical research will be han-dled separately under the specific areas in this discussion, such as Chinese, Japanese, Korean, and Filipino. These include the scattered nature of the sources, the lack of complete catalogs and inventories, problems with multiple names and name identification, problems of dating and the different dating systems, the thorny problem of relating older place names to recent jurisdictions, and problems with access to and preservation of records.

Because the research process has been poorly articulated in most instances, Asian Americans who contemplate research should be aware that they will face difficulties that will seem insurmountable. While, as mentioned, the problems are formidable, it is worth noting that many Asian Americans have done successful research. They have had to seek language assistance and have found out for themselves the best approaches. Some groundwork has been done and knowledge gained, thus making this process considerably easier than it once was. While no comprehensive resources are available thus far, a few suggestions and a bibliography should provide direction enough for beginners. Because of the number of different situations, more specific suggestions about the records and research processes will be handled in this chapter under separate geographic and language headings.

The many obstacles notwithstanding, Asian Americans have some advantages in research: some excellent records can be tapped; fewer immigrants and closer group affinities exist; and many of these immigrants have arrived recently enough to have ties in the country of origin. If these advantages are exploited, research can be much easier.

IMMIGRANT GROUPS AND SETTLEMENT PATTERNS

Immigration is one of the major themes of American history. A steady flow of immigrants from Europe arrived on the East Coast prior to the American Revolution and continuing through this century. Until the discovery of gold in California, however, Asian immigration was negligible. Labor demands on the West Coast and in Hawaii brought thousands of Asians, but never anywhere near the numbers which came from Europe. Nonetheless, the first efforts to control immigration were brought about by the so-called "yellow peril." Distrust of the Chinese "coolies," who were willing to work for low wages and who kept to themselves, was responsible for legislation by Congress in 1882 to restrict Chinese immigration. Japanese laborers, who began to replace the Chinese, were also met with suspicion and sometimes outright hostility.

The Gentleman's Agreement in 1907 with Japan to curtail labor immigration was followed by discriminatory legislation in a number of states and the eventual bar against Orientals legislated by Congress in 1924. The racial bar was retained until 1952. A new phase of Asian immigration began in 1965, when restrictions on national origins were dropped in favor of quotas for relatives of immigrants and those with priority skills.

Because of the different phases and immigrant groups involved, there are wide differences in research approaches and problems. Some Koreans, for example, immigrated to Hawaii just after the turn of the century, but much larger numbers have arrived since the 1965 immigration changes. The largest number of Japanese came in the 1886 through 1924 period, while many Chinese came between 1852 and 1882.

The recent influx of Vietnamese, Koreans, Thais, and Chinese from Taiwan and Hong Kong has also altered traditional immigration patterns. Newly arrived immigrants may still have close ties to their native countries (except those from Indochina who fled as refugees) and most likely have a capability in their native languages. To do effective research, it is important that one be able to place his or her own family and the immigrant generation in historical perspective. The following synopsis of the immigrant groups and settlement patterns is intended merely as an outline. For further details, refer to specific volumes in the bibliography.

Chinese

The opening of the West, which was greatly hastened by the discovery of gold in California and the development of the plantation system in Hawaii, created demands for cheap labor. But equally important were the conditions within China that contributed to the exodus. Severe economic dislocations and political unrest stemming from the Opium War (1839–40) and heightened by the T'ai-p'ing Rebellion (1850s) made life difficult in many areas of south China. In addition, intense local feuds in the Pearl River delta forced many people along and near the coast adjacent to present-day Hong Kong to seek a better life.

Some came under contract, and some were forced against their will as "coolies," but the majority arrived under the credit ticket system, in which an advance was made for the ticket across. This was to be paid back to the sponsoring firm, which also helped find a job and settle the immigrant in the new country. Once the exclusion legislation was passed in 1882, and because only the offspring of American citizens were allowed entry, the system of "paper sons" was used to bring Chinese to the New World. Slots were very valuable, and a thriving business ensued until regulations were further tightened.

San Francisco's Chinatown began to flourish soon after the discovery of gold. California was referred to as the "gold mountain" or the "golden hills" because of the relatively high wages and news of the precious metal. Many Chinese worked in the mining camps, assisted in building the Western railroads, and were active in business ventures and the trades. Some were also involved in handicrafts and in the fishing industry. It is estimated that all but one percent of the Chinese on the West Coast came from Kwangtung Province. Certain districts of the province, such as Sze Yap, Sam Yap, and the Chung Shan districts near the mouth of the Pearl River, produced the majority. *A History of the Chinese in California*, published by the Chinese Historical Society of America, discusses the geographical background of the immigrants and their early activities. It notes that Chinese commonly grouped themselves in family name associations, depending on their Chinese origins. These associations were grouped together as benevolent organizations to protect rights of members and to promote ethnic solidarity.[1]

A series of nuisance laws was passed in California against the Chinese. Finally, California's second constitution, adopted in 1879, made it illegal for corporations and governments to employ Chinese. By 1882 advocates of total exclusion were able to push a law through the U.S. Congress. The 1880 census, just prior to exclusion, indicates that 105,000 were listed as Chinese in the United States. Of that number, about 80,000 lived in California, where the anti-Chinese movement was centered, while nearly 10,000 lived in Oregon. Labor organizations were behind much of the movement, and for the next two decades they continued to push anti-Chinese ordinances.

Even though "paper sons" and offspring entered, by 1920 the number of Chinese in the continental United States had dropped because of deaths and departures to 60,000. There was a slow increase thereafter, but it was not until 1943, when President Franklin D. Roosevelt repealed the Chinese Exclusion Act as a gesture of friendship to our allies abroad, that immigration was once again allowed.

The first Chinese to arrive in the Hawaiian Islands arrived in small numbers as early as the 1820s. Efforts to import plantation workers in the 1850s increased the number of arrivals dramatically. The majority came on contract but left the plantations at the first opportunity. With the increased demand for sugar after the Civil War, the Board of Immigration actively sought workers in China. Again the majority came from Kwangtung, though the distribution included wider geographical areas than the distribution of immigrants to California. Roughly 30 percent in Hawaii were of Hakka origin, while only about 3 percent in the West Coast were Hakka.

The largest surge of immigration came after the 1876 reciprocity treaty between the Kingdom of Hawaii and the United States. Because sugar was allowed duty-free entry, the demand for it rose immediately. By 1880 there were nearly 20,000 Chinese in Hawaii, about 30 percent of whom were working on the plantations. While a few chose to renew their contracts, the majority left to enter retail businesses or returned to China when their contracts expired. As in the United States, agitation against the Chinese, who had increased to 20 percent of the population by the 1880s, began to grow. In 1888 legislation banning labor immigration was passed in Hawaii. Other Chinese still were eligible, but they were to be screened by the newly formed Chinese Bureau.

The Chinese in Hawaii also organized through district associations, some clan organizations, trade guilds, and benevolent associations. The United Chinese Society, founded in 1884, protected the interests of Chinese in Hawaii. The Chinese Civic Association was also founded to increase awareness of the ethnic heritage and to promote Chinese advancement in the larger community. Chinese in the 1890s became more aware of their rights and began to protest the harsh measures and poor working conditions on the plantations.

Japanese, considered more servile, were brought in to supplement the work force and to weaken Chinese resistance. Many of the Chinese moved into Honolulu's Chinatown, but much of Chinatown was destroyed when fires set to control the bubonic plague raged out of control. The Chinese were able to rebuild, and many prospered. Hawaii was annexed to the United States in 1900, and gradually many of the immigration restrictions were applied to territories, including Hawaii. In 1932 there were 24,000 Chinese in Hawaii, only about 3 percent of whom were connected with plantations. The majority were retailers, and some were even entering professional occupations.

After the lifting of exclusion legislation in 1943, a small number of Chinese entered the United States each year, mostly relatives of professionals leaving Mainland China, where the Communists were steadily gaining control. The numbers have swelled considerably since 1965. Yearly averages have been in the vicinity of 20,000, with the distribution more widespread than before. While major Chinatowns still exist in San Francisco and New York City, where Cantonese has been spoken for several generations, many of the new immigrants settle wherever opportunities for advancement are present. A large percentage of Chinese Americans are well-educated professionals. There seems to be a preference for California life, for in 1980 there were an estimated 150,000 Chinese Americans in the Los Angeles area, with 15,000 living in the Los Angeles Chinatown.[2]

There are probably between 700,000 and 800,000 Chinese in the United States at present, though recent trends toward intermarriage and some illegal immigration make it difficult to arrive at a precise figure.

Japanese

Japan was under a tightly controlled feudal government until 1868. Emigration was strictly forbidden. A few Japanese left or accidentally landed abroad, but these cases were rare. After the modern state was established in 1868, a few overseas ventures were allowed but emigration was still piecemeal. By 1885, however, with the agreement with the Hawaiian government, emigration was allowed on a much larger scale. Many emigration companies in Japan actively recruited contract workers for the Hawaiian sugar plantations. The focus of the recruiting was in southwestern Japan, where famine and a depressed economy made the promise of income in Hawaii an enticing offer. Most hoped to save some money and return to their villages more esteemed and more financially secure.

Certain villages in Hiroshima, Yamaguchi, Kumamoto, and Fukuoka prefectures provided large numbers of workers. Other areas, however, such as Niigata, Fukushima, Okayama, and the island of Shikoku, also had groups of emigrants. After the turn of the century, a number from Okinawa left for Hawaii. Most, though not all, were plantation workers.

The first attempt to import Japanese labor to Hawaii, in 1868, was a failure. Most of the 153 recruits were from the back streets of Tokyo and Yokohama and were unable to adjust to conditions in the hot sugar cane fields. As a result the Japanese received bad publicity. Because of fears in Hawaii regarding the Chinese, pressures mounted to find another source of cheap labor. The Contract Convention of 1886 was the result of several years of lobbying by the Hawaiian government and sugar interests. By 1894, when the convention was revised to allow for individual immigration, nearly 30,000 Japanese laborers had arrived in Hawaii.

While many Japanese returned home at the end of their contracts, some remained on the plantations, while others chose to move into the cities and seek other occupations. Despite increasing restrictions, there were over 100,000 Japanese in Hawaii by 1920. At the time of Japanese exclusion in 1924, Japanese made up 43 percent of the population of the islands. They still number roughly one-third, though some of these have come from Japan just in the past few years.

A small party of Japanese tried to start an agricultural colony in northern California in 1869, but this experiment failed. By the time the Japanese began to arrive in larger numbers on the West Coast in the mid-1880s, there was already a hostile attitude against Orientals due to the Chinese problem. Many Japanese settled on marginal agricultural land and were employed in mining and labor jobs. By 1900 around 40,000 Japanese lived in the continental United States, about two-thirds of them settling in California. Some of these had left Hawaii, while others had followed relatives and friends from Japan to opportunities in the United States. While some of the early arrivals settled in San Francisco, the Los Angeles area soon had the largest concentration. By 1930 around 35,000 Japanese Americans lived in this area; the majority farmed, were in the vegetable trucking business, or were involved in nurseries or gardening, while those in the *Nihon machi* (Japan town) in the city center were in retail trades and related occupations. There were small Japanese sections in many cities in the West during this period.

The majority of Japanese immigrants on the West Coast arrived between 1900 and 1915. There was a traffic in picture brides from 1910 through 1921 that provided wives for many of those already here, but the end of immigration in 1924 meant that many Japanese men never married, since many states banned interracial marriages. Restrictions on owning land and obtaining citizenship also hampered the progress of Japanese Americans in this country.

Animosity between Japan and the United States grew after 1924, peaking in 1941 with the tragedy of Pearl Harbor. Japanese Americans on the West Coast were forced to move to designated camps in the interior, because they were considered by some a security threat. Even native-born citizens were encamped. About 110,000 Japanese Americans were sent to the internment camps in one of the most shameful episodes in our nation's history. Because of the numbers in Hawaii and logistics problems, similar actions were not pursued. Japanese Americans proved to be loyal. Because they were allowed to take only a few belongings to the camps and had to relinquish their property, Japanese Americans on the mainland had to start over again after the Second World War. This interruption makes genealogical research all the more difficult.

After the war Japanese Americans generally moved to the suburbs. Many took white collar and technical jobs. With the passing of the McCarren-Walter Act of 1952, exclusion was ended and citizenship was finally allowed. About 25,000 "war brides" entered the United States under special provisions, both during and after the occupation of Japan (1945–50) and the Korean War (1950–53), when U.S. troops were stationed in Japan. Although immigration restrictions were eased considerably in 1965, the number of Japanese entering has been proportionately less than the number of immigrants from other Asian groups because of the economic boom and excellent fringe benefits in Japan. Approximately 700,000 Japanese reside in the United States at present, with the states of California and Hawaii having the majority (nearly 300,000 each).

The Japanese have had very closely knit community organizations, including regional associations. There have also been Japanese newspapers, churches, funeral homes, and many businesses which have served the ethnic community. Since World War II the Japanese American Citizen's League has become prominent in promoting the rights of Japanese Americans and in serving the ethnic community. Before the war the Japanese consulates kept the people aware of their legal and political rights and tried to protect the interests of citizens in the deteriorating situation.

Koreans

Until this century Korean immigration to the United States was practically insignificant. About 7,000 Koreans immigrated to Hawaii between 1903 and 1905, during a time of political strife and domestic turmoil. Many of these were initially employed on the sugar plantations. A number of political refugees also came to Hawaii after Japan annexed Korea in 1910. From Hawaii, a few thousand came to the West Coast, settling mainly in California. Still, there were only 6,000 Koreans in Hawaii in 1930 and a few thousand in California.

Since the lifting of racial quotas in 1965, an influx of large proportions has occurred. In the ten-year period from 1965 to 1975, 3 percent of all immigrants to the United States were Korean. By 1975 the Korean-American community in the United States numbered around 400,000. Present estimates are in the range of 600,000 or more. Over 150,000 live in the Los Angeles area, while an estimated 30,000 Korean Americans reside in the Washington, D.C., area. Chicago, Honolulu, San Francisco Bay, and Seattle also have Korean communities. Many of the Koreans are professionals or small business operators. Since over 90 percent have arrived in the past two decades, most are very closely tied to Korea, as well as to Korean associations in the larger cities. Since Koreans are continuing to apply and to come to the United States because of the opportunities here, the number will continue to grow as fast as immigration laws permit.

Indochinese

The Indochinese group is composed primarily of refugees from Vietnam, Cambodia and Laos (the area formerly known as French Indochina). Since the fall of Indochina to the Communists in the spring of 1975, there has been a steady flow of refugees, approximately 200,000 of whom have been resettled in the United States. Some refugees fled overland to Thailand, while others escaped by small boats into the South China Sea. Many died during these escape attempts, while others were treated harshly or plundered. Most of those who reached the United States had very few possessions and were in need of relief aid. About 20,000 Indochinese people settled in the United States during the Vietnam War (1966–75). About 40 percent of these immigrants are Catholics, many of whom had gone to South Vietnam when the Communists gained the North in 1954 by defeating the French. Many of these refugee groups have been sponsored by organizations. The refugees have been widely dispersed, though there are certain places where they are more numerous, such as in California, Texas, and the Washington, D.C., area. They range from educated professionals to primitive tribespeople.

Other Asians

Approximately 150,000 immigrants have come from the Indian subcontinent, which comprises the present countries of India, Pakistan, and Bangladesh. About 20,000 U.S. residents of this background are comparatively old residents or descendents of those who arrived in the first two decades of this century, before the door was closed on Asian aliens. The larger portion has arrived since the easing of immigration quotas in 1965. Many of these are professionals or business operators. Although they are somewhat dispersed, there is a preference for urban areas: about 30,000 live in the New York metropolitan area; roughly the same number in the Los Angeles and San Francisco areas; and about 10,000 in the Chicago area. Philadelphia and Boston also have East Indian communities, as does the Washington, D.C., area.

Approximately 10,000 Indonesians also live in the United States, many of whom left their original country during the turmoil of the 1960s. Most are professionals and live in widely scattered areas.

While over 20,000 Thais are reported to live in the United States, the number might be considerably higher if illegal aliens were counted. It is highly probable that many live in the Los Angeles area alone, while there are also groups in the New York City and Chicago areas. Several thousand Thai women married U.S. servicemen in the 1960s and early 1970s, when U.S. forces were stationed in Thailand.

In recent years other groups on the fringe of Asia have also arrived. Since the Revolution of 1979, many Iranians have chosen to stay in the United States or have left their native land as political exiles. The majority of these are students or professional people. A few Afghans have also arrived since the Soviet occupation of their country.

The so-called Asian-American community is really a number of ethnic communities with diverse backgrounds and traditions.[3] Some of their members can trace their families through five generations in America, while others have just arrived and are just beginning to taste the common American experience.

RECORDS IN THE CONTINENTAL UNITED STATES AND HAWAII

The offspring of more recent immigrants may be able to proceed directly to records abroad, which are covered in the next section, by searching out home sources and utilizing family contacts. Many Asian Americans, however, are now several generations removed from the old country. Ties in the home country may have lapsed. Research must be broadened at this point to include possible record sources in the continental United States and Hawaii. Hawaii is mentioned separately because it was an independent island nation until annexation to the United States in 1900. Its record-keeping traditions are different enough to require separate treatment as the various record categories are presented.

One must keep in mind that record sources for Asian Americans in the various states (and preannexation Hawaii) rarely go beyond the immigrant. Still, these records can provide important information, or at least clues, in helping the researcher arrive at that point. As the generations pass, the importance of these records should increase. The emphasis here will be mainly on the Asian context; further details about genealogical research methods within this country can be found in the other chapters of this book and in other books on genealogy and the research process.

Vital Records

Vital records are essentially records of vital events: births, deaths, marriages, and divorces. A discussion of those records and their value is contained in chapter 2.

Members of Asian ethnic groups have sometimes failed to understand the regulations and procedures governing the creation of vital records. While third parties sometimes submitted information, the immigrants and their children often neglected to do so. Immigrants and children in Hawaii were encouraged to submit the details, even if years later. A record category called "delayed birth certificates" was created in the 1890s and continued for several decades. These records are available from the Hawaii State Department of Health from 1896 and from the Hawaii State Archives before that time, and they are on film through 1903 at the Genealogical Society of Utah (or LDS) Library and its branches.

There are also some records that contain vital information pertaining to Japanese immigrants to Hawaii. For example, for the period 1885–1910 the Japanese Consulate General in Honolulu has records which give the name of the immigrant and family members, birth and death dates, and the former family residence in Japan. A series of cards by household head from 1885 to the present also includes this information.

Census Records

Census records are essentially surveys at a point in time; they are made at intervals and include information on the composition of families and about certain individuals; however, since the information is generally given orally and subsequently transcribed, it is not always reliable. This is particularly apparent in the case of Asian Americans. The names are frequently incomplete or reversed; misspellings are common; and other parts of the schedules are often blank or vague. Despite limitations, census records may answer some research questions and provide clues for further research.

The key to using a census is knowing where the family resided at the time. A few Chinese appear in the U.S. census beginning in 1850; the numbers increase in 1870 and 1880. As mentioned earlier in this volume, the 1880 census is indexed roughly by the sound of the surname (Soundex) and by the name of the head of the household in each state and locality. Most of the 1890 census was lost by fire. Japanese immigrants appear in the 1900 U.S. census, which also includes the newly added territory of Hawaii. Few Koreans and Filipinos appear before 1910. There are also Hawaiian census reports from 1890 and 1896, but these censuses appear to be incomplete. Some Chinese and Japanese appear in the urbanized areas and towns, but the larger group, plantation workers, were generally neglected.

The Hawaiian censuses are at the Hawaii State Archives and on film at the LDS Genealogical Department Library. The U.S. censuses are at the National Archives in Washington, D.C., and its branches. The LDS Genealogical Department Library and some other genealogical libraries also have full copies or portions of the censuses prior to 1900. The 1910 census has just become available at the National Archives. As discussed in chapter 2 of this book, the censuses at ten-year intervals since that time must be searched by personnel of the Bureau of Census in Pittsburg, Kansas.

Immigration Records

Immigration records deal with the arrival and registration of immigrants. Since 1906 the Immigration and Naturalization Service (INS) and its predecessors has been charged with keeping track of immigration and naturalization matters. It deals with requests from families of immigrants, submitted on Form G-641 (figure 8.1). This form is available at local INS offices in major U.S. cities and is submitted to the office with a fee for an INS search.

The INS searches the arrival records in its archives of the Western ports and post-1900 Hawaii. The ports include San Francisco (from 1892, but with some records missing before 1906), Seattle (from 1894), and Honolulu (from 1900). If the necessary information is provided, the INS will also search Alien Registration Records (from 1940) and Naturalization Records (from (1906), though many Asians were unable to gain citizenship until the restrictions were lifted in 1952. These records include dates of birth, ages at arrival, places of origin (sometimes incomplete), destinations in the United States, details on arrival, occupations, dates, and courts of naturalization.

Hawaii has its own set of records for the period before 1900, when it became a territory of the United States. These include ship manifests (1743–1890) and passenger manifests (1879–1900). These have been indexed, and there are separate indexes for Chinese and Japanese. The index cards are a finding aid to the respective manifests, but one must be aware of problems with spelling and the reversal of names. While the index cards abstract the information from the manifests, checking the manifests is well worth the effort. The manifests include information such as the ship's name, probable occupation or assignment, group affiliation or emigrant company, family relationships, in some cases a place of

Figure 8.1
Application for Verification of Information from Immigration and Naturalization Service Records

UNITED STATES DEPARTMENT OF JUSTICE
Immigration and Naturalization Service

Form approved
OMB No. 1115-0088

Fee Stamp

**APPLICATION FOR
VERIFICATION OF INFORMATION FROM
IMMIGRATION AND NATURALIZATION SERVICE
RECORDS**

TYPE OR PRINT THE NAME AND MAILING ADDRESS OF THE PERSONS TO WHOM
INFORMATION OR COPIES OF RECORD SHOULD BE RETURNED IN THE BOX BELOW:

NAME	
STREET ADDRESS	
CITY, STATE ZIP CODE	

PERSON CONSENTING
NAME AND ADDRESS

SIGNATURE OF PERSON CONSENTING

1. CHECK TYPE OF VERIFICATION REQUESTED:
   - ☐ LAWFUL ADMISSION FOR PERMANENT RESIDENCE
   - ☐ AGE OR DATE OF BIRTH
   - ☐ NATURALIZATION OR CITIZENSHIP
   - ☐ GENEALOGICAL INFORMATION *(See instructions #6 and 7.)*
   - ☐ OTHER (CERTIFICATE OF BIRTH DATA, ETC.)

2. STATE PURPOSE FOR WHICH DESIRED

2A. NAMES OF BENEFICIARIES

3. NUMBER OF COPIES DESIRED, IF ANY:

4. IF INFORMATION IS FOR SOCIAL SECURITY BENEFITS, SHOW SOCIAL SECURITY NUMBER:

DATA FOR IDENTIFICATION OF THE RECORD TO BE VERIFIED

5. FAMILY NAME	GIVEN NAME	MIDDLE NAME	6. ALIEN REGISTRATION NUMBER
7. OTHER NAMES USED, IF ANY		8. NAME USED AT TIME OF ENTRY INTO UNITED STATES	
9. PLACE OF BIRTH	10. DATE OF BIRTH	11. PORT ABROAD FROM WHICH LEFT FOR UNITED STATES	
12. PORT OF ENTRY INTO UNITED STATES	13. DATE OF ENTRY	14. NAME OF VESSEL OR OTHER MEANS OF ENTRY	

GIVE THE FOLLOWING INFORMATION FOR VERIFICATION OF NATURALIZATION OR CERTIFICATE OF CITIZENSHIP

15. NAME ON CERTIFICATE	16. CERTIFICATE NUMBER	17. DATE ISSUED
18. ADDRESS WHEN CERTIFICATE WAS ISSUED	19. NAME AND LOCATION OF NATURALIZATION COURT OR IMMIGRATION OFFICE ISSUING CERTIFICATE OF CITIZENSHIP	

20. SIGNATURE OF APPLICANT

**DO NOT COMPLETE THIS BLOCK —
RESERVED FOR GOVERNMENT USE ONLY**

THE RECORDS OF THE IMMIGRATION AND NATURALIZATION SERVICE REFLECT THE FOLLOWING:
VERIFICATION OF INFORMATION REQUESTED WAS MADE ON THIS DATE SHOWN AT RIGHT

DATE:

- ☐ LAWFUL ADMISSION FOR PERMANENT RESIDENCE ON _____ AT _____ CLASS _____
- ☐ NATURALIZATION INFORMATION AS SHOWN ABOVE IS CORRECT.
- ☐ NATURALIZATION IN (COURT) _____ ON (DATE) _____
   - AT (LOCATION) _____
- ☐ DATE OF BIRTH _____
- ☐ ARRIVAL RECORD DATED _____ SHOWED SUBJECT'S AGE AT TIME TO BE _____
- ☐ UNABLE TO IDENTIFY ANY RECORD
- ☐ COPIES ATTACHED AS REQUESTED

SIGNATURE _____

TITLE _____

PRIVACY ACT IDENTIFICATION (WHEN REQUIRED)		Approved By:	DATE

☐ IDENTITY ESTABLISHED IN PERSON

DOCUMENTS ATTACHED   ☐ G-652 Affidavit   ☐ OTHER (List)

FORM G-641 (REV. 6-1-81) Y

Courtesy U.S. Department of Justice, Immigration and Naturalization Service.

origin, and the port of departure. The problem, however, is that the information is rarely complete and it is frequently misinterpreted. In many cases Chinese names were Romanized with the ''Ah'' preface and the surname last. There are over 55,000 Japanese men listed and some 12,000 women. There is also a large number of Chinese. Koreans, Filipinos, and other Asians are rare; for the most part these groups came after 1900 and are in INS records. The manifests and indexes are available at the Hawaii State Archives and on film at the LDS Genealogical Department Library.

There are a number of other records bearing on immigration and registration at the Hawaii State Archives. The Genealogical Society of Utah has filmed many of these as well. These include records of the Bureau of Immigration (Department of the Interior in pre-1900 Hawaii) and Chinese Bureau (Department of Foreign Affairs). The latter bureau was created in 1890 to restrict and control Chinese immigration. The Bureau of Immigration kept records of arrival of Chinese (1847–80), death records (1898–1902), lists of Chinese on Honolulu streets, departures of Chinese from Hawaii (1752–1900; some left for the West Coast), certificates of identification for Chinese (1895–98), certificates of registration (1890), photograph books (ca. 1890; 2,277 entries), index to naturalizations (1842–92, 1901–02), and correspondence regarding immigration. The Chinese Bureau (1890–1900) kept records of Chinese naturalizations (1844–72), Chinese work permits, Hawaiian-born children of Chinese parentage (1893–98), entry permits for women (1893–98), entry permits for merchants and students, passports (1884–95), and applications to enter (1892–97). Some of these records are in Chinese and some in English or Hawaiian.

There is also a record group (No. 85) at the National Archives, referred to as the ''segregated Chinese files,'' that contains a considerable amount of correspondence and records related to the immigration and movement of Chinese from the time of exclusion (1882) to the law barring Asians (1924).

Records of entry (1885–1910) and departure (1909–41) are also available on the Japanese at the Japanese Consulate General in Honolulu. The UCLA Japanese project was able to acquire (at the university library in Los Angeles) over 100 reels from the Japanese Foreign Ministry relating to immigration from Japan to the United States. A specialized Japanese immigrants' section in the Bishop Museum in Honolulu is also collecting materials, but an inventory list is not yet available. In the future this will probably be the main repository for materials on Japanese immigrants to Hawaii.

Community and Ethnic Records

Because of the attitude of the larger society, most of the Asian immigrants preferred to live in close proximity with those of their own ethnic groups. Ethnic communities sprung up wherever the immigrants settled. An ethnic community is a racially and culturally distinctive group of people in a locality, organized by common interests and goals. Because assimilation and acceptance in the larger society has generally been more difficult for Asians, many of these communities have endured.

In many of the larger cities in the United States and Hawaii, Asians clustered into communities. The Chinese had built a thriving Chinatown in Honolulu by the 1880s. A Chinatown was started in San Francisco in the 1850s, while one prospered in New York City beginning a few decades later. A major Chinatown exists in Los Angeles, while a few communities have Chinese sections or areas. Japan towns or *Nihon machi* were also common. Outsiders referred to the one in Los Angeles as "Little Tokyo." There were Japanese sections in Honolulu and in cities on the West Coast. In smaller towns the Japanese would congregate on a street or two in the older part of town. While the evacuation of the Japanese on the West Coast uprooted most of these settlements, a few Japanese ethnic communities have been established in the post-World War II period. Korean and Filipino communities of long standing also exist, as do more recent Korean and Vietnamese enclaves.

Asian ethnic communities were and still are generally well organized and have a number of potential record sources. While many of the communities are moving toward English, the native languages of the immigrants thrive in what are often combined business and residential areas. Many of the ethnic communities have directories of local ethnic businesses and residents and publish newsletters.

Chinese communities are self-contained and clannish. Their traditions and culture resemble old China at the time the immigrants came. Many of their organizations are based on village and district affiliations and show little relationship to what exists in cities in China. These communities represented the origins of the Chinese immigrants and helped them adjust to the new country. Clan associations, generally of people with the same surname who considered themselves related, also played an important role in maintaining Chinese traditions and group solidarity. There were also fraternal organizations, called Tongs, that assisted the early immigrants. While some of these early immigrant organizations have disappeared or been replaced by larger organizations such as the United Chinese Society, the Chinese Consolidated Benevolent Association, and others, it may be worthwhile to locate their directories and publications. In these ethnic organizations, there are no societies with an interest in genealogy and history, but individual members can supply valuable information if sought out and consulted.

Japanese communities also were highly organized. Japanese regional associations in the United States and Hawaii; prefectural associations, made up of immigrants from the same prefecture in Japan; and the more recent Japanese American Citizen's League and United Japanese Society of Hawaii have played important roles as ethnic organizations. To find group affiliations and information about the existence of records bearing on one's own family, family members and friends should be consulted. The records of some of these organizations can provide important clues to the origins of the immigrants and to various aspects of individual members' lives.

Other groups have their ethnic associations as well. University and public libraries usually have some of their materials in collections, especially for groups in their respective areas. There are special collections, such as oral history tapes of some Asian immigrants, at UCLA. The University of Southern California has a special Korean project. Okinawans and Filipinos are the subjects of collections at the University of Hawaii. These, the existing organizations and potential contacts with those of past organizations, may be worth checking if the researcher lives nearby or plans to visit the particular area.

Newspapers

Ethnic newspapers generally covered their respective communities in depth. The papers were read faithfully by the immigrants and by their offspring, who read the English section that appeared in later years. The newspapers covered deaths, funerals, births, marriages, anniversaries, new arrivals in the community, and other items of a biographical or historical nature. Valuable information such as age at death, prefecture of origin, and names of relatives and survivors may be in an obituary or a news item. Advertisements and announcements also have their value in reconstructing the family history.

In Karl Lo and Him Mark Lai's annotated list of Chinese newspapers, 254 are listed.[4] About a third of these were published in San Francisco while 65 were published in New York City. Honolulu also had a number of Chinese papers. These papers are in Chinese and/or English. English papers became popular among the offspring of the immigrants. Rather than try to list the details, I suggest that the Lo and Lai book be consulted, since it contains the newspaper names, dates, and repositories.

Although there is no comprehensive book of this type on Japanese ethnic newspapers, I have compiled a tentative list of newspapers and known collections. (See end of chapter.) Some of the older newspapers in Hawaii, such as the *Nippon Jiji* (from 1896) and the *Hawaii Hochi* (also *Times*, from 1912) published items on the arrival of immigrants and their origins. The newspapers with English-language sections and their approximate beginning dates are also listed. The list is organized by city rather than title for genealogical research purposes.

The Korean communities in Honolulu and California, as well as the Filipino communities in these locations, also had ethnic newspapers. Many of these are still active. For example, the *Korean Pacific Weekly* (from 1913), the *Korean Dongji Hoi* (*1937*), *The Philippine Mail* (monthly from 1930), and *The Filipino Forum* (from 1928).

Cemetery and Funerary Records

The practice of honoring the dead with tablets and monuments is many centuries old in the Orient. The location of gravesites in China and Korea was carefully done according to geomantic principles. Cemetery plots in Japan often adjoined Buddhist temples, which handled the funeral arrangements.

Provisions allowing ethnic cemeteries were specified in agreements allowing Chinese and Japanese laborers to come to Hawaii. Many of these cemeteries were close to the plantations. As the cities grew, cemeteries also were purchased in the suburbs. Cremation also was a method of disposing of the dead, especially among the Japanese, while the Chinese sometimes exhumed bodies and returned them to their native villages in China when circumstances allowed.

Scattered about the islands of Hawaii are many ethnic cemeteries and some public ones where Asians were buried. The Hawaii Chinese History Center has encouraged the copying of tombstone inscriptions of Chinese ethnics. Other groups have also copied inscriptions and made transcript lists of them. The Chinese ones are in the collections of the history center, while libraries in Hawaii have some. The LDS Genealogical Department Library also has a few lists. There are relatively few lists for the continental United States, even though a number of ethnic cemeteries exist. It may be appropriate to visit the cemetery and copy the information.

The tombs or markers may contain useful inscriptions, such as birth dates, death dates, ages at death, sometimes specific places of birth and even biographical information. Some contain posthumous names (see section below on Buddhist death registers) and religious information. Markers in English may be side by side with markers in a native language.

A number of funeral homes cater to an ethnic clientele. Some Japanese funeral homes, for example, have kept records of cremation and burial and even some personal records of the deceased. In earlier times Buddhist temples made mortuary tablets for deceased Japanese and Chinese, and Chinese temples had ancestral tablets. These practices have almost disappeared, however, in this country.

Local Records

A great many records pertain to the general population: criminal and civil judgments, land records, wills, probates, sales, settlements, adoptions, agreements, and many other court or legal cases. Many of these are found at the county level, and some at federal and state courts. Guides and inventories to county records may also show specific local records. Special taxes on groups such as the Chinese were common in some California counties; these included business taxes, miners' taxes, fishermen's taxes, and police taxes.

The Hawaiian Bureau of Conveyance has records involving land transfers and adoptions (to 1915). Records prior to 1900 are in the State Archives; the Circuit Court of Record has the later settlements. The Interior Department kept labor contract books on Chinese (1880–86) and Japanese (1868–1900), as well as immigrant lists and passport applications. These are also in the Hawaii State Archives.

The Hawaiian Sugar Planters' Association (HSPA) has records (1906–46) of sugar plantation workers, while the individual companies, such as the Hawaiian Commercial Sugar Company and Wailuku Sugar Company, have records with names, dates, assignments, camp and house numbers, and information on family members. School records are also a possibility. Formerly some ethnic-language schools existed, but many of these were legislated away or closed due to local pressures. Declarations of intentions for those seeking citizenship were also filed at federal courts until racial quotas were tightened beyond hope.

City directories can also be quite useful for finding out whether a family or individual has lived in a certain area at a particular time. The given name of an individual may also be ascertainable. Some of the earliest directories were published in the late 1800s. These exist both for the overall community and for some ethnic groups in San Francisco, Honolulu, New York, Los Angeles, Seattle, and Chicago. Maps can also be of great value in locating streets and smaller towns. These places can be visited and researched in more detail.

Personal Records

While many personal records relate to home sources, a number fall outside that category. These are individual work permits, applications, certificates of identification, voter registrations, and a variety of other sources. The papers illustrate the types of records which are available. A brief list of Japanese papers and documents (table 8.1) also illustrates types of records which are extant. These types of papers also exist for other ethnic groups, though the list might be expanded considerably. Some of these documents are in English, but many are also in the immigrant's native language. For example, figure 8.2, in Japanese, is a document which permits the bearer to travel abroad. It carries the stamp of the governor of Hiroshima Prefecture, dated 27 September of the 5th year of Taisho (1916). Permission is granted to the bearer to go to the United States. The name of the person is listed (Jiro Yabumoto), his home in Japan (Kumano Village), his height (4'8"), his birth date (7 November 1878), and other data, including the name of his father (Okuji), his class (farmer), and order of birth (eldest son).

Other Records

There are also church records at ethnic churches, Buddhist death registers for Japanese in Hawaii (refer to the section below on records abroad regarding this source), records of travel agencies and hotels handling the immigrants' itineraries and paperwork (particularly Japanese travel agencies in Hawaii), and military records. Although the records of many Asian ethnic groups have yet to be adequately inventoried, the reverence for the printed word and appetite for it among most Asian ethnic groups hold promise that substantial sources will be discovered. Of course, many sources will also be discarded or neglected, by offspring or others who may not know the language or recognize the value of many of these items.

RECORDS ABROAD

Except for the Chinese who came to the United States before exclusion in 1882, almost all Asian immigrants have arrived in the United States and Hawaii within the past century. While some Asian Americans are into the third and fourth generations, a number have just arrived. This makes it imperative, therefore, to know something of the sources abroad and how to tie into them.

Table 8.1. Personal Papers and Documents (Japanese)

Document	Purpose	Contents	Authorization
Labor emigration permit or exit permit	permission to work abroad or leave Japan	name, date of departure, address in Japan (in Japanese)	by signature or seal of prefectural governor
Local identification card or paper	local identification	name, head of house, registered domicile and/or address in Japan, and usually a picture of the individual and a description (in Japanese)	from village official or mayor of city or town
Passport	foreign travel or residence	name, passport number, registered domicile and/or address in Japan, date passport issued, age and/or birthdate, date of admittance, ship, stamp of immigration inspector, head of house, etc. (in Japanese)	by Japan Foreign Office and Minister of Foreign Affairs
Labor contract	employment conditions and guarantees	name, employer, terms and duration of contract, wages, etc. (in English and Japanese)	by parties involved, namely representatives of immigration bureaus and companies

To make the proper connections, several pieces of information are essential. First, one must determine the place from which the family or ancestors came. This can be a native village, town, or city. There may still be some ties to the so-called native area, but these gradually vanish as people move about and generations pass on. While many of the younger generation may have only vague ideas of family origins, some of the older members of the ethnic community may know considerably more. They should, of course, be approached for information or clues about past addresses and specific information on localities abroad. The previously cited sources in the United States and Hawaii may also provide clues or valuable information. It is helpful, too, if one can find the proper characters or at least the proper spelling of the names of various geographic jurisdictions.

It is also crucial to know the name (and characters) of the immigrant or

Figure 8.2
Document Granting Permission to Travel Abroad

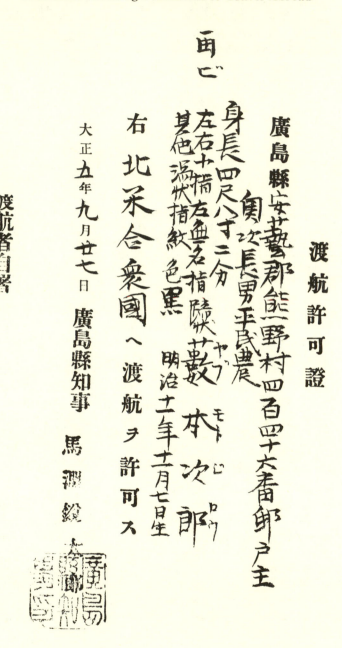

immigrant ancestor if that person immigrated several generations ago. That name may also appear in records abroad, though sometimes in slightly different form. By making this connection, one may be able to proceed to other lines and extend the genealogy and the scope of the family history. It is helpful to have some idea of various dates (birth, emigration, and so forth), usually the more specific the better. This will make it easier to reconstruct the family history and lines and find the proper record abroad.

Since there is relatively little knowledge of what records exist abroad and their value, this general introduction may at least suggest some approaches to research abroad. More detailed information about the sources and research procedures is contained in the works cited in the bibliography or in some cases is not yet available. This information is categorized by the geographic origins of the various ethnic groups.

Mainland China, Taiwan, and Hong Kong

One of the most momentous events in Asian if not in world history was the Communist takeover of China just over thirty years ago. There were immediate antagonisms between the United States and China because of U.S. involvement in the Korean War (1950–53) and support of the expatriate Nationalist government on Taiwan. These antagonisms continued unabated for two decades until reconciliation with the People's Republic began in the early 1970s. While the present government on the mainland is still cautious, there is considerably more access than has been allowed in the past, and there are signs that restrictions may be relaxed even further. But these changes will probably occur gradually and will be carefully weighed in terms of their effect on the regime's control over the populace. The Chinese greatly fear a return to the anarchy and weakness that plagued China during the so-called "century of humiliation" that began with Chinese concessions to the West after the Opium War (1839–40) and ended with the eventual takeover in 1949.

Because conditions in China were so bad during this tumultuous period, many Chinese left their homeland. Most continued to have a strong sentimental attachment to their homeland and the land of their ancestors. This was in large part due to the strong Confucian emphasis on piety toward the fathers, the related beliefs in ancestor veneration and lineage continuity, and traditional Chinese feelings toward the soil and the native village. The dream many had of returning was upset by the conditions in China. First, there was the collapse of the Ch'ing dynasty in 1912, followed by the disruptive warlord period (1916–27). Conflict with Japan and open warfare (1937–45) followed, culminating in civil war (1947–50) and eventual Communist control. Rather than return home, many more left China to sanctuaries in Taiwan, Hong Kong, the countries of Southeast Asia, the United States, and other sympathetic nations around the world.

Although they have left China, the Chinese abroad are still considered Overseas Chinese (*hua chiao*) by the Peking government, and efforts have been made to win their support or at least sympathy. The People's Republic generally has allowed correspondence to continue between relatives under specific conditions. Such contacts and now visits to the ancestral village are being encouraged. The government recognizes the obvious economic benefits, including much-needed foreign exchange. Allowing visitors is still largely in the experimental stage and is approached most cautiously. A structured itinerary and a guide or attendant are prerequisites for visitors. Someone must assume responsibility for the visitor, and no one is free to roam as he or she pleases. As a result of these policies, official attitudes toward genealogical research vary considerably. There is a degree of arbitrariness, which when coupled with the somewhat uncertain state of record preservation can produce a variety of results. Some visitors are extremely successful in their research, while others meet frustrations. This can also be true for those who correspond with relatives in China. Some have managed to get complete genealogies, albeit a portion at a time, while others have relatives who either avoid the issue or seem unwilling or unable to conduct a search.

FAMILY REGISTERS AND VITAL RECORDS

While most of the Chinese in Taiwan are the offspring of immigrants, they comprise two basic groups: those who fled the mainland during and after the Civil War (1947–50) and those who have lived on the island for a number of generations. While some of the recent group were able to flee with records, including genealogies, there are clans or families in Taiwan that have maintained genealogies for several centuries, with the portions predating their arrival being copied from originals at their former mainland homes. Taiwan is a bastion of Chinese tradition, especially in light of attacks on that tradition on the mainland in recent years. There are, moreover, some lingering Japanese influences after fifty years of Japanese occupational control. During this period, household or family registers similar to those used in Japan were used to record changes in the status of family members. The system was continued after 1945, but with slight modifications reflecting Chinese preferences.

These registers, begun in 1896, contain information on births, deaths, marriages, and other changes of consequence. Reports are made to the local registration office, where the information is entered into the appropriate household or family register. Since the complete family and frequently the extended family (or household) is entered on one multipage record, genealogical research is greatly facilitated, at least until these records end. Heads of houses or successors can be followed back through entries made in the compilation of the registers. These registers usually include all those still alive from 1896 and usually also the names of the parents before them.

Hong Kong, though largely Chinese in population makeup, remains a colonial outpost of the British. Hong Kong Island was originally ceded in the 1840s, while the New Territories were acquired by lease (for ninety-nine years) in 1898. While the New Territories are geographically part of the mainland, this area and the adjoining islands are under British administrative control. The types of records, therefore, reflect British methods. The Registrar General's Department of

Hong Kong maintains vital records, including birth and death records from 1873 and marriage records from 1946. A more precise summary of the genealogical records in Hong Kong is contained in a Genealogical Society of Utah paper.[5] Although these records are in English, many also include the Chinese characters. A birth certificate usually includes the name, when and where born, sex, names of parents, profession of father, name and address of informant, date of registration, and additional names (Western or Christian) added or used since birth. These are among the few records in East Asia that follow the Western mode.

These modern records, as well as the registration records in the People's Republic of China, about which there seem to be few precise data as yet, have certain limitations. Some of the records may be useful to three and four generations, yet research beyond this point requires an altogether different approach. Instead of the government office, traditional sources require a thorough search of the original village. Outside of China, in spite of the excellent collection at the LDS Genealogical Department Library, it is usually a matter of chance to tie directly into a genealogy, find mention of the family in a local history, or the like. Even in China proper, where records preservation generally has been erratic, finding records can be an unpredictable venture.

GENEALOGIES

Foremost among the traditional records are the Chinese genealogies. These are excellent sources of information of exceptional generational depth. They contain segments that branch from common ancestors, the earliest one of which may be the founder of the clan or the first to take the surname. Chinese genealogies follow the patrilineal line or the generations of male successors from the original ancestor. The genealogy fans out as additional branches are created with the births of additional sons and their offspring. Branches eventually break off when the lineage becomes too cumbersome or moves to another place.

Chinese genealogies range in scope from surname genealogies covering countless branches to genealogies covering particular families. Most are clan genealogies or genealogies that cover the branches of a particular clan residing in a specific locality, such as the Huang (uses the character for "yellow") family of Ch'ang-shan district, Hunan Province, or the Wang (means "king") family of Hsin-huang, Chia-hsing district, Chekiang Province. Since lineage members are identified by the surname, lineage organization, and geographic location, it is necessary to know where the ancestors originated and lived. Chinese are usually aware of the home of the ancestor even though they may be living abroad. They may not, however, be aware of the jurisdictional changes over the decades or since their branch moved away. Many of the former villages in Kwangtung Province, from which many Chinese emigrated, are now communes or have been reorganized into different districts or towns. If contacts with relatives in China have been severed or lost, it may be necessary to search for the current addresses and names of relatives who may be of assistance.

Clan genealogies are graphic representations of Confucian traditions in which ancestor veneration and concern for lineage continuity are paramount. They show the male successors in genealogical sequence and record brothers as branches. Women are only peripheral in the genealogy, and when they are mentioned, it is usually as wives under their family names. Many of these genealogies are printed according to a particular format, though some are in manuscript form. The tradition of clans compiling genealogies is nearly 1,000 years old, while linkage genealogies originated 2,000 to 3,000 years ago. Since there is a tendency to dovetail, the older portions or segments predating A.D. 1000 should be approached with some skepticism.

The Chinese genealogy usually includes more than just genealogical charts and tables. Notes on the compilation or revision, on the origins and history of the clan or lineage organization, on lineage rules and regulations, on ancestral rites and clan property, on individual clansmen and gravesites, and so on are among the items found. The genealogical portion, however, usually comprises the bulk of the material, though the proportion varies among sources. The pedigree charts are usually a skeletal view of the lineage and can be an excellent finding aid, especially in the larger genealogies. While most genealogies are limited to a few volumes, the genealogy of the descendants of Confucius takes up about 150 volumes. The more detailed and structured portion of the genealogies is the tables. The most popular style, that of Ou Yang-hsiu (A.D. 1007–1072) has five generations or variations of this in vertical sequence from top to bottom on a page. Branches extend to the left and are found separately further down the genealogy. Figure 8.3 gives an example of a small portion of a pedigree chart in translated form.

The information in the tables can vary considerably. Illustrious ancestors and clansmen of note receive considerable attention, while others are barely mentioned. An example of the type of information in genealogies and the variation from a genealogy of the Kuan family of T'o-Fu follows:

Twenty-first generation ancestor (case 1): Pi-ch'iu (no information on wife); they begot sons (no information given); moved to San-pu-shui.

Twenty-first generation ancestor (case 2): The venerable Chun-yen; also known as Ch'i-chuan; posthumous name—Yen-pin; wife from Chou family. A first-degree graduate in the district examinations, he was placed in the ninth rank among civil officials. He was born about 8 P.M. on the twentieth day of the twelfth month of the first year of the Shun-chih (1644) in the Ch'ing period. He died at about 6 A.M. on the fourteenth day of the twelfth month of the year Chin-shen (1704), during the reign of the Emperor K'ang Hsi of the Ch'ing dynasty. He was buried at Chiao-liu, Hai-tu-t'ou, Ho-mei-k'an-t'ien, by the side of ancestors Chun-k'uan and Ju-hai. His wife was born about 2 A.M. on the twenty-third day of the sixth month of the second year of Shun-chih (1645); she died at about 2 P.M. on the twenty-third day of the eighth month of the year Yung-cheng (1732); she was buried on the west side of Ma-ling Mountain at Sha-ti-tung.

They begot three sons: Ju-hai (first), Ju-shao (second), and Ju-t'ung (third). They moved from San-men, Lu-ts'un, to T'ang-li-ts'un, Shang-shen, Chi'ih'k'an.[6]

Figure 8.3
Chinese Pedigree Chart

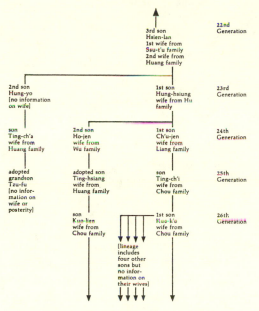

From the author's collection.

As can be seen, some entries list even the hour and precise location, while others mention only the name.

CLASSICAL LANGUAGE

Several noteworthy features of traditional Chinese sources must be considered in research. First, the language is Classical Chinese. In order to handle it, familiarity with a large number of characters (sometimes over 10,000) and a knowledge of local names and history can be extremely helpful. Because the classical language differs from the present colloquial style and is somewhat cryptic, translating can be difficult at times. The use of multiple names in some entries can also make it difficult to compare genealogies and identify individuals. Several names are usually used at stages in a man's life, and posthumous names are used as well. Fortunately, the use of *p'ai ming* (generational names) and the inclusion of other information clarifies most situations. Dates are usually listed according to the Chinese sixty-year cyclical calendar and/or the reign year of an emperor. These are in the lunar calendar; it is considerably easier to approximate the date than to try to figure out the Western equivalent, unless, of course, one has conversion charts. Many entries have no dates. Dates can be calculated or estimated if necessary.

ANCESTRAL TABLETS AND TOMBSTONE INSCRIPTIONS

Another traditional source with genealogical information is the ancestral tablet. These tablets were traditionally kept on household altars and in clan temples. While they are now more difficult to find, they should be included in the search for records. Some ancestor tablets are simple wooden sticks, while some are highly ornate. Some of the more contemporary ones even have pictures of the deceased. Some include interior compartments with birth and death information written on slips of paper or strips of wood. Many have information written on them, but they should be approached cautiously because they are considered sacred by the family.

Tombstone inscriptions are another traditional source worth checking. They are found near the native village or in clan burial areas. Names, burial dates, sometimes the names of children, and occasionally even more extensive information may be included.

LOCAL HISTORIES

Another traditional source with possibilities is the Chinese local history pertaining to the native district or specific area in China. Editions and volumes close to the time and locality of the period and geographic area of interest should be consulted. There are about 10,000 local histories in libraries and archives both in the United States and abroad. Chinese local histories are actually more than just historical narratives of the local area. They include genealogical tables of prominent families, biographical essays on many prominent people, and tables which list categories of people (officials, successful examination candidates, aged persons, filial sons, chaste widows, outstanding women, and so on), and they give extensive information about the history and geography of the district and local areas. The writing of local histories was strongly encouraged by the Chinese government in the eighteenth century, and the practice was widespread until the collapse of Imperial China in 1912.

Histories are kept at many levels in China: empire (*kuo*), province (*sheng*), prefecture (*fu*), subprefecture (*t'ing*), district (*hsien*), market town (*chen*), and village (*hsiang*). It is the local histories (*difang-chih*) at the subprefectural and district level and below that are of the most value to genealogists. They are useful in identifying the lineage organizations in a particular area; they provide clues as to where the people resided; and sometimes they provide clues on clan or family history.

OTHER SOURCES OF GENEALOGICAL VALUE

A number of other records and documents can be surveyed: land records, church records (if ancestors or family members were Christian), marriage contracts, adoption agreements, agreements regarding household division, leases and cultivation contracts, eulogies and merit tables, and even horoscopes and records of offerings. Letters and correspondence may also provide useful clues.

More detailed information on Chinese sources is contained in the major source papers on Hong Kong and Taiwan listed in the bibliography to this chapter, as well as in several papers of the World Conference on Records. While finding the clan or family genealogy may be a major breakthrough, some of these other sources may also shed more light on the family history and on individuals within the family group. Although the language and culture may be unfamiliar to the offspring of the Chinese immigrant to America, with the help of family members and relatives it is possible to reconstruct the family history and determine one's lines and origins.

Japan

FAMILY REGISTERS

For Japanese Americans research in Japan ordinarily begins with the family or household register (*koseki*). Because many of the immigrant Japanese were unable to become American citizens, at least until 1952, they continued to make reports on changes of status on themselves and their offspring to the Japanese consulates nearest them. The consulate would forward this information to the proper office in Japan. Registry in the *koseki* implied Japanese citizenship.

The Japanese *koseki* is essentially a family or household civil register; it covers, in theory at least, all Japanese born or living in Japan or of Japanese nationality since inception of the modern record in 1872. Because changes in status for the entire family or household are entered into the record, it is a convenient source for genealogy. Separate documents and certificates are replaced by a single, easy to reference family record. The record is filed by the name of the head of house (*koshu*) or since 1947 the "first one entered" (*hittosha*) and the registered locality or permanent address (*honseki*). This record is illustrated in figure 8.4.

To obtain copies of the *koseki* or the withdrawn registers (*joseki*), it is necessary to determine the name of the family head and the local office with jurisdiction over the record. Because many of the place names have changed because of amalgamations and changes in jurisdiction, Japanese Americans sometimes find it difficult to find the present name of a village or area from which their parents, grandparents, and others emigrated some seventy or eighty years ago.

There are several reference volumes in Japanese that list the names of older units and the addresses of present local offices. Dai Ichi Hoki's *Zenkoku shichoson yoran* (a directory of Japanese cities, towns, and villages), published annually, is one of the most useful. Another extremely valuable volume is the annual detailed atlas published by Kokusai Chigaku Kyokai, entitled *Dai Nippon bunken chizu narabi ni chimei soran* (Japanese maps grouped by prefecture with a comprehensive list of present-day place names). The addresses of government offices are also in this volume. Unfortunately, there is nothing in English that can provide this detailed information, though it may be possible to make one, since the immigrants generally came from certain areas.

Figure 8.4
Brief Approximation of 1886-Type *Koseki*

		右瞻本ハ戸籍原本ト相違ナキコトヲ認證ス	以下余白	戸主平民乙原菊右衛門四女婚姻届出同日受付入籍 印	大正元年参月弐拾日〇〇郡〇〇村〇〇〇番屋敷			明治弐拾六年参月壱日死亡 印 以下余白	以下余白	大正元年参月弐拾日乙原カズエ婚姻届出同日受付 印	明治拾九年参月九日相續	〇〇縣〇〇郡〇〇村参百弐拾四番屋敷
	大正九年弐月七日											平民
〇〇縣〇〇郡〇〇村長 〇原〇〇												前戸主亡父甲野新平
印				妻		姉		戸 主			亡父甲野新平	
				明治弐拾年八月拾参日生	カズエ	父乙原菊右衛門ッネ四女 母	明治六年参月拾壱日生	ぬみ	亡父新平長女	明治九年四月拾五日生	甲野新平	亡父新平長男

From the author's collection.

268

An individual can usually be traced from birth to death through entries in the *koseki*. Compilation entries also enable one to proceed to other registers—to earlier or collateral records for those who left for marriage, adoption, or other reasons. Family and household members are entered in a prescribed sequence beginning with the head of house. The name of the former head of house is normally cited; his record is usually the next generation back. Records can be ordered until access is no longer possible. Since there is an eighty-year retention rule, at least, for the office servicing requests, registers are usually removed from circulation after they have been withdrawn for the stipulated period. Then they become *joseki* records—namely, records of all members deleted or crossed off because of death, forfeiture of citizenship, marriage, and so forth. Records prior to 1886 are also closed for political purposes, since they have an open format and contain personal and class information. Until 1975 it was relatively easy to obtain copies of *koseki* and even to pursue volumes at local offices. Privacy laws enacted as a result of abuses have made it more difficult to obtain records and require a statement or reason for requesting copies. It may be necessary to ask parents, grandparents, uncles and aunts, and so forth to help obtain copies, since they are more closely related to the person whose record is being requested and the request would have a better chance of being accepted.

Most Japanese government offices try to be helpful to Japanese Americans. They will accept requests provided sufficient funds are included (send U.S. currency of from five to ten dollars, using an international money order available at the local U.S. post office), with enough information to enable these offices to find the proper record. Write clearly and in simple English.

The *koseki* includes information from a variety of notification reports submitted by the family. Most reports were submitted within a week to ten days of the event or change. Family names, the domicile address (*honseki*), birth dates, order of birth, information on marriages, place and date of death, family relationships, adoption information, transfers to other registers, and many other items are recorded as appropriate. Once the copies arrive, it will be necessary to have the information translated and entered on pedigree charts and family group sheets. Naturally, friends and relatives are the best resources if this cannot be done by one's self.

BUDDHIST DEATH REGISTERS

Although the *koseki* covers the population almost completely, except for gaps because some records could not be reconstructed after the bombings of World War II, it will only take the researcher so far. One of the most universally available alternative sources in Japan is the *kakochō*, or Buddhist death register. Because it is basically a Buddhist-style obituary record, there are some drawbacks. The prominent entry is a Buddhist posthumous, or vow, name. The nature of the name—a series of characters indicating Buddhist other-world hopes or individual virtues, along with the sex and status of the deceased—and the lack of ascertainable relationships can sometimes make it difficult to find specific individuals. But as most entries include a complete death date, the record has advantages. The real key to utilizing *kakochō* is the quality of the source. Some include notes on relationships, the common name of the deceased or a close relative, and even the age at death.

The custom of assigning Buddhist names and memorializing them was almost universal in Japan by 1700 (death was the province of the Buddhists). The practice is still strong, yet probably less widespread. There are about 80,000 Buddhist temples in Japan, and most have *kakochō*. Some records are incomplete, and some have been lost or have deteriorated over the decades. Nonetheless, taken together, an enormous amount of information is available.

To find the proper temple, one must ascertain the family's historical temple affiliation. Telephone books in Japan, directories of temples, home sources, or interviews and/or correspondence with family members or relatives are some of the ways of finding the addresses. The next step is to set up an appointment with the priest, if in Japan, to enlist the assistance of a relative there, or to try to obtain the information through correspondence. Some of the smaller temples are more intimate, and the search is not too difficult if the information is there. It is helpful if the priest has as much information as possible, and it is proper to donate some money for his services. Since a number of people have extended their family lines considerably by using this source, *kakochō* are worth considering even with the often lengthy, cumbersome Buddhist name. While it may seem unwieldy in Romanization, the meaning in characters may be sublime and highly appropriate for the deceased. A copy of a page from a *kakochō* (figure 8.5) illustrates the language and basic format.

MORTUARY TABLETS AND TOMBSTONE INSCRIPTIONS

Kakochō are not the only records used to memorialize the dead in Japan. Japanese also place *ihai* (mortuary tablets) on the family altar (*butsudan*), while those of contributors are placed in the local parish temple. While the information is similar to that in the *kakochō*, and indeed can be used to cross-check information, there are some differences. The tablets are usually discarded after several generations or when no longer needed. Some *ihai* have biographical information on the reverse side. Most are oblong in shape, made of wood, with characters in gold or black ink. (See figure 8.6.)

Tombstone inscriptions of the family or ancestral grave (*o-haka*) are also worth checking if one is able to make a trip to the native village in Japan or have a relative assist with research. Some of the tombstones are built for the collective dead, but many are for individuals. The inscriptions contain Buddhist names, death dates and often common names. Some of the wealthier people or feudal officials have large stone monuments with biographical information inscribed. Some inscriptions are extremely old and therefore difficult to decipher. Special rubbing techniques may be utilized for those that have weathered.

Figure 8.5
Page from a *Kakochō*

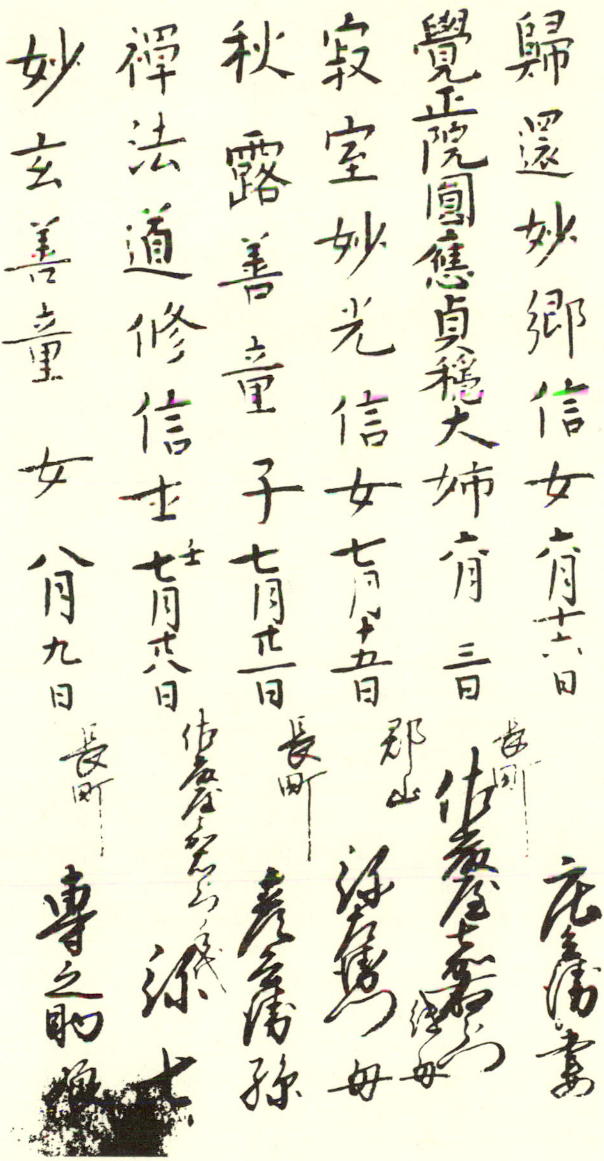

帰還妙郷信女 有十六日

覺正院圓應貞穩大姉 有 二日

寂室妙光信女 七月十五日

秋露善童子 七月廿一日

禅法道修信士 廿月廿六日 八月九日

妙玄善童女 八月九日

From the author's collection.

271

Figure 8.6
Ihai (Mortuary Tablet)

From the author's collection.

GENEALOGIES

A smaller percentage of Japanese Americans may be able to tie into Japanese compiled genealogies (*keizu* or *kafu*) if they have samurai or aristocrats as ancestors. Many of these are very elaborate and often extend many generations on the surname line. The further these genealogies go back, the more critically they must be viewed, since many were written by professional genealogists to legitimize claims to status and office. In theory all these lines run into the Imperial line and the Sun Goddess, showing that the Japanese people all stem from divine origins. Separating fact from fiction is difficult, because there are usually no primary sources to verify the various connections.

OTHER SOURCES

Locating and identifying source materials beyond those discussed above can be very difficult, even though a few exist that have genealogical information. Materials from the pre-1868 feudal period are usually scattered, diverse, and fairly hard to use. Another problem of considerable import is the lack of surnames in feudal sources; commoners did not have the privilege of using surnames until the 1870s. Because of the rather haphazard way in which surnames were taken once the use of such names became mandatory, it is difficult to make connections into the feudal period. Japan has an inordinately large number of surnames at present; estimates number the total at over 110,000. Some of the names are extremely common, such as Satoh and Suzuki; over 2,000,000 or so people have each of these surnames. Others are extremely rare, being limited to a few hundred people in a small area.

Japanese families usually have family crests or marks. These are worn on clothing and appear on many family possessions. Called *kamon* or *iemon,* some of the crests are extremely rare while others are more widespread. Some families have had *kamon* for several centuries; others for only a few generations. The designs can vary between branches of families by slight modifications, or the same motif can be retained. Favorite designs are plants, birds, animals, characters, and geometric figures. If the crest is unusual or special, it may also help to identify related families. But one must use caution, as some crests are quite common, and a hasty conclusion may result in an improper connection. There are estimates that there are over 10,000 family crests, but a few hundred of these are extremely common.

The other sources of feudal Japan depend largely on the class status of the ancestors in the feudal period. Those of samurai ancestry, for example, had a number of records on stipends, rosters, fief grants, and genealogies that legitimized them as retainers of feudal lords. These genealogies were submitted to the domain and subsequently the shogunate. The merchant class had financial records and census records, and were in town records. The peasants or commoners were recorded in census records, in some land records, and in some records denoting religious affiliation. The latter records were created as a sort of inquisition against Christianity in the seventeenth century and remained despite the elimination of the threat. Periodic censuses were taken of families to show their religious affiliations, the given names and relationships of family members, and usually their ages at the time of the census. Although only a fraction of what originally was a large number of records still exist, there are a few of these sources in the diverse areas of Japan.

RESEARCH PROBLEMS

There are a number of roadblocks that make Japanese research beyond the *koseki* very difficult. As noted, there is the basic problem of finding the sources and making connections due to the lack of surnames. The older Japanese written language, itself, is one of the hardest to deal with, not only because of the traditional problem of multiple readings but also because of the frequent use of cursive and of variant characters (*hentaiji*) in the respective regions of Japan. Some feudal records are extremely hard to decipher and can be what Japanese call *nazo* (puzzles). Sometimes it takes a thorough grounding in local history and handwriting styles to decipher these texts.

The changes in place names also can be perplexing. A century and a half ago there were roughly 70,000 villages in Japan, but now there are only a few thousand. Accurately identifying places in the feudal period can be even more difficult, because at that time there were over 250 or so semiautonomous domains instead of the present 47 prefectures (similar to but smaller than most of our states). Older Japanese dates are according to the reign-title and year, but the

Western solar calendar has been used since 1872. Before that time the lunar calendar and sexagenary cycle were the basis for dates. The most vexing of problems, however, is that of names. Because readings are sometimes very personal and multiple readings are possible in many cases, this is a very troublesome area. Sometimes it is necessary to ask the family the appropriate reading. Although names are more stable in the modern period, the use of multiple given names and titles sometimes makes it difficult to determine which is which. Feudal sources also neglect females except in the death registers and census records. In summary, it usually takes a number of specialized dictionaries and research aids, as well as expert help, to proceed beyond the modern period. Few Japanese Americans or even Japanese in Japan can handle this transition. In a country where making contacts is vital, however, almost anything can be accomplished with effort, some cost, and the assistance of the right person.

Korea

Most people are aware that Korea is divided north and south of the 38th parallel. This division occurred after World War II. The Korean War (1950–53) was an attempt by North Korea to conquer South Korea and accomplished nothing except the destruction of much of the country. Korea has a rich heritage of record keeping, and even though many records were destroyed in the Korean conflict, those remaining are worth checking as genealogical sources. How successful one will be, however, will depend largely on where the family lived, on its class status, and on the element of chance.

MODERN AND TRADITIONAL RECORDS

There are two main groupings of Korean records; the modern and the traditional. The main genealogical source for the modern period is the family or household register (*hojuk*), similar to the Japanese *koseki* already mentioned. The Japanese annexed Korea officially in 1910 and ruled until the end of World War II. Traditional records, on the other hand, show a strong Chinese influence, paralleling the acceptance of Chinese ideas in Korea. This influence increased steadily throughout the Yi dynasty (1392–1910), particularly among the upper class *yangban* (scholar-officials) who dominated Korean society during this period.

The natural place to begin one's research in Korea is at the appropriate government office, where the family was registered in the past. These offices are found at the *ku*, or ward, levels in the larger cities and in *myon* offices in rural areas. The records extend back to the beginning of the Japanese period and have continued to the present time in South Korea. There was also a register of households from the early seventeenth century to the Japanese takeover, but only a small percentage of this record remains.

GENEALOGIES

Many Korean clans and families, especially those of *yangban* origin, still maintain genealogies in the south. The genealogies, usually called *chopko* in

Korean, are very similar to the Chinese ones except that they evolved somewhat differently. They are written in classical Chinese but read in Korean. A knowledge of the characters is thus a prerequisite for research in this source. Because of the increased use of phonetic *han'gul* (simplified Korean phonetic script), many Koreans are finding it hard to stay versed in the classical language.

These genealogies are found through the surname and the *pon'gwan* (clan seat). The clan seat is the name of the county-level administrative district where the clan resided in the latter part of the Yi dynasty. Because certain surnames, such as Kim (about 22 percent of the population) and Yi (or Lee, about 15 percent of the population), are so common, it is usually crucial to know the family seat; for example, the Kim clan of Yanggun or the Yi clan of Haenam.

Most Korean genealogies are accurate for twenty or so generations but are less certain as they approach the remote past. Male successors are listed by generation and women only as wives and occasionally as daughters. The genealogy stems from a founding ancestor and branches out as lineage organizations divide. Most genealogies include a short history of the clan and information on gravesites, illustrious ancestors, and clan matters. Figure 8.7 shows an example of the contents of a Korean genealogical table.

OTHER TRADITIONAL RECORDS

Koreans also have local histories similar to the Chinese and *pangmok* (examination rosters) that have genealogies of civil service examination candidates. There are also biographies and epitaphs in sources such as *munjip* (literary collections). While an inventory of Korean genealogical records has been made recently, it has not been published as yet.

Prior to 1910, Korean society was highly stratified. There were three main classes of people. The *yangban* (scholar-officials) were found at the local, provincial, and national levels. Their status varied depending on their access to privilege, wealth, and particular posts. Naturally, their families and relatives benefitted by the success of one of their group in the examinations and by the rise to prominence of family members. The *yangban* are the best-recorded group, by far. Because of intermarriage in the modern period and the breakdown of the old society, probably as many as a quarter of Koreans can tie into one of these lines. The largest group, however, was the commoners. There is considerably less in the way of records available. At the bottom of Korean society were slaves. These were privately owned or people of low occupations. Some masters listed slaves as part of their own families in Yi dynasty *hojuk* and in other records. They are, however, not too well recorded there either. It is therefore difficult for the lower classes to do genealogical research. A combination of luck and skill is needed to extend one's lines in Korea beyond the turn of the century. Those with *yangban* lines have a definite advantage.

The Philippines

The history of the Philippines can be divided roughly into the Spanish era (from about 1570 to 1900), the American era (1900 to 1947), and the period of

Figure 8.7
Korean Genealogical Table

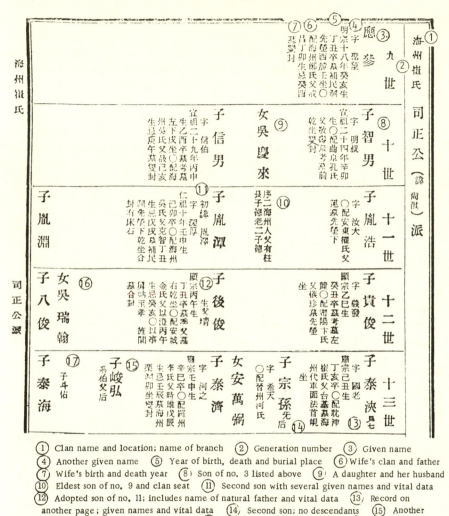

(1) Clan name and location; name of branch   (2) Generation number   (3) Given name
(4) Another given name   (5) Year of birth, death and burial place   (6) Wife's clan and father
(7) Wife's birth and death year   (8) Son of no. 3 listed above   (9) A daughter and her husband
(10) Eldest son of no. 9 and clan seat   (11) Second son with several given names and vital data
(12) Adopted son of no. 11; includes name of natural father and vital data   (13) Record on
another page; given names and vital data   (14) Second son; no descendants   (15) Another
second son; adopted out to his uncle   (16) A daughter and her husband   (17) Son of no. 16

From the author's collection.

independence since then. There was, of course, a brief and destructive interlude of Japanese rule (1942–45).

In the Spanish era the Catholic Church played a dominant role. Parish registers in the Spanish language or sometimes in the dialect of the locality were kept in the churches throughout the Philippines. The earliest ones began in 1572 and cover events such as baptisms, marriages, deaths, and burials. In the American era, English was used in many of the parishes as use of the language spread. A list of the parishes and records available in the Philippines can be found in the detailed book by Lee W. Vance, *Tracing Your Philippine Ancestors*. This is a landmark volume and is by far the best single source available.[7]

The Catholic Church also was very much involved in keeping civil and judicial records in the Spanish era. Permissions to marry or to remove graves and records that recorded land deeds were kept by the church or the Spanish administration. The earliest local vital records outside the church began only in the 1880s. Many were kept in the American era, though only about one-third survived World War II. Since 1946 the local civil registrar has been responsible for keeping records of births, marriages, and deaths. Copies of these can be requested by mail, but unless the researcher provides enough information, the search may take considerable time.

The national archives in Manila has immigration and naturalization records, including passports (1918–29) and some records of departure. Some of the earlier civil registers (1919–35) are also on file there. The HSPA also has records of many Filipino laborers in Hawaii. A number of the HSPA records and parish registers have been filmed by the Genealogical Society of Utah and are available at the main library in Salt Lake City or through branch libraries. The best index to the majority of these holdings and the nature of the records is again the Vance book.

Vietnam

The wave of recent arrivals from Vietnam has brought many refugees with few personal belongings. Most would also be unable to gain access to records back in Vietnam. It is hard to know anything about the records situation in Vietnam after many years of civil war and the eventual complete Communist takeover. There were civil records during the long French administration (1860–1954), and some families had genealogies similar to those of the Chinese. Chinese influences were strong in Vietnam for over 1800 years until the French seized control.

Vietnamese names are in the Oriental order. The surname is first, followed by the generational name and given name; for example, Nyugen Van Thieu. Nyugen, not Thieu, is the surname. Nyugen, Li, Lei, Tran, Houng, Vo, and Fhaan are among the more common surnames in Vietnam. Also common are Pham, Troung, Trinh, Nac, Lieu, Ngo, Bui, and Do. Each of these names has a Chinese character equivalent. Chinese characters read in Vietnamese were used in Vietnam until the latter part of the eighteenth century, when the French Romanized the language.

Thailand and Indonesia

There are very few Thai records from before the 1920s. What records exist are mostly local civil records, but the coverage is incomplete. Civil records began as early as 1828 in Indonesia under Dutch influence, but most of the early registers included mainly Europeans. Christian church records were among the earliest records kept, though converts represented only a small percentage of the population. Some of the families in Indonesia have genealogy books, especially those related to the sultans. Oral genealogies were common among many tribes in the outlying areas; the LDS Genealogical Department Library is presently collecting some of these. Because there are so few sources available in Southeast Asia for the average person, it is usually necessary to conduct interviews with family members abroad to extend one's lines.

India

The records of India, on the other hand, are very diverse and by and large unexplored. Civil registration was largely voluntary from the time it was started in the 1880s; it was finally required officially in 1969. Some areas have extensive records while others have very few. Among the traditional records, one of the most intriguing sources is the pilgrimage record. Genealogical information was imparted to Hindu priests during visits to sacred religious centers in many areas of India. These pilgrimages have been going on for centuries. Since relatively few records from this part of the world are in libraries and archives in the West, research must be done in India. It is very difficult, because by and large these are uncharted waters.

A TYPICAL CHINESE- AND JAPANESE-AMERICAN SEARCH

Because Chinese and Japanese Americans are two of the larger Asian-American ethnic groups, the examples and suggestions that follow will be aimed primarily at these groups. Some of the more general information, however, is useful for other Asian groups as well.

Chinese

Talk or write to older members of the family to learn about addresses in the United States, names of family members, pertinent dates, and possible home sources. See if these older relatives know the place of origin abroad, the address or location of relatives in China, and the particular name of the clan or lineage to which the family traditionally belonged. The name and location of the ancestral temple, family gravesite, and other items of historical and genealogical significance should also be recorded, either by cassette or into a research notebook.

A search of individual record sources will be necessary either to eliminate each possibility or to add the information to the research. From the information, establish the lineage connections and add to the skeletal outline. The types of sources and the information these sources contain have already been summarized. Since most of these records are in Chinese, translation and Romanization will probably be necessary to make the genealogy or family history more meaningful to future generations in this country.

To avoid confusion, write the name in the Chinese order, using all-capital letters to show the surname. If the Western order is preferred, capitalize or underline the surname: for example, "LI, Ming-ch'eng," "Ming-ch'eng LI," or "Ming-ch'eng Li." A clan or lineage can be identified more accurately by noting the ancestral home: "the LI clan of Fu-an" or "the HUANG clan of Chin-shan."

Dates prior to 1912 are normally assumed to be lunar dates. Rather than convert, it is usually easier to use a capital "L" to refer to lunar. Dates since 1912 are usually solar calendar dates, though many Chinese continue to use the lunar calendar. A Western date would be recorded as, for example, 25 March 1921, while a lunar date may be recorded as 8 D (D for day) 6 M (M for month) 1875 (conversion of the Chinese year). An L can be added to clarify the date: 7 D 6 M 1875 L. Some may prefer to write 7 June 1875, but that would be misleading. If dates are unavailable, one may either calculate or approximate the date (ca. 1820) or enter the generation number. Some entries include the intercalary month, or extra month added every few years to make the lunar calendar conform to the seasons. After the M (for month), this can be shown with a plus (+) sign, the word "intercalary," or some other notation. The year can be converted using a sixty-year cyclical calendar or with a calendar showing the reign-years of the emperors.

Place names can usually be handled with the use of a few simple rules. If the Western order is used, list the town or city, the county, the state, and then the country; for example, "Chicago, Cook, Illinois, U.S.A.," or "Tsuen Wan, New Territories, Hong Kong, B.C.C." The Chinese order would reverse these: country, province, county, and city or village: for example, "China, Kwangtung, Tai-shan, Shinlie," or "Republic of China (Taiwan), Taichung, Shalu."

In many instances the jurisdiction has changed. The former or, if known, the present jurisdiction can be used, depending on what is available. With older records, only the ancestral home or place of residence is listed. In these cases it may be necessary to indicate with the word "of" that a family is from a certain place: "HUANG family of Ch'angsha, Hunan Province." This place may be a burial place or merely a place where the family lived for many generations. This can be noted in parentheses.

Two Chinese pedigree charts are included. One is left blank (figure 8.8), and the other (figure 8.9) is partially completed to illustrate how this can be done. Also included is a family group sheet (figure 8.10).

An example of a card catalog entry from the LDS Library for a Chinese clan

Figure 8.8
Chinese Pedigree Chart (Blank)

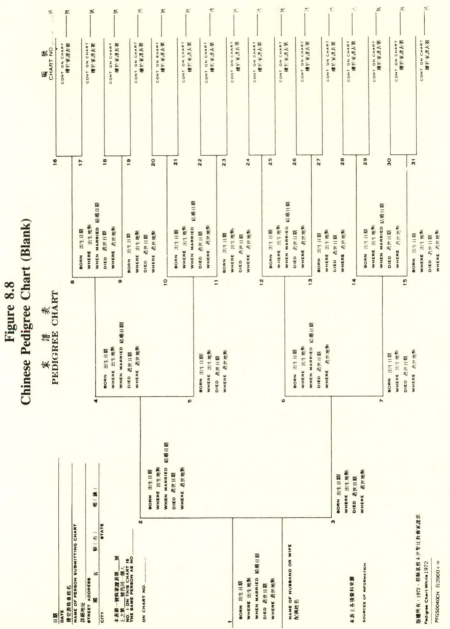

Figure 8.9
Chinese Pedigree Chart (Partially Completed)

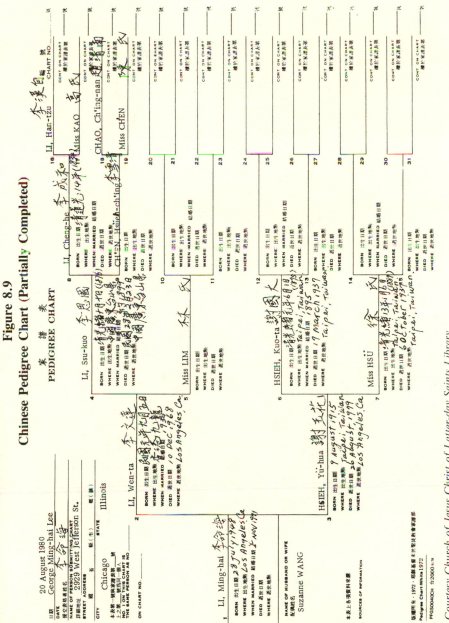

Courtesy *Church of Jesus Christ of Latter-day Saints Library.*

281

Figure 8.10
Chinese Family Group Sheet

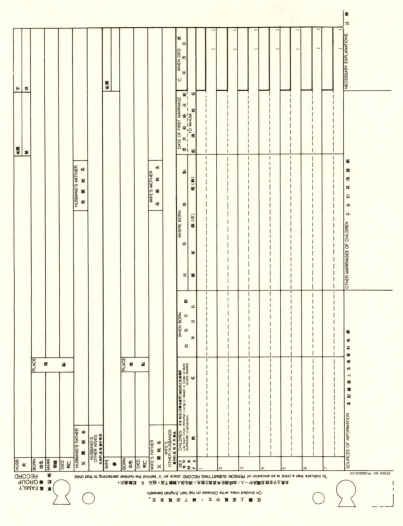

Courtesy Church of Jesus Christ of Latter-day Saints Library.

282

genealogy also illustrates how Chinese records can be referenced and found (figure 8.11). Because the records are in Chinese, it is presupposed that those searching for the records should be able to handle content notes in Chinese.

Japanese

The immigrant generation, or *issei* as they are known to Japanese Americans, is becoming harder to find as time passes. The *issei* should be approached while they are still alive. Because of language problems, it may be necessary to seek out help in conducting a thorough interview. The interview should begin with the native place in Japan and trace the journey across. Subsequent jobs, addresses, and family matters of interest should also be among the items one should seek. If there are no surviving *issei*, the next generation, *nisei*, should be able to provide some clues.

Japanese community and ethnic records, though often in Japanese, may be very useful for genealogy and family history. Japanese newspapers, for example, contain detailed references to residents. Obituaries and other individual news items may also prove valuable. Besides the information on the deceased, the names of relatives and family members may also be helpful.

The focus of the research should be on finding the native place in Japan. By tying into Japanese records, the genealogy and family history can be extended. The *koseki*, or family register, may add two or three generations, while the *kakochō* may add as many as a half dozen more. Other records in Japan are more difficult to tie into and harder to decipher and use, especially those of the feudal period.

The Japanese also use the surname first, followed by the given name. In some Western records the proper order is reversed. The usual ways of recording the name follow: "ADACHI, Nobuo," "Nobuo ADACHI," or "Nobuo *Adachi*." The reading can be written over the name if characters are used in *furigana*, Japanese phonetic syllabary. Most dictionaries with Romanized entries use the modified Hepburn system, though there are other Romanization schemes.

There are several special name situations encountered in Japanese research. One of the more common problems is adoption of a male heir to the wife's family, in which case the husband takes the surname of her family. This situation can be shown in the following way: "MARUYAMA or KANDA, Eikichi." Kanda was the husband's surname before marriage. Another problem is the use of multiple names. A Japanese might have several in different stages of life. These names could be explained in the "necessary explanations" area on a family group sheet, put in parentheses, or inserted in the proper order: "Tekeshi was also known as Tengu, (George) Nobuyuki *Asano*, or Kaneko (Yoshinaka) KIKUCHI." If a given name is unknown, simply use a Mr. or Miss, followed by the surname: "Miss TANAKA." Where the wife's surname and given name are unavailable and a wife did exist, the name of the husband can be used: "Mrs. Mitsuo *Tabata*."

The problem of recording Japanese dates is slightly different from that of

Figure 8.11
Catalog Card Entry for Chinese Records

```
ASIA
Film
1,211,004
Item 8      Lai, I-tsun.
                  (Ying-ch'uan Lai shih tsu p'u)
```

潁川賴氏族譜／賴以尊重修．一美國猶他州
鹽湖城：猶他家譜學會攝影，１９７９．

微捲１捲；３５釐米．

```
            Genealogy of the Lai family of Ying-
      ch'uan, Taiwan branch.
                              19 Dec 1979      DAG
      TAI 1A/7                Card 1 of 3
```

```
ASIA
Film
1,211,004
Item 8      Lai, I-tsun.        ...
```

受姓始祖：賴叔潁（周）
臺灣始遷祖：賴廷右
散居地：臺灣省基隆市
珍藏者：賴陳蔥女士
原書：寫本．民國乙酉〔１９４５〕記事．
〔５８〕面：插圖，家譜表．

```
                              19 Dec 1979      DAG
      TAI 1A/7                Card 2 of 3
```

```
ASIA
Film
1,211,004
Item 8      Lai, I-tsun.        ...




            1. Lai family of Ying-ch'uan, Taiwan
      branch.  2. China, Taiwan, Chi-lung Shih -
      Genealogy.

                              19 Dec 1979      DAG
      TAI 1A/7                Card 3 of 3
```

Asian Collection, Church of Jesus Christ of Latter-day Saints Library.

recording Chinese ones. The Japanese converted to the solar calendar earlier (in 1872) and in only rare instances have used lunar dates since. This clarifies the month and day, but the year still must be referenced to the year in the reign of the emperor. For example, Taisho 8, or the 8th year of the Taisho era, is 1919. Before 1868 the eras were proclaimed more often; some lasted a year or two, while others lasted twenty. Because of the changes and lack of communications, there was always some overlap. Intercalary months were also used every three or four years. The sixty-year Chinese sexagenary cycle (five related cycles of twelve years each) was also used quite frequently in the feudal period.

Place names are also troublesome, since the system of designation has evolved considerably. Presently, the prefecture; county or municipal district; and city, town, or village are the designations. Previous designations (before 1870) were the *han* (feudal domain), *kuni* (county or province), and the present town (*machi*) and village (*mura*). Some of these changes can be explained, if known. For example, Narumi, Aichi, Owari no Kuni, is now Narumi-cho Midoru-ku, Nagoya-shi, Aichi-ken, Japan. Place names can be written as follows: Joyo-machi (township), Yame-gun (county or district), Nagano-ken (prefecture), Japan.

Two Japanese pedigree charts follow. One (figure 8.12) is purposely left blank, and the other (figure 8.13) partially completed. A family group sheet is also included (figure 8.14), as is an example of a catalog card for a Japanese genealogy, again from the LDS Genealogical Department Library (figure 8.15).

In summary, while a step-by-step explanation of how to do research might be preferable, it would be misleading because of the diverse research situations Asian Americans face. The emphasis is on solving problems and compiling the genealogy. It is hoped that this brief glimpse may suggest some possible approaches. For the details and background information, consult specific volumes in the bibliography.

NOTES

1. Thomas W. Chinn, ed., *A History of the Chinese in California: A Syllabus* (San Francisco: Chinese Historical Society of America, 1969).

2. "Chinatown Struggles," *Los Angeles Times,* 13 April 1980.

3. These are largely general observations since no detailed inventories are as yet available. Some of the figures are from Tsuen-Hsuin Tsien, "Research Notes: Current Status of East Asian Collections in American Libraries," *Journal of Asian Studies* 36 (May 1977): 499–514.

4. Karl Lo and Him Mark Lai, comps., *Chinese Newspapers Published in North America, 1854–1975* (Washington, D.C.: Center for Chinese Research Materials, 1977).

5. "Major Genealogical Record Sources in Hong Kong," Research Paper, series J, no. 4 (Salt Lake City, Utah: Genealogical Society of the Church of Jesus Christ of Latter-day Saints, 1975).

6. From a manuscript copy of the Quan family genealogy on file at the LDS Library; translation assistance from Basil Pei-nai Yang.

7. Lee W. Vance, *Tracing Your Philippine Ancestors* (Salt Lake City, Utah: published by author, 1980).

Figure 8.12
Japanese Pedigree Chart (Blank)

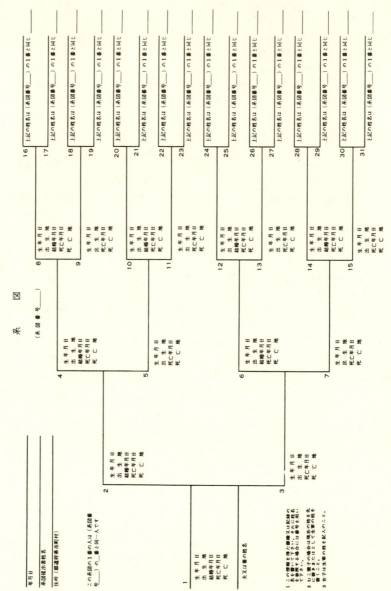

Courtesy Church of Jesus Christ of Latter-day Saints Library.

Figure 8.13
Japanese Pedigree Chart (Partially Completed)

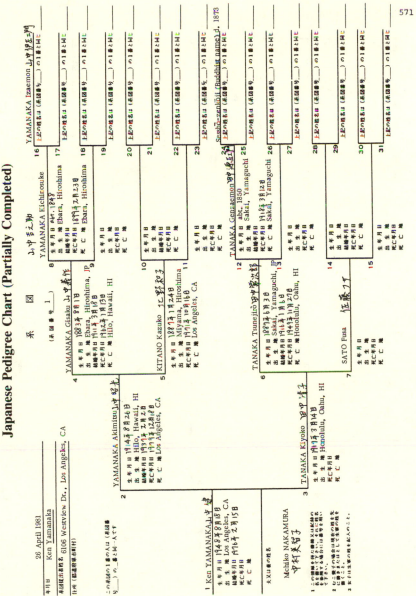

Courtesy Church of Jesus Christ of Latter-day Saints Library.

Figure 8.14
Japanese Family Group Sheet

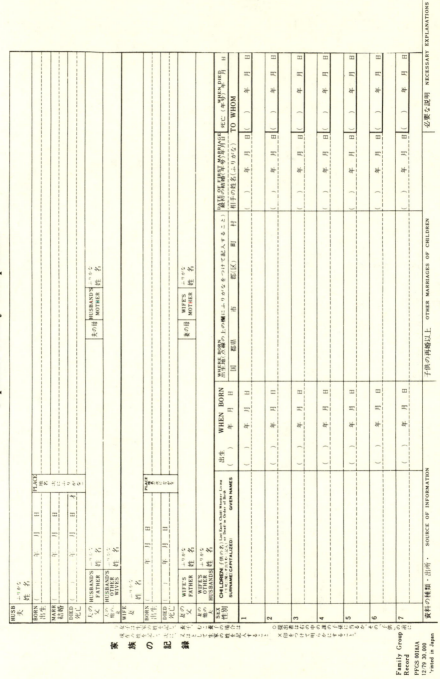

Courtesy Church of Jesus Christ of Latter-day Saints Library.

Figure 8.15
Catalog Card for a Japanese Genealogy

```
ASIA
Film
1,250,906
Item 11
```
かのう　け　ごかふ

狩野家　五家譜．ーユタ州ソルトレーク市：系図協
会撮影，１９７９．ーマイクロ・フィルム１リール；３５㎜．

原図書：写本　文化９〔１８１２〕　国立国会図書館
蔵．〔３７〕丁：図解

１.日本一系図　２.狩野家

```
JPNC 4-4C/44          19 May 1980          DBC
RN : 20558
```

Asian Collection, Church of Jesus Christ of Latter-day Saints Library.

BIBLIOGRAPHY

General Works

Fuchs, Lawrence H. *Hawaii Pono: A Social History.* New York: Harcourt, Brace and World, 1961.
    A historical account of the various ethnic groups in Hawaii and the problems each faced in the
    islands. Useful for historical background and for comparisons of assimilation.
Hundley, Norris, Jr., ed. *The Asian American: The Historical Experience.* Santa Barbara: ABC, Clio
    Press, 1976.
    Includes essays from past issues of the *Pacific Historical Review* on Asian-Pacific commu-
    nities and the problems of assimilation of the immigrants. Focus is mainly on the sociohistori-
    cal aspects of immigration.
Isaacs, Harold R. *Images of Asia: American Views of China and India.* New York: Harper and Row,
    1972.
    Formerly entitled *Scratches on Our Minds,* this book explores the vascillating attitudes of
    Americans toward China and India. Also has some interesting views on the immigrants.
Lind, Andrew. *Hawaii's People.* Rev. ed. Honolulu: University of Hawaii Press, 1980.
    A study of Hawaii's ethnic groups and their characteristics. Discusses the distribution, social
    norms, employment trends, and attributes of the major ethnic groups. Useful for background
    and for its bibliography of social and demographic studies of Hawaiian groups.
Lyman, Stanford M. *The Asian in North America.* Santa Barbara: ABC, Clio Press, 1977.
    Focuses primarily on the Chinese and Japanese experience in North America. A collection of
    articles and essays on the historical aspects of immigration and the problems of adjustment.
    Good for historical background and for an understanding of the social problems Asian
    immigrants faced.
Melendy, H. Brett. *Asians in America: Filipinos, Koreans and East Indians.* Boston: G. K. Hall and
    Co., Twayne Publishers, 1977.

A volume in the *Immigrant History of America Series*. Focuses on immigrants from the Philippines, Korea, and the Indian subcontinent. Focuses primarily on immigration before the law was changed in 1965. Discusses the prejudice encountered, immigrant political activities, and the various immigrant communities.

————. *The Oriental Americans*. Boston: G. K. Hall and Co., Twayne Publishers, 1972.
Concentrates on the Chinese and Japanese immigrants and the historical aspects of their settlement in America. Also discusses the legislation and climate of the times. Focuses mainly on the pre-World War II period.

Nordyke, Eleanor C. *The Peopling of Hawaii*. Honolulu: East-West Center, 1977.
Treats the trends and problems of immigration to Hawaii. Fairly concise, with an excellent bibliography of more specific works on the various ethnic groups.

Palmer, Spencer, ed. *Studies in Asian Genealogy*. Provo, Utah: Brigham Young University Press, 1972.
This volume is composed of papers from the Asian portion of the 1969 World Conference on Records held in Salt Lake City, Utah. Some of these papers are listed individually in this bibliography by the particular countries. The papers on records are especially valuable, though some of these are dated.

Thernstrom, Stephen, and Orlov, Ann, eds. *Harvard Encyclopedia of American Ethnic Groups*. Cambridge, Mass.: Belknap Press, Harvard University Press, 1980.
A comprehensive directory of ethnic groups in the United States. Includes brief historical and bibliographic treatment of the following Asian ethnic groups: Chinese (pp. 217–34), Japanese (pp. 561–71), Korean (pp. 601–6), Filipino (pp. 354–62), Indochinese (pp. 508–13), Indonesian (p. 513), East Indian (pp. 296–301), and Thai (p. 990).

Chinese Americans and China

BOOKS

Baker, Hugh R. D. *Chinese Family and Kinship*. New York: Columbia University Press, 1978.
An academic study of the traditional Chinese family and kinship relations, mainly in south China, the origin of most Chinese emigration. Discusses the composition of the family, the nature of the clan, the importance of lineage and ancestor worship, and the traditional relationship of the clan to the community and the state.

Barth, Gunther. *Bitter Strength: A History of the Chinese in the United States, 1850–1970*. Cambridge, Mass.: Harvard University Press, 1964.
A detailed account of the initial period of Chinese immigration. Discusses the reasons for immigration and the methods and life of the early immigrants. Analyzes social and political problems and developments leading to immigration restrictions.

Char, Tin-Yuke, comp. *The Sandalwood Mountains: Readings and Stories of the Early Chinese in Hawaii*. Honolulu: University of Hawaii Press, 1975.
An excellent account of some of the early Chinese immigrants to Hawaii. Includes a number of interesting anecdotes and insights on the nineteenth-century Chinese settlers. Also has some references to the Chinese cemeteries on the islands, a section on Chinese organizations and groups (pp. 145–80), and a section entitled "Family Histories, Lineage and Genealogy" (pp. 223–66).

Chen, Jack. *The Chinese of America*. New York: Harper and Row, 1980.
A recent synthesis of views of the history of the Chinese in America and the Chinese contribution.

Chinn, Thomas W., ed. *A History of the Chinese in California: A Syllabus*. San Francisco: Chinese Historical Society of America, 1969.
An excellent volume on the immigration and settlement of the Chinese in California. Explains the reasons for immigration, places of settlement, occupations, and organization. Also includes a thorough bibliography, footnotes, and maps.

Coolidge, Mary Roberts. *Chinese Immigration.* New York: Holt and Co., 1909. (Reprint edition available through Chinese Materials Center, published by Cheng Wen, Taipei, Taiwan, 1969.)

> An original detailed study of Chinese immigration and the exclusionary laws that affected it.

Fan, Tin-chiu. *Chinese Residents in Chicago.* Saratoga, Calif.: R and E Research Associates, 1974.

> Basically a copy of an original work on the Chinese in Chicago submitted as a thesis at the University of Chicago. Contains details of Chinese settlement in the Chicago area.

Glick, Clarence E. *Sojourners and Settlers: Chinese Migrants in Hawaii.* Honolulu: University of Hawaii Press, 1980.

> A study of the Chinese experience in Hawaii. Focuses on the sociohistorical aspects. Discusses the struggle of Chinese for acceptance, the role of immigrant organizations, and settlement patterns. Includes a few photographs of the early Chinese.

Hsu, Francis Lik. *The Challenge of the American Dream: The Chinese in the United States.* Belmont, Calif.: Wadsworth Publishing Co., 1971.

> Discusses the struggles and successes of the immigrants.

Kingston, Maxine Hong. *China Men.* New York: Alfred A. Knopf, 1980.

> A novel about the author's Chinese ancestors and family growing up in America. A sequel to *The Woman Warrior,* which focused more on the author herself. The dialogue and atmosphere are presented in a very articulate and interesting manner.

Lee, Calvin. *Chinatown U.S.A.* Garden City, N.Y.: Doubleday and Co., 1965.

> Provides interesting insights into the life and customs of America's Chinatowns. Focuses mainly on the San Francisco Chinatown but includes information on the one in New York and on some of the smaller Chinatowns. Illustrated with historic and contemporary photographs.

Lee, Rose Hum. *Chinese in the United States.* London: Oxford University Press, 1964.

> An academic study of Chinese immigration to the United States and of the immigrants themselves.

Li, Dun J. *The Ageless Chinese: A History.* 3rd ed. New York: Charles Scribner's Sons, 1978.

> A general overview of the four thousand years of Chinese history. Also includes some mention of traditions, the language, and important historical figures. Useful mainly for background on Chinese history.

Lo, Karl, and Lai, Him Mark, comps. *Chinese Newspapers Published in North America, 1854–1975.* Washington, D.C.: Center for Chinese Research Materials, 1977.

> A pioneer attempt to identify ethnic Chinese newspapers and the locations of existing copies. Lists 254 titles, about a third of which were published in San Francisco. New York follows with 65 titles.

Lyman, Stanford M. *Chinese Americans.* New York: Random House, 1979.

> Discusses the Chinese Americans as an ethnic group and describes their settlements and traditions.

Meltzer, Milton. *The Chinese Americans.* New York: Harper and Row Publishers, Har-Row, 1980.

> A recently published volume intended as a concise history and study of Chinese Americans.

Miller, Stuart C. *Unwelcome Immigrant: The American Image of the Chinese, 1785–1882.* Berkeley and Los Angeles: University of California Press, 1969. (Also in paperback.)

> Primarily discusses anti-Chinese feelings and their roots. Interesting to see the early American impressions of China and the myths and hysteria during the first century of contact.

Morton, Scott. *China: Its History and Culture.* New York: McGraw, 1981.

> Useful for background information on China proper and her culture.

Nee, Victor, and Nee, Brett de Bary. *Longtime California: A Documentary Study of an American Chinatown.* New York: Pantheon Books, 1973.

> Explains the traditions and life in San Francisco's Chinatown. Includes translated documents and narratives on experiences there.

Sih, Paul K. T., and Allen, Leonard B. *The Chinese in America.* New York: St. John's University Press, 1976.

> Focuses on Chinese immigration and achievements of the Chinese in America.

Steiner, Stanley. *Fusang, the Chinese Who Built America.* New York: Harper and Row, 1979. (Also in paperback.)

> Expounds on the Chinese-American experience and contribution to the building of this country. Contains references to little-known aspects of the Chinese in America and includes notes on their struggles.

Sung, Betty Lee. *Mountains of Gold: The Story of the Chinese in America.* New York: Macmillan Co., 1967.

> Basically an overview of Chinese immigrant history in the United States. Also notes some of the customs and traditions of China that were perpetuated by the Chinese in the new land. Mentions Chinese occupations, the spread of Chinese laundries and restaurants, and some of the outstanding achievements of the immigrants.

————. *The Story of the Chinese in America.* New York: Collier Books, 1974.

> Paperback version of *Mountains of Gold* with minor updating.

Telford, Ted A.; Thatcher, Melvin; and Yang, Basil P. N., comps. *An Annotated Bibliography of Chinese Clan Genealogies.* Taipei, Taiwan: Cheng Wen Publishing Co., 1981.

> This volume in Chinese includes over 3,000 titles of Chinese clan genealogies arranged by surname and location. The great majority are in the Chinese collection of the LDS Genealogical Department Library.

Tung, William L., comp. *The Chinese in America, 1820–1973: A Chronology and Fact Book.* Dobbs Ferry, N.Y.: Oceana Publications, 1974.

> Includes facts and statistics in basic chronological order on the immigration and achievements of Chinese. Also given are some of the important documents relating to immigration restrictions, treaties, and judicial decisions on immigration. A useful bibliography is also included.

Young, Nancy Foon, comp. *The Chinese in Hawaii: An Annotated Bibliography.* Honolulu: Social Science Research Institute, University of Hawaii Press, 1973.

> An inventory of the books, periodicals, pamphlets, and manuscripts then available on the Chinese experience in Hawaii. The entries, arranged alphabetically by author and title, include descriptive annotations and notes on the location of the materials. Lists archival material and documents of value in research on Chinese immigration and the settlement of individual immigrants. Some notes on vital and census records are also included.

MONOGRAPHS AND ARTICLES

"Chinese Local History as a Source for the Genealogist." Rev. ed. Genealogical Research Papers, series J, no. 3. Salt Lake City: Genealogical Society of the Church of Jesus Christ of Latter-day Saints, 1975.

> A brief paper showing the context and value of Chinese local histories in genealogical research. Includes several examples of categories and entries in these histories.

Chinn, Thomas W. "Genealogical Sources for Chinese Immigrants to the United States." *World Conference on Records and Genealogical Seminar,* area H-3. Salt Lake City: Genealogical Society of the Church of Jesus Christ of Latter-day Saints, c1969.

> Explains Chinese naming customs, Chinese immigration, and a few of the sources for research. Appears in entirety in Palmer, *Studies in Asian Genealogy.*

Eberhard, Wolfram. "Scholastic Application of the Chinese Clan Genealogies, Part 1: Chinese Genealogies as a Source for the Study of Chinese Society." *World Conference on Records and Genealogical Seminar* areas H-9, 10b. Salt Lake City: Genealogical Society of the Church of Jesus Christ of Latter-day Saints, c1969.

> Shows how Chinese clan genealogies can be used in research and discusses their content. Also appears in Palmer, *Studies in Asian Genealogy.*

Gubler, Greg. "Characters and Ancestors: The Case of China and Korea." *Genealogy Digest* 9 (Winter 1978): 5–11.

> An introductory look into Chinese and Korean sources and some of the customs on which they are based. Shows several examples and traces the historical outlines.

Hayes, James. "Chinese Clan Genealogies and Family Histories: Chinese Clan Genealogies as Local and Family History." *World Conference on Records* (2d, 1980) vol. 11, no. 824. Salt Lake City: Corporation of the President of the Church of Jesus Christ of Latter-day Saints, c1980. The author shares his experiences of inventorying records in the British Crown Colony, where he is a government administrator. Provides insights into the record-keeping traditions, availability of sources, and the ways clan genealogies can be used in family history research.

Joint East-Asian Center. "A Checklist of Chinese Local Histories." Series 4. Stanford and Berkeley: Joint East-Asian Center Publication, East Asian Library, 1980. Basically an inventory of Chinese local histories in participating libraries; contains over 2,500 titles. Arranged by locality.

Lau, Chau-mun. "The Chinese in Hawaii: A Checklist of Materials in the Asia and Hawaiian Collections of the University of Hawaii Library." Honolulu: University of Hawaii Library, 1973. An inventory of about 250 entries of materials in libraries of the University of Hawaii relating to the Chinese.

Leng, Tsun. "The Content and Use of Chinese Local History (Fang-Chih)." *World Conference on Records and Genealogical Seminar*, area H-6. Salt Lake City: Genealogical Society of the Church of Jesus Christ of Latter-day Saints, c1969. Similar in content to *Chinese Local History as a Source for the Genealogist*. Contains descriptions of uses and gives the types of information in the sources. Also appears in Palmer, *Studies in Asian Genealogy*.

Lin, Tien-Wei. "Chinese Clan Genealogies and Family Histories: Clan Genealogies as They Relate to Local History." *World Conference on Records* (2d, 1980) vol. 11, no. 824c. Salt Lake City: Corporation of the President of the Church of Jesus Christ of Latter-day Saints, c1980. Describes the relationship of Chinese clan genealogies to local histories and the information found in both.

Lo, Hsiang-lin. "The Extent and Preservation of Genealogical Records in China." *World Conference on Records and Genealogical Seminar, area H-8*. Publication no. H8. Salt Lake City: Genealogical Society of the Church of Jesus Christ of Latter-day Saints, c1969. A glimpse of China's record-keeping traditions and the impact of the Communist takeover on the mainland. Also appears in Palmer, *Studies in Asian Genealogy*.

———. "Scholastic Application of the Chinese Clan Genealogies, pt. 2: History and Arrangement of Chinese Genealogies." *World Conference on Records and Genealogical Seminar*, areas H-9, 10a. Salt Lake City: Genealogical Society of the Church of Jesus Christ of Latter-day Saints, c1969. Discusses the historical origins of clan genealogies and their content and gives examples of the types of information the genealogies contain. Also appears in Palmer, *Studies in Asian Genealogy*.

"Major Genealogical Record Sources in Hong Kong." Research Paper, series J, no. 4. Salt Lake City: Genealogical Society of the Church of Jesus Christ of Latter-day Saints, 1975. Describes genealogical sources found in Hong Kong, their availability, and the time coverage and content of the respective sources, both traditional and British.

"Major Genealogical Record Sources in Taiwan." Rev. ed., 1976. Research Paper, series J, no. 2. Salt Lake City: Genealogical Department, Church of Jesus Christ of Latter-day Saints, 1976. Lists genealogical sources in Taiwan; describes their coverage, availability, and content; and provides a brief historical introduction.

Ohai, Jean. "Chinese Genealogy and Family Book Guide: Hawaii and Chinese Sources." Honolulu: Hawaii Chinese History Center, 1975. A brief (fourteen pages) but excellent guide on how to do research and compile a genealogy using Hawaiian and Chinese sources. One of the very few publications that provides insight into the research process.

———. "Family History for Chinese Americans." World Conference on Records (2d, 1980) vol. 11, no. 807. Salt Lake City: President of the Church of Jesus Christ of Latter-day Saints, c1980.

Describes the sources and techniques available in family history research. Defines some basic settlement patterns, lists supplemental sources and background materials, and suggests some approaches to family history research. An excellent introductory paper.

Telford, Ted A. "East Asian Family Sources: The Genealogical Society of Utah Collection—China." *World Conference on Records* (2d, 1980) vol. 11, no. 814. Salt Lake City: Corporation of the President of the Church of Jesus Christ of Latter-day Saints, c1980.

Describes the collection at the LDS Library or on call. Emphasis is on the large clan genealogy and local history collections. Information is included on distribution of these records.

———. "Women and Traditional Sources: Chinese Clan Genealogies: Tracing the Female Line." *World Conference on Records* (2d, 1980) vol. 11, no. 831a. Salt Lake City: Corporation of the President of the Church of Jesus Christ of Latter-day Saints, c1980.

Although women were peripheral in the patrilineal Chinese genealogies, in some cases they can be traced to the original family. Telford shows the variations in this source from place to place and the problems of linkage. He also notes the instances in which linkage is possible.

Wang, Shih-ching. "Chinese Clan Genealogies and Family Histories: Historiography of Chinese Genealogies—Taiwan." *World Conference on Records* (2d, 1980) vol. 11, no. 824a. Salt Lake City: Corporation of the President of the Church of Jesus Christ of Latter-day Saints, c1980.

Explains the origins of the genealogies, outlines the content and information included, and suggests some of their strengths and limitations.

———. "Contracts and Other Old Documents as Sources for Family History and Genealogy in Taiwan." *World Conference on Records* (2d, 1980) vol. 11, no. 812. Salt Lake City: Corporation of the President of the Church of Jesus Christ of Latter-day Saints, c1980.

Lists a number of records of genealogical value in Taiwan and evaluates their content and value in research.

Japanese Americans and Japan

BOOKS

Conroy, Hilary. *The Japanese Frontier in Hawaii, 1868–1898.* Berkeley and Los Angeles: University of California Press, 1953.

A thorough study of the early period of Japanese immigration, focusing mainly on the political and social ramifications and the historical aspects.

———, and Miyakawa, T. Scott, eds. *East Across the Pacific: Historical and Sociological Studies of Japanese Immigration and Assimilation.* Santa Barbara: ABC, Clio Press, 1972.

A series of essays and articles on Japanese immigration, on the problems of assimilation, and on family and generational interaction. Most useful are the sections dealing with the historical background of labor immigration and with the institutions and methods used to facilitate immigration.

DeFrancis, John. *Things Japanese in Hawaii.* Honolulu: University of Hawaii Press, 1973. (Available in paperback.)

A synopsis of Japanese influences in Hawaii. Includes pictures, a brief glossary of Japanese terms, and an appendix containing Japanese addresses of note.

Fukui, Budd. *The Japanese American Story.* Minneapolis, Minn.: Dillon Press, 1976.

An account of the life and experience of Japanese Americans by a *nisei* who was raised in prewar Seattle. Provides an especially good insight, therefore, into Seattle's ethnic community.

Herman, Masako, comp. *The Japanese in America, 1843–1973: A Chronology and Fact Book.* Dobbs Ferry, N.Y.: Oceana Publications, 1974.

Includes the historical highlights and successes of a century of the Japanese in America. Also includes documents and statistics pertinent to immigration and a small bibliography.

Hosokawa, Bill. *Nisei: The Quiet Americans.* New York: William Morrow, 1969.

> A narrative account on Japanese in this country. Focuses primarily on the *nisei* and their achievements.

Ichihashi, Yamato. *Japanese in the United States.* American Immigration Collection, Vol. 28. Stanford: Stanford University Press, 1932; reprint ed. New York: New York Times/Arno Press, 1969.

> A thorough account justifying Japanese immigration and illustrating Japanese activities in America. Includes considerable statistical data and gives the historical background behind various issues.

Ichioka, Yuji; Sakata, Yasu; and Tsuchida, Nobuya. *A Buried Past: An Annotated Bibliography of the Japanese American Project Collection.* Berkeley and Los Angeles: University of California Press, 1974.

> Lists approximately 1,500 sources on Japanese immigrants to the United States both in Japanese and English; also sociological and historical studies, interviews, and Japanese government archival documents deposited in the research library at the University of California, Los Angeles.

Matsuda, Mitsugu. Revised by Dennis M. Ogawa with Jerry Y. Fujioka. *The Japanese in Hawaii: An Annotated Bibliography of Japanese Americans.* Hawaii Series, no. 5. Honolulu: University of Hawaii Press, 1975.

> An excellent annotated bibliography of both published and manuscript sources in various locations in Hawaii. Discusses the titles, content, and repositories of the respective sources. Includes records pertaining to immigration, vital events, and individuals. Also includes directories, annuals, and periodicals.

Modell, John. *The Economics and Politics of Racial Accommodation: The Japanese of Los Angeles, 1900–1942.* Urbana: University of Illinois Press, 1977.

> An academic study of the reaction of the large community and struggles of the Japanese in prewar Los Angeles County. Includes some statistical information.

Ogawa, Dennis M. *Jan Ken Po: The World of Hawaii's Japanese Americans.* Honolulu: University of Hawaii Press, 1973. (Also in paperback.)

> Deals with Hawaii's Japanese-American subculture and gives some interesting anecdotes.

———, with Grant, Glen. *Kodomo no Tame Ni: For the Sake of the Children, The Japanese Experience in Hawaii.* Honolulu: University of Hawaii Press, 1978.

> The first part of the book outlines the historical aspects of Japanese immigration. The book discusses the origins of the immigrants, why they came, and their destinations. Also includes an anthology of articles on the Japanese in Hawaii and their culture.

Okahata, James H., ed. *A History of the Japanese in Hawaii.* Honolulu: United Japanese Society, 1971.

> A survey of the Japanese experience in Hawaii. Discusses the early immigrants, their struggle for acceptance, and the later successes of Japanese in Hawaii.

Okubo, Kiyoshi, ed. *Hawaiito ni okeru Nihorojin no iminshi* (A history of Japanese immigrants on the island of Hawaii). Hilo, Hawaii: Hilo *Times,* 1971.

> Discusses the phases of immigration, immigration procedures, and where the immigrants settled. Includes a directory of Japanese and their native prefecture. Published in Japanese.

Ota, Ryo. *Kakeizu no nyumon* (guide to the study of family lineages). Tokyo: Jinbutsu Oraisha, 1967.

> An excellent but traditional Japanese-language guide to research in Japanese-language sources. Discusses the strengths and weaknesses of the various sources.

———. *Seishi to kakei* (surnames and lineages). Tokyo: Sogensha, 1942.

> A monumental volume in Japanese which traces the origins of Japanese surnames and lineages. Used as a guide to Japanese family names and, in particular, to the lines of samurai and aristocratic families.

Papinot, E. *Historical and Geographical Dictionary of Japan.* 1910; reprint ed., Rutland, Vt.: Charles E. Tuttle Co., 1968.

A reference work particularly useful for understanding some of the names and places of feudal (pre-1868) Japan. Also included are some social terms and brief sketches of a few historical figures.

Patterson, William. *Japanese Americans: Oppression and Success.* New York: Random House, 1971.

A discussion of Japanese immigrants to the United States, their difficulties and achievements.

Reischaur, Edwin O. *Japan: The Story of a Nation.* 6th ed. New York: Alfred A. Knopf, 1980.

Useful mainly as a background source on Japan proper.

Shirota, Jon H. *Pineapple White.* Los Angeles: Ohara Publications, 1972.

The story of an immigrant Japanese who came to Hawaii in 1906 to work on a sugar plantation. Disenchanted, he later left for California, where he lived in the Los Angeles Japan Town.

Spicer, Edward H., et al. *Impounded People.* Tucson: University of Arizona Press, 1969.

Discusses the internment camp experience and the conditions involved. Included is information on the respective camps, on the decisions leading to internment, and on the eventual release. Includes some accounts by participants.

Webb, Herschel. *Research in Japanese Sources: A Guide.* New York: Columbia University Press, 1965.

Written primarily for those doing research in Japanese sources, but includes some useful observations on Japanese naming customs, geographic jurisdictions, and dating methods and for the more advanced, suggests some research tools and aids.

Wilson, Robert A., and Hosokawa, Bill. *East to America: A History of the Japanese in the United States.* New York: William Morrow, 1980.

Recently published. Discusses the reasons for immigration, the settlements, and the struggles of Japanese in the United States. An excellent, thorough account.

MONOGRAPHS AND ARTICLES

Brown, L. Keith. "Samurai and Merchant Family History: The Family in Japan." *World Conference on Records* (2d, 1980) vol. 11, no. 822. Salt Lake City: Corporation of the President of the Church of Jesus Christ of Latter-day Saints, c1980.

Introduces sources for the study of Japanese family history and outlines the changing structure of the Japanese family as observed from field research in Mizusawa (Iwate Prefecture) and the study of family registers (*koseki*).

Gubler, Greg. "Characters and Ancestors: And Then There is Japan." *Genealogy Digest* 10 (Spring 1979): 3–9, 17.

Briefly traces the historical development of a few major Japanese sources and discusses some of the obstacles and options in Japanese genealogical research.

———. "Family History for Japanese Americans." *World Conference on Records* (2d, 1980) vol. 11, no. 805. Salt Lake City: Corporation of the President of the Church of Jesus Christ of Latter-day Saints, c1980.

A brief introduction to the basic sources and research approaches both in this country and in Japan.

———. "Looking East: The Realities of Genealogical Research in Japan." *Genealogical Journal* 8 (March 1979): 43–50.

Deals with some of the myths and realities of research in Japanese sources. Introduces a number of sources and discusses a few of the research problems encountered once one enters the feudal period.

Hiraga, Noboru. "The Extent and Preservation of Original Historical Records in Japan." *World Conference on Records and Genealogical Seminar,* area H-2. Salt Lake City: Genealogical Society of the Church of Jesus Christ of Latter-day Saints, c1969.

Discusses some of the very old Japanese documents and the preservation problems in Japan.

Suggests possible research approaches and problems. Also includes examples of some of the sources and the character equivalents.

Hirata, Kin-itsu. "The Search for My Japanese Roots: Using Buddhist and Local Sources to Reconstruct Family History." *World Conference on Records* (2d, 1980) vol. 11, no. 802. Salt Lake City: Corporation of the President of the Church of Jesus Christ of Latter-day Saints, c1980. Hirata, a medical doctor and avid genealogist from Mino City in Japan, has spent many years trying to reconstruct his family lines and history. With the help of his family, he was able to use Buddhist death registers and local sources to reconstruct the lines of seventy-five families having a common ancestor in fifteenth-century Japan. This paper is a synopsis of the methodology and sources used, the details of which are in a Japanese volume published recently.

―――, and Gubler, Greg. "Family and Local History in Japan: Breaking the Impasse: Sources and Options in Japanese Family History Research." *World Conference on Records* (2d, 1980) vol. 11, no. 818b. Salt Lake City: Corporation of the President of the Church of Jesus Christ of Latter-day Saints, c1980.

Introduces a number of traditional sources in Japan, including Buddhist death registers, mortuary tablets, tombstone inscriptions, and some of the feudal records predating the Meiji Restoration of 1868.

"Major Genealogical Record Sources in Japan." Rev. ed., 1974. research paper, series J, no. 1, Salt Lake City: Genealogical Society of the Church of Jesus Christ of Latter-day Saints, 1974. This paper includes more than just the major sources. It introduces most of the genealogical sources of Japan and includes notes on coverage, availability, and content. A concise list form is used, but the list neglects source priorities.

Moore, Ray. "Family Records and Social History in Tokugawa Japan." *World Conference on Records and Genealogical Seminar*, area H-3. Salt Lake City: Genealogical Society of the Church of Jesus Christ of Latter-day Saints, c1969.

Concentrates mainly on samurai and aristocratic records and genealogies. Discusses the roles of these classes and the content of the records. Also appears in Palmer, *Studies in Asian Genealogy.*

"Nihon no koseki" (The Japanese household register). Genealogical Research Paper, series J, no. 5. Salt Lake City: Genealogical Department, Church of Jesus Christ of Latter-day Saints, 1979. Although originally written in English, this paper deals with the Japanese family or household register, the basic source for beginning Japanese research. The types of registers, the content, and access problems and the procedures for ordering copies, as well as suggestions on reading the entries, are among the topics covered in this paper. Includes examples of the records as appendix.

Nordyke, Eleanor C., and Matsumoto, Y. Scott. "The Japanese in Hawaii: A Historical and Demographic Perspective." *Hawaiian Journal of History* 11 (1977): 162–74.

Outlines the phases of immigration and the number of arrivals. Also gives statistical breakdowns of the Japanese ethnic group, including information on sex, occupations, and age groups.

Suzuki, Kenji. "East Asian Family Sources: The Genealogical Society of Utah Collection, Japan." *World Conference on Records* (2d, 1980) vol. 11, no. 814c. Salt Lake City: Corporation of the President of the Church of Jesus Christ of Latter-day Saints, c1980.

Describes the types of sources being collected and the status of acquisition programs in the various prefectures of Japan. Includes information on the amount of material filmed and the value of the respective record sources.

COMMUNITY NEWSPAPERS (LISTED BY CITY)

Chicago

Chicago Shimpo. Biweekly mimeographed paper for Midwest area, 1945 to present; copies of file at newspaper office, 3744 North Clark Street, Chicago, IL 60613.

Denver

Kakushi Jiji (Colorado Times). Small Japanese daily/biweekly, 1918–43; portions at University of
Illinois Library (1918–21) and Library of Congress (1940–43).

Rocky Mountain Jiho. Japanese weekly, 1962 to present; predecessors were the *Rocky Mountain Post*
(1896–1941?) and the *Rockii Shimpo* (1942–61); there are a few copies at the Library of
Congress and at the University of Colorado Library.

Hilo, Hawaii

Hawaii Mainichi Shimbun. Small Japanese daily, 1909–41; some later copies (1935–41) at *Hilo
Times*. Semiweekly Japanese paper, 1955 to present; copies on file at newspaper office, 636
Kilauea Avenue, Hilo, HI 96720.

Holualoa, Hawaii

Kona Hankyo. Weekly paper for Kona coast area on island of Hawaii, 1897–1926; copies at *Hilo
Times*.

Honolulu

Hawaii Hochi (Herald). Japanese daily, 1912–42 and 1942 to present; copies at Bishop Museum and
at newspaper; filming of earlier copies was done by the Genealogical Society of Utah.

Hawaii Shimpo. Japanese daily, 1894–1926; some copies at *Hilo Times*.

Honolulu Star and Advertiser. Index and selected obituaries of Japanese Americans, 1929–?. Not an
ethnic newspaper, but a collection; available at Hawaii State Archives.

Nippu Jiju (later called *Hawaii Times*). Japanese daily with English, 1906–41, 1942 to present.
Nearly complete set at Bishop Museum; earlier portions filmed by Genealogical Society of
Utah; copies also at University of Hawaii Library (1936–41, 1942 to present) and Hawaii
State Archives (1942 to present).

Yamato and Yamato Shimbun. Bi- and triweekly, 1895–1905; became the *Nippu Jiji;* a few copies at
the University of Hawaii Library (1904–05) and at Bishop Museum.

Los Angeles

Kashu Mainichi (California State Daily). Japanese-language daily with English section, 1931–42,
1946 to present; UCLA Library has an almost complete set.

Pacific Citizen. English-language publication of Japanese American Citizens League; scattered
monthly issues from 1931 to March 1942, weekly from June 1942 to present. Formerly
published in other cities, presently published at 125 Weller Street, Los Angeles, CA 90012.
Microfilm copies at Library of Congress and copies at San Diego State University Library.

Rafu Shimpo (Los Angeles Daily Japanese News). Japanese daily with English section, 1903–42,
1942 to present. Nearly complete sets on microfilm at UCLA and University of Southern
California libraries; partial set (from 1937) at Los Angeles Public Library.

New York City

New York Nichibei (Japanese American News). Weekly Japanese paper with English section; successor to *Nichibei Jiho* (1902–41) and *New York Shimpo;* copies of more recent papers at
newspaper office, 260 West Broadway, New York, NY 10013.

Portland

Oregon News. Small Japanese daily/weekly, 1902–42; some copies at University of Illinois Library
(1917–23).

Sacramento

Ofu Nippo (Sacramento Daily News). Japanese daily, 1907–41; copies at California State Library
(1909–16) and University of Illinois Library (1917–25); later copies at University of California, Berkeley, Library.

Salt Lake City

Utah Nippo. Japanese daily/triweekly, 1914–42, 1942 to present; English section since 1940; pre-
dated by the *Rocky Mountain Times* (c1900–14). Microfilm copies at University of Utah
Library (1917–75) and Library of Congress (1942–45).

San Francisco

Hokubei Asahi (North American Sun). Japanese daily, 192?–35; merged with *Shin Sekai* in 1935;
had English supplement. Some copies at University of California, Berkeley, Library
(1932–35).

Hokubei Mainichi (North American Daily). Japanese daily with English supplement, 1948 to present.
Microfilm copies at University of California, Berkeley, Library (1948–74) and California
State Library (1962 to present).

Nichibei (Japanese American News). Japanese daily, 1895–1942; started first English-language
section in 1925. Copies at California State Library (1919–25) and University of California,
Berkeley, Library (1927–42).

Nichibei Times. Japanese daily with English section, 1946 to present; copies on file at newspaper
office, 1375 Eddy Street, San Francisco, CA 94119, and at the Library of Congress
(1957–67).

Shin Sekai (New World Daily News). Japanese daily, 1897–1935; English section added in 1930.
Microfilm copies at University of California, Berkeley, Library (1899–1935).

Shin Sekai Asahi (New World–Sun). Japanese daily with English section, 1935–41; merger of *Shin
Sekai* and *Hokubei Asahi*. Microfilm copies at University of California, Berkeley, Library
(1935–41) and Library of Congress (1940–41).

Seattle

Asahi News (Sun). Japanese daily, 1905–18. Portions preserved in Washington State University
Library (1918) and University of Illinois Library (1917–18).

Hokubei Hochi (North American Post). Daily since 1950; 1946 to present. Copies at University of Washington Library and on file at newspaper office, 517 South Main Street, Seattle,
WA 98104.

Hokubei Jiji (North American Times). Japanese daily, 1902–42. Microfilm copies at Library of
Congress (1916–35).

Japanese American Courier. Weekly paper in English, 1928–42. On microfilm at University of
Washington Library (1928–42).

Taihoku Nippo (Great North Daily News). Japanese daily, 1909–41. Copies on microfilm at University of Washington Library (1917–41) and Library of Congress (1940–41).

Toronto

Continental Times. Biweekly Japanese paper with English section, 1948 to present. Copies on file at
newspaper office in Toronto.

Vancouver

Continental Daily News. Japanese daily, 190?–42. Extent of preservation unknown.

Korean Americans and Korea

BOOKS

Choy, Bong-Yang. *Koreans in America*. Chicago: Nelson-Hall Publications, 1979.
A study of the Korean ethnic communities in America and the Korean immigrants' problems of adjustment. Also includes a historical treatment of immigration and of the successes of individual Koreans.

Gardner, Arthur L. *The Koreans in Hawaii: An Annotated Bibliography*. Hawaii Series, no. 2. Honolulu: University of Hawaii Press, 1970.
A descriptive bibliography of various Korean-language and ethnic sources. Notes the locations of both published and manuscript sources and their content.

Kim, Hyung-chan, ed. *The Korean Diaspora: Historical and Sociological Studies of Korean Immigration and Socialization in North America*. Santa Barbara, Calif.: ABC, Clio Press, 1977. (Also in paperback.)
A collection of articles on the various facets of Korean immigration and assimilation. Covers the early and more recent periods of Korean immigration. Talks about the organizations that assisted immigrants and the immigrants' problems of adjustment.

————. *The Koreans in America*. Minneapolis, Minn.: Lerner Publications, 1977.
A brief synopsis of Korean immigration and settlement in America. Also describes the achievements of Koreans and Korean immigrant organizations.

————, and Patterson, Wayne, comps. *The Koreans in America, 1882–1974: A Chronology and Fact Book*. Dobbs Ferry, N.Y.: Oceana Publications, 1974.
Includes articles relating to Koreans and Korean immigration to the United States, documents on immigration and the Korean liberation movement, and a chronology of historical events.

Wagner, Edward W. "The Korean Chopko as a Historical Source." *World Conference on Records and Genealogical Seminar*, area H-12. Salt Lake City: Corporation of the President of the Church of Jesus Christ of Latter-day Saints, c1969.
Introduces the Korean type of clan genealogy and its content. Also discusses its research potential.

MONOGRAPHS

Patterson, Wayne. "The Korean Frontier in America: Immigration to Hawaii, 1896–1910." Ph.D. diss., University of Pennsylvania, 1978.
(Available from University Microfilms, Ann Arbor, Mich.)
An academic study of the early period of Korean immigration to Hawaii. Also discusses the reasons for emigration from Korea and the political situation.

Peterson, Mark. "Women and Traditional Sources: Sources for Genealogies for Women in Korea." *World Conference on Records* (2d, 1980) vol. 11, no. 831b. Salt Lake City: Corporation of the President of the Church of Jesus Christ of Latter-day Saints, c1980.
Discusses sources that include genealogical data about women and how they can be used in some instances to supplement the male-centered Korean clan genealogies. Also refers to the genealogies and their compilation, as well as to some aspects of traditional Korean society.

Song, June-ho. "An Interpretative History of the Yangban Family Records in Korea." *Family History in Korea: Yangban Family History*. *World Conference on Records* (2d, 1980) vol. 11, no. 816. Salt Lake City: Corporation of the President of the Church of Jesus Christ of Latter-day Saints, c1980.
A scholarly study of the origins and historical development of Korean clan and family genealogies. Discusses how the genealogies were compiled, their content and distinguishing characteristics, and the Korean clan system. Also includes a number of actual examples of Korean genealogies.

Yang, Basil. "East Asian Family Sources: The Genealogical Society of Utah Collection: Korea."

World Conference on Records (2d, 1980) vol. 11, no. 814a. Salt Lake City: Corporation of the President of the Church of Jesus Christ of Latter-day Saints, c1980.

Discusses the microfilm and book holdings of the LDS Genealogical Department Library in Salt Lake City. Focuses on the large Korean clan genealogy collection, on exam rosters, and on Korean local histories. Includes a list by surname and branch of the genealogies and a list by locality of the local histories. Also mentions several other sources.

Filipino Americans and the Philippines

BOOKS

Alcantara, Reuben, with Alconcel, Nancy S.; Berger, John; and Wycoco, Cesar S. *The Filipinos in Hawaii: An Annotated Bibliography.* Honolulu: University of Hawaii Press, 1977.

Completed as a project of the Social Sciences and Linguistics Institute of the University of Hawaii, this volume contains 164 pages detailing sources and publications on and of the Filipinos in Hawaii. Extremely useful for those contemplating research on Filipino immigration and settlement. Also includes sources on the assimilation of Filipinos in multiethnic Hawaii.

Dorita, Mary. *Filipino Immigration to Hawaii.* San Francisco: R and E Research Associates, 1975.

Originally produced in 1954 as a master's thesis. Outlines the attempts of HSPA to recruit Filipino labor and the stages of immigration to Hawaii.

Lasker, Bruno. *Filipino Immigration to the Continental United States and to Hawaii.* Chicago: Institute of Pacific Relations, University of Chicago Press, 1931; reprint ed., New York: New York Times/Arno Press, 1969.

A detailed study of the reasons and makeup of Filipino immigration. Extremely useful for information on prewar immigration and the origins and distribution of the immigrants.

Saito, Shiro. *Filipinos Overseas: A Bibliography.* New York: Center for Migration Studies, 1977.

Includes 1,232 entries, many on immigration. Has a list of Philippine newspapers in American libraries and Philippine research material at the University of Hawaii Library.

Vance, Lee W. *Tracing Your Philippine Ancestors.* Salt Lake City: published by author, 1980.

An excellent guide to records in the Philippines. Includes comprehensive lists of various archives and parishes as well as maps. Also includes instructions on Philippine research and historical background material. The first volume of its kind. Available from the author at P.O. Box 8614, Salt Lake City, UT 84108.

MONOGRAPHS

Smith, Peter C., with Cullinane, Michael, and Ng, Shui-Meng. "Sources for Family History in the Philippines: Content and Uses." *World Conference on Records* (2d, 1980) vol. 10, no. 828. Salt Lake City: Corporation of the President of the Church of Jesus Christ of Latter-day Saints, c1980.

Based on a survey of Filipino parish registers. Discusses their distribution, content, and research value.

Other Asian or Related

BOOKS

Conrad, Agnes. "Sources for Family History in Hawaii." *World Conference on Records* (2d, 1980) vol. 10, no. 819. Salt Lake City: Corporation of the President of the Church of Jesus Christ of Latter-day Saints, c1980.

A concise introduction of the records in Hawaii by the state archivist. Discusses state record-keeping traditions, the value of the records, and how to obtain them. Also mentions the respective Asian ethnic groups and what basically is available on them.

Goswamy, B. N. "Pilgrimage Records of India: A Rich Source for Genealogy and Family History." *World Conference on Records* (2d, 1980) vol. 11, no. 907. Salt Lake City: Corporation of the President of the Church of Jesus Christ of Latter-day Saints, c1980.

Describes India's record-keeping traditions and the institution of pilgrimages. Relates the way these records are made and the type of information in them.

Jagchid, Sechin, and Heyer, Paul V. "Genealogy and Family History in Mongolia." *World Conference on Records* (2d, 1980) vol. 11, no. 809. Salt Lake City: Corporation of the President of the Church of Jesus Christ of Latter-day Saints, c1980.

Discusses the unique genealogical traditions of the Mongol people and how the system evolved. These records were mainly limited to Mongol heads and their families and were used to show lineage continuity.

Mazzaoui, Michael M. "Tradition of Genealogy Among the Moslems." *World Conference on Records* (2d, 1980) vol. 11, no. 911. Salt Lake City: Corporation of the President of the Church of Jesus Christ of Latter-day Saints, c1980.

Since Moslems are scattered throughout much of the southern part of Asia, this paper is useful in understanding Moslem genealogical traditions and the reasons behind them.

Tirmizi, S.A.I. "Genealogical Records of Medieval India." *World Conference on Records* (2d, 1980) vol. 11, no. 912. Salt Lake City: Corporation of the President of the Church of Jesus Christ of Latter-day Saints, c1980.

A brief paper by the national archivist of India on some of the earlier genealogical sources and traditions. Tirmizi concludes that medieval India "bequeathed to us a fairly rich heritage of genealogical records," but most of the records are male-centered and little known in the West.

MONOGRAPHS

"Genealogical Records of Value for Korea." Unpublished research paper, Series J, no. 7. Salt Lake City: Genealogical Department, Church of Jesus Christ of Latter-day Saints, 1979.

An inventory of the genealogical record types in Korea. In list format, includes information on the availability, content, and general location of each source. Also includes an introduction and some explanatory notes.

"Tracing Your Ancestors to Japan: A Guide for Japanese Americans and Canadians." Unpublished research paper, Series J, no. 6. Salt Lake City: Genealogical Department, Church of Jesus Christ of Latter-day Saints, 1979.

A comprehensive guide to research in Japanese-American sources. Written in question-and-answer format, this unpublished volume is available at the LDS Geneological Department Library. Discusses a wide range of sources and research strategies. Also includes information on sources in Japan proper.

PERIODICALS

Amerasia Journal, 3232 Campbell Hall, Los Angeles, CA 90024

Published yearly by the Asian American Studies Center. Most articles relate to Asian-American experience.

Bulletin, 17 Adler Place, San Francisco, CA 94133

Published most months by the Chinese Historical Society of America. Includes insights and publications on Chinese Americans.

Gum Saan, 993 Isabella Avenue, Monterey Park, CA 91754

Published periodically by the Chinese American Historical Society of Southern California. Mentions publications on Chinese.

Hawaii Journal of History, 560 Kawaiahao Street, Honolulu, HI 96813

Published yearly by the Hawaiian Historical Society. Some articles and book reviews.

Newsletter, 111 North King Street, Room 410, Honolulu, HI 96817
Periodic information about genealogy and publications.

Pacific Citizen, 355 East First Street, Los Angeles, CA 90012
Published weekly by the Japanese American Citizen's League. Occasional notes about publications and historical items.

Pacific Historical Review, University of California Press, Berkeley, CA 94720
Published bimonthly by the Pacific Coast Branch of the American Historical Association. Articles and book reviews.

MAJOR REPOSITORIES

California

Asian Foundation Library, 105 Market Street, San Francisco, CA 94102
Some books on Asian Americans and on respective Asian countries.
California Historical Society Library, 209 Jackson Street, San Francisco
Research on early California Chinese; some books and manuscripts.
California State Archives, Room 200, 1020 "O" Street, Sacramento, CA 95814
Manuscripts, archival material and publications on early settlers, particularly the Chinese among Asians.
California State Library, 914 Capitol Mall, Sacramento, CA 95809
Some early Asian ethnic newspapers and books on Asian Americans.
California, University of, Berkeley, Bancroft Library, Berkeley, CA 94720
Rare manuscripts and books pertaining to the early Chinese in California in Bancroft Library; small Chinese genealogy and larger local history collection in East Asian Library; also in Bancroft an Asian-American collection with materials on early Chinese, ethnic newspapers and publications, and school records and donor lists.
California, University of, Davis, CA 95616
University library: materials collected through Asian-American project.
California, University of, Los Angeles, 405 Hilgard Avenue, Los Angeles, CA 90024
Undergraduate and research libraries, Oriental and Asian-American collections. The latter includes materials on Japanese, Chinese, Korean, and Filipino ethnics. Strength of collection is Japanese area, due to Japanese American Research Project; includes diaries and tapes of immigrants, collection of Japanese-language newspapers, books and articles written by immigrants or on Japanese in California, and Japanese Foreign Ministry archival materials (about 100 reels of microfilm) related to emigrants departing to the United States.
Los Angeles Federal Archives and Records Center, 2400 Avila Road, Laguna Niguel, Los Angeles, CA 92677
Records of federal courts and local federal paperwork; 1900 and earlier censuses.
Los Angeles Public Library, 630 West Fifth, Los Angeles, CA 90017
Collection of local ethnic newspapers; also books and publications on Asian Americans in Los Angeles area.
San Diego State University, San Diego, Miramar Road, Box 2367, La Jolla, CA 92037
University library: collection of some Asian Pacific materials, including ethnic newspapers.
San Francisco Federal Archives and Records Center, 1000 Commodore Drive, San Bruno, CA 94066
Federal court records; early tax records of Chinese; some federal materials for Hawaii, 1900 and earlier censuses.
San Francisco Public Library, Civic Center, San Francisco, CA 94102
Main library: Californiana and rare books rooms contain manuscripts and books relating to the early Chinese in the Bay Area; materials collected by the Chinese Historical Society of America on Chinese Americans.

Southern California, University of, Los Angeles, University Park, Los Angeles, CA 90007
Recent efforts to collect Korean materials by the Korean Studies Center.

District of Columbia

Library of Congress, 1st-2nd Streets, S.E., Washington, DC 20540
General section has many ethnic newspapers and books on ethnic groups; Orientalia division has large collection of Chinese local histories (3,750 titles) and some Chinese clan genealogies; also a large collection of Japanese publications, including histories and a few genealogies.

National Archives, Pennsylvania Avenue and 8th Street, N.W., Washington, DC 20408
Immigration and customs records as well as censuses (1900 and prior); also Chinese immigration records, including correspondence, certificates of residence, and special entries from 1882 to about 1925.

Hawaii

Bernice P. Bishop Museum, 1355 Kalihi Street, Honolulu, HI 96819
Building a Japanese immigrants section; collections of immigrant records, Japanese ethnic newspapers, papers and manuscripts relating to Japanese in Hawaii, and Japanese government documents and materials. A rapidly expanding, well-supported collection.

Bureau of Conveyance, 403 Queen Street, Honolulu, HI 96813
Land records and deeds since annexation.

Hawaii Chinese History Center, 111 North King Street, Room 410, Honolulu, HI 96817
Actively collecting sources on the Chinese in Hawaii, including materials on Chinese societies and organizations. Transcribes gravestones in Chinese cemeteries, clips pertinent articles, tapes oral histories, and so forth. Collection and research help are available to members.

Hawaii State Archives, Iolani Palace Grounds, Honolulu, HI 96817
Records from the Kingdom and Republic eras and from early days of the Territory of Hawaii; includes passenger and ship manifests (1843–1900), regular and delayed birth registrations and vital records (to 1903), records of the Bureau of Immigration (to 1900), records of the Chinese Bureau (1890–1900), Hawaiian censuses (to 1900), Hawaiian tax records (to 1900), Hawaiian court records (1900), correspondence with overseas governments and other documents.

Hawaii State Department of Health, 1250 Punchbowl Street, Honolulu, HI 96813
Vital records and appropriate certificates (post-1900).

Hawaii State Library, 1390 Miller Street, Box 2360, Honolulu, HI 96804
Maintains collection of ethnic newspapers in Hawaii and of publications dealing with each of Hawaii's ethnic groups.

Hawaii Sugar Planter's Association, HSPA, P. O. Box 2450, Honolulu, HI 96804
Maintains files of records of individuals who worked for various sugar companies from about 1906 to 1941; includes some Chinese and Japanese, but the majority are Filipinos.

Hawaii, University of, Manoa Campus, 2550, the Mall, Honolulu, HI 96822
Some general materials and microfilms at Hamilton Library. Asian Collection and Hawaiian and Pacific Collection at Sinclair Library include some Chinese local histories for Kwangtung Province and a few genealogies, 176 titles of Korean local history and other Korean works; strong collections related to Filipinos and Okinawans, and a number of early works of the respective Asian ethnics in Hawaii, including those in the native languages.

Japanese Consulate General, 1742 Nuuanu Avenue, Honolulu, HI 96813
Maintains registry of family households and of those leaving Hawaii (1885 to present), of entries in family household registers (on cards or notifications 1885 to present), of some births and deaths (1890–1913), and of domiciles in Japan of Japanese in Hawaii as of 1900. Requests must be made through the consulate. There are some interruptions in the records.

Japanese travel agencies, various locations in Honolulu

Records of immigrants and travel arrangements made for groups and individuals; researchers must approach the appropriate travel agency and request.

U.S. Immigration and Naturalization Service, 595 Ala Moana Boulevard, Honolulu, HI 96813
Will search its post-1900 records on request.

Illinois

Chicago, University of, Chicago, 1100 East 57th Street, Chicago, IL 60637
Far Eastern library: about 2,700 titles of Chinese local histories and a few Chinese genealogies; some Japanese feudal records.

Illinois, University of, Urbana, IL 61801
University library; a collection of some of the Asian ethnic newspapers.

Kansas

Personal Census Service Branch, Bureau of Census, Pittsburg, KS 66767.
For searches of censuses (1920–80) taken at 10-year intervals, a completed form (BC-600) and fee are required.

Massachusetts

Harvard University, Cambridge, MA 02138
Harvard-Yenching library: some Chinese genealogies and local histories (3,525 titles); Korean genealogies (523 titles), local histories and exam roster (233 titles); and Japanese genealogies, and a good collection of histories.

Michigan

Michigan, University of, Ann Arbor, MI 48104
Asia Library: Chinese local histories (2,291 titles); documents from some of Japan's feudal domains; a number of Japanese-language histories and documents.

Missouri

Military Personnel Records Center, 9700 Page Boulevard, St. Louis, MO 63132
Service and military records; information on request and on certain conditions.

New York

Chinatown Cultural Center, 10 Confucius Plaza, New York, NY 10007
Collection of materials centered on Chinese in New York.

Columbia University, 535 West 114th Street, New York, NY 10027
East Asian Library: Chinese genealogies (over 1,000 titles in original) and local histories (1,622 titles).

Cornell University, Ithaca, NY 14850
Olin Research Library: largest collection of materials on Southeast Asia in the United States.

New York Public Library, Fifth Avenue and 42nd Street, New York, NY 10018
Collection of Oriental books, a number of books on Asian Americans.

Oregon

Oregon, University of, Eugene, OR 97403
University Library: some materials related to Asian Americans in Oregon.

Pennsylvania

Pennsylvania, University of, 3420 Walnut Street, Philadelphia, PA 19104
South Asian Collection: a large, specialized collection related to the countries of the Indian Subcontinent.

Utah

Genealogical Department Library (LDS), 50 East North Temple Street, Salt Lake City, UT 84150
  A specialized collection of genealogical and historical records, most of which are microfilm copies of originals; Asian-American records on film include many of the archival sources in Hawaii, HSPA records, two major Japanese papers (to 1941), Hawaiian church records, and a number of volumes relating to specific ethnic groups and cultures; the LDS Genealogical Department Library also has strong collections of Chinese genealogies (nearly 5,000 titles) and local histories (5,500 titles), of Korean clan genealogies (3,670 titles) and local histories (326 titles), and of Japanese genealogies (about 1,500 reels). The Japanese collection also includes some Buddhist death registers and examinations of religion/census registers, along with many reference works. Parish registers from the Philippines and records (including oral genealogies) from Southeast Asia are also being obtained. Efforts are underway to expand into other parts of Asia as well.

Washington

Seattle Public Library, 1000 Fourth Avenue, Seattle WA 98104
  Some materials relating to Asian Americans in the Seattle area.
Washington, University of, Seattle WA 98105
  University Library: some materials on Asian Americans of the Pacific Northwest; there are also some Chinese and Japanese genealogical sources in the University's East Asia library.

MAJOR SOCIETIES AND ETHNIC ORGANIZATIONS

American Siam Society, 633 24th Street, Santa Monica, CA 90302
  Has a library and newspaper collection of Thai materials; promotes Thai cultural and common interests.
Asia Society, 112 East 64th Street, New York, NY 10021
  Promotes the study of Asian culture and the Asian countries; maintains a library and publishes a newsletter, *Asia*.
Buddhist Churches of America, Headquarters, 1710 Octavia Street, San Francisco, CA 94109
  The headquarters of a large number of ethnic Japanese Buddhist congregations in America. For individual affiliated congregations, the headquarters should be contacted. The individual churches continue to promote Japanese culture and ways.
Chinese Historical Society of America, 17 Adler Place, San Francisco, CA 94133
  Founded in 1963 to promote study of the Chinese in America. Maintains a museum, holds seminars, and collects publications and oral histories.
Chinese Historical Society of Southern California, 1648 Redcliff Street, Los Angeles, CA 90026
  Founded in 1975 to encourage study of the Chinese in California and to assist the Asian American Center at UCLA in finding and collecting materials of value on the Chinese in the area.
Chinese Institute in America, 125 East 65th Street, New York, NY 10021
  Promotes an understanding of China, offers Chinese language and cultural classes, and maintains a research library of materials relating to the Chinese in America, especially New York.
Filipino American Community of Los Angeles, 1740 West Temple Street, Los Angeles, CA 90026
  Actively promotes the culture of the area's Filipino group and collects materials on Filipino Americans.
Hawaii Chinese History Center, 111 North King Street, Room 410, Honolulu, HI 96817
  Founded in 1971. Collects materials and promotes the study of the Chinese in Hawaii, holds

occasional seminars on genealogical research, and encourages the preservation of both written and oral histories.

Japanese American Citizen's League, 765 Sutter Street, San Francisco, CA 94115
Maintains branches in many areas where Japanese live. Supports efforts to collect materials and to promote and understand the culture and contributions of the *issei*.

Japanese American Society of Southern California, 125 Weller Street, Los Angeles, CA 90012
One of the older immigrant organizations, concerned with maintaining heritage and with the collection and preservation of records.

Japan Society, 333 East 47th Street, New York, NY 10017
Promotes an understanding of Japan and the Japanese people; has a library and some publishing activities.

Korean National Association, 1368 West Jefferson Boulevard, Los Angeles, CA 90007
Headquarters of the national Korean association; branches are in major cities and areas of Korean settlement. Groups foster Korean culture and some historical and research activities.

BOOKSTORES AND SUPPLIERS

Asian American Studies Center, 3232 Campbell Hall, University of California, Los Angeles, CA 90024
Publishes the magazine *Amerasia* and has also published several bibliographies on Asian-American ethnic groups and a number of historical and sociological studies.

Cellar Book Shop, 18090 Wyoming Street, Detroit, MI 48227
Inventory includes many books on Southeast Asia and some on Asian Americans.

Center for Chinese Research Materials, 1527 New Hampshire Avenue, N.W., Washington, DC 20030
Supplier of books from Taiwan; also produces research aids and language materials for Chinese studies.

Cheng & Tsui Company, P. O. Box 328, Cambridge, MA 02139
Supplier of books on East Asia; includes dictionaries, language aids, and histories, principally of China.

China Books and Periodicals, West Coast Center, 2929 24th Street, San Francisco, CA 94110
Supplier of publications from the People's Republic of China; includes some dictionaries, language aids, maps and historical items.

Everybody's Bookstore, 840 Kearny Street, San Francisco, CA 94108
Specializes in rare Asian books and books on China and on Asian Americans.

Genealogical Department, Jesus Christ of Latter-day Saints Library, 50 East North Temple Street, Salt Lake City, UT 84150
Distributes Genealogical Society of Utah publications and World Conference on Records papers. The research papers of the Genealogical Society vary in price according to the size and production cost; 1980 World Conference papers are presently $1.00 each or $7.00 per volume or complete set of area papers.

Hawaii, University Press, 2840 Kolowalu Street, Honolulu, HI 96822
Publishes several bibliographies on Hawaii's Asian groups and books on the Asian experience in Hawaii and on the culture and history of the respective Asian countries.

Kinokuniya of America, Japan Center-West Building, 1581 Webster Street, San Francisco, CA 94115
Books on Japan and on the Japanese language, culture, and history. Most are published in Japan.

Kodansha International, 10 East 53rd Street, New York, NY 10022
Another supplier of books on Japan.

R & E Research Associates, 4843 Mission Street, San Francisco, CA 94112

Collects and publishes reprints, including theses and regional materials, relating to Asian Americans. Also has sponsored some research. Many of these items are useful for more detailed studies.

Tuttle, Charles E., Company, P. O. Drawer F, Rutland, VT 05701

Books on Japan and its culture; some language and Japanese-American items.

9

Black American Records and Research

CHARLES L. BLOCKSON

Increasing numbers of articles are being published within the rapidly developing field of black genealogy, creating the need for a precise guide to the subject. Additionally, the interdisciplinary nature of the concept of black genealogy has made it difficult to obtain a concise, workable reference guide for scholars and the general public. The purpose of this chapter is to offer a solution to that problem and to direct the reader quickly and informatively to methods which are relevant in tracing black genealogy.

For a definition of black American genealogy, the reader is referred to James D. Walker's *Black Genealogy: How to Begin,* in which it is identified as "the history of the person or family, slave or free, whose ancestry included at least one person of African blood."[1] Black genealogy is the ultimate puzzle. As bits and pieces of the black American's life are put together, the pattern becomes increasingly interesting and revealing, especially when the search involves locating records which are difficult to obtain.

Black genealogy has been popularized by several fairly recent presentations of histories of people with African blood. The fictional autobiography of Miss Jane Pittman[2] had a tremendous impact on the public when that powerful drama was beamed across the nation via television. Miss Pittman, a black woman, related her family life from the time of slavery, through the Reconstruction, to the time of the civil rights movement. This history of one black family's efforts to overcome adversity captured the interest of many Americans. Likewise, the television adaptation of Alex Haley's book *Roots* drew considerable attention to the genealogy of the Afro-American family. Black genealogy is in fact much older than some researchers recognize, for many blacks had a tradition of searching or preserving their family histories long before "Miss Jane Pittman" and *Roots* appeared, though the literature of genealogy which subsequently has been published generally agrees that these two sagas popularized black genealogy and spurred blacks and other groups to pursue their genealogies.

Researchers who pursue black family history may encounter tremendous difficulties. Perhaps the most significant obstacle to its recovery has been slavery and
the separations that the institution imposed on families. Other problems in successful black genealogical research include illiteracy, geographical separation
through migration, changes of name, segregation, miscegenation, absence of
records, and especially the shame that has long been associated with Africa and
slavery and that has caused some people (black and white) to distort the past,
deny their heritage, destroy records, or engage in other acts which hamper
genealogical research. Maxwell Whiteman, an early writer on black genealogy,
wrote in 1972 that, in a world of white genealogists, various generations of
persons who came from African ancestors had been neglected in genealogical
research. The genealogical societies up to that time showed little or no interest in
this branch of America's family tree and collected almost nothing about black
genealogy. Headings which one would seek when examining catalogs of genealogical collections, such as "Negro," "Afro-American," or "black," rarely
were found. Whiteman declared further that, as most genealogists patently
avoided the subject of black genealogy, any discussion of it "has to meet
historical and bibliographical frustrations as well as the social forces that strongly
militate against its investigation."[3]

It is indeed encouraging to see publications pertaining to black family life
included in libraries and archival institutions which in the past failed to deal
properly with black historical and cultural records. The diversity of materials
cited points to the need for research in many virtually untouched areas in Afro-
American genealogy. The range and significance of black historical records
require additional research and pursuit by many genealogists, sociologists, historians, and others. Yet it is important today that dispersed members of the universal Afro-American community come together, as can happen through genealogical investigation.

IN PURSUIT OF BLACK GENEALOGY

Although there are major problems involved in pursuing information on one's
ancestors, black researchers, many of whom have multiethnic backgrounds,
must learn to stem the tide of frustration and leads that seemingly come to a dead
end. As mentioned earlier in this work, such a researcher must contact relatives
and record what is known now. While most blacks came to America during the
period of legal (and also illegal) slavery and documents of this heritage may be
lacking, with determination practically every black pedigree can be traced back
at least until 1825. In addition, one-seventh of all blacks in the United States in
1863 were free. This means that now living in the United States are a great
number of blacks who have free antebellum ancestry which can be traced to
about 1800, and in another generation there will be very few blacks who will be
unable to trace at least one of their lines to that date.

After emancipation, whether it occurred during slavery or with the Emancipation Proclamation of 1865, the reunion of separated families was difficult at best, and numerous factors continued to mitigate against family stability. Yet neither the vast power of slavery nor its legacy of racism could quench the thirst for freedom or the struggle of black families for knowledge of their history. This freedom and this knowledge are integral parts of life for a free people. Thus genealogy and history, in the passing of family ancestries and histories from one generation to the next (most often by word of mouth), have been a central concern of black Americans throughout their existence.

Obstacles to Research

The stumbling blocks which the researcher in black genealogy will encounter need not mean that one's family lines cannot be pursued successfully. At the outset, however, it is well to identify some of the problems which one may face during the research process. With the assistance of those knowledgeable on the subject, supported by the appropriate historical documents, what initially appears to be a hopeless situation may well result in a stimulating and rewarding experience. The potential successes notwithstanding, the researcher also should be reminded that some of the obstacles may remain and that one's family lines may well come to rather early and abrupt ends.

EARLY NAMING PRACTICES

Since the days of their captivity and subsequent arrival in this country, blacks have been aware of the importance of the written record. This research may have been important to them only as they were able to make a mark, perhaps an ''x''. For many blacks, the second immediate response to freedom was to change their names. Some wanted to shed their masters' surnames which they also carried or to shed classical names like Caesar, Pompey, or Venus. The use of classical names is illustrated in figure 9.1, a detailed receipt for estate property which was transferred from the original administrator to another. Along with the livestock, farm implements, and other items, the document lists ''thirteen named slaves,'' which includes Pompy (or perhaps Pompey).

In the matter of classical names, I comment further on such naming practices in my book *Black Genealogy,* as research found that frequently slaves as well as free blacks had classical names. These might have included names such as Scipio, Caesar, Pompey, or Cato. When the name was assigned, the master probably did so in jest or arbitrarily, as when naming a pet. This assigning of a single name and perhaps adding to it the master's family name impedes genealogical research and may obliterate any trace of a black's true heritage. As slaves were sold from one master to another, frequently they were assigned new names (both first and last), so that in a series of sales or transfers over the years, M'chiba might well have become Cato, then Caesar, then George, and even Little Buck. When subsequently freed, many blacks discarded their slave names and adopted other names of their choice. A flood of George Washingtons and Thomas Jeffersons emerged.[4]

Debra L. Newman's *List of Free Black Heads of Families in the First Census*

Figure 9.1
Illustration of Use of Classical Names for Slaves

I James Scully Administrator of the Estate of Stephen Palmer, have Received of James L Denson former Administrator of the said Estate. the following named property, to wit. Negroes thus. Patty, Frances, George Washington. Lydia, old Jack, ~~[crossed out]~~, Malissa, Pompy. Hannah Lucinda, Catharine, Isaac, Ginny & Joe. Also 500 Bush corn. 4 stacks fodder, 1 oats. 13 Bush Potatoes, 28 sheep, 2 cows & calves, 2 cows without calves 4 yearlings, 10 Pork hogs, 8 sows, 32 shoats, 10 Pigs 2 Spining wheels & cards, Mule Suly, Bay Mare Nancy, Mule Dolly, Mule Kate, 2 turn plows, 4 solid sweeps of scuters, 4 Bolts & clevises, a pr harness, 1 Iron wedge 9 weeding hoes, 200 lbs Spining cotton 1 Pot, 126 yds Spun Yarn, 1 Pot, copper skimmer. 1 Large strainer, 1 Grid iron 2 Sythe-Blades, 1 Small Pot, 1 Spider & lid, 1 Griddle. Also In note. Francis Luster of 5. dated Jy 25th 1828. one on Muns Chadwells note 25" Jay 1824 one on Thos Stanford of 9.19 cts dated 30" Dec 1826 one on Dan H Green dated 12" Jay 1824 for $4. one on John Wilks for $4. dated 21" dec, 825. one on James Jay for $2.43. dated 7." 1825. one on Rodrick Modard for $30. dated 28th April 1841. one on Alfred early. for $5 dated 6 Jay 1827. one on John Travis for $43.36 cts dated 24 dec 1842. one on John L L Moorer for $44 May 1" 1842. one on Alfred ... for $10 Jay 6" 1842.

Courtesy of John L. Heflin, Jr., Brentwood, Tennessee.

of the United States, 1790 (discussed in the bibliography for this chapter) further illustrates the use of classical names and shows a variety of naming practices. Not only were the names Cato, Caesar, Pompey (Pomp and Pompy) used, but frequently names such as Auguster Caesar, Sambo, Belfast, Bristol, Cambridge, Durham, Tobe (as in Haley's *Roots*), and even Poor House and Tobacco Port. Those who were mulatto were so identified.[5]

Slaves were also named after political leaders; the receipt in figure 9.1 also includes a slave by the name of George Washington. Thus naming practices, name changes, and in some instances geographical relocations of slaves and newly freed slaves help to compound the research problems.

LOST ANCESTORS AND MIXED ANCESTRY

After emancipation, the reunion of separated families was still difficult at best, and numerous factors continued to work against family stability. Frequently ancestors crossed racial lines, and among other difficulties, this may have meant that an ancestor was lost because parenting could not be documented. Miscegenation or racial mixing, with all of its stigmas, is commonplace in black genealogy and has created monumental problems. The complex relationships of the native white population and the vast numbers of blacks, Spaniards, and American Indians and the intermingling of bloodlines from the time of the founding fathers to the present day are obstacles of which searchers of family lines must be aware. Today more than 60 percent of black Americans have a mixture of Indian blood in their veins. Obviously persons of such a mixture must search the genealogical records of the American Indian.

Some records of an early black/white admixture during slavery were kept in a document known as the "Bastardy Case Book"; figure 9.2 illustrates the type of information contained. These books were commonly used in Delaware, and other states sometimes kept similar records, copies of which are extant. The book records illegitimate children who were born of slave fathers and white mothers, white fathers and black mothers, and free black fathers and free mulatto mothers.

Another significant segment of the American population is the Creoles, or persons of mixed black, Spanish, and French heritage, who settled in Louisiana. The Creoles' influence is visible and can still be felt within the structure of many black families. Cape Verdeans, a mixture of African and Portugese, originated in the Azores and settled primarily in two areas: New Bedford, Massachusetts, and Brunswick, Georgia. Another group is the Geeches, a concentration of Afro-Americans who settled in the Sea Islands of South Carolina and Georgia. They retain many of the traditions of the Yoruba cultures in West Africa and speak a mixture of broken English and their own African dialect.

Passing

Tracing of black ancestry is also hindered by the phenomenon of "passing." Some blacks, as well as whites, will discover family members who found it necessary or advantageous to "pass" into Caucasian society. As a result, their

Figure 9.2
Sample Page from a Bastardy Casebook Showing Mulatto Mother and Free Negro Father

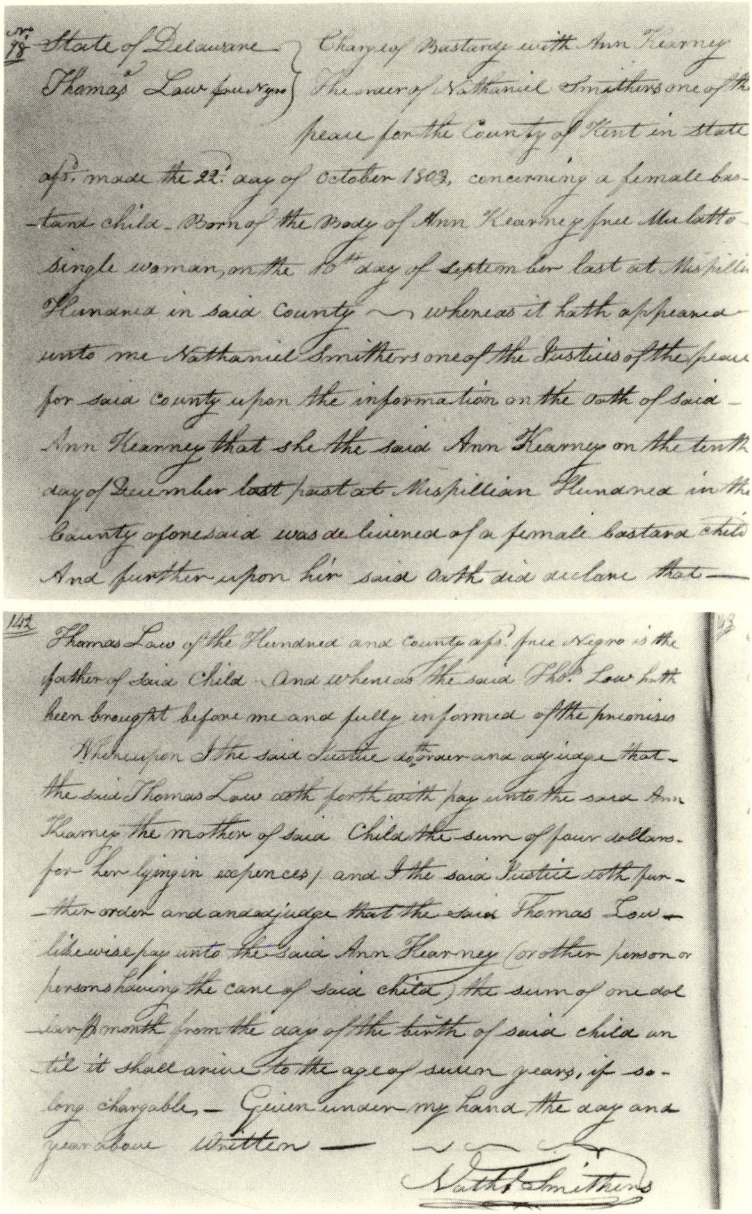

No. 78 State of Delaware v. Thomas Law free Negro } Charge of Bastardy with Ann Kearney
The order of Nathaniel Smithers one of the [illegible]
peace for the County of Kent in state
afs. made the 22d day of October 1803, concerning a female bas-
-tard child - Born of the Body of Ann Kearney free Mulatto
single woman, on the 10th day of september last at Mispillion
Hundred in said County — whereas it hath appeared
unto me Nathaniel Smithers one of the Justices of the peace
for said county upon the information on the oath of said
Ann Kearney that she the said Ann Kearney on the tenth
day of December last past at Mispillian Hundred in the
County aforesaid was delivered of a female bastard child
And further upon her said oath did declare that —

142 Thomas Law of the Hundred and County afs. free Negro is the
father of said Child And whereas the said Thos. Law hath
been brought before me and fully informed of the premises
Whereupon I the said Justice do order and adjudge that
the said Thomas Law doth forthwith pay unto the said Ann
Kearney the mother of said Child the sum of four dollars
for her lying in expences, and I the said Justice doth fur-
-ther order and adjudge that the said Thomas Law
likewise pay unto the said Ann Kearney (or other person or
persons having the care of said child) the sum of one dol-
-lar pr month from the day of the birth of said child un-
-til it shall arrive to the age of seven years, if so
long chargable, — Given under my hand the day and
year above written —
Nathl Smithers

Courtesy Division of Historical and Cultural Affairs, Hall of Records, State of Delaware.

present-day descendants may find themselves protecting this knowledge about their family structure; if those who are searching for their heritage are to be successful in their quest, they must overcome any hesitance or anxiety in looking to sources other than the ordinary ones.

The current wave of genealogists with mixed ancestry and who visually are white are beginning to acknowledge their black ancestors, to document their heritage through black records, and even to attend reunions of their black relatives. On the other hand, some whites and blacks find it much more desirable to have Indian blood and often boast of the admixture whether or not documentation is forthcoming.

Confusing or Inaccurate Records

Compounding the problem of black genealogical research are types of records which have been maintained and the fact that they were often erroneous. A 1912 article entitled "Enumeration of Mulattoes by Census Bureau Causes Genealogical Mix-up" included in its headline the following information:

Statistics Show That Thousands of Citizens of African Descent Did Not Class Themselves as Negroes and are Referred to in Census Report Under "Foreign and Mixed Parentage"—Instructions to Negroes Confusing—Race Loses Numerically Throughout the Country—List Made Public by Census Bureau Giving Negro Population in States and Various Cities.

In the body of the article, the discussion is continued as follows:

Because the Bureau of Census at Washington insisted that mulattoes be enumerated in the last census there has been a genealogical mix-up, the Negro being the loser from a numerical standpoint.

Investigations made by The Age show that the statistics just issued for publication by the Department of Commerce and Labor class thousands and thousands of Negroes with what has been officially designated as "foreign or mixed parentage." Had the Bureau of Census designated all of African descent under the heading of "Negro" figures would show that Negroes constitute a much larger percentage of population.

For instance, Greater New York is put down as having a Negro population of 91,709, when, all told, there are at least 100,000 citizens of color in the various boroughs. The claim [is made] that there are 22,000 Negroes in Brooklyn, although it was conceded by those familiar with the population of this city that from 27,000 to 30,000 Negroes reside across the bridge. . . .

The Census Bureau in its statistics specifies the country's population under the following divisions: "Native parentages," "foreign or mixed parentage," "foreign born whites," "Negro" and "all other." Thousands of citizens in the State of New York and throughout the country have been classed under "foreign or mixed parentage," because mulattoes were enumerated, when they should have been put down as Negroes.[6]

The article continues by defining the term Negro and explaining how those who were mulatto and those who were more visibly Negro were confused and applied various interpretations to the census definitions. Thus blacks who trace their ancestors may well face a problem with records which are misleading in their interpretations or in what appears to be fact.

The Oral Tradition

Because of the historical absence of systematic records and because slaves were forbidden to read or write, blacks who are tracing their family histories must to a degree depend on oral history. The implementation of oral history techniques must be an integral part of the search for genealogy. Bobby L. Lovett's discussion on oral history in chapter 4 of this book guides the researcher in developing such techniques and lists numerous sources of additional information. In his *Black Genealogy: How to Begin*, Walker lists the major concerns one should have in a black genealogy interview. These are

1. The physical description and racial origin of the subject of the interview;

2. Whether the subject's parents, grandparents or great-grandparents were slaves or free;

3. Whether the subject's parents, grandparents or great-grandparents were house or field slaves;

4. Methods by which marriages were performed (religious, civil, slave, or Indian);

5. Children born to a particular female or sired by a particular male family member;

6. Owners of the slaves;

7. Dates of death of family members;

8. Affiliations with churches, benevolent societies, and other groups and detailed information on the church, its pastor, its cemetery, its school, and so on;

9. Employers of the subject and type and length of job held;

10. Whether or not the subject owned property;

11. Whether or not the subject was involved in infringements of the law;

12. The subject's educational background;

13. Admixtures with other races and how these admixtures were known; and

14. Naming practices: how the name was acquired and how altered or completely changed.[7]

Some genealogists are quite skeptical about consulting senior citizens within their families for information. Some have observed that the adequacy of recall of these senior citizens is questionable, as time has taken its toll on their memory or on their ability to interpret what they remember. Nonetheless, senior family members must be interviewed as soon as possible, before their memory and indeed their presence have gone. In spite of the possibility of error, there is much that is valuable in the information that they may provide. Often various persons present accounts which appear to be entirely unconnected with each other, but which turn out to be based originally upon a single source. In such a case all of the accounts have to depend upon the reliability or unreliability of the first source.

If the subject's information is halting, or varies widely from what the researcher knows to be true, the dependability of the senior citizen's other information should also be questioned. The phenomenal success of recording information from senior citizens has rekindled interest in family reunions among black Americans, sometimes creating more widespread interest in the search for family lines.

From this point the researcher must acknowledge that oral history is only a minor tool of research work. Through careful analysis of various recorded documents, generations must be searched from one to another, going back to fourth, fifth, sixth, and seventh generations or more whenever possible.

GENEALOGICAL RECORDS

Records useful for the study of black genealogy vary in type and scope. Walker's list and description of some of these records are given throughout his monograph, while specific ones are grouped under the heading "Sources of Black Genealogical Records" and indicate whether the document is useful for tracing a free black or a freed slave.[8] My book (previously cited) also discusses some of the types of records needed for research in black genealogy. These include plantation records; records of sharecropping, breeding, slave collars, and branding; and insurance policies.[9] The researcher should consult these two publications, as well as examine the documents described in the following sections.

Family Bibles

Distant relatives may provide the researcher with valuable historical gems such as family Bibles. It is not easy to determine what values were transmitted between generations and by which institutions, but the genealogical records in old family Bibles bear testimony to the importance of family in shaping those values. They may also be used to determine dates of birth, death, and marriage and may furnish other information on family members that is sometimes missing from public records.

Even in slaveholding territories, masters made sure that certain types of records were maintained in family Bibles, as well as in special account books kept for business purposes. Interestingly enough, it was the combined efforts of blacks and whites that established the family Bible as a valued source of information. Figure 9.3 shows the type of information on slaves which the masters kept in their Bibles.

Church Records

Early church records are another source of public information, that is, if the records can be found. Throughout the years many churches have rotated minis-

Figure 9.3
Bible Record Showing Names of Slaves

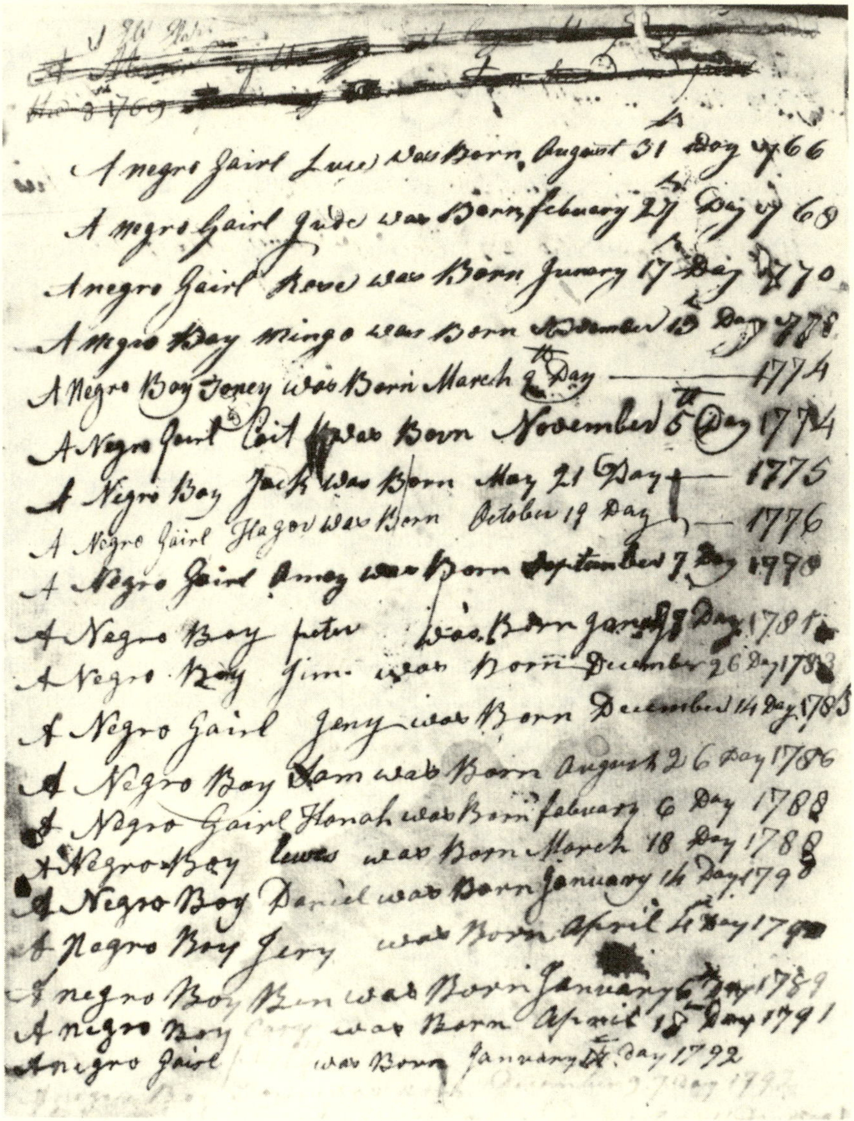

A negro Gairl Luce was Born August 31 Day 1766
A Negro Gairl Jude was Born february 27 Day 1768
A negro Gairl Rose was Born Jenuary 17 Day 1770
A Negro Boy Mingo was Born November 13 Day [illegible]
A Negro Boy Toney was Born March 2th Day 1774
A Negro Gairl Cait was Born November 5th Day 1774
A Negro Boy Jack was Born May 21 Day 1775
A Negro Gairl Hagar was Born October 19 Day 1776
A Negro Gairl Amey was Born September 7 Day 1778
A Negro Boy peter was Born [illegible] Day 1781
A Negro Boy Jim was Born December 26 Day 1783
A Negro Gairl Jeny was Born December 14 Day 1785
A Negro Boy Sam was Born August 26 Day 1786
A Negro Gairl Hanah was Born february 6 Day 1788
A Negro Boy Lewis was Born March 18 Day 1788
A Negro Boy Daniel was Born January 14 Day [illegible]
A Negro Boy Jery was Born April 4 Day [illegible]
A negro Boy Ben was Born January 6 Day 1789
A negro Boy Cary was Born April 18 Day 1791
A negro Gairl was Born January [illegible] Day 1792

Courtesy Tennessee State Library and Archives.

ters frequently, and others have changed their locations. Some church records have been lost by fire or flood, or have been discarded as useless refuse. Sometimes the records are temporarily inactive because they have been placed in the keeping of various members of the congregation. The researcher will find great differences among the various denominations regarding their records; however, difficulty with church records is no reason not to persevere in the quest for a family history.

Church records may contain only basic information about family history. Most church registers, however, include the dates of birth, baptism, marriage, death, and burial. Church anniversaries offer valuable historical and genealogical information and sometimes lead to the discovery of photographs. Within some churches, groups such as benevolent societies, literary societies, social clubs, and schools were sustenance for the family. Thus, when found, the church records give important insights into family history, church history, and also community history.

Church records of the WPA survey (1939–41) provide valuable genealogical information. This very resourceful investigation was carried out on a county-by-county basis, based on the results of a four-page questionnaire which was uniformly employed. In addition to the questionnaire returns, miscellaneous information was sometimes included. The WPA records on black churches and on white churches which accepted black members are generally available in state libraries and archives. Figure 9.4 is a sample page from a WPA record and identifies those members of the church congregation who were black. Note that the name Pompy appears on the membership roll.

Unfortunately, many churches have little respect for the value which such records hold for historians and researchers and have simply neglected them. Some churches, however, have donated their records to county and state historical societies to insure their preservation. In recent years the churches have begun to use their records, regardless of the records' location, to write their own histories.

Cemetery Records

During slavery it was not unusual to find blacks buried on the back sides of white cemeteries. The black churches, established somewhat later, may provide documentary evidence for the genealogist who pursues black family lines. Records of black cemeteries, for example, provide a historical link with the colonial past. Scattered through the nation, these cemeteries were established because blacks could not be buried alongside their white masters. Consequently, black cemeteries could be found near black churches. Researchers should also investigate records of white church burial grounds, for many of these denominations, such as the Quakers, Catholics, and Moravians, have kept excellent records on blacks since the colonial period. More recently, the Genealogial Society of Utah has undertaken an extensive microfilming program for the collecting of Afro-American genealogy, in which records of black churches are included. Roger

Figure 9.4
Church Record, Works Projects Administration, 1939–41, Showing Black Members of White Congregation

M	Page		Page
Melone, Elizabeth	11	Parker, Richard	5,8,19
Melone, Robert	17,35	Parker, Sarah	5
Montgomery, Maj.	73	Parker, Wm	9,10,12
Moore, Cloey	11,17,35,37,39	Parker, Wm Jr.	13,14,15,18,19 23,26,28,34
Moore, Nancy	11,17,35		
Moore, Shadrick	11,17,35,39	Parker, Wm Sr.	5,108
Mosley, Drury	25,35	Perry, Bro	83,84,86,87,96
N		Perry, Tilmon	60
Nancy (Negro)	34,108	Peytons Creek	9
No Carolina	44,53	Phillips, Wm	2,3
Norvel, Robert	35	Pickits, Elizabeth	63,97
Norvel, Sarah	35	Pompy, (Negro)	34,108
Novls, Drusilla	95	Puncheon Camp Creek Church	87
Novls, Robt	20	**Q (No Q's)**	
Novell, Bro	42	**R**	
Nunley, Branch	19,67,71	Roark,	17
O		Roark, Mrs	35
Orinder, Wm	83,84,85,86,87	Roundlick	40,45,48
P		Rucks, Bro	38,52
Pampy, (Negro)	34,108	Roundlick Church	12
Parker, Arthur	19	Rucks, Josiah	6,9,10,13,17,27 30,34,36,46,58
Parker, Bro	21	**S**	
Parker, D.	21	Sally (Negro)	35
Parker, Dan	19	Salt Lick	62,100
Parker, Drusella	39	Salt Lick Church	98
Parker, Lucy	34,108	Sarah (Negro)	34,106
Parker, Rhode	39	Shaw, Cary	20

Courtesy Tennessee State Library and Archives.

Scanland gives an account of the LDS Genealogical Department Library and its holdings of black American records in chapter 6 of this book. Bobby L. Lovett explores cemeteries as a source of genealogical information, in chapter 4.

Tombstones found in the black cemeteries often give important information on the family. In addition to birth and death dates, tombstone epitaphs often provide information on occupations and causes of death, marriage dates, names of wives and children, and other data.

Census Records

Another record source for black genealogy is the federal census. The year 1790 was the date of the first federal census, while the most recent record publicly available is for the year 1910. In the census reports, names are alphabetized under each state. Each entry includes the number of people in the family and the application page number from the 1790 census volume. Both Jean Elder Cazort (chapter 2 of this book) and James D. Walker (chapter 5) discuss the various census reports and their content. These discussions should be consulted for more detailed information.

In the early censuses, slave schedules were made for every state, a practice that continued until 1860. Each state listing was further broken down by county, with slaves listed under their owners' names. Unfortunately, many of these early records are incomplete. For an illustration of the slave schedules, see figure 9.5.

Two books by the eminent black historian Carter G. Woodson, *Free Negro Heads of Families in the United States in 1830* and *Free Negro Owners of Slaves in the United States in 1830,* provide excellent sources for genealogical pursuit. These volumes list names and sections of the country where blacks lived and other pertinent data. The researcher is also able to identify free blacks who lived in certain states; for example, in Georgia, Maryland, North Carolina, and Virginia.[10] Those who lived in the District of Columbia can also be identified in a separate publication.[11] The bibliography for this chapter lists the publications that identified free blacks in these states. Every free black or mulatto who lived in Virginia in 1793 reportedly is listed in "Registration of Free Negroes Commencing September Court 1822" and "Register of Free Blacks 1835, Book 3." Such persons were required to register with the county clerk for the district in which they lived. Included also are physical description (age, height, identifying marks, and scars), mother's name (if she was freeborn), or name of the emancipator (if the person was freed). Thus the researcher whose black ancestors were free, were free heads of families, or were slaveowners is able to identify these relatives and capture a picture of the position they held in history.[12]

Plantation Records

Thousands of detailed records covering every aspect of plantation operation during the eighteenth and nineteenth centuries were unavoidably lost or destroyed, but fortunately a number of similar records survived and are waiting to reveal their secrets to the diligent researcher.

Figure 9.5
U.S. Census Report, Slave Schedule, 1850

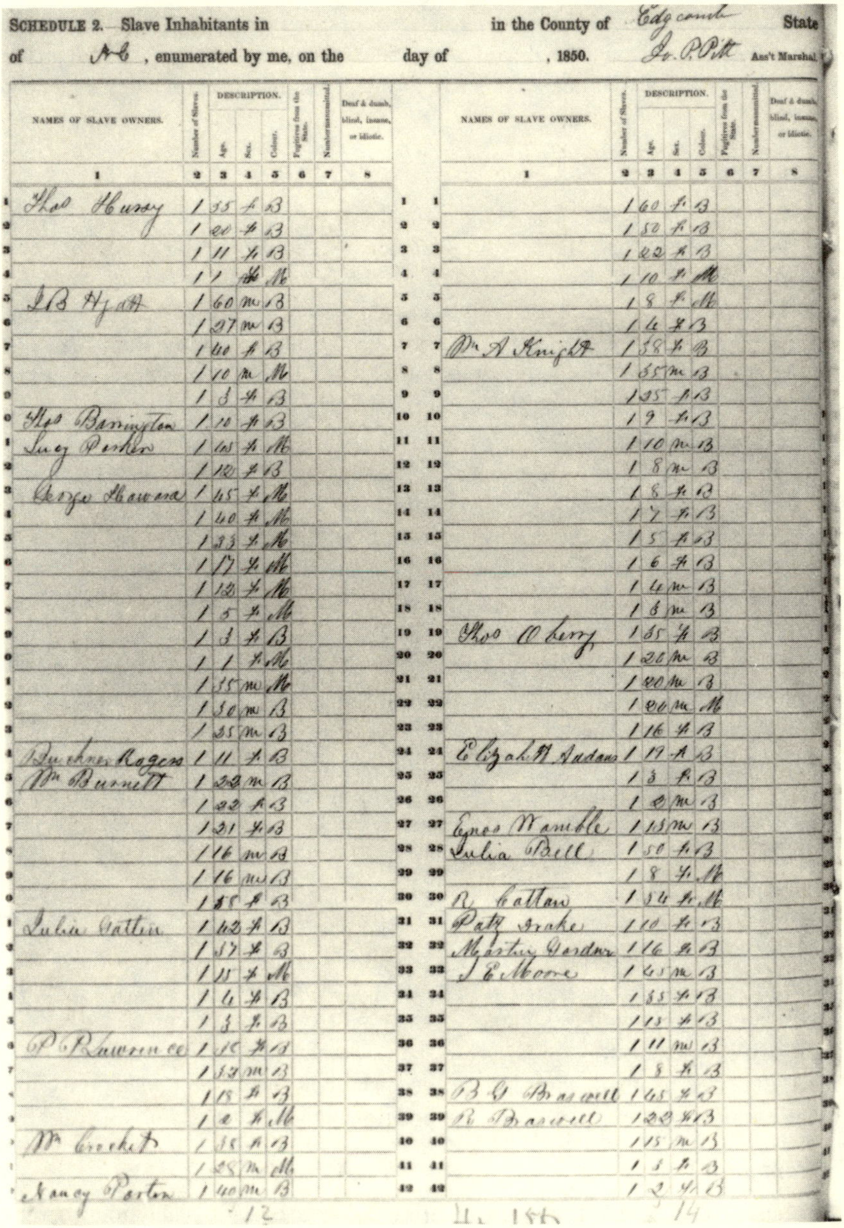

SCHEDULE 2.—Slave Inhabitants in in the County of Edgcomb State of NC, enumerated by me, on the day of , 1850. Jo. P. Pitt Ass't Marshal.

	NAMES OF SLAVE OWNERS.	Number of Slaves.	DESCRIPTION. Age.	Sex.	Colour.	Fugitives from the State.	Number manumitted.	Deaf & dumb, blind, insane, or idiotic.
	1	2	3	4	5	6	7	8
1	Thos Hussy	1	35	f	B			
2		1	20	f	B			
3		1	11	f	B			
4		1	1	f	M			
5	J B Hyatt	1	60	m	B			
6		1	27	m	B			
7		1	40	f	B			
8		1	10	m	M			
9		1	3	f	B			
10	Thos Barrington	1	10	f	B			
11	Lucy Parker	1	45	f	M			
12		1	12	f	B			
13	George Howard	1	45	f	M			
14		1	40	f	M			
15		1	33	f	M			
16		1	17	f	M			
17		1	12	f	M			
18		1	5	f	M			
19		1	3	f	B			
20		1	1	f	M			
21		1	35	m	M			
22		1	30	m	B			
23		1	25	m	B			
24	Buckner Rogers	1	11	f	B			
25	Wm Burnett	1	32	m	B			
26		1	22	f	B			
27		1	21	f	B			
28		1	16	m	B			
29		1	16	m	B			
30		1	58	f	B			
31	Julia Cotten	1	42	f	B			
32		1	37	f	B			
33		1	15	f	M			
34		1	4	f	B			
35		1	3	f	B			
36	P P Lawrence	1	15	f	B			
37		1	32	m	B			
38		1	18	f	B			
39		1	2	f	M			
40	Wm Crocket	1	38	f	B			
41		1	28	m	M			
42	Nancy Porter	1	40	m	B			
		12						

	NAMES OF SLAVE OWNERS.	Number of Slaves.	DESCRIPTION. Age.	Sex.	Colour.	Fugitives from the State.	Number manumitted.	Deaf & dumb, blind, insane, or idiotic.
	1	2	3	4	5	6	7	8
1		1	60	f	B			
2		1	50	f	B			
3		1	22	f	B			
4		1	10	f	M			
5		1	8	f	M			
6		1	4	f	B			
7	Wm A Knight	1	38	f	B			
8		1	35	m	B			
9		1	25	f	B			
10		1	9	f	B			
11		1	10	m	B			
12		1	8	m	B			
13		1	8	f	B			
14		1	7	f	B			
15		1	5	f	B			
16		1	6	f	B			
17		1	4	m	B			
18		1	3	m	B			
19	Thos O Berry	1	55	f	B			
20		1	26	m	B			
21		1	20	m	B			
22		1	20	m	M			
23		1	16	f	B			
24	Elizabeth Adams	1	19	f	B			
25		1	3	f	B			
26		1	2	m	B			
27	Enos Wamble	1	15	m	B			
28	Julia Bell	1	50	f	B			
29		1	8	f	M			
30	R Cotten	1	54	f	M			
31	Patz Drake	1	10	f	B			
32	Martin Gordon	1	16	f	B			
33	J E Moore	1	45	m	B			
34		1	35	f	B			
35		1	13	f	B			
36		1	11	m	B			
37		1	8	f	B			
38	B G Braswell	1	45	f	B			
39	R Braswell	1	23	f	B			
40		1	15	m	B			
41		1	3	f	B			
42		1	2	f	B			
		14						

Record Group 29, National Archives Microfilm Publications M652, n.p.

To find specific records the researcher must know both the name of the slaveowner and the location of the plantation, for the records may be filed under either entry. Employment records; wills, estate inventories, and records of auctions, breeding, branding; and insurance are examples of documents which prove that slaves were valuable assets to their owners. Figure 9.6, a labor voucher, shows that in 1864 five slaves were hired for $535.00. In some cases slave labor contracts were drawn up for work which a state office or state department needed to have done. Such a contract is illustrated in figure 9.7, which, unlike the first labor voucher, includes no sum of money for the labor.

BONDAGE RECORDS

There exist documents which show when some blacks were bound into servitude. This is illustrated in figure 9.8, a printed form from North Carolina which shows that "one negro boy slave known by the name of Jack of the value of two hundred pounds" is bound into servitude in Orange County.

OWNERSHIP RECORDS

With care, one may be able to trace the transfer of ownership of a slave ancestor from one family member to another or from one family to another. This may be achieved by tracing records that show who owned the slave ancestor at a particular time. Transfer of ownership by sale, will, or disposition of estate property was common practice. Figure 9.9 shows legal transactions pertaining to one female and one male slave. Accordingly, the illustration is a list submitted to probate by the administratrix of an estate. Dated "March 19th/64," the document lists seed cotton, ginned cotton, pigs, buggy, harness, and other farm inventory and includes "Shepherd & Isabella, a boy & girl," whose value was $8,000. Further research into the series of transactions revealed a document dated 15 July 1864, a petition to the judge of a probate court for permission to sell named slaves, "Shepherd about 22 years old and Isabella about 16 years of age," and later a petition from the administratrix of a husband's estate to the judge of probate, Wilcox County, Alabama, for authority to sell "for division among the heirs" certain itemized property including hogs, seed cotton, gin cotton, a buggy and harness, and "1 molatto Girl Isabel, 1 molatto boy Sheppard." The various documents examined are related and were prepared in the mid-1860s. Thus the documentation concerning Isabella (or Isabel) and Shepherd (or Sheppard) shows variations in the spelling of their names and further describes them as "molatto" (mulatto). Assuming that the researcher has identified either of these two slaves as his or her ancestor, note should be made of the variations in spelling of both names and, if not previously assumed or known, that they were the offspring of black and white parents.

Bills of sale of slaves, as illustrated in figure 9.10, also are important documents for tracing slave ownership and relocation from plantation to plantation and from one county or state to another.

Figure 9.6
Slave Labor Contract for Private Employer

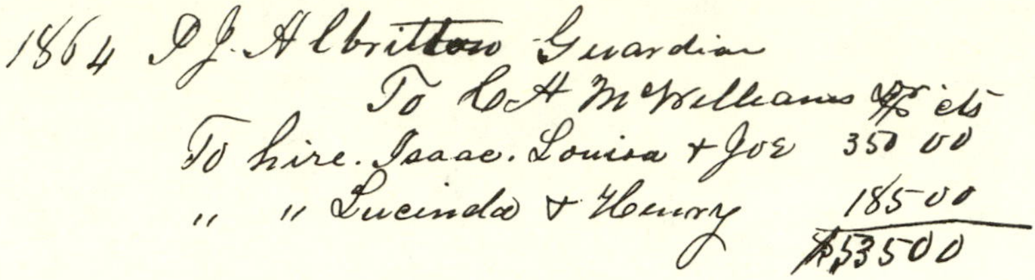

1864 D.J. Albritton Guardian
To C.H. McWilliams & etc
To hire. Isaac. Louisa + Joe   350 00
"   " Lucinda + Henry   185 00
$535 00

Courtesy John L. Heflin, Jr., Brentwood, Tennessee.

WILLS

Wills may be examined to determine legal transactions regarding slaves and, if other documentation is available, may show migration patterns. Here again in Wilcox County, Alabama, figure 9.11, the last will and testament of W. C. Gray, which is dated 10 June 1847, bequeaths all of his property to his wife. Included in the will is "one negro girl named Ellen."

ESTATE INVENTORIES

Estate inventories, prepared many times for the purpose of appraising property and for dividing property to settle an estate, identify many slaves by name.

Figure 9.7
Slave Labor Contract for Work in State Office

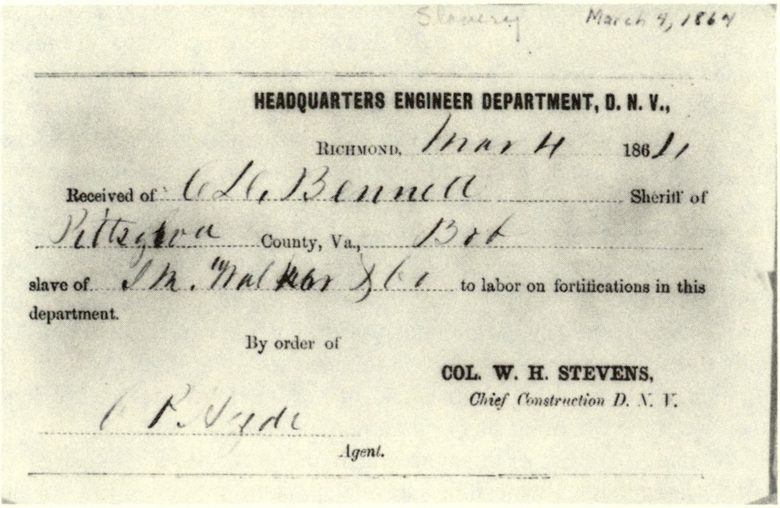

Courtesy Fisk University, Special Collections, Fisk University Library.

Figure 9.8
Bondage Record for Black Bound in Servitude

[ST]ATE OF NORTH-CAROLINA,
Orange County.

Know all Men by these Presents,

That we Joseph Street & Simpson Tate & Peter Mawkins all of the County aforesaid, are held and firmly bound unto Thomas Hart of the County aforesaid, in the just and full sum of Two Thousand four Hundred Pounds Current Money of the State aforesaid, to be paid unto the said Thomas Hart his Heirs, Executors, Administrators or Assigns. For the true Performance whereof, we bind ourselves, our Heirs, Administrators, Executors and Assigns, jointly, severally, and firmly, and by these Presents, sealed with our seals, and dated this 17th Day of Feby 1804

THE Condition of this Obligation is such, that if the above bounden Joseph Street do well and truly make his personal Appearance at our next County Court, to be held for the County aforesaid, on the 4th Monday of Feby next, then and there to answer unto Susannah Leath of a Plea that he detains from her one negro boy slave known by the name of Jack of the Value of three or two hundred pounds damage fifty pounds

and then and there to stand to and abide by the Judgment of the said Court and not depart the said Court without Leave, then the above Obligation to be void; otherwise to remain in full Force and Virtue.

Signed, sealed, and delivered, in the presence of us,
Jesse B[illegible]

Joseph Street (Seal)
Simpson Tate (Seal)
Peter his x mark Mawkins (Seal)

I Saml Turrentine Sheriff of the County of Orange do hereby assign over the within Obligation and Condition, to Susannah Leath the Plaintiff therein named, his Executors, and Administrators, to sue for and recover, agreeably to an Act of Assembly in such case made and provided. Given under my Hand and Seal, this 17th Day of Feby 1804

Thos Witherd (Seal)
for Samuel Turrentine

Courtesy John L. Heflin, Jr., Brentwood, Tennessee.

Figure 9.9
Receipt for Sale of Estate Property Showing Value of Slave Boy and Girl

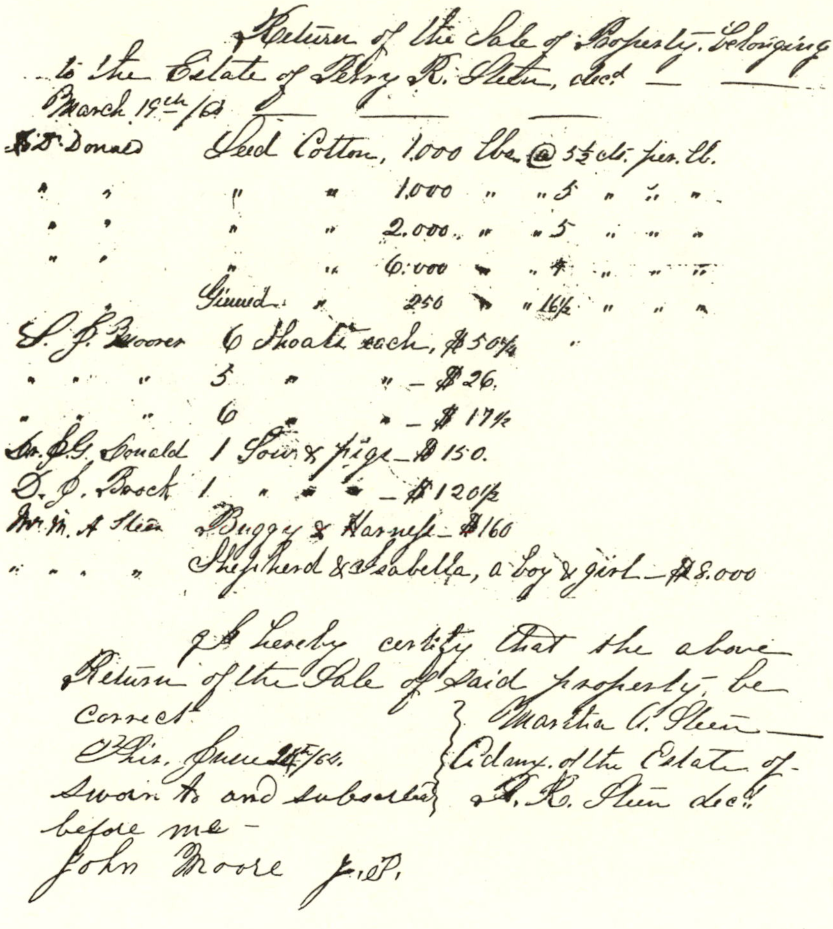

Return of the Sale of Property belonging to the Estate of Perry R. Steen, dec'd

March 19th/61

Wm. Donald — Seed Cotton, 1,000 lbs. @ 5½ cts. per. lb.

" " " " 1,000 " " 5 " " " "

" " " " 2,000 " " 5 " " " "

" " " " 6,000 " " 4 " " " "

" Ginned " 250 " " 16½ " " " "

S. P. Brown — 6 Shoats each, $50½ "

" " " 5 " " — $26.

" " " 6 " " — $17½

Jn. P. G. Donald — 1 Sow & Pigs — $150.

D. P. Brock — 1 " " " — $120½

Mr. Wm. A. Steen — Buggy & Harness — $160

" " " " Shepherd & Isabella, a boy & girl — $8.000

I hereby certify that the above Return of the Sale of said property, be Correct

This, June 24/61.

Martha A. Steen —
Admr. of the Estate of
P. R. Steen dec'd

Sworn to and subscribed before me —

John Moore J.P.

Courtesy John L. Heflin, Jr., Brentwood, Tennessee.

Figure 9.10
Bill of Sale of Slaves

November 12, 1836

Know all men by these presents that I Francis T
Reid of the County of Henry and State of Tennessee have this
day bargained and sold to Benjamin C Brown of the County
and State aforesaid, one negro man named Moses aged about
forty five years, one negro woman named Amanda aged
about thirty eight years, and one negro child aged about
three years. for and in consideration of the sum of
sixteen hundred and fifty dollars. to me in hand
paid the receipt whereof is hereby acknowledged and
I do hereby warrant the said negroes to be sound
healthy and slaves for life – In testimony whereof
I have hereunto set my hand and affixed my seal
this twelfth day of November AD 1836

F T Reid

State of Tennessee } Personally appeared before me Thomas K Porter Clerk
Henry County } of the County Court of said County Francis T Reid the
above named bargainor with whom I am personally acquainted and
who acknowledged that he had executed the foregoing bill of sale to Benjamin C Brown for the purposes therein mentioned. Witness my hand
at office November the 12th 1836.

Thos K Porter clk

State of Tennessee } Registers office November the 15th 1836
Henry County }
Then the foregoing bill of sale from Francis T Reid to Benjamin
C Brown & certificate of acknowledgment were duly Registered in my office in Book E
page 410.

James Leeper Register
of Henry County

Courtesy Fisk University, Special Collections, Fisk University Library.

327

Figure 9.11
Will Showing Disposition of Slave Girl

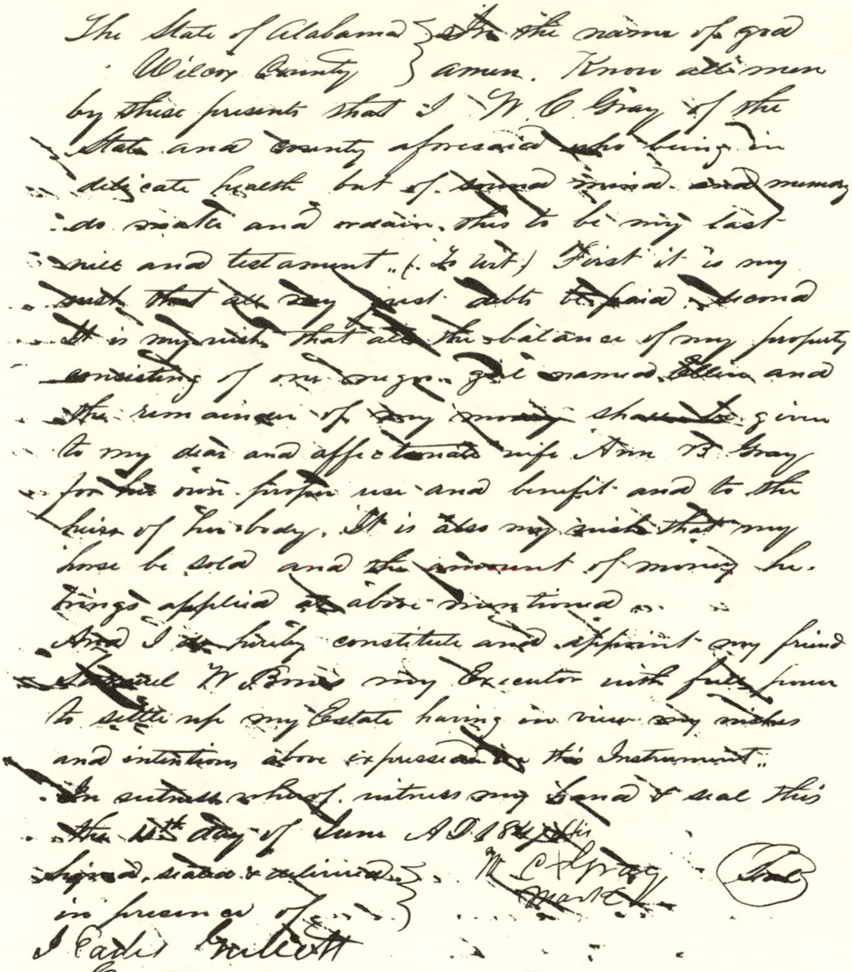
The State of Alabama } In the name of god
Wilcox County } amen. Know all men
by these presents that I W. C. Gray of the
State and County aforesaid who being in
delicate health but of sound mind and memory
do make and ordain this to be my last
will and testament (to wit) First it is my
wish that all my just debts be paid. Second
It is my wish that all the balance of my property
consisting of one negro girl named Ellen and
the remainder of my money shall be given
to my dear and affectionate wife Ann B. Gray
for her own proper use and benefit and to the
heirs of her body. It is also my wish that my
horse be sold and the amount of money belonging applied as above mentioned.
And I do hereby constitute and appoint my friend
Samuel W. Bones my Executor with full power
to settle up my Estate having in view my wishes
and intentions above expressed in this Instrument.
In witness whereof witness my hand & seal this
the 15th day of June A.D. 184[illegible]
Signed, sealed & delivered } W. C. his X Gray mark (Seal)
in presence of
J. Eades Walcott
S. W. Bones

Courtesy John L. Heflin, Jr., Brentwood, Tennessee.

Usually, the larger the named list, the larger the plantation. Figure 9.12 illustrates an estate inventory which includes nineteen named slaves ranging in value from $300 to $1,300. Their value reflects the larger portion of the estate, which has a total value of $17,703. Among those named are a woman (Lydia) and two children (Phyllis and May Ann); Pompei (or Pompey, the writing is illegible), a man; Hanna and child Laura; and other slaves who, with one exception, are identified as man, woman, boy, or girl. Here again the researcher may determine the likelihood that one of these slaves was his or her ancestor if the person was at that time a youth or an adult. Because some slave documents refer to adults as boy or girl even after they reach maturity (as was seen with Shepherd, about twenty-two), caution must be exercised when making that determination.

INSURANCE RECORDS

Insurance records may contain information which will enable the researcher to determine the slave's owner, the state in which the estate was located, and the slave's age at the time. Figure 9.13, an insurance policy from the Mutual Life Insurance Company, Columbia, South Carolina, was especially prepared to cover slaves, as it reads "do insure the life or lives of the within named slave or slaves" and goes on to identify Rosalie, fourteen years, and Virgil, twelve years. Thus the researcher who has determined that either Rosalie or Virgil was his or her ancestor will have proof of that ancestor's approximate date of birth, the name of the slaveowner, and the plantation's location.

MEDICAL RECORDS

Some researchers may be interested in the health or medical histories of their ancestors. Often bills of sale or advertisements of slaves for hire indicate that the slave is healthy (whether that was really the case cannot be determined with certainty). In other cases plantation records show that a slave has received medical treatment and may or may not indicate the health problem.

EMPLOYMENT RECORDS

Great numbers of free blacks labored in the North as charcoal and iron workers, both during slavery and after. Their work may be documented in employment records spanning three centuries. Such records often include day books, time books, ledgers, payroll books, journals, cash books, and entries specifically on the black workers. There are also entries on blacks purchasing goods and on the condition of their health, the number of children they had, and occasionally the region of Africa where they were born.

EMANCIPATION RECORDS

Plantation records, as well as papers of black families, may contain free papers for blacks who either were emancipated for whatever reason or were never bound in servitude. Figure 9.14, dated 12 July 1850, shows that slaves Martha and her three children, boys George, Sam, and Mark Jackson, are "hereby Emancipated

Figure 9.12
Inventory and Appraisal of Estate Property, Including
Nineteen Named Slaves

Dec the 4th 1856   A List of property appraised of the Est of Stephen Plalmer upon a division as had this day between Dabny Palmer and John Palmer Legatees of Said deceas To Wit

	$
Jinay a woman	800.00
Jack a man	350
Lydia & two children Phillis & May and,	1250
Pompe aman	1200
Hanna & child Laura	1100
Lucinda a girl	500
Cathrine a girl	350
Patty a girl	250
Dillis a girl	175
Joe aman	1300
Isaad a man	1150
George a Boy	850
Patty a woman	1100
Fannis a woman	1050
Ritta a girl	900
Malissa	475
amount of Negro Property	$ 12300
Horses Mules Stock and Farming tools & Wagon	10 25
Money	$ 13,3 25
	26 28
Amount of cotton	259 53
	4,1 50
Expenses deducted	174 03
	3 16
Amount of Dabnys share first	17,3 88
	1,000
	19 3,3 88
	6.6 94

Courtesy John L. Heflin, Jr., Brentwood, Tennessee.

and Set free and granted all the rights and priviledges of Free Persons of Color by this law now in force in this State upon condition that she the said Martha with her three Children George, Sam and Mark Jackson forthwith remove themselves without the Jurisdiction of the State of Tennessee unless upon cause Showen to the proper Court they be allowed to remain." The document shows further that Martha and her three sons petitioned and were granted permission to remain in Tennessee but were required to post bond to receive that privilege.

The researcher in black genealogy will find plantation records in a number of libraries, such as the University of North Carolina, Chapel Hill; the University of Virginia; and some state libraries. Sometimes the records are scattered and sold separately, thus fragmenting black genealogical research resources. The black genealogist may need to search the records of private collectors and dealers who sell such documents. Those plantation records which are legal documents are also in the records of public offices and frequently find their way to state libraries and archives.

Sharecropping Records

While many sharecropping records have been destroyed, or, if they exist, are financially inaccurate, they can at least provide verification of residence. In the sharecropping South (1890–1930 and even later), large numbers of blacks were nonlanded and constituted what should be considered a broad rural proletariat. In per capita terms, two in five whites and only one in nine blacks owned land. Many sharecroppers moved every year to another "plantation." Genealogical researchers may experience difficulty in tracing and locating relatives who were sharecroppers, who moved frequently, and sometimes who moved back to an original farm site. Because counties changed names, care must be exercised to account for the variation in naming of the townships and county areas where the relatives lived.

War Records

Black participation in wars is one of the most neglected aspects of American history. Because blacks have served in wars from the Revolution to the present, those who are searching for genealogical information can find a wealth of information at the National Archives as well as in various state archives. The U.S. Army War College at Carlisle, Pennsylvania, has an extensive collection of materials relating to the black military. Three references are especially valuable. The first, *List of Black Servicemen Compiled from the War Department Collection of Revolutionary War Records*, gives the names of Revolutionary War servicemen known or presumed to have been black. It was compiled from three sources in the War Department Collection of Revolutionary War Records. The work is arranged alphabetically by name, with reference to the fuller source where more information can be obtained.[13] The second is entitled *The Negro in the Military Services of the United States, 1639–1886* and is a collection of records and papers,[14] and the third is *Index to Compiled Service Records of*

Figure 9.13
Insurance Policy for Slaves

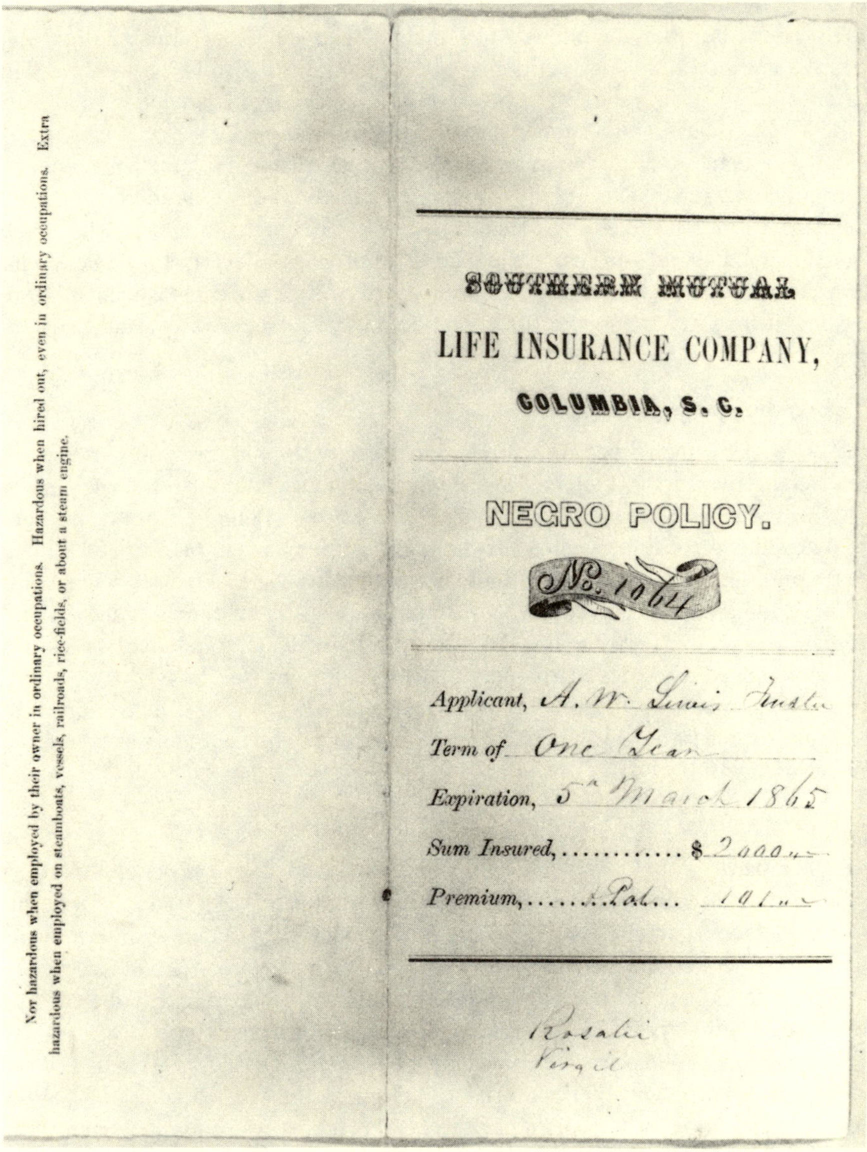

SOUTHERN MUTUAL

LIFE INSURANCE COMPANY,

COLUMBIA, S. C.

NEGRO POLICY.

No. 1064

Applicant, *A. W. Lewis, Trustee*

Term of *One Year*

Expiration, *5ᵗʰ March 1865*

Sum Insured, ... $2000

Premium, ... I Pol... *191*

Rosalie
Virgil

Nor hazardous when employed by their owner in ordinary occupations. Hazardous when hired out, even in ordinary occupations. Extra hazardous when employed on steamboats, vessels, railroads, rice-fields, or about a steam engine.

(*continued*)

Figure 9.13—*Continued*

SOUTHERN MUTUAL LIFE INSURANCE COMPANY,
COLUMBIA, SOUTH-CAROLINA.

No. 1061

This Policy of Insurance witnesseth, That the SOUTHERN MUTUAL LIFE INSURANCE COMPANY, in consideration of *one hundred* Dollars, to them in hand paid by *C. W. Lewis Smith* do insure the life or lives of the within named slave or slaves belonging to *C. W. Lewis Smith of said of Augusta* in the State of *Georgia* in the amount set opposite his, her or their name, as below, viz:

NAMES.	AGE.	AMOUNT INSURED.
Rosetta	*44 Years*	*1000 Dollars*
Virgil	*12*	*2000 Dollars*

amounting to the total sum of *Three Thousand* Dollars, for the term of *One Year* from the date of this Policy.

And the said Company do hereby promise to pay to the said *said Insured* within sixty days after due proof of the death of any of the above named slaves, (if the death shall occur within the time for which this insurance is effected,) the amount insured in this Policy, set opposite the name or names of the deceased.

Provided always, (and it is hereby declared to be the true intent and meaning of this Policy,) That if the application signed by the said *C. W. Lewis Smith* and dated *fifty February 1861* shall be in any respect fraudulent or untrue; or if the said slave or slaves, or any of them, shall die by his, her or their own hands, or by intemperance, or by the hands of justice, or in the violation of law, or by or in consequence of a mob, a riot, a foreign invasion, a civil war, or an insurrection, or any military or usurped power, or by the mal-treatment or neglect of the owner, or of any person to whom he, she or they may be entrusted ; or if the said slave or slaves, or any of them, are now, or shall be hereafter insured in any other Company, or shall abscond or be kidnapped, or shall, without the written consent of the said Company, either be sold or given to a new owner, or be removed fifty miles from their present residence, or be employed in a more hazardous occupation than their present one, the degree of hazard to be estimated by the said application and the scale endorsed on this Policy, whenever it is applicable, or if, in case of the sickness of the said slave or slaves, or any of them, he, she or they shall fail to receive all due and proper care, promptly, and without delay, or if this Policy shall be assigned, without the written consent of the said Company ; then, and in all such cases, the said Company shall not be liable to pay the sum insured and set opposite the name or names of the said slave or slaves, deceased, or any part thereof, and this Policy, so far as relates to such payment, shall be utterly void. And it is further agreed, That the said Company shall not be bound to pay more than two-thirds of the value of such of the said slaves as may die during the continuance of this Policy, the said value to be estimated as at the beginning of the last illness.

IN WITNESS WHEREOF, the said Company have, by their President and Actuary, and by *Charles Hall* their Agent at *Augusta Ga.* signed this Policy at twelve o'clock (at noon,) this *fifth* day of *March* one thousand eight hundred and fifty *forty-seven*.

W. F. de Saussure President,
F. W. McMaster Actuary,
Charles Hall Agent.

Courtesy Fisk University, Special Collections, Fisk University Library.

333

Figure 9.14
Manumission, or "Free," Papers for Former Slaves

State of Tennessee / July Term 1850
Shelby County / SS

Britt Hines /
Ex Parte / To the Honorable County Court
Petition / of Shelby County July Term
1850.

This cause coming on this day to be hea
=rd before the County Court of Shelby County
the Chairman and Nine others Justices present
up on the petition of Britt Hines It was
Ordered and decreed by the Court that the ma
=tters & things therein set forth be referred to
the Chairman of this Court who shall report
thereon at the present term whether according
to the prayer of said petition it will be consist=
ent with the interest and policy of this State

And thereupon the said Chairman
Makes his report which is as follows to wit

State of Tennessee /
Shelby County / I John B Hodges Chairman
of the County Court of Shelby County to whom
was referred the matters and things Contained
in the petition of Britt Hines do hereby report
that they have been examined by myself and the
other members of the Court and that we believe
that to grant and allow the same will be con
=sistant with the interest and policy of the State
of Tennessee

John B Hodges Chairman

said No Exception being taken thereto it is
ordered that the same be in all things Confirmed
and it appearing to the Court that said
petitioner has entered into bond and security,

334

as the law directs and conditioned as the law requires It is therefore ordered adjudged and decreed by the Court that the Slaves Martha and her three children viz George Sam and Mark Jackson named in said petition be and they are hereby Emancipated and Set free and granted all the rightes and preveledges of Free Persons of Color by the laws now in force in this State upon condition that She the said Martha with her three Children George Sam and Mark Jackson forthwith remove themselves without the Jurisdiction of the State of Tennessee unless upon cause Shown to the proper Court they be allowed to remain

And thereupon the said Martha for herself and her three children George Sam and Mark Jackson files her petition therein praying that this Court will allow them to remain in the State of Tennessee and upon Satisfactory Sufficient cause being Shown to the Court from said petitioner and other proof It is Ordered that the prayer thereof be granted and the Said Martha with her three Children George Sam and Mark Jackson be allowed the preveledge of remaining in this State upon Condition of her Complying with the Acts of the General Assembly in Such cases made and provided.

And thereupon the said Martha came into Court and Entered into bond and Securety for herself and Children in the Sum of $1000 Conditioned as the law requires which Bond is approved by the Court.

(continued)

335

Figure 9.14—*Continued*

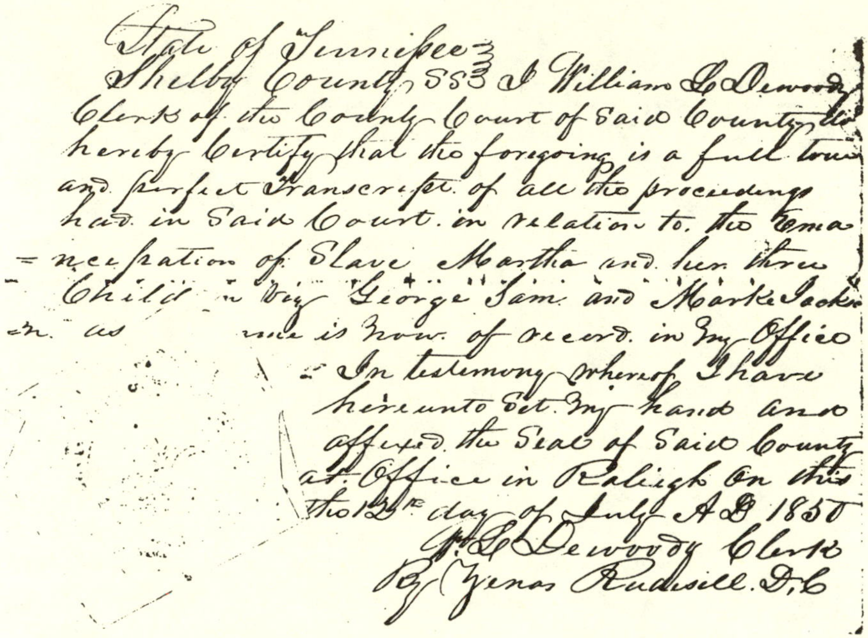

State of Tennessee
Shelby County, SS I William L Dewood
Clerk of the County Court of said County do
hereby Certify that the foregoing is a full true
and perfect Transcript of all the proceedings
had in Said Court in relation to the Ema
= ncipation of Slave Martha and her three
Child in viz George Sam and Marke Jacks
on as ... is now of record in My Office
In testimony whereof I have
hereunto Set My hand and
affixed the Seal of Said County
at Office in Raleigh On this
the 12th day of July AD 1850
W L Dewoody Clerk
By Zenas Rudisill. D.C

Courtesy Fisk University, Special Collections, Fisk University Library.

Volunteer Union Soldiers Who Served with United States Colored Troops. This microfilm publication reproduces alphabetical cards which give the name of the soldier, his rank, and the unit in which he served. Cross-references are made for names that appear in the records under more than one spelling and also for names of men who served in more than one unit or organization.[15] Walker gives a fuller account of military records and their usefulness for black genealogical research in chapter 5 of this book.

PENSION BUREAU

Records of soldiers who have drawn pensions are in the Pension Bureau in Washington, D.C., which furnishes transcripts of applications or other forms relating to pensions. Some of these documents contain only meager information but may be helpful. State libraries and archives also house pension records, especially for pensions the particular state provided for soldiers.

Good unofficial sources are the publications of the DAR and Sons of the American Revolution (SAR), groups which have been active for nearly one hundred years. More than 5,000 black soldiers fought in the Continental Army of George Washington. Today only three acknowledged black women are members of the DAR and two black men are members of the SAR.

DEPARTMENT OF MILITARY AFFAIRS AND THE ADJUTANT GENERAL

This subgroup contains a sizable volume of materials relevant to the Civil War, including Muster and Descriptive Rolls, Department of Men and Substitutes. These records span the entire conflict and include information on hundreds of draftees and enlistees from all over the nation. The information provided on black soldiers includes name, rank, place of birth, age, occupation when drafted, place of enrollment, district, period of service, physical traits, date of commencement of services, and notes.

Debra L. Newman, an archivist in the Industrial and Social Branch of the National Archives, has done extensive research in a neglected but important segment of Afro-American genealogy. Her investigation of 300 free black women who left the British in the evacuation of Philadelphia in 1788 and went to Canada provides another facet of Afro-American heritage. Newman describes what is contained in a unique document, "The Inspection Roll of Negroes, Taken on Board Sundry Vessels at Staten Island and Bound for Nova Scotia," and describes this document as a record of the destination of British ships departing American waters for Canada with blacks aboard. The document provides personal information on some 3,360 blacks.

Slave Advertisements and Newspapers

From earliest colonial days, cases involving runaway slaves frequently appeared as advertisements in newspapers throughout the North and South. Runaway slave advertisements provide vital information for black genealogists. The broadsides and posters were distributed to taverns and displayed on trees, walls, or in any place that guaranteed a lot of attention. The advertisements generally included a description of the escaped slave, the name of the owner, the amount of reward offered, and any other incidental fact that might help the owners retrieve their human property, such as whether the runaway was crippled, had a scar or brand, was defiant or obedient, spoke other languages, was accompanied by others, or had a particular skill.

Underground Railroad Records

A secret and complex network of free blacks, former slaves, and white abolitionists helped many slaves escape from the South. Underground railroad historians William Still and Wilbur H. Siebert have both written notable works on escaped slaves and the underground movement in general. Still's work, entitled *The Underground Railroad,* was published in 1872 and preceded by twenty-six years Seibert's work, entitled *The Underground Railroad from Slavery to Freedom.* Both books include hundreds of names of station keepers and passengers in this mysterious network.[16]

In Pennsylvania the Philadelphia Vigilant Committee's *Underground Railroad Journal* records include newspaper advertisements as well as vital written information on fugitive slaves passing through its office.

Newspapers

One can hardly overestimate the importance of newspapers as a source of genealogical information. They are a primary source of national and local history. From *Freedom's Journal* (1827) to the present day, black newspapers have played a leading role in the struggle for freedom of black people.

Editors of the early black press at first relied on newsletters, editorials, meeting notes, columns on race elevation, news about important legal cases, and news about social events. These publications have always contained obituaries, births, business advertisements, reports of athletic events, and other items important to the shaping of local and family history.

Many state historical societies and libraries have been assiduous in recent years in persuading newspapers of every locality to send a copy of each issue to them for preservation. Perhaps the most important general collection of newspapers can be found at the Library of Congress. Researchers need not go that far to obtain copies of discontinued papers from their local black publishers; it is likely that their state libraries and archives also have collected and microfilmed them. For black genealogical research, such small, short-lived papers may provide the missing link in tracing one's family lines. A selected list of black newspapers is included in the bibliography to this chapter.

City Directories

Genealogists and writers of family histories have discovered a great deal of information on blacks in city directories. Early directories contained heads of families, places of residence, and occupations. As early as 1811, several directories referred to blacks with asterisks, crosses, or daggers. Much later, additional family members were added to these municipal directories. Many of these works, however, can be consulted only in libraries and historical societies containing large genealogical collections.

Commercial, fraternal and religious organizations such as the Masons, Odd Fellows, Links, Inc., and Elks often published directories of their memberships. These are likely to be in the hands of the secretaries of the organizations concerned, yet old volumes may turn up almost anywhere. Certain ones may be preserved in special black collections in libraries, and it is possible that members have copies in their private papers.

Other important sources of information for the researcher in black genealogy are *Who's Who in Colored America, The Negro Yearbook, Men of Mark, Directory of Afro-American Resources* and similar works, which are included with details in the bibliography for this chapter. While some of these works are out of print, they are available in special black collections and in many state libraries.

Photographs

Family researchers must consider the use of photographs in their investigations; however, it is imperative that a senior member of the family identify those photographs which are lacking in names and dates. Flea markets and antique shops, which are flourishing today, often yield well-preserved photographs of World War I soldiers, family albums (both black, and white with black slaves or servants), unidentified groups, and others. Here, too, what could be a wealthy resource for black genealogy is becoming scattered among private collectors. Fortunately, however, sometimes these items finally rest in state libraries and with local historical or genealogical societies.

Freedmen's Bureau Records

The Freedmen's Bureau records have been placed on microfilm and are available to researchers through the National Archives. Among the documents the records contain are letters to the bureau commissioners, reports from bureau schools, assistant commissioners' reports, and an assortment of orders and circulars. The papers are an important source of information on newly freed slaves, whose needs the bureau was created to address. Established by the federal government immediately before the Civil War ended, the bureau's work was performed in southern and border states as well as the District of Columbia. The bureau's activities ended in 1869, and by 1872 it was officially discontinued.

Bank Records

From 1865 to 1874 the Freedmen's Savings and Trust Company operated and maintained accounts for blacks. The researcher may find it profitable to search these early bank records by reviewing *Registers of Signatures of Depositions in Branches of the Freedmen's Savings and Trust Company, 1865–1874*. These records are available on microfilm in the National Archives and are arranged in alphabetical order by state, then by city within the state, and then by account number.[17]

Many black-owned and -operated banks were founded during the last century and in the present century as well. Their records also are important sources for the researcher, for the information given on the family member and for information on the importance of the bank as a black business enterprise in the community. The board members of these banks often included influential black leaders, one of whom might be the family member whose life the researcher is tracing.

Negro Court and Criminal Court Records

Negro court records were established during the colonial period to handle cases involving blacks. The name, nature of the case, judicial proceedings, and trial outcome were a matter of record in the quarterly sessions. By the very nature of these courts, the information collected was comprehensive. Such records included notes of arbitration, detailed descriptions of both civil and criminal cases, statements of witnesses, references to previous cases, settlements, and verdicts. After determining that an ancestor had a criminal record, the researcher should find out where the trial was held and then locate the appropriate court and criminal records for additional details.

PRISON, WORKHOUSE, AND INEBRIATE ASYLUM RECORDS

Some prison records, including those of local jails, have been turned over to their respective state archives. There is no way to tell in advance whether the records the researcher needs have been preserved; however, a record of the trial should be available in the court records.

Among the best sources in many state archives for insights into the social conditions of blacks during the later nineteenth century are prison, almshouse, and workhouse records. Many of these records provide detailed information on black inmates. The registers call for the following information: name, when received, age, sex, nativity, complexion, height, weight, parental relation, school attended (and whether illiterate, semiliterate, or well educated), industrial relations, occupation before conviction, habits, marital status, and religious instructions.

INSTITUTION POPULATION RECORDS

In addition to some similar information found in penal records are the institution population records, which include entries for the admissions, discharges, and deaths of patients or inmates. These items usually include detailed descriptions of the individual's psychological state upon commitment.

DISCHARGE AND DESCRIPTIVE DOCKET RECORDS

Discharge and descriptive docket records list the number of times the person was punished, education received in the institution, amount of money earned from overwork during imprisonment, intended residence, and remarks. Such records are now considered a vital source for genealogical searches.

Other Institutional Records

The range and scope of institutional records that are useful to the searcher are wide and varied. Among these are physicians' records, which some states have recorded in the *Register of Practitioners of Medicine and Surgery*.[18] Included in these documents are records for every county, recording the physician's name, date and county of registration, sex, race, place of birth, residence, medical degree, places of continuous practice, and removal or death. When such records are examined in connection with those mentioned earlier as slave documents, the researcher may be able to develop a picture of the family member's medical history.

YOUNG MEN'S CHRISTIAN ASSOCIATION AND PHYLLIS WHEATLEY ASSOCIATIONS

By the late 1890s, separate "colored branches" of the Young Men's Christian Association (YMCA) had emerged in cities throughout the nation. The YMCA issued an annual yearbook and official roster. These volumes give basic information on the size of membership, property, activities, and financing of "Colored Men's Associations."

Named in honor of black America's first nationally known poet, the Phyllis Wheatley Associations often contained a number of photographs and genealogical data pertaining to its members.

The Canadian Connection

Blacks resided in Canada as early as the 1720s and were slaves under the French and English. The Maroon descendants of black slaves (and perhaps of Arawak Indian women) were transported by the British to Nova Scotia upon the Maroons' surrender after years of violent rebellion against the British government.

The black population grew in numbers as a substantial influx of slaves who had fled the United States escaped on the underground railroad. Migration to Canada reached its peak during this period, with blacks, both slave and free, settling in southern Ontario communities then called Dawn, Colchester, Elgin, Dresden, Windsor, Sandwich, Bush, Wilberforce, Hamilton, St. Catherine, Chatham, Riley, Auberton, London, Malden, Buxton, and Confield.[19]

Records of such black Canadian communities can be traced through a number of sources. Names and addresses of historical societies and archives can be obtained from the researcher's local or state library. Abolitionist newspapers of the time provide excellent information pertaining to community life within these settlements.

For additional genealogical data on blacks in Canada during this early period, the researcher should consult Benjamin Drew's *A North-Side View of Slavery*.[20]

Miscellaneous Records

If used in combination with other genealogical material, the record list which follows will provide valuable links to the black past.

MANUMISSION RECORDS

As earlier noted, some families still have freedom papers in their possession. Many other freedom papers are in special collections of academic and public libraries. A manumission record, or freedom paper, is a formal document which illustrates that a slave has been freed or will be freed at a specific time. (As an example, see figure 9.14 shown earlier.) These records vary in format. Some were prepared as part of a will or as a separate document written by the master and given to the slave when that person was freed. Manumission records are generally filed under titles which facilitate their use; for example, "Manumission Records of North Carolina." They also may be found under the specific master's name or in separate court records. The Society of Friends kept excellent records of their manumitted slaves. Sometimes these records were deposited in state archives.

CLEMENCY FILES AND FILES OF FORFEITED ESTATES

Clemency files are arranged alphabetically. The references to black inhabitants which they include can be found in the county's courthouse. Records on forfeited estates and abandoned lands are also located with the courthouse records.

HABEUS CORPUS CASE RECORDS

A compilation of writs and responding memoranda concerning detained black men, women, and children can be found in various northern and southern archives and courthouses. Questions of slave status and ownership are addressed. Marriage and divorce records sometimes are included with this grouping.

Helen T. Catterall's *Judicial Cases Concerning American Slavery and the Negro* is an excellent and extensive work which contains many thousands of court records on blacks. For a description of the work, see the bibliography for this chapter.

SHIPPING RECORDS

Shipping records sometimes provide valuable information on merchants who were persistent participants in the commerce of slaves. The commercial firm of Morris and Willing, a prominent Revolutionary-period Philadelphia establishment, was one of the largest slave trading firms in Colonial America. This firm in 1761 advertised the sale of 170 blacks who had just arrived from the Gold Coast of Africa. Throughout the firm's mercantile and financial correspondence, 1774–1800, there is valuable information for genealogists. The Willing family founded Wilmington, Delaware, and Robert Morris was one of the major financiers of the American Revolutionary War. Later he was confined to debtor's prison.

BREEDING RECORDS

To increase the supply of slaves, whether they were scarce in number or a master chose to expand his labor force, in many parts of the South slaves were bred through the use of studs. Sometimes slaves of different backgrounds were mixed deliberately, with the idea of producing a specific breed. While documentation may be lacking, some historians claim that the sole purpose of certain plantations was the breeding of slaves. It is known that slave breeding was accepted as a natural course on many plantations.

In some instances slave women received incentives for producing children for their white masters. One incentive may have been freedom once a certain number of children had been born. White men, too, were known to breed their own slaves to increase the work force. Some breeding records are extant and contain the slave's age, national background, health status, and other data. Other breeding records give various details, such as the number of children a stud sired by each woman he serviced, the nature of work in which his parents were engaged, general comments about the stud's "attitude," a statement about the stud's value as a laborer, and other data. The researcher should consult certain courthouses and historical societies for leads to breeding records. As earlier noted, the Bastardy Case Book is a form of breeding record, copies of which also are extant.

BRANDING RECORDS

As demonstrated in the television adaptation of *Roots,* frequently slaves were branded, in a manner similar to that used for cattle. Such branding was used as a means of identity in case the slave attempted to escape and live as a free person. Even before they left Africa, slaves frequently were branded before being put aboard the ship; thus the brand mark identified the ship which carried the person into servitude. Branding might also have occurred at the landing point. The practice of branding a slave more than once was not uncommon. The use of brands was a legally accepted practice; courthouses are known to have recorded branding records as a measure of discouraging slave runaways. Thus it is likely that their archives include such records. In many cases information pertaining to tribal markings the slaves had received in Africa was also recorded and may be found in these archives.

AMERICAN INDIAN RECORDS

American Indians, like black American slaves, relied primarily on their own system of oral history; they left few written records behind. Because single names often were used in intermarriage between blacks and Indians, this information alone may seem of little importance to someone on a genealogical search. The only way to approach this problem from the Indian side is through the existing records of the Bureau of Indian Affairs or other records described in chapter 7 of this book. The tracing of black ancestry into the mixed black-Indian relationship can be difficult because of poor record-keeping practices. Above all, however, the researcher must know the tribal affiliation of the Indian ancestor.

Sometimes blacks who were runaway slaves found their way to Indian reservations, where they might have been retained as slaves or as free persons or found and returned to the master. Figure 9.15 shows that a runaway lived with Indians for approximately one year, subsequently was jailed in Hardeman County, Tennessee, and later offered to his possible owner upon proof of ownership.

In the case of group mixings, examples may also be seen in the West Indies, where offspring are sometimes grouped in a single community; thus the researcher is able to complete the family's history in a relatively short period. Some mixed families who lived in the United States tended not to migrate but to settle in close proximity to the original home once they married. Researchers may know of such communities within their states, in which case they can proceed without difficulty in tracing particular family lines.

CREOLE RECORDS

In New Orleans blacks of mixed parentage were placed in rigid categories, strictly according to the racial makeup of their parents during the nineteenth century. My previous research produced the list which follows. The list progresses from the lowest class to the highest, depending on the amount of black blood, as the blood mixture declines proportionately from term to term as follows:

Parents	Child
black and white	mulatto
mulatto and white	quadroon
quadroon and white	octoroon
mulatto and mulatto	cascos
octoroon and white	mustifee
mustifee and white	mustifino
mulatto and black	sambo
sambo and black	mango

This mixed society produced many interesting groupings, such as the Cordon Bleu, a class of wealthy free blacks who were the offspring of French-black liaisons and were commonly called Creoles.[21]

COUNTY ORPHAN COURT RECORDS

During the middle half of the nineteenth century, large numbers of county schools for "colored orphans" existed in both northern and southern states. The records from the schools include valuable antebellum materials for genealogical research. The information they provide on black orphans includes name, age,

Figure 9.15
Letter Regarding Runaway Slave on Indian Reservation

Bolivar Tennessee
July 10. 1833.

Mr. James Meadows.

Sir,

On the 8th Instant a Negro Man who says his name is John & that he belongs to you was committed to Jail as a Runaway — the boy is a Black stout built fellow says he is 41 years old, says he can read and write a little and has been Run away since Christmas 1831 — and was apprehended in the Chickasaw Nation south of this where he says he has been for more than a year — if you have lost such a fellow you will make legal proof of ownership, pay charges & take him away —

Your Obt Svt

Wm M Shackelford
Jailor
of Hardeman County Te.

Courtesy John L. Heflin, Jr., Brentwood, Tennessee.

sex, previous place of residence, health, physical traits, period of arrival, and names of parents when possible.

BLACK GENEALOGY: A CASE STUDY

While black genealogical research may lead to numerous roadblocks, clearly some blacks in this country are able to trace their ancestry back to very early periods. The discussion of the Jamestown Group which follows illustrates what can be done.

The Jamestown Group

The first black immigrants to the United States arrived in 1619 as slaves or, as some historians suggest, as immigrants. I have been able to make only a superficial search regarding two members of the Jamestown Group and extracted the following information:

Antoney Negro: Isabell Negro: William their child baptised
were living at the muster of Captain William Tucker in 1625.

This is documented on page 49 of Lester's *Adventures of Purse and Persons in Virginia 1607–1624,* which abstracts all of the patents issued in Virginia for the period 1666–95. In searching in this book for the Johnsons, I learned that the land which Antoney Johnson, Negro, owned in Northampton County, Virginia, escheated in 1645 and was regranted. Although Antoney Johnson, who was mentioned in the census of 1624–25 in Virginia, had married Isabell and by then had a son, William (and possibly other children later), it seems that he survived his family and died without heirs. Escheat was a term used only when a person died leaving no heirs and the land reverted to the crown. When the land was deserted and was not planted, the patent was reissued as a "lapsed" patent to another grantee. Needless to say, I was very disappointed to learn that Antoney Johnson died without leaving heirs.

The reference on page 296 is most interesting, for it reads

Rich. Johnson (Johnson—also given as John) Negro, 100 acres. Northampton Co., 21 Nov. 1654, P. 294. On S. side of Pungoteague River, Ely. upon Pocomock Nly. upon land of John Johnson, Negro Wly. upon Anto. Johnson, Negro, and Sly. upon Nich. Waddilow. Trans. of 2 pers: Wm. Ames, Wm. Vincent.

Subsequently (page 413), the document reveals the following:

John Jenkins, 250 acres, N'ampton, adj. lands of Thomas Teagle, Jno. Johnson, Negro, and Antoney Johnson, Negro. p. 53 (501) (17 March 1655 to John Williams, who assigned same sd. Jenkins.)

The reference on page 532 shows

Francis and Mary Vincent, 100 acres. N'ampton Co., 20 Mar. 1660, p. 425, (501) S. side Pungoteague River., Ely, upon a br. of same called Pocomock, Nly. upon land of Jno. Johnson, Negro, and Sly. Upon land of Nicolas Waddilow. Granted to Richard Johnson Negro 21 Nov. 1654.

Records show the black family of Johnson lived and owned land as late as the year 1660.[22]

While the Northampton County records provided vital information, this researcher found in "Torrence" that sixty-two people of the name Johnson died in that county between 1658–1800, leaving wills and inventories. No Antoney was listed, but if he disposed of his property before his death, it would have been expected and logical that he left no will and inventory. But the very great number of Johnsons makes a detailed search absolutely necessary. Evidence can be built not only on the positive notes but also on statements that documentation has not been found; for example, if a Johnson is found owning land which was part of the tract once owned by a member of Antoney Johnson's family and no deed is found showing how he acquired it, the conclusion genealogically would be that the person was a descendant of Antoney Johnson.

All of this would require hours of checking and cross-checking. One way to make this kind of research more rewarding would be to publish all wills, deeds, and orders (in abstract form) for Northampton County, Virginia, from about 1632 to about 1800. With this information in print (indexed), studies could continue for a long period trying to identify distinctly the various Johnsons.

In addition to the Johnsons, I have located another early black landowner in Virginia. He was Emanuel Cambow, who was granted fifty acres in James City County on April 18, 1667; however, the James City records have been almost totally destroyed and there is little hope of tracing his descendants.

Although there are major problems involved in pursuing information on the descendants of the first black English-speaking settlers in America, the researcher must keep in mind that where genealogy is concerned, with persistence many of these problems can be solved.

SUMMARY

A lay person can do some independent searching and need not be an expert in this field or a historian. The most important thing is to go back as far as possible in the searching, which is occasionally painful and requires infinite patience. Black searchers may find it helpful to understand some of the history that has provided the resources that will aid them. I have found a vast amount of strength and stability in my own black family, from its arrival in America to this day. Evidence of my successful research on the Blockson family is demonstrated in the book, *Black Genealogy*.[23]

NOTES

1. James D. Walker, *Black Genealogy: How to Begin* (Athens: The University of Georgia Center for Continuing Education, 1977), p. 2.

2. This drama was a television adaptation of Ernest J. Gaines, *The Autobiography of Miss Jane Pittman* (New York: Dial Press, 1971).

3. Maxwell Whiteman, "Black Genealogy: Problems, Sources, Methodology," *RQ* 11 (Summer 1972), p. 311.

4. Charles L. Blockson, with Ron Fry, *Black Genealogy* (Englewood Cliffs, N.J.: Prentice-Hall, 1977), p. 4.

5. Debra L. Newman, *List of Free Black Heads of Families in the First Census of the United States, 1790*, Special List no. 34 (Washington, D.C.: National Archives and Records Service, 1973).

6. *New York Age*, 25 July 1912.

7. Walker, *Black Genealogy: How to Begin*, pp. 11–12.

8. Ibid., pp. 42–49.

9. Blockson, *Black Genealogy*, pp. 69–77.

10. Carter G. Woodson, ed., *Free Negro Heads of Families in the United States in 1830* (Washington, D.C.: Association for the Study of Negro Life and History, 1925); *Free Negro Owners of Slaves in the United States in 1830, Together with Absentee Ownership of Slaves in the United States in 1830* (Washington, D.C.: Association for the Study of Negro Life and History, 1924; reprint ed., New York: Negro Universities Press, 1968).

11. Meredith Bright Colket and Frank T. Bridgers, *Guide to Genealogical Records in the National Archives* (Washington, D.C.: National Archives and Records Service, 1964). See also recent updated edition, *Guide to Genealogical Research in the National Archives*.

12. "Registration of Free Negroes Commencing September Court 1822" and "Register of Free Blacks 1835, Book 3 (1822–61)," edited and indexed by Donald Sweig (Providence, R. I.: Black Heritage Society, n.d.).

13. Debra L. Newman, *List of Black Servicemen Compiled from the War Department Collection of Revolutionary War Records*, Record Group 93 (Washington, D.C.: National Archives and Records Service, 1974).

14. United States Adjutant General's Office, *The Negro in the Military Services of the United States, 1639–1886: A Compilation of Official Records, State Papers, Historical Extracts, Etc., Relating to His Military Status and Service from the Date of His Introduction into the British North American Colonies*, Record Group 94, Adjutant General (Washington, D.C.: National Archives and Records Service, 1973, available on microfilm).

15. United States Adjutant General's Office, *Index to Compiled Service Records of Volunteer Union Soldiers Who Served with the United States Colored Troops* (Washington, D.C.: National Archives and Records Service, 1964; microfilm publication).

16. William Still, *The Underground Railroad* (Philadelphia: Porter and Coates, 1872; reprint ed., New York: Arno Press, 1969); Wilbur H. Seibert, *The Underground Railroad from Slavery to Freedom* (New York: Macmillan Co., 1898; reprint ed., New York: Russell and Russell, 1967).

17. Freedmen's Savings and Trust Company (Washington, D.C.), *Registers of Signatures of Depositors in Branches of the Freedmen's Savings and Trust Company, 1865–   * (Washington, D.C.: National Archives and Records Service, 1969; available on microfilm).

18. *Register of Practitioners of Medicine and Surgery*, Records of the Department of Internal Affairs, 1859–1969, Record Group 14, Pennsylvania State Archives.

19. Blockson, *Black Genealogy*, p. 93.

20. Benjamin Drew, *A North-Side View of Slavery: The Refugees, or The Narratives of Fugitive Slaves in Canada Related by Themselves, with an Account of the History and Condition of the Colored Population of Upper Canada* (Boston: J. P. Jewett and Co., 1856).

21. Blockson, *Black Genealogy*, pp. 115–16.

22. Annie L. Jester, ed., *Adventures of Purse and Persons in Virginia, 1607–27*, 2d ed. (Richmond, Va.: Order of First Families of Virginia, 1964).

23. Reference to the Blockson family appears on pages 7–9 and 20–21 of *Black Genealogy*.

BIBLIOGRAPHY

Books, Articles, and Monographs

Abajian, James de T., ed. *Blacks in Selected Newspapers, Censuses and Other Sources; an Index to Names and Subjects*. Boston: G. K. Hall and Co., 1977.

Extracts names of blacks listed in certain newspapers, census reports and other documents.

The American Slave: A Composite Autobiography. Edited by George P. Rawick. 19 vols. Westport, Conn.: Greenwood Press, 1972.

A collection of transcriptions of slave narratives prepared by the Federal Writers' Project in the 1930s and deposited in the Library of Congress.

Amistad Research Center, Fisk University. *Author and Added Entry Catalog of the American Missionary Association Archives*. 3 vols. Westport, Conn.: Greenwood Press, 1970.

The Amistad Center is now located at Dillard University, New Orleans. The catalog guides the researcher to the valuable archives of the American Missionary Association and its early activities with blacks.

Atlanta University, Trevor Arnett Library. *Guide to Manuscripts and Archives in the Negro Collection of Trevor Arnett Library, Atlanta University*. Atlanta, Ga., 1971.

Useful guide to the library's notable collection of primary source materials.

Beard, Timothy Field. "Black American Ancestry." In *How to Find Your Family Roots*. New York: McGraw-Hill Book Co., 1977, pp. 125–34.

A brief description of how the researcher traces black ancestry through the slavery period, with a discussion of free blacks. Several important published sources, black societies, and black history organizations are identified.

———. "Black Ancestry." In *How to Find Your Family Roots*. New York: McGraw-Hill Book Co., 1977, pp. 274–88.

A list of sources to help the researcher. Includes guides, general sources, and a state-by-state list of selected resources on black genealogy.

Beasley, Delilah L. *The Negro Trail Blazer of California*. Los Angeles: Times Mirror Printing and Binding House, 1919.

A compilation of records of the California archives, Bancroft Library, and University of California, Berkeley, as well as diaries, old papers, and conversations of pioneers in California.

Beltran, G. Aguirre. "Tribal Origins of Slaves in Mexico." *Journal of Negro History* 31 (July 1946): 269–352.

Useful to the genealogist in locating records and accounts of slaves in Mexico and their origins. How the ancient Roman practice of indicating on slave contracts the origin of their captivity survived, and accounts of such record-keeping practices relating to African slaves in Mexico.

Bentley, George R. *A History of the Freedmen's Bureau*. Philadelphia: Octagon Books, 1970.

Provides useful information on the Bureau of Refugees, Freedmen, and Abandoned Lands. Records include marriage, birth, and other vital information on blacks.

Berlin, Ira. *Slaves Without Masters*. New York: Pantheon Books, 1974.

Contains information on blacks as slaves and a bibliography which leads the researcher to additional information useful for black genealogy.

Blassingame, John W. *The Slave Community: Plantation Life in the Ante-Bellum South*. New York: Oxford University Press, 1972.

Describes and analyzes the life of the black slave and the slave's African heritage, culture, religion, behavior, family, and personality. Good selected bibliography (pp. 239–54). Useful for understanding what slave communities were like.

Blockson, Charles L. *Pennsylvania's Black History*. Philadelphia: Portfolio Associates, 1975.

A history of blacks in Pennsylvania.

———. *The Underground Railroad in Pennsylvania*. Jacksonville, N.C.: Flame International, 1980.

A county-by-county delineation of the black role in the underground railroad operations of a key state. Pennsylvania State University is preparing a film based on the work.

————, with Fry, Ron. *Black Genealogy*. Englewood Cliffs, N.J.: Prentice-Hall, Inc., 1977.

An explanation of the steps which the researcher should take in discovering his or her family's roots. Includes tracing ancestors through an eventful past, as far back as a specific African kingdom. Sources which should be used and problems which one may encounter in the search are included. The appendixes give sources by state and by African country (in a single alphabet), a list of newspapers, and a bibliography on black genealogical sources.

Brigano, Russell Carl. *Black Americans in Autobiography: An Annotated Bibliography of Autobiographies and Autobiographical Books Written Since the Civil War*. Durham: Duke University Press, 1974.

Excellent biographical information. Some slave narratives.

Brown, Barbara W., and Rose, James M. *Black Roots in Southeastern Connecticut, 1650–1900*. Detroit: Gale Research Co., 1980.

An alphabetical list (one with black surnames and one for blacks who had no surnames), as well as a section on unidentified blacks (arranged by town). Gives numerous records and resources.

Brown, Letitia Woods. *Free Negroes in the District of Columbia, 1790–1846*. New York: Oxford University Press, 1972.

Traces the history of free blacks in the District of Columbia.

Burger, Michele. "How to Trace Your Family Tree." *Ebony* 32 (July 1977): 52–54.

Instructs the researcher on how to begin a genealogical study and advises that patience, skill, and luck are the keys to successful pursuit. Well illustrated with pictures of family trees, a slave shack, a black family reunion, and other scenes.

Campbell, Stanley W. *The Slave Catchers: Enforcement of the Fugitive Slave Law, 1850–1860*. Chapel Hill: University of North Carolina Press, 1970.

Gives names of some slaves.

Catterall, Helen T., ed. *Judicial Cases Concerning American Slavery and the Negro*. Carnegie Institution of Washington, publication no. 374. Papers of the Division of Historical Research. 5 vols. Washington: Carnegie Publications, 1926–37; New York: Negro Universities Press, 1968.

Includes numerous manumission records, court records on blacks, and other information which relates to slavery.

Chicago Public Library, George Cleveland Hall Branch. *The Chicago Afro-American Union Analytic Catalog: An Index to Materials on the Afro-American in the Principal Libraries of Chicago*. Housed in the Vivian G. Harsh Collection of Afro-American History and Literature at the George Cleveland Hall Branch of the Chicago Public Library. 5 vols. Boston: G. K. Hall and Co., 1972.

Extensive analytical guide to black resources in the Hall Branch of the Chicago Public Library.

Clifton, Lucille. *Generation*. New York: Random House, 1976.

A story of the author's ancestors from Dahomey.

Conneau, Theophile. *A Slaver's Log Book, or Twenty Years' Residence in Africa: The Original Manuscript*. Englewood Cliffs, N.J.: Prentice-Hall, 1976.

A transcribed personal narrative of the African slave trade.

Day, Beth Feagles. *Sexual Life Between Blacks and Whites*. New York: World Publishing Co., 1972.

Describes miscegenation.

Donald, Henderson H. *The Negro Freedman: Life Conditions of the American Negro in the Early Years After Emancipation*. New York: Cooper Square, 1952.

Discusses marriage and family life, learning how to earn a living, social classes and traits, religious customs and other activities, and situations blacks encountered once they were freed.

Donnan, Elizabeth, ed. *Documents Illustrative of the History of the Slave Trade in America.* 4 vols. Carnegie Institute of Washington Publication no. 409. Washington, D.C.: Carnegie Institute 1930–   ; reprint ed., New York: Octagon Books, 1965.

An excellent reference to slave trade information, including some slave ship manifests.

Dover, Cedric, *Half-Caste.* London: Martin, M. Secker and Warbury, 1937.

Discusses miscegenation and race problems.

Drew, Benjamin. *A North-Side View of Slavery: The Refugee, or The Narratives of Fugitive Slaves in Canada Related by Themselves, with an Account of the History and Condition of the Colored Population of Upper Canada.* Boston: J. P. Jewett and Co., 1856.

An account of slavery in the United States and the condition of fugitive slaves in Canada.

DuBois, W.E.B. *The Philadelphia Negro.* Philadelphia: published for the University of Pennsylvania, 1899.

An inquiry into the condition of blacks in Philadelphia, as gleaned from field work in meetings, churches, and schools and visits with families. Important for early history of blacks in Philadelphia.

Eichholz, Alice, ed. *Free Black Heads of Households in the New York State Federal Census, 1790–1830.* Detroit: Gale Research Co., 1981.

By 1830 all blacks who lived in New York were counted as free. This work is an alphabetical index of names of all free black heads of households in New York who are recorded in census reports for 1790, 1800, 1810, 1820, and 1830.

Fisk University. *Dictionary Catalog of the Negro Collection of Fisk University Library.* 6 vols. Boston: G. K. Hall and Co., 1974.

A catalog of one of the nation's most important collections of black resources. Primary resources which are included in the library are omitted from the list.

Flanders, Ralph Betts. *The Free Negro in Ante-Bellum Georgia.* Bell and Howell Black Culture Collection, no. 564–2. Wooster, Ohio: Bell and Howell, 1938.

A history of free blacks in Georgia.

Franklin, John Hope. *The Free Negro in North Carolina, 1790–1860.* 1942; reprint ed., New York: W. W. Norton Co., 1971.

A history of free blacks in North Carolina.

Frazier, Edward Franklin. *The Free Negro Family.* Nashville, Fisk University Press, 1932; reprint ed., New York: Arno Press, 1968.

Gammon, Tim. "The Black Freedmen of the Cherokee Nation." *Negro History Bulletin* 40 (July 1977): 732–35.

Reviews the 1866 treaty between the United States and the Cherokee Indians, which had great ramifications for the freedmen. Subsequent provisions of the act are also related. Important in the study of the relationship between blacks and Indians.

Gordon, Taylor. *Born to Be Free.* New York: Covici-Friede, 1929.

A story of the author's life in a black community in White Sulphur Springs, Montana.

A Guide to the Microfilm Publication of the Papers of the Abolition Society. Prepared by Jeffery Nordlinger Bumbrey. Philadelphia: Pennsylvania Abolition Society and Historical Society of Pennsylvania, 1976.

An important source for locating papers of abolition societies. The work of these societies, represented in their papers, preserved many experiences of slaves and free blacks.

Haley, Alex. "Black History, Oral History and Genealogy." *Oral History Review* (1973): 1–25.

Discusses black genealogical research and use of oral history in the research process.

———. "How to Trace Your Heritage to Africa: The Voice of Experience." *World Conference on Records* (2d, 1980) vol. 11, no. 903. Salt Lake City: Corporation of the President of the Church of Jesus Christ of Latter-day Saints. c1980.

The author relates his experiences in tracing his ancestors to Africa.

———. "My Furthest-Back Person—The African." *New York Times Magazine,* 16 July 1972, pp. 13–16.

Describes the steps used in tracing the author's ancestry.

————. *Roots: The Saga of an American Family.* New York: Doubleday and Co., 1976.

A saga of the author's family, which illustrates how one can trace a family back to Africa. Sources and types of records researched and the use of oral history in the genealogical search are especially important.

————. "What Roots Means to Me." *Reader's Digest* 110 (May 1977): 73–76.

An account of the author's feelings about the significance of the book *Roots* and its popularity among readers, including beginning and experienced genealogists.

Hampton Institute, Collis P. Huntington Memorial Library. *Dictionary Catalog of the George Foster Peabody Collection.* 2 vols. Westport, Conn.: Greenwood Press, 1972.

Valuable guide to the library's special black collection. Important slavery pamphlets, manuscripts, archives, and oral interviews with former slaves are in the collection but excluded from the catalog.

Harper, C. W. "House Servants and Field Hands: Fragmentation in the Antebellum Slave Community." *North Carolina Historical Review* 55 (January 1978): 42–59.

Useful for study of slave life.

Harris, Mark. "America's Oldest Interracial Community." *Negro Digest* 6 (July 1948): 21–24.

An account of a group known as the Jackson Whites, who lived in and around northern Westchester County, New York, and in eastern New Jersey in the 1790s. The group included Indians, West Indians, American blacks, Germans, and British.

Howard University. *A Catalogue of the African Collection in the Moorland Foundation.* Boston: G. K. Hall and Co., 1970.

Guide to the library's collection of Africana.

————, Founders Library, Moorland Foundation. *Dictionary Catalog of the Arthur B. Spingarn Collection of Negro Authors.* 2 vols. Boston: G. K. Hall and Co., 1970.

Important guide to works by black authors.

————. *Dictionary Catalog of the Jesse E. Moorland Collection of Negro Life and History.* 9 vols. Boston: G. K. Hall and Co., 1970. First supplement. 3 vols., 1976.

An index to the secondary resources on blacks which are in the library's special collections. The collections are now located in the Moorland-Spingarn Research Center within the library facility. The extensive collection of manuscripts and archives, including the black press archives, is omitted from the catalog.

Index to Black Newspapers: First Quarter, 1980. Wooster, Ohio: Indexing Center, Bell and Howell, 1980.

Especially important for historians and genealogists. Compiled from the final editions of several black newspapers, such as the *Amsterdam News, St. Louis Argus, Atlanta Daily World, Baltimore Afro-American, Chicago Bililian News, Chicago Defender, Cleveland Call and Post, Los Angeles Sentinel, Michigan Chronicle,* and *Pittsburgh Courier.* In two parts— Subject and Personal Names. Local, regional, state, national, and international news articles are indexed. Available from Indexing Center, Micro Photo Division, Bell and Howell, Old Mansfield Road, Wooster, OH 44691.

Jacobs, Donald M., ed., assisted by Paley, Heath, et al. *Antebellum Black Newspapers: Indices to "New York Freedom's Journal" (1827–29), "The Rights of All" (1829), "The Weekly Advocate" (1837), and "The Colored American" (1837–41).* Westport, Conn.: Greenwood Press, 1976.

Contains subject and name indexes. Useful for genealogical information on early blacks.

Johnson, James Weldon. *Black Manhattan.* New York: Alfred A. Knopf, 1930.

Etches the background of blacks in New York, including Harlem. Covers slaves and freedmen, education, religious life, the Civil War, and other topics. Important for a view of early black life in New York.

Johnston, James Hugo. "Documentary Evidence of the Relations of Negroes and Indians." *Journal of Negro History* 14 (January 1929): 21–43.

Useful for tracing mixtures of blacks and Indians in various states.

Kemble, Frances Anne. *Journal of a Resident on a Georgian Plantation in 1838–1839*. New York: Harper's and Brothers, 1863.

A diary which records conditions of slaves. Useful for a view of slave life.

Landon, Frank. "The Negro Migration to Canada After the Fugitive Slave Act." *Journal of Negro History* 5 (January 1920): 22–36.

Discusses exodus of fugitive slaves to Canada after President Millard Fillmore signed the Fugitive Slave Bill on 18 September 1851.

Lewis, Shawn. "A Journey Back Home." *Ebony* 31 (August 1976): 74.

Relates the story of Gladys Pinderhughes, an eighty-three-year-old great-grandmother who traced her roots back to Africa.

The National Union Catalog of Manuscript Collections. Ann Arbor, Mich.: J.W. Edwards, 1959–61.

Guides the researcher to manuscript collections and some oral histories in various libraries in the United States.

"The Negro Boy Alfred." In "Everybody's Search for Roots." *Newsweek* 90 (July 4, 1977): 28.

A brief account of Alfred Low, a slave and the great-grandfather of a persistent black researcher who identified her relative after searching the county clerk's office in Athens, Georgia, and also the records in the University of Georgia Library.

The Negro Soldier: A Select Compilation. New York: Negro Universities Press, 1970.

Discusses the loyalty and devotion of blacks in the Revolution and the War of 1812, employment of blacks in the army of the Revolution, and services of blacks in other early U.S. wars, 1641–1815.

Negro Year Book and Annual Encyclopedia of the Negro. Tuskegee, Ala.: Negro Year Book Co., 1912–52.

Slight variations appear in titles of the editions. The yearbooks are useful to the genealogist for their accounts of the achievements of blacks as well as for a discussion of the social conditions of blacks in the United States, in Africa, in Europe, and in Latin America.

Newman, Debra L. *List of Free Black Heads of Families in the First Census of the United States, 1790*. Special List no. 34. Washington, D.C.: National Archives and Records Service, 1973.

A list of free black heads of families compiled mainly, though not entirely, from the printed volumes of the 1790 census. Arranged alphabetically by state and then alphabetically by name of head of the family. Also indicates number of persons in the family.

Nichols, Charles H. *Many Thousands Gone: The Ex-Slaves' Accounts of Their Bondage and Freedom*. Bloomington: Indiana University Press, 1969.

A collection of slave narratives.

North Carolina Central University, School of Library Science, African-American Materials Project. *Newspapers and Periodicals by and About Black People: Southeastern Library Holdings*. Boston: G. K. Hall and Co., 1978.

A preliminary listing of Afro-American historical materials such as newspapers and periodicals, pre-1950 imprints, archival collections, manuscripts, theses in certain academic libraries, collections in state departments of archives and history, public libraries, historical societies, museums, and some military installations. Six southern states are represented: Virginia, North Carolina, South Carolina, Georgia, Alabama, and Tennessee.

Olmsted, Frederick Law. *The Cotton Kingdom: A Traveller's Observations on Cotton and Slavery in the American Slave States. Based upon Three Former Volumes of Journeys and Investigations*. 2 vols. New York: Mason Brothers, 1861.

An account of slavery, economic conditions, and cotton manufacturing in southern states. Also discusses life on the plantation.

———. *A Journey in the Seaboard Slave States, with Remarks on Their Economy*. New York: Mason Brothers, 1861.

A discussion of slavery and economic conditions in the South, based on data gathered during travels there.

Peebles, Minnie. "Black Genealogy." *North Carolina Historical Review* 55 (April 1978): 164–73.

Instructs the beginning researcher on how to proceed with genealogical study. Explains how to trace free blacks and where such records are located in North Carolina, also how to trace descendants of slaves and where the necessary information can be found. Concludes with a discussion of the problems the author encountered in tracing her father's lines.

Penn, Irvine G. *The Afro-American Press and Its Editions.* 1891; reprint ed., New York: Arno Press, 1969.

Useful for early history of the black press and for biographies and photographs of the journalists. Blacks who wrote for white as well as black newspapers and periodicals are included.

Philadelphia Library Company. *Afro-Americans, 1553–1906: Author Catalog of the Library Company of Philadelphia and the Historical Society of Pennsylvania.* Boston: G. K. Hall and Co., 1973.

Lists works on slavery, blacks in the United States, and other important bibliographies.

Porter, Dorothy, comp. *Early Negro Writing, 1760–1837.* Boston: Beacon Press, 1971.

Useful for examples of works of early black societies and organizations, including early speeches, sermons, and slave narratives.

————, comp. *The Negro in the United States, a Selected Bibliography.* Washington, D.C.: Library of Congress, 1970.

A selective bibliography on a variety of topics, such as the urban Negro, race relations, politics, education, religion, social conditions, biography, and history in the collection at the Library of Congress. Entries are in alphabetical order under broad subject headings, and in most instances brief annotations are given.

Porter, Kenneth Wiggins. "John Caesar: Seminole Negro Partisan." *Journal of Negro History* 31 (April 1946): 190–207.

An account of black participation in the Seminole War. Presents the work of Negro chiefs and warriors and documents the mixture of blacks and Indians.

Puckett, Newbell Niles, comp. *Black Names in America: Origins and Usage.* Edited by Murray Heller. Boston: G. K. Hall and Co., 1975.

Gives black names and naming practices. Useful for developing an understanding of the social values related to naming of blacks. Includes lists of early names (1619–1799) and names of slaves and free blacks (1804–64), a dictionary of African origins, an index of unusual names, and a bibliography that includes the principal sources used to select the names.

"Registration of Free Negroes Commencing September Court 1822" and "Register of Free Blacks 1835, Book 3" (1822–61). Edited and indexed by Donald Sweig. Providence, R.I.: Black Heritage Society, n.d.

"Every free negro or mulatto" in Virginia in 1793 was required to register with the county clerk for the district in which he or she lived. Registration included a physical description, with such details as age, height, identifying marks, and scars. The mother's name (if free-born) or the name of the emancipator (if freed) was also given. A useful resource in tracing one's roots in Virginia.

"A Remarkable Negro Family." *Southern Workman* (October 1925):449–59.

Presents the story of a farm family (the Hubert family of Springfield, Georgia) which contributed significantly to the material progress of Georgia and of the nation. Well illustrated. Important example of the progress of a black family.

Reuter, Edward B. *The Mulatto in the United States: Including a Study of the Role of Mixed-Blood Races Throughout the World.* Boston: R. G. Badger, 1918; New York: Johnson Reprint, 1970.

Lists numerous persons who were identified as mulattoes during the early part of the twentieth century.

Roderick, Thomas H. "Negro Genealogy." *American Genealogist* 47 (1971): 88–91.

Rose, James, and Eichholz, Alice. *Black Genesis.* Detroit: Gale Research Co., 1978.

Designed to stimulate an interest in black family ancestry among novices, to encourage black genealogical research, and to help researchers reexamine history. Includes some narratives of various records and record sources, but is basically a state-by-state list of primary and secondary resources useful for black genealogy.

Russell, John. "The Free Negroes in Virginia." Johns Hopkins University Studies no. 8. Baltimore: Johns Hopkins University, 1913, pp. 9–194.

An account of free blacks in Virginia.

Sanders, Edith Green. *Black Genealogy: An Annotated Bibliography*. Atlanta: Samuel Williams Special Collections, Atlanta Public Library, 1978.

Gives steps for tracing black heritage through genealogy and explains classification numbers for locating genealogical materials in the Williams Collection. Includes an annotated list of books and periodical articles on black genealogy, audio-visual aids, related sources outside the library, and a brief list of organizations and associations on black genealogy.

Savage, W. Sherman. "The Negro on the Mining Frontier." *Journal of Negro History* 30 (January 1945): 30–46.

Useful account of frontier history and the presence of blacks in the early West. The genealogist will find several names mentioned in this article.

Scarupa, Harriet Jackson. "Black Genealogy." *Essence* 7 (July 1976): 56.

A beginner's guide to searching for black ancestry and other information about the past. Includes information on how to prepare for the search, where to begin, and how to utilize various resources.

Schatz, Walter, ed. *Directory of Afro-American Resources*. New York: R. R. Bowker Co., 1970.

Arranged geographically by state, then by city, then by institution within the city. Describes manuscript, archival, and book collections on black subjects in academic, public, and special libraries. Useful for locating primary resources for black genealogical research.

Seibert, Wilbur H. *The Underground Railroad from Slavery to Freedom*. New York: Macmillan, 1898; reprint ed., New York: Russell and Russell, 1967.

A comprehensive history of the underground railroad. Includes a list of important fugitive slave cases.

Simmons, William Johnson. *Men of Mark*. Cleveland: G. M. Rewell and Co., 1887; reprint ed., New York: Arno Press, 1968.

Gives biographies of prominent black men of the nineteenth century.

Slave Testimony: Two Centuries of Letters, Speeches, Interviews, and Autobiographies. Edited by John W. Blassingame. Baton Rouge: Louisiana State University Press, 1977.

Presents testimonies of blacks on the slave condition. Combines in one volume several different kinds of slave sources, such as letters written between 1736 and 1864, speeches, interviews conducted by journalists and others between 1824 and 1938, and autobiographies which appeared in periodicals and rare books between 1828 and 1878. Well illustrated with photographs of some slaves.

Smith, Jessie Carney. *Black Academic Libraries and Research Collections*. Westport, Conn.: Greenwood Press, 1977.

Some sections of the work are especially important for the genealogist. These include chapter 5, "Special Collections of Black Literature in Black Colleges," pp. 156–205; examples of black periodicals and newspapers, pp. 195–96; and bibliography, pp. 281–90.

Still, William. *The Underground Railroad*. 1872; reprint ed., New York: Arno Press, 1968.

A classic work on the history of the underground railroad.

Taylor, Quintard; Coleman, Ronald G.; and Lombard, R. T. J. "African Families: Black and White." *World Conference on Records* (2d, 1980) vol. 11, no. 902. Salt Lake City: Corporation of the President of the Church of Jesus Christ of Latter-day Saints, c1980.

Thompson, Era Bell. "The Vaughn Family: A Tale of Two Continents." *Ebony* 30 (February 1975): 53–58.

Presents the saga of some African and American descendants of former slaves who for over one hundred years have remained in contact with each other.

Uchendu, Victor; Kilson, Marion; and Thom, Derrick J. "West African Cultures: Past and Present." *World Conference on Records* (2d, 1980) vol. 11, no. 905. Salt Lake City: Corporation of the President of the Church of Jesus Christ of Latter-day Saints, c1980.

U.S. Library of Congress, Catalog Publication Division. *Newspapers in Microfilms: United States, 1948–1972.* Washington, D.C.: Library of Congress, 1973.

This extensive list includes black newspapers which have been microfilmed. Arranged by state and then by city. Title index included.

Voorhis, Harold Van Buren. *Negro Masonry in the United States.* New York: H. Emmerson, 1940.

History of the Freemasons in the United States. Provides important social and cultural documentation.

Walker, James D. *Black Genealogy: How to Begin.* Athens: University of Georgia, Center for Continuing Education, 1977.

Designed as an independent study course for television but serves as a useful and important guide to black genealogical research. Instructs the researcher on methodology, presents general research resources and sources of black genealogical records, and includes forms which the genealogist must use.

————. "U.S. Black Family History Resources: An Overview." *World Conference on Records* (2d, 1980) vol. 3 pt. 1, no. 304. Salt Lake City: Corporation of the President of the Church of Jesus Christ of Latter-day Saints, c1980.

Washington, Booker, T. *Up from Slavery.* New York: A. C. Burt, Page and Co., 1915.

Autobiography of a former slave who became a noted educator.

West, Earl H., comp. *A Bibliography of Doctoral Research on the Negro, 1933–1966.* Washington, D.C.: Xerox, 1969.

Though somewhat dated in terms of research on black Americans, the list is an excellent guide to studies on blacks, many of which are useful for genealogical research.

Woodson, Carter G., ed. *Free Negro Heads of Families in the United States in 1830.* Washington, D.C.: Association for the Study of Negro Life and History, 1925.

Lists free black heads of household.

————. *Free Negro Owners of Slaves in the United States in 1830, Together with Absentee Ownership of Slaves in the United States in 1830.* 1924; reprint ed., New York: Negro Universities Press, 1968.

Lists free blacks who owned slaves.

Periodicals

The following selected list of black periodicals will aid the researcher in obtaining information on individual blacks and their families, history, and medical problems, and on similar topics. This listing supplements the journals given later in this chapter as publications of various organizations.

CLA Journal, Morehouse College, Atlanta, GA 30314

Official publication of the College Language Association. Founded 1957. Important source for examples of black writing. Quarterly.

The Crisis, 1790 Broadway, New York, NY 10019

Organ of the National Association for the Advancement of Colored People. Founded 1910. Publications include biographical information and other genealogical and historical information. Monthly from October to May and bimonthly June-July, August-September.

Ebony, Johnson Publishing Company, 820 South Michigan Avenue, Chicago, IL 60605

Founded 1945. Includes articles on genealogy, black history, book reviews, and other information on black Americans. Monthly.

Journal of Negro Education, Howard University, Washington, DC 20009

Founded 1932. Publishes articles on black education, history, and culture; book reviews. Quarterly.

The Journal of Negro History, Association for the Study of Afro-American Life and History, 1401 14th Street, N.W., Washington, DC 20005

> Founded 1916. Publishes articles on black themes. Especially good for relationship between blacks and other ethnic groups. Good for the genealogist. Quarterly.

Journal of Afro-American Historical and Genealogical Society, Box 13086, T Street Station, Washington, DC 20009

> Founded 1980. Free with membership in the Afro-American Historical and Genealogical Society. Presents materials on Afro-American history and genealogy and includes reviews of books and periodicals related to the society's interests.

The Negro History Bulletin, Association for the Study of Afro-American Life and History, 1401 14th Street, N.W., Washington, DC 20005

> Founded 1937. A news organ; publishes brief articles on or about the black American experience. Monthly except June, August, and September.

Opportunity

> A journal of the National Urban League. Vols. 1–27 published 1923–49. Although discontinued, this periodical is especially useful for articles by black Americans. Also gives information on housing and other problems blacks encountered during the existence of the publication.

Newspapers

One of the most important sources of information on black genealogy is the black newspaper. The work of the black press was launched in 1827, when John B. Russwurm and Samuel E. Cornish published the first black newspaper, *Freedom's Journal,* as an organ aimed toward eradicating slavery. From that time forward the number of black newspapers increased; however, many have since ceased publication. Black newspapers have been influential in both black and mainstream America and have addressed a variety of themes including race relations and the progress of the black race, black life, black society, and black accomplishments in the arts and in sports. In particular, those areas which help to identify names, events, and dates useful for tracing one's ancestry or for assessing the flavor of the country and of black life in earlier times include black churches, colleges, and schools; black lodges and fraternal organizations; and biographical information on black people. For a full account of the black press, its influence, and the contents of early black newspapers and periodicals, the following works should be consulted.

Detweiler, Frederick G. *The Negro Press in the United States.*
> College Park, Md.: McGrath Publishing Co., 1968.

Oak, Vishnu V. *The Negro Newspaper.* New York: Negro Universities Press, 1948.

Penn, I. Garland. *The Afro-American Press and Its Editors.* 1891; reprint ed., New York: New York Times/Arno Press, 1969.

Wolseley, Ronald E. *The Black Press, U.S.A.* Ames: Iowa State University Press, 1971.

The chronological listing of selected black newspapers which follows parallels that given in Oak's *The Negro Newspaper.* The list includes some newspapers which were affiliated with church denominations (and supported by church members) and others which were published for commercial reasons or to meet the needs of other special groups. Dates of founding and demise are included in parentheses; some post–Civil War newspapers are still published.

ANTEBELLUM NEWSPAPERS

For the most part, black newspapers published during this period were founded by influential black men. These newspapers were short-lived and were published from two months to five years. Only the *North Star* survived for a longer period of time.

Freedom's Journal (1827–30); subsequently changed to *Rights of All.* Founded by John B. Russwurm and Samuel E. Cornish.

Weekly Advocate (1837–42); subsequently changed to the *Colored American*. Founded by Phillip A. Bell and edited by Samuel R. Cornish. Continued the work of *Freedom's Journal* in the crusade against slavery.

Elevator (1842). Published in Albany by Stephen Myers.

Clarion (1842). Successor to the *National Watchman;* published in Troy, New York, by Henry Highland Garnett.

National Watchman (1842). Published in Troy, New York, by William G. Allen and Henry Highland Garnett.

Mystery (1843). Published in Pittsburgh by Martin R. Delaney.

Genius of Freedom (1846?). Published in New York by David Ruggles.

North Star (1847–64). Founded in Rochester by Frederick Douglass; in 1850 renamed *Frederick Douglass' Paper*. Published weekly.

Imperial Citizen (1848). Founded in Syracuse by Samuel Ringgold Ward.

Colored Man's Journal (1851). Founded by Louis H. Putnam in New York.

Alienated American (1852). Founded in Cleveland, Ohio, by W.H.H. Day.

Mirror of the Times (1855). Founded in San Francisco by Mifflin W. Gibbs; later merged into the *Pacific Appeal* (1862).

Colored American (1865). The name by which the *Weekly Advocate* was known from two months after its founding. The paper is more commonly known under the title *Colored American*. It was the first black newspaper founded in the South.

POST–CIVIL WAR (1866) TO WORLD WAR I

Black newspapers founded during the 1866–1918 period emerged in almost every state. Like their forerunners, some were short-lived, but some lasted for many years and a few of these are still published. Examples of these newspapers are

Savannah Tribune (1875).

Philadelphia Tribune (1884 to date).

New York Age (1885).

Colorado Statesman (1890).

Afro-American (national, 1882 to date).

Dallas Express (1892).

Houston Informer (1893).

Indianapolis Recorder (1893).

California Eagle (1897).

Kansas City Plaindealer (1899).

Norfolk Journal and Guide (1900 to date).

Boston Guardian (1901).

Chicago Defender (1905 to date).

Nashville Globe and Independent (1906).

Amsterdam News (1909 to date).

Pittsburgh Courier (1910 to date).

St. Louis Argus (1912).

Carolina Times (1919).

Kansas City Call (1919 to date).

WORLD WAR I TO PRESENT

The rise and fall of black newspapers continued during the post–World War I era. Several which had been established during the post-Civil War–World War I period continued, and some are in existence today. Some became dailies, and several joined affiliates which helped to preserve them as successful business ventures. Examples are

Oklahoma Eagle (1920).

Cleveland Call and Post (1921 to date).

Detroit Tribune (1922).

Florida Times (1923).

Atlanta World (1928). Subsequently changed to *Atlanta Daily World;* became a semiweekly, then a
triweekly, and finally a daily.

Louisville Defender (1933 to date).

Harlem Heights Daily Citizen (1934). Suspended after three months.

Los Angeles Sentinel (1934 to date).

Iowa Observer (1936).

Informer and Sentinel (New Orleans, 1939).

Los Angeles Tribune (1940).

CONFERENCES AND TRAINING PROGRAMS

Research indicates that a number of libraries, museums, historical societies, genealogical societies, and other organizations and institutions sponsor public programs to train persons in genealogical research methods, to discuss local and family history projects, and to review topics of interest.
Some focus on basic genealogical study and offer sections or courses on black or Afro-American
genealogy. Programs of this nature are offered at Stamford University; the World Conference on
Records (both of its conferences to date), sponsored by the Genealogical Society of Utah; the
National Genealogical Society; the National Archives; Brigham Young University; and others previously discussed in chapter 2.

Among the courses sponsored in recent years, or continuing, which focus or have focused wholly
on black genealogy, are those sponsored by the Afro-American Genealogical and Historical Society
(Chicago), The Afro-American Historical and Genealogical Society (Washington), The Fred Hart
Williams Genealogical Society (Detroit), and the Rhode Island Black Heritage Society (Providence).
Others are listed as follows.

Afro-American Family History Association, 2077 Bent Creek Way, S.W., Atlanta, GA 30338
Carole Merritt, President
Maintains a Genealogical Study Group for the beginning as well as for the experienced
researcher in black genealogy. (See also list of Afro-American Historical Societies which
follows this discussion.)

Afro-American Family History Project, Grassroots Genealogy Workshop, Afro-American Genealogy, North Carolina Agricultural and Technical State University, Greensboro, NC 27411
Tommie M. Young, Director
Funded by the North Carolina Humanities Committee. Designed to assist in "grassroots"
genealogy with a series of statewide workshops, lectures, discussions, and practical activities
related to tracing and documenting Afro-American family history. Focuses on African family
traditions, social forces and the African descendant in America, the role of the family in
confirmation of the sense of self-identity, and other topics.

Ethnic Materials Project, Burton Historical Collection, Detroit Public Library, 5201 Woodward
Avenue, Detroit, MI 48202
Margaret Ward, Field Archivist
Through a special fund, the library holds workshops on black genealogy, microfilms the
registers of Detroit's oldest black churches, has organized the Fred Hart Williams Genealogical Society to promote black family history, maintains oral history programs to record the
black experience in Detroit, collects photographs of black families, and engages in similar
activities.

Institute on Ethnic Genealogy for Librarians, Fisk University Library, Fisk University, Nashville,
TN 37203
Jessie Carney Smith, Director
Through a special fund the Fisk University Library in 1979 sponsored a training program for

librarians and library researchers and trained the participants to work with the public in locating materials on ethnic genealogy that are housed in libraries. Participants also became familiar with genealogical resources in various repositories. While the training program ended in 1980, the library continues to collect and disseminate information on similar training conferences, particularly those of special interest to librarians.

GENEALOGICAL SOCIETIES

Afro-American family history and genealogical societies merit thorough investigation by the researcher. Many local organizations which restrict themselves to community activities conduct vital work in the preservation of black history. Listed below are several societies which are becoming more popular and which serve as examples of the work that is being done to preserve and to promote black family history and genealogy.

Afro-American Family History Association, 2077 Bent Creek Way, S.W., Atlanta, GA 30338

Carole Merritt, President

Founded in May 1977. The first organization of its kind in Georgia, the association seeks to promote interest in African-American family history and genealogy through a series of programs of study, through collection and preservation of historical materials and publications, and through education. To meet its goals, the association sponsors numerous activities and ongoing projects. These include the following.

1. Quarterly meetings (January, April, July, and August) which focus on topics such as problems and concerns in black genealogy, uses and techniques of oral history, the black family in historical and sociological perspective, and black landownership.

2. Bills of Sale Project, initiated in 1978 as one of the association's first major activities. The project identifies slave bills of sale and other historical materials that refer to slaves, which are located in the archives of various libraries, agencies, and historical organizations in Georgia. Inventories and indices will be developed from the project to assist the researcher in locating originals and copies of bills of sale. Publication of the first index was scheduled for 1981.

3. Exhibition on the Black Family, scheduled for late 1981 at the Atlanta Public Library, the Atlanta Historical Society, and the Georgia Department of Archives and History. Funding for the planning phase was provided by the National Endowment for the Humanities. The exhibit's purpose is to demonstrate the significance of the black family's heritage through the display and interpretation of items such as photographs, written documents, and objects. Involved in the search for exhibit materials are individuals, families, church groups, institutions, and other organizations.

4. Genealogy Study, a forum for persons who are active in genealogical research which permits them to share their experiences and concerns with others. The Study Group is designed for persons with little or no genealogical research experience as well as for the seasoned researcher.

5. Tours, held during the July quarterly meetings and designed to provide participants with information and insights about historical cities that are excluded from or limited in commercial tours. The tours provide a unique perspective of the city visited by focusing on black historical sites and events. Quarterly newsletter.

The Afro-American Genealogical and Historical Society of Chicago, % DuSable Museum, 740 East 56th Place, Chicago, IL 60637

Contact Muriel B. Wilson

Founded August 1977 and focuses on black, and black and Indian family history and genealogy. Aims to preserve and perpetuate records of blacks and their ancestors, to encourage study of black family history and genealogy, to work in conjunction with the DuSable Museum and other black genealogical societies and black history organizations, to promote and publish genealogical materials and articles, to conduct research in black genealogy, to identify black landmarks (buildings), to hold conferences and workshops on black genealogy and history, to conduct programs on social and cultural events for children, and to establish a data bank on black American genealogical information, including a library on black genealogy. Newsletter.

Afro-American Historical and Genealogical Society, P.O. Box 13086, T Street Station, Washington, DC 20009

Charles Johnson, President

A chartered nonprofit organization founded in 1977 to promote scholarly Afro-American historical and genealogical endeavors. Presents workshops, seminars, and lectures for people of all ages and backgrounds who are interested in Afro-American history and genealogy. Meetings held six times a year, open to the public. Newsletter and journal, each published in winter, spring, summer, and fall.

Afro-American Institute of Ancestry, 10215 South Lafayette Avenue, Chicago, IL 60628

Contact Tony Burroughs

Founded September 23, 1976, but currently inactive. Activities scheduled to resume.

The Fred Hart Williams Genealogical Society, Burton Historical Collection, Detroit Public Library, 5201 Woodward Avenue, Detroit, MI 48202

De Witt S. Dykes, Jr., President

Has been functioning officially since November 1979. Promotes interest in, and makes available, information on researching and preserving Afro-American family history. Presents lectures by members and nonmembers with genealogical experience. Explores research and preservation projects which will be sponsored by the society, with particular emphasis on families and on establishment of black communities in Michigan. Solicits documents, newspapers, clippings, and family photographs for the Burton Historical Collection.

The society was named in honor of Fred Hart Williams (1882–1961), a descendant of a family which came to Detroit on the underground railroad. Williams was a pioneer in collecting and interpreting historical materials on black Americans in Michigan. Considered the Renaissance man of his era, he dedicated his many talents to civic, social, and cultural affairs and served his community as newspaperman, author, historian, and patron of the arts. Williams founded the E. Azalia Hackley Collection of the Detroit Public Library. Newsletter.

Parting Ways, The Museum of Afro-American Ethnohistory, Inc., P.O. Box 1976, 130 Court Street, Plymouth, MA 02360

Marjorie E. Anderson, Director

Preserves and promotes black family history.

The Rhode Island Black Heritage Society, One Hilton Street, Providence, RI 02905

Rowena Stewart, Director

Promotes and preserves study of black family history and black life and culture. Conducts exhibits and special projects which reflect traditional life styles and customs of the black community. Publishes the *Bulletin!* quarterly.

ORGANIZATIONS

Archives of older black organizations are important research resources for black genealogy. These resources may be housed in libraries or may remain in the hands of officers of the organizations. Examples of black American organizations follow.

Alpha Kappa Alpha Sorority, Inc., 5211 South Greenwood Avenue, Chicago, IL 60615

Founded 1908. A social organization which promotes the ideals of service and scholarship among college women and encourages high achievement among black women. Its quarterly publication, *The Ivy Leaf,* as well as its special series of profiles of black women, highlight the contributions of black women. Archives are in the Moorland-Spingarn Research Center, Howard University, Washington, D.C.

Alpha Phi Alpha Fraternity, Inc., 4432 Martin Luther King Drive, Chicago, IL 60653

Founded 1906. A fraternal organization for men which emphasizes social service, encourages high social, economic, and intellectual achievement, and prepares its members for usefulness in the cause of humanity. Publishes the *Sphinx* monthly.

Association for the Study of Afro-American Life and History (formerly the Association for the Study of Negro Life and History), 1401 14th Street, N.W., Washington, DC 20005

Founded 1915. Open for membership to historians, students, scholars, and others who are interested in the study of black and Afro-American history. Promotes scholarship and educational activities, racial unity, and publication and research on black themes. Publishes the *Negro History Bulletin* and the quarterly *Journal of Negro History*. Earlier issues of the journal often included genealogies of black families and other biographical information. In 1977 the association published "A Proposal for Local Genealogy Search" as a part of its Genealogy Search Program.

Delta Sigma Theta Sorority, Inc., 1707 New Hampshire Avenue, N.W., Washington, DC 20009

Founded 1913. Maintains a public service five-point program: educational development, economic development, community and international development, housing and urban development, and mental health. Also promotes scholarship and social action programs. Local programs are aimed toward community needs. Publishes *The Delta Journal*.

Frontiers International, Inc. (formerly Frontiers of America), 1901 West Girard Avenue, Philadelphia, PA 19130

Founded 1936. Dedicated to the basic concept of service to others. Engages in many activities, such as service to the needy and promotion of leadership in the community. Its "buddy" project aids in the cultural, scholastic, moral, and spiritual development of boys. Publishes *The Frontiersman*.

Kappa Alpha Psi Fraternity, Inc., 2320 North Broad Street, Philadelphia, PA 19132

Founded 1911. Unites college men in promoting spiritual, social, intellectual and moral welfare and in inspiring service in public interest. Publishes *Kappa Alpha Psi Journal*.

National Association for the Advancement of Colored People (NAACP), 1790 Broadway, New York, NY 11213

Founded 1909. Civil rights organization which aims to "end all barriers to racial justice and guarantee full equality of opportunity and achievement in the United States." Works to eliminate discrimination in housing, employment, education, legislation, sports, and other areas. Its numerous branches are concerned with problems in such areas of the community as health, education, youth, and labor. Archives are maintained in its various regional branches and at the Moorland-Spingarn Research Center, Howard University. Publishes *The Crisis*.

National Association of Negro Business and Professional Women's Clubs, Inc., 2861 Urban Avenue, Columbus, GA 31907

Founded 1935. Promotes and protects the business and professional interests of black women; unites women in action toward improved social and civic conditions; develops youth through scholarships; and promotes black heritage, world peace, and universal brotherhood.

National Bar Association, 1314 North 5th Street, Kansas City, KS 66101

Founded 1925. Advances the science of jurisprudence; works toward more equitable representation of racial groups in the judiciary of the nation's cities; promotes legislation to improve economic conditions of all peoples; and aids citizens of all races to achieve freedom and the conditions provided for in the Constitution.

National Council of Negro Women, Inc., 1346 Connecticut Avenue, N.W., Washington, DC 20036

Founded 1935. Represents the concerns of women on issues which affect the welfare of the black community. Collects archives, especially those that relate to black women, and promotes programs and projects on black women, genealogy, and other black themes. Newsletters and reports.

National Dental Association, P.O. Box 197, Charlottesville, VA 22902

Founded 1913. Promotes the field of dentistry among blacks and works to eliminate discrimination and segregation in America's dental institutions, clinics, and organizations. Publishes *The Quarterly*.

National Medical Association, 1717 Massachusetts Avenue, N.W., Washington, DC 20036
> Founded 1895. Bonds together for mutual cooperation and helpfulness people of African descent who practice medicine, surgery, pharmacy, and dentistry. Publishes *The Journal.*

National Urban League, 55 East 52nd Street, New York, NY 10022
> Founded 1910. Works to secure equal opportunity for blacks and other economically and socially disadvantaged groups. Areas of concern include housing, employment, education, health, welfare, law, and business. Publishes *Urban League Housing News* and *Urban League News* (both monthly) and *Black Executive Exchange Program Newsletter* and *The Builder* (both quarterly).

Omega Psi Phi Fraternity, Inc., 2714 Georgia Avenue, N.W., Washington, DC 20001
> Founded 1911. Supports the fraternal concepts of social action and scholarship. Focuses on community uplift and undertakes various projects to achieve its purposes. Publishes the *Oracle,* the *Omega Bulletin,* and various books.

10

Hispanic-American Records and Research

LYMAN DE PLATT

Hispanic-American records, for purposes of this publication, will be defined as those which deal with Americans of Spanish and Mexican origin, giving particular emphasis to those records found in the United States and Mexico. However, the vast repositories of Spain will also be mentioned in the appropriate places as they deal with Spaniards who came directly to the United States or who passed into this country through Caribbean or Mexican ports.

Genealogical and historical research on Hispanic Americans can be successfully pursued throughout the United States and the other countries mentioned. It is not always possible to trace every ancestor across the border or through the extant records, but it is certainly just as easy, if not more so, as trying to trace an Anglo-European, black, or Oriental pedigree. The key to success among all these modern genealogies is to get the living family to record immediately all the available information it can on its ancestry, traditions, and origins.

POPULATION MOVEMENTS

During most of the colonial period in Mexico, it was a closely guarded law that but few foreigners (non-Spanish) were to be allowed into the country. The several courts, the holy office of the Inquisition, or at times the viceroys themselves, would occasionally order reviews of the territory to see if foreigners were encroaching beyond controllable levels. It was also Spanish law that persons moving into different areas of the territory had to have passports approved by the government. Thus the ancestry of most Hispanic-Americans is very seldom mixed with that of other European races or admixtures prior to 1775.

There were many attempts made to colonize Mexico, or New Spain as it was then called, particularly the northern provinces. The isolated and limited case of twenty-one orphan children is a particularly moving example. All of the children had the last name of Lorenzana, in recognition of the Archbishop of Mexico. The details of their preparation, travel, suffering, and arrival in California are recorded in the Archivo General de la Nación (AGN) in Mexico City.[1] The families they were assigned to in California are also given. Many of these children became outstanding citizens and the ancestors of thousands of people today.[2]

Numerous attempts were made, some successfully, others not, to persuade large groups—families—to immigrate en masse into California, New Mexico, Arizona, and Texas. An example of this kind of record reads: "Jose Vicente Moxica, Spaniard, aged 30, married, carpenter of Gudalajara; married to Victoria de Luna, with five children: Jose Maximo age 14, Jose Candelario age 8, Maria Josefa age 15, Maria Eustaquia age 7, and Polonia age 3.[3]

In 1775 Charles III, King of Spain, granted permission to all Spaniards to settle wherever they chose in Spanish America, which at that time included most of the present-day United States west of the Mississippi. These early immigrants usually traveled from Spain to the Canary Islands, where many of them stayed for a time. From there they proceeded to Havana or Santo Domingo, ultimately reaching New Orleans or ports in Mexico. The emigration records for these people were kept in Spain at Cadiz and Seville. Today they are housed at the Archivo General de Indias (AGI) in Seville.[4]

After the United States gained its independence in 1776 and up until the early 1900s, there were no quota restrictions on Spaniards or Mexicans entering the United States. Prior to 1903, those entering through Mexico were subject to no registration requirements.

For the period 1903–1953, there are recorded at the Immigration and Naturalization Service (INS) office in El Paso, Texas, approximately 1,500,000 individual legal entries into the United States across the border of Mexico. About 600,000 of these are entries made prior to July 1, 1924. These documents relate to aliens immigrating to the United States who were granted border-crossing privileges all along the border, from California to Texas; they also include records of some U.S. citizens living in Mexico. However, each year tens of thousands of Mexicans also entered the United States illegally. This has occurred ever since 1847, when the Mexican government offered to resettle persons living in California, Arizona, New Mexico, and Texas in the northern Mexican states of Baja California, Sonora, Coahuila, Durango, Nuevo Leon, and Tamaulipas. In the Archivo Histórico de Sonora (AHS) is a copy of the legislation dealing with this transfer. It reads in part:

Article 1. A fund was established June 14, 1848, to transfer Mexican families that wish to emigrate from the territory lost by the peace treaty of Guadalupe Hidalgo.

Article 2. All persons finding themselves in this situation will advise the nearest Mexican consul or agent of their intentions, giving them their name, age, residence, profession, and if they have a family the number of members comprising it with the same information being given for each one.

Article 3. The government will name three individuals to form a commission, one to New

Mexico, another to Upper California, and another to Matamoros in Tamaulipas, to take charge of the transfer of these families.

. . .

Article 5. The families of New Mexico to pass to Chihuahua; those on the left bank of the Bravo River to pass to the states of Tamaulipas, Coahuila, or Nuevo Leon; and those in Upper California to pass to Baja California or the state of Sonora.

. . .

Article 7. The governments of Chihuahua, Coahuila, Nuevo Leon, Tamaulipas, and Sonora and the highest political authority of Baja California will regulate the organization of the civil colonies to be founded by these immigrants.[5]

In May of 1856 the same archive records the movement of some 500 emigrants from California near the Colorado River en route to Sonora, destined to Ures, Hermosillo, Guaymas, and Alamos.[6] This is the last mention of any immigration into the western area of Mexico. It is possible that some did immigrate, but unlikely. Once the first decisions had been made, the borders were technically closed, although they in fact have remained open to anyone who really wanted to cross either way.

The number of people who crossed from Mexico into the United States without any identification papers or with forged documents increased at sometimes alarming rates. An influx was especially noted following the overthrow of Porfirio Díaz in 1911. As an indication, 3,201,371 Mexicans were turned back at the borders between 1946 and 1953 because of inability to identify themselves properly.[7]

Spaniards or Mexicans entering the United States by boat between 1820 and 1903 usually did so through Galveston, Texas; New Orleans, Louisiana; and San Diego and San Francisco, California. People entering in this manner were required to "state their name, age, sex, country of birth, . . . where they intended to settle, and their occupation. Lists of the names of those entering as passengers were furnished the Bureau of Customs by the Captain of the ship."[8]

Spaniards immigrating through New Orleans have been studied by Charles R. Maduell, Jr.,[9] from the original passenger lists housed at the New Orleans Public Library. Microfilm copies of these lists covering the time period of 1820–1903 can be consulted at the LDS Genealogical Department Library in Salt Lake City.[10] The earliest lists (1820–23) have also been published in a two-volume work by Milton P. Rieder, Jr., and Norma Gaudet Rieder.[11]

Records of immigrants to the United States through Texas, New Mexico, Arizona, and California are found in a wide variety of collections and places. Of particular value to the researcher is the AGN in Mexico, in which are contained most of the documents dealing with the northern part of Mexico during the colonial period. Examples of the types of material that might be found are given in the following paragraphs.

There are literally hundreds of lists of garrisons, detachments, crews, and so on throughout the vast holdings of the AGN. The following list was submitted by Felipe Barrios from the Presidio of Loreto on October 5, 1773, detailing those

individuals who had been assigned to the new establishments at San Diego and
San Carlos de Monterrey in Upper California.

1.	Sargento Mariano Carrillo	single
2.	Cavo Josef María Gongora	single
3.	Cavo Guillermo Carrillo	single
4.	Juan Josef Dominguez	single
5.	Manuel Robles	married in Sinaloa
6.	Alexandro de Soto	single
7.	Alexo Antonio Gonzalez	single
8.	Josef Anastacio Camacho	single
9.	Pablo Antonio Cota	single
10.	Miguel Yslas	doubtfully married
11.	Josef Manuel Perez Nieto	married at this place
12.	Josef María Soberanes	single
13.	Josef Marcelino Brabo	single
14.	Josef María Verdugo	single
15.	Juan Esteban Rocha	single
16.	Rafael Villavicencio	single
17.	Juan María Olibera	single
18.	Luis Gonzaga de Lugo	single
19.	Josef Julian Morillo	single
20.	Juan Antonio Labra	single
21.	Claudio Victorio Feliz	single
22.	Josef Francisco Sinoba	single
23.	Josef Ramon Noriega	married in the South
24.	Josef Antonio Ontiveros	single
25.	Sevastian Alvitre	single
26.	Francisco Avila	single
27.	Francisco Cordero	single
28.	Asencio Francisco Avila	married at this place
29.	Francisco Maria Peña	single
30.	Josef Antonio Peña	single
31.	Luis Peña	single
32.	Rafael Gerardo	single
33.	Francisco Lopez	single
34.	Alexandro Duarte	single
35.	Josef Maria Duarte	single
36.	Juan Maria Ruiz	married in Monterrey
37.	Juan Antonio Coronel	married in Culiacan
38.	Martín Reyes	single
39.	Manuel Antonio Robles	single
40.	Juan Antonio Rubio	married in the South
41.	Fernando Roelas	single
42.	Antonio Cota	single
43.	Francisco Reyes	single
44.	Josef Mariano Yepes	single
45.	Juan Pablo Servantes	single

46.	Juan de la Cruz Verdugo	single
47.	Francisco Rafael Marquez	single
48.	Juan Alvarez	single
49.	Nicolas Gonzalez	single
50.	Mariano Verdugo	single[12]

As an example of the crew lists, the following one for October 1770 of the *San Carlos* shows the type of information available in these records.

Commandant Don Vizente Vila
Pilot Joseph Cañisares
Marines:

Joseph, el Viejo
Ygnacio Maria Lugo
Joseph Francisco Marillo
Diego Guainamota
Baptista Carabajal
N. Balensuela
Un Negro Cosinero (a negro cook)

This crew being insufficient to man the ship, the commandant asked for men from my Captain and was provided with the following:

Joseph Camacho, soldier
Juan Joseph Carpio Basquero, Indian
Juan Antonio Carpio, Indian
Narsizo Berdugo, muleteer
3 Indians of California from the Mission of San Ygnacio

October, 1770[13]

To settle the northwest territory of the viceroyalty, it was necessary to assign some individuals with special talents to tours of duty in the area.[14] Lists such as the following were submitted to the government, this one from Monterrey, dated 1 January 1797 by Diego de Borica.

Class	Profession	Name	No. of Years	Date of Contract
Master	Weaver	Antonio Henriquez	4	1 Feb. 1794
Official	Bricklayer	Toribio Ruiz	4	1 Nov. 1795
Master	Tailor	Joaquin Botello	5	22 Oct. 1795
Master	Ribbon maker	Manuel Muñoz	5	22 Oct. 1795
Master	Broad weaver	Mariano Mendoza	5	22 Oct. 1795
Master	Bricklayer	Manuel Ruiz	6	23 Jan. 1791

Henriquez and Manuel Ruiz were assigned to the ship *San Carlos;* Mendoza to the *San Juan;* Toribio to the settlement at San Diego; and Botello and Muñoz to the one at Monterrey.

As pertains to the foreigners mentioned earlier, many good records are available on them in the AGN. Take for example this review of the people in Zacatecas in 1794–95.

Intendency of Zacatecas, depositions taken of the *French* living in this Province. Individual notices of the foreigners found within this jurisdiction with their names, ages, nationalities, civil statuses, occupations, dates of entry into this Kingdom, how this was verified, years they have resided in their present locations, goods they possess, and by what permission they reside in these Dominions. [Examples follow:]

. . .

Phelipe Casas, age 42, native of the city of Rome, married in the city of Sombrerete, without known occupation he works at whatever he can, does not remember when he came here or how he was permitted to enter, resides in Sombrerete where he has lived for the past 20 years, has no possessions or means, of honorable conduct.

Juan Safiro, age 53, native of Sarra in the Duchy of Saboya, married in the village of Sombrerete, cook, does not remember when he came here or how he was permitted to enter, resides in Sombrerete for the last eight years, has no possessions or means, maintains himself through his employment.

Juan Samuel Suhur, of more than 40 years of age, native of Germany, married, carpenter, came to this Kingdom with the miners from Germany contracted for by His Catholic Majesty for these parts in the quality of operator in said mines, converted to our Religion four years ago in the village of Sombrerete during which time he resided there, has no possessions.

Juan Gotfried Adler, age about 35 years, German, married in the village of Sombrerete, potter, came to this Kingdom with royal permission as one of the German miners, converted to our Religion some three years ago in Sombrerete where he has lived for two years.

Juan Eizfel Sajon, age 38, single, servant of Don Federico Sonneschmid, resident in the capital of Mexico, finding himself transient in this place for his health.

Juan Bastan, of more than 50 years, Italian, married, employed at the Liquor Control Commission [*Ministerio de Asentista del Real Estanco de Vinos Mescales*] of the Nieves mine, came to this Kingdom some 30 years past as a relative of a governor that entered into the Province of New Mexico, resident in the city of San Miguel del Mesquital where he has lived for the past 20 years, having no possessions except the small salary of his employment.

Gasper Pasquareli, age 40 years, Italian, married, businessman, he estimates he has been here for ten years having forgotten how he entered the Kingdom, resides at the Nieves mine where he has lived for the past five years and worked with equipment.

Thomas Mazas, 33 years old, native of the city of Genova, married in Mexico, baker for 18 years, has been in this Kingdom six months having come from Cadiz with the same profession in the ship *La Carlota,* living at present in Zacatecas where he has been transient for the last five months, having his residence in Mexico City, having no known possessions.

Zacatecas, 31 Oct. 1794[15]

There are many other records like these available for different parts of the country. Some of them contain information on people that later lived in the border states of the United States.

Some passports and passport information are also available at the AGN. The following are some examples.

Arrival at Tampico of the American schooner *Antelope* with twenty-two passengers, 5 August 1822

List of foreigners who arrived at Tampico, 21 July 1822

List of foreigners who were transient in Tamaulipas in June, 21 July 1822

List of some foreigners established in Mazatlan, 27 July 1822

List of foreigners residing in the territory of New Mexico, 4 August 1822

List of foreigners who arrived in Chihuahua, 21 August 1822

Details of the foreigners in New Mexico in July, 2 September 1822

Details of foreigners transient in Queretaro in August, 2 September 1822

Details of foreigners transient in Puebla in July, 5 September 1822

Details of foreigners in the Federal District, 9 September 1822

Details of foreigners in Jalisco, 9 September 1822

Details of foreigners in San Luis Potosi in August, 12 September 1822

Details of foreigners in Coahuila in August, 20 September 1822

Details of foreigners residing in Chihuahua, 21 September 1822

Details of foreigners residing in New Mexico, 29 September 1822

April 22, 1823

The Supreme Executive Power has decided that all foreigners that present themselves at the ports of the provinces of this country shall observe strictly the formalities relating to passports, not allowing any to enter that do not have their papers in proper order.

The government of New Mexico announced shortly thereafter receipt of said order and accepted responsibility for enforcing the order. Similar acknowledgments are on file for Veracruz, Guadalajara, Sonora, the Internal Provinces of the East, the Internal Provinces of the West, Acapulco, Durango, and Monterrey.

On 1 October 1823 the Supreme Executive Power ordered that from this date on, port commanders will no longer have the authority to issue passports, but that this power will lie with the *jefe político* of the area, or the mayor as the case may be. This order was sent to the *jefes políticos* at Veracruz, Guadalajara, San Luis Potosi, Tabasco [Villa Hermosa], Tixtla, Tejas, Nuevo Santander, Acapulco, Oaxaca, Sinaloa, and Chiapas.[16]

Following these stricter measures established by the central government, more orderly records of immigration and emigration began to be kept. Several examples of this follow.

List of nineteen individuals that need passports, subjects of Her Royal British Majesty, and employees of the Compañía Anglo Mexicana, 13 January 1829.

5052   Eduardo Williams
5053   Ricardo Magor

5054   Jose Pascoe
5055   Alexandro Petrie
5056   Juan Adams
5057   Jayme Baird
5058   Diego Fraser
5059   David Williams
5060   Eduardo Edwards
5061   David Davies
5062   Walter Gerdell
5063   Diego Gerdell
5064   G. Howel
5065   Diego Lees
5066   Juan Hosking
5067   David Jones
5068   Enrique Pemberthy
5069   Samuel Richardson
5070   Dr. Guillermo Cheyne
5071   Captain Don Jaime Vetch, subject of Her Royal British Majesty, returning to England, 15 January 1829
5072   Juan Francisco Soldano, Spaniard, solicits passports for New Orleans, 15 January 1829: I came to this Kingdom in 1814 concerning a will of my uncle who was the archdeacon of Valladolid of Michoacan.
5073   Diego Carrillo, notably poor, asks for a passport to remove himself and his wife to France, 15 January 1829
5074   Vicente Sedano, Spaniard, married, businessman, says that in 1799 he entered business in this Republic and desires now to go to Europe for four years to develop mercantile establishments there, solicits passports for himself and family, 14 January 1828.[17]

SPANISH CENSUS RECORDS

The Spanish took many censuses during the colonial period. Literally thousands of these are extant, scattered through the archives of Spain, Mexico, and the United States. Some have been lost or are at least temporarily undiscovered. Interesting for its statistical summaries and historical perspective is the 1790 census of Mexico. Following is a representative sampling of some of the northern provinces of New Spain. The rest of the census is also available.[18]

General Census ordered to be taken by his Excellency the Viceroy of this Kingdom on 25 March 1790.
New Mexico
General Summary: 30,953 persons; 28 Franciscans

    3   villages
   26   pueblos
    3   parishes
   19   missions
    1   hacienda

Regional Summary:

Santa Fe and its Royal Presidio

3,733 persons
- 1 village
- 2 pueblos
- 2 parishes
- 2 missions
- 4 Franciscans

San Felipe

3,790 persons
- 6 pueblos
- 2 missions
- 2 Franciscans

Santa Cruz de la Canada and Pueblo de Taos

8,895 persons
- 1 village
- 8 pueblos
- 6 missions
- 7 Franciscans

Zuni and Laguna

3,320 persons
- 3 missions
- 3 Franciscans

Albuquerque and Alameda

5,956 persons
- 1 village
- 2 pueblos
- 2 missions
- 1 hacienda
- 3 Franciscans

Paso del Rio del Norte

5,253 persons
- 5 pueblos
- 5 missions
- 9 Franciscans

Military:

Company at the Presidio of Santa Fe	121
Retired officials	2
Retired officials at El Paso	2
Invalids	13
Soldiers, half pay	2
Interpreters of the Nations	6
TOTAL	146

Upper California

General Summary: 8,590 persons
- 1 pueblo

4 presidios
12 missions
26 priests

Regional Summary:

Royal Presidio of San Diego

Age	Single		Married		Widowed	
	Male	Female	Male	Female	Male	Female
0–7	307	262				
7–16	298	251	1	13		
16–25	50	42	213	256	1	10
25–40	24	13	370	339	11	34
40–50	8	11	108	121	12	28
50–	2	17	72	33	16	34
TOTAL 2,957	689	596	764	762	40	106

Royal Presidio of San Francisco plus 2 missions & 4 priests

Age	Male	Female	Male	Female	Male	Female
0–7	293	300				
7–16	236	147		18		
16–25	31	2	84	102	11	1
25–40	8	3	106	88	4	1
40–50	6	6	35	29	5	1
50–	3	1	30	15	5	16
TOTAL 1,587	577	459	255	252	25	19

Royal Presidio of Monterrey plus 3 missions and 9 priests

Age	Male	Female	Male	Female	Male	Female
0–7	302	306				
7–16	319	224	5	27		1
16–25	55	4	177	136	4	10
25–40	20		272	273	11	26
40–50	5		33	72	4	22
50–	1		54	29	16	87
TOTAL 2,615	702	534	601	597	35	146

Royal Presidio of Santa Barbara plus 1 pueblo, 3 missions, and 5 priests

Age	Male	Female	Male	Female	Male	Female
0–7	182	195				
7–16	192	91	6	24		1
16–25	55	26	153	163	5	4
25–40	27	7	99	87	5	9
40–50	2	4	31	22		2
50–	9	15	11	4	3	3
TOTAL 1,431	461	338	300	300	13	19

The censuses for Upper California have been published by the Historical Society of Southern California in its quarterly.[19] In Upper California in 1790 the following professions and occupations were being pursued:

Military	268	Silversmiths	2
Navy	19	Blacksmiths	3
Miners	5	Tailors	6
Farmers	38	Bricklayers	2
Ranchers	19	Tanners	1
Day workers	123	Shoemakers	8
Manufacturers	2	Doctor	1
Carpenters	5		

The censuses for Lower California and Sonora were as follows:

Lower California
General Summary: 4,076 persons
1 pueblo and its presidio
16 missions
1 hacienda
9 dependent ranches
7 independent ranches
1 hospital attendant
23 priests

	Single		Married		Widowed	
Age	*Male*	*Female*	*Male*	*Female*	*Male*	*Female*
0–7	398	375				
7–16	390	292	2	55		
16–25	185	43	124	244	12	7
25–40	76	2	339	358	58	18
40–50	22	2	239	176	39	22
50–	11	5	254	123	109	96
TOTAL 4,076	1,082	719	958	956	218	143

Sonora
General Summary: 38,305 persons
13 major pueblos
9 presidios
29 priests

	Single		Married		Widowed	
Jurisdiction	*Male*	*Female*	*Male*	*Female*	*Male*	*Female*
Arispe	2,109	1,799	1,597	1,597	232	288
Cieneguilla	319	285	249	249	9	33

Jurisdiction	Single		Married		Widowed	
	Male	*Female*	*Male*	*Female*	*Male*	*Female*
Sonora	2,010	1,585	1,227	1,227	107	206
Hostimuri	4,153	3,504	3,865	3,865	237	381
San Carlos	264	174	145	145	20	40
Pitic	336	308	197	197	15	42
Altar	1,458	285	348	348	9	29
Tucson	129	106	154	154	50	51
Fronteras	115	80	110	110	14	26
Santa Cruz	324	167	193	193	13	41
Bacoachi	58	44	84	84	3	0
Bavispe	40	17	70	70	9	3
San Rafael	119	27	61	61	21	11
TOTAL	11,434	8,381	8,300	8,300	739	1,151

The military establishments in Sonora had the following troop strength.

San Carlos	71
Pitic	74
Altar	88
Tucson	102
Fronteras	105
Santa Cruz	103
Bacoachi	91
Bavispe	91
San Rafael	83
	808
Invalids	15
TOTAL	823[20]

Spanish censuses tend to be informative much earlier than those of the English-speaking world. Excellent details on family names, ages, relationships, and civil status are available in many of the extant censuses for the northern areas from the beginning of civilization there. References to many of these records are found in the studies mentioned in the bibliography at the end of this chapter. The Genealogical Society of Utah has filmed many of these records, as have the major universities and archives mentioned in the section below on archives and libraries. To date no complete reference has been compiled itemizing those records; however, I have one in preparation.

MILITARY RECORDS

Foremost among the record sources that contain valuable data on families of this area are the collections of military information, which can be found in all the major archives mentioned in this chapter and in many of the minor ones. Of particular note is the set of service records for the Americas from the Archivo de Simancas in Spain. The records are divided into sections: Florida and Louisiana, Cuba, New Spain (including some records from Florida, Louisiana, and Mississippi and of course from Texas, New Mexico, and California), and a separate section for Yucatan, Campeche and Quintana Roo.

These records are on microfilm at the LDS Genealogical Department Library and elsewhere. An index to them is available.[21] These service records are for the late 1700s and early 1800s and are very valuable because of the amount of biographical detail they give. An example of one is given below in the history of Manuel Peru.

Other types of records are available as mentioned. Taking just one collection as a sampling, the following material shows the variety that exists:

1817. Corps of the Internal'Provinces. The subinspector-general remits sixty-four invalid records for individuals.

1773–75. The mine of San Alfonso de Cieneguillas. *Padrón* (census) of the residents of the mine as ordered by the governor, Don Francisco Crespo. Also Lieutenant Don Pedro Tueros solicits an increase in his subsistence allowance in order to stay alive in said place.

1820. Militia of Coahuila and Texas. Report directed to Field Marshal Don Alejo García Conde by Captain Don José Gaspar de Ochoa, who before returning to his post in Durango describes the activities of the troops under his command in the provinces and frontier outposts. He also requests the advancement of a group of distinguished officers.

1789. Militia of Sonora and New Vizcaya. Proposal of candidates to cover the vacancies of militial officials in the presidios of Sonora and Nueva Vizcaya.[22]

1780s. Troop reviews of the veteran units stationed in New Spain.[23]

1798–99. Military review of the two militia companies of Spaniards and Pardos of the village of Sinaloa.[24]

1780. Joaquin Cañete, lieutenant of the Royal Presidio of Loreto, California, requests an increase in salary.[25]

1778–80. Document concerning the capturing of deserters from the presidio of San Diego, Matias Vega and Francisco Ramirez, and from the presidio of San Francisco, Ignacio Castro and Felipe Ochoa.[26]

1785. Document compiled by the temporary commander of San Blas, Don Francisco Antonio Mourelle, concerning whether Mass should be recited in the arsenal on holidays which were not observed.[27]

1839. Status of the military strength of the permanent company of San Francisco.[28]

1808. Service record of Antonio Aguilar, son of Pedro Aguilar and Manuela Estrada of Chama (New Mexico). Farmer. Five feet, one inch tall. No age given. Black hair and eyebrows, dark eyes, straight nose, thin beard, mole in right eyebrow. Signed by mark.[29]

Putting these military records together into a research effort directed towards one person's history, it is possible to come up with the following details.

In American Fork, Utah, there is a Mexican-American family that has been in the United States for five generations. They descend from a family that dead ends in the parish registers of Casas Grandes, Chihuahua, Mexico. The earliest entries in that parish begin in 1852. José Perú, one of their ancestors, was married in Casas Grandes and was given as being from Janos, the son of Manuel Perú. Extensive research in local records has turned up no further information.

Janos was one of the frontier presidios. It was established in 1686, nearly 200 years prior to the beginning of the Casas Grandes parish and civil records. In Janos, however, nothing is left in the way of records. Do they still exist? Where are they? What do they contain?

In a recent book, Henry Putney Beers locates and describes some of these records as follows:

1. Eight feet of presidial and parish records covering the years 1707–1858 are in the University of Texas Library at Austin.

2. Numerous documents on Janos are found in the *Archivo General de Indias* in Seville, Spain.

3. In 1969 the University of Texas at El Paso microfilmed the presidial archives which were then in the church at Janos. This collection of 36 rolls dating from 1778 to about 1900 includes many service records and military review lists. Copies of these records are available at the Genealogical Society of Utah Library, the University which filmed them, and several other major repositories.[30]

In the Military Archives of Simancas, Spain, is a service record of Manuel Perú, second ensign (*alferez*), belonging to the Presidio of Principe, Nueva Vizcaya, in 1800.[31] The AGN contains a later service record for the same individual, as do the Janos records.[32]

Records used elsewhere in this writing include descriptions of the Janos Presidio, the Principe Presidio, the San Buenaventura Presidio, and descriptions of life and its duties in the frontier areas of northern New Spain. From these records one can consider the following biographical sketch of Manuel Perú.

Manuel Perú was born in the year 1772 and is given as being Spanish. The surname Perú being very uncommon, it is quite likely that Manuel was related to the three other soldiers of that name stationed in the same area. An analysis of the birthplaces given on later service records for men serving in this area shows that most of them were from Sonora, Chihuahua, and Durango.

On 1 July 1788, at the age of sixteen, Manuel became a soldier in the 4th Flying Company of Nueva Vizcaya, which had been created as a veteran light cavalry company by Hugo O'Coner in 1773 with 100 men. The company was supposed to maintain four squads of 20 to 25 men under one officer. Their main assignments consisted of fighting Indians and protecting convoys and roads. Their expeditions were to last for fifteen days each, following a given route. Within twenty-four hours of their return, another squad was to be back in the field. It would follow the same course. If it found less than a hundred Indians, it could attack; if there were more, it was to contact another squad from a neighboring presidio or from home base and join forces. The officers were to keep diaries of these expeditions which were to be sent to headquarters in Chihuahua for reports to the viceroy.

These presidial troops were armed with a broadsword, dagger, lance, rifle, and pistol. Their campaign uniforms consisted of knee-length trousers, a short waistcoat with gold buttons, a blue bandana with the reverse side red, a blue cape, a cartridge box, a leather jacket, and a bandoleer on which was embroidered the name of the presidio.

Manuel advanced to the rank of cadet on 26 April 1789. Sometime after that he married and began his family. For awhile he served in the 2nd Flying Company of Nueva Vizcaya, stationed at Namiquipa, and was then stationed at Principe, where he was advanced to the rank of ensign. From Principe he was moved to Janos for several years and then to San Buenaventura, where he apparently spent the rest of his service. He was advanced to the office of lieutenant on 3 May 1807.

Manuel served in seventeen campaigns against the Indians and local bandits, killing twenty-two and capturing fourteen of both sexes. His valor was held in high repute and his conduct was good. However, Manuel's reporting officer felt that he did not apply himself in other than a normal manner and that he lacked some leadership capacities. Manuel was still in San Buenaventura serving as a lieutenant in December 1817. He may have retired in 1818, with thirty years of service, at the age of fifty-six.

Manuel's descendants stayed in the area around San Buenaventura for several generations, after which many of them began moving into the United States, particularly around El Paso, Tucson, and Los Angeles.

ARCHIVES AND LIBRARIES

Up to this point we have examined records of a general nature that are found in state, regional, or national archives. Other libraries and archives with major holdings of these types of records include the following:

Archivo General de Indias, Seville, Spain

Genealogical Society of Utah (LDS) Library, Salt Lake City, Utah

Bexar Archives, University of Texas Library, Austin, Texas

Biblioteca Nacional de Mexico, Mexico City, Mexico

Bancroft Library, University of California, Berkeley, California

State Records Center and Archives, Sante Fe, New Mexico

Archivo Historico de Sonora, Hermosillo, Sonora, Mexico

Archivo Historico de Durango, Durango, Mexico

Archivo Historico del Estado, Culiacan, Sinaloa, Mexico

Archives of the Archdiocese of Santa Fe, Santa Fe, New Mexico

Huntington Library, San Marino, California

Texas History Research Library, the Alamo, San Antonio, Texas

Polytechnic Archives, Monterrey, Nuevo Leon, Mexico

Nacogdoches Archives, Texas State Library, Austin, Texas

Laredo Archives, Special Collections, St. Mary's University Library, San Antonio, Texas

For the most complete work on materials housed in the United States, consult Henry Putney Beers's recent, but nevertheless somewhat out of date, book entitled *Spanish and Mexican Records of the American Southwest*.[33] For a general overview of the records repositories and collections dealing with immigrants, see my book *Genealogical-Historical Guide to Latin America* or its Spanish-language edition, *Una Guía Genealógico-Histórica de Latinoamérica*.[34]

TYPICAL PROBLEMS IN RESEARCH

The single most difficult problem in doing research is to extend a pedigree when the origin of the family is unknown. Many Mexican and Spanish lines in the United States go back two or three generations and then leave the country. Few U.S. records give the whereabouts of the ancestry. There are, however, two records which are becoming increasingly valuable as their ability to solve this problem becomes known. The first is the 1900 national census of the United States, which records the birthplaces of all members of the family and indicates the birthplaces of the parents as well. The second is a secondary source, but because of its size it must be considered. It is called the International Genealogical Index and is available at the LDS Genealogical Department Library and all of its more than 350 branch libraries. It now contains the names of more than 60 million persons, including many millions from the northern and central states of Mexico, whose names have been taken from the parish registers of the Catholic Church.

The other single most difficult problem when working with Hispanic-American genealogy is the fact that many children were born of unions that were not legally recorded. When this occurs, many times the lineage of the father is permanently lost. Occasionally the father is known but is omitted from earlier records. Later records, such as marriages or deaths, may include this information. Every attempt should be made to identify the father before giving up on his ancestry.

One must also consider the deliberate falsification of information that appears in some records. A detailed comparison of dates, places, and historical perspectives must be made to insure that everyone is the right age to have a feasible connection on the pedigree; for example, a child born to a mother who is twelve years old or to one aged fifty-five to sixty is unlikely. A couple's marriage ages are important as a clue to possible former marriages. Census records are notorious for incorrect ages and must be used with caution in judging approximate birth dates.

FAMILY SOURCES

As genealogy is a study of family units, it stands to reason that the home of the nuclear family and the homes of children and grandchildren of the nuclear couple should contain the most extensive materials available pertaining to the family's genealogy and history.

In Hispanic-American homes in the United States, and in homes in Mexico and Spain, the best place to begin investigations is with older family members and relatives. It is usually possible to get names, dates, and family traditions from these people that may extend as far back as five generations. Normally, they are at least able to give some details on their parents and grandparents.

Almost every family has something of value to the researcher. Many times, in an effort to obtain this information, and before establishing a trustworthy relationship with the interviewee, the investigator will begin asking questions which are too personal. It has been my personal experience that a sincere feeling of kinship expressed through letters or various visits will open untold treasures of historical data that would remain hidden to the insincere fact finder. Even kinship is not an absolute prerequisite to success in this area if a proper deference to and respect for age is cultivated. Examples of this will be given in one of the case studies recorded later in this chapter.

A careful investigation will uncover some, if not all, of the following types of genealogical and historical material: vital and church records; photographs and picture albums; biographies; citizenship papers; diaries; family histories; legal papers on homes, land, and so forth; military documents; school and occupational records; newspaper clippings; and others. If these materials are unavailable in the home in question, then the homes of friends, neighbors, and relatives should be visited, as should local libraries, archives, and museums.

Case Study 1

In one case a person writes:

I am interested in having research done in Mexico, beginning in the state of Sonora, on the family of Francisco Bustamente. He and his wife Loreta appear in the 1850 census of Los Angeles with three children: Josefa, age 15; Jesus, age 10; and Merced, age 6. Merced is the direct ancestor. The place of birth for all of them is given as Mexico, which could mean California, but I have family letters, written in Spanish, concerning property in Sonora State and around Tucson. Francisco's occupation was given as teacher.

This was all that was known by the family about its ancestor, but even after 150 years, some family material was still available. A search of the Los Angeles Mission records, of the *Historical and Biographical Record of Los Angeles and Vicinity*,[35] of a book entitled *Los Angeles from the Mountains to the Sea*,[36] of the annual publications of the Historical Society of Southern California, and of similar publications in Sonora begin to add flesh to the skeleton. More family members are identified. Francisco Bustamente is identified as the Francisco Bustamente who in 1850 signed a contract to teach children first, second, and third lessons and likewise to read script, write, count, and "so much as I may be competent, to teach them orthography and good morals."

Bustamente was the first paid schoolteacher in California. He was a former soldier. He arrived in San Diego in August 1842 with Manuel Micheltorena, who had served under Santa Ana in the Texan War and who had been appointed as commander general of California. Military records in the AGN further identify Bustamente as a lieutenant who had been stationed in Sonora and Chihuahua. They show his service record, his physical description, and the campaigns in which he served against the Indians and against the United States. Land records in Tucson and Hermosillo further tie the family to a history on both sides of the border and to many other families. Much more is available, but the initial clues were gathered from sketchy family records.

Case Study 2

Another case study begins:

I am anxious to begin research on my mother's lineage. Her parents were members of the Catholic Church. Her father was Jose Joaquin Yslas, born October 1863 in Hermosillo, Sonora, Mexico, and her mother was Maria del Carmen Romo (taken from the French name "Rambeau" and changed around the time of Maximillian because of prejudice against the French). She was born September 1880 in Pueblo de Aconchi, Sonora, Mexico.

A request was made of the family to check around its home to see what was available that might add information to this material, and relatives were also to be contacted, to learn what might be still available in their memories. A baptismal certificate was found for Jose Joaquin Yslas and his marriage record. Both of these were copies made in 1955 and 1974 for the family by local Catholic officials. The baptismal certificate, from Mexico, proved to be an accurate transcription, but the marriage record, recorded in Phoenix, Arizona, and copied for the family by a non-Spanish-speaking priest, was highly inaccurate. He recorded the mother-in-law of Jose Yslas as his wife, but recorded the real wife's parents on the transcript. A second request for the same record, made in 1977, identified the correct couple but no parents for either, even though they exist on the original. This little exercise shows the problems that develop when those familiar with the pedigree are unable to copy or look at the original without interference from those in charge of the records. Of course, many records are deteriorating and must be placed out of the reach of the public, but every attempt should be made to see a true copy—microfilm, photocopy, or verbatim transcription by a qualified individual—of all vital records in the researcher's pedigree.

Besides these two documents, some handwritten notes taken in the 1950s during an interview by a granddaughter with Maria del Carmen Romo Yslas were found. From these notes it was learned that the parents of Jose Joaquin Yslas were Jose Yslas Yslas and Remedios Alegria and that the grandparents were Augustin Yslas and Isabel Yslas. This latter couple apparently returned to Spain. The notes revealed that Maria del Carmen's parents were Francisco Romo and Beatrice Ochoa. Francisco Romo was also known as Francisco Lopez and as Francisco Rambeau. According to family tradition, Francisco's mother, Estephana Larez, was married to Manuel Lopez but had three children by Nicholas Romo, whom she later married. This Nicholas was apparently a large landowner. Maria del Carmen's brothers all went by the name of Lopez as adults. Her mother's mother was named Raphaela.

From a telephone conversation with one of the daughters of Jose and Maria, all that could be learned was that Ochoa was not the real surname of Maria's mother. When the interviewer asked her whether she could substantiate a rumor that Beatrice was part Indian, the answer was an emphatic no.

Despite further attempts, this was all the information that was obtained from this family in the way of family records, tradition, and so forth. As can be seen from further analysis of this information, some of it is inaccurate. It points up the problem found in nearly all families—inaccuracy increases dramatically after the death of the older generation. Those who record the traditions and facts that still exist and preserve for the future the precious documents of the past, should do so as accurately as possible, recording what is handed down as it was given, without prejudice. A small clue here and there in the future will provide others with openings into broad, well-lighted avenues of information as more and more records become available that are now lost, inaccessible, or unknown to present researchers.

RECORDS

There are many publications available that deal with people and records within the United States. In researching Hispanic Americans, one must deal with their U.S. pedigrees in the same way as with any other nationality. This includes searches in vital records, censuses, land records, cemeteries, probates, military archives, and local histories. The extension of these pedigrees into Mexico and Spain has been dealt with locally, but much of what has been done has not been published or referenced for general use. Some good materials exist that shed light on the records, problems, processes, and so forth that are needed or encountered in the research process. The bibliography at the end of this chapter contains references to the books I am familiar with and have used in my studies. There are many others, but I hope this bibliography will contain many references with which the majority of the readers are unfamiliar.

Let us now turn to the use of the more commonly available record sources and take the second case study as a base from which to begin.

Civil

The recording of births, marriages, and deaths began in Mexico in 1857 and in Spain in 1870. These records are kept on a municipal level and are valuable for many administrative and legal matters, such as establishment of the rights of inheritance and citizenship, eligibility for school attendance, entitlement to other benefits, and eligibility for military service. For the genealogist the records provide the information necessary to reconstruct entire family units. Many times birth records in Mexico and Spain give the names of grandparents as well as parents. Civil registration is considered the best single existing source for genealogical research in the modern time period.

In the United States these records are called vital records. There are birth records available in Gila and Yavapai counties in Arizona for nearly all of the children of Jose Joaquin Yslas and Maria del Carmen. Very little use can be made of this record in this particular case study, as most of the information needed begins prior to the commencement of civil registration. These records are kept on a municipal basis in all the border states. Some of them have been microfilmed by the Genealogical Society of Utah, while others must be searched in their original archives. Some archives will answer correspondence requests if enough accurate data can be supplied.

Ecclesiastical

The principal church records available throughout Spain and Mexico are parish registers of baptisms, marriages, and burials. Generally speaking, the oldest parish registers provide the least information, and the most useful records are those later ones that precede the introduction of printed forms in the late nineteenth century, when once again the amount of information begins to diminish.

In parts of Mexico, separate parish registers were kept for Spaniards, Indians, Negroes, and their admixtures. This was done for tax purposes and for facility in providing dispensations to contracting parties in a marriage when necessary. Also, it was unlawful for many years for Spaniards to marry Negroes or anyone who had any Negro ancestry.

Some ecclesiastical *padrones,* or censuses, exist in diocesan archives and, when available, are invaluable in establishing entire family units. These censuses were usually taken for the purpose of elevating rural chapels to the category of parish churches or for erecting convents. Other records found in diocesan archives include marriage investigations, disputes, cancellations, ecclesiastical trials, chaplaincy records, wills, tithing records, and property titles.

Non-Catholic records are practically nonexistent because of the late starts of most other sects in Mexico and Spain and because of the little attention which most of them gave to record keeping. There are limited possibilities of finding non-Catholic information as early as 1880, but it is usually necessary to go to the church which still houses the original records.

Many Catholic records have disappeared from the original parishes. To determine where the existing records are today, it is necessary to understand a little of the jurisdictional structure of the Church. Parishes are the smallest ecclesiastical division. Even though a parish may consist of vice-parishes and isolated chapels, the parish registers are usually found at the parish archive. Parishes have always been under the jurisdiction of a diocese or archdiocese, as they are today. If a parish ceases to function, its records are normally placed in the bishop's or archbishop's archive. The bishop's archive usually only contains records of a diocesan nature, administrative in format, together with these records of defunct parishes. Most parish records of Mexico have been microfilmed by the Genealogical Society of Utah and are available throughout its library system. Those for Spain are beginning to be preserved by this same library.

In our case study some useful records were found for the families in question, while other records appear not to exist. The baptismal record of Jose Joaquin Yslas is as follows:

In the parish of Hermosillo on the 22nd of October of 1863 I the priest Dr. D. Juan Perez Serrano . . . baptized . . . a child of two days old to whom I have the name Jose Joaquin legitimate son of Jose Yslas and Remedios Alegria. The godparents were Joaquin Yslas and Susana Dias. . . .[37]

With the names of the parents positively established from this baptismal record, the next step was to try and find the parents in a marriage record. With only the year 1863 as a reference point, it was necessary to examine the records from that point backwards. The parents were finally found in 1851 in the following entry.

In Hermosillo on 9 December 1851 were married Jose Yslas, single, native of Horcasitas and resident of this city, natural-born son of Francisco Yslas and Maria Isabel Yslas, and Maria Remedios Alegria, single, native of Hermosillo, legitimate daughter of the legitimate marriage of Jose Antonio Alegria and Maria _____ Flores, the latter being deceased.[38]

This entry provided good information for future research. To do proper research into the pre-1850s, however, it is necessary to become acquainted with the local history and how it affected the keeping and moving of records. Even though the records of Hermosillo go back far enough, the marriage of Jose Antonio Alegria and Maria Lorenza Flores is not recorded there. It should be noted at this point that the above marriage record disproves part of the material given by Maria del Carmen in her interview. She said that the parents of Jose Yslas Yslas were Agustin Yslas and Ysabel Yslas. Certainly both the parents had

Yslas as their surname, but the above record shows that the father is Francisco Yslas, not Agustin. Perhaps both names are his, but that is not apparent at this point. The mother is Isabel, even though Maria is given as her first name. The full name of the mother of Maria Remedios Alegria was not decipherable in the parish register.

In many areas of the Catholic world, on the diocesan level, prenuptial investigations have been kept for several centuries. In this case study they were looked for and found, and they added information not recorded in the actual marriage record. These prenuptial investigations are usually four to seven pages long, and only a summary of this one is given here.

1. Jose Yslas was age thirty-three at marriage, meaning that he was born about 1818.
2. Maria Remedios Alegria was age twenty at marriage, meaning that she was born about 1831.
3. Jose Yslas had been a resident of Hermosillo for six years at the time of his marriage in 1851, or that is to say, he had lived there from about 1845, having been twenty-seven at the time he moved to the city.
4. Jose Yslas is described professionally as a *jornalero*, which translates to "day laborer" or one who hires out on a daily basis.[39]

According to family records, Maria del Carmen Romo was born in Aconchi, a small village in the state of Sonora. An initial investigation of that area shows that the parishes are intermixed. The towns of Aconchi, Baviacora to the north, and Banamichi to the south were rotated as parish headquarters. An exhaustive search of the parish registers does not reveal the baptismal entry of Maria del Carmen even though her family is there—the Romos, Ochoas, and Lares. Her parents are recorded in the records as having children as early as 1859. Despite limited success in the parish registers, therefore, the information contained therein forces the search to continue in other records.

Mexican Census

The national censuses of Mexico are unavailable for use, while those for Spain are available for certain time periods only. The U.S. federal censuses are all available up through 1910. In Mexico and Spain and the Spanish portions of the American Southwest, many local censuses of civil and ecclesiastical origins are available and can provide the links needed to continue back into the past. It was to this group of records that it was necessary to turn to find the missing information for the second case study. In the Archivo Historico de Sonora in Hermosillo are many local censuses, many of them uncataloged. There are none for Hermosillo or Horcasitas but several for Arispe, Ures, Baviacora, and Aconchi. There is an 1868 census for the towns of Aconchi, Arispe, Banamichi, Baviacora, Rayon, and Sinoquipe. No Yslas families appeared in the census in any of these places, but in Aconchi an exciting find was made which added much to the little found in the parish registers and began to substantiate a great deal of the information provided in the interview with Maria del Carmen Romo recorded earlier.

In this census, living side by side are the parents of Maria del Carmen, along with two of their children, as follows:

Francisco Lopez	age 30	married	can write
Beatriz Ochoa	age 29	married	
Refugio Lopez	age 7		
Trinidad Lopez	age 5		

Living next door to this family are the parents and two younger siblings of Beatrice Ochoa, as follows:

Francisco Ochoa	age 60	married	cannot write
Rafaela Lopes	age 50	married	
Jesus Ochoa	age 27	single	
Dolores Ochoa	age 25	single[40]	

This was a great addition to the material needed to complete information on the families in the case study. However, an even greater addition than this was the material found in the uncataloged 1848 census of Aconchi. It should be realized as this material is studied that it predates by twenty years any information available in the parish registers of the area.

A search through the census of the city of Aconchi in 1848 revealed nothing. The census continues with records for outlying areas, however, so the search continued. A few pages into the record of outlying areas, under the heading of San Pablo Mission, is the following information:

Don Nicolas Romo	age 60	married	worker
Dona Estefana Lares	53	married	
Jesus Romo	32	married	worker
Maria Romo	30	married	
Dionisio Romo	28	single	
Maria Felipa Romo	26	single	
Maria Ursula Romo	24	single	
Francisco Romo	20	single	worker
Nicolas Romo	8	single	
Manuel Romo	6	single	
Jesus Maria Romo	2	child[41]	

A few of the entries had Don or Dona attached to them. This indicates that although the family was probably engaged in farming, they were most likely well respected by the local populace. The first Maria was probably the wife of the first

Jesus. The last three individuals were probably their children. Francisco, age 20, would become the father of Maria del Carmen Romo. This record verifies part of the family tradition concerning Estefana Lares and her two husbands. She appears to have had a normal family here, but at a later date several of her boys are found in the parish registers using the surname Lopez, indicating a previous relationship with one who, from other records, proves to be Manuel Lopez.

Three pages later under the same San Pablo mission is the following excellent material:

Don Francisco Ochoa	age 49	married
Dona Rafaela Lopes	44	married
Maria del Carmen Ochoa	16	single
Francisco Ochoa	15	single
Javier Ochoa	14	single
Maria Dolores Ochoa	13	single
Beatriz Ochoa	12	single
Jesus Ochoa	10	child
Jose Refugio Ochoa	8	child[42]

Besides these discoveries there were other Romo, Lopes, and Ochoa families in Aconchi which were copied for future study. Following these discoveries a trip was made to the area surrounding Aconchi. Detailed geographical notes were taken for inclusion in the historical compilations to be made later. Cemetery records were copied. Each little town was visited that had any connection with the families in question. Interviews were carried out with the oldest individuals in each town, some of whom provided additional excellent biographical materials for future use, and there was also some very interesting storytelling (lies) by a few of the more colorful citizens. The major facts that were learned are the following:

1. The Ochoa family was from San Felipe.
2. The Lopez family lived at La Estancia, San Pablo, and Baviacora, this latter being the place from which it spread.
3. The Romo family lived at Rodeo and San Pablo.
4. Rafaela Lopes's first husband was Manuel Romero. She died in about 1930. The Romo and Romero families were related.
5. Francisco Ochoa and Rafaela Lopes lived at San Pablo and worked in the local mill. Most of the people worked for the mill at that time.
6. The Romo family did in fact rent land. Nicolas Romo and Estefana Lares lived at La Estancia at one time.
7. Nicholas died at Baviacora before the revolution.
8. In Baviacora there were a number of Lares families. They apparently spread from there. Estephana Lares may have died there.
9. Nicholas left San Pablo about 1912–14 (this does not agree with number 7 above)

to work at the mine called Las Cabezas. Many people left San Pablo to work in the mine at that time.

10. Beatriz Ochoa died at San Felipe.
11. Francisco Lopez may have died at San Felipe.

Monumental Inscriptions

There is a variety of types of burial grounds in the United States, Mexico, and Spain, and they contain different degrees of information, some of which is completely valueless. Prior to 1 March 1794 all cemeteries in Mexico and Spain were maintained by the local churches. Nearly all of these churchyard burial grounds have disappeared because of the normal deterioration of time or because of the modernization of the areas in which they once existed. Some indications of the type of material that is still available can be seen from the transcriptions that follow.

In the Horcasitas cemetery, which was in reasonably good condition considering the poor state of affairs of the city, the early inscriptions had disappeared. What was available on the Yslas families was copied.

1. QEPD (*Que en paz descanza*). Dolores P. de Islas died 8 November 1931 at age seventy-seven; plaque placed by her children.
2. QEPD. Jose Yslas P. died 20 May 1917 at age seventy-four; plaque placed by wife and children.
3. Jose Islas P. died 4 January 1962 at age eighty-one, DEP (descansa en paz); plaque placed by wife.
4. Margarita Islas, widow of Tapia, born 22 July 1877, died 3 January 1951; plaque placed by her children.
5. Jose Luis Badilla Islas, 19 April 1909 to 5 May 1975.
6. Richardo Badilla Islas, died 12 January 1973, age 58.

At the time of the visit the caretaker was placing the cover on the grave of "Jose Luis Badilla Isla." It was pointed out to him that the "s" had been left off the surname Isla. He instructed his assistant to add it. From the caretaker the location was learned of a lady who directed the search to Trinidad Ibarra Islas y Alvarez. She and her brothers and sisters are children of Henriqueta Islas, who was the daughter of Trinidad Urias and Ramon Yslas. A member of this family, Agustin Yslas, aged 70 in 1975, was living in Tucson at that time. He was later visited and additional information on the family was obtained.

One of the reasons for the disappearance of cemetery information is that the graves are not bought in perpetuity and after a certain time period are used again by other families, or by the same family for other deceased relatives. In the judicial archives at Hermosillo, for example, in the intestate proceedings of Don Francisco Yslas is found the following information:

On 13 August 1885 at Hermosillo permission was given to Don Eduardo Yslas to construct a grave (boveda) on top of that of his brother, Ramon Yslas, in perpetuity, for his father don Francisco Yslas, who died of a nervous attack today at the age of 75 (born about 1810), married to Maria Bernal; native of this city, businessman, son of Teodoro Yslas and dona Anna Ansar. Children: Ramon Islas (who died 13 August 1880, age 27), Elena, Francisco, Eduardo, Florencio, Carmen, Alfredo, Teresa, Adelaida, Emila, Guadalupe, and Teodora. He left no will. Wife and children survive him.[43]

As this very good, although directly unrelated, information on the specific Yslas family was traced, other information was obtained by going back to the parish registers. "On 9 September 1823 Don Manuel de Ainsa, native of Manila, the Philippines, married Dona Filomena Yslas, native of Arispe, daughter of Don Teodora Yslas and Dona Ana Anza." This Filomena was sister to Francisco, above. She must have been born about 1803 or so, possibly in Arispe. "Francisco Yslas, single, native of Arispe, son of Teodora Yslas, now deceased, and ana Maria Anza, married Maria Bernal, daughter of Ramon Bernal and Lorensa A., both deceased.[44]

One can see from the above information that it was finally the cemetery records that put researchers onto the right track in finding the origins of the Yslas family. Some burial information still exists prior to 1600 but is usually found in the walls and floors of the churches, where it has been protected from the elements.

On 1 March 1794 King Charles IV ordered the establishment of civil cemetries in the urban areas of the principal cities of his kingdom. Most public cemeteries, however, were established in the early to mid-eighteenth century, usually in conjunction with the formation of civil registration in any given municipality. These cemeteries normally kept records of burials, exhumations, and sales of plots, niches, crypts, and so on. Many of the older records have been transferred from the cemeteries' offices to the archives of the local public health offices or similar repositories. These records contain valuable information on relationships and vital data on the deceased.

Notarial

After the records already mentioned, the next most important and informative are the notarial records. Everything of a public or legal nature pertaining to individuals that was recorded during the colonial period usually found its way into the notarial books. These books include wills, land transactions, dowry information, contracts, bonds, powers, mortgages, complaints, charges, and payments.

Some notarial records have been destroyed for various reasons, but for the most part they are still available in good condition in the original archives of the province, department, or state or in the national or general archives of the nation. In northern Mexico both state archives and local archives exist. In Mexico City there is also a large notarial archive, which contains many records from around the country.

Although some of the more conscientious scribes did so, it was not customary to make indexes of the notarian books. More of these records began to be indexed following the independence period, as local officials realized the absolute value of the information contained in their records.

Wills are by far the most important of the records contained in notarial registers. Wills are found in other places as well: in ecclesiastical archives, municipal archives, public registries, judicial archives, private homes, museums, and elsewhere.

Land

Of all the records best suited to genealogical and historical research in Mexico, Spain, and the United States, those that deal with land are found in more assorted places than any other. During the initial years of the conquest, large land grants, called *encomiendas,* were distributed to those who assisted in pacification and conquest. The records today are kept at the AGN. An index to this collection begins in the *Boletin* of the archive, volume 1, number 1, published in 1960. The section in the archives itself is called Tierras. There are 3,832 volumes in this collection. Included in the archives are many records for northern Mexico and the southwestern part of the United States.

A great deal of land passed into the possession of the Catholic Church through gifts during the hundreds of years of the colonial period. Wealthy Spaniards would bequeath their property to the custody of a chaplain who would administer the estate from year to year, taking proceeds from its production to pay his salary, say Masses in behalf of the deceased benefactor, and provide other Christian services, both to individuals and to organizations. These records, called *capellanias,* exist in large numbers in the section by that name at the AGN. They begin in 1524.

Another section of this same archive, entitled Ramo de Vinculos, contains many hereditary estate records from 1557 to 1814. There is an index to this section which gives excellent relationship information for two and three generations per document.

Finally, one of the largest repositories for land record information must be the notarial archives already referenced. The wills contained therein, the mortgages of property, the disputes between relatives for one item or another, all contain rich details concerning the land records of the country. In the AGN there are similar intestate probate records in the Ramo de Intestados for the seventeenth, eighteenth, and nineteenth centuries. These certainly must be considered, along with the other sources mentioned, in dealing with the lands of Mexico.

Space will not permit sample documents from the last records discussed, but they have also been used to compile the second case study and must be considered a necessary part of the research process for anyone attempting to reconstruct a family tree or do research of a similar nature.

Compilation of Hispanic-American genealogies is not easy, but it is easier than reconstructing such other ethnic genealogies as those of Anglo-Europeans, blacks, or Orientals, provided it is possible to travel to the areas where the ancestral families lived and to the archives that contain their records. If this is impossible, then one should preserve those records on the family which are more readily available; at a future time or in a future generation this material will prove invaluable in tracing the local clues. Without this personal family information, it is many times impossible to break through the barrier into the archival repositories that contain further information.

NOTES

1. Archivo General de la Nación (AGN), Mexico City, Ramo de Californias, bundle 41, pp. 115–216.

2. For a more detailed history of the orphanage in Mexico City, see Martiniano T. Alfaro, *Reseña Histórica Descriptiva del Hospicio de Mexico* (Mexico: Tip. y Lit. La Europa, 1910); also the 1811 census of the Casa de Hospicios, AGN, Ramo de Padrones (microfilm copies at the University of California, Berkeley, and University of Texas, Austin).

3. AGN, Ramo de Californias, bundle 49A, p. 138; see also bundle 66, p. 397; bundle 67, p. 185; and bundle 69, p. 63, for a few additional references of this type.

4. Three volumes of the earliest records have been published by the Archivo General de Indias (AGI) under the directorship of Don Cristobal Bermudez Plata: *Catálogo de Pasajeros a Indias,* vol. 1, 1509–34; vol. 2, 1535–38; and vol. 3, 1539–59 (Seville: Imprenta de la Gavida, 1940–46). The staff of the AGI is presently working on an index up to 1800, which may be consulted by correspondence. Peter Boyd-Bowman has also published some excellent general references to this early time period: *Indice Geobiográfico do Cuarenta Mil Pobladores Españoles de América en el Siglo XVI,* vol. 1, 1493–1519 (Bogota: Instituto Caro y Cuervo, 1964); vol. 2, 1520–39 (Mexico: Editorial Jus, 1968).

5. Archivo Histórico de Sonora (AHS), drawer 3–4, 414.6, bundles 1–2.

6. Ibid.

7. John Myers Myers, *The Border Wardens* (Englewood Cliffs, N.J.: Prentice-Hall, 1971), p. 79.

8. Charles R. Maduell, Jr., comp., *Index of Spanish Citizens Entering the Port of New Orleans Between January 1840 and December 1865* (New Orleans: Charles R. Maduell, Jr., 1966).

9. Ibid.

10. "Register of Film Numbers for Passenger Lists and Indexes of Vessels Arriving in the United States" (Salt Lake City: Genealogical Society of Utah, 1980).

11. Milton P. Rieder, Jr., and Norma Gaudet Rieder, eds., *New Orleans Ship Lists,* 2 vols. (Metairie, La.: privately published, 1968).

12. AGN, Ramo de Californias, bundle 66, pp. 400–400v.

13. Ibid., bundle 76, p. 273.

14. Ibid., bundle 69, p. 63.

15. Ibid., Ramo de Historia, bundle 503, p. 4.

16. Ibid., Ramo de Pasaporte, vol. 1, vol. 57, and various other minor consultations.

17. Ibid., nos. 5052–74.

18. Ibid., Ramo de Historia, vol. 522, pp. 244–79.

19. Marie Northrup, ed., *Historical Society of Southern California Quarterly* (March 1961): 107–8, for San Diego. See indexes of *Historical Society of Southern California Quarterly* for additional census of 1790 plus others for the nineteenth century.

20. AGN, Ramo de Historia, vol. 522, p. 266.

21. Archivo de Simancas, *Catálogo XXII del Archivo de Simancas, Secretaría de Guerra* (eighteenth century), Valladolid, 1958.

22. AGN, Ramo de Provincias Internas, vol. 227, 15: 284–91; vol. 247, 20: 349–70; vol. 252, 23: 232, 235; vol. 250, 7: 373–409.

23. AGI, Mexico, bundles 2463–67, pp. 244, 1386, and others.

24. AGN, Ramo de Inquisiciones, bundle 1282, pp. 423–26.

25. AGN, Ramo de Californias, vol. 2A, folio 13, pp. 235–38.

26. Ibid., vol. 2, folio 12, pp. 313–22.

27. Ibid., vol. 10, folio 7, pp. 88–93.

28. Doris Marion Wright, *A Guide to the Mariano Guadalupe Vallejo Documents for the History of California, 1780–1875* (Berkeley: University of California Press, 1953), p. 129.

29. Virginia L. Olmsted, "Spanish Enlistment Papers of New Mexico, 1732–1820," *National Genealogical Society Quarterly* 67: 229.

30. Henry Putney Beers, *Spanish and Mexican Records of the American Southwest* (Tucson: University of Arizona Press, 1979), p. 203.

31. Archivo de Simancas, *Catálogo,* p. 239.

32. AGN, Ramo de Provincias Internas, bundle 233, p. 515.

33. Beers, *Spanish and Mexican Records of the American Southwest,* p. 203.

34. Lyman De Platt, *Genealogical-Historical Guide to Latin America* (Detroit: Gale Research Co., 1978); *Una Guía Genealógico-Histórica de Latinoamérica* (Ramona, Calif.: Acoma Books, 1978).

35. James Miller Guinn, *Historical and Biographical Record of Los Angeles and Vicinity* (Chicago: Chapman Pub. Co., 1901).

36. John Steven McGroarty, *Los Angeles: From the Mountain to the Sea* (Chicago and New York: American Historical Society, 1921).

37. Hermosillo Cathedral, vol. 8 of baptisms, pp. 393v–94, no. 1021.

38. Ibid., vol. 3 of marriages, p. 43v, no. 269.

39. Ibid., prenuptial investigations, book no. 11, pp. 41–42v.

40. AHS, padrón Aconchi, 1868, carpeton 409, p. 4v.

41. AHS, padrón Aconchi of 15 March 1848, carpeton 258, p. 9.

42. Ibid., p. 12.

43. Archivo Judicial de Hermosillo, folder 55/1892, Juzgado Segundo de la Primera Instancia de Hermosillo.

44. Hermosillo Cathedral, vol. 1 of marriages, p. 54v, 161v.

BIBLIOGRAPHY

Books, Articles, and Monographs

Bancroft, Hubert H. *California Pastoral, 1769–1848.* San Francisco: History Co., 1884–90.
    General history.
———. *California Pioneer Register and Index, 1542–1848.* Baltimore: Genealogical Publishing Co., 1964.
    Biographical.
———. *History of Arizona and New Mexico, 1530–1888.* San Francisco: History Co., 1889; Albuquerque, N.M.: Hornand Wallace, 1962.
    General history.
———. *History of California.* 7 vols. San Francisco: History Co., 1884–90.
    General history.
———. *History of the North Mexican States and Texas.* 2 vols. San Francisco: History Co., 1886–89.
    General history.
Bannon, John Francis. *The Spanish Borderlands Frontier, 1513–1821.* New York: Holt, Rinehart and Winston, 1970.

General history.

Beck, Warren. *New Mexico: A History of Four Centuries*. Norman: Oklahoma University Press, 1962.

General history.

Beers, Henry Putney. *Spanish & Mexican Records of the American Southwest*. Tucson: University of Arizona Press, 1979.

Guides to record sources and bibliographies for all of the states of the Southwest.

Bolton, Herbert E. *Guide to Materials for the History of the United States in the Principal Archives of Mexico*. Washington D.C.: Carnegie Institution, 1913; New York: Kraus Reprint Corp., 1966.

Guide to record sources.

————. *The Spanish Borderlands: A Chronicle of Old Florida and the Southwest*. New Haven: Yale University Press, 1921.

General history.

————. *Spanish Exploration in the Southwest, 1542–1706*. New York: n.p., 1916.

General history.

————. "The Spanish Occupation of Texas, 1519–1690." *Southwestern Historical Quarterly* 16 (July 1912): 1–26.

General history.

————. *Texas in the Middle Eighteenth Century: Studies in Spanish Colonial Administration*. Berkeley: University of California Press, 1915; reprint ed. New York: Russell and Russell, 1962.

History of Texas, town histories, biographies, and other information.

Bowan, Jean Donald. "The Spanish of San Antonio, New Mexico." Ph.D. diss., University of Texas, 1960.

Local history.

Bowden, Jocelyn J. *Spanish and Mexican Land Grants in the Chihuahua Acquisition*. El Paso: Texas Western Press, University of Texas at El Paso, 1971.

Land records, local and regional history, some biographical data on local residents.

Brinckerhoff, Sidney R. "The Last Years of Spanish Arizona, 1786–1821." *Arizona and the West* 9 (Spring 1967): 5–20.

General history, Arizona history, some local history.

Burma, John H., ed. *Mexican-Americans in the United States*. Cambridge, Mass.: Schenkman Publishing Co., 1970.

Ethnic history, migration information, case studies.

Cabildo of New Orleans. *Spanish Census of New Orleans, 1791*. New Orleans: n.p., n.d.

Biographical, family history.

Casteñeda, Carlos E. *Our Catholic Heritage in Texas, 1519–1936*. 7 vols. Austin, Tex.: Von Boeckmann-Jones Co., 1936.

Ecclesiastical, social, and local history.

————. *A Report on the Spanish Archives in San Antonio, Texas*. San Antonio: Yanaguana Society, 1937.

Guide to record sources, indexes, inventories, and so on. Assists in finding and using the part of the Béxar Archives not transferred to the University of Texas in 1896.

Céliz, Fray Francisco. *Diary of the Alarcón Expedition into Texas, 1718–1719*. Translated by Fritz L. Hoffman. 2 vols. Los Angeles: Quivira Society, 1935.

Local history, biographical material.

Chapman, Charles E. *The Alta California Supply Ships, 1773–1776*. Austin: Texas State Historical Association, 1915. Reprinted from the *Southwestern Historical Quarterly* 19 (October 1915): 184–94.

General history.

————. *The Founding of Spanish California; the Northwestward Expansion of New Spain,*

1687–1783. New York: Macmillan Co., 1916. Ph.D. diss., University of California, 1915.
General history.

———. *A History of California: The Spanish Period.* New York: Macmillan Co., 1921.
General history.

Chávez, Angelico. *Archives of the Archdiocese of Santa Fe.* Washington, D.C.: Academy of American Franciscan History, 1957.
Guide to record sources, indexes, and inventories.

———. *Origins of New Mexico Families in the Spanish Colonial Period.* Santa Fe, N.M.: Historical Society of New Mexico, 1954; Albuquerque: University of New Mexico, 1973.
Local history, biographical.

Conrad, Glenn R. *The First Families of Louisiana.* 2 vols. Baton Rouge, La.: Claitor's, 1970.
Local history, biographical.

Cook, Warren L. *Flood Tide of Empire: Spain and the Pacific Northwest, 1543–1819.* New Haven, Conn.: Yale University Press, 1973.
General history.

Cowen, Robert G. *Ranchos of California: A List of Spanish Concessions, 1775–1822, and Mexican Grants, 1822–1846.* Fresno, Calif.: Academy Library Guild, 1956.
Local history, land records.

Cox, Isaac J. "The Early Settlers of San Fernando." *Quarterly of the Texas State Historical Association* 5 (October 1901): 142–60.
Local history, census information, biographies.

Coy, Owen C. *Guide to County Archives of California.* Sacramento: n.p., 1919.
Guide to Spanish and early California archival materials, listings, indexes, and other information.

Curley, Michael J. *Church and State in the Spanish Floridas, 1783–1822.* New York: AMS Press, 1940.
Ecclesiastical and general history.

Denis, Alberta Johnston. *Spanish Alta California.* New York: Macmillan Co., 1927.
Documentary history, using many original source quotations, but without identifying the sources.

Ericson, Carolyn R. *Nacogdoches—Gateway to Texas: A Biographical Directory, 1773–1849.* Fort Worth: Arrow-Curtis Printing Co., 1974.
Local history, biographies.

Farish, Thomas E. *History of Arizona.* 8 vols. San Francisco: n.p., 1915–18.
General history.

Gamio, Manuel. *The Mexican Immigrant.* New York: New York Times/Arno Press, 1969.
General history, immigration.

———. *Mexican Immigration to the United States.* New York: New York Times/Arno Press, 1969.
General history, immigration.

Garcia, Genaro, ed. *Historia de Nuevo León: Con Noticias Sobre Coahuila, Texas y Nuevo México.* México, D.F.: Librería de la Vda. de Ch. Bouret, 1909.
General and local history.

Garcia, Richard A., comp. and ed. *The Chicanos in America, 1540–1974: A Chronology and Fact Book.* Dobbs Ferry, N.Y.: Oceana Publications, 1977.
Statistical, biographical, and general history.

Geary, Gerald J. *The Secularization of the California Missions, 1810–1846.* Washington, D.C.: Catholic University of America, 1934.
Ecclesiastical and general history.

Gomez Canedo, Lino. *Primeras Exploraciones y Poblaciones de Texas, 1686–1694.* Monterrey, Mexico: Publicaciones del Instituto Tecnológico y de Estudios Superiores, 1968.
General history.

Greenleaf, Richard E., and Meyer, M. C. *Research in Mexican History: Topics, Methodology,*

Sources and a Practical Guide to Field Research. Lincoln: University of Nebraska Press, 1973.
  Instructional guide, perhaps the best that exists on how to do research in Mexico and the borderlands. This guide and my own (also listed here) cover most of the information needed for a systematic approach to research in the area.

Hackett, Charles W., ed. *Historical Documents Relating to New Mexico, Nueva Vizcaya, and Approaches Thereto, to 1773*. 3 vols. Washington, D.C.: Carnegie Institution, 1923–27.
  Local history.

Haigh, Roger M., ed. *Finding Aids to the Microfilmed Manuscript Collection of the Genealogical Society of Utah: Preliminary Survey of the Mexican Collection*. Salt Lake City: University of Utah Press, 1978.
  Guide.

Hammon, George Peter. *The Rediscovery of New Mexico, 1580–1594*. Albuquerque: University of New Mexico Press, 1966.
  Local history.

Hatcher, Mattie Austin. *The Opening of Texas to Foreign Settlement, 1801–1821*. Austin: University of Texas Press, 1927; reprint ed., Philadelphia: Porcupine Press, 1976.
  Local history.

Holmes, Jack D. L. *Honor and Fidelity: The Louisiana Infantry Regiment and the Louisiana Militia Companies, 1766–1821*. Birmingham, Ala.: Jack Holmes, 1965.
  Military history, local history, biographical information.

Hughes, Ann E. *The Beginnings of Spanish Settlement in the El Paso District*. Berkeley: University of California Press, 1914.
  Local history, biographical information.

Hutchinson, Cecil A. *Frontier Settlement in Mexican California: Hijar-Padres Colony and Its Origins, 1769–1835*. New Haven, Conn.: Yale University Press, 1969.
  Local history, including a complete list of the colonizers.

Jenkins, John H. *Cracker Barrel Chronicles: A Bibliography of Texas Towns and County Histories*. Austin, Tex.: Pemberton Press, 1965.
  Reference book.

Jenkins, Myra Ellen. *Calendar of the Spanish Archives of New Mexico*. Santa Fe, N.M.: State of New Mexico Records Center, 1968.
  Indexes, guides, bibliographic references.

Jones, Oakah L., Jr. *Los Paisanos, Spanish Settlers on the Northern Frontier of New Spain*. Norman: University of Oklahoma Press, 1979.
  Local history, general history.

Kielman, Chester V. *Guide to the Microfilm Edition of the Béxar Archives, 1717–1803*. Austin: University of Texas Archives Microfilm Publication, 1967.
  Bibliographic references, guides, indexes, and other information.

————. *The University of Texas Archives: A Guide to the Historical Manuscripts Collections in the University of Texas Library*. Austin: University of Texas Press, 1967.
  Bibliographic references, guides, indexes, and other information.

Leonard, P. H. *The Decline of the Californias: A Social History of the Spanish-Speaking Californias, 1846–1890*. Berkeley: University of California Press, 1966.
  General history.

Lo Buglio, Rudecinda. *The Archives of Northwestern Mexico*. Salt Lake City: Genealogical Society of Utah, 1980.
  Bibliographic references, guides, indexes, general history.

————. *Survey of Pre-Statehood Records: A New Look at Spanish and Mexican-Californian Genealogical Records*. Salt Lake City: Genealogical Society of Utah, 1980.
  Bibliographic references, guides, indexes, general history.

Lowery, Woodbury. *The Spanish Settlements Within the Present Limits of the United States, 1513–1561*. New York: Russell and Russell, 1959.

General and local history.

McConville, J. Lawrence. "A History of Population in the El Paso-Ciudad Juárez Area." Master's thesis, University of New Mexico, 1966.

Local history, statistics, biographical data, and other information.

McWilliams, Carey. *North from Mexico: The Spanish-Speaking People of the United States.* Philadelphia: J. B. Lippincott Co., 1949; reprint ed., Westport, Conn.: Greenwood Press, 1968.

Ethnic studies, general history.

Maduell, Charles R., Jr., comp. *Marriage Contracts, Wills and Testaments of the Spanish Colonial Period in New Orleans, 1770–1804.* New Orleans: Charles Maduell, 1970.

Martínez, Pablo L. *Guía Familiar de Baja California, 1700–1900.* México, D.F.: Imprenta "Laura," 1965.

Vital records for most of Baja California, biographical information.

Mechan, J. L. "The Northern Expansion of New Spain, 1522–1822: A Selected Descriptive Bibliographical List." *Hispanic American Historical Review* 1 (1927): 233–76.

General history, bibliographical references.

Moquín, Wayne, and Van Doren, Charles, eds. *A Documentary History of the Mexican Americans.* New York: Praeger Publishers, 1971.

Ethnic history, bibliographic references, biographical information.

Morefield, Richard Henry. "Mexicans in the California Mines, 1848–1853." *California Historical Society Quarterly* 35 (March 1956): 37–46.

Local history.

Morgan, Dale L., and Hammond, George P., eds. *A Guide to the Manuscript Collections of the University of California.* Berkeley: University of California Press, 1963.

Indexes, guides, bibliographic references.

Mullins, Marion D. *The First Census of Texas, 1829–1836.* Washington, D.C.: National Genealogical Society, 1962.

Census materials, biographical information, family history.

Mundo Lo, Sara de. *Bibliography of Hispanic American Collective Biography.* Boston: G. K. Hall and Co., 1980.

Bibliographic references to much of the important material available on Mexican-American culture.

Nasatir, Abraham Phineas. *Spanish War Vessels on the Mississippi, 1792–1796.* New Haven, Conn.: Yale University Press, 1968.

Military history, local history.

Navarro Garcia, Luis. *Sonora y Sinaloa en el Siglo XVII.* Seville: Publicaciones de la Escuela de Estudios Hispano-Americanos de Sevilla, 1967.

General history.

New Mexico State Records Center and Archives. *Guide to the Microfilm of the Spanish Archives of New Mexico, 1621–1821, in the Archives Division of the State of New Mexico Records Center.* Santa Fe: Records Center and Archives, 1967.

Indexes, lists, bibliographical information.

Nogales, Luis G. *The Mexican-American: A Selected and Annotated Bibliography.* Stanford, Calif.: Stanford University Press, 1971.

Bibliographic information.

O'Gorman, Edmundo. *Historia de las Divisiones Territoriales de México.* 4th ed. México, D. F.: Editorial Porrúa, 1968.

Excellent guide to state boundary changes during the Spanish domination of Mexico.

O'Rourke, Thomas P. *The Franciscan Missions in Texas, 1690–1793.* Washington, D.C.: Catholic University of America, 1927.

Ecclesiastical and local history.

Oswandel, J. Jacob. *Notes of the Mexican War, 1846–1848.* Philadelphia: n.p., 1885.

General history.

Parker, J. Carlyle. *Sources of California: From Padron to Voter Registration.* Salt Lake City:

Genealogical Society of Utah, 1969.

Bibliographic materials, indexes, local history, and similar information.

Patronato Nacional de Archivos Históricos. *Catálogo XXII del Archivo de Simancas, Secretaría de Guerra (siglo XVIII), Hojas de Servicios de America*. Valladolid, España: Patronato, 1958.

Military service records for the eighteenth century of Spanish soldiers serving throughout Latin America, including the modern southwestern United States.

Peplow, Edward H. *History of Arizona*. 3 vols. New York: Lewis Historical Publishing Co., 1958.

Family, personal, local, and general history.

Platt, Lyman De. *Genealogical-Historical Guide to Latin America*. Detroit: Gale Publishing Co., 1978.

Guide to record sources in Mexico and other countries. Indexes, lists, tables, how-to information on research in Spanish records.

——. *Una Guía Genealógico-Histórica de Latinoamérica*. Ramona, Calif.: Acoma Books, 1978.

Spanish edition of the *Genealogical-Historical Guide*.

——. "Hispanic American Records and Research." *World Conference on Records* (2d, 1980) vol. 9, no. 708. Salt Lake City: Corporation of the President of the Church of Jesus Christ of Latter-day Saints, c1980.

Bibliographic reference, general history, general reference.

——. "The Mexican Military." *World Conference on Records* (2d, 1980). vol. 9, no. 713. Salt Lake City: Corporation of the President of the Church of Jesus Christ of Latter-day Saints, c1980.

Military history of Mexico from 1760s to 1820s, including detailed information about the border area.

Polzer, Charles William, et al. *The Documentary Relations of the Southwest Project Manual*. Tucson: University of Arizona, 1977.

Archival references, bibliographic materials, local history, indexes, lists, and similar information.

Pompey, Sherman L. *Genealogical Records of California*. Fresno, Calif.: n.p., 1968.

General and local history, census and tax records, military records, and similar information.

Pourade, Richard F. *Anza Conquers the Desert: The Anza Expedition from Mexico to California and the Founding of San Francisco, 1774–1776*. San Diego, Calif.: Union Tribune Publishing Co., 1971.

General history.

Richardson, Rupert N. *Texas: The Lone Star State*. New York: Prentice-Hall, 1943.

General history.

Richman, Irving B. *California Under Spain and Mexico, 1535–1847*. New York: Cooper Square Publications, 1965.

Documentary history.

Robles, Vito Alessio. *Coahuila y Texas en la Epóca Colonial*. México, D.F.: Editorial Cultural, 1938.

General history.

Rodriguez Casado, Vicente. *Primeros Años de Dominación Española en la Luisiana*. Madrid: n.p., 1942.

General history.

Roel, Santiago. *Nuevo León: Apuntes Históricos*. 4th ed. Monterrey, México: Universidad de Nuevo León, 1952.

General history.

Rowland, Leon. *Los Fundadores de California, 1769–1785*. Academy of California Church History, publication no. 3. Fresno: the Academy, 1951.

General and local history, biographical information.

Scott, Florence J. *Historical Heritage of the Lower Rio Grande*. 3rd ed. Rio Grande City, Tex.: La Retama Press, 1972.

Biographical data on early settlers, historical data on the development of the towns and ranches under Spanish, Mexican, and Texan control between 1747 and 1848.

Secretaria de Gobernación. *Indice del Ramo de Provincias Internas*. 2 vols. México, D.F.: Archivo General de la Nación, 1967.

Censuses, military records, land records, local and general history, correspondence, biographical information, family history, and similar information for the northern areas of Mexico and the U.S. Southwest.

Simmons, Marc Steven. "Spanish Government in New Mexico at the End of the Colonial Period." Ph.D. diss., University of New Mexico, 1965.

General and local history.

————. "Tlascalans in the Spanish Borderlands." *New Mexico Historical Review* 39 (April 1964): 101–10.

Local history.

Sonnichsen, C. L. *Pass of the North: Four Centuries on the Rio Grande*. El Paso, Tex.: Texas Western Press, 1968.

General history.

Temple, Thomas Workman, III "Sources for Tracing Spanish-American Pedigrees in the Southwestern United States, Pt. 2: California and Arizona." *World Conference on Records and Genealogical Seminar*, area F-14b. Salt Lake City: Genealogical Society of the Church of Jesus Christ of Latter-day Saints, c1969.

Biographical references, local and family history sources.

Texas General Land Office. *An Abstract of the Original Titles of Records in the General Land Office of Texas*. Austin: Pemberton Press, 1964.

Identifies all colonies and the settlers of each for the time period 1791–1836. Excellent early history reference source.

Timmons, W. H. "The El Paso Area in the Mexican Period, 1821–1848." *Southwestern Historical Quarterly* 84 (July 1980): 1–28.

Local and family history.

————. "The Population of the El Paso Area—A Census of 1784." *New Mexico Historical Review* 52 (October 1977): 311–16.

Census material, biographical information, local and family data.

Twitchell, Ralph E. *The History of the Military Occupation of the Territory of New Mexico from 1846–1851 with Biographical Sketches of Men Prominent in the Conduct of the Government During that Period*. Chicago: Rio Grande Press, 1963.

Military and general history, biographical information.

————. *Old Santa Fe: The Story of New Mexico's Ancient Capital*. Chicago: Rio Grande Press, 1925, 1963.

General history.

————. *The Spanish Archives of New Mexico*. Cedar Rapids, Iowa: Torch Press, 1914.

Guide to record sources, indexes.

————, comp. *The Twitchell Archives, 1685–1898*. 6 microfilm reels. Filmed 1955–57 by the University of New Mexico Library, Albuquerque.

Land grants, disputes, wills, judgments, mine claims, inventories, indexes, and other information.

Vásquez, Nadine M. *Sinaloa Roots: An Account of the 1781 Expedition to Alta California and Ancestral Records of Early California Settlers, 1723–1808*. Carmichael, Calif.: Nadine M. Vásquez, 1974.

General, local, and family history; biographical material.

Villa, Eduardo W. *Historia del Estado de Sonora*. 2d ed. Hermosillo: Editorial Sonora, 1951.

General history.

Villaseñor Espinosa, Roberto, and Garza, Beatriz Artega. *Indice del Ramo de Californias*. 2 vols. México, D.F.: Archivo General de la Nación, 1977.

Censuses, military records, land records, local and general history, correspondence, biographical information, family history, and so forth for the northern areas of Mexico and the U.S. Southwest, particularly upper and lower California.

Villeré, Sidney L. *The Canary Islands Migration to Louisiana, 1778–1783*. Baltimore: Genealogical Publishing Co., 1972.

Weddle, Robert S. *San Juan Bautista: Gateway to Spanish Texas*. Austin: University of Texas Press, 1968.
Local history, biographical information.

————. *The San Saba Mission: Spanish Pivot in Texas*. Austin: University of Texas Press, 1964.
Local history, biographical information.

Whitaker, A. P. *The Spanish American Frontier, 1783–1795: The Westward Movement and the Spanish Retreat in the Mississippi Valley*. Gloucester, Mass.: Peter Smith, 1962.
General history.

White, Gifford E. *The 1840 Census of the Republic of Texas*. Austin: Pemberton Press, 1966.
Census materials, family history, local history.

Woods, Richard D. *Reference Materials on Mexican Americans: An Annotated Bibliography*. Metuchen, N.J.: Scarecrow Press, 1976.
Annotated bibliography of reference sources on Mexican Americans. Includes works on archives, guides to genealogical records, first families, vital statistics, newspapers, periodicals, and other subjects.

————, and Alvarez-Altman, Grace. *Spanish Surnames in Southwestern United States: A Dictionary*. Boston: G. K. Hall and Co., 1978.
Dictionary.

Wright, Doris M. *A Guide to the Mariano Guadalupe Vallejo Documentos Para la Historia de California, 1780–1875*. Berkeley: University of California Press, 1963.
Correspondence, military records, biographical information, local and general history, and other information.

Periodicals

Antepasados. San Francisco: Los Californianos.
Founded 1970. Indexes, guides, genealogies, history, and other information.

Archivo General de la Nación. *Boletín*. México, D.F.
Founded 1930. Indexes; guides; genealogies; general, local, and family history; lists of records; transcriptions of documents; census records; land records; and so on. All genealogical material contained in the collection is available at the Genealogical Department Library in Salt Lake City, Utah. Many indexes to the archive have been published separately. Those that deal specifically with the frontier areas are listed in the preceding section of this bibliography.

Austin Genealogical Society. *Quarterly*. Austin, Tex.
Founded 1960. Local and family history, genealogy, indexes, guides, and similar information.

Duke University Press. *Hispanic American Historical Review*. Durham, N.C.
Founded 1920. Indexes, biographical information, bibliographies, references, and local and general history.

Historical Society of Southern California. *Quarterly*. Los Angeles, Calif.
Founded 1884. Local and family history, genealogy, indexes and guides, and similar sources.

Houston Genealogical Forum. *The Genealogical Record*. Houston, Tex.
Founded 1958. Indexes, guides, local history, family history, and genealogy.

Journal of Mexican American History. Santa Barbara, Calif.
Founded fall 1970. General, local, and family history; indexes; guides; and other information.

Local Historical and Genealogical Society. *Quarterly*. Dallas, Tex.
Founded 1955. Local and family history, genealogy, and similar information.

New Mexico Genealogical Society. *New Mexico Genealogist*. Albuquerque, N. Mex.
Founded 1962. Census records, cemetery records, biographical information, indexes, lists, local history, and other information.

San Antonio Genealogical and Historical Society. *Our Heritage*. San Antonio, Tex.
Founded 1959. General, local, and family history; biographical and genealogical materials; indexes; and guides.

San Diego Historical Society. *Journal of San Diego History* (formerly *San Diego Historical Quarterly*). San Diego, Calif.
Founded 1955. Censuses; general, local, family, and oral history; indexes; guides; and other information.

Southern Arizona Genealogical Society Magazine. Tucson, Ariz.
Founded 1965. Local and family history, genealogy, indexes, guides, and other information.

Southern California Genealogical Society. *The Searcher*. Long Beach, Calif.
Founded 1965. Marriages, cemetery inscriptions, Bible records, local history.

South Texas Genealogical and Historical Society. *Quarterly*. Gonzales, Tex.
Founded 1966. Local and family history, genealogy, indexes, guides, and similar information.

Southwestern Genealogical Library. *The Southwestern Genealogist*. El Paso, Tex.
Founded 1963. Local and family history, genealogy, indexes, and other information.

Texas State Genealogical Society. *Stirpes*. Fort Worth, Tex.
Founded 1961. General, local, and family history; genealogy, indexes, guides, and other information.

Texas State Historical Association. *Southwestern Historical Quarterly*. Austin, Tex.
Founded July 1897. General and local history, indexes, guides, and other information.

Index

Academic libraries, 59; alumni records in, 70; basic reference sources for genealogists, 68; collecting practices, 68; college and university archives, 69–70; institutional records, other types of, 70; mission statements, 61; needs of family historians and genealogists, 68; primary research materials, 68; resources of, 68–70; special collections and genealogy, 69; student records in, 69

Accuracy, importance of, 24

Adoptees, 24, 48

Adoption Liberation Movement, 48

Adoption records, 48

African heritage, 4

African Star, The, 98

Afro-American family history, 96

Afro-American family history association, establishment of, 95

Afro-American Family History Grassroots Genealogy Workshop, 95

Alabama State Department of Archives and History, 72, 81

Allen County Historical Society, 86

Almanach de Gotha, 78

American and British Genealogy and Heraldry, 65

American Antiquarian Society, 54, 75; indexing of early newspaper, 47

American Antiquarian Society Library, 84

American Countries, 76

American family, history of, 91

American Indian Historical Society, 75

American Indian Movement, 232

American Indians

allotment period: allotment register, 221; allotted Indian, death of, 221; and genealogical records, 221; General Allotment Act, 221; Indian and English names, 221; Register of Families, 221; reservations and allotments, 214; traditions and kinship system, 221

background: attitudes of, 209, 229–32; attitudes toward, 209, 211, 229; bibliography, 235–38; crimes, 108; Doris Duke Oral History Project, 234; education of, 108; history of, 108; interest in roots, 93; naming customs and kinship system, 211; "non-paper Indians," definition of, 232; and oral history, 103; "paper Indians," definition of, 232; religion of, 108; research, 209–38 *passim*; tribal activities, 108

American Indians (*cont.*)
   intermingling, or conversion, period,
      211–12; heads of families, 212;
      land records, 212; tribal groups,
      heads of, 212
   removal, or concentration, period: cen-
      sus information, 212; 1832 cen-
      sus, Creek Nation, 212; 1835
      census, Cherokee Nation, 212;
      National Archives, records of,
      212; removal, 212; removal mus-
      ter rolls, 212–13
   reservation period: Act of 4 July 1884
      and annual census, 214; annuity
      rolls, 213; Bureau of Indian Af-
      fairs, records of, 214; census, an-
      nual, 214; census records, school,
      214; census rolls, 214; conditions
      on, 108; definition of, 212; educa-
      tion of, 214; and the federal gov-
      ernment, 232; Indian or English
      name, 214; Navajo reservation,
      census of, 214; Plains Indians,
      213; treaties with tribes, 213–14
   tribes, concept of, in *Handbook of
      American Indians North of Mex-
      ico,* 210
   types and locations of records:
      BIA: agents, attitudes of, 233; com-
         missioners' reports, 108; land or
         lease records, 233; levels of of-
         fices, 233; National Archives, 233
      churches: Mormon, and Indian
         tribes, 234; Quaker, and Indian
         tribes, 234
      family: Arizona, University of (Tuc-
         son), 234; California, University
         of (Los Angeles), 234; Florida,
         University of, 234; and genealogi-
         cal research, 232; Illinois, Univer-
         sity of, 234; LDS Library, 234;
         New Mexico, University of, 234;
         Oklahoma Historical Society, 234;
         problems in gathering informa-
         tion, 232; South Dakota, Univer-
         sity of, 234; Utah, University of,
         234
      miscellaneous: BIA reports, 229;
         Bureau of American Ethnology,

229; Cherokee claims, 226; Cher-
         okee Claims Commission Rec-
         ords, 226; Congressional Reports
         of Committees, 229; Continental
         Congress, journals of, 229; Court
         of Claims, Indian tribes and court
         cases with, 229; National Ar-
         chives, 226–29; National Records
         Center, 229; Sanitary Record of
         Sick, Injured, Births, Deaths,
         226; tribal records, 101, 229; vital
         records, 221; Wheeler-Howard
         Act, 226; wills, 229
      National Archives: and agency re-
         cords, 233; annuity rolls, 233;
         BIA records in, 233; collection of
         American Indian records, 233;
         correspondence of agents, 233; as
         largest holder of records, 233; re-
         gional archives, 233; reports, 233;
         wills, 233
      private collections: as custodian of
         records, 234; genealogical librar-
         ies, 234; historical societies, 234;
         Oklahoma, University of, collec-
         tion, 234; universities, 234
      tribal offices: as custodian of re-
         cords, 233; Wheeler-Howard Act
         (Indian Reorganization Act), 233
American Legion, 48
American Library Association: genealogi-
      cal conference, 66; and geneal-
      ogy, 65–67; and promotion of
      genealogy, 59; publishing, 65–66;
      training genealogical reference li-
      brarians, 66; 1978 yearbook, 6
American Society for Genealogists, 12
Ancestor chart. *See* Pedigree chart
Archives, 97; college and university,
      69–70
Arizona Branch Genealogical Library, 81
Arizona State Department of Libraries
      and Archives, 81
Arkansas Genealogical Society, 16
Arkansas State History Commission, 81
Ark-La-Tex Genealogical Association,
      56
Arnold, Cynthia, 16
Ashton, Rick, 8

Asian Americans
  background: Buddhist tradition, 240;
    Confucian tradition, 240; defini-
    tion of, 239; Hindu tradition, 240;
    immigrants, 239; Islamic tradi-
    tion, 240; Pacific migration, 239
  genealogy: advantages of, 244; clues to
    research, 243; immigrant groups
    and settlement patterns, 244–50;
    immigrants, 240; immigration re-
    strictions, 244; labor demands,
    244; obstacles to research,
    243–44; "yellow peril," 244
  Chinese Americans: ancestral venera-
    tion, 242; anti-Chinese move-
    ments, 246; businesses, 246; in
    censuses, 252; Chinatown,
    245–47, 255; Chinese benevolent
    associations, 246; Chinese Bureau
    in Hawaii, 246; Chinese Civic As-
    sociation, 246; Chinese Consoli-
    dated Benevolent Association,
    255; Chinese Exclusion Act, 246;
    clan organizations and associa-
    tions, 246, 255; communities, tra-
    ditions, and culture, 255; contract
    convention, 247; "coolies," 245;
    district associations, 246; 1880
    census, 245–46; and emigration,
    247; employment, 245, 247; em-
    ployment restrictions in Califor-
    nia, 245; exclusion legislation,
    245, 247; and filial piety, 242; of
    Hakka origin, 246; in Hawaii,
    246–47; Kingdom of Hawaii,
    treaty, 246; laborers and the
    Board of Immigration, 246; lan-
    guage, transliteration of, 242; lin-
    eage and continuity, 242; nuisance
    laws in California, 245; Opium
    War, 245; "paper sons," 245–46;
    Pinyin system, 242; T'aip'ing Re-
    bellion, effects of, 245; trade
    guilds, 246; United Chinese Soci-
    ety, 255; Wade-Giles system, 242
  immigration, 244–45; applications to
    enter, 254; arrivals, 254; Bureau
    of Immigration, records on, 254;
    certificates of identification, 254;
    certificates of registration, 254;
    Chinese Bureau, Department of
    Foreign Affairs and, 254; death
    records, 254; departures, 254; en-
    try permits (for merchants and
    students), 254; entry permits (for
    women), 254; Hawaii, restrictions
    in, 246; Hawaiian-born children
    of Chinese parentage, 254; A His-
    tory of the Chinese in California,
    245; on Honolulu streets (lists of),
    254; immigration patterns,
    changes in, 244; immigration peri-
    od, research in, 245; in the Na-
    tional Archives, 254;
    naturalization indexes, 254; pass-
    ports, 254; photograph books,
    254; restrictions and control, 244,
    254; "segregated Chinese files,"
    254; in the United States, 241,
    247
  records and resources: adoptions,
    257; agreements, 257; ancestral
    tablets, 257; applications, 258;
    bibliography (Chinese Americans
    and China), 290–94; Buddhist
    temples, 257; certificates, indi-
    vidual, 243; certificates of identi-
    fication, 258; chia-p'u or tsu-p'u
    (clan or family genealogies), 243;
    criminal and civil judgments, 257;
    Department of Interior, 257; ex-
    clusion, 254; family registers,
    243; gravesites (China), 256;
    guides and inventories (county re-
    cords), 257; Hawaii Chinese His-
    tory Center, 257; Hawaiian
    Bureau of Conveyance, 257; Ha-
    waiian Circuit Court of Records,
    257; Hawaiian Commercial Sugar
    Company, 257; Hawaiian State
    Archives, 257; Hawaiian Sugar
    Planters Association, 257; immi-
    gration records, 243; laborers in
    Hawaii, 256; land records, 257;
    LDS Genealogical Department Li-
    brary, 257; local records, 257–58;
    mortuary tablets, 257; news-
    papers, annotated list of, 256; per-

Asian Americans
  Chinese Americans
    records and resources (*cont.*)
      sonal records, 258; probates, 257;
      sales, 257; settlements, 257;
      taxes, 257; temples, 257;
      tombstones, information on, 257;
      voter registrations, 258; Wailuku
      Sugar Company, 257; wills, 257;
      work permits, 258
    typical search: conducting the
      search, 278–83; dates, 279; inter-
      calary month, 279; lunar calendar,
      279; pedigree charts, 279–81;
      place names, method of use, 279;
      recording names, 279; solar calen-
      dar dates, 279
  Filipinos and the Philippines: American
    era, 275, 277; Catholic Church,
    impact on records, 277; census,
    252; civil registers, 277; deaths
    and burials, 277; departures, 277;
    Filipino communities, 255; Fil-
    ipinos in the United States, 241;
    graves, removal of, 277; immigra-
    tion and naturalization records,
    277; laborers, legislation against,
    241; laborers in Hawaii, records
    of, 277; marriages, 277; parish
    registers, 277; passports, 277;
    Spanish era, 275, 277; *Tracing
    Your Philippine Ancestors*, Fil-
    ipinos in, 277
  resources: bibliography, 301; com-
    munity newspapers, 256; Filipino
    collection, at the University of
    Hawaii, 256; *The Filipino Forum*,
    256; Genealogical Society of
    Utah, filming, 277; Hawaii Sugar
    Planter's Association, 277; Ma-
    nila, national archives, 277; *The
    Philippine Mail*, 256
Japanese Americans and Japan
  background: businesses, 249; com-
    munities, traditions and culture,
    255; *dekasegi* (working away
    from home), 241; employment in
    the United States, 248; in Hawaii,
    246, 248; immigrants, West
    Coast, 248; immigration re-
    strictions, removal of, 248–49; in-
    ternment camps, 248; Japanese
    American Citizen's League, 249;
    Korean War, U.S. troops in Ja-
    pan, 248; laborers in Hawaii, 256;
    McCarren-Walter Act and, 248;
    Nihon machi (town), 255;
    pre-1868 feudal period, 272; pri-
    vacy laws, 269; regional associa-
    tions, 249; and surname origins,
    242; in the United States, 241,
    249; "war brides" in the United
    States, 248; U.S.-Japanese rela-
    tionship, 248
  records and research: adoptions,
    269; ancestral grave (*o-haka*),
    270; bibliography of, 294–97;
    births, 269; Buddhist death regis-
    ters, 258, 269–70; Buddhist
    names, 270; censuses, 252, 273;
    cities, towns, and villages (direc-
    tory of) (*Zenkoku shichoson
    yoran*), 267; common names,
    272–73; death, place and date of,
    269; domicile address (*honseki*),
    269; family crests (*kamon* or
    iemon), 242–43; family gene-
    alogies (*kafu* or *keizu*), 243; fami-
    ly names, 269; family registers
    (*koseki* or *joseki*), 243, 267; fami-
    ly relationships, 269; genealogies,
    272; genealogies, compiled (*keizu*
    or *kafu*), 272; Hawaii prefectural
    association (Japanese), 255;
    household or family register
    (*koseki*), 267; *ihai* (mortuary tab-
    lets), 270, 272; immigration, 254;
    Japanese American Citizen's
    League, 255; Japanese Consulate
    General (and immigration), 254;
    Japanese Foreign Ministry, 254;
    joseki (withdrawn registers), 267;
    kakachō (Buddhist death register),
    269–71; *koseki*, definition of,
    267; maps, 267; marriages, 269;
    merchant class, records of, 273;

Asian Americans
 Japanese Americans
  records and research (*cont.*)
    mortuary tablets, 243; mortuary
    tablets and tombstones, 270–72;
    motifs in mortuary tablets, 273;
    peasants or commoners, records
    of, 273; permit to travel abroad,
    258; personal record of Jiro
    Yabumoto, 258, 260; regional as-
    sociations, 255; requests for infor-
    mation, 269; research in Japan,
    267; retention of records, rules
    for, 269; samurai ancestors, re-
    cords on, 272; tombstone inscrip-
    tions, 270; transfers to other
    registers, 269; United Japanese
    Society of Hawaii, 255; with-
    drawn registers, 267 (see also
    joseki); *Zenkoku shichoson yoran*
    (directory of Japanese cities,
    towns, and villages), 267
  research problems: dates, older, 273;
    feudal period, 272; *koseki*, re-
    searching beyond, 273; language,
    difficulty in deciphering, 273;
    place names, changes in, 273;
    surnames, lack of, 273
  typical search: common problems,
    283; conducting the search, 283;
    dates, recording of, 283, 285;
    Hepburn (modified) system, use
    of, 283; intercalary months, 285;
    language problems, 283; lunar
    dates, 285; names, arrangement
    of, 283; place names, changes in
    and use, 285; records, use of,
    283; Romanization of names, 283;
    solar calendar, 283
 Korean Americans and Korea, 243;
    Chinese influence, 274; com-
    moners, 275; communities, 249,
    255; Confucian influences, 242;
    Japanese influence, 274; Korean
    ethnic communities, 255; Korean
    War, 274; Koreans, immigration
    of, 244, 249; racial quotas, 249;
    slaves, 275; in the United States,
    241; *yangban* (scholar-officials),
    274–75; Yi dynasty, 274
  resources: accuracies and inac-
    curacies, 275; bibliography,
    300–301; biographies, 275; in ·
    censuses, 252; *chopko* (gene-
    alogies), 274–75; clans and fami-
    lies, 243, 274–75; classical
    Chinese, use of, 275; community
    newspapers, 256; destroyed re-
    cords, 274; dictionaries, spe-
    cialized, use of, 274; family
    registers (Japanese era), 243;
    females, neglect of, 274; *ga-jung*
    (clan or family genealogies), 243;
    gravesites, 256; *han'gul* (lan-
    guage), 240; *hojuk* (household
    register), 243, 274; immigration
    records, 243; Japanese-era *hojuk*
    (family registers), 243; *Korean
    Dongji Hoi*, 256; *Korean Pacific
    Weekly*, 256; local histories, 275;
    pangmok (examination rosters),
    275; records, inventory of, 275;
    records, language of, 240; re-
    cords, location of, 274; records,
    modern, 274; research in Korea,
    274; surnames, common, 275; tra-
    ditional records, 274; University
    of Southern California, Korean
    project, 256; Western solar calen-
    dar, 274; *yangban* origin, 274
 Mainland China, Taiwan, and Hong
    Kong: ancestor veneration, 261;
    ancestral tablets and tombstone in-
    scriptions, 266; biographical es-
    says, 266; categories of people,
    266; China, conditions in, 261;
    Ch'ing dynasty, 261; Civil War,
    262; clan genealogies, 263; classi-
    cal language, 265; Communist
    takeover of China, 261; Confucian
    emphasis and traditions, 261,
    263–64; correspondence between
    relatives, 261–62; district (*hsien*),
    266; empire (*kuo*), 266; family
    registers, 262–63; feelings, tradi-
    tional, 261; genealogical research,

Asian Americans
  Mainland China (*cont.*)
    attitudes toward, 262; Genealogi-
      cal Society of Utah, 263; genea-
      logical tables, 266; genealogies,
      262, 263–65; Huang family, 263;
      Kuan family genealogy, 264–65;
      library and archival collections,
      266; LDS Genealogical Depart-
      ment Library, 263; lineage con-
      tinuity, 261; local histories
      (*difang-chih*), 266–67; lunar cal-
      endar, 265; market town (*chen*),
      266; marriage records, 263;
      names, generational (*p'ai ming*),
      265; names, multiple, 265;
      names, posthumous, 265; Opium
      War, 261; Overseas Chinese (*hua
      chiao*), 261; People's Republic
      of China, 261–63; politics, 262;
      prefecture (*fu*), 266; province
      (*sheng*), 266; Registrar General's
      Department of Hong Kong,
      262–63; sixty-year cyclical calen-
      dar, 265; subprefecture (*t'ing*),
      266; Taiwan, clans or families in,
      262; Taiwan household or family
      registers, 262; United States and
      the Korean War, 261; U.S.-Chi-
      nese relations, 251; village
      (*hsiang*), 266; villages, reorga-
      nization of, 263; vital records,
      262–63; Wang family, 263;
      women in clan genealogies, 264
    other Asians in the United States:
      Afghans, 250; from Bangladesh,
      250; from India, 250, 278; Indo-
      chinese (refugees from Cambodia,
      Laos, Vietnam), 249–50; Ira-
      nians, 250; from Pakistan, 250;
      from Thailand and Indonesia,
      244, 250, 278
    records, United States and Hawaii
      cemetery and funerary: funeral
        homes, 257; the Orient, tablets
        and monuments, 256
      community and ethnic: Asian com-
        munities, 255; Asian immigrants,
        254; assimilation, 254; languages,
      255; newspapers, ethnic, 256;
      newspapers in Hawaii (*Hawaii
      Hochi, Nippon Jiji*), 256; in pub-
      lic libraries, 255; UCLA, Asian
      collections in, 256; in university
      libraries, 255; University of
      Hawaii, Okinawan collection, 256
    Hawaii, records of: Chinese names,
      Romanized, 254; Chinese names
      in, 254; Filipinos in, 254; Hawaii
      State Archives, 254; immigration
      and registration records, 254; in-
      dexes, Chinese and Japanese, 252;
      Koreans in, 254; LDS Genealogi-
      cal Department Library, 254;
      other Asians in, 254; passenger
      manifests, 252; ship manifests,
      242–54
    other sources: adoption agreements,
      266; church records, 266; eulogies
      and merit tablets, 266; horo-
      scopes, 266; household agree-
      ments, 266; land records, 266;
      leases and cultivation contracts,
      266; letters and correspondence,
      266; marriage contracts, 266; of-
      ferings, records of, 266; World
      Conference on Records, 267
    records abroad: ancestors, 259–61;
      Asian immigrants in the United
      States, 258; origin, place of, 259
    research in: alien registration re-
      cords, 252; Bureau of Census,
      Pittsburg, Kansas, 252; census re-
      cords, 251–52; Consulate Gener-
      al, Honolulu, 251; delayed birth
      certificates, 251; Genealogical So-
      ciety of Utah Library, 251–52;
      Hawaiian censuses, 252; Hawaii
      State Department of Health, 251;
      Immigration and Naturalization
      Service, 252; immigration re-
      cords, 252–53; inaccuracies in,
      251; National Archives, 252; oral
      information, 251; vital records, 251
    research problems and approaches:
      assimilation, 239–41; Chinese
      language, characters in, 240; Chi-
      nese language, classical, 240; ge-

Asian Americans
  records, U.S. and Hawaii
    research problems (*cont.*)
      nealogical and family history,
      value of, 242; genealogical re-
      search, requirements in education,
      243; Gentlemen's Agreement,
      purpose of, 244; home sources,
      243; immigrant laborers, 108; im-
      migration records, spellings in,
      241; Japanese laborers, re-
      strictions, 244; language and cul-
      tural differences, 241; language
      barriers, 240; librarians, and
      available resources, 242; library
      materials, lack of, 242; Roman
      alphabet, conversion of scrips,
      242; Romanization, 240–41
  resources, supplies, and organizations
    bibliography, 289–97; other Asian
    or related, 301–3
    bookstores and suppliers: Asian
      American Studies Center, 307;
      Cellar Book Shop, 307; Center for
      Chinese Research Materials, 307;
      Cheng & Tsui Company, 307;
      China Books and Periodicals, 307;
      Everybody's Bookstore, 307; Ge-
      nealogical Department, LDS Li-
      brary, 307; Hawaii, University
      Press, 307; Kinokuniya of Amer-
      ica, 307; Kodansha International,
      307; R & E Research Associates,
      307; Tuttle, Charles E., Com-
      pany, 308
    major repositories, list of: Asian
      Foundation Library, 303; Bernice
      P. Bishop Museum, 304; Bureau
      of Conveyance, 304; California
      Historical Society Library, 303;
      California State Archives, 303;
      California State Library, 303;
      Chinatown Cultural Center, 305;
      Columbia University, 305; Cornell
      University, 305; Genealogical De-
      partment Library, LDS, 306; Har-
      vard University, 305; Hawaii
      Chinese History Center, 304;
      Hawaii State Archives, 304;
      Hawaii State Department of
      Health, 304; Hawaii State Li-
      brary, 304; Hawaii Sugar Plant-
      er's Association, 304; Japanese
      Consulate General, 304; Japanese
      travel agencies, 304; Library of
      Congress, 304; Los Angeles
      Federal Archives and Records
      Center, 303; Los Angeles Public
      Library, 303; Military Personnel
      Records Center, 305; National Ar-
      chives, 304; New York Public Li-
      brary, 305; Personal Census
      Service Branch, Bureau of Cen-
      sus, 305; San Diego State Univer-
      sity, 303; San Francisco Federal
      Archives and Records Center,
      303; San Francisco Public Li-
      brary, 303; Seattle Public Library,
      306; University of California
      (Berkeley), 303; University of
      California (Davis), 303; Univer-
      sity of California (Los Angeles),
      303; University of Chicago, 305;
      University of Hawaii (Manoa
      Campus), 304; University of Illi-
      nois, 305; University of Michi-
      gan, 305; University of Oregon,
      305; University of Pennsylvania,
      305; University of Southern Cal-
      ifornia, 304; University of Wash-
      ington, 306; U.S. Immigration
      and Naturalization Service, 305
    societies and organizations: Ameri-
      can Siam Services, 306; Asia So-
      ciety, 306; Buddhist Churches of
      America, 306; Chinese Historical
      Society of America, 306; Chinese
      Historical Society of Southern
      California, 308; Chinese Institute
      of America, 306; Filipino Ameri-
      can Community of Los Angeles,
      306; Hawaii Chinese History Cen-
      ter, 306; Japanese American Cit-
      izen's League, 307; Japanese
      American Society of Southern
      California, 307; Japan Society,
      307; Korean National Association,
      307

Asian Americans (*cont.*)
  Vietnam: Chinese influence, 277; civil
    records, 277; French influence,
    277; genealogies, 277; immigra-
    tion, 244; names, Chinese charac-
    ters and equivalents, 240, 277;
    names, order of, 277; refugees
    and resources, 243
Atlanta Historical Society, 74
Atlanta Public Library, 83
Atlases, examples of, 76
Atlas of the World, 76

Bailey, William Shreve, 64
Baker Memorial Library (Dartmouth Col-
    lege), 68
Bangor Public Library, 84
Baptist records: in Baptist historical li-
    braries, 46; in ministers' journals,
    46
Barrow, Geoffrey, 66
Barzun, Jacques, 109
Baum, Willia, K., 104
Beard, Timothy Field, 67, 80
Bell, James B. *See* Doane, Gilbert H.
Beloit Historical Society, 88
Bennington Museum—Genealogical Li-
    brary, 88
Berkshire Athenaeum, 84
Beverly Historical Society, 84
Bible records, 93
Bibliographies: as aid to research, 31.
    See also under each ethnic group
Bibliography: basic genealogical texts,
    50–51; periodicals, list of, 53–54;
    reference words, 50–52
Bicentennial celebration, 9, 92
Bills of sale (of slaves), 40, 98
Biographical history, 95
Biographical information, 25
Birmingham Historical Society, 74
Birmingham Public Library, 81
Black American family history, 75, 107;
    and the Civil War, 92; migration
    of families, 107; researchers, 106
Black American family history associa-
    tions, 75

Black American history, 107
Black Americans
  and American Indians, records of: Bu-
    reau of Indian Affairs, 343; mixed
    black-Indian relationships, 344;
    runaway slaves and Indians, 344;
    slaves and oral history, 343;
    slaves on Indian reservations, 343
  background: black American geneal-
    ogy, definition of, 309; *Black Ge-
    nealogy: How to Begin*, in, 309;
    black genealogy, popularization
    of, 309; and family history, 309;
    "Miss Jane Pittman," 309; pre-
    serving family histories, 309;
    Roots, 309
  bank records: black-owned and -oper-
    ated, 340; Freedmen's Savings
    and Trust Company, 339; Na-
    tional Archives, 340; *Registers of
    Signatures of Depositions in
    Branches of the Freedmen's Sav-
    ings and Trust Company*,
    339–340
  branding: purpose of, 343; records,
    317, 343; in *Roots*, 343
  breeding: Bastardy Case Book, 313,
    343; information on slaves, 343;
    purpose of, 343; records, 317,
    343
  Canada, blacks in: and Arawak Indian
    women, 341; free blacks in, 341;
    locating records, 341; Maroons,
    341; migration, 341; *A North-Side
    View of Slavery*, 341; settlements
    in, 341; slaves in, 341; under-
    ground railroad, 341
  case study: *Adventures of Purse and
    Persons in Virginia 1607–1624*,
    346; black landowners in Vir-
    ginia, 347; black migration, 346;
    Jamestown Group, 346; Johnson,
    Antoney, 346–47
  cemetery records, 319, 321; black
    cemeteries, 319, 321; Catholics,
    319; Genealogical Society of
    Utah, 319, 321; Moravians, 319;
    Quakers, 319; slave, 104;

Black Americans
  cemetery records (*cont.*)
    tombstone information, 321; white
      churches, and, 319
  census: free black ancestors, 321; free
    blacks, locating, 321; free heads
    of families, 321; *Free Negro
    Heads of Families in the United
    States in 1830*, 321; *Free Negro
    Owners of Slaves in the United
    States in 1830*, 321; mulatto, 321;
    "Register of Free Blacks 1835,
    Book 3," 321; "Registration of
    Free Negroes Commencing Sep-
    tember Court 1822," 321; slave
    schedules in, 321; Virginia, free
    blacks in, 321
  church records: baptism, 319; benev-
    olent societies in, 319; birth dates,
    319; black church, 319; death and
    burial, 319; family history in,
    319; literary societies in, 319;
    marriage, 319; and photographs,
    319; registers, 319; schools, 319;
    social clubs in, 319; WPA, church
    records of, 319
  clemency files, 342; courthouse re-
    cords, 342
  conferences and training programs, list
    of: Afro-American Family History
    Association, 359; Afro-American
    Family History Project, Grassroots
    Genealogy Workshop, 359; Brig-
    ham Young University, 359; Eth-
    nic Materials Project, Burton
    Historical Collection, Detroit Pub-
    lic Library, 359; Genealogical So-
    ciety of Utah (world conferences
    on records), 359; Institute on Eth-
    nic Genealogy for Librarians (Fisk
    University), 359–360; National
    Archives, 359; National Genea-
    logical Society, 359; Samford
    University, 359; World Con-
    ference on Records, 359
  county orphan court, information on
    black orphans, 344
  court and criminal records, 340–41

Creole records, 313; Cordon Bleu
    class, 344; mixed parentage, re-
    sults of, 344
family Bible, use of, 317
Freedmen's Bureau: activities of, 339;
    estates, forfeited, 342; information
    on freed slaves, 339; National Ar-
    chives, 339
genealogical societies: Afro-American
    Family History Association, 360;
    Afro-American Genealogical and
    Historical Society of Chicago,
    360–61; Afro-American Historical
    and Genealogical Society (Wash-
    ington, D.C.), 361; Afro-Ameri-
    can Institute of Ancestry, 361;
    Parting Ways, The Museum of
    Afro-American Ethnohistory, 361;
    Fred Hart Williams Genealogical
    Society, 361; Rhode Island Black
    Heritage Society, 361
Habeus Corpus case records: divorce,
    342; *Judicial Cases Concerning
    American Slavery and the Negro*,
    342; marriage, 342; slave status
    and ownership, 342
institution population records: Phyllis
    Wheatley Associations, 341; phy-
    sicians' records, 341; *Register of
    Practitioners of Medicine and
    Surgery*, 341; Young Men's
    Christian Association, 341
manumission: definition of, 342; man-
    umitted slaves, 342; Society of
    Friends, records of, 342
military: blacks in the, 331, 337; Civil
    War, 337; Continental Army, 337;
    Daughters of the American Revo-
    lution, publications of, 337; De-
    partment of Military Affairs, and
    the Adjutant General, 337; *Index
    to Compiled Service Records of
    Volunteer Union Soldiers Who
    Served with United States Colored
    Troops*, 331, 337; *List of Black
    Servicemen Compiled from the
    War Department Collection of
    Revolutionary War Records*, 331;

Black Americans
  military (*cont.*)
      Muster and Descriptive Rolls, De-
      partment of Men and Substitutes,
      337; National Archives, 331, 337;
      *The Negro in the Military Services
      of the United States, 1639–1896,*
      313; participation in wars, 331;
      Pension Bureau, 337; Revolution-
      ary War servicemen, list of
      blacks, 331; soldiers, information
      on, 337; Sons of the American
      Revolution, publications of, 337;
      U.S. Army War College, 331
  mixed ancestry: blacks and Indians,
      343–44; black/white admixture,
      313; Cape Verdeans, definition
      of, 313; Geeches, definition of,
      313; multiethnic background, 310;
      West Indies, mixed families in,
      344
  newspapers: *Afro-American Press and
      Its Editors,* 357; black news-
      papers, list of (antebellum to pre-
      sent), 355–59; early black press,
      338; *Freedom's Journal,* 338; in
      historical societies and libraries,
      338; importance of, 338; informa-
      tion contained in, 338; Library of
      Congress, 338; *The Negro News-
      paper,* 357; *The Negro Press in
      the United States,* 357
  organizations: Alpha Kappa Alpha So-
      rority, Inc., 361; Alpha Phi Alpha
      Fraternity, 361–62; Association
      for the Study of Afro-American
      Life and History, 362; Delta Sig-
      ma Theta Sorority, 362; Frontiers
      International, 362; Kappa Alpha
      Psi Fraternity, 362; National As-
      sociation for the Advancement of
      Colored People, 362; National As-
      sociation of Negro Business and
      Professional Women's Clubs, 362;
      National Bar Association, 362;
      National Council of Negro Wom-
      en, 362; National Dental Associa-
      tion, 362–63; National Medical
      Association, 363; National Urban
      League, 363; Omega Psi Phi Fra-
      ternity, 363
  other records, sources of: bibliography,
      349–56; city directories, 338–39;
      *Directory of Afro-American Re-
      sources,* 339; Elks, 339; Links,
      Inc., 339; Masons, 339; *Men of
      Mark,* 339; *The Negro Yearbook,*
      339; Odd Fellows, 339; organiza-
      tions, published directories of,
      339; special black collections, 339
  photographs: of slaves, 339; use in
      family albums, 339
  plantation records: auction, 323; bills
      of sale of slaves, 323; bondage,
      323; branding, 323; breeding,
      323; emancipation, 329–31; em-
      ployment, 323, 329; estate in-
      ventories, 323–24, 329–30; free
      blacks, 329; genealogical sources,
      fragmenting, 331; insurance pol-
      icies and slaves, 317, 323, 329;
      medical, 329; mulatto, 323–24;
      location of, 323; libraries, records
      in, 331; ownership of slaves, 323;
      in public offices, 331; "Shep-
      herd" and "Isabella" (slaves),
      323; slave ancestor, 323; slave
      labor, 323–24; slaves in estate in-
      ventories, 339; tracing ownership
      of, 323; University of North Car-
      olina (Chapel Hill), 331; Univer-
      sity of Virginia, 331; wills,
      323–24
  prison, workhouse, and inebriate
      asylum records: black inmates,
      340; description of inmates, 340;
      discharge and descriptive docu-
      ments, 340–41
  research procedures in: bibliography,
      349–56; black genealogical re-
      cords, 317–46; *Black Genealogy:
      How to Begin,* 316; Blockson
      family, 347; Emancipation Procla-
      mation, 310–11; genealogical re-
      search, 315; *List of Free Black
      Heads of Families in the First
      Census of the United States,* 311,
      313; oral tradition, techniques of,

Black Americans
    research procedures in (*cont.*)
        316–17; researchers, 310; re-
        unions, 311, 313, 317
    researching problems in: ancestors, Af-
        rican, 310; ancestors, lost, 313;
        ancestors, mixed, 313; *Black Ge-
        nealogy,* 311; confusing or inac-
        curate records, 315–16;
        "Enumeration of Mulattoes by
        Census Bureau Causes Genealogi-
        cal Mix-up," 315–16; foreign or
        mixed parentage, 315; free blacks,
        313; genealogy, neglect of, 310;
        illiteracy, 310; migration, 310;
        miscegenation, 310, 313; names,
        change of, 310–11; names, classi-
        cal, 311; racial mixing, 313;
        "passing," 313, 315; records, ab-
        sence of, 310; segregation, 310;
        separation, geographical, 310;
        slaves, and selling of, 311, 313;
        tracing free blacks or freed slaves,
        317
    sharecropping, 331; use of, 331
    shipping: Africa, Gold Coast, 342;
        Morris and Willig (firm) and,
        342; slaves, commerce of, 342
    slave advertisements: broadsides, 338;
        description of slaves, 338; post-
        ers, 338; runaway slaves, 337–38
    slavery: advertisements for em-
        ployment, 329, 337–38; bills of
        sale, 329; breeding, 343; census
        schedules, slave, 321; commerce
        of slaves, 342; estate inventories,
        329; impact of black genealogy
        on, 310; on Indian reservations,
        341; legal transactions regarding,
        342; runaways, 337–38; sale of
        slaves, 323, 342; slave collars,
        317; slave owners and ownership,
        323, 329; slaves and the oral tra-
        dition, 316; slaves in Canada, 341
    underground railroad: definition, 338;
        former slaves and, 338; free
        blacks and, 338; Philadelphia Vig-
        ilante Committee, 338; *The Un-
        derground Railroad,* 338;

Underground Railroad Journal,
    338; *The Underground Railroad
    from Slavery to Freedom,* 338;
    and white abolitionists, 338
    women, black: free blacks, 337; "The
        Inspection Roll of Negroes Taken
        on Board Sundry Vessels at Staten
        Island and Bound for Nova
        Scotia," 337
Black Genealogy: How to Begin, 12, 76,
    94
Black historical societies, 75
Black Oral History Project, 103
Black Women Oral History Project, 102
Blake, James, Jr., 5
Blind and physically handicapped, 49
Blockson, Charles, 94
Bluffton College—Mennonite Historical
    Library, 85
Board for Certification of Genealogists,
    12
Bollinger family, genealogical records of,
    5
Boltwood, Lucius M., Genealogical and
    Historical Collection, 84
Bookcraft, 56
Books in Print, and genealogical mate-
    rials, 62
Boston Evening Transcript: genealogy
    column, 47; index to, 47
Boston Public Library, 84
Brick Store Museum, 84
Bridgers, Frank E. *See* Colket, Meredith
Brigham Young University Library, 68;
    and training in genealogy, 57
Bristol Historical and Preservation Soci-
    ety, 87
*British Colonial Office Manuscript Re-
    cords of Early Indian Affairs,
    The,* 108
Brooklyn College, Department of Black
    and Puerto Rican Studies, 103
Brown v. *Board of Education,* 93
Brummel, Leendert, 78
Bucks County Historical Society, 87
Buffalo and Erie County Public Library,
    86
Bureau of the Census (Pittsburg, Kan-
    sas), 44

Burgan, John S., 11
Burial records, 45. *See also* Vital records
Burke's Genealogical and Heraldic History of the Landed Gentry, 78
Burton Historical Collection, 13. *See also* Detroit Public Library

Cache Genealogical Library, 29
Caesar, Julius, 31
Calhoun County Museum, 87
California Historical Society, 81
California State Library, 72, 81
California State Library—Sutro Library, 81
Cambria County Historical Society, 87
Cameron County Historical Society, 87
Canton Historical Society, 84
Cape Ann Historical Association, 64
Cape May County Historical Society and Museum, 85
Carnegie Library of Pittsburgh, 87
Catalogs of genealogical collections, examples of, 77
Cemeteries: *Cemetery Transcribing: Preparations and Procedures,* 105; locating, 104; loss of, 104; records, 8, 32, 46–47, 93, 104; registers of the dead, 104; slave, 104; as sources of genealogical information, 46; WPA compiled lists of, 104
Census: data, locating, 44; federal, 14; manuscripts, 98; mortality schedules, 44; population, changes and growth of, 43; records, location of, 43; reports, published, 78–79; as sources for verification, 24
Census Bureau, 79
Census taking, history of, 43
Chadwell, Patricia, 14
Chase, Ellen, 10, 17
Chattanooga Public Library, 87
Chemung County Historical Society, 86
Chinese Americans. *See* Asian Americans, Chinese Americans
Chinese Historical Society of America, 75

Church and other records, types and content of, 80
Church archives, 46
Church College of Hawaii, 83
Church denominations, published directories of, 46
Church records, 8, 45–46, 93; disciplinary action, 46; locating, 45; loss of, 104; membership lists of, 45; minutes, 45; value of, 45; variations in ways of handling, 45
Cincinnati, University of, Library, 68
City historical societies, examples of, 74
City University of New York libraries, 68
Civil court records, locating, 42
Civil Rights Movement, 103; and family origins, 93
Cleveland Public Library, 86
Coats of arms, 91
Computerized surname reference files, 93
Colket, Meredith, 45
College of William and Mary Library, 68
Colonial Dames of America, formation of, 5
"Colored" Americans. *See* Black Americans
Columbia Lippincott Gazetteer of the World, 76
Columbia University: libraries, 68; and oral history, 103
Columbian Centinel of Boston, 47
Composite Autobiography of Slavery, A: The Slave Narratives, 101
Computer banks: and analyzing records, 105; as historical methodology, 105; use of, 105
Connecticut State Library, 82
Correspondence: organization and record keeping, 25; records, 25
Cossitt-Goodwyn Library, 87
County historical societies, examples of, 74
County records: contracts (land records), 38; deeds, 38; land and property records, 38; leases, 38; liens and mortgages, 38, 40
County sources, 49

Courthouses, 59
Court proceedings, 8
Cowan, Robert, will of, 41–42
Cox Library, The, 81
Criminal court records, locating, 42
Czech Americans, genealogical guides to, 108

Dallas Public Library, 87
Daniels, Thomas E., 16
Data, alternative sources of, 100
Daughters of the American Revolution, 4, 8, 10–11, 47, 92; and collected gravestone inscriptions, 47; and compiled cemetery records, 47; formation of, 6
Daughters of the American Revolution Library, 75
Daughters of the Barons of Runnemede, formation of, 5
Daughters of the Confederacy, 11
Dates, authentication of, 109
Dating practices, 25; double dating, 31–32; Julian and Gregorian calendars, 31
Davis, Allen F. See Watts, Jim
Deaths, registration of, 44
Debrett's Peerage of England, Scotland, and Ireland, 78
Dedham Historical Society, 64
Deeds, 8, 93, 98
Delaware State Archives, 72, 82
Denver Public Library, 82
Deseret Book Company, 57
Detroit Historical Society, 74
Detroit Public Library, 8, 13–14, 16, 54; Burton Historical Collection of, 8, 85
Detroit Society for Genealogical Research, 14, 16
Diaries: overseers', 101; planters', 98
Directories: of foreign archives, 78; types of, 79
Directory of European Associations, 78
Disciples of Christ Historical Society, 75
District of Columbia Public Library, 82
Divorce records: content of, 38; locating, 38

Dixon, Janice T., 76, 95
Doane, Gilbert H., 12, 76
Draznin, Yaffa, 12
Duke, Doris, Oral History Project, 103

Eastern Kentucky University Library, 68, 83; guide to genealogical materials, 68
Elements of Style, The, 109
Elks (organization), 48
Emancipation, 93
Encyclopedia of Associations, The, 77–78
Encyclopedias of associations, examples of, 77
Enoch Pratt Free Library, policy regarding genealogy, 6, 11
Essex Institute, 84
Estates, settlement of, 40
Ethnic cemeteries: location of, 104; and urbanization, 105
Ethnic family history, 62, 106; language barriers, 106; origins of, 93–94; records, absence of, 106; research problems in, 106; study of, 96
Ethnic family history researcher, 107; and oral history interviewing, 101
Ethnic genealogical research materials, preservation of, 74
Ethnic genealogy, 62; research into, 21
Ethnic groups: and genealogical search, 11; genealogy works for, 66; study of, 94
Ethnic historical associations, examples of, 75
Ethnic history, 91, 96, 106–8; evaluation of accuracy, 107; interest in, 94; publications on, 93; researching, 91
Ethnic records, 108
Ethnic studies, published catalogs, 107
European ethnic groups: research problems, 108
European family history, 93–94
European immigrants, 4
Everton, George B., 67, 81
Everton Publishers, 57
"Everybody's Search for Roots," 9

Fadden, Grace J., 103
Fairfield Historical Society, 82
Family Bibles, as source for verification, 24
Family genealogy, study of, 102
Family group record, 23, 24; filing, 25
Family group sheets, 24
Family historian, as detective, 98
Family Historian's Handbook, The, 12
Family histories, 43; published, 5, 6, 8; tools for writing, 77
Family history, 30, 97; bibliography on, 115–20; biography, 97; chronological approach to, 97; creating from a genealogy, 97–98, 100; definitions of, 95–97; historical methodology in, 98; information needed to develop, 94; narrative, content of, 94; origins of, 91–93; as prepared by genealogists, 11–12; publishing, patterns in, 65; research, teaching of, 63, 94–95; research, value in, 44; research handbooks for, 94; research process, 98–100; study of, 93, 102; texts for teaching, 94; topical approach, 97; writing of, 97, 110–12
Family papers, white, 101; as source for identifying blacks, 101
Family pedigree chart, verifying data, 32
Family relationships, graphic representation of, 23
Family sources, 23–24, 49
Family traditions and history, preservation of, 4
Farmer, John, 91
Farmer, Karen: and the DAR, 10; as descendant of William Hood, 10
Federal Land Series, 65
Federal records, 43–45
Federal Writers' Project, 93
Fees for service: genealogists', 16; in record offices, 28
Ferguson, John L., 16
Filby, P. William, 65, 80, 89
Filson Club, 75

Finding Our Fathers: A Guidebook to Jewish Genealogy, 12
Finding Your Roots: Every American Can Trace His Ancestors—At Home and Abroad, 12
Fisk, Reverend Photius, 64
Fisk University, 64; Fisk Jubilee Singers, 64
Fisk University Library, 64, 103; Special Collections, 64; and slave narratives collection, 101
Flack, Dora D. *See* Dixon, Janice T.
Flint Public Library, 85
Florida State Library, 83
Forbes Library, 84
Fordham University Library, 68
Foreign genealogical handbooks, examples of, 78
Foreign genealogical registers, examples of, 78
Foreign histories, importance of, 79
Fort Worth Public Library, 88; Southwest and Genealogy Department, 14
Franklin, John Hope, 107
Freedmen, 93
Freedmen's Bank records, and ethnic family history, 101
Freedmen's Bureau, marriage records of, 101
Freedmen's Savings and Trust Company, 101
Free Negro Heads of Families in the United States in 1830, 79
Free Negro Owners of Slaves in the United States in 1830, 79
Free Public Library (Middletown, Ohio), 86
Friends Historical Association, 75
From Slavery to Freedom: A History of Negro Americans, 107
Fry, Ron. *See* Blockson, Charles

Gardner, David E., 78
Gazetteer, 76
Gazetteers and dictionaries of places, 76
Genealogical and family associations, periodicals of, 43

Genealogical and Local Histories in the St. Louis Public Library, 77
Genealogical collections, historians and genealogists, 61
Genealogical Helper, 14
Genealogical-Historical Guide to Latin America, 12
Genealogical Index, 67
Genealogical librarianship, 65
Genealogical Library for the Blind and Physically Handicapped, 49
Genealogical materials, collecting, 59
Genealogical pattern, 100
Genealogical Periodical Annual Index, The, 79
Genealogical periodicals, major, 13
Genealogical Periodicals Library, 84
Genealogical process, 59
Genealogical Register of the First Settlers of New England, A, 91–92
Genealogical repositories, list of major, 54–55
Genealogical research, 59; beginning the search, 21–30; and historical research, 61; in the South, 23
Genealogical Research in England and Wales, 78
Genealogical societies, 14; libraries in, 59; list of, 55–56
Genealogical Society of New Jersey, 85
Genealogical Society of Pennsylvania, 87
Genealogical Society of Utah Library, 54, 88
African records
  Malawi, 194; citizenship records of, 194
  other African countries: gazetteers, 196; histories, general, 196; other printed works, 196
  South Africa: government archives (Capetown), 195; Natal Archives Depot (Pietermaritzburg), 195; Orange Free State Archives (Bloemfontein), 195; Transvaal Government Archives (Pretoria), 195
  South West Africa (Namibia): blacks in, 195; Keetmanshoop, 195;

Lutheran church registers, 195; Okahandja, 195; Rehoboth, 195; state archives, records of, 195; tribal records, 195
Zambia, early records of residents, 195
Zimbabwe: blacks, coloureds, and whites, 195; Church of England parish registers, 196; citizenship rolls, 196; marriage registers, 196; vital records, 195–96; voter rolls, 196
American Indian collections: Aleut Indians, 184; baptisms, 185; book collection, 185; burials, 185; California mission registers, 185; census rolls, 184; Cherokees, 185; confirmations, 185; deaths, 185; 1860 census of, 184; Five Civilized Tribes, 184–85; freedmen (Indian), 184; genealogical research on, 184–85; heirship records, 184; homesteaders, 184; "Indian Lands West of Arkansas," 184; land rolls, microfilmed, 184; marriage records, 184–85; in National Archives Record Group 75, 184; New England, records of, 185; Oklahoma, records from, 185; *Our Native Americans and Their Records of Genealogical Value*, importance of, 184; records, research, and resources, 175–76, 184–85; schools, 184; Sioux materials, 184; Southwestern tribes, 185; tribal enrollments, 184; tribes, histories of, 185; vital records, 184; in white society, 185; wills, 184. *See also* Eskimos
background: access to, 178; Africa-Asian (and Polynesia) collection, 176; assistance to researchers, 180; bibliography on, 203–4; books in, 179; branch library system, 175, 180–83; British (Australia and New Zealand) collection, 176; catalogs, 177;

Genealogical Society of Utah Library
  background (*cont.*)
        chronological coverage, 179; col-
        lection depth, 180; Continental
        Europe collection, 176; ethnic and
        minority groups, resources for,
        175, 183–203; Family Group Re-
        cord Archives, 176, 177; films,
        little-used, 183; foreign language,
        reference service in, 176; genea-
        logical reference service, 176; Ge-
        nealogical Society of Utah and,
        16, 74–75, 179; Genealogical So-
        ciety of Utah Library microfilm-
        ing program, 175–205 *passim;*
        General Reference and United
        States collection, 176; Interna-
        tional Genealogical Index, 177,
        180–81; Latin America and
        Iberian Peninsula collection, 176;
        location of, 180; LDS Church Re-
        cord collection, 176; main library,
        175–205 *passim;* microfilms,
        177–78; the Mormons, 176; oral
        genealogy collections of, 175,
        179; organization of, 176; the,
        Orient, collection, 176; periodi-
        cals (bound), 179; records, micro-
        filmed, 175; record type (catalog
        entries), list of, 182–83; reference
        staff specialists, 176; Scandinavia
        collection, 176; services and fees,
        176; Special Collections, 176;
        training programs, 176; United
        States, genealogical resources for,
        184–91; utilizing the main library,
        180–83; "Where to Write for
        Birth and Death Records, United
        States and Outlying Areas," 181;
        "Where to Write for Birth and
        Death Records of U.S. Citizens
        Who Were Born or Died Outside
        of the United States and Birth
        Certifications for Alien Children
        Adopted by U.S. Citizens," 181;
        "Where to Write for Marriage
        Records, United States and Outly-
        ing Areas," 181

black American collections: 175, 185;
        Afro-American genealogies, 187;
        Afro-Americans as heading, 185;
        Bible records, 186; birth, mar-
        riage, and death records, 185;
        Black Genealogy, 187; *Black
        Genesis,* 187; *Blacks in Selected
        Newspapers, Censuses and Other
        Sources: An Index to Names and
        Subjects,* 187; book collection,
        187; cemetery records, 186; cen-
        sus and tax rolls, 185; census re-
        cords, blacks in, 186; census,
        slaves named in, 187; censuses of
        Union veterans, Civil War (1890
        census), 187; church records,
        185–86; court records, 185; death
        registers, 185; deeds, 185–86; *Di-
        rectory of Afro-American Re-
        sources,* and back research, 187;
        1860 population schedules (Kear-
        ney County), slaves in, 187; 1860
        slave schedules, 186; family re-
        cords, lack of, 185; free blacks,
        listing of, 186; freedmen's re-
        cords, lack of, 185; genealogical
        research, 185–86; Genealogical
        Society of Utah microfilming,
        187; *Index to Compiled Service
        Records of Colored Troops,* 187;
        marriage books, 185; military re-
        cords, 187; mortality schedules,
        186–87; National Archives, re-
        cords of, 187; "Negroes" as
        heading, 185; newspapers,
        185–86; pension records, 187;
        post-Civil War records, 185; Rev-
        olutionary War records, 186–87;
        slave lineages, 186; slave narra-
        tives, published, 187; southern
        black research, 186; states repre-
        sented in, 185; wills, 186; World
        War I discharge records, 187. *See
        also* Black Americans
Canadian records: black settlements,
        191; blacks in, 191; Blood Indi-
        ans, 191; Canadian Indians, 191;
        census records, 191; church re-

Genealogical Society of Utah Library

Canadian records (*cont.*)

cords, 191; Indians of Alberta, 191; Jewish settlements, 191; land records, 191

Carribean records: Anglican registers, 192; Barbados, 192; Bermuda, 192; blacks and the Anglican records, 192; Catholic parish registers, 192; cemetery records, 192; church records, 192; civil registers, 192; Dominican Republic, 192; Guadeloupe, 192; Haiti, 192; Jamaica, 192; Jewish (vital registers, circumcision, synagogue) records, 192; Martinique, 192; notarial records, 192; Puerto Rico, 192

Central American records: book collection, 193; Costa Rica, 193; El Salvador, 193; Guatemala, 193; Honduras, 193

Central Asian records: British period, 197; civil registers, 197; delayed birth certificates, 197; Dutch period, 197; English records of, 197; India, 197; Sri Lanka, 197

Eskimo collections: 1910 census of Alaska, 188; at Point Barrow, 188

European records: Basque region, 193; book collection on, 193; Catholic Church records (Diocese of Barcelona), 193; Madeira (island), 193; marriage records (*informaciónes matrimonales*), 193; Spain and Portugal, 193

European Jewish records: Austria, 194; England, 194; France, 194; German, Polish, and Hungarian collection, Jews in, 194; Greece, Greek Orthodox parish registers in, 194; Hungarian Jewish records, 194; *Preliminary Survey of the German Collection,* 194; *Toledot: The Journal of Jewish Genealogy,* 194

Hispanic American collections, 175–76; in Arizona and New Mexico, 189; in Arkansas, 188; in California, 189; California book collection in, 189; California mission records and Spanish colonizers, 185; censuses, Spanish, 188; censuses, state and federal, 189; census indexes, 189; census records, 189; church records in, 189; in Colorado, 189; Florida, Alabama, and Mississippi, records of, 188; genealogical source materials, 188–89; local histories, 189; Louisiana and Cabildo records, 188; marriage and church records, 189; parish records, 188–89; San Luis Valley, 189; Spanish missions, records of, 189; tax lists, 189; Texas, 188–89; vital records, 189; Worth S. Ray Collection, 189

Jewish records: business, 190; cemetery records, 190; census rolls, 190; deeds, 190; genealogies, 190; Jewish-American archives, 190; Jewish-American book holdings, 190; Judah L. Magnes genealogical collection, 190; local, county, state, and federal records, 190; military service, 190; probate records, 190; synagogue and cemetery records, 190

Mexican records: book collection, 192; church records, 192; civil censuses, 192; civil registers, 192; notarial records, 192; *padrones* (church censuses), 192; parish registers, 192; *Preliminary Survey of the Mexican Collection,* 192

Middle East, Israeli, and Palestinian records: Arab historical and genealogical research, 196; Aziz S. Attiya Library for Middle East Studies, 196; civil registers, 196; foreigners, registers of, 196; German consulate records, 196; German Jews, records of, 196; military registers, 196; Muhktars' registers, 196; Nūfūs records, 196; University of Utah, 196

Genealogical Society of Utah Library
(*cont.*)
Oriental American genealogical research: ancestry, 191; biographical
and historical accounts, 190; census records, 190–91; genealogies,
191; inaccuracies and incompleteness, 190
Oriental records: Central National Library (Seoul, Korea), 199; Harvard-Yenching Library, materials
from, 199; National Diet Library,
199; Oriental clan genealogies,
199; Oriental genealogies, 199
China: book collection, 200; civil
records, 199–200; clan genealogies, 199; household registration, 200; local histories, 199;
Ming Dynasty, civil records of, 200
Hong Kong: clan publications, 200;
genealogies, 200; wills, 200
Japan: clan genealogies, 200; examination registers, individual, 200;
family group records, 200; *kafu*
(compiled genealogies), 200; kakochō (Buddhist death records),
200; *koseki* (household registration) records, 200; local histories,
200; Register of Five-Man Units,
200; religious registers, 200
Korea: biographies, 201; civil service examination rosters, 201;
clan genealogies, 199–200; epitaphs, 201; local histories, 200;
obituaries, 201; records of, 175;
World Conference on Records
(1980), 200
Macao: church records, 201
Philippines: church directories, 201;
gazetters, 201; general histories,
201; Hawaiian sugar cane plantation, immigration records of, 202;
migration to Hawaii, 201–202;
parish registers, Spanish, 201;
Philippine book collection, 201;
Tracing Your Philippine Ancestry,
201. *See also* Pacific Islands
records

Settlements abroad: Chinese censuses (Philippine collection), 201;
delayed birth registration, 201;
Hawaiian collection, records on,
201; marriage records, 201; migration records, 201; *padrones de
Chinos* (Chinese censuses), 201;
vital records, 201
Pacific Islands records:
Cook Islands: civil registers, 202;
land court records, 202; oral genealogies, 202
Fiji: civil registers, 202; European
births, marriages, deaths, 202; Fijian births, marriages, deaths,
202; Indian births, marriages,
deaths, 202
French Polynesia: civil registers,
202; court records, 202; family
records, 202; marriages, 202; oral
genealogies, 202
Hawaii: emigration, 202; census of,
203; church records, 203; Father
Damien's leper colony, 203; emigration, 202; Kingdom period,
202; newspapers (English and Hawaiian), 203; vital records, 202
Maori, the: Maori-language newspapers, 203; New Zealand materials on, 203; oral genealogies,
203; *whakapapa* (genealogy)
books, 203
Micronesia, 203
Samoa, 175, 203; American and
Western, 203; civil registers, 203
Taiwan, library collections in, 199
Tonga, 175; oral genealogy, 203;
whakapapa (genealogy), manuscripts and books, 203
Trust Territories of the Pacific, medical records of, 203
South America: Argentina, 193;
Bolivia, 193; Brazil, 193; Chile,
193; Paraguay, 193; Peru, 193;
records of Brazilian slaves, 193
Southeast Asian records:
Indonesia: book collection, 198;
Catholic parish registers (Diocese

Genealogical Society of Utah Library
  Southeast Asian records
    Indonesia (*cont.*)
        of Semarang), 198; civil records,
        198; Dutch dominion period, 198;
        genealogical records, mis-
        cellaneous, 198; oral genealogies,
        198; parish registers, 198; popula-
        tion registers, 198; records of,
        175; Yogyakarta Sultanate re-
        cords, 198
    Malaysia: Chinese in, 198; civil re-
        cords, 198; Dutch period, 198;
        oral genealogies, 198; parish re-
        cords, 198
    Singapore, clan genealogies, 198
    Thailand: Chinese families in, 199;
        Thais, biographies and gen-
        ealogies of, 199
    Western Asian records: Armenian
        Catholic Church, 197; Armenian
        censuses, 197; Armenian Gene-
        aological Records Search Founda-
        tion, 197; Armenian genealogical
        research, 197; Armenians,
        196–97; India, 197; Lebanon,
        197; Roman Catholic parish regis-
        ters (Istanbul), 197; Turkey, 197
Genealogical source materials, 9
Genealogical suppliers, list of, 56–57
Genealogical works, out of print, 13
Genealogies in the Library of Congress,
    67, 77
Genealogist, 11; as historian, 96; in-
    terpreting genealogical materials,
    60; and librarians, 60
Genealogist's Guide, The, 66
Genealogy: absurdities and atrocities of,
    10; as area of library activity, 61;
    defined, 96; and heraldry, 66; his-
    torical development of, 91; gene-
    alogists and librarians, 15–18;
    interest in, 94; in libraries, 11;
    publishing in, 65; pursuing, 9–11;
    study of, 5, 93; workshops and
    training, 15, 95
"Genealogy As It Relates to Library Ser-
    vice," 6

Genealogy as Pastime and Profession, 12
"Genealogy Beginner's Manual," 15
Genealogy Club of America, 56
"Genealogy for All People," 9
Genealogy librarian, service to patrons,
    15–16
General Society of Colonial Wars, forma-
    tion of, 5
*Generations: Your Family in Modern
    American History*, 95
Genessee County Department of History,
    86
Georgia Department of Education, Public
    Library Service, 15
Georgia Historical Society, 83
Germans, migration of, 107
Glassboro State College, 85
Godfrey Memorial Library, 82
Goodspeed's Book Shop, Inc., 57
Gottschalk, Louis, 100
Government record offices, 23
Graff, Henry F. *See* Barzun, Jacques
Grand Rapids Public Library, 85
Greenwich Public Library, 82
Greenwood, Val D., 81
*Guide to Genealogical Records in the
    National Archives*, 45
*Guide to Union Catalogues and Interna-
    tional Loan Centers*, 78

Haley, Alex, 9, 16, 94, 97, 98–100,
    111–12; and the search process,
    100
Hampton Institute, slave narratives col-
    lection in, 101
*Handbook of Genealogical Correspon-
    dence*, 29
Handbooks on genealogy, examples of,
    76
Handy Book for Genealogists, The, 67,
    81
Haverhill Public Library, 84
*Heads of Families at the First Census,
    1790*, 79
Helmbold, F. Wilbur, 95
Hereditary and patriotic societies, 5
Hill, Ellen, 16

Hispanic Americans
archives and libraries: Archives of the
Archdiocese of Santa Fe, 380; Archivo General de Indias, 366,
379; Archivo General de la Na-
cion, 366–67, 371; Archivo Historico de Durango, 379; Archivo
Historico del Estado, 379; Archivo Histórico de Sonora, 366;
Bancroft Library, University of
California (Berkeley), 379; Bexar
Archives, University of Texas Library, 379; Bibliotheca Nacional
de Mexico, 379; Genealogical Society of Utah (LDS), 367,
379–80; Huntington Library, 380;
Loredo Archives (Special Collections), St. Mary's University Library, 380; Nacogdoches
Archives, Texas State Library,
380; New Orleans Public Library,
367; Polytechnic Archives (Monterrey), 380; State Records Center
and Archives, Santa Fe, 379;
Texas History Research Library,
380
background: ancestry, 365; bibliography, 380–400; Bureau of
Customs, 367; emigration records,
location of, 366; family records,
preservation of, 392; garrisons, attachments, and crews, lists of,
368–69; genealogies, compilation
of, 391; immigration and emigration records, 371–72; Immigration
and Naturalization Service and aliens, 366; immigration records,
366–67; Lorenzana (surname),
366; Mexican origin, 365; Mexicans in the United States, 366;
Mexico, immigration, 367; passenger lists, 367; passports and
passport information, examples
of, 371; periodicals, 400–401;
Porfiro Diaz, overthrow of, 367;
records, types of, 367; resettlement legislation, 366–67; Spaniards, immigration of, 367;
Spaniards or Mexicans, ports of
entry of, 367; Spanish America,
settlement of, 366; Spanish origin,
365; U.S. citizens in Mexico, 366
case studies: Francisco Bustamente
family, 381–82; Jose Joaquin
Yslas, 382; Maria del Carmen
Romo, 382–83
census, Mexican: Beatrice Ochoa, 387;
Estefana Lares, family tradition
of, 388; local, 386; Lopes family,
388–89; national, 386; Ochoa
family, 388–89; parish register
and census information, 386–87;
problems in research, 387; Romo
family, Maria del Carmen and,
387–88; San Pablo Mission census, 387–88
census, Spanish, 372–74; AHS, census
information in, 386–87; American
Southwest and local censuses,
386; content of, 376; Genealogical
Society of Utah and, 376; lower
California and Sonora, censuses
for, 375–76; military establishments, Sonora, 376; 1790 census
of Mexico, 372–74; Spain, 386;
Upper California, census of, 375;
U.S. federal censuses, 386
civil records: births, 384; deaths, 384;
Genealogical Society of Utah,
384; location in Mexico, 384;
marriages, 384; recording in Mexico, 384; value of, 384. See also
Vital records
collections, information on: Genealogical Historical Guide to Latin
America, 380; Spanish and Mexican Records of the American
Southwest, 380; Una Guia Gene-
alogico de Latinoamerica, 380
ecclesiastical records: archbishop's archives, 385; bishop's archives,
385; diocesan archives, 384; and
family records, 386; Genealogical
Society of Utah, 385; Indians in

Hispanic Americans
  ecclesiastical records (*cont.*)
      Mexico, 384; Joseph Joaquin
      Yslas, baptismal record, 385–86;
      location of records, 384; Maria
      del Carmen Romo, 386; marriage
      records, 385; in Mexico, 384;
      Negroes in Mexico, 384; non-
      Catholic records, 384–85; in
      padrones (censuses), 384; parish
      registers, content of, 384–85; pre-
      nuptial investigation, summary of,
      386; racial mixing, 384; in Spain,
      374; Spaniards in Mexico, 384;
      Yslas family, 385–86
  family sources: biographies, 381;
      church records, 381; citizenship
      papers, 381; diaries, 381; family
      histories, 381; genealogical and
      historical material, 381; legal pa-
      pers on homes and land, 381;
      military documents, 381; news-
      paper clippings, 381; occupational
      records, 381; in other locations,
      381; photographs and picture al-
      bums, 381; school records, 381;
      vital records, 381
  land records: in the AGI, 392n; in the
      AGN, 391; *Boletin,* of AGN ar-
      chive, 391; *capellanias,* location
      of, 391; Catholic Church, as land
      owner, 391; disposition of land,
      391; disputes between relatives,
      391; hereditary estate records,
      391; index to AGN collection,
      391; land grants (*encomiendas*),
      391; location of, 391; mortgages,
      391; Ramo de Vinculos, 391;
      wills, as source of, 391
  military records: Archivo de Simancas,
      377; Archivo General de Indias
      and index to, 377–78; LDS Gene-
      alogical Department Library, 377;
      Manuel Peru, biographical infor-
      mation on, 377–79; service re-
      cords for the Americas, 377; troop
      strength, list of, 376; University
      of Texas Library, 378; University
      of Texas (El Paso), 378
  monumental inscriptions: cemetery re-
      cords, 390; Don Francisco Yslas
      and Yslas family, 389–90; Hor-
      casitas cemetery, 389; judicial ar-
      chives, 389; Mexico, cemeteries
      in, 389; Spain, cemeteries in, 389
  notarial records: bonds, 390; charges,
      390; complaints, 390; contracts,
      390; dowry information, 390; in-
      dexes to records, 391; land trans-
      actions, 390; location of, 390;
      mortgages, 390; parish registers,
      390; payments, 390; powers, 390;
      wills, 390
  parish registers: Janos (former pre-
      sidio), 378; location and descrip-
      tion of, 378
  population movements: in AGN re-
      cords, 370; crew list (*San Car-
      los*), 369; Diego de Borica, 369;
      Felipe Barrios, 367; Loreto pre-
      sidio, 367–68; Monterrey, 369;
      San Carlos (ship), 369; *San Juan*
      (ship), 369; tours of duty, assign-
      ments of, 369; Zacatecas, records
      of, 370
  problems in research: births, unre-
      corded, 380; family origin, un-
      known, 380; inaccuracies in
      records, 380–81; *International
      Genealogical Index,* 380; later re-
      cords, content of, 380; 1900 cen-
      sus, 380
  U.S. records (general): cemeteries,
      383; censuses, 383; land, 383; lo-
      cal histories, 383; military ar-
      chives, 383; pedigrees in Mexico
      and Spain, extension of, 383; pro-
      bate, 383; vital, 383
Historical Commission of Charleston, 74
Historical development of genealogy,
      5–6
Historical research: and genealogical re-
      search, 61; methodology of,
      100–106; objective of, 96

Historical societies, 23, 74–75; establishment of, 6; libraries in, 59; number of, 74; purpose and activities of, 74; records in, 46; types of materials collected, 75
Historical Society of Delaware, 74, 82
Historical Society of Frederick County (Maryland), 74
Historical Society of Hudson County (New Jersey), 74
Historical Society of Old Newbury, 84
Historical Society of Pennsylvania, 87
Historical Society of York County (Pennsylvania), 74, 87
Histories, local, 8, 93; importance of, 77; out of print, 13
History, local: collecting and preserving, 13; and genealogy, 6; patterns in publishing, 65
History for genealogists, 30–32
Hood, William, 10
Holland Society of New York, 86
Houston Public Library, 88
How to Find Your Family Roots, 67, 80–81
"How to Use the Card Catalog of the LDS Genealogical Library for Polish Research," 13
How to Write the History of a Family: A Guide for the Genealogist, 77
Huguenot Society of South Carolina, 87
Hunterdon County Historical Society, 85

Idaho State Historical Society, 83
Illinois State Library, 83
Immigrants, European, 93
Immigration: policies and restrictions, 94; records and passenger lists, guide to, 80
Index-Gazetteer of the World, 76
Index to Genealogical Periodical Literature, 79
Index to Genealogical Periodicals, 79
Indiana Historical Society, 74
Indianapolis Public Library, 83
Indiana State Library, 83
Information requests by mail, 28

Institute on Ethnic Genealogy for Librarians, 95
Inventories, 42
Inventories, registers, and indexes, importance of, 77
Iowa Historical Society Library, 17
Iowa State Department of History and Archives, 72, 83

Jackson, Martha, 64
Jacksonville Free Public Library, 83
Jacobus, Donald Lines, 10–12, 79
Japanese-American families, concentration of, 107
Japanese-American history, 107
Japanese Americans. See Asian Americans, Japanese Americans and Japan
Japanese family history, 107
John Hay Library (Brown University), 68

Kaminkow, Marion H., 67, 77
Kane, Joseph H., 76
Kansas State Historical Society, 83
King, Kenneth, 14
Kinte, Kunta, 4, 111; descendants of, 99–100; as example in family history, 98
Kirk, Jeffrey, 94
Kirkham, E. Kay, 46
Kucera, Zdenka, 13
Kyvig, David E., 95

Land, court, and tax records, use of, 80
Language dictionaries (English and foreign), examples of, 78
La Porte Public Library, 83
Latter-day Saints, Church of Jesus Christ of, 68, 74, 176; and collecting genealogical records, 8–9; and genealogical research, 9. See also Genealogical Society of Utah Library; LDS Church, Genealogical Department of
Lawson, McGhee, Memorial Library, 87
LDS branch libraries, 17
LDS Church, Genealogical Department of: patrons, number of, 16, 17; patrons, service to, 16

LDS Genealogical Society, microfilming of church records, 46

Legislative records, 43

Librarians: assistance to genealogists, 63; attitude toward genealogy, 3, 12; attitude toward genealogy patrons, 10; and fees for service, 17; and genealogical collections, 17; and genealogists, 60; interpreting materials, 60; referrals, 63; service to genealogists, 17

Libraries: acquisitions for genealogists, 15; administration of, 65; aids to genealogical research, 75–80; and archives, 23; barriers to information access, 60; basic materials for researchers, guides to, 67; card catalog, use of, 67; circulation of materials, restrictions on, 60–61; classification systems, 67; collecting practices, 67; collection development, 60–65; and family histories, 67; genealogical holdings, deficiencies in, 60; and genealogical reference interview, 63; genealogical reference materials, core collection of, 66; and genealogical resources, 67–75; and genealogy, 6–9; and historical societies, list of, 80–88; interlibrary loan, 60, 63; library literature and genealogical material, 62; networks, 62; policy statement, user 61–62; professional assistance, 67; reference assistance, 15, 63; reference books and sources in, 67; reference interview, 67; reference service in genealogy, 63–65; research and genealogy, 67–68; as resource centers, 60, 62; types of resources, 67–68; use of, 97

Library Literature, 79

Library of Congress, 8, 47, 54; Genealogy and Local History Collection, 82; and slave narratives collection, 101

Library profession, 60

Library records and research, 59, 67–80

Library service: to genealogical researchers, 59–60; to genealogists, 15; in genealogy, 67; to users, 64–65

Library Service to Genealogists, 65

Library's role in local history and genealogy, 65

Lincoln, Abraham, and Lincoln family history, 5

Litigation records, 42

Long Island Historical Society, 86

Lord Ligonier (ship), and cargo of slaves, 99

Los Angeles Public Library, 82

Louisiana State University, and family history, 94

Lowell Historical Society (Massachusetts), 74

Lunar time, 91

Lynn Public Library, 84

McCoy, F. N., 109

McMurray College Library, 88

Madison County Historical Society (Nebraska), 74

Magna Charta Dames, formation of, 5

Main State Library, 16, 84

Major Council Meetings of American Indian Tribes, The, 108

Marriage banns, 45–46

Marriage records, 32, 45, 93; as source for verification, 24; date, 23

Marriages, multiple, 24

Marty, Myron A. *See* Kyvig, David E.

Maryland Gazette, 99

Maryland Historical Society, 74, 84

Maryland State Library, 84

Masons (organization), 48

Massachusetts State Library, 84

Mayflower Society, formation of, 5

Membership Rolls and Register of Ancestors of the Georgia State Society of the DAR, 78

Memoirs of Roger Clap, 5

Memphis/Shelby County Public Library and Information Center, workshops in genealogy, 15

Methodist records, regional centers, 46
Mexican Americans, 93–94; and family
    history, 92. *See also* Hispanic
    Americans
Meyer, Mary K., 10
Miami-Dade Public Library, 93
Michigan Historical Commission, 74
Migration patterns, 31, 107; of families,
    61; of non-Europeans, 93
Milbourn and Tull Genealogical Library,
    84
Military records: compiled service re-
    cords, 45; content of, 108; early,
    44; later service, 44; medical, 45;
    *Military Service Records in the
    National Archives of the United
    States,* 45, 108; mortality sched-
    ules and, 44; muster rolls, 43, 45;
    pension applications, 43; prison,
    45; rosters, 8; service records,
    43–45; volunteer soldiers, 44–45
    Civil War: centennial celebration, 92;
        Confederate Army, 92; genealogi-
        cal value of records, 45; and ge-
        nealogy, 92; listing of the dead,
        101; in the National Archives, 44;
        The Roll of Honor, contents of,
        104–5; service records of, 45;
        Union soldiers in national ceme-
        teries, 105; U.S. Colored Troops
        in national cemeteries, 105
    Revolutionary War, 91–92; and gene-
        alogy, 4; pension applications, 14
    Spanish-American War, 92
    World War I, 92
    World War II, 92
Military sources, importance of, 80
Milwaukee Public Library, 88
Minnesota Historical Society, 85
Minorities: and genealogical study, 9; in-
    visible, 93
Mississippi State Department of Archives
    and History, 72, 85
Missionary society reports (Northern),
    101
Missouri Historical Society, 74, 85
Mistresses' journals, 101
MLA Style Sheet, 109

Modern Researcher, The, 109
Monmouth County Historical Associa-
    tion, 85
Mormons, the, 8
Mount Clemens (Michigan) Public Li-
    brary, 14
Museum and Library of Maryland His-
    tory, 10

National Archives and Records Service,
    8, 10, 13–14, 43, 55, 68, 108,
    123–73 *passim*
    Afro-Americans: African immigrants
        (free), 155; Africans, as imported
        slaves, 155; Afro-American fami-
        lies, 155; *Afro-American History:
        Sources for Research,* 153; Afro-
        American military units, 155; cen-
        sus, southern states, 156; in cen-
        sus enumerations, 134–35; census
        records, 156; Continental Con-
        gress, papers on, 155; Freedmen's
        Bureau, 155; Freedmen's Savings
        and Trust Company, 155; inter-
        coastal slave manifests, 155; *Jour-
        nal of the Afro-American
        Historical and Genealogical Soci-
        ety,* 156; ship manifests, 155;
        slave and free, 156; slavery peri-
        od, 156; slaves (male and
        female), 155; slave trade ship
        documents, 155; Staten Island,
        evacuations, 155; U.S. Army
        Commands, records of, 156; U.S.
        Bureau of Customs, 155
    Bureau of Refugees, Freedmen, and
        Abandoned Lands, 156
    Civil War records: Afro-Americans
        in the Union Army, 152; Con-
        federate Conscription Acts, 159;
        Confederate records series, 159;
        conscription, entitlement to, 159;
        draft, 156; enrollment, 159;
        Freedmen's Bureau, responsibility
        for, 156–57; Freedmen's Savings
        and Trust Company, 156; guides
        to, 156; slaves, freed, 157; U.S.
        Colored Troops, 156; U.S. courts,

National Archives and Records Service
Afro-Americans
  Civil War records (*cont.*)
    156; U.S. Department of the
    Treasury, Civil War Districts,
    156; U.S. Veterans Administra-
    tion, 156
  Confederate states, records on: Afro-
    Americans in the Confederate
    States Army, 160; Afro-American
    units (military), 160; American
    Indians in the Confederate States
    Army, 160; Confederate States
    government records, 160–61; con-
    scription laws, 160–61; freedmen,
    employment of, 160; French ori-
    gin, persons of, 161; German ori-
    gin, persons of, 161; *Guide to
    Federal Archives Relating to the
    Civil War,* 156; *Guide to the Ar-
    chives of the Government of the
    Confederate States of America,*
    156; immigrants as servicemen,
    160–61; Italian origin, persons of,
    161; mixed nationalities, units of,
    161; *North Carolina Troops,
    1861–1865: A Roster,* 160; Scan-
    dinavian origin, persons of, 161;
    Scotch origin, persons of, 161;
    slave claims, records of, 160;
    "Slave Records" series, 161;
    slaves, employment of, 160;
    slaves, escaped, 160; slaves, fugi-
    tive, case files of, 160; slaves on
    military fortifications, 161; U.S.
    Colored Troops, 160; Welsh ori-
    gin, persons of, 161
  District of Columbia slave records:
    *Guide to Federal Archives Relat-
    ing to the Civil War* and, 160;
    *Journal of the Afro-American His-
    torical and Genealogical Society*
    and, 160; slave records, 160;
    slaves, compensation for loss of,
    160; slaves, manumission of, 160;
    U.S. District Court for the District
    of Columbia, 160; U.S. General
    Accounting Office, 160

  Freedmen's Bureau, inventory of re-
    cords: arrangement, 157; basic re-
    cord series, 158; claims (for
    freedmen), 158; court records of,
    158; destroyed records, 158; di-
    vorce records, 157; education and
    school records of freedmen, 158;
    freedmen, labor contracts for,
    157; health care records of freed-
    men, 158; Kentucky State Ar-
    chives and the, 157; land records
    of, 158; marriage records of, and
    slavery, 157
  Freedmen's Savings and Trust Com-
    pany: content of, 159; depositors'
    signature books, 158–59; location
    of, 159
American Indian Records
  Bureau of Indian Affairs, 161; Indi-
    an affairs, responsibility for, 161;
    series of, 161
  census records: arrival rolls, 162;
    churches, 162; departure rolls,
    162; enrollments, 162; enumera-
    tions, 135; quasi-censuses, 162;
    removal of, 162; reservations
    schools, 162; tribal records, 135;
    tribes, list of, 162; tribes, state or
    federal control of, 162; tribes, un-
    recognized, 162
  Cherokee Indian records, 161
  claims: Cherokee claims, 163; Civil
    War service, 163; Dawes Act,
    163; General Accounting Office,
    records of, 163; *Guide to Records
    in the National Archives Relating
    to American Indians,* 161; military
    service benefits, 163; names, An-
    glicized, 163; regional archives,
    records in, 163; reimbursements
    from military service, 163; Treas-
    ury agencies records, 163; Vet-
    erans Administration records, 163;
    War Department, records of, 163;
    whole companies and regiments,
    163
  military service records: Alaska Indi-
    ans, 164; Bureau of Indian Af-

National Archives and Records Service
  American Indian Records
    military service records (*cont.*)
      fairs, 164; Five Civilized Tribes,
      163–64; Maine Indians and the
      Revolutionary War, 163; service
      in major foreign wars, 163
    treaty records series: Bureau of Indi-
      an Affairs, 162; Department of
      State, 162; Department of the In-
      terior, 162; Treasury Department,
      162; tribal members, names of,
      162; War Department, 162
  American Trust Territories: Alaska,
    164; Dominican Republic, 164;
    Guam, 164; Hawaii, 164; Mar-
    ianas, the, 164; Puerto Rico, 164;
    territorial records, 164
  background: Afro-Americans, guides to
    records of, 125; Alex Haley, 123;
    Cherokee Indians, guides to re-
    cords of, 125; ethnic groups, re-
    search on, 128; ethnic origin,
    records on, 123, 134; family his-
    tory and genealogy, study of, 123;
    family history records, 128–29;
    Federal Records Centers, 123; ge-
    nealogical tools in, 125; general
    information leaflets, 125; German
    government, guide to records,
    125; guides to records and use,
    125–29; *Guide to Federal Ar-
    chives Relating to the Civil War,*
    125; *Guide to Records in the Na-
    tional Archives Relating to the
    American Indian,* 125; *Guide to
    Genealogical Research in the Na-
    tional Archives,* 125; *Guide to the
    Archives of the Government of the
    Confederate States of America,*
    125; *Guide to the National Ar-
    chives of the United States,* 124;
    Italian government, guide to re-
    cords of, 125; locations and areas
    served, list of, 126–28; microfilm
    reading room, 139; pamphlets,
    124; presidential libraries, 123;
    reference information papers, 124;
      record group format, definition,
      system, and use, 124–25; records
      inventory, 124; regional branches
      of, 125–28; responsibility for re-
      cords, 123; special publications,
      124; staff information papers,
      124; subject guides, 125; utilizing
      the archives, 128–29
  census information: Afro-Americans
    in, 130; aliens, 129; American In-
    dians in, 129–30, 134; American
    Indians not taxed, 129; Bureau of
    Refugees, Freedmen, and Aban-
    doned Lands, census schedules in,
    134; Bureau of the Census, 125,
    129; Civil War information, 134;
    Daughters of the American Revo-
    lution, 133; ethnic family re-
    search, 134–35; free persons,
    129–30; health statistics, 129; lit-
    eracy, 129; military pensioners,
    129; prisoners of war, political,
    129; problems and inaccuracies of
    records, 134–35; slave owners,
    133; slave schedules, 133; slaves
    in, 129–30; Virginia, tax list of,
    129; welfare status, 129
  census schedules: 1790–1840, 129–30;
    1790–1870 Census Microfilm
    Catalogue, 131; 1810–1840
    schedules, 129; 1820 Census of
    Manufacturers, 129; 1850–60
    schedules, 130; 1870 schedules,
    130; 1880 schedules, 130–31;
    1885 schedules, 131; 1890 sched-
    ules, 131; 1900 schedules, 131;
    1910 schedules, 131
  census schedules (state): 1790 Recon-
    structed Census of Delaware, 129;
    1830 Indiana, 132; 1850 Michi-
    gan, 132; 1860 Ohio, 132
  census schedules, Soundex to: 132–33;
    American Indians, coding, 133;
    Orientals, coding, 133
  census schedules, supplementary: 1820
    Census of Manufacturers, 129,
    133; 1850–1880, content of, 133;
    non-population schedules, 133;

National Archives and Records Service
census schedules (*cont.*)
other enumerations, 134; Revolutionary War pensioners, 133; veterans' schedules, 133
civilian personnel records: content of, 153–54; Freedom of Information regulations on, 154; indexes or finding aids, 154; locating, essentials for, 154; National Personnel Records Center, 153–54; native-born citizens, 153; post-Civil War applications, 154; *Register of U.S. Government Employees, 1815–1933*, 154; terminated employees, 154; twentieth-century employment records, 154; Union Army service, 154; unnaturalized citizens, 153; U.S. Department of State records, 153
Department of Justice, 139
federal immigration records: aliens, information and registration, 135; Boston, port of, 136; "City Passenger Lists for the Port of Baltimore, 1820–66," 138; crew lists, 135–36; ethnic origin of immigrants, 135–36; indexes, immigration records, 136–38; "Miscellaneous East Coast and Gulf Port Records," 136; New Orleans, port of, 136; New York, port of, 136; passenger arrival records, 136; passenger lists, East Coast, 136; passenger lists, German, 135; passenger lists, Gulf region, 136; ship manifests, 135–36; U.S. Department of State, and aliens, 135
military records: service
Branches: Regular Army, 45; Revenue Cutter Service, 142; U.S. Air Force, 45, 141; U.S. Army, 141, 145–47; U.S. Coast Guard, 45, 141–42, 149; U.S. Marine Corps, 45, 141; U.S. Merchant Marine, 149; U.S. Military Academy, 146; U.S. Naval Academy, 148; U.S.

Navy, 45, 141–42, 147–48
military records, types of: aliens, 141; compiled military service, 143; consolidated officers' files, 146–47; Continental Congress, 142; continuous service, 148; courts-martial, 146, 148; destroyed records, 149; enlistment papers, 146, 148; ethnic origin of servicemen, 147; Freedom of Information Act, 149; identifying the records, 146; immigrants, 148; indexing the records, 147; medical records, 146, 148; National Personnel Records Center, 148–49; officers' records, 147–48; personnel records, 148; prisoner-of-war, 148; Privacy Act, 149; race and religion, records on, 148; racial and ethnic mixing, 146; Seamen's Protection Certificates, 149; ship and station, 148; Ships' records, 148; superior army commands, 147; unit, 147; unnaturalized residents, 141; U.S. War Department, 142, 147; veterans' homes, state, 142; volunteer units and volunteers, 141–43, 147
military records, wars
Civil War (Union), 142–45; Afro-Americans in, 144; American Indians in, 144; Canadians in, 144; Confederate records in, 143; immigrants for the war, 145; Irish in, 144; Italians in, 144; Norwegians in, 144; Polish in, 144; Spanish in, 144; Swiss in, 144; Turkish in, 144; Union Army, 145; unnaturalized aliens in, 145; volunteers in, 144
Indian wars, 142–43; Afro-Americans (free and slave) in, 144; Afro-American units in, 144; American Indians in, 144; ethnic origin of troops, 144; immigrants in, 144; records of, 144; series, indexes to, 144; unnaturalized citizens in, 144

National Archives and Records Service
   military records (*cont.*)
      Mexican War, 142; ethnic group-
         oriented units, 144; records, 144;
         series, indexes to, 144
      Philippine Insurrection, 142–43, 145
      post-Revolutionary War, 143; series,
         indexes to, 144; 1784–1811 wars,
         143
      Revolutionary War, 142; Afro-
         Americans (slave and free) in,
         143; American Indians in, 143;
         Canadians in, 143; French in,
         143; Polish in, 143
      Spanish-American War, 142–43,
         145; "colored" regiments in,
         145; Puerto Rican regiments in,
         145; volunteers in, 145
      War of 1812, 143–44; series, index-
         es to, 144
   naturalization: African descent, 138;
      aliens, naturalization of, 138;
      court records and proceedings,
      138; declaration of intent,
      138–39; federal court records, lo-
      cation of, 139; Federal Records
      Center, 139, 140; Freedom of In-
      formation Act, 139; Immigration
      and Naturalization Service, 139;
      Indiana State Archives records,
      140; Mississippi, naturalization re-
      cords of, 140; New Jersey, natu-
      ralization records of, 140; New
      York City, naturalization records
      of, 140; Philadelphia, naturaliza-
      tion records of (1800–1899), 130;
      U.S. laws and, 138; Works Pro-
      jects Administration and, 139;
      WPA inventories, 140
   other ethnic groups: Alaskans, 164;
      Chinese, 164; Danes, 164; Free-
      dom of Information Act, 165;
      *Guide to Genealogical Research
      in the National Archives,* 165n;
      *Guide to Materials on Latin
      America in the National Archives
      of the United States,* 165; intern-
      ment camps, 165; Japanese, 164;
         Japanese in Hawaii, 164; Latin
         Americans, 164; United States
         and Latin America, relationships
         with, 165
   passport records: laws governing, 140;
      quasi-war with France, 141; sea-
      men's passports (Bureau of Cen-
      sus), 141; Seamen's Protection
      Certificates, 1798–1866;
      1916–1947, 140, 141; War of
      1812, 141
   publications, National Archives:
      guides, 166; conference papers,
      125, 173; indexes, 166; leaflets,
      general information, 172–73; mi-
      crofilm catalogs, 172; non-na-
      tional Archives publications, 173;
      preliminary inventories, 167–71;
      reference information papers, 167;
      special lists, 171–72
   special series for ethnic family history,
      154–65; immigrant groups, 155;
      U.S. Department of State records,
      155
   veterans benefit records: arrangement
      of files, 151; benefits, 149,
      152–53; bounty land warrant ap-
      plication files, 151; Continental
      Congress, 151; Civil War and
      later series, 150; Civil War vet-
      erans, 152; domiciliary care and
      hospitalization, 152; ethnic infor-
      mation, 152; Freedom of Informa-
      tion, 150, 152; General Land
      Office, 151; home records (ear-
      lier), contents of, 152; homes,
      state and federal, 152; indexes to
      files, published and unpublished,
      150; Indian War series, 150; laws,
      151; locating records, 151; Mex-
      ican War series, 150; National
      Homes for Disabled Volunteer
      Soldiers, 152; Old War series,
      150; pension application files,
      149–50; pension claims series,
      150; Philippine Insurrection ser-
      vice, 150; privacy regulations,
      152; Revolutionary War series,

National Archives and Records Service
veterans benefit records (*cont.*)
150, 151; Spanish-American War
records, 150; Veterans Administration, 150; veterans' homes
and hospitals, 152; War of 1812
series, 150; War War I service,
150
National Atlas of the U.S.A., The, 76
National Center for Health Statistics, 37
National directory of funeral home direc-
tors, 105
National Genealogical Society, 5, 9,
55–56; code of ethics, 12; Con-
ferences in the States, 57; Jubilee
Conference, 15
National Genealogical Society Library,
75, 82
National Genealogical Society Quarterly,
13
National Geographic Society, 76
National Personnel Records Center,
44–45
National Society of Colonial Dames of
America, 8
National Society of Daughters of the
American Revolution Library, 55,
82
National sources, 50
New Bedford Free Public Library, 85
Newberry Library, 8, 10, 15, 17, 55, 67;
Local and Family History Collec-
tion, 83
New Cassell's French Dictionary, The,
106
*New England Historic and Genealogical
Register,* 92
New England Historic Genealogical Soci-
ety, 5, 47, 55, 85, 92
New Hampshire State Library, 85
New Jersey Historical Society, 85
New Jersey State Department of Educa-
tion, 85
New London County Historical Society,
82
Newman, John J., 105
New Orleans Public Library, 83
"New school of genealogists," 10

"New School" of genealogy, 11–12
Newspaper advertisements (for runaway
slaves), 101
Newspapers, 47–48; genealogical column
in, 47; genealogical information
in, 47
Newsweek, 9
New York Genealogical and Biographical
Society, 86
New York Historical Society, 74, 86
New York Public Library, 47, 55; Local
History and Genealogy Division,
86
New York State Library, 72, 86
New York University Library, 68
North Carolina Department of Cultural
Resources, Division of Archives
and History, 72. *See also* North
Carolina State Library
North Carolina State Library, 86
Notices to creditors, 42

Ohio Genealogical Society, 14
Ohio State Library, 86
Oklahoma Historical Society, 74
Olstead County Historical Society, 85
Opportunities for study, list of formats,
57
Oral evidence in research, 63
Oral history: collections, examples of,
102; collections and use, 102–3;
notes, 99; projects, examples of,
102; reference tools, 63; sources,
101
Oral interviewing, 100
Oral interview process, 103–4; steps in
conducting, 103–4
Oral interviews, 99
"Oral Recollections of Black South Car-
olinians, The," 103
Order of the Crown of Charlemagne
(U.S.), formation of, 5
Organization of American Historians, 94
Oriental immigrants, 4
*Original Roget's Thesaurus of English
Words and Phrases, The,* 109
Otis Library, 82
Oxford English Dictionary, 78

Paleography manuals, examples of,
    79–80
Parker, J. Carlyle, 65
Parker, Jimmie B., 13
Pasadena Public Library, 82
Passenger and Immigration Lists Index,
    80
Patrick, Lucia, 15
Peabody Institute Library, genealogical
    collection, 11
Pedigree, definition of, 96
Pedigree chart, 21–24, 93
*Pen and Sword: The Life and Journals of
    Randal W. McGavock,* 111
Pennsylvania State Library, 87
Pension applications, 8
Periodical indexes, examples of, 79
Personal name indexes (city directories),
    108
Phillimore, W. P., 77
Photoanalysis: as historical research
    method, 105; importance in fami-
    ly history research, 105
*Photoanalysis: How to Interpret the Hid-
    den Psychological Meaning of
    Personal and Public Photographs,*
    106
Photographs, 23, 29; identification of,
    30; of relatives in the Civil War,
    92
Pickaway County District Library, 86
Pikes Peak Regional District Library, 82
Plainfield Free Public Library, 86
Platt, Lyman De, 12
Polish Genealogical Society, 56
Pomona Public Library, 82
Pope Gregory, 32
Portsmouth Athenaeum, 85
"Preserving Our Heritage," 9
*Preserving Your Past: A Painless Guide
    to Writing Your Autobiography
    and Family History,* 76, 95
Private and special genealogical or histor-
    ical society libraries, 74–75
Private organizations, and genealogical
    records, 48
Probate records, abstracts of, 8; content

of, 40–42; indexes of, 8; letters
    of administration, 42
*"Professional Code for Genealogical Li-
    brary and Librarians, A,"* 15
Professional genealogist. *See* Genealogist
Public libraries: basic research tools, 30;
    collecting practices, 71; collection
    development, 62; collections in,
    62; and genealogical collections,
    6, 59; and genealogical collec-
    tions, types of, 71–72; and gene-
    alogy, 8, 14; important collections
    in, 71; and local genealogists, 16;
    mission statements of, 61; policy
    toward genealogical research, 15;
    purpose of, 70–71; resources of,
    12–14; response to users, 13
Public library, and genealogy, 14
Public Library of Cincinnati and Hamil-
    ton County, 86
Public Library of Fort Wayne and Allen
    County, 8, 15, 55, 83
Public library service, and genealogy, 11
Puerto Ricans: oral history interviews of,
    103. *See also* Hispanic Americans

Quakers, genealogical information in re-
    cords, 46
Queensborough Public Library, 86

Radcliffe College, Schlesinger Library,
    102–3
Rawick, George P., 101
Readers' Guide to Periodical Literature,
    79
Records and services, listing of: from
    historical societies, 29; from li-
    braries, 29; from public archives,
    29
Records centers, 59
Reference and Adult Services Division,
    History Section (ALA): con-
    ference on genealogy, 66; state-
    ment on publishing newsletters,
    66–67, 89n
Reference librarian, and basic works in
    genealogy, 12

Regional historical associations, 74
Registers of patriotic societies, examples of, 78
Reliability of sources, 109
Research exchange files, importance of, 76
Research records, 25
Research register, 75
Research steps, 96–97
Researcher's Guide to American Genealogy, The, 81
Researching and Writing History: A Practical Handbook for Students, 109
Researching facts about individuals, 98
Researching family history, 91–120 *passim*
Resources for advanced research, 77
Reynolds, Fred, 8
Reynolds, Leighton D., 79
Rhode Island Historical Society, 87
Roberts, Gary Boyd, 15
Rochester Public Library, 86
Rogers, Ellen Stanley, 79
Rogers, Ely Russell. *See* Rogers, Ellen Stanley
Rogers (Lauren) Library and Museum of Art, 85
Roget, Peter M., 109
Roots, 4, 16, 94, 97, 111–12; publication and dramatization of, 9; publication and televising of, 11
Roots of America, 4–5
Roster of Revolutionary Soldiers and Patriots in Alabama, 78
Rottenberg, Dan, 12
Royal Bastards, 5
Rubincam, Milton, 9
Rutherford B. Hayes Library, 87

Saint Louis Public Library, 77, 85
Samford University, genealogical training institute, 57
San Antonio Public Library, 88
Sanchez-Korrol, Virginia, 103
San Diego Public Library, 82
San Francisco Public Library, 82

Santa Barbara Historical Society, 74
Santa Barbara Mission Archive/Library, 82
Scandinavians, migration of, 107
School records, 48
Scribes and Scholars: A Guide to the Transmission of Greek and Latin Literature, 79
Search and Research, 29, 67
Searching for Your Ancestors, 12, 76
Seattle Public Library, 88
Shipping in the Port of Annapolis, 99
Shreve Memorial Library, 18
Sinko, Peggy Tuck, 15
Slave cemeteries, 104
Slave narratives collection, 101
Slave papers, 64
Slaves: in census documents, 101; former, 93
Slaves, African, records on, 108
Slave ship records, computerized list of, 105
Slovak Americans, genealogical guides to, 108
Smith, Clifford Neal, 65
Smith, Frank. *See* Gardner, David E.
Smithsonian Institution, course in, genealogical research, 57
Smithtown Public Library, 86
Society of Descendants of the Illegitimate Sons and Daughters of the Kings of Britain, 5
Society of Mayflower Descendants, 8
Society of the Cincinnati, 8
Solar time, 31
Sons and Daughters of the Confederacy, 92
Sons of the American Revolution, 4, 92; formation of, 5
Sons of the American Revolution Library, 82
Sources: local, 49; primary, 59; state, 50
"Sources for American Genealogists and Family Historians," 12
Southern Arizona Genealogical Society, 56
Southern Historical Association, 74

Sparks Quarterly, and serial publications, 13
Sperry, Kip, 12, 79
Spokane Public Library, 88
State historical societies, examples of, 74
State Historical Society of Iowa, 83
State Historical Society of Wisconsin, 88
State histories, 8, 43
State libraries: and archives, 43, 72–74; function of, 72; genealogical holdings in, 73–74; and local historical societies, 72; resources in, 43; use of, 72
State organizations, libraries in, 59
Stevenson, Noel C., 28–29, 67
Strunk, William S., Jr., 109
Survey of American Church Records: Major Denominations Before 1860, A, 46
Survey of American Genealogical Periodical Indexes, 12
Syracuse Public Library, 86

Tax lists, 43
Tax rolls, 42–43
Tennessee State Library and Archives, 61–62, 72, 87
Tennessee State University, study of family history, 94
Texas State Library, 88
Times of London (author), 76
"Today" show, 9
Toledo-Lucas County Public Library, 87
Tombstones: information on, 47; inscriptions, 93, 104–5
"Tonight" show, 16
Tools for research, basic, 30; atlases and gazetteers, 31; city directories, 31; federal census schedules, searching, 31; genealogical guides, 30; maps and atlases, 30
Town histories, 8
Tracing Your Ancestry: Step by Step Guide to Researching Your Family History, 95
Transcribing and Editing Oral History, 104

Tulsa City-County Library, 87
Tuttle, Charles E., Company, 57
"Typical Genealogical Research Problems and Reference Questions," 65

Understanding History: A Primer of Historical Research, 100
University of Pennsylvania Library, 68
University of South Carolina, Instructional Services Center, 103
University of Utah Library, 68
University of Wisconsin, computerized slave ship records, 105
Unitarian and Universalist Genealogical Society, 56, 84
U.S. Board of Geographical Names, 76
U.S. Geological Survey, 76

Verification, sources of, 23–24
Vesterheim Genealogical Center, 56
Virginia State Library, 88
Vital records: contents of, 32–38; filing order, 37; indexing and abstracting, 13; published, content of, 79
Vital statistics: sources of information, 37; where to write, 37
Vital statistics registration: in Massachusetts, 37; in Georgia, 37
Voter registration records, content of, 42

Wagenknecht, Robert E., 61
Wasp, 8
Walker, James D., 12, 76, 94; and the National Genealogical Society, 9–10
Watts, Jim, 95
Waukesha County Historical Museum, 88
Welles, Albert, 10
West Chester County Historical Society, 74
Western Reserve Historical Society, 75, 87
West Hartford Public Library, 82
Westin, Jeane Eddy, 12
West Virginia University, West Virginia Collection, 88

Whartenby, Wrenette, 18
"Where to Write for Birth and Death
    Certificates for Alien Children
    Adopted by U.S. Citizens," 37
"Where to Write for Birth and Death
    Records: United States and Outly-
    ing Areas," 27
"Where to Write for Divorce Records:
    United States and Outlying
    Areas," 37
"Where to Write for Marriage Records:
    United States and Outlying
    Areas," 37
White, E. B. *See* Strunk, William S., Jr.
Wichita Public Library, 83
Wills, 93; dying intestate, 42; language

of, 42; locating, 42; "quiet the
    title," 38
Wilson, Nigel G. *See* Reynolds, Leighton
    D.
World Conference on Records, 9
World War II, 8
Works Projects Administration, 37, 93;
    guides, 77; inventory of church
    records, 46
Woodson, Carter G., 79
Wyoming State Library, 88

Yanchisin, Daniel A., 15
Yeshiva University Library, 68
*Your Family History: A Handbook for
    Researching and Writing,* 95

About the Contributors

RUSSELL B. BIDLACK, Dean of the School of Library Science at the University of Michigan, holds A.B.L.S., A.M.L.S., Ph.D., and Litt.D. degrees. He has made notable contributions to librarianship, for which he received the Beta Phi Mu Award for Distinguished Service to Education for Librarianship in 1977 and the Melvil Dewey Medal for Recent Creative Professional Achievement of a High Order in 1979.

Active in professional associations, Bidlack has chaired American Library Association committees such as the Nominating Committee, the Committee on Accreditation, and the American Library History Roundtable. He has served as president of the Technical Services Section of the Michigan Library Association and as chairperson of the Deans and Directors Group, Association of American Library Schools.

Bidlack's research and publications (over fifty monographs and articles) have related to both librarianship and to local history. His principal hobby since 1939 has been genealogy, when his favorite professor in college instructed him in beginning the study of family history. He is a recognized authority on the family association and the family periodical and has spoken on these subjects at both the 1969 and the 1980 World Conference on Records in Salt Lake City. *The Sparks Quarterly,* which he has edited since 1954, is considered a model for other family periodicals. He is also editor of the *Bidlake/Bidlack Family Periodical.*

CHARLES L. BLOCKSON was educated at Pennsylvania State University and serves as consultant in human rights for the Norristown, Pennsylvania school district. Villanova University awarded him an honorary doctorate in 1975, and Blockson was honored again in 1981 by Pennsylvania State University as University Alumni Fellow.

For more than thirty years Blockson has collected books, documents, manuscripts, and other items on the black experience from colonial times to the present. He is author of *Pennsylvania Black History, Black Genealogy, The Underground Railroad in Pennsylvania*, and other works, and lectures frequently on black history and culture.

JEAN ELDER CAZORT, Associate Librarian for Technical Services at Fisk University, holds M.A. and M.A.L.S. degrees. She has been Librarian of Meharry Medical College and Visiting Lecturer, Peabody Library School. Her memberships include the Tennessee Library Association, the Southeastern Library Association, the Tennessee Artist-Craftsman's Association, and she is a founding member of Women in the Arts.

Cazort teaches an honors colloquium on genealogical research at Fisk and lectured in the Fisk Institute on Ethnic Genealogy for Librarians. Exploration into her roots led her to the discovery of noted pianist Hazel Harrison, and spurred her to coauthor with Constance Tibbs Hobson the Greenwood title *Born to Play: The Life and Career of Hazel Harrison*.

GREG GUBLER is Assistant Professor of History and Asian Studies at Brigham Young University, Hawaii Campus, Laie, Hawaii. From 1976 to 1982 he was Research Specialist for East Asia at the Genealogical Society, Salt Lake City. He has done extensive research and writing on Asian sources and genealogical research procedures and has presented papers and lectures at conferences and seminars, including the 1980 World Conference on Records.

Gubler holds a Ph.D. in East Asian history, formerly taught on the history faculty at the University of Florida, was a Fulbright Scholar at Nanyang University in Singapore, and for five and one-half years resided and traveled extensively in Asia.

CASPER LEROY JORDAN is Deputy Director of the Central Library of the Atlanta Public Library. His career has touched a number of facets of librarianship: academic libraries at Wilberforce and Atlanta universities; the public library system in New York State, and library education at the Atlanta University School of Library and Information Studies. Jordan has been active in state, regional, and national professional associations and has held offices in many of these groups. He is a contributor to professional literature and for more than thirty years edited *The Free Lance*, a magazine of poetry and prose. Jordan is a graduate of Case Western Reserve and Atlanta universities. He was the 1981 recipient of the American Library Association's Black Caucus Library of the Year Award. He was a founding member of the Afro-American Family History Association and is active in the Association's research projects.

BOBBY L. LOVETT is Associate Professor of History and Acting Chairperson of the History Department at Tennessee State University. He received his Ph.D. degree from the University of Arkansas, Fayetteville in 1979. Lovett is author of numerous works, including *The Atlantic Slave Trade: A Computer Instructional*

Package for Afro-American History, "Memphis Riots: White Reaction to Blacks in Memphis, May 1865–July 1866," *Tennessee Historical Quarterly* (1979); "The Negro's Civil War in Tennessee, 1861–1866," *Journal of Negro History* (1976); "West Tennessee Colored Troops in Combat, 1864," *West Tennessee Historical Quarterly* (1980); and "The Negro in Tennessee, 1861–1866: A Socio-Military History of the Civil War Era" (Ann Arbor: University Microfilms, 1978). Lovett is a specialist in black history and actively pursues research on early black cemeteries, black newspapers, and black families.

JIMMY B. PARKER, Coordinator, Library Publications and Accreditation, Genealogical Department of the Church of Jesus Christ of Latter-day Saints, is an Accredited Genealogist (A.G.) in midwestern United States, eastern United States, and New England areas. He also has a special interest in American Indian genealogy.

Parker was cochairperson of the Program Committee, World Conference on Records, Salt Lake City, 1980, and has lectured at numerous genealogical seminars. His memberships include Board of Trustees and Executive Secretary, Association of Professional Genealogists; Board of Trustees and Fellow, Utah Genealogical Association; and Board of Trustees, Board for Certification of Genealogists. In 1978 he received the Award of Merit, National Genealogical Society.

Parker's writings include "American Indian Genealogical Research," which appeared in the *National Genealogical Society Quarterly;* "Sources of American Indian Genealogy," in the *Genealogical Journal;* and numerous books, pamphlets, and articles on United States genealogy and family history as well as several biographical works.

LYMAN DE PLATT, Senior Reference Consultant in the American section, Jesus Christ of Latter-day Saints Library, has been employed by the library's Genealogical Department since 1969. Throughout his employment there he has specialized in Latin America but also has worked with the Administration Division in publications. He has also had experience in the area of family organizations.

Between 1962 and 1965 Platt worked as a missionary in Peru for the LDS Church. He served in the United States Air Force between 1965 and 1968 and was decorated with honors several times during the Vietnam conflict, both by the U.S. and by the Vietnamese air forces.

Platt is the author of seven books and a number of articles on genealogy, family, and Latin American history and has written seventeen publications on record sources in each of the major countries of the Spanish-speaking world. He has traveled throughout the United States and Latin America representing the Genealogical Department of the library as negotiator, researcher, seminar participant, and guest lecturer. He has over twenty years of personal experience in the records sources of England, Wales, the United States, and Latin America.

ROGER SCANLAND received his M.L.S. degree from Brigham Young University in 1971. From 1971 through 1980 he was a staff member of the Genealogical Society of Utah Library in Salt Lake City. While there he held positions in public services, technical services, and administration. In 1980 he joined the faculty of Harold B. Lee Library, Brigham Young University.

Scanland was one of the founding trustees of the Association of Professional Genealogists and the founding editor of its *APG* Newsletter. He is also a contributing editor of *Genealogical Journal*. In addition to his library duties, he teaches a university course in North American sources for family and local history. He has lectured at the genealogical research seminars held each summer at Brigham Young and at several of the Utah Genealogical Association's annual conventions. For the past several years Scanland has pursued interests in black genealogy and in other aspects of ethnic family history.

JAMES DENT WALKER is a research consultant in genealogy, the National Archives, and American history before 1917. From 1944 to 1979, he held various positions with the National Archives and Records Service. He has served as Director of Local History and Genealogy, Research Consultant (General Reference Division), and Supervisor of Military Service Records at the Archives.

Walker was educated at the American University, George Washington University, and the U.S. Department of Agriculture Graduate School. He also received archival training at the National Archives Institute on Genealogical Research and the Institute on Genealogical and Historical Research, Samford University.

From 1965 to 1979, Walker was Lecturer, Assistant Director, and Director, National Institute on Genealogical Research. Later he directed the National Archives Conference on Local History and lectured in the Archives' Conference on Afro-American History. He has also lectured extensively on areas of genealogy. Both in 1969 and in 1980 he lectured at the World Conference on Records, Salt Lake City; the National Genealogical Society; American Library Association's Annual Conference; and numerous additional professional and state genealogical and historical society programs.

Walker is a member of the Historic Records Advisory Board, City Museum Board, and the Council of the Afro-American Historical and Genealogical Society. Formerly he has served as Vice-President, National Genealogical Society, and as member and first Vice-Chairperson, Board for Certification of Genealogists. He founded and served as President of the Afro-American Historical and Genealogical Society.

A fellow of the National Genealogical Society in 1978, Walker has received numerous honors from genealogical and historical societies. He has also published articles in various national periodicals and has served as editor of the National Archives Conference on Local History Papers. Walker is author of *Black Genealogy: How to Begin.*